UNESCO Report

Engineering:
Issues
Challenges and
Opportunities
for Development

Produced in conjunction with:

- World Federation of Engineering Organizations (WFEO)
- International Council of Academies of Engineering and Technological Sciences (CAETS)
- International Federation of Consulting Engineers (FIDIC)

UNESCO
Publishing

United Nations
Educational, Scientific and
Cultural Organization

Published in 2010 by the United Nations Educational, Scientific and Cultural Organization
7, place de Fontenoy, 75352 Paris 07 SP, France

ISBN 978-92-3-104156-3

Cover photos: Drew Corbyn, EWB-UK; Paula West, Australia; flickr garion007ph; Angela
Sevin, Flickr; imageafter; Tony Marjoram; SAICE; UKRC; Joe Mulligan, EWB-UK.

All full-page images from chapter introduction pages are by kind courtesy of Arup.

Typeset and graphic design: Gérard Prosper
Cover design: Maro Haas
Printed by: UNESCO

Printed in France

This landmark report on engineering and development is the first of its kind to be produced by UNESCO, or indeed by any international organization.

Containing highly informative and insightful contributions from 120 experts from all over the world, the report gives a new perspective on the very great importance of the engineer's role in development.

Advances in engineering have been central to human progress ever since the invention of the wheel. In the past hundred and fifty years in particular, engineering and technology have transformed the world we live in, contributing to significantly longer life expectancy and enhanced quality of life for large numbers of the world's population.

Yet improved healthcare, housing, nutrition, transport, communications, and the many other benefits engineering brings are distributed unevenly throughout the world. Millions of people do not have clean drinking water and proper sanitation, they do not have access to a medical centre, they may travel many miles on foot along unmade tracks every day to get to work or school.

As we look ahead to 2015, and the fast-approaching deadline for achieving the United Nations' eight Millennium Development Goals, it is vital that we take the full measure of engineering's capacity to make a difference in the developing world.

The goal of primary education for all will require that new schools and roads be built, just as improving maternal healthcare will require better and more accessible facilities. Environmental sustainability will require better pollution control, clean technology, and improvements in farming practices.

This is why engineering deserves our attention, and why its contribution to development must be acknowledged fully.

If engineering's role is more visible and better understood more people would be attracted to it as a career. Now and in the years to come, we need to ensure that motivated young women and men concerned about problems in the developing world continue to enter the field in sufficient numbers. It is estimated that some 2.5 million new engineers and technicians will be needed in sub-Saharan Africa alone if that region is to achieve the Millennium Development Goal of improved access to clean water and sanitation.

The current economic crisis presents challenges and opportunities for engineering. The risk is great that cuts in education funding will reduce training opportunities for potential engineering students. However, there are encouraging signs that world leaders recognize the importance of continuing to fund engineering, science and technology at a time when investments in infrastructure, technology for climate change mitigation and adaptation in such areas as renewable energy may provide a path to economic recovery and sustainable development.

Engineering is often the unsung partner to science – I hope *Engineering: Issues Challenges and Opportunities*, UNESCO's first report on engineering, will contribute to changing that.

Irina Bokova

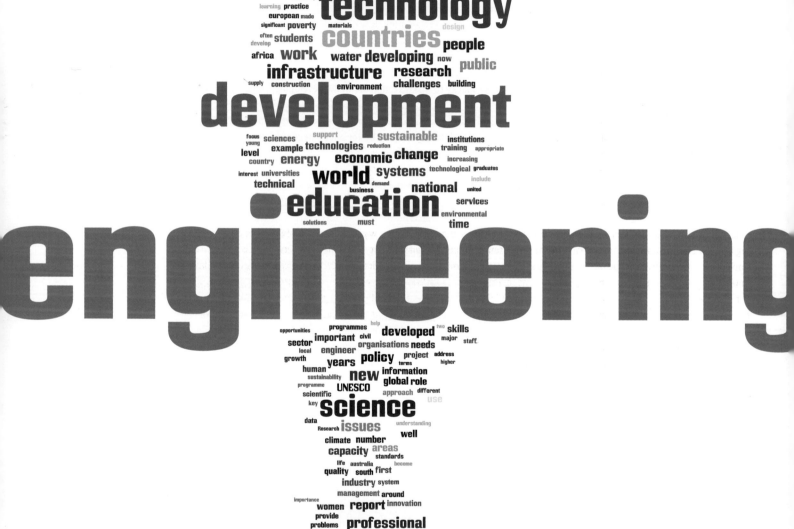

The critical roles of engineering in addressing the large-scale pressing challenges facing our societies worldwide are widely recognized. Such large-scale challenges include access to affordable health care; tackling the coupled issues of energy, transportation and climate change; providing more equitable access to information for our populations; clean drinking water; natural and man-made disaster mitigation, environmental protection and natural resource management, among numerous others. As such, mobilizing the engineering community to become more effective in delivering real products and services of benefit to society, especially in the developing world, is a vitally important international responsibility.

Engineering as a human endeavour is also facing numerous additional challenges of its own, including attracting and retaining broader cross-sections of our youth, particularly women; strengthening the educational enterprise; forging more effective interdisciplinary alliances with the natural and social sciences and the arts; enhancing our focus on innovation, entrepreneurship and job creation, and; promoting increased public awareness and support for the engineering enterprise. This volume, the first UNESCO Report on engineering, is an attempt to contribute to greater international understanding of the issues, challenges and opportunities facing engineering, with a particular focus on contributions of our discipline to sustainable development.

The Report, one of the most cost-effective reports UNESCO has published, is based almost entirely on voluntary contributions from the international engineering community. I would like to begin by thanking the over hundred contributors. I would also like to commend the coordinating and editorial team for their efforts – Tony Marjoram, Andrew Lamb, Francoise Lee, Cornelia Hauke and Christina Rafaela Garcia, supported by Maciej Nalecz, Director of UNESCO's Basic and Engineering Sciences Division. I would also like to offer my heartfelt appreciation to our partners – Tahani Youssef, Barry Grear and colleagues in the World Federation of Engineering Organisations, Peter Boswell, John Boyd and colleagues in the International Federation of Consulting Engineers, Bill Salmon, Gerard van Oortmerssen and colleagues in the International Council of Academies of Engineering and Technological Sciences. I also thank the members of the editorial advisory committee, and especially the co-chair, Kamel Ayadi, for their help in getting the Report off the ground.

This Report is a worthy partner to four UNESCO Science Reports, the first of which was published in 1998. Although engineering is considered a component of "science" in the broad sense, engineering was not prominent in these reports. This opened the door to increasing calls from the international engineering community for an international study of engineering, and particularly of the role of engineering in international development. This Report helps address the balance and need for such a study. As the Director-General has noted, the future for engineering at UNESCO is also looking brighter following the proposal for an International Engineering Programme that was adopted at our recent Executive Board and General Conference in October 2009.

Given its pervasiveness, engineering is indeed a deep and diverse topic, as this report illustrates. We have tried to cover the breadth and depth of engineering as best we can, given the constraints we faced, and indeed Tony Marjoram and his team have done a wonderful job in pulling it all together. We hope the Report will prove useful to a broad community, and are committed to continue to work together with our partners in the design of appropriate follow-up activities.

An agenda for engineering

This is the first UNESCO report on engineering, and indeed the first report on engineering at the international level. With a focus on development, the Report has been produced in response to calls to address what was perceived as a particular need and serious gap in the literature. The Report has been developed by UNESCO, the intergovernmental organization responsible for science, including engineering, in conjunction with individual engineers and the main international engineering organizations: the World Federation of Engineering Organizations (WFEO), the International Council of Academies of Engineering and Technological Sciences (CAETS) and the International Federation of Consulting Engineers (FIDIC). Many distinguished engineers and engineering organizations were invited to contribute to the Report, and responded overwhelmingly with articles, photographs and their time on an entirely voluntary basis – underlining the commitment and enthusiasm of the engineering community to this pioneering enterprise.

The Report is a platform for the presentation and discussion of the role of engineering in development, with particular reference to issues, challenges and opportunities. Overall global issues and challenges include: the need to reduce poverty, promote sustainable social and economic development and address the other UN Millennium Development Goals; globalization; and the need to bridge the digital and broader technological and knowledge divides. Specific emerging issues and challenges include: climate change mitigation and adaptation and the urgent need to move to a low-carbon future; the recent financial and economic crisis and recession – the worst since the 1930s; and calls for increased investment in infrastructure, engineering capacity and associated research and development. At the same time, many countries are concerned about the apparent decline in interest and enrolment of young people, especially young women, in engineering, science and technology. What effect will this have on capacity and development, particularly in developing countries already affected by brain-drain?

The Report sheds new light on the need to:

- develop public and policy awareness and understanding of engineering, affirming the role of engineering as the driver of innovation, social and economic development;

- develop information on engineering, highlighting the urgent need for better statistics and indicators on engineering (such as how many and what types of engineers a country has and needs – which was beyond the scope of this Report);

- transform engineering education, curricula and teaching methods to emphasize relevance and a problem-solving approach to engineering;

- more effectively innovate and apply engineering and technology to global issues and challenges such as poverty reduction, sustainable development and climate change – and urgently develop greener engineering and lower carbon technology.

The Report shows that the possible solutions to many of these issues, challenges and opportunities are interconnected. For example, a clear finding is that when young people, the wider public and policy-makers see information and indicators showing that engineering, innovation and technology are part of the solution to global issues, their attention and interest are raised and they are attracted to engineering. The Report is an international response to the pressing need for the engineering community to engage with both these wider audiences and the private sector in promoting such an agenda for engineering – and for the world.

World Federation of Engineering Organizations

Barry J. Grear AO, President WFEO 2007–09

This Report presents an important opportunity. As the first ever international report on engineering, it gives the world's engineering community a chance to present the significant contribution that engineering makes to our world.

The Report explores the main issues and challenges facing engineering for development – for the development of engineering and the crucial role of engineering in international development.

The concerns, ideas and examples of good practice captured in this Report provide valuable information for government policy-makers, engineering organizations, international development organizations, engineering colleagues and the wider public to understand the future of engineering, capacity needs, engineering and technical education, and engineering applications.

I congratulate and thank all who have contributed to the development of the book and particularly the editor, Dr Tony Marjoram, who has been an encourager to the engineering community through his role at UNESCO.

The World Federation of Engineering Organizations was founded by a group of regional engineering organizations and in 2008 we celebrated forty years of its existence as an international non-governmental organization. WFEO brings together regional and national engineering organizations from more than ninety countries, representing approximately fifteen million engineers; we are honoured to be associated with the production of this first UNESCO Engineering Report.

International Council of Academies of Engineering and Technological Sciences

Gerard van Oortmerssen, President CAETS, 2008

CAETS, the International Council of Academies of Engineering and Technological Sciences, recognizes the importance of revitalizing engineering as a profession.

Engineers are responsible for technological development that has created our modern society; they have built infrastructure, industrial production, mechanized agriculture, modern transportation systems, and technological innovations such as mass media, computers and communication systems. Technological development is continuing at an ever-increasing pace, especially in new areas such as information and communication technology, nanotechnology and biotechnology. These developments are exciting, require increased engineering capacity and deserve public acclaim. Technological innovations have created wealth, facilitated our life and provided comfort.

For some. But not for all.

Prosperity and economic development are not distributed equally over the world. Realization of the United Nations Millennium Development Goals will require significant effort by engineers, but also creativity because the contexts of developing countries often requires new ways of doing things or the rediscovery of traditional techniques.

In addition, there are new challenges for engineers. Our society is facing problems, which, to some degree, have been caused by

developments for which engineers are responsible: the depletion of natural resources, environmental problems and climate change. Talented engineers are needed to provide solutions for these problems through greater efficiency in production processes and transportation systems, new sustainable energy sources, more efficient use of materials, the recovery of materials from waste... the list is long.

There is growing demand for engineering talent from a growing and developing global population. And the nature of engineering is changing. Engineering has always been multi-disciplinary in nature, combining physics, chemistry and mathematics with creative design, invention and innovation; but its scope is increasing. Engineers, more and more, have to be aware of the social and environmental impacts of technology, and have to work in complex teams, interacting and cooperating with society.

It is unfortunate that, under these circumstances of growing need for multi-talented engineers, the interest in engineering among young people is waning in so many countries. Awareness of the importance and the changing nature of engineering should be raised in circles of government as well as the general public.

CAETS therefore very much welcomes this UNESCO effort to explore the current state of engineering, and the issues and challenges for its development and for global development.

International Federation of Consulting Engineers

John Boyd, President FIDIC 2007–09

The International Federation of Consulting Engineers (FIDIC) is the international organization that represents the business of consulting engineering worldwide. This Report deals with issues that are key to the ongoing success of our industry, profession and society, and we are very pleased to have participated in its preparation. It comes at an important time. The profession of engineering is diminishing particularly in developed countries where our services, like our profession, have become invisible. We have in many ways created this problem ourselves. Ironically, this has come at a time when the need for engineering innovation has never been more apparent.

Issues of sustainable development, poverty reduction and climate change are fundamentally engineering issues. We have to learn to broaden our design brief beyond the traditional objectives of schedule, cost and conventional scope. We have to learn to include broader societal necessities such as minimizing water, energy and materials use, respecting human and cultural rights, and looking out for health and safety, not only within the work but also in its impacts.

This is a challenge that needs true engineering innovation. Leadership in this issue requires us to go beyond our comfort zone, to engage in the debates of our society, and to stand up for values regardless of their popularity.

This is our challenge, and this is our opportunity.

◊ *Wright brothers, first powered aircraft flight, 1903.*

The inception, development, and production of this UNESCO Report was facilitated, supported, and promoted by more than 150 individuals, organizations and institutions in the professional, public and private sectors. Without their voluntary generosity, commitment and support, this world-first international Report may not have been possible. All are to be warmly congratulated on behalf of the engineering and wider communities for their enthusiastic patronage of a project attempting to fill the gap in the paucity of information regarding the important role of engineering in sustainable social and economic development. Initial acknowledgements are therefore due to the Executive Board and colleagues of the World Federation of Engineering Organizations (WFEO), including Bill Rourke, Peter Greenwood and Barry Grear, who discussed and endorsed the idea of an international engineering report in 2005, to Kamel Ayadi, WFEO President in 2006–07, who presented a proposal for a UNESCO Engineering Report to UNESCO in 2006, and to Koïchiro Matsuura, former Director-General of UNESCO, who approved the proposal, leading to the beginning of work on the Report in October 2006. Barry Grear, WFEO President in 2008–09, and Maria Prieto-Laffargue, President from 2010, are also acknowledged as enthusiastic supporters of the Report, as is Director-General Irina Bokova, who has emphasized the important role of engineering in sustainable social and economic development.

Work on the Report began with invitations to and discussions with Bill Salmon and colleagues from the International Council of Academies of Engineering and Technological Sciences (CAETS), Peter Boswell and colleagues at the International Federation of Consulting Engineers (FIDIC), whose support as partner organizations is gratefully acknowledged. An editorial advisory committee was then formed, drawn from engineering organizations around the world, and consulted on an actual and virtual basis regarding the structure and format of the Report. The editorial advisory committee consisted of co-chairs Walter Erdelen, then Assistant Director-General for Natural Sciences at UNESCO and Kamel Ayadi, together with Peter Boswell (FIDIC), George Bugliarello, Brian Figaji, Monique Frize, Willi Fuchs, Issié Yvonne Gueye, Charlie Hargroves, Yumio Ishii, Paul Jowitt, Andrew Lamb, Eriabu Lugujjo, Najat Rochdi, Bill Salmon (CAETS), Luiz Scavarda, Mohammed Sheya, Vladimir Yackovlev, Tahani Youssef, Miguel Angel Yadarola, Zhong Yixin and Lidia Żakowska. Many were also invited to contribute and all are thanked for their help in organizing the Report.

The Report consists essentially of invited contributions, submitted on an honorary basis, and the generous support of the following contributors is highly appreciated: Menhem Alameddine, Sam Amod, Felix Atume, Margaret Austin, Kamel Ayadi, Gérard Baron, Conrado Bauer, Jim Birch, Peggy Oti-Boateng, Nelius Boshoff, Peter Boswell, David Botha, John Boyd, Damir Brdjanovic, George Bugliarello, Lars Bytoff, Jean-Claude Charpentier, Tan Seng Chuan, Andrew Cleland, Regina Clewlow, Daniel D. Clinton Jr., Jo da Silva, Mona Dahms, Cláudio Dall'Acqua, Darrel Danyluk, Irenilza de Alencar Nääs, Erik de Graaff, Cheryl Desha, Allison Dickert, Christelle Didier, Gary Downey, Xiangyun Du, Wendy Faulkner, Monique Frize, Willi Fuchs, Jacques Gaillard, Pat Galloway, P.S. Goel, Barry Grear, Phillip Greenish, Peter Greenwood, Yvonnne Issié Gueye, Leanne Hardwicke, Charlie Hargroves, Rohani Hashim, Sascha Hermann, Bob Hodgson, Hans Jürgen Hoyer, Youssef Ibrahim, Azni Idris, Yumio Ishii, Mervyn Jones, Russ Jones, the Jordan Engineers Association, Paul Jowitt, Jan Kaczmarek, Marlene Kanga, Anette Kolmos, Sam Kundishora, Andrew Lamb, Allyson Lawless, Leizer Lerner, Antje Lienert, Simon Lovatt, Juan Lucena, Eriabu Lugujjo, Takaaki Maekawa, Don Mansell, Tony Marjoram, Petter Matthews, Jose Medem, Jean Michel, James R. Mihelcic, Ian Miles, Victor Miranda, Włodzimierz Miszalski, Mokubung Mokubung, Jacques Moulot, Johann Mouton, Solomon Mwangi, Douglas Oakervee, Gossett Oliver, Rajendra Pachauri, Beverley Parkin, Stuart Parkinson, Waldimir Pirró e Longo, Arvind K. Poothia, Krishnamurthy Ramanathan, Tony Ridley, Badaoui Rouhban, Bill Salmon, Luiz Scavarda, David Singleton, Vladimir Sitsev, Jorge Spitalnik, Catherine Stansbury, Neill Stansbury, Don Stewart, Mario Telichevsky, Leiataua Tom Tinai, Susan Thomas, K. Vairavamoorthy, Charles Vest, Kevin Wall, Iring Wasser, Ron Watermeyer, Philippe Wauters, Andrew West, John Woodcock, Vladimir Yackovlev, Miguel Angel Yadarola and Zhong Yixin. Gunnar Westholm and Alison Young consulted on the complexities of statistics and indicators relating to science and engineering, and their contribution helped identify some of the issues and challenges regarding the urgent need for more detailed data collection and disaggregation. The UNESCO Institute of Statistics provided data for this Report, and their role in developing data is of obvious importance. Further details of the contributors are listed separately.

Several of the above and other contributors also contributed photographs and other materials to illustrate the text, and special thanks in this context go to Arup, a global technical consulting company, for the use of photographs of some of their projects around the world and their *Drivers of Change* publication, developed to help identify and explore issues facing and affecting our world, to the South African Institution of Civil Engineers (SAICE) and the UK Institution of Civil Engineers (ICE) – no report on engineering would be complete without a photograph of Isambard Kingdom Brunel – one of the most famous founders of modern engineering.

The editorial team was based in the Engineering Sciences programme of the Basic and Engineering Sciences Division in the Natural Sciences Sector of UNESCO, and consisted of Tony Marjoram, Senior Programme Specialist responsible for the engineering sciences as coordinator and editor, Andrew Lamb, consultant technical editor and editorial advisor,

Cornelia Hauke and Christina Rafaela Garcia, administrative editorial assistants, and Françoise Lee, programme secretary. In the Natural Sciences Sector, this team was supported by Walter Erdelen, former Assistant Director-General for Natural Sciences, Maciej Nalecz, Director of Basic and Engineering Sciences, Badaoui Rouhban, Mohan Perera, Guetta Alemash, Rosana Karam, Djaffar Moussa-Elkadhum, Sylvie Venter, Eloise Loh, Pilar Chiang-Joo and Patricia Niango. Ian Denison, Marie Renault, Isabelle Nonain-Semelin, Gérard Prosper and colleagues at the UNESCO Publications Unit in the Bureau of Public Information helped develop, arrange copy-editing, layout and printing of the Report, and manage over 120 individual contracts that were required for the Report. Particular thanks go to Andrew Lamb, whose assistance in putting together and editing a diversity of styles and lengths of contribution into the 200,000 words of the Report has been invaluable, and to Tomoko Honda, for her understanding and support as the Report has developed over the last two years. Finally, acknowledgement is due to the many thousands of engineers and the engineering community – present and past – whose work and enthusiasm we hope is reflected in this Report. Their spirit and commitment in overcoming issues and challenges has created opportunities for development that we hope more of us will be able to enjoy.

© ARUP

Contents

Introduction
to the Report

This is the first report at the international level on engineering, and the first with a specific focus on engineering in the context of human, social, economic and cultural development in developed/industrial countries and particularly in lower-income, developing countries.

Engineering has given us the world we live in. It is an incredibly diverse activity covering many different areas and levels. Engineering is regarded differently in different places and at different times. This diversity, and the constraints of size and the resources available to produce this first Report, requires that such a potentially comprehensive study must have a certain focus.

The Report is therefore intended as a platform for the better understanding of engineering around the world, and was conceived to meet this urgent and overdue need. The Report is a health-check rather than a 'state of the profession' review with reflections from more than one hundred distinguished engineers and engineering organizations from around the world. It highlights the links between engineering, economic growth and human development, and aims to bring engineering out of the shadows for policy-makers and the public. It positions engineering as a central actor in the global issues and challenges – such as poverty reduction, climate change and the need for sustainable development – that we face around the world. Technology is often emphasized by world leaders as providing the solutions to global problems; engineers need to get involved in the conversation and help to put words into practice. Governments for example, might be encouraged to have chief engineering advisors.

Another idea behind the Report was to present engineering as a human and social as well as a scientific, technological and innovative activity, in social, economic and cultural contexts; engineering is one of the few activities that connects with almost all others. It is intended to be a human rather than a technical report on engineering. It aims to discuss human as well as engineering issues and to try to understand and address some perceptions about engineering such as engineering is a boring and difficult subject which is poorly paid and environmentally negative. These are vital issues and engineering is vital in sustainable development,

addressing climate change mitigation and adaptation, and the reduction of poverty. As a problem-solving profession, engineering needs to focus on these issues in a rigorous, problem-solving approach. In an attempt to understand how it might do this better in the future, this Report also considers engineering education suggesting that it might benefit from less formulaic and more problem-based, project-based and just-in-time approaches in order that the next generation of engineer can rise to the challenges and opportunities that they are inheriting.

To examine these issues and challenges, a wide variety of people were invited to contribute to this Report, including engineers, economists, scientists, politicians, policy-makers and planners, from the public and private sectors, and from the profession and universities. Amid busy lives, almost all invited contributors responded to our requests for shorter contributions, which they wrote on a voluntary basis. This Report is a tribute to their commitment to engineering and a testament to their shared, heartfelt need for such a document.

Given the issues and challenges facing the Report itself, while many issues and challenges facing engineering have been identified and discussed, others have only become more apparent. As the Director-General observes, this Report raises almost as many questions as it answers.

There is, in particular, a need for improved statistics and indicators on engineering. It was hoped, for example, to compare the number of engineers per capita around the world, as can be done for doctors and teachers. Rather surprisingly, this was not possible due to fact that such data collected at the international level aggregates 'scientists and engineers' together (although such data does exist at the national level in some countries). UNESCO data shows that developed, industrialized countries have between twenty and fifty scientists and engineers per 10,000 population, compared to around five scientists and engineers on average for developing countries, down to one or less for some poorer African countries. Given the importance of engineering, science and technology in development, this lack of information is a serious constraint to the development and future of developing countries.

This Report therefore highlights that there is a clear need for the introduction of disaggregated data for engineering as an input to policy making and planning, together with different types and levels of engineer (for which clearer definitions would also be useful). There is also a need for better data on the important contribution of engineering to innovation, and the importance of engineering, innovation and entrepreneurship to development. This would be of particular relevance for developing countries given the estimate that around 90 per cent of the world's engineers work for 10 per cent of the world's population (the richest 10 per cent).

○ *Blériot XI.*

The Airbus A380 – the world's largest passenger aircraft.

This Report appears at an important time of need, challenge and opportunity for engineering. This is reflected in the proposal for an International Engineering Programme that was adopted at UNESCO's Executive Board and General Conference in October 2009. In this new decade it is hoped that this Report will help to mobilize interest in finding answers to the questions it poses, to emphasize the need for future editions of this UNESCO Report on engineering, to renew awareness of the importance of engineering in development, and to help find solutions to the problems of human development itself.

Background

The idea for a UNESCO report on engineering, developed through the 1990s and into the 2000s, was partly a response to calls from the engineering community regarding the need for such a report, and partly to comments from the engineering and broader science and technology communities that the *World Science Report* (published by UNESCO in 1993, 1996, 1998 and superseded by the *UNESCO Science Report* in 2005) contained very little reference to engineering and technology. These calls reinforced the need for a specific report on engineering by UNESCO as the United Nations organization responsible for science, including engineering. It was regarded that the founders of UNESCO intended the 'S' in UNESCO to be a broad definition of science, including engineering and technology, and therefore that UNESCO should report on the whole of this noble knowledge enterprise.

This reflects the decision of a United Nations Conference for the establishment of an educational and cultural organization (ECO/CONF) convened in London in November 1945, where thirty-seven countries signed the constitution that founded the United Nations Educational, Scientific and Cultural Organization that came into force after ratification in November 1946. In November 1945, this Conference accepted science in the title of the organization and in the content of its programmes, reflecting the proposal of Joseph Needham, supported by Julian Huxley, that 'science and technology are

now playing, and will increasingly play, so predominant a part in all human civilization.' Engineering was also included from the beginning; this Conference took place at the Institution of Civil Engineers in London, with Julian Huxley becoming the first Director-General and Joseph Needham becoming the first Head of the Natural Sciences Section of UNESCO. Needham, a biochemist, is best known for his *Science and Civilisation in China* series that began in 1954 and is now in twenty-seven volumes, and includes engineering and technology as a central component of science and civilization. Without Needham and Huxley this Report may not have been possible.

The need for a UNESCO Report on engineering is based on the importance of engineering in social, economic and human development, the particular importance of engineering in poverty reduction, sustainable development, climate change mitigation and adaptation, and the importance of better communicating this to policy-makers, decision-takers and the wider public audience. This need increases as these issues increase in importance, and as the pace of change in engineering also increases; the rate of knowledge production and application has increased dramatically in terms of the amount of knowledge created and the speed of application. From the first wave of the Industrial Revolution from 1750–1850, to the fourth wave when we went from early steam to internal combustion engines and the crossing of the 34 km of the English Channel by Louis Bleriot in his 20 kW monoplane in 1909. Sixty years later, in 1969, the 140,000,000 kW Saturn V rocket took the Apollo 11 mission across 400,000 km of space – a giant leap for mankind, and for engineering. The 230,000 kW Airbus A380 was introduced thirty years later in 2009, and routinely carries up to 850 passengers a distance of 15,000 km taking people of all backgrounds across continents at 900 km/h.

And yet, despite such achievements and feats, engineering is routinely overlooked in many countries around our world. Why is there such a poor general understanding and perception of engineering around the world, and what impact is this having? Is this perhaps even related to the awe-inspiring impact of engineering as a complicated, sometimes fearful entity, appealing to complicated people? Perhaps engineering also needs to become more human and humane to develop a wider appeal. This is at a time when there is an urgent need for engineers to develop the technologies that will be essential in the next wave of innovation based on environmentally sustainable 'green' engineering and technology that we will need if we are to address climate change mitigation and adaptation – if we are to save spaceship Earth.

Following the development of the idea for such a report on engineering in the 1990s and into the 2000s, as mentioned above, the Executive Board of the World Federation of Engineering Organizations (WFEO) – the main international umbrella organization for national engineering organizations based at UNESCO and established at UNESCO in 1968 – discussed the idea of an engineering report with the UNESCO Engineering Programme in 2005, and a proposal for such a report was prepared by the Engineering Programme. This proposal was presented to the (then) UNESCO Director-General, Koïchiro Matsuura, in October 2005, with the initial response that the next UNESCO Science Report could perhaps include a chapter on engineering. The President of WFEO, Kamel Ayadi, then requested a meeting with the Director-General, whom he met in March 2006. Following further discussions, and the submission of a revised proposal, production of the Report was approved in October 2006 with work beginning in January 2007. This Report is an attempt to address the above needs, and to at least begin to fill a critical gap at the international level.

◖ *Girl at rope well.*

© EWB-UK

Production and presentation of the Report

An Editorial Board and Advisory Committee for the Report were formed, with meetings in March 2007 in Paris and in November 2007 in Delhi. These soon merged into an Editorial Advisory Committee. The outline of the Report was developed, with particular reference to the contents and possible contributors. It was decided that the Report be as comprehensive as possible, covering the many fields of engineering around the world, with a particular emphasis on issues, challenges and opportunities for development – using the term development in a broad sense to refer to both national and international development, and the development of engineering itself. This decision in favour of a thematic focus was also in response to the regional reports focus of the *UNESCO World Science Report*. In view of the desire to be as comprehensive as possible, and cognisant of the limited human and financial resources available to produce the Report, it was also decided to invite relatively short voluntary contributions from around one hundred contributors in different fields and areas of engineering around the world in order to produce a Report of around 250 printed pages. An initial round of one hundred contributions and potential contributors were identified by December 2007 and they were invited to contribute in early 2008. By mid-2008, a total of 115 contributions had been identified and collected, with eighty contributions received and twenty promised contributions in the pipeline.

For the remainder of 2008 and into 2009, contributions were reviewed to check for gaps in content to see where further contributions were required. Gaps were identified, further contributions invited and remaining contributions encouraged. The Report was presented at a soft launch at the World Engineers Convention in Brasília in December 2008. A first draft of the Report was prepared in June 2009. In all, a total of over 120 contributions have been made. Only three invited contributors were unable to contribute, due to time pressure and other activities. This underlines the commitment of the engineering community around the world to this Report, and the rather ambitious initial schedule given the scale of the project. In November to December 2009 a second draft was prepared for copy-editing, design, layout and printing in time for publication in mid-2010 and a planned launch at the UNESCO Executive Board in October 2010.

The range of perspective and variety of approach of over 120 contributions has enabled a richness and depth that would not have been achieved with fewer contributors. Contributions for example include both personal reflections and academic presentations. A greater effort has been needed in editing to consider a length, consistent style, overlap and balance, whilst at the same time attempting to retain the original flavour of the contributions, allowing for some overlap. This approach has also restricted the space available for reporting at regional and national levels, with a focus on some national perspectives rather than full country reports. The diverse availability of comparable statistics and indicators also occasioned this approach. It is to be hoped that these issues – especially the need for better statistics and indicators on engineering – will be addressed in forthcoming editions of the Report. However, this first Report would not have been possible without such an approach, and the contributors are to be warmly thanked for their commitment and contributions, with apologies for the limited time available for feedback and discussion in the editing process.

Objectives of the Report

The overall objectives of the Report are to identify and explore the main issues and challenges facing engineering around the world, with particular reference to issues and challenges for development, and the opportunities for engineering to face and address them. External issues and challenges facing engineering include: the need for better public and policy-level understanding of what engineering is and what engineers do; how engineering and technology drive development; how many engineers a country or industry needs and in what areas and levels; why young people are turning away from engineering; what the consequences are of not having enough engineers; and why it is that engineering is so often overlooked. These external factors link to internal issues and challenges within engineering, including such questions as how can engineers promote public awareness and understanding of engineering, how does this reflect the changing needs for engineering and need for engineering and engineering education to change, regenerate and transform, and what can we do. These external and internal factors are further linked – the poor public perception of engineering reflects the urgent need to understand and address these issues and challenges as well as the need for engineering to face the challenge of change. Failure to do so will have obvious impacts on capacity and the application of engineering and technology for development.

The main target audience for the Report includes policy-makers and decision takers, the engineering community, the wider public and young people. The Report is intended to share information, experience, practical ideas and examples with policy-makers, planners and governments, and promote the engagement and application of engineering to important global challenges of poverty reduction, sustainable development and climate change. These are connected, and provide an opportunity for change and the engagement of young people, who are concerned about such issues and are attracted to the engineering challenge to address them.

Layout of the Report

In addition to this introduction on the background, main focus, objectives and target audience of the Report, the first chapter includes discussion of what engineering is and what engineers do, and the differences between engineers, technologists and technicians. The second chapter focuses on engineering and human development and includes sections on the history of engineering and engineering at UNESCO: engineering, innovation, social and economic development; engineering, technology and society; engineers and social responsibility, and includes a review of the big issues and pieces on engineering and social responsibility and corporate social responsibility. The third chapter examines engineering and emerging issues and challenges and includes sections on foresight and forecasts of the future, emerging and future areas of engineering and engineers of the future, getting the engineering message across and engineering and technology in the third millennium.

The fourth chapter is one of the main chapters and attempts to give an overview of engineering. It begins with a review of statistics and indicators on engineering followed by field reviews covering civil, chemical, environmental, agricultural and medical engineering. The engineering profession and its organization is then discussed, with reference to the organization of the profession, international cooperation and reference to leading organizations including the World Federation of Engineering Organizations (WFEO), the International Council of Academies of Engineering and Technological Sciences (CAETS), the International Federation of Consulting Engineers (FIDIC), the European Federation of National Engineering Associations (FEANI), the Federation of Engineering Institutions of Asia and the Pacific (FEIAP), the Association for Engineering Education in Southeast and East Asia and the Pacific (AEESEAP), the Asian and Pacific Centre for Transfer of Technology (APCTT) and the African Network of Scientific and Technological Institutions (ANSTI). International development and engineering organizations are discussed in sections on Practical Action, Engineers Without Borders, Engineers Against Poverty and Engineers for a Sustainable World. The following section introduces engineering studies and gives an overview of engineering, science and technology policy and the transformation of national science and engineering systems, with reference to New Zealand and South Africa. Key issues of engineering ethics and anti-corruption efforts are described, with the concluding section focusing on women and gender issues in engineering.

The fifth chapter presents perspectives of engineering around the world. It begins with an introductory overview and regional perspectives on Africa, the Arab States, Asia and the Pacific, Europe, the Americas and the Caribbean. Several country perspectives are offered from Africa in Côte d'Ivoire, Uganda, Ghana and Nigeria; from the Arab States in Tunisia, Lebanon and Jordan; from Asia and the Pacific in China, India, Malaysia, Japan, Australia and the South Pacific; from Europe in Germany, France, the United Kingdom, Russia and Poland, and from the Americas and the Caribbean in the USA, Canada, Brazil, Venezuela, Argentina and the Caribbean.

The sixth chapter is a more in-depth look at the main theme of this report – engineering for development – with reference to development applications and infrastructure. Engineering and the Millennium Development Goals and related international development goals, including particular references to: poverty reduction (with a case study from South Africa); sustainable development (and study on the MDGs, sustainable development and standards); climate change technology, mitigation, adaptation; disaster risk reduction; engineering in emergencies; and appropriate technology (with a case study on appropriate building technologies). Sections on engineering infrastructure include water and sanitation, energy, transportation, communications, asset management and maintenance, and infrastructure development in developing countries as well as a look at Infrastructure Report Cards (with case studies on South Africa, USA and Australia).

The seventh and last substantive chapter is on engineering capacity in education, training and mobility, and begins with a discussion of engineering education. The discussion of engineering capacity includes an introductory discussion of needs and numbers (demand and supply of engineers), followed by contributions on: technical capacity-building and the WFEO; capacity-building for sustainability in Africa; a case study on needs and numbers in civil engineering in South Africa; enrolment and capacity in Australia; and continuing engineering education, professional development and the brain drain, gain, circulation and the diaspora. A section on the transformation of engineering education includes contributions on: problem-based learning; sustainability and the engineering curriculum in Australia; rapid curriculum renewal; and the evolution of environmental education in engineering and research in engineering education. A section on engineering education for development includes case studies on centres for engineering and technology for international development in Australia, Botswana and Ghana. This chapter concludes with a discussion on engineering accreditation, standards, and mobility of engineers, with particular reference to the Washington Accord, Engineers Mobility Forum, APEC Engineer and European perspective on the Eur Ing and Bologna Accord.

Recent issues and challenges - economic crisis and climate Change

Since this Report was conceived and many contributions were invited and submitted, the world was overtaken by the financial and economic crisis. This began with the collapse of a housing bubble, peaking in the United States in 2006 fuelled by the easing of credit and sub-prime lending, deregulation and the increasing complexity of financial markets. The financial crisis peaked in September and October 2008 with immediate impacts on financial institutions and the banking sector. The NASDAQ, the largest trading stock exchange in the world (originally, the National Association of Securities Dealers Automated Quotations), is based particularly on 'technology' stocks and suffered large losses. There were also broader consequent impacts on economies around the world with the possibility that the burden of economic impact will fall particularly – directly and indirectly – on poorer people and countries. As noted in the discussion of science and engineering policy, many bank loans, especially smaller loans by development banks and other forms of microfinance in developing countries, are for technology such that a decline in the finance available for these loans would have a particular impact on development in developing countries. This Report therefore provides support for the view that, at a time of economic downturn, it is important for all countries to invest in technology and innovation.

The underlying cause of the crisis relates to increasingly complex financial 'innovations' and derivatives, and by changing attitudes toward risk based on mathematical modeling that is increasingly undertaken by young people using tools which are less well understood by senior bankers. Young engineers in particular were attracted into the financial sector; leading to an impact on engineering in terms of the brain drain. Following the initial emergency response and support for bank bailouts or quantitative easing, attention focused on engineering as regards longer term solutions to the economic crisis. In the 'American Recovery and Reinvestment Act' of 2009, President Barack Obama – in one of his first actions as President – emphasized the importance of investing in infrastructure for economic recovery and growth with a total infrastructure investment of US$80.9 billion, with particular importance in engineering. President Obama's action was echoed around the world. United States and European governments spent US$4.1 trillion on bank bailouts giving these companies forty-five times more funding than the US$90.7 billion that US and European governments spent on aid to all developing countries in 2007[1] (Institute for Policy Studies, 2008) – about the same order of magnitude to the US$135–195 billion per year that is estimated by Jeffrey Sachs to be required over the next twenty years to end extreme poverty, although there is a debate on Sachs' 'costing' of poverty (The End of Poverty, 2005[2]).

A FIDIC survey of economic stimulus packages around the world, reported in the introduction to chapter six estimates an additional demand of US$20 billion for engineering consultancy services

As regards climate change, the Intergovernmental Panel on Climate Change (IPCC) has emphasized the importance of technology and investment in response to climate change mitigation and adaptation that echoes the emphasis on engi-

---

1   Institute for Policy Studies, 2008

2   Jeffrey D. Sachs. 2005. *The End Of Poverty, Economic Possibilities For Our Time*. Penguin Press, 416p.

neering in the context of investment in infrastructure in the recovery from the financial and economic crisis. The major and agreed findings of the IPCC are as follows:

- The planet has warmed
- Most warming is due to greenhouse gases
- Greenhouse gases will continue to increase through the twenty-first century

The IPCC also recognizes that climate models have greatly improved, and estimates a rise in the average global temperature of 1.8 – 4.0°C over the twenty-first century, and warns that a temperature rise of anything over 2.0°C is likely to be catastrophic for the world. Immediate action is therefore needed to prevent catastrophic and irreversible change to the world's climate.

Engineering is one of the most important activities in the context of climate change mitigation and adaptation and, as noted elsewhere, one of the major areas of need and growth for engineering is in the area of sustainable or green engineering. Many countries have already introduced policies and initiatives for climate change mitigation and adaptation prior to the 2009 United Nations Climate Change Conference in Copenhagen, and together with the specific outcomes of COP15, this will be one of the areas of greatest demand and challenge that engineering has ever faced. One of the first challenges is to make sure that there will be enough appropriately qualified and experienced engineers to meet this demand – this will require the development of new courses, training materials and systems of accreditation. This will also hopefully encourage young people into engineering.

Photo by Robert Howlett

○ *Isambard Kingdom Brunel – a founding father of modern engineering.*

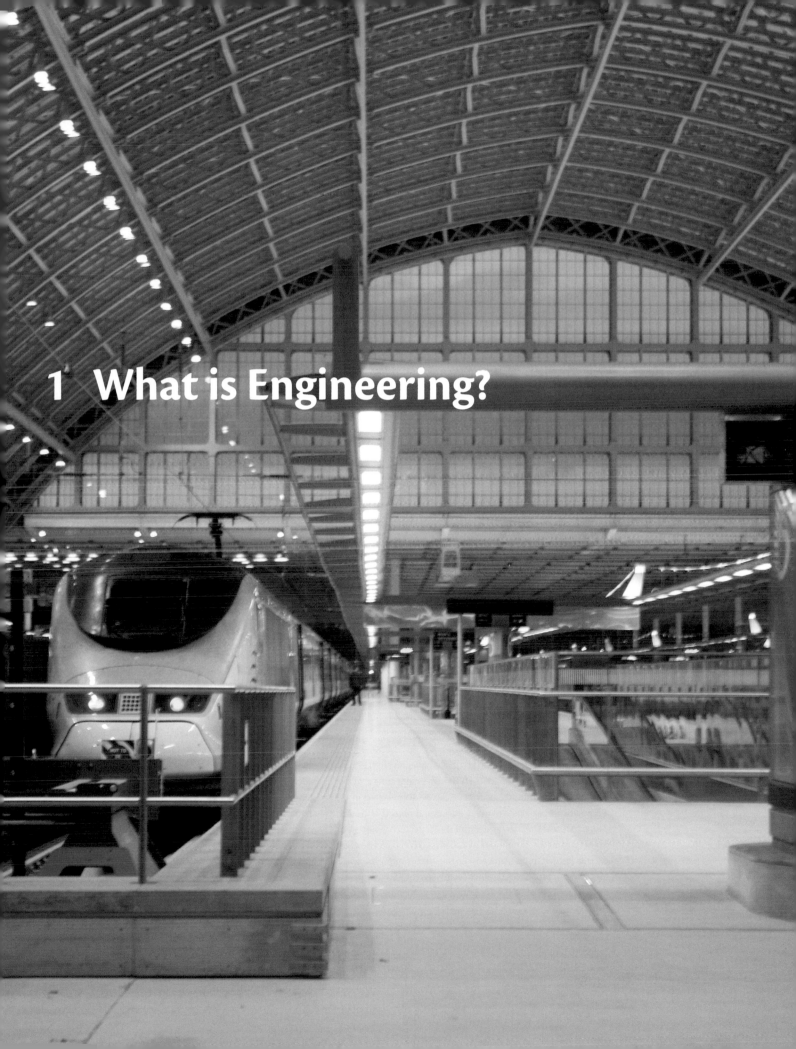

1 What is Engineering?

1.1   What engineering is, what engineers do

Tony Marjoram and Yixin Zhong

Engineering

While meanings change, the concept of engineering derives from the dawn of human history as our ancestors developed and designed tools that were essential for their survival. Indeed, human beings are defined by their tool-making, designing and engineering skills, and the socialization and communication that facilitated the invention, innovation and transfer of technology such as the axe, hammer, lever, wedge, pulley, wheel and so on. Although based on trial and error, this activity is similar to the modern idea of engineering where trial and error is still an important part of innovation.

Engineering is the field or discipline, practice, profession and art that relates to the development, acquisition and application of technical, scientific and mathematical knowledge about the understanding, design, development, invention, innovation and use of materials, machines, structures, systems and processes for specific purposes. There are of course many definitions. The term 'engineering' derives from the word 'engineer' used in the 1300s for a person who operated a military engine or machine – such as a catapult or, later, a cannon. The word 'engine' in turn derives from the Latin *ingenium* for ingenuity or cleverness and invention. The terms 'art' and 'technical' are important because engineering also arranges elements in a way that may, or may not, appeal to human senses or emotions, and relates also to the Greek *technikos* relating to art, craft, skill and practical knowledge and language regarding a mechanical or scientific subject. Prior to the development of the different fields of engineering, engineering and 'technical' were originally closely connected,. The military connotation declined giving way to civil engineering, mechanical, chemical, electrical and electronic and later, fields that continue to develop with the development of knowledge (apart from some curious exceptions such as the Army Corps of Engineers in the USA).

While meanings change, the fact that engineering in the modern sense also relates to art, even though engineering may not commonly be regarded as artistic, can be appreciated in the creativity and elegance of many engineered objects and structures (witness the increasing appearance of such objects and structures as art exhibitions in galleries). As noted elsewhere in this Report, humans live in engineered economies, societies and technocultures. Almost every area of human interest, activity and endeavour has a branch of engineering associated with it.

Engineering also connects to the natural sciences, and to the social and human sciences. Science, from the Latin *scientia* for knowledge, relates broadly to a systematic approach to the observation of phenomena and the development of hypoth-esis, experimentation and theory regarding these phenomena, and the production of knowledge upon which predictions or predictable outcome may be based, i.e. the scientific method, dating from the early 1600s and largely accredited to Francis Bacon (who died of pneumonia after testing the hypothesis that it may be possible to preserve a chicken by stuffing it with snow). In this broad sense, science includes engineering as a highly skilled technique or practice, and also includes much of what many scientists also do today. In a narrower, contemporary sense, science is differentiated into the basic and applied sciences, following the linear model of innovation – that research in the basic sciences leads through applied research and development in engineering to technological application, innovation and diffusion. As discussed elsewhere, while this model endures with scientists and policy-makers on grounds of simplicity and funding success, many observers regard the 'linear model' as descriptively inaccurate and normatively undesirable partly because many innovations were neither based on nor the result of basic science research. The social and human sciences emulate the natural sciences in the use of empirical scientific methods. Technological change and innovation is one of the major drivers of economic, social and human change, so engineering and technology and the social sciences are more closely connected.

Engineers

People who are qualified in or practice engineering are described as engineers, and may be licensed and formally designated as professional, chartered or incorporated engineers. As noted above, the broad discipline of engineering includes a range of specialized disciplines or fields of application and particular areas of technology. Engineering itself is also differentiated into engineering science and different areas of professional practice and levels of activity. The engineering profession, as with other professions, is a vocation or occupation based upon specialized education and training, as providers of professional advice and services. Other features that define occupations as professions are the establishment of training and university schools and departments, national and international organizations, accreditation and licensing, ethics and codes of professional practice. Surveying is closely professionally connected to engineering, especially civil engineering, and it is interesting to note that George Washington, Thomas Jefferson and Abraham Lincoln were all surveyors before going into politics.

Apart from a degree or related qualification in one of the engineering disciplines and associated skill sets, which includes design and drawing skills – now usually in computer-aided design (CAD) and continued professional development (CPD) and awareness of new techniques and technologies – engineering education also seeks to develop a logical, practical, problem-solving methodology and approach that includes soft social as well and technical skills. These include motivation, the ability to perform, rapid understanding, communication and leadership under pressure, and social-technical skills in training and mentoring.

Engineering is one of the oldest professions, along with divinity, medicine and law. While the linear model has lead to the perception of engineers as applied scientists, this is a further distortion of reality related to this model, as engineering is distinct from but related to science, and in fact predates science in the use of the scientific method – engineers were the first scientists. This debate is, however, rather misleading and diverts attention away from the need for a better public and policy understanding of the role of engineering and science in the knowledge society and economy. Science and engineering are essentially part of the same spectrum of activity and need to be recognized as such. Engineers use both scientific knowledge and mathematics on the one hand to create technologies and infrastructure to address human, social and economic issues, and challenges on the other. Engineers connect social needs with innovation and commercial applications. The relationship among science, technology and engineering can be roughly described as shown in the figure below.

Fields of engineering

There are a diverse and increasing range of areas, fields, disciplines, branches or specialities of engineering. These developed from civil, mechanical, chemical, electrical and electronic engineering, as knowledge developed and differentiated as subjects subdivided, merged or new subjects arose. The emergence of new branches of engineering is usually indicated by the establishment of new university departments, new professional engineering organizations or new sections in existing organizations.

To illustrate the scope and diversity of engineering, it is useful to conclude this section with a list of engineering branches[3] illustrating various disciplines and sub-disciplines in engineering; an important presentation of the diversity of engineering that space dictates can only appear once in the Report. The list is intended to be illustrative rather than exhaustive or definitive, as descriptions and definitions differ from country to country, often overlapping and changing over time. Further suggestions will, no doubt, be forthcoming.

Agricultural engineering

- Engineering theory and applications in agriculture in such fields as farm machinery, power, bioenergy, farm structures and natural resource materials processing.

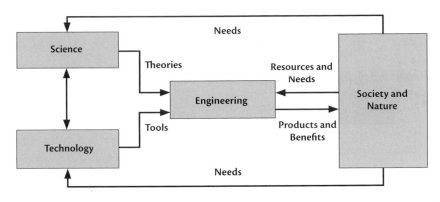

Chemical engineering

- Analysis, synthesis and conversion of raw materials into usable commodities.
- Biochemical engineering – biotechnological processes on an industrial scale.

Civil engineering

- Design and construction of physical structures and infrastructure.
- Coastal engineering – design and construction of coastline structures.
- Construction engineering – design, creation and management of constructed structures.
- Geo-engineering – proposed Earth climate control to address global warming.
- Geotechnical engineering – behaviour of earth materials and geology.
- Municipal and public works engineering – for water supply, sanitation, waste management, transportation and communication systems, hydrology.
- Ocean engineering – design and construction of offshore structures.
- Structural engineering – design of structures to support or resist loads.
- Earthquake engineering – behaviour of structures subject to seismic loading.
- Transportation engineering – efficient and safe transportation of people and goods.
- Traffic engineering – transportation and planning.
- Wind engineering – analysis of wind and its effects on the built environment.

Computer and systems engineering

- Research, design and development of computer, computer systems and devices.

Electrical engineering and electronic engineering

- Research, design and development of electrical systems and electronic devices.
- Power systems engineering – bringing electricity to people and industry.

3   Source: http://en.wikipedia.org/wiki/List_of_engineering_branches

Medical use of engineering.

- Signal processing – statistical analysis and production of signals, e.g. for mobile phones.

Environmental engineering

- Engineering for environmental protection and enhancement.
- Water engineering – planning and development of water resources and hydrology

Fire protection engineering

- Protecting people and environments from fire and smoke.

Genetic engineering

- Engineering at the biomolecular level for genetic manipulation.

Industrial engineering

- Analysis, design, development and maintenance of industrial systems and processes.

Instrumentation engineering

- Design and development of instruments used to measure and control systems and processes.

Integrated engineering

- Generalist engineering field including civil, mechanical, electrical and chemical engineering.

Maintenance engineering and asset management

- Maintenance of equipment, physical assets and infrastructure.

Manufacturing engineering

- Research, design and planning of manufacturing systems and processes.
- Component engineering – assuring availability of parts in manufacturing processes

Materials engineering

- Research, design, development and use of materials such as ceramics and nanoparticles.
- Ceramic engineering – theory and processing of oxide and non-oxide ceramics.
- Textile engineering – the manufacturing and processing of fabrics

Mechanical engineering

- Research, design and development of physical or mechanical systems such as engines.
- Automotive engineering – design and construction of terrestrial vehicles.
- Aerospace engineering – design of aircraft, spacecraft and air vehicles.

- Biomechanical engineering – design of systems and devices such as artificial limbs

Mechatronics

- Combination of mechanical, electrical and software engineering for automation systems.

Medical and biomedical engineering

- Increasing use of engineering and technology in medicine and the biological sciences in such areas as monitoring, artificial limbs, medical robotics.

Military engineering

- Design and development of weapons and defence systems.

Mining engineering

- Exploration, extraction and processing of raw materials from the earth.

Naval engineering and architecture

- Research, design, construction and repair of marine vessels.

Nanotechnology and nanoengineering

- New branch of engineering on the nanoscale.

Nuclear engineering

- Research, design and development of nuclear processes and technology.

Production engineering

- Research and design of production systems and processes related to manufacturing engineering.

Software engineering

- Research, design and development of computer software systems and programming.

Sustainable engineering

- Developing branch of engineering focusing on sustainability and climate change mitigation.

Test Engineering

- Engineering validation and verification of design, production and use of objects under test.

Transport Engineering

- Engineering relating to roads, railways, waterways, ports, harbours, airports, gas transmission and distribution, pipelines and so on, and associated works.

Tribology

- Study of interacting surfaces in relative motion including friction, lubrication and wear.

1.2 Engineers, technologists and technicians

Ron Watermayer

Engineering encompasses a vast diversity of fields. It also encompasses a diversity of types and levels of engineer – from engineers in universities more concerned with research and teaching what is sometimes described as the 'engineering sciences' (rather than engineering practice), to practicing, professional and consulting engineers, to engineering technologists and technicians. These are fluid concepts. As engineering changes, so does the idea and definition of what it means to be an engineer. There is also a significant overlap; many involved in the engineering sciences also practice and consult. Definitions of engineers, technologists and technicians also differ around the world.

In the United Kingdom, for example, the UK Inter Professional Group defines a profession as 'an occupation in which an individual uses an intellectual skill based on an established body of knowledge and practice to provide a specialised service in a defined area, exercising independent judgment in accordance with a code of ethics and in the public interest." The engineering profession shapes the built environment, which may be defined as "the collection of man-made or induced physical objects located in a particular area or region."[4] It creates the physical world that has been intentionally created through science and technology for the benefit of mankind.

The UK Institution of Civil Engineers reports that the purpose of regulating a profession is 'to assure the quality of professional services in the public interest. The regulation of a profession involves the setting of standards of professional qualifications and practice; the keeping of a register of qualified persons and the award of titles; determining the conduct of registrants, the investigation of complaints and disciplinary sanctions for professional misconduct.'[5]

There are a number of approaches to the regulation of a profession around the world. Broadly speaking, these include:

- Licensing: to authorize eligible persons to practise in a specific area.

- Registration: to recognize demonstrated achievement of a defined standard of competency.

- Specialist lists: to indicate peer-recognized competence in a particular area.

All these forms of regulation are linked to codes of conduct. Serious breaches of a code of conduct can lead to the withdrawal of a license, the loss of a title or the removal of the transgressor's name from a specialist list, either on a temporary or permanent basis.

Engineering qualifications and professional registration with regulatory bodies may in many countries be categorized as falling into one of three generic tracks, namely:

- Engineer
- Engineering Technologist
- Engineering Technician

The precise names of the titles awarded to registered persons may differ from country to country, e.g. the Engineering Council UK registers the three tracks as Chartered Engineer, Incorporated Engineer and Technician Engineer, whereas Engineers Ireland registers Chartered Engineer, Associate Engineer and Engineering Technician. In some countries, only the engineer or the engineer and engineering technologist tracks are registered. In others, the registration of engineering technicians has only recently been embarked upon.

Other approaches can also be taken. Researchers at Duke University in the USA[6] have put forward a slightly different view regarding engineering tracks:

- Dynamic Engineers: those capable of abstract thinking, solving high level-problems using scientific knowledge, thrive in teams, work well across international borders, have strong interpersonal skills and are capable of leading innovation.

- Transactional Engineers: possess engineering fundamentals but are not seen to have the experience or expertise to apply this knowledge to complex problems.

The Duke University researchers observed that one of the key differentiators of the two types of engineers is their education. Most dynamic engineers have as a minimum a four-year engineering degree from nationally accredited or highly regarded institutions whereas transactional engineers often obtain a sub-baccalaureate degree (associate, technician or diploma awards) rather than a Bachelor's degree, in less than four years but in more than one. They do however point out that educational background is not a hard and fast rule because in the

---

4   ISO 15392

5   Study Group on Licensing, Registration and Specialist Lists (2005)

6   Report on Framing the Engineering Outsourcing Debate: Placing the U.S. on a Level Playing Field with China and India, 2005. http://www.soc.duke.edu/globalengineering/papers_outsourcing.php (Accessed: 10 August 2010)

last fifty years a number of science and technology leaders have emerged with little or no traditional education.

How many engineers, technologists and engineers does a country require?

The engineering profession plays a major role not only in the growth and development of a country's economy but also in improving the quality of life for its citizens. The engineering profession is also playing an ever-increasing role in enabling a country to participate in the global economy and in the protection of the environment. The linkage between a country's indigenous engineering capacity and its economic development is understood. It is also understood that more engineering professionals will be required to address the sustainable development issues of the day – for example, the development of renewable energy sources, advancements in technology, solutions for sustaining the environment and improving healthcare. What is not understood is how many engineers, technologists and technicians are required to drive economic growth and sustainable development objectives within a country.

There is no simple answer to this question as it is not simply a numbers game; more engineering professionals are needed if the number of engineers, engineering technologists and engineering technicians per capita is below the figures of a country's competitors. Furthermore, increasing the number of engineering graduates is not necessarily a solution as there may be a shortfall in the job market for such graduates or the attractiveness of other non-engineering professions requiring problem-solving skills might entice graduates away from engineering. These issues are discussed later in this Report.

Three main approaches to professional regulation:

1) Licensing: In this approach, an area of engineering work is linked to those persons who have demonstrated competence to perform such work. Licensing on a statutory basis prohibits unlicensed persons from performing such work. Non-statutory licensing provides the public with lists of persons competent to perform work within an area of engineering, which may also be undertaken by non-licensed persons.

2) Registration: In this approach, those persons who demonstrate their competence against a standard and undertake to abide by a code of conduct, are awarded titles and are admitted to a register. Such registration may be governed by the laws of a country (statutory register) or the regulations or the rules set by the governing body of the profession, which oversees the registration process and maintains the register (non-statutory register). Where governing bodies operate non-statutory registration, they may only use civil action to prevent non-registrants from using the title and are not empowered to restrict any area of work to registrants. (Statutory registration linked to the reserving of an area of work for registered persons has the same effect as statutory licensing.)

3) Specialist lists: In this approach, a professional or trade body administers a non-statutory voluntary listing of professionals who have met a defined standard of competence in a specialist area.

Engineering professional tracks

The 'engineer' track is typically aimed at those who will:
- use a combination of general and specialist engineering knowledge and understanding to optimize the application of existing and emerging technology;
- aply appropriate theoretical and practical methods to the analysis and solution of engineering problems;
- provide technical, commercial and managerial leadership;
- undertake the management of high levels of risk associated with engineering processes, systems, equipment, and infrastructure; and
- perform activities that are essentially intellectual in nature, requiring discretion and judgement.

The 'engineering technologist' track is typically aimed at those who will:
- exercise independent technical judgement at an appropriate level;
- assume responsibility, as an individual or as a member of a team, for the management of resources and / or guidance of technical staff;
- design, develop, manufacture, commission, operate and maintain products, equipment, processes and services;
- actively participate in financial, statutory and commercial considerations and in the creation of cost effective systems and procedures; and
- undertake the management of moderate levels of risks associated with engineering processes, systems, equipment and infrastructure.

The 'engineering technician' track is typically aimed at those who are involved in applying proven techniques and procedures to the solution of practical engineering problems. They:
- carry supervisory or technical responsibility;
- are competent to exercise creative aptitudes and skills within defined fields of technology;
- contribute to the design, development, manufacture, commissioning, operation or maintenance of products, equipment, processes or services; and
- create and apply safe systems of work.

2 Engineering and Human Development

The development and application of knowledge in engineering and technology underpins and drives sustainable social and economic development. Engineering and technology are vital in addressing basic human needs, poverty reduction and sustainable development, and to bridge the 'knowledge divide'. This chapter focuses on the vital role of engineering and innovation in human, social and economic development. It includes a very short history of engineering, referring particularly to engineering education and how the history of engineering has affected its future. The history of engineering at UNESCO discusses how the engineering sciences programme was once the largest activity in the Natu-ral Sciences Sector at UNESCO, but declined with the rise of the environmental sciences, and is now hopefully poised for a resurgence in recognition of the importance of engineering as a core and underpinning an area of knowledge application and innovation in such areas as climate change mitigation and adaptation. This chapter includes sections on engineering, technology and society, engineers and their social responsibility in such areas as military technology and pollution on the one hand, and the design and construction of environmentally sustainable infrastructure, living and working spaces on the other, as well as the broader corporate social responsibility of engineers and engineering.

2.1 History of engineering; engineering at UNESCO

Tony Marjoram

2.1.1 A very short history of engineering

The history of engineering in the context of the way we live, and interact with nature and each other is very much the history and pre-history of humanity itself. Human beings are partly defined as tool designers and users, and it is this innovation and the design and use of tools that accounts for so much of the direction and pace of change of history. Most of the broader history of civilization, of economic and social relations, is also the history of engineering, engineering applications and innovation. The Stone Age, Bronze Age, Iron Age, Steam Age and Information Age all relate to engineering and innovation shaping our interaction with the world; 'the Stone Age did not end because we ran out of stones!' The Pyramids, Borobudur, El Mirador, the civilizations linked to metal smelting at Zimbabwe and water engineering at Angkor, the medieval cathedrals and Industrial Revolution are all testament to the engineering skills of past generations. Engineering is also vital in the surveying and conservation of our cultural heritage; the famous work of UNESCO in conserving Borobudur and Abu Simbel were essentially engineering projects.

The history of engineering as a profession, where payment is made in cash or kind for services, began with tool- and weapon-making over 150,000 years ago – indicating that engineering is one of the oldest professions. Military engineering was soon joined by civil engineering in the quest for defence and development of early infrastructure. The professionalization of engineering is illustrated by Imhotep who built the Step Pyramid at Saqqara in 3000 BC and was one of the few commoner mortals to be accorded divine status after his death. Engineering professionalization continued with the development of craft and guild knowledge, and the formalization of associated knowledge and education. Simple patriarchal forms of engineering education existing in ancient societies developed into vocational technical schools of different types in the Middle Ages and particularly during the Renaissance and the Scientific Revolution of the sixteenth and seventeeth centuries. Leonardo da Vinci, for example, had the official title of *Ingegnere Generale* and his notebooks reveal an increasing engineering interest in how things worked. Galileo Galilei developed the scientific approach and method to the understanding of the natural world and analysis of practical problems – a landmark in the development of engineering, mathematical representation, structural analysis and design that continued into

Figure 1: **Waves of Innovation**

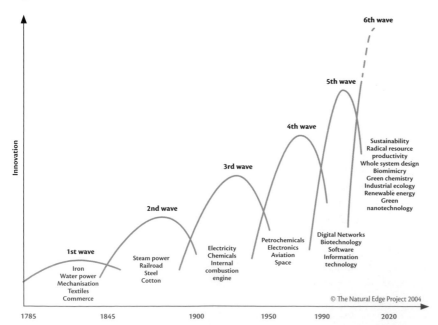

© The Natural Edge Project 2004

the Industrial Revolution – and the replacement of muscle by machines in the production process.

Engineering powered the so-called Industrial Revolution that really took off in the United Kingdom in the eighteenth century spreading to Europe, North America and the world, replacing muscle by machine in a synergistic combination between knowledge and capital. The first Industrial Revolution took place from 1750–1850 and focused on the textile industry. The second Industrial Revolution focused on steam and the railways from 1850–1900 and the third Industrial Revolution was based on steel, electricity and heavy engineering from 1875–1925. This was followed by the fourth Industrial Revolution based on oil, the automobile and mass production, taking place between 1900–1950 and onward, and the fifth phase was based on information and telecommunications and the post-war boom from 1950. These waves of innovation and industrial development have become known as Kondratiev waves, K-waves, long waves, supercycles or surges, and relate to cycles in the world economy of around fifty years duration consisting of alternating periods of high and low sectoral growth. Most analysts accept the 'Schumpeter-Freeman-Perez' paradigm of five waves of innovation since the first Industrial Revolution, although the precise dates, phases, causes and effects of these major changes are hotly debated, as is the nature of the sixth wave based on new knowledge production and application in such fields as IT, biotechnology and materials beginning around 1980, and the possible seventh wave based on sustainable 'green' engineering and technology seen to have begun around 2005.

A very short history of engineering education

The most crucial period in the development of engineering were the eighteenth and nineteenth centuries particularly the Iron and Steam Ages the second Kondratiev wave of innovation and successive industrial revolutions. Early interest in the development of engineering education took place in Germany in the mining industry, with the creation in 1702 of a school of mining and metallurgy in Freiberg. One of the oldest technical universities is the Czech Technical University in Prague founded in 1707. In France, engineering education developed with the creation of the *École Nationale des Ponts et Chaussées* (1747) and *École des Mines* (1783). The *École Polytechnique*, the first technical university in Europe teaching the foundations of mathematics and science, was established in 1794 during the French Revolution – the revolution in engineering education itself began during a 'revolution'. Under Napoleon's influence, France developed the system of formal schooling in engineering after the Revolution, and engineering education in France has retained a strong theoretical and military character. The French model influenced the development of polytechnic engineering education institutions around the world at the beginning of the nineteenth century, especially in Germany in Berlin, Karlsruhe, Munich, Dresden,

Stuttgart, Hanover and Darmstadt between 1799 and 1831. In Russia, similar schools of technology were opened in Moscow (1825) and St. Petersburg (1831) based on a system of military engineering education. The first technical institutes appeared at the same time in the USA including West Point in 1819 (modelled on the *École Polytechnique*), the Rensselaer School in 1823 and Ohio Mechanics Institute in 1828. In Germany, polytechnic schools were accorded the same legal foundations as universities.

In Britain, however, engineering education was initially based on a system of apprenticeship with a working engineer following the early years of the Industrial Revolution when many engineers had little formal or theoretical training. Men such as Arkwright, Hargreaves, Crompton and Newcomen, followed by Telford, George and Robert Stephenson and Maudslay, all had little formal engineering education but developed the technologies that powered the Industrial Revolution and changed the world. In many fields, practical activity preceded scientific understanding; we had steam engines before thermodynamics, and 'rocket science' is more about engineering than science. Britain tried to retain this lead by prohibiting the export of engineering goods and services in the early 1800s, which is why countries in continental Europe developed their own engineering education systems based on French and German models with a foundation in science and mathematics rather than the British model based on artisanal empiricism and laissez-faire professional development. Through the nineteenth and into the twentieth centuries however, engineering education in Britain also changed toward a science- and university-based system and the rise of the 'engineering sciences', partly in recognition of the increasingly close connection between engineering, science and mathematics, and partly due to fears that Britain was lagging behind the European model in terms of international competition.

By the end of the nineteenth century, most of the now industrialized countries had established their own engineering education systems based on the French and German 'Humboldtian' model. In the twentieth century, the professionalization of engineering continued with the development of professional societies, journals, meetings, conferences, and the professional accreditation of exams, qualifications and universities, facilitating education, the flow of information and continued professional development. These processes will continue with the development of international agreements relating to accreditation and the mutual recognition of engineering qualifications and professional competence, which include the Washington Accord (1989), Sydney Accord (2001), Dublin Accord (2002), APEC Engineer (1999), Engineers Mobility Forum (2001) and the Engineering Technologist Mobility Forum (2003), and the 1999 Bologna Declaration relating to quality assurance and accreditation of bachelor and master programmes in Europe.

© Hochtief

⸫ *Engineering constructs and preserves our heritage, as at Abu Simbel.*

How engineering's history affects its future

The Humboldtian model is also, ironically, one of the factors that lead to the contemporary decline of interest in engineering at university level; the fact that the mathematical base is regarded as too abstract, out of touch, hard work and boring by many young people. This is turn has lead to a questioning of the Humboldtian model and increasing interest in problem- and activity-based learning. The Humboldtian model also underpins the linear model of innovation. The linear model of innovation is the first and major conceptual model of the relation between science and technology, and economic development. This model has become the accepted worldview of innovation and is at the heart of science and technology policy, although the linear model of innovation overlooks engineering, to the continued discredit of engineering in the context of science and technology policy. The model is based on the Humboldtian notion that pure, disinterested, basic scientific research, followed by applied research and development, leads to knowledge applications, production and diffusion. While the precise origins of the model are unclear, many accredit Vannevar Bush's *Science: The Endless Frontier* published in 1945. This reflects particularly on the role of science (rather than engineering) in wartime success, underpinned by statistics based on and reinforcing the linear model. This became the model for peacetime economic development as embodied in the Marshall Plan and later the OECD and its work on Science and Technology indicators, despite various criticisms (e.g. that the linear model overlooks engineering), modifications, alternative models and claims that the linear model is dead (Godin, 2005).[1]

Engineering therefore has a particular need to overcome the Humboldtian notions underlying the 'fundamentals' approach to education and linear model of innovation, and to position itself more effectively in the development dialogue and bring fun into the fundamentals of engineering education through such approaches as problem-based learning. For the future of engineering, an obvious goal is the need to focus specifically on the important role engineering will play in addressing the UN Millennium Development Goals, especially poverty reduction and sustainable development, and the vital role of engineering in climate change mitigation and adaptation in the development of sustainable, green, eco-engineering and associated design, technology, production and distribution systems and infrastructure. Fortunately, the promotion of public understanding and interest in engineering is facilitated by presenting engineering as a part of the problem-solving solution to sustainable development and poverty reduction.

The usefulness of promoting the relevance of engineering to address contemporary concerns and help link engineering with society in the context of related ethical issues, sustainable development and poverty reduction is demonstrated by the growth of Engineers Without Borders and similar groups around the world, and such activities as the Daimler-UNESCO Mondialogo Engineering Award, which attract students through its connection to poverty reduction and sustainable development and appeals to the urge of youth to 'do something' to help those in need. University courses can be made more interesting through the transformation of curricula and pedagogy using such information and experience in more activity-, project- and problem-based learning, just-in-time approaches and hands-on application, and less formulaic approaches that turn students off. In short, relevance works! Science and engineering have changed the world, but are professionally conservative and slow to change. We need innovative examples of schools, colleges and universities around the world that have pioneered activity in such areas as problem-based learning. The future of the world is in the hands of young engineers and we need to give them as much help as we can in facing the challenges of the future.

2.1.2   Engineering at UNESCO

Engineering was part of UNESCO from the beginning. It was the intention of the founders of UNESCO that the 'S' refer to science and technology, and that this include the applied sciences, technological sciences and engineering. The engineering and technological sciences have always played a significant role in the Natural Sciences Sector at UNESCO. Indeed, UNESCO was established during a conference that took place in London in November 1945 at the Institution of Civil Engineers – the oldest engineering institution in the world. This reflects the stark realization and emphasis of the importance of science, engineering and technology in the Second World War when many new fields and applications were developed in such areas as materials, aeronautics, systems analysis and project management, as well as the success of the Marshall Plan to rebuild capacity and infrastructure after the war. This emphasis was mirrored in the support for programme activities at UNESCO by other UN agencies of the basic, applied and engineering sciences and technology (before the development of operational activities by UNDP in the mid-1980s).

Background

In the history of the engineering and technological sciences at UNESCO, it is interesting to note the similarities and resonances between the programme priorities in engineering today and those of the 1960s, 1970s and intervening years. It is also interesting to note the importance of engineering in those earlier years when engineering was the biggest activity in the Science Sector – in terms of personnel and budget – before the rise of the environmental sciences. There has also been long-term interest in renewable energy, beginning with an international congress in 1973. There has been close cooperation with the social sciences in the field of science and society

◑ *Mondialogo Engineering Award project from Japan and Nepal on low-cost food.*

© Mondialogo

---

1   B. Godin. 2005. *Measurement and Statistics on Science and Technology: 1920 to the Present*, London: Routledge.

with the journal *Impact of Science on Society*, which was published from 1967–1992. The reform of engineering education and the need for greater interdisciplinarity and intersectoral cooperation, women and gender issues in engineering, innovation and the development of endogenous technologies are other recurrent themes, and are as important today as they were in the 1970s. It is also interesting to note that programme activities appear to have been more interdisciplinary twenty years ago than they are today.

Apart from these similarities, there are of course differences between programme activities over the last forty years and also differences in definition and context over time and in different places, for example the meaning behind 'engineering', the 'engineering sciences' and 'technology' (which today is often narrowly regarded as synonymous with Information and Communication Technologies, ICTs). The difficulties of defining 'engineering' and 'engineering science', and of engineers, technologists and technicians, is illustrated by the discussions over the Bologna Accord in 1999 regarding the harmonization of graduate and postgraduate education in Europe by 2010 (in Germany, for example, there are over forty definitions of an engineer). This problem is therefore not unique to UNESCO but is faced by society and governments around the world.

The context of 'development' has also changed, although development specialists continue generally to overlook the role of engineering and technology in development at all levels at the macroeconomic level and at the grass roots where small, affordable technologies can make a tremendous difference to people's lives and poverty reduction. This, again, is not unique to UNESCO. Most development specialists have a background in economics and continue to view the world in terms of the three classical factors of production: capital, labour and natural resources, where knowledge, in the form of engineering, science and technology, are not easily accommodated. This is unfortunate given the obvious importance of engineering, science and technology in development, particularly in the Industrial Revolution for example, as recognized by some commentators at the time and in the work of economists such as Schumpeter and Freeman on the role of knowledge and innovation in economic change, and the fact that we now live in 'knowledge societies'.

The context of UNESCO has also changed from the early days when engineering was the main activity area in the Science Sector (largely supported by UNDP special funding) to the decline of such funding for engineering and the sector in terms of both personnel and budget. UNESCO faced a crisis from the mid-1980s with the decline of UN funding and the withdrawal of the United States and UK in 1984, and the consequent budget cut of 25 per cent. UNESCO has not really recovered from this cut as the budget has remained constant, even with the return of the UK in 1997 and the United States in 2003.

Engineering programme

The engineering programme at UNESCO, as the main programme in the Science Sector until the 1980s, has been active in a diverse range of initiatives and include the implementation of multi-million dollar projects supported by UN special funds, project development and fund raising, networking, cooperation and support of international professional organizations and NGOs, conferences and symposia, training, workshops and seminars, information and publications, consultancy and advisory activities and programme activity areas (including engineering education and energy). The primary focus of the engineering programme, until the late 1980s, was on core areas of engineering education (what would now be called human and institutional capacity-building), where the emphasis turned increasingly toward renewable energy (see later). The focus on core areas of engineering education and capacity-building is presently returning with the new millennia (albeit with much less human and financial resources). Much of this activity was conducted in close cooperation with the five main science field offices, which were established to facilitate implementation of projects supported by the UNDP special funds. With the decline of funds in the 1990s, the field network has declined with fewer specialists in engineering in the field and at headquarters.

The field of energy was an increasing emphasis in the engineering programme that developed in the late 1970s and 1980s. Energy activity at UNESCO began effectively in the early 1970s with the International Congress on the 'Sun in the Service of Mankind', held in Paris in 1973, organized by UNESCO with WMO, WHO and ISES (the International Solar Energy Society), when the International Solar Energy Commission was also created. In the late 1980s and 1990s interest on renewable energy continued with the creation of the World Solar Programme (WSP), during the 1996–2005, and associated World Solar Commission (WSC), which clearly borrowed from the earlier activity of ISES. It is useful to note that WSP/WSC activity accounted for a total of over US$4 million of UNESCO funds, with over US$1 million alone supporting WSP/WSC activity in Zimbabwe, including the World Solar Summit held in Harare in 1996 that lead to the creation of the World Solar Programme and World Solar Commission chaired by President Mugabe. Declining funds in the late 1980s and 1990s gave rise to increasing creativity. Unfortunately, the historical record for the World Solar Programme and World Solar Commission is lost as all programme files disappeared at the end of 2000. This is discussed in *Sixty Years of Science at UNESCO 1945–2005* (UNESCO, 2006).[2]

From the early 1960s until the late 1980s the engineering programme – the largest of the three activity areas of in the Natural Sciences Sector – peaked with over ten staff at head-

© Mondialogo

◯ *Mondialogo Engineering Award project from Malaysia and India on bio-solar technology.*

2   Go to: http://upo.unesco.org/details.aspx?Code_Livre=4503 (Accessed: 29 May 2010)

⌒ *Adobe building is an early example of civil engineering.*

quarters, another ten staff in five main regional field offices that were developed over this period, and a budget of up to US$30 million per biennium. A diverse range of activities and initiatives were implemented, including the establishment and support of engineering departments at universities, research centres, standards institutions and similar bodies in numerous countries. Most of this activity is what we would now call human and institutional capacity-building. It is therefore interesting to reflect on the current emphasis on technical capacity-building and the lessons we may learn from the past.

Engineering programme activities

The engineering programme at UNESCO has focused essentially on two areas of activity: engineering education and capacity-building, and the application of engineering and technology to development, including such specific issues as the Millennium Development Goals (especially poverty reduction and sustainable development) and, most recently, climate change mitigation and adaptation. Overall activities include networking, cooperation and the support of joint activities with international professional organizations and NGOs, and the organization, presentation and support of conferences and symposia, workshops and seminars, as well as the production of information and learning/teaching materials, identification and commissioning of publications, project development and fundraising.

Other programme activities that have continued since the establishment of engineering in UNESCO include expert advisory and consultancy services. In recent times this includes participation in the UN Millennium Project Task Force 10 on Science, Technology and Innovation, and a contribution to the TF10 report *Innovation: Applying Knowledge in Development*. Pilot projects have also been supported, most notably relating to energy, with mixed results. Interest in the promotion of university-industry cooperation and innovation developed at UNESCO in the early 1990s reflecting increasing academic interest, and the university-industry-science partnership (UNISPAR) programme was created by the engineering programme in 1993. This activity included an innovative International Fund for the Technological Development of Africa (IFTDA), which was established with an investment of US$1 million and supported the development of many small-scale innovations before the IFTDA project was closed as the capital was required for other priorities.

Networking, international professional organizations and NGOs

The engineering programme has been continuously active in the development and support of networking, international organizations and NGOs in engineering, and helped create the World Federation of Engineering Organizations, the main 'umbrella' organization for national and regional engineering institutions and associations in 1968. UNESCO also helped create such regional organizations as the Federation of Engineering Institutions in SE Asia and the Pacific (FEISEAP, which continues as FEIAP), the Association of Engineering Education in South East Asia and the Pacific (AEESEAP) and the African Network of Scientific and Technical Institutions (ANSTI) in 1979. Network support activity continues with UNESCO supporting networking activities for technology and development, Engineers Without Borders, Engineers Against Poverty, Engineering for a Sustainable World and the International Network for Engineering Studies.

Conferences and symposia, workshops and seminars

The organization and support of various international and regional conferences and symposia is an important and long-term activity of the engineering programme, usually in cooperation with WFEO. Most recently the programme was involved in organizing and supporting the 2008 World Engineers' Convention (WEC 2008) in Brazil. This followed on from WEC 2004 in Shanghai and the first World Engineers' Convention, WEC 2000, in Hanover. The engineering programme was particularly active in the organization and presentation of training and seminars in the 1960s–1980s with UNDP Special Funds. Although this activity has inevitably declined since those golden years, there has been a recent resurgence that includes conferences and workshops on engineering and innovation, sustainable development, poverty reduction, engineering policy and planning, gender issues in engineering, standards and accreditation. Activities are being planned on technology and climate change mitigation and adaptation, and an international engineering congress is to be held in Buenos Aires in 2010 and the 2011 World Engineers' Convention (WEC 2011) 'Engineers Power the World: Facing the Global Energy Challenge' is to be held in Geneva.

Information and publications

The production of information and publications, in hard cover and electronic formats, is a vital part of capacity-building, and the engineering programme continues to be very active in this domain. Important early activities included the development of the UN Information System for Science and Technology (UNISIST) programme, based at UNESCO, publication of the first international directory of new and renewable energy information sources and research centres in 1982, and the UNESCO Energy Engineering Series with John Wiley beginning in the 1990s (some titles are still in print and others have been reprinted). More recent publications include *Small is Working: Technology for Poverty Reduction* and *Rays of Hope: Renewable Energy in the Pacific*, which also included short film productions. UNESCO toolkits of learning and teaching materials also published by UNESCO Publishing include *Solar Photovoltaic Project Development* and *Solar Photovoltaic Systems: Technical Training Manual, Technology Business Incubators* (this has proved so popular it has almost sold out and has been translated and published in Chinese, Japanese and Farsi) and *Gender Indicators in Science, Engineering and Technology*. The establishment of the Sudan Virtual Engineering Library project at the University of Khartoum has also been most successful; serving as a mirror service for the MIT Open Courseware project in Sudan, forming part of the open courseware programme of the University of Khartoum and a model for the Sudanese Universities Virtual Library. Several publications are in press, including forthcoming titles on technology policy and poverty reduction, innovation and development.

Project development and fundraising

Engineering programme staff have long been active in the development of new project proposals; in the earlier days primarily for UNDP funding. More recent project development activity includes the Daimler-UNESCO Mondialogo Engineering Award – one of the three pillars of the UNESCO partnership with Daimler to promote intercultural dialogue, in this case between young engineers and the preparation of project proposals to address poverty reduction, sustainable development and the MDGs. Proposals that did not go forward include a low-orbit satellite project designed to promote education in Africa using Russian military rockets to launch satellites (an idea borrowed from Volunteers in Technical Assistance in the USA, which they continued to develop with limited success, leading to the near collapse of VITA in 2001 and transformation into the Volunteers for Prosperity initiative in 2003 under President Bush), and a proposal for a World Technological University.

↻ *Easter Island is also an engineering achievement.*

The rise and fall of engineering and prospects for resurgence

Engineering at UNESCO rose in the early years to be the largest of the three initial and continuing theme areas of UNESCO, together with the basic sciences and the environmental and ecological sciences. Over the last fifty years the engineering programme has had around one hundred professional and support staff, a regular programme budget of over US$50 million and extra-budgetary funding of over US$200 million (mainly UNDP special funds in the mid-1960s to the early 1990s). Engineering at UNESCO began to decline in real terms in the 1990s (in terms of staff and budget), which reflected the decline of the Science Sector and indeed of UNESCO over this period, and was attributed to various external and internal factors. The 1980s marked a general decline in overseas aid, the withdrawal of the US and the UK in 1984 that precipitated a funding crisis in UNESCO, the fall of the Berlin Wall in 1989 that led to the end of the Cold War and changing international climate, and UNDP special funds began to decline from the late 1980s with the establishment and development of the Operations Division of UNDP. There were also various internal factors at UNESCO. The Natural Sciences Sector is perhaps the least well understood sector in UNESCO, and engineering – for various reasons – is less well understood than science. Engineering is distinct from science, though it is considered as part of science in UNESCO, and with a declining science budget, science issues, priorities and 'science' policy have tended to predominate (even though engineering policy is a significant part of science policy, as discussed in section 4.5.2). This situation reflects the limited numbers of scientists and engineers in the decision-making bodies of UNESCO such as the Executive Board and General Conference where education interests tend to predominate. In this way, the status and challenges faced by engineering at UNESCO mirrors those faced by engineering in governments, organizations and societies worldwide.

Other internal factors leading to the decline of engineering at UNESCO include the choice of programme priorities based on personal interaction and lobbying rather than a strategic approach based on broader policy issues and a more democratic determination of needs and priorities. This was compounded in the late 1980s and 1990s by the focus on the World Solar Programme. While the idea to focus is eminently understandable, adequate human and financial resources and significant substantive results are required, and should not be to the exclusion of other programme interests, otherwise programme activities may become theme areas with little real substance, peripheral to core engineering issues, with the risk, perhaps not surprising, of limited programme achievements. This contributed significantly to the decline of engineering and the administrative merger of engineering into the Basic and Engineering Sciences Division in 2002, with obvious potential consequences for the future of engineering in UNESCO. It is clear that the programmes in UNESCO, with the most secure budgets and effective lobbying, are those linked to international and intergovernmental programmes such as the Man and the Biosphere Programme (created in 1971), the International Hydrological Programme (1975) and the Intergovernmental Oceanographic Commission (1960). While this advantage for programmes to have such an international background is acknowledged, there is also a disinclination to create new international programmes due to human and financial resource constraints.

In this context, it is certainly noteworthy that a proposal for a feasibility study for an 'International Engineering Programme' was made by South Africa and adopted with significant support in the 2009 General Conference and Executive Board as part of the effort to continue and develop engineering activities at UNESCO into the new millennium (which itself has significant external support). This follows and reinforces a proposal from the United States for the development of 'Cross-Sectoral Activities in Technical Capacity Building', presented to and approved unanimously at the Executive Board in April 2005, in order to focus on capacity-building in the basic sciences and mathematics, engineering and the water sciences (with a focus in engineering on activities that included 'strengthening of the existing engineering programme, including training educators for developing countries, support of workshops for educators in curriculum development, best practices, and quality assurance, and development of appropriate collaborations with industry.' This was the first proposal from the United States since its return to UNESCO in 2003. It is to be hoped that these proposals will support a resurgence and strengthening of engineering in UNESCO and around the world, with the development of international programme activities in capacity-building and engineering applications for poverty reduction and sustainable development, climate change mitigation and adaptation. UNESCO has a unique mandate and mission in the natural sciences, including engineering and technology, to assist Member States, and especially developing countries.

Mondialogo Engineering Award – promoting cooperation for development

The Mondialogo Partnership

The Mondialogo Engineering Award is part of a partnership initiative that was launched by DaimlerChrysler (as it then was) and UNESCO in 2003. The overall aim of the Mondialogo partnership is to promote international cooperation, dialogue and understanding among young people around the world to promote living together and as a basis for developing mutual understanding, respect and tolerance. The partnership has its origins in a discussion between DaimlerChrysler and the German National Commission for UNESCO regarding possible activity to promote intercultural dialogue and understanding. This included reference to the Associated Schools Project of UNESCO, related with other possible activities at the tertiary/university level. Following an internal request for proposals an 'Intercultural Dialogue through Engineering Applications' (IDEA) project was proposed by the Engineering Programme of UNESCO, creating a link between a company built on quality engineering and the UN organization responsible for science and engineering. The proposal was agreed and the Mondialogo initiative developed.

The Mondialogo initiative consists of three pillars: the Mondialogo Engineering Award; the Mondialogo Schools Contest; and the supporting Mondialogo Internet Portal. The Mondialogo Engineering Award promotes cooperation between student engineers at universities around the world, with a focus on the development of engineering project proposals between universities in developing and developed countries that address poverty reduction, sustainability, the other UN Millennium Development Goals and climate change mitigation and adaptation. The Mondialogo School Contest is for school students between fourteen and eighteen years of age, with a focus on developing projects around one of three core themes: peace, sports and fair play, elimination of discrimination; sustainable future; identity and respect for cultural diversity. The multilingual Mondialogo Internet Portal complements and supports these project activities with an internationally accessible information and dialogue platform focusing on intercultural exchange. Since 2003, there have been three rounds each of the Schools Contest and Engineering Award, with the first round of the Mondialogo Engineering Award in 2004–2005, the second in 2006–2007 and the third in 2008–2009. Over this time, the Mondialogo partnership has itself won several awards as an exemplar of corporate social responsibility and public-private partnership in the promotion of international cooperation and dialogue among young people.

The Mondialogo Engineering Award

The Mondialogo Engineering Award is in essence a design exercise for student engineers from developing and developed countries who form international teams and develop project proposals together. The projects must address issues of poverty, sustainable development and climate

Mondialogo Engineering Award medals.

change. One of the driving ideas is that international cooperation on such projects is one of the best ways to promote intercultural dialogue and understanding.

Each round of the Award has commenced with an advertising campaign and mailout of posters and information to every university with an engineering faculty around the world. Interested student engineers were encouraged to form local university teams and were invited to register themselves and any ideas they had for possible project proposals on the Mondialogo website. They then formed international teams of at least two local teams from developing and developed country universities, and registered projects on which they would work to produce proposals for submission to the Award. Project proposals were then developed collaboratively by the teams over the course of around six months. The available time period was complicated by the fact that universities in the southern and northern hemispheres have different academic years, examination schedules and periods when students have more or less time.

Project proposals were then developed and submitted, short-listed and finalised by an independent Jury. The project proposals are assessed on criteria of technical excellence, focus on poverty reduction, sustainable development and the UN Millennium Development Goals, feasibility and demonstration of intercultural dialogue between teams within each project group. Each round of the Award concluded with a Mondialogo Engineering Award Symposium and Ceremony. These have taken place in Berlin in 2005, Mumbai in 2007 and Stuttgart in 2009. The Award Symposium is considered an important component of

Mondialogo Engineering Award finalists.

Mondialogo Engineering Award – promoting cooperation for development *(continuation)*

the Award activity enabling representatives of the finalist teams of young engineers to present their project proposals to the other finalists, the Daimler and UNESCO organizers, Jury members and the media. The Symposium was followed by a Mondialogo Award Ceremony where the Awards were presented.

The 2009 Award – pursuing dreams into reality

The 2009 Award Ceremony was hosted by Daimler CEO, Dieter Zetsche, and Walter Erdelen, Assistant Director-General for Natural Sciences at UNESCO, at the Daimler Museum in Stuttgart, and featured a keynote presentation by Lewis Hamilton, the youngest ever Formula One World Champion in 2008. Hamilton's informal comments were moving, encouraging and very inspirational, and emphasized the vital role engineers play in F1, and how young engineers should pursue their commitment and translate their dreams into reality – as he had done himself – to create solutions to some of the most serious problems facing the world. One of the young engineers later reported that the whole cooperative design process, award symposium and ceremony, including Hamilton's comments, just 'blew my mind' – underlining the importance of activities and events that one can sometimes overlook when in the midst of things. One of the judges also mentioned that the commitment of the students almost brought a tear to his eye. Their commitment is most reassuring – as our future is indeed in their hands!

Thirty gold, silver and bronze Mondialogo Engineering Awards were presented at the Award Ceremony worth a total of €300,000. The prize money is intended to help facilitate and implement the proposed projects, although it is apparent that most of the students participate because they think it is a good thing to do. This is evident in the many weblogs of project proposals from the 2009 and previous awards that are being implemented. The diverse range of engineering project proposals addressing world problems was truly impressive and included proposals focusing on water supply and sanitation, waste management, food production and processing housing and shelter, transportation and mobility, energy, emergency, disaster response and reconstruction and multi-sector proposals.

Organization of the Award

The Mondialogo Engineering Award (MEA) is organized and managed by the Engineering Programme at UNESCO and Corporate Sponsorship department at Daimler, supported by Daimler's communications consultant, Experience (formerly Schmidt und Kaiser).

The Mondialogo Engineering Award Jury, who selected the winners from the shortlist, was co-chaired by Herbert Kohler, Vice-President E-Drive and Future Mobility and Chief Environmental Office at Daimler, and Walter Erdelen, Assistant Director-General for Natural Sciences at UNESCO, and included Peggy Oti-Boateng from the Technology Consultancy Centre at the University of Kumasi in Ghana, Shirley Malcom from the American Association for the Advancement of Science, Ali Uddin Ansari from the Centre for Environment Studies and Socio-responsive Engineering at Muffakham Jah College in Hyderabad, Paul Jowitt from Heriot-Watt University in Edinburgh, and Barry Grear, President of the World Federation of Engineering Organizations (who succeeded previous Presidents Kamel Ayadi and Dato Lee Yee Chong).

Between 2004 and 2009 nearly 10,000 engineering students from more than half the countries in the world took part in the Mondialogo Engineering Award. In the 2008–2009 Award, thirty winning proposals were selected from ninety-seven project proposals from student teams in fifty-five countries with a total of 932 registered project ideas from nearly 4,000 student engineers in ninety-four countries. There were eight gold, twelve silver and ten bronze awards, worth €15,000, €10,000 and €5,000 respectively (a total of €300,000), with one Contin-

uation and one Community Award. In the second Award in 2006–2007, thirty award winners were selected from ninety-two project proposals from student teams in fifty-four countries with a total of 809 registered project ideas from over 3,000 student engineers in eighty-nine countries. There were ten Mondialogo Engineering Awards and twenty Honourable mentions, each worth €10,000 and €5,000 respectively, and one Continuation Award. In the first Mondialogo Engineering Award in 2004–2005, twenty-one winning proposals were selected from student teams in twenty-five countries with a total of 111 project proposals submitted by 412 teams from 1,700 student engineers in seventy-nine countries. Twenty-one Mondialogo Engineering Awards each worth €15,000 were made, with five awarded special Jury recognition.

This shows how the Mondialogo Engineering Award has gone from strength to strength in terms of total numbers of registered teams, interest in the Award and in the interest and commitment of young engineers to work together in the preparation of project proposals that address major issues and challenges facing the world, especially poverty reduction, sustainable development, climate change mitigation and adaptation. It is hoped that the MEA will continue to help turn the dreams of young engineers into reality, and improve the quality of life of some of the world's poorest people. This is particularly important following the financial and economic crisis. Unfortunately, this downturn lead to a dramatic change in the business environment for Daimler, and a cut in corporate sponsorship, including the Mondialogo partnership. The search is on for new sponsors to help support and develop the Mondialogo partnership and Engineering Award.

⊃ *The Mondialogo Engineering Award involved young engineers to address global issues.*

© UNESCO

2.2 Engineering, innovation, social and economic development

Paul Jowitt

The Great Age of Engineering?

It's easy to think, from the Western perspective, that the great days of engineering were in the past during the era of massive mechanization and urbanization that had its heyday in the nineteenth century and which took the early Industrial Revolution from the eighteenth century right through into the twentieth century which, incidently, simultaneously improved the health and well-being of the common person with improvements in water supply and sanitation. That era of great engineering enjoyed two advantages: seemingly unlimited sources of power, coal, oil and gas, and a world environment of apparently boundless capacity in terms of water supply, materials and other resources relative to human need.

Now we know differently. We face two issues of truly global proportions – climate change and poverty reduction. The tasks confronting engineers of the twenty-first century are:

- engineering the world to avert an environmental crisis caused in part by earlier generations in terms of energy use, greenhouse gas emissions and their contribution to climate change, and

- engineering the large proportion of the world's increasing population out of poverty, and the associated problems encapsulated by the UN Millennium Development Goals.

This will require a combination of re-engineering existing infrastructure together with the provision of first-time infrastructure at a global scale.

And the difference between now and the nineteenth century? This time the scale of the problem is at a greater order of magnitude; environmental constraints are dangerously close to being breached; worldwide competition for scarce resources could create international tensions; and the freedom to power our way into the future by burning fossil fuels is denied.

Resolving these issues will require tremendous innovation and ingenuity by engineers, working alongside other technical and non-technical disciplines. It requires the engineer's ability to synthesize solutions and not simply their ability to analyse problems. It needs the engineers' ability to take a systems view at a range of scales, from devices and products through to the large-scale delivery of infrastructure services.

This means that the great age of engineering is NOW.

Let us briefly examine the key issues.

© P. Jowitt

⌒ *Civil engineering construction.*

'Poverty is Real'

The immediate prospects for both the urban and rural poor in many parts of the world is bleak with little or no access to even the most basic of infrastructure, education and healthcare, and with little or at best tenuous, legal rights to land or property.

Six of the eight UN Millennium Development Goals[3] (MDGs) are directly concerned with the human condition; physical health, their economic and social well-being and the capacity to play a full and useful role in the world. The remaining two relate to the environmental limits within which we have to operate and the partnerships we need to build to deliver the infrastructure that underpins civilization on which we depend; infrastructure that achieves real, pro-poor outcomes in the process of its planning, construction and operation. Working towards the UN MDGs therefore requires engineers to become involved.[4] The critical role of underpinning infrastructure for development was stated at the outset by Calestous Juma[5] (Chair of the UN Science, Technology and Innovation Task Force):

'At least three key factors contributed to the rapid economic transformation of emerging economies. First, they invested heavily in basic infrastructure, which served as a foundation for technological learning. Second, they nurtured the development of small and medium-sized enterprises, which required the development of local operational, repair and maintenance expertise. Third, their governments supported, funded and nurtured higher education institutions, academies of engineering and technological sciences, professional engineering and technological associations, and industrial and trade associations.'

---

3   The Millennium Development Goals were recognized by the UN General Assembly as being part of the road map for implementing the UN's Millennium Declaration. There are eight overall Goals (on Poverty, Education, Gender, Child Mortality, Maternal Health, HIV/AIDS, Environment, Global Partnership).

4   This was underlined at a meeting with the British Chancellor of the Exchequer at 11 Downing Street, London, on 30 November 2005.

5   Calestous Juma (ed.) *Going for Growth: Science, Technology and Innovation in Africa.* Published by the Smith Institute, 2005.

◐ *The Pelamis Wave Energy device generates renewable electricity.*

© P. Jowitt

Pre-requisites for development

The pre-requisites for development, without which attempts to improve livelihoods in the developing world will be unlikely to succeed, include reasonable governance structures, a functioning civil society, and freedom from persecution, conflict and corruption.

The impact of global politics, trade and conflicts on development is immense. These include trade rules, tariffs and western subsidies, local and regional conflict, oil diplomacy, governance, and the roles of transnational companies. But a functioning local business sector can also help deliver poverty-reduction outcomes through direct involvement in the development of effective and sustainable infrastructure, which in turn is of critical importance for three reasons:

- It underpins communities by providing the basic needs and services of shelter, access to safe water/sanitation, energy, transport, education and healthcare.

- It provides an internal demand for local skills and employment through its delivery.

- It provides a vital platform for the growth of the local economy and small and medium sized enterprises through improved access to infrastructure services, local skills, and the stimulation of and better access to both internal/local and external/national markets.

But infrastructure delivery also requires investment.

Those mired in poverty do not have and cannot afford all the resources necessary to resolve their plight. They will need external investment from governments, businesses and international agencies, and assistance from the worldwide engineering community. There will be no spectators as the future unfolds, but there are implications for civil engineers in particular.

'Climate Change is Real'

In June 2005, the National Science Academies of eleven countries issued a Joint Statement.[6] Its opening line was, 'Climate change is real'. It went on to say, 'The task of devising and implementing strategies to adapt to the consequences of climate change will require worldwide collaborative inputs from a wide range of experts, including physical and natural scientists, engineers, social scientists, medical scientists, those in the humanities, business leaders and economists.'

They called on the G8 Leaders – due to meet in Gleneagles in July 2005 – to acknowledge the threat and identify cost-effective steps to contribute to substantial and long-term

---

6   Joint Science Academies' Statement, *Global Response to Climate Change.* June 2005. http://royalsociety.org/Joint-science-academies-statement-Global-response-to-climate-change/ (Accessed: 2 May 2010).

reductions in net global greenhouse gas emissions. The same message is contained in the Stern Report.[7] Yet political progress on binding international measures for climate change mitigation and adaptation is still slow. At the recent climate change conference in Bali, US agreement on a roadmap for negotiations on a replacement for the Kyoto Protocol came only after the barbed comment by the delegate from Papua New Guinea to some of the western nations, 'Either lead, follow or get out of the way.'

It is now almost universally accepted that global climate change is a reality, its effects are locked in, and the activities of the human race – principally through the release of greenhouse gases – are a contributory factor. The work of building acceptance and understanding of climate change was recognized with the Nobel Peace Prize in 2007.

Whatever their precise spatial and temporal effects, the consequences of climate change (such as sea level rise, changes in rainfall patterns, drought and flooding) will mostly impact on the most impoverished and therefore vulnerable people of the world, while those least susceptible are in fact those responsible for the bulk of causative emissions.

With urbanization increasing apace, the greatest risks to humanity will be found in lesser-developed countries whose urban infrastructure is often either fragile or non-existent. By 2025, the world's population will have increased by about 1.5 billion to a total of around 6.6 billion and the percentage of those living in urban environments will have increased from 40 per cent to 60 per cent.[8] The planet has just passed the point at which more people live in cities and towns than in rural areas. The demand for effective infrastructure services is therefore immense.

Energy and climate change

The world is currently powered by a predominantly fossil-fuelled, carbon-based energy system based on coal, oil and gas. All these resources are non-renewable and out of balance within the timescales of the human race, and we are now aware of their wider environmental impacts.

The patterns of worldwide energy use are disproportionate, and with them the sources of CO_2 emissions. But the patterns are changing with the emerging economies, such as China and India, and their growth as car-ownership, consumer societies. China is the world's largest user of coal and the second largest consumer of oil and gas,[9] though still a relatively small

consumer on a per capita basis. By 2020, China's energy use is predicted to double.[10]

The achievement of a sustainable energy economy requires a strong energy-research base that addresses the basic demands placed on the energy system for heat, power and mobility. Whether at work or leisure, people are at the centre of the energy system and demand-side solutions need to be innovated as well as supply-side and infrastructure fixes. While market forces may act to resolve some aspects of the energy equation, there are others where the limitation is not technological but suffer from a lack of clear leadership and policy development.

There is no magic bullet. There are just three approaches:

1. Change our behaviour

2. Change the technology

3. Change the fuel

Demand-side innovations are just as important as supply-side fixes. Demand for energy needs to be reduced by a combination of changes in personal/corporate behaviours, increased energy efficiency in buildings and transportation systems, and in the energy ratings of plant, equipment and machinery in the home, offices and factories.

One way or another, the urban infrastructure of developed countries needs to be re-engineered to provide sustainable and fulfilling environments for their inhabitants. And the new, first-time infrastructure that is urgently needed in developing countries needs to be based on those same principles, learning from the mistakes of the developed countries.

On the supply side we need to shift to carbon-free sources of energy. Wind has become a well-established, carbon-free energy source (at least in its operational phase) but is not without its detractors, including those who still doubt its economics;[11] those against it argue on environmental, aesthetic, noise pollution grounds, and not least by its intermittency. The availability of wind energy tends to be in the more remote parts of the world, distant from centres of demand, and with poor grid and interconnector access. Wave and tidal energy systems are still very much still in development and will be required to operate in even more hostile and remote environments. Nuclear power brings with it a range of issues that need to be addressed, ranging from nuclear safety, public acceptability locally, and access to nuclear technology internationally.

7   Stern Report, http://www.hm-treasury.gov.uk/independent_reviews/stern_review_ economics_climate_change/sternreview_index.cfm (Accessed: 2 May 2010).

8   David Cook and John Kirke, *Urban Poverty: addressing the scale of the problem*, Municipal Engineer 156 ME4, 2003.

9   *BP Statistical Review of World Energy*, June 2005. http://www.bp.com/statisticalreview (Accessed: 2 May 2010).

10   Gregory A Keoleian; School of Natural Resources and Environment; Co-Director, Center for Sustainable Systems; University of Michigan

11   David Simpson, *Tilting at Windmills: The Economics of Wind Power*, April 2004. The David Hume Institute, Hume Occasional Paper No. 65.

⤳ *Slums are often at the margins of engineered infrastructure.*

© P. Jowitt

The construction of large-scale hydropower schemes has declined, primarily due to concerns over their social and environmental impacts. There are exceptions, the most significant example is the Three Gorges Dam on the Yangtze River which contains a storage reservoir of some 600 km in length, providing flood control, producing 18 GW of hydropower, but also displacing almost two million people and resulting in the loss of valuable archaeological and cultural sites, biodiversity loss and environmental damage.[12] Projects such as the Three Gorges Dam inescapably place the engineer in a difficult situation. Engineering is not an apolitical activity and may never have been so, and the engineer needs all the skills of discernment, judgement and conflict resolution.

An energy supply for Africa is a prize worth seeking, 'In many African countries, lack of energy security feeds into a cycle of poverty. At the beginning of the twenty-first century, it is unacceptable for millions of people to live without access to electricity!' (Claude Mandil, IEA).[13]

Delivering the Millennium Development Goals

The energy needs of the developing world bring us back to the issues of world poverty. Lack of access to basic infrastructure is at the root of world poverty and the human tragedies

associated with it. Two billion people lack access to a basic power supply and an equivalent number lack access to safe water. The UN target is to halve that number by 2015. Safe water for one billion people by 2015 means connecting more than one third of a million people per day, every day, for the next eight years. Can it be done? And if so, how? What limits our response?

The limiting factors are not a lack of engineering knowledge and technology, or knowing what needs to be done, but finding ways of applying that engineering technology, building local capacity to ensure its effective delivery, managing and financing it, and ensuring that its application is maintained.

Infrastructure development offers a vital opportunity for capacity-building, technological learning, and the development of local businesses, 'Infrastructure uses a wide range of technologies and complex institutional arrangements. Governments traditionally view infrastructure projects from a static perspective... they seldom consider that building railways, airports, roads and telecommunications networks could be structured to promote technological, organizational and institutional learning.'[14]

Building the infrastructure to deliver the UN MDGs is not about a single project, but about the delivery of many; each one is complex in itself, but at the right scale and with the right planning, is perfectly feasible. The UN MDGs will only be met if they are treated as a series of projects, each of which needs a project management plan and which the engineering profession is well placed to help deliver.

Is there a model for this? Are there development models that have been successful in dealing with issues akin to those of the developing world? Perhaps there are. For example, in many deprived inner city areas in the developed world, the issues are broadly similar: run down infrastructure, high unemployment, an economically disadvantaged local population, high crime rates and drug use, and a dysfunctional local economy. One solution to such cases was the establishment of special purpose development corporations, financially independent of the local municipality but ultimately accountable. There will be other models as well.

So this is the challenge:

'To develop an action-based project plan, to ensure that the UN MDGs are met while achieving sustainability worldwide.'

Yes, the Great Age of Engineering is NOW!

---

12   The International Rivers Network, Three Gorges Dam, see http://www.irn.org/programs/threeg/

13   Claude Mandil, Executive Director, The International Energy Agency. http://www.iea.org/textbase/papers/2003/african_energy.pdf (Accessed: 29 May 2010).

14   Professor Tony Ridley and Yee-Cheong Lee, Infrastructure, innovation and development, chp 5, *Going for Growth: Science, Technology and Innovation in Africa*, Calestous Juma (ed.) Published by the Smith Institute, 2005.

2.3 Engineering, technology and society

George Bugliarello

From the earliest times of human civilization, the activity that has come to be called engineering has impacted on society through the technological artefacts – both tangible and intangible – that it creates. Products of engineering surround us and affect virtually every aspect of our lives, influencing culture, art and religion in a tightening circle of reciprocal interactions. Roads, aqueducts, pumps and canals have made urban life possible, electricity has illuminated and helped power the world, industries and communications have fostered global affluence and weapons of increasing power are shaping the interactions among nations. Modern music, paintings, and architecture, automobiles and modern bridges embody both art and technique as did the Pyramids and the Parthenon.

Every major engineering innovation, from metal-making to electronics, has brought about changes in society. The development and practice of engineering is affected, in turn, by significant changes in society's goals, customs and expectations. To respond to society's demands, the very education of engineers is becoming more interdisciplinary, including courses in the humanities, the social sciences and biology. At times, however, society has overlooked the potential of engineering to help address some of its most pressing problems and has responded slowly to engineering innovations, which frequently require new organizational patterns, new laws, the development of new perceptions, and the evolution of customs. Societal entities that respond faster and more intelligently to engineering innovations usually have the advantage. The American and French revolutions eventually enhanced technological development by opening up their societies to the opportunities offered by the Industrial Revolution; the Russian Revolution greatly accelerated the pace of industrialization in that country.

The fact is that engineering and technology are processes that require the synergy of individuals, machines (artefacts) and social organizations (Bugliarello, 2000)[15]. An important facet of that synergy is the ever-closer interaction with science. Engineering is basically about the modification of nature through the creation of tangible and intangible artefacts and has at times preceded a scientific understanding of the process. Science is about the understanding of nature. Often, to do so, it needs to create artefacts. Thus, although different in intent, the two endeavours have become indispensable to each other – engineered instrumentation, computers, software and satellites to the pursuits of science, and science to advances over the entire spectrum of engineering.

Society is today making ever-greater demands on engineering, from those caused by exploding urbanization and by the endemic poverty of a quarter of the world's population in the face of overall global affluence, to the mounting concerns about availability of critical resources, the consequences of climate change and increasing natural and man-made disasters. This confronts engineering and society not only with unprecedented technical challenges, but also with a host of new ethical problems that demand the development of global engineering ethics. How far should engineering pursue the modifications of nature? What are engineering's roles and responsibilities in society? How should engineering address problems of equity in terms of the availability of resources and services of and between current and future generations? Should concerns about global warming take precedence over the urgent problem of poverty, or how can they be addressed together? What should be the engineering standards in an increasingly globalized enterprise, e.g. the around-the-clock design teams operating synergistically in locations across the world? These questions cannot be addressed without considering the need for some fundamental engineering tenets such as the upholding of human dignity, the avoidance of dangerous or uncontrolled side effects, the making of provisions for unexpected consequences of technological developments, and asking not only about the 'hows' but also the 'whys' in the creation of artefacts.

The synergy of engineering with other societal activities is the root cause of the material prosperity of many societies and is a key to improving the condition of many developing countries. The rapidly developing interaction of engineering with biologi-

Engineers can be artists – Coimbra footbridge.

© Arup

15   Bugliarello, George, The Biosoma: The Synthesis of Biology, Machines and Society, *Bulletin of Science, Technology & Society*, Vol. 20, No. 6, December 2000, pp. 452–464.

cal and medical systems is beginning to dramatically increase the health of vast sectors of the world population, and the synergy of engineering and education through advances in information and telecommunications technology, to improve skills and job opportunities globally. At the same time, however, developments in mechanization and automation may tend to diminish both employment opportunities and person-to-person, face-to-face interactions by interposing machines. Also, as dependency on technology grows – and as technology becomes less well understood and operated to its maximum capacity – society is placed at increasing risk by technological failures and design faults, whether of logistical supply systems for water, food, energy and vaccine, or of other critical infrastructures and systems. The risk is aggravated by the ever-greater interdependencies of our engineered world. Engineering in its entirety is, in effect, a social enterprise that has made modern society possible, with all its potentials and risks, and is nurtured in turn by society (Sladovich, 1991)[16]. It extends the physical and economic capacity of society by enhancing the reach of society's components and capabilities of its members, and by creating new methods and instruments for agriculture, the production of goods, communication, defence, offence, exploration of space and the oceans, and of the preservation and utilization of nature's resources from land to energy, water and materials. Engineering's evolving and deepening interaction with the other components of society and its increasing ability to intervene in biological processes have become a key factor in determining the future of our species.

16   Sladovich, H.E. (ed.). 1991. *Engineering as a Social Enterprise*, National Academy Press, Washington, DC.

2.4   Engineers and social responsibility

2.4.1   The big issues

Stuart Parkinson

Engineering has immense capacity to help provide benefits to society – as the other contributions in this Report demonstrate – but it also has a similarly large capacity to be used to cause harm. It helps to provide basic needs such as water, food, shelter and energy, and does so on the scale necessary for industrial society to function. But engineering has also contributed to the huge increase in the destructiveness of weaponry and warfare seen over the centuries, to increases in inequality and to the global damage inflicted on the world's ecosystems.

As an engineer, it is crucial to understand this dual nature of the profession and to be vigilant regarding your own role and that of your employers so that you maximize the chances of a positive contribution to society. In essence this is what it means to be a socially responsible engineer.

Engineering and war

In promoting engineering as a career, the professional institutions are quick to point out the critical role that engineering plays in helping to provide benefits to society, for example:

> 'Today, it is true to say that virtually every aspect of our daily lives is enabled or aided in some way by engineers. Engineers make things happen, they turn ideas into real products and they provide the solutions to life's everyday practical problems.'[17]

However, they are less quick to highlight the ways in which technology has been engineered – in close collaboration with the sciences – to contribute to many of society's ills. Perhaps the starkest example of this is demonstrated by the increase in the lethality of weapons over the twentieth century. Researchers at the University of Buenos Aires have estimated that the 'lethality index' – defined as the maximum number of casualties per hour that a weapon can inflict – increased by

◑ *Tsunami reconstruction housing.*

© Arup

17   Young Engineers website. http://www.youngeng.org/index.asp?page=66 (Accessed: 4 May 2010).

a staggering sixty million times over the course of the century, with thermonuclear warheads mounted on ballistic missiles representing the zenith of destructiveness.[18] Indeed, as is well known, these weapons have given us the power to destroy human civilization and much of the natural world in a very short space of time.

However, the controversies that surround military technology are related to a much broader set of issues than just the raw power of a given weapon. For example, it is important to realize that most people who die in wars are actually killed by smaller, simpler technology such as guns and other small arms – and war still kills hundreds of thousands of people across the world each year.[19] While many engineers justify their work on military technology by arguing it contributes to national security, the situation is far more complex. For example, regulation of international arms sales is generally poor, with weapons finding their way – both legally and illegally – to governments with bad human rights records and to war zones. With about 75 per cent of war casualties being civilians, this is especially disturbing.[20]

One overarching issue related to military technology especially relevant to engineers is what economists call the 'opportunity cost', i.e. the loss of skills and resources from other important areas that are currently used by the military. Indicators of this opportunity cost are not hard to find. In 2006, global military spending was a massive US$1.2 trillion.[21] This is greater than the combined size of the economies of the world's 110 poorest countries,[22] and nearly twelve times the global level of official development aid[23] – a level of aid which still falls well short of that needed to achieve the Millennium Development Goals.[24] Indeed, resolutions proposed annually at the UN General Assembly since 1987 have highlighted the desire of the majority of the world's governments for cuts in military spending to be used to help fund international development. This has become known as 'disarmament for development'.[25]

Another comparison of particular relevance to engineers is spending on research and development (R&D). In 2006, the governments of the world's wealthiest countries[26] spent US$96 billion on military R&D compared with only US$56 billion on R&D for health and environment protection combined.[27]

Engineering and pollution

Engineering and technology is also a key contributor to global environmental problems, such as climate change and loss of wildlife. For example, industrial society now emits the equivalent of about 50 billion tonnes of carbon dioxide each year[28] – with the burning of fossil fuels being the main culprit. The resulting climate change is predicted to have huge impacts on both humans and wildlife over the coming decades and beyond – with many millions of people at risk. Indeed, a recent report by the World Health Organization estimated that climate change could already be responsible for 150,000 extra deaths every year.[29]

Engineering and technology are also key contributors to the global loss of wildlife through their role in activities ranging from industrial deforestation to industrial fishing. The rate of species extinction across the world is now estimated to be more than 100 times the natural level, with the consequence that we are now in the midst of a 'major extinction event' – something that has only happened five times before in the five billion year history of planet Earth.[30]

But of course engineering is playing a key role in helping to understand and tackle global environmental problems as well. For example, in the case of climate change, energy efficiency and renewable energy technology are playing increasingly important roles in helping to cut greenhouse gas emissions – and so mitigate the threat – while other technologies such as flood defences are allowing society to adapt to some of the changes which are already happening. Other examples can be found elsewhere in this Report, many showing that technology and innovation alone cannot save us; such solutions must be engineered to suit society.

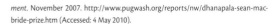
⊙ *Waste management.*

18 Lemarchand, G. 2007. *Defense R&D Policies: Fifty years of history*. INES Council and Executive Committee meeting, June 2–4 2007. Berlin, Germany. http://www.inesglobal.com/ (Accessed: 4 May 2010).

19 Smith, D. 2003. *The Atlas of War and Peace*. Earthscan, London. pp. 38.

20 Ibid. 22.

21 Stalenheim, P., Perdomo, C., Skons, E. 2007. *Military expenditure*. Chp. 8 of SIPRI (2007). SIPRI Yearbook 2007: Armaments, Disarmament and International Security. Oxford University Press/SIPRI. http://yearbook2007.sipri.org (Accessed: 4 May 2010).

22 This was calculated using figures from International Monetary Fund (2007). *World Economic Outlook database*. http://www.imf.org/external/pubs/ft/weo/2007/02/weodata/index.aspx (Accessed: 4 May 2010).

23 This was calculated using figures from UN (2007). *The Millennium Development Goals Report 2007*. UN, New York. pp.28. http://www.un.org/millenniumgoals/pdf/mdg2007.pdf (Accessed: 4 May 2010).

24 The eight Millennium Development Goals (MDGs) include trying to halve extreme poverty by 2015. For a discussion on the shortfalls in development aid needed to achieve the MDGs (See footnote 23).

25 Dhanapala, J. 2007. Disarmament and development at the global level. Statement at the IPB conference, *Books or bombs? Sustainable disarmament for sustainable develop-*

ment. November 2007. http://www.pugwash.org/reports/nw/dhanapala-sean-macbride-prize.htm (Accessed: 4 May 2010).

26 Countries of the Organisation for Economic Co-operation and Development (OECD).

27 OECD. 2007. *Main Science and Technology Indicators 2007*. OECD, Paris. http://www.oecd.org/

28 Emissions of greenhouse gases (GHGs) are generally expressed in tonnes of 'carbon dioxide equivalent' as different GHGs have different warming properties. Figures are from the Intergovernmental Panel on Climate Change (2007). *Climate Change 2007: Synthesis Report*. Fourth Assessment Report. Summary for Policymakers. http://www.ipcc.ch/pdf/assessment-report/ar4/syr/ar4_syr_spm.pdf (Accessed: 4 May 2010).

29 World Health Organization. 2003. *Climate Change and Human Health – risks and responses*. http://www.who.int/bookorders/anglais/detart1.jsp?sesslan=1&codlan=1&codcol=15&codcch=551 (Accessed: 4 May 2010).

30 UNEP. 2007. *Global Environmental Outlook 4*. Chp. 5. United Nations Environment Programme. http://www.unep.org/geo/geo4/media/ (Accessed: 4 May 2010).

However, a lack of resources is again impeding the speed at which the world faces up to these urgent environmental problems. And again, a comparison with military spending is a useful reminder of the resources which could be made available. For example, the Institute for Policy Studies recently published a report comparing the United States government budget allocated to 'military security' with that allocated to 'climate security'. It found that the military budget was 88 times the size of that devoted to tackling the climate problem.[31] The UK organization, Scientists for Global Responsibility, carried out a similar comparison, this time between the government R&D budgets of the world's wealthiest countries. They found a very similar imbalance between military and renewable energy R&D spending.[32]

Is the engineering profession doing enough?

Given such disturbing facts, it is worth asking whether the engineering profession is doing enough to fulfil its obligations in terms of social responsibility. As entries in this Report show, there is a great deal of positive activity across the profession, but there remain areas where there is a need for improvement.

The most obvious example is arguably the close relationship between the engineering profession and the military. Given the controversies discussed above, related to military technologies and the size of military budgets, one might expect to hear more criticism from within the profession about how its skills are deployed. Yet it is very hard to find cases of, for example, professional engineering institutions criticizing the government policies that cause such problems.

For example, during the recent debate in the UK over proposals to replace the Trident nuclear weapons system – proposals criticized by the then UN Secretary General[33] – the main comment from the Royal Academy of Engineering (RAE)[34] was simply that there needed to be sufficient investment in skills and infrastructure to ensure timely delivery of the US$40 billion project. Such a muted response sits uncomfortably with the RAE's recently launched 'Statement of ethical principles' which encourages engineers to have 'respect for life… and the public good.'[35]

Indeed, with the active encouragement of UNESCO, professional engineering and scientific institutions have in recent years begun to adopt and promote ethical codes for the profession, which highlight the importance of principles such as social justice and environmental sustainability. Yet, when there are clear conflicts between these goals and the military and commercial interests, which are so intertwined with the engineering profession, the principles seem quickly to be compromised.

Standing up for social responsibility

Over the years there have been a number of engineering and science organizations which have, in frustration with governments and professional institutions, tried to promote greater social responsibility within the science and technology arenas.

In 1957, the Pugwash Conferences on Science and World Affairs was formed in response the early nuclear arms race.[36] These conferences – which continue today – bring together scientists, engineers and others from across the world to discuss solutions to global problems. These discussions have been important in sowing the seeds of major arms control treaties.

A more radical organization, the International Network for Engineers and Scientists for Global Responsibility (INES), was set up in 1991 arguing that the professions should play a much greater role in supporting peace, social justice and environmental sustainability.[37] It has over seventy member organizations in more than thirty countries.

Influential individuals from the engineering and scientific communities have also spoken out urging the professions to adopt a more radical position. For example, in 1995 former Manhattan Project scientists, Prof. Hans Bethe and Prof. Joseph Rotblat called on all engineers and scientists to refuse to work on nuclear weapons projects.[38] More recently, Jayantha Dhanapala, a former UN Under-Secretary General and currently Chair of the UN University Council, called on engineers and scientists (among others) to refuse to work for the world's top twenty-five military corporations, until the 'disarmament for development' agenda is seriously acted upon.[39]

Becoming an active member of, or otherwise engaging with, one or more of the engineering campaigning groups or non-governmental organizations would be an important contribution to the social responsibility agenda for any engineer, and it should be recognized as such in career and professional development schemes.

31 Pemberton, M. 2008. The budgets compared: military vs climate security. Institute for Policy Studies. http://www.ips-dc.org/getfile.php?id=131 (Accessed: 4 May 2010).

32 Parkinson, S. and Langley, C. 2008. Military R&D 85 times larger than renewable energy R&D. SGR Newsletter, No. 35, pp.1. http://www.sgr.org.uk/

33 Annan, K. 2006. Lecture at Princeton University. 28 November 2006. http://www.un.org/News/Press/docs/2006/sgsm10767.doc.htm (Accessed: 4 May 2010).

34 RAE. 2006. Response to The Future of the Strategic Nuclear Deterrent: the UK manufacturing and skills base. http://www.raeng.org.uk/policy/responses/pdf/Nuclear_Deterrent_Consultation.pdf (Accessed: 4 May 2010).

35 RAE. 2007. Statement of ethical principles. http://www.raeng.org.uk/policy/ethics/principles.htm (Accessed: 4 May 2010).

36 Pugwash Conference on Science and World Affairs. http://www.pugwash.org/

37 International Network for Engineers and Scientists for Global Responsibility (INES). http://www.inesglobal.com/

38 Rotblat, J. 1995. Remember your humanity. Nobel lecture, Oslo. December 10. In: Braun et al (2007). Joseph Rotblat: Visionary for peace. Wiley-VCH, Weinheim, Germany. pp. 315–322.

39 Dhanapala, J. 2007 (See footnote 25).

Indeed, a key aspect of being an engineering professional is to actively seek opportunities that have a positive impact on global problems such as war, pollution, poverty or climate change. This is the heart of social responsibility in engineering.

2.4.2   Engineering Social Responsibility

David Singleton

As engineers of the built environment, we have a significant impact upon the world around us. This is both an opportunity and a responsibility. The way that all of the world's inhabitants live, and the living standards that we have come to expect form a part of our quality of life, which in turn is influenced by the infrastructure around us; much of that infrastructure is shaped by our engineering.

Our challenge as engineers, now and in the future, is to provide infrastructure to rural and semi-rural communities in the developing world. Also, with increasing urbanization, we face additional challenges in terms of how we can economically provide infrastructure in new urban areas; how do we retrofit existing infrastructure, and how do we accomplish all this in a responsible and sustainable manner?

With half of the world's population now living in urban areas, urbanization has been and will continue to be a rapid process with virtually all the forecasted population growth in coming years taking place in urban areas in less developed countries. Forecasts for 2050 show that 70 per cent of the world's population will be urban; some 6.4 billion people will live in urban areas (the equivalent of the world's total population in 2004) and most of this population will be concentrated in Asia (54 per cent) and Africa (19 per cent). China will have the largest urban population at 1 billion in 2050.

Urbanization is generally defined as the process of growth as a proportion of a country's resident urban population. The terms 'urban areas' and 'cities' are often taken to mean the same thing, but urban areas include towns and other smaller settlements. For example, half of the world's urban population lives in settlements of fewer than 500,000 people, while megacities – generally defined as having rapid growth and a total population in excess of 10 million people – house only 9 per cent of urban inhabitants.

Arup[40] has carried out significant research into the forces of urbanization and we have a clear understanding of the impact of urbanization on society and the positive role that it can play in social and economic development. Concentrating the

© Stephen Jones, EWB-UK

↶ *Kyzyltoo water supply, South Kyrgyzstan – infrastructure in rural and semi-rural areas.*

world's population into urban settlements gives sustainable development a better chance through economies of scale on various fronts. By contrast however, cities can draw together many of the world's environmental problems. Cities provide both an opportunity and a challenge in terms of infrastructure provision.

It is important to understand the challenges associated with urbanization and to see these in terms of opportunities for change. Long-term planning for urban areas needs to be considered holistically. Any town or city has many components or urban 'ingredients' and there are complex relationships between them such as: facilities, in terms of physical infrastructure; systems and utilities required by an urban area to function; services that urban residents need; and the desirable attributes an urban area should possess.

Whether in developing or developed countries, the physical infrastructure associated with urbanization is concerned with much more than basic services; infrastructure can make people's lives better, especially when viewed in terms of the service it provides. It is not simply about putting pipes and drains in the ground but about 'public health' through the provision of clean and safe water and sanitation, it is not just about designing and constructing good, safe and reliable transport but about providing 'accessibility' or even 'mobility' to employment and education and about determining and meeting the need to transport people and freight more efficiently. Good infrastructure makes people's lives better in the here and now. Accessible highways better connect towns and cities, effi-

---

40   A global firm of consulting engineers, designers and planners. http://www.arup.com

cient railway lines and stations mean we can commute to work or escape to places where we choose to spend our leisure time, and good design creates residential areas and houses that are comfortable, safe places to live. Sustainable development also ensures that this will not be at the expense of future generations or the environment.

While good engineering provides good infrastructure, which can make people's lives better, as engineers we also have a responsibility to create solutions that are not only effective, but contribute positively to our environment. Sustainable design objectives should run through everything that we do as engineers; we should always be thinking about how we can make people's lives better tomorrow, as well as today.

As stated above, the urbanization challenge is not just about providing infrastructure in developing worlds but also about retrofitting existing ones. By adopting an integrated approach to managing our existing cities, we can dramatically increase their chances for environmental, social and economic success in the years to come.

However, the challenge of retrofitting cities to be more sustainable is complex. Fortunately, small steps can deliver large benefits, and change does not need to be radical. Unlocking value from present inefficiencies is just one opportunity, for example, information technology can be used for real-time journey planning, making existing transport networks more efficient.

We need to find city-specific solutions that provide a higher quality of life at lower economic cost and help cities to deal with risks such as climate change and access to clean water and food. Despite the size of the challenge, the rising cost of resources like energy and food and the resultant economic benefits of sustainable development will drive the reinvention of our cities.

Arup is committed to achieving integrated design solutions that balance social, economic, physical and temporal parameters, creating unique and authentic new urban environments. The firm's intrinsic agenda addresses efficient landuse, infrastructure efficiency, urban economics and matters of microclimate, sociology, ecology, hydrology and energy usage. These agendas allow us to focus our desire to create sustainable communities, for example in achieving the potential to 'unlock' new life from 'brownfield' sites.

The new environments we create should facilitate human interactions without being prescriptive, allowing chance and spontaneity to occur in interesting and fulfilling places in which to live, work and play. Thoughtfully planned and designed infrastructure can achieve all of this. But we must manage the risks to the environments that surround us, including those

The PlayPump – children have fun and help with water supply.

© David Singleton

that we create by our designs and their implementation. As engineers, we can manage these risks by applying 'precautionary principles', planning buildings and infrastructure to cope with the worst likely outcome rather than hoping for the best. Taking into account of major forces such as climate change, water shortages and energy issues means constantly thinking about the overall sustainability of our designs. Our aim is to set a standard of sustainable design that benefits the environment in both the short and the long term. We have a significant impact on the world around us and there is an opportunity, and indeed a moral obligation, for us to set a standard of design that benefits the environment and the people who live within. We must constantly think about the overall sustainability of our designs, how we build them, and how they affect the surrounding environment.

To do this effectively, we should ensure our innovation and design solutions meet people's needs and allow them to live the way they choose without creating a negative legacy for generations to come. This is what we might call 'Engineering Social Responsibility'.

One of the challenges for the engineering profession is to develop sustainable urban infrastructure that recognizes, rather than resists, the inevitability of migration to urban centres and makes provision for these rapidly growing populations. As engineers we must work effectively in collaboration with our colleagues and other development-focused professionals and community leaders to implement sustainable solutions to challenges such as urban poverty. However, we need to ensure that these solutions are well integrated into wider decision-making, planning and institutional development processes to improve living conditions for all.

Sustainability and corporate responsibility are having an increasing influence on how organizations behave, operate and do business. There are many reasons why sustainability should be at the top of everyone's business agenda, not least because the continued survival of future generations depends on finding solutions to the combined issues of climate change, finding an alternative to carbon-emitting fossil fuels for energy and transport needs, and ensuring widespread access to clean water.

The environment in which businesses operate is starting to reward sustainability in business, and a clearer definition is emerging. Sustainability represents a challenge to business, but embracing it is fundamental to managing a company's risk profile, and is essentially good business practice. The engineering industry is no exception. In fact, the engineering industry has a greater responsibility towards meeting government legislation, self- or industry- imposed governance, the demands of customers to demonstrate we are acting responsibly, and to educate clients of the need to change behaviour and be more environmentally aware.

The sustainability agenda can be pursued in a number of ways. At Arup we do so through researching sustainability issues, identifying opportunities to operate in a more sustainable way, evaluating projects on their sustainability performance, creating methodologies to embed sustainability considerations in all our work and promoting sustainability to clients, educating all those we deal with on sustainability. We can also promote sustainability in the training and education of design professionals in the built environment.

Training and education is not a unique vision, many others have highlighted the need for changes in engineering education to support the sustainability agenda. In 2003, an ICE Presidential Commission, 'Engineering without Frontiers' asked what was expected of an engineer by society in the twenty-first century. This had been answered in part in 2000 at the 'Forum for the Future' where thirty-two young engineers developed a vision of the engineer for the twenty-first century (partly sponsored by The Arup Foundation), including roles in sustainable development.

Our vision is of an engineer who demonstrates through everyday practice:

- An understanding of what sustainability means.

- The skills to work toward this aim.

- Values that relate to their wider social, environmental and economic responsibilities, and encourages and enables others to learn and participate.

(Forum for the Future, 2000)

In 2003, a second phase of the work of the Forum saw another twelve young engineers from partner companies and organizations assess what progress had been made in particular areas identified for progress in the initial phase completed in 2000. The record of progress results was not encouraging, and the report noted four key areas where consistent effort was needed if change is to be driven through effectively:

- Make choosing a sustainability option cheaper and easier for clients and contractors.

- Build the capacity of teachers and trainers to integrate sustainability into courses.

- Make specifying sustainability criteria in materials and processes an effective tool for change in procurement chains.

- Embed sustainability thinking and practices into the culture of organizations and across different professional groups.

(Proceedings of the ICE: Briefing: Engineers of the 21st Century – partnerships for change)

A third phase of the programme began in 2005 to promote sustainable development within the engineering profession. This is focused on the identification of barriers and influencing change, and directly addresses the four areas for change identified in 2003. Overall, the programme emphasized the commitment and enthusiasm young engineers have for promoting sustainable development.

So it seems that the industry is responding, and at least realizes this is an important subject for engineers to address and lead on. In 2007, The Chartered Institution of Building Services Engineers (CIBSE) published a sustainability toolkit setting out some fundamental principles and providing online tools to support engineers in meeting the demands for sustainable buildings, and to respond to the sustainability agenda.

The UK Green Build Council (UK-GBC) was also launched in February 2007 to provide clear direction on sustainability for the sector as a whole, something that had previously been lacking. With members drawn across the industry, including NGOs, academic institutions and government agencies, it aims to provide a joined-up and collaborative approach to sustainability and building engineering.

Designing in a sustainable way also requires us to investigate those trends, which are most likely to have an impact upon the world in the future. In order to anticipate future change, Arup conducted a series of scientific reviews and surveys, which we call the 'Drivers of Change' that explore the major drivers that most affect society's future. The three most important factors identified by our clients were climate change, energy resources and water, with urbanization, demographics and waste not far behind. Detailed research on these six 'Drivers of Change' was then undertaken and our current focus is to embed them into Arup's design, methodologies and evaluation processes. For engineers, tackling these issues must embrace every aspect of design and planning. This cannot be separated from other key considerations and requires a holistic and sustainable approach across all the different facets of a new development. There also needs to be a strong vision for leadership with clear strategies for the emergence of new leaders in engineering.

As an organization, Arup has promoted sustainability for decades. Our company's culture includes a commitment to shape a better world through our work. The ethical dimension of engineering is a subject of lively discussion within the firm, and there are many issues and questions under continuous debate. Should we be refusing work that could be characterized as unsustainable? Or should we take on such work and try to make them as sustainable as possible, educating our clients in the process? The answer is not straightforward. If we are to contemplate turning away unsustainable work, we must balance this with the need to educate our clients, and to maintain our own business and provide employment for our staff.

Sustainability at Arup

- 1946: Arup founded by Ove Arup, Danish philosopher and engineer, proponent of a multi-disciplinary approach to design that included societal factors as well as design and technical issues.

- 1970: In a seminal speech to the firm, Ove Arup articulated his vision of the firm's obligation to our environment. The speech is still relevant today.

- 1998: Arup adopts as its mission 'we shape a better world'. It underlines the significant impact the firm has on almost all aspects of the built environment.

- 2001: Arup's first sustainability forum at Boston's Massachusetts Institute of Technology.

- 2005: *Forum for the Future* sustainability presentation to Arup's global strategy meeting.

- 2007 (September): Sustainability policy is ratified, recognizing the wider influence we have in the work we do for our clients, as well as by running our business in a sustainable way.

- 2008 (March): Sustainability Statement published.

The author's aspiration is that eventually, over time, we will not talk about sustainable design because it will be simply a part of what we always do as 'business as usual'. It's the only way we can fulfil our obligation towards social responsibility within our field as engineers.

2.4.3 Corporate Social Responsibility

Petter Matthews

Corporate Social Responsibility (CSR) has moved from the margins to the mainstream, from a preoccupation with public relations and philanthropy, to a concern with a range of strategic issues that are of critical importance to policy-makers and practitioners. It has become inextricably linked with the key global challenges of our time including governance, climate change, security and international development. And most importantly, CSR is now seen as a mechanism through which the skills, technology, economic power and global reach of the private sector can be applied to the challenges of fighting poverty and achieving the Millennium Development Goals (MDGs).

Given these developments, it is perhaps surprising that CSR remains so poorly understood and that there are still so few examples of it having directly contributed to poverty reduction. CSR as a discipline still lacks well elaborated methodologies to capture its effects, and for many companies it is no more than a gloss on what is essentially 'business as usual'. The private sector has benefited from improved markets access in recent years, but has not yet fully understood that these benefits are accompanied by new social responsibilities. Business as usual is a wholly inadequate response given the critical challenges that we face. Systemic change is necessary. This means developing new and innovative business models, transforming business management systems and building genuine cross-sectoral partnerships. In effect, the challenge is to develop a 'second generation' of approaches to CSR.

This paper focuses on the implications of this for the engineering industry. While recognizing the crucial role of small and medium enterprises, it is concerned primarily with the role of large international companies. It begins by summarizing the objections to CSR that in themselves constitute barriers to progress. It goes on to explain why CSR is especially relevant to the engineering industry, and discusses a practical method for selecting opportunities. The paper concludes by considering the implications of failure of CSR for business and for society.

Objections to CSR

Objections to CSR are made by opponents to it from across the institutional spectrum. Those opposed to CSR from a 'campaigning' perspective dismiss it as a corporate-driven distraction that diverts attention from the need for proper enforceable regulation.[41] They argue that only the state is mandated to protect the public interest, and question the legitimacy of corporate influence over public policy. It is of course true that regulation is often very weak, particularly in developing countries, and this situation is sometimes exploited by irresponsible companies. In fact, it is the absence of regulation that has acted as a driver of CSR in many circumstances, as responsible companies have sought to compensate for the governance deficit.[42] However, a problem with the campaigning perspective is that it tends to pitch business interests against society. Of course there are tensions, but there is also interdependence. A more fruitful strategy is to use this interdependence to build symbiotic relationships so that business and societal interests become mutually reinforcing.

Critics of CSR from the 'market economy' perspective argue that business fulfils its role in society simply by pursuing its own self-interest.[43] They reject measures to manage a company's social impacts beyond those required by law and mar-

---

41 See for example the work of the Corporate Responsibility Coalition (Core) at http://www.corporate-responsibility.org

42 Marsden, C. and Grayson, D. 2007. *The Business of Business is . . .? Unpicking the Corporate Responsibility Debate*, The Doughty Centre for Corporate Responsibility, Cranfield School of Management.

43 Hopkins, M. 2006. *Corporate Social Responsibility & International Development*, pp. 17–19, Earthscan, London.

ket forces. This view is often associated with the economist Milton Friedman in his influential article, *The social responsibility of business is to increase its profits.*[44] The problem with this perspective is that it overlooks the social contract that exists between the corporation and the state. The primary responsibility of business is the production and distribution of the goods and services that society needs. The right to make a profit from this social function is granted to corporations by the state and demands justification. CSR is an attempt to justify this right by responding to society's changing expectations of business.

The objections to CSR from campaigning and market economy perspectives both have important lessons. Robust regulation is necessary to curb unrestrained corporate behaviour and ensure compliance with minimum standards. This is particularly important in the developing world where workers and poorer communities are especially vulnerable. But unlocking the full potential of the private sector also requires incentives that encourage companies to go beyond compliance with minimum standards and innovate in delivering high standards of social and environmental performance. Getting this combination of regulation and incentives is of critical importance in developing the second generation of CSR.

CSR and the engineering industry

The engineering industry and its clients have been at the forefront of the development of CSR in recent years. There are two important reasons for this. First, the markets for its goods and services are increasingly shifting towards the developing world. A number of factors have combined to boost government expenditure and increase demand for infrastructure and services. These include several years of record economic growth in many low and middle-income countries prior to the current economic crisis, sustained increases in natural resource commodity prices over the long term and higher levels of development assistance. The OECD estimates that through to 2030, telecommunications, road, rail, water, electricity and other energy related infrastructure will require investment equal to 3.5 per cent of global GDP.[45] This means we should expect approximately US$2.6 trillion dollars to be needed annually for constructing new and maintaining and replacing existing infrastructure by 2030. Developing countries will be major growth centres for the engineering industry in the next twenty to thirty years.

Second, the core activities of the engineering industry, such as building, maintaining and operating infrastructure, exploiting natural resources and large-scale manufacturing, impact directly on the lives of poor people and are often conducted in close proximity to them. Companies must manage their relationships with the disadvantaged who are either directly or indirectly affected by their operations, as well as a range of other stakeholders who tend to prioritize poverty reduction including governments, NGOs and international agencies. CSR offers companies a way of managing these complex relationships and building a 'social license to operate'.

Of course there are a range of additional factors that are also driving the need for a second generation of CSR that apply across industrial sectors. These include pressure from campaigners, shareholders and ethical investors, the demand for new technologies, compliance with global frameworks such as the UN Global Compact[46] and the growing recognition that responsible companies tend to attract and retain the best employees.

Identifying opportunities

When fully integrated into corporate strategy, CSR can become a source of opportunity and competitive advantage, and a driver of innovation. Jane Nelson has proposed a framework of four strategies for individual firms to strengthen their contribution to local development and poverty reduction (Figure 1). Three of these strategies, compliance with regulation, charitable contributions and managing costs, risks and negative impacts, represent the conventional corporate responses to managing social issues. The more innovative fourth strategy 'creating new value' combines improved social outcomes with competitive advantage and is a critical principle that underpins the second generation of CSR. Porter and Kramer refer to outcomes based on this principle as 'shared value'. They argue that the most valuable corporate societal contributions, '…occur when a company adds a social dimension to its value proposition, making social impact integral to the overall strategy.'[47]

46 See http://www.unglobalcompact.org/

47 Harvard Business Review, December 2006, Harvard University, Cambridge MA. pp. 10.

44 Friedman, M. *The Social Responsibility of Business is to Increase its Profits*, The New York Times Magazine, September 13, 1970.

45 Organisation for Economic Cooperation and Development (2008) *Infrastructure to 2030*, OECD, Paris.

© Arup

◠ *Evinos Dam, Greece.*

Figure 1: **Strategies to strengthen the contribution to development by the individual firm**[48]

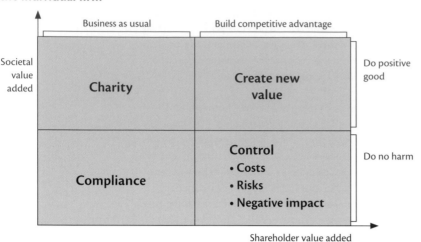

The ESPF encourages companies to seek a detailed understanding of the local environment and those using it are encouraged to consult with local stakeholders. The knowledge that is acquired and the relationships built tend to discourage thinking about the companies' interaction with society as a zero sum game. The opportunities that emerge are measured against their potential to create value that is meaningful to local stakeholders and provide competitive value for the company. The ESPF also encourages companies to think about CSR as a driver of innovation. Poverty, sustainability and climate change have become 'market shaping' issues that are unlikely to disappear even during periods of economic downturn.

The second generation of CSR has to have a firm theoretical underpinning, but it also requires practical methods, such as the ESPF, to implement improvements and measure their effects. This is where the engineering industry can excel and lead the development of the second generation of CSR.

Opportunities for creating 'new value' or 'shared value' are particularly strong in the engineering and construction sector. Its activities are of great societal importance, e.g. the creation and maintenance of essential social and economic infrastructure. Also, engineering and construction activities tend to have a large physical, social and economic 'footprint' that creates a wide range of opportunities for creating new value. However, the opportunities will vary between sectors and geographical regions and even between the individual operations of a particular company. It is important therefore to adopt a systematic approach to identifying and selecting opportunities. The Economic and Social Performance Framework (ESPF) developed by Engineers Against Poverty is an example of a practical tool designed for this purpose.[49]

The consequences of failure

That CSR is such a prominent issue is evidence of a deficiency in the relationship between business and society. If this relationship can be reconstituted on the basis of shared value, the interests of the company and of society can become mutually reinforcing. And the activities that we currently refer to as CSR will become indistinguishable from the core business of the company.

Business should not be expected to lead the fight against poverty, which is the role of governments and multilateral agencies, but simply increasing aid and writing off debt are unlikely to deliver cost effective and sustainable solutions in the long term. Unlocking the development potential of the private sector represents what is probably the single greatest opportunity to step-up the fight against poverty. A window of opportunity exists for business to innovate and lead the necessary changes and if they fail, they will probably come to regret the disruptive social, environmental and economic consequences that are likely to result from a failure to meet the Millennium Development Goals.

---

48 Adapted from Nelson, J., *Leveraging the Development Impact of Business in the Fight Against Global Poverty*, Working Paper 22, John F. Kennedy School of Government, Harvard University, Cambridge MA.

49 Go to: http://www.engineersagainstpoverty.org

Figure 2: **Schematic of an Economic and Social Performance Framework (ESPF) for the oil and gas industry**[50]

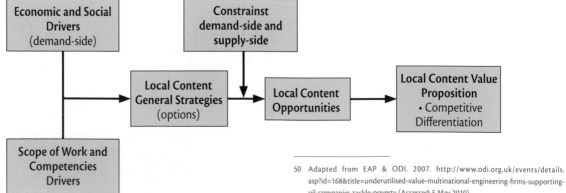

---

50 Adapted from EAP & ODI. 2007. http://www.odi.org.uk/events/details. asp?id=168&title=underutilised-value-multinational-engineering-firms-supporting-oil-companies-tackle-poverty (Accessed: 5 May 2010).

3 Engineering:
Emerging Issues and Challenges

Emerging issues, challenges and opportunities for engineering relate to internal and external factors. Internally, the decline of interest and enrolment of young people, especially women in engineering is a major concern for future capacity. Externally, in the development context, emerging issues, challenges and opportunities relate to the Millennium Development Goals, especially poverty reduction and sustainability, and increasingly to climate change mitigation and adaptation. This chapter has a focus on external issues, challenges and opportunities, with enrolment issues covered later in the chapter on engineering education. The chapter begins with a section on foresight and forecasts of the future, providing a background in foresight of science and technology and innovation, and drawing on the many foresight exercises that have been con-

ducted around the world. A section on emerging and future areas of engineering emphasizes the increasing importance of engineering and sustainability, urbanization and globalization, and increasingly important domains of engineering relating to materials, energy, information and systems, and bioengineering. The theme of sustainability is developed in the section on the changing climate and increasing need for engineers and engineering of the future – beginning in the present – to focus on areas relating to climate change mitigation and adaptation. The following section examines the issues of information and advocacy, public and policy awareness and influence, and how to get the engineering message across from a professional communications viewpoint. The chapter concludes with a view of engineering and technology in the third millennium.

Ariane 4 rocket.

3.1 Engineering, foresight and forecasts of the future

Ian Miles

Futures studies have been with us for a long time, but the term 'foresight' has only come into wide use in recent years. A striking development in the last decade of the twentieth century was the growing prominence of large-scale foresight exercises conducted at national and international levels. This trend was amplified in the new millennium. These exercises, usually funded by governments and intended to provide insights for innovation policy, priorities for research and development funding, and the like,[1] frequently went by the name 'Technology Foresight'. The Japanese experience from the 1970s onwards (using technology forecasting to help build shared understandings of how science and technology might better meet social needs and market opportunities) was the initial inspiration for early efforts in Europe. These large-scale European experiences were widely diffused in turn.

Common to foresight, as opposed to many other futures studies, is the link of long-term analysis (beyond the usual business time horizon) to policy-making (often to specific pending decisions about research or innovation policies) and the emphasis on wide participation (involving stakeholders who may be sources of knowledge not available to the 'great and good', whose engagement may provide the exercise with more legitimacy and whose actions may be necessary complements to those taken by government).

Several factors converged to foreground foresight. First was the need to prioritize research budgets – choices needed to be made as to where to invest, as governments were not able to

continue increasing funding across the whole spectrum. The legitimacy of huge funding decisions being made effectively by the very scientists and engineers that benefitted from them was also in doubt, not least because some emerging areas seemed to be neglected (the Japanese 'Fifth Generation' programme in the 1980s was a wake-up call,[2] triggering a wave of large public research and development programmes in information technology throughout the industrial world). Foresight, and other tools like evaluation studies, was seen as providing ways of making more knowledge-based and transparent decisions.

Second, there were growing concerns about the implications of science and technology and how to shape development so that new technologies could prove more socially and environmentally beneficial. A succession of environmental concerns (pesticides, nuclear accidents, ozone depletion and climate change), food panics (in the UK alone there were, in quick succession, scares around salmonella and listeria, BSE, foot-and-mouth disease, and avian flu – all of them implicating modern farming and food processing techniques, and with huge economic costs even when human mortality was low), and social and ethical concerns, mainly around biomedical issues in human reproduction and the use of tissues and stem cells, with emerging problems over decisions about death, applications of new neuroscience and technology, enhancement of human capabilities, and the prospect of artificial intelligence in the not-so-distant future. Nanotechnologies, or their treatment in the media, are also contributing to unease about how technology decisions are made and where they may be taking us. Foresight can contribute to creating visions of future

---

1 For documentation of a large number of foresight activities, see the European Foresight Monitoring Network at http://www.efmn.eu – the overview report is particularly helpful for statistical analysis. R. Popper *et al.*, 2007. *Global Foresight Outlook 2007* at http://www.foresight-network.eu/files/reports/efmn_mapping_2007.pdf (Accessed: 5 May 2010).

2 Feigenbaum, A. and McCorduck, P. 1983. *The Fifth Generation: Artificial Intelligence and Japan's Computer Challenge to the World* London, Michael Joseph. This book had an electrifying impact here.

possibilities, and as well as positive visions there are warnings about dangers and barriers to the realization of opportunities.

A third set of factors concern innovation. Innovation has come to be recognized as a key element in competitiveness, national performance and achieving socio-economic objectives. More precisely, many countries have come to feel that there are weaknesses in their innovation systems – the institutions, and relationships between institutions, that generate and apply knowledge (in science and technology laboratories, applied engineering, design, higher and vocational public services, commercial enterprises, policymaking, finance and so on). Foresight was seen to provide tools that could help connect and integrate components of innovation systems, and indeed some exercises (e.g. France's FUTURIS)[3] have been explicitly aimed at informing decisions about restructuring national laboratories and the innovation system more generally.

Many countries have embarked on large-scale foresight exercises, and in several cases we are now into the third or even later round of such exercises. In some cases, it remains a specialized activity impelled by one part of government; in others foresight approaches have been embedded much more widely. Expertise has been developed in using techniques such as road-mapping, scenario analysis, Delphi surveys and trend analysis, and there are interesting developments in the application of information technology to support these approaches and provide new means of decision support.

One lesson learned early on during these exercises was that it is important to bring together expertise in social affairs, business management, financial issues and policy, together with expertise possessed by scientists and engineers.[4] Exercises that neglected this found themselves hastily having to plug these knowledge gaps. Foresight activities – in the most successful exercises – proved a valuable setting to enable experts of many kinds to share and fuse their knowledge, to break away from their standard presentations and immediate preoccupations, to articulate their understandings about longer-term developments and to explore how these did or did not align with those of experts in adjacent and related areas.

What has proved to be at a premium is the capability to possess (and share) highly specialized knowledge, but also to be able to relate this understanding to the issues raised in a wide range of other fields; people with 'T-shaped skill profiles' (people with in-

depth knowledge of their own domain as well as competence in a much broader spectrum of managerial, interpersonal and other skills). Additionally, foresight required open-minded people; the experts have to be able to participate on the basis of the knowledge they possess, not simply to argue positions that reflect corporate or sectional interests. Thus a combination of cognitive, social, professional and ethical capabilities are required. This sort of profile is liable to be in demand in any engineering work where relations with customers and users, and perspectives that go beyond immediate project management, are required.

Foresight exercises have addressed a multitude of topics[5] but an inescapable feature is that, across the board, we are continuing to move toward a world in which more and more of our social and economic activities are instrumented:[6] where we use new technologies to transform the material world and design and simulate these transformations; where technologies mediate our interactions and help us codify and collate our knowledge; where we have increasingly powerful tools to intervene in both tangible and intangible elements of complex systems, and to help us understand such systems. New forms of engineering are emerging (service engineering and bioengineering being two examples), as are new approaches to education and lifelong learning. There is probably no single future for engineering; new specialisms will emerge, new skill profiles and hybrid combinations will be required and new professions will develop that have a greater or lesser engineering component. Personal foresight will be an asset that should enable individuals to make informed choices in these shifting landscapes.

Meanwhile, foresight programmes underline the central role played by engineers and engineering in creating the future. Hopefully, such activities will continue to be diffused and institutionalized so that the essential links between engineering and social and environmental concerns can be deepened and made more effective.[7] In this way, debate and action around long-term opportunities and threats will be informed by knowledge of the strengths and limitations of engineering capabilities and of the structure and urgency of social concerns.

○ The Vizcaya Bridge in northern Spain – designed by de Palacio in 1887 and UNESCO World Heritage site.

---

3 See R. Barré Foresight in France, Chp. 5 in L. Georghiou et al. (eds, 2008) The Handbook of Technology Foresight, Cheltenham, UK and Northampton, MA, USA: Edward Elgar (This Handbook provides much more depth on many of the issues discussed in the present text). A good account is also available at: http://forlearn.jrc.ec.europa.eu/guide/7_cases/futuris_operation.htm (Accessed: 5 May 2010).

4 See the study of 'industrially-oriented foresight, J. Molas-Gallart et al. (2001). A Transnational Analysis of the Result and Implications of Industrially-oriented Technology Foresight Studies, ESTO Report, EUR No: EUR 20138 EN available at: http://www.p2pays.org/ref/05/04160.pdf (Accessed: 5 May 2010).

5 See the EFMN database. Even one country's activities can span a vast range, for example recent projects in UK Foresight have concerned themes as various as Flooding, Obesity, Drugs and Brain Science, Exploiting the Electromagnetic Spectrum, Detection and Identification of Infectious Diseases, and Intelligent Infrastructures. Go to http://www.foresight.gov.uk for details of these and many more projects.

6 This term is borrowed from IBM's Samuel J. Palmisano in his paper A Smarter Planet: The Next Leadership Agenda available at http://www.ibm.com/ibm/ideasfromibm/us/smartplanet/20081106/sjp_speech.shtml (Accessed: 5 May 2010). Much of this is also described in terms of being 'informated' or 'infomated', but other technologies are being employed alongside information technology, for example, genomics and nanotechnologies.

7 An interesting step here is the introduction of 'Engineering Foresight' modules into engineering courses, for example a course for third year mechanical engineering students at Manchester University intended to equip them for the sort of projects they may be working on in the future. The course, with a horizon of several decades, particularly explores "step change, disruptive technology and scientific breakthrough rather than incremental product and process development", and locates mechanical engineering in relation to future markets, societies and technologies by training in students in various forecasting techniques. Go to: http://www.manchester.ac.uk/

3.2 Emerging and future areas of engineering

George Bugliarello

In the last five decades a set of increasingly urgent global issues has emerged that call for an unprecedented move across the broad engagement of engineering, ranging from how to make the world sustainable in its social, economic and environmental dimensions, to how to cope with urbanization and globalization. Many of these challenges are underscored by a recent study on *Grand Engineering Challenges* by the National Academy of Engineering in the USA.[8]

An incipient broadening of the traditional frontiers of engineering that encompass interactions with sociology, economics, political science and other social sciences and processes, with healthcare and with the agricultural sciences, is beginning to enable engineers to play a more effective and integrated role in addressing these issues. At the same time, the emergence of several fundamental new engineering endeavours, closely interwoven with science, from nanotechnology to bioengineering has the potential to revolutionize engineering and to impact on global issues in not yet fully fathomed ways.

Economic, Social and Environmental Sustainability

In the area of engineering for economic sustainability, the challenges are to design technologies and systems that can facilitate global commerce, foster technological innovations and entrepreneurship, and help generate jobs, while minimizing environmental impacts and using resources efficiently.

In the social domain, engineering is challenged to design systems that can facilitate education and healthcare, enhance the quality of life, help eliminate global poverty, and help humans preserve their humanity in a world increasingly paced by machines. In each of these areas, the engineering contribution is indispensable, but bound to fail without a close synergy with political and economic forces. An emerging challenge to engineering is also to develop technological approaches that can help prevent or mitigate hostile acts, reduce the impact of natural disasters, and motivate humans to reduce their draw on the resources of the planet.

The traditional role of engineering in the quest for resources – from water to food, energy and materials – needs to be reinforced and expanded by new approaches, as well as in the increasingly important role of engineering in resource conservation and waste management.

The uneven distribution of water across continents and regions and its limited availability make enormous demands on engineering skills, from devising more effective systems for water and wastewater treatment and for recycling, to desalination, reducing evaporation losses in reservoirs, stanching the large amount of leakage from old distribution systems and building new recirculation systems.

Food supply, doubled by the green revolution in the last quarter of the previous century, is again threatening to become insufficient because of the increasing demands of rapidly growing populations and economies, the increasing use of agricultural land for the development of biofuels, and the depletion of fish stocks. This calls for new engineering approaches, including aquiculture and applications of genetics. In many countries, the large percentage of food spoiled in storage and transport is a problem that we can no longer defer. Neither can the threats to food security that are heightened by climate change, affecting 30 per cent of farmers in developing countries (Brown and Funk, 2008),[9] and wich will place new demands on agricultural engineering and global logistics.

In energy, engineering is challenged to continue to improve technologies for the collection, in all its manifestations, of the inexhaustible but widely dispersed solar energy, for the extraction of oil, for tapping thermal energy from the interior of the Earth, and for providing environmentally sustainable power and light to large segments of the world's population. Integration into power grids of large amounts of intermittent solar and wind power is a major challenge, and so is the devising of economical storage mechanisms – large and small – that would have widespread utility, including also the reduction of power plant capacities required to supply power at peak hours. Improvement in efficiency of energy utilization to reduce the large percentage (about 50 per cent) of global energy supply wasted is a global engineering challenge of the first magnitude, and so is the decarbonization of emissions from fossil fuel power plants, e.g. through underground gasification and deep coal deposits. The need to replace liquid hydrocarbons, which power much of the world's transportation systems, is particularly urgent, and the prospect of doing so by biomolecular engineering of plant microbes or by hydrogen fuel cells is emerging as a more desirable possibility than making biofuels from agricultural biomass.

The challenges in the area of material resources are to find more sustainable substitutes (as in the structural use of composites, soil, plastic refuse and agricultural byproducts), so as

8   NAE (National Academy of Engineering), February 15, 2008. Go to: http://www.engineeringchallenges.org

9   Brown, M. E. and C. C. Funk. 2008. Food security under climate change, *Science*, Vol. 319, pp. 580–581, 1 February.

to reutilize those in scarce supply, such as copper, to recycle them and to develop effective closed cycles of materials flow between production and utilization.

In the area of environment, engineering is challenged to help reduce the encroachment of the footprints that human habitats and activities leave on it, from the destruction caused by expanding human habitats and by conflicts, to the indiscriminate mining and transformation of resources, the impact of dams on wildlife, the emissions to the atmosphere of health-threatening and global warming gases, as well as the higher atmospheric temperatures over cities that also contribute to global warming; the 'heat island' phenomenon. Increased efficiencies in the use of all resources, moderation of consumption, recycling of materials, conflict resolution, containment of sprawl, and alternative forms of energy become ever more imperative engineering challenges. So is the ever greater waste disposal problem, including the thorny problem of nuclear waste, to protect human health and the environment. The preservation of the integrity of critical habitats of other species to enable them to coexist with human activities demands careful infrastructural design and site planning. All these challenges can only be overcome through the synergy of new technologies and public understanding of the necessity of new policies.

Urbanization

Urbanization is a second urgent, emerging global development issue with now half the global population living in cities. In the developing world, that percentage is projected to continue to rise explosively in the foreseeable future, while the developed world is already largely urbanized. This makes global sustainability increasingly affected by the impact of cities, large and small. The rapidly changing demographic profiles of cities challenge engineering to address the needs of the massive wave of young populations in cities of the developing world, without neglecting their eventual greying as their life expectancy increases, already a burgeoning problem in the developed world. This will require rethinking the design of many interfaces between humans and artefacts to facilitate their use. The urban engineering challenges are to help find ways to provide for this tidal wave of urban growth with solutions for adequate housing, mobility, water, sanitation, electricity, telecommunications, and clean air for all citizens by using local resources as much as possible to develop infrastructure systems that can follow the expansion of urban areas, and thus help reduce the horrendous blight of urban poverty by creating new job opportunities (Bugliarello, 2008).[10] Urbanization also requires the improvement of quality of life in cities by managing congestion and reducing pollution and noise – in any country.

With the continuing expansion of cities over areas at risk from earthquakes and volcanic eruptions, inundations, devastating storms and tsunamis, and with cities becoming frequent targets of hostile activities, engineering is ever more challenged to find ways to enhance the protection of the populations at risk through more robust and resilient infrastructures, more effective warning systems, and more realistic evacuation or shelter-in-place plans.

Throughout the range of urban sustainability needs of the developing world, good enough solutions will have to be engineered that are more affordable than the traditional ones of the developed world, and that can rapidly satisfy a majority of needs. They range from cheaper and faster construction, to simpler maintenance and repair, 'green' energy-, material- and environment-saving technologies, more flexible urban mobility solutions (as in bus rapid transport (BRT) systems) and telecommunications systems that provide broadband interconnections without expensive land links.

Globalization

Globalization of the world economy presents engineering with a third major set of challenges: to help provide populations, regions and individuals with access to global knowledge, markets and institutions by enhancing transportation systems, the diffusion of information and fast Internet technologies, the provision of technical training required to participate in the global economy, and through the development of common standards to facilitate the synergies of engineering capacities across the globe.

New fundamental engineering endeavours

New and prospective challenges in four fundamental engineering domains: materials, energy, information and systems, as well as bioengineering, offer vast new possibilities for the future.

In the domain of materials: it is becoming increasingly possible through nanotechnology and bionanotechnology to create, ion-by-ion, atom-by-atom, or molecule-by-molecule, materials with a broad range of capabilities, from enhanced structural strength (Dzenis, 2008)[11] to sensing, transferring energy, interacting with light at the scale of light's wavelength, and changing characteristics on command (Vaia and Baur, 2008).[12] This will have the effect of revolutionizing manufacturing, construction and infrastructures. Composite materials, also utilizing a variety of natural materials, make it possible to create strong, lightweight structures. Large-scale self-assembly of materials and microstructures is a more distant but important possibility. Materials and energy are linked in the emerging

The Eastgate Centre in Harare, Zimbabwe, designed from a termite mound for natural ventilation.

10 Bugliarello, G. 2008. Urban sustainability and its engineering challenges. *Journal of Urban Technology*, April.

11 Dzenis, Y. 2008. Structural nanocomputers. *Science*, Vol. 319, pp. 419–420, 25 January.

12 Vaia, R. and J. Baur. 2008. Adaptive composites. *Science*, Vol. 319, pp. 420–421, 25 January.

concept of deconstructable structures and in the development of recycling, so as to reuse as much as possible the materials and the energy embedded within them.

In the energy domain: developments in fuel cells, biomass and waste incinerators, bacterial electricity generators, biofuel engines, photovoltaic generators and thermal collectors with greater efficiencies, in both large and small scale advanced wind turbines and in micro-hydro turbines, all have immediate applications to development. High-voltage superconducting direct current lines offer the prospect – by reducing long distance power losses – to capture distant sources of energy and to transmit energy globally. Also of considerable potential impact is the demonstrated possibility of using the energy from walking in order to generate a current sufficient enough to power low wattage electronic devices. A future challenge responding to a universal need is the design of batteries with greater specific storage capacity per unit weight. Advanced new lighting systems can replace CO_2 generating fuel burning lamps and fires as well as inefficient incandescent bulbs. Nuclear fusion is still a hope of distant realization, but building a large number of advanced, inherently stable fission reactors with a safe proliferation-proof fuel cycle to supply base power will become increasingly necessary to reduce greenhouse emissions, and in the absence of other kinds of energy supply.

In the information domain: personal portable devices, which are revolutionizing individual communications and access to the internet, will become ever more integrated into single multi-function, multi-purpose devices combining voice, data, and imaging thanks to the future development of billion transistor microchips and universal open standards. This will have great impact on areas not reached by traditional telephone systems for reasons of geography, cost or organization. Continuing advances in semiconductor electronics and computer architecture (Ferry, 2008)[13] will make ever more powerful (pentaflops and more) computers possible, with enormous impact on engineering analysis and design and the study of biological, social and environmental phenomena. Information is key to increasing the efficiency in the use of energy and materials. It is also key – in synergy with systems engineering – to globally improving the performance of healthcare systems, social services, manufacturing, transportation and other infrastructural systems, agriculture and geophysics, and mineral prospecting and extraction, all major development challenges.

In every major global challenge, from the eradication of the endemic blight of poverty, to universal and effective healthcare, economic development, urbanization, security and global warming, *systems engineering* of the highest order is called for as it must encompass and harmonize social, political and economic systems, healthcare and nutrition issues, as well as the more traditional engineering systems that deal with water and energy supply, construction, infrastructures and production. To respond to many of these systems engineering challenges, the incipient developments of agent-based and multi-scale modeling offer the possibility of including more realistic behavioural components as well as encompassing in a model dimensions that range from the nano- to the macroscale. A promising systems engineering frontier is also the creation of more sophisticated robots and robotic systems for use in a wide range of applications, from helping the disabled to manufacturing and the performance of dangerous tasks.

Bioengineering

Bioengineering, the interaction of engineering with biology and medicine, will be of increasing significance in healthcare, industry and agriculture, and in everyday life. A host of emerging achievements encompasses for instance biological treatments of drinking water (Brown, 2007),[14] tissue engineering for the replacement of diseased biological tissues and the creation of new tissues, the engineering of all sorts of sophisticated artificial organs (including artificial limbs and ocular prostheses), advances in instrumentation, sensors, as well as more powerful and faster diagnostic approaches and drug delivery to the organism, accelerated vaccine production (Heuer, 2006),[15] and the engineering of proteins, genes and organisms. Many of these advances, of potentially great significance for development, are made possible by progress in miniaturization (e.g. the laboratory or the factory on a chip), computational soft- and hardware, imaging and visualization, and by mechatronics – the combination of mechanical devices and electronics.

An emerging but still largely unfathomed aspect of bioengineering is biomimesis, the search for new ideas and 'proofs of concept' for engineering designs stemming from research in the characteristics of living systems. It can be expected to lead to cheaper or more efficient and effective solutions, as in the simple example of ventilation systems inspired by the design of termite mounds, or in the great structural strength achieved in nature by the synergy of multiple hydrogen bonds.

A new branch of engineering

Out of all these new challenges and possibilities, a new interdisciplinary thrust of engineering can be expected to emerge, what can perhaps be called engineering for development – and would not just be for developing countries. Engineering for development would respond to the global need for engineers who understand the problems of human development and sustainability, and can bring to bear on them

13 Ferry, D. K. 2008. Nanowires in nanoelectronics. *Science*, Vol. 319, pp. 579–580, 1 February.

14 Brown, J. C. 2007. Biological treatment of drinking water, *The Bridge*, Winter, pp. 30–35.

15 Heuer, A. H. (Ed.). 2006. Engineering and vaccine production for an influenza pandemic. *The Bridge*, Vol. 36, No. 3, Autumn.

their engineering knowledge. They are motivated by a sense of the future, and are able to interact with other disciplines, with communities and with political leaders, to design and implement solutions. In this context, an often overlooked but essential responsibility of engineering is to help recognize, prevent or mitigate possible unwanted consequences of new technological developments, such as the onset of tropical disease arising from the damming of rivers in tropical regions, the destruction of thin soils created by mechanized farming equipment, or the social instabilities caused by too rapid an introduction of automation.

Training a sufficient number of engineering professionals focused on development should become a high priority as a critical ingredient in the ability of the global community to deal with the emerging and urgent issues that confront it today.

3.3   A changing climate and engineers of the future[16]

Charlie Hargroves

In his closing words to the Australia 2020 Summit, Prime Minister Kevin Rudd said that 'Climate change is the overarching moral, economic, scientific, and technological challenge of our age.' Responding to the challenge of climate change provides both the greatest challenge and the greatest opportunity the engineering profession has ever faced, and this dual nature may turn out to be the most important 'convenient truth' ever realized.

When considering The Intergovernmental Panel on Climate Change's statement from 2007 that 'the world has less than eight years to arrest global warming or risk what many scientists warn could be catastrophic changes to the planet', it would be easy to despair. However this is balanced by a growing realization of the vast opportunities such a focus can deliver, such as that 'Creating the low-carbon economy will lead to the greatest economic boom in the United States since it mobilized for the Second World War', as stated by the former US President Bill Clinton in late 2007.

In the last two years there has been a significant shift in the global conscience on these issues and few now believe that not taking action is a viable approach; some even consider it a disastrous, costly and amoral one. The daunting question that many are now asking is 'are we actually destroying the world we are creating?' These messages are not new, however, in light of compelling evidence of both the challenges and opportunities for over thirty years now there is still hesitancy; there is still a lack of action on a broad scale, there are even efforts to block such progress. Much of this results from a lack of understanding, a lack of education and competency in the proven economic policies, scientific knowledge, and technological and design solutions currently available.

Rather than seeking a 'silver bullet' solution – the one engineering answer to save the world – it is becoming clear that what we need is more like a 'silver shotgun' approach, an integrated solutions-based engineering portfolio of options, all travelling in the same direction. The engineering profession must now focus the creativity and ingenuity that has delivered today's incredible levels of human and industrial development on the task of delivering sustainable engineering and development solutions.

Engineers of the future will focus on leading efforts to reduce pollution, first by reducing material flows and then by creating critical knowledge and skill sets to redesign technologies, processes, infrastructure and systems to be both efficient, productive and effective.

The challenge for engineers of the future is to understand the science, engineering and design issues vital to a comprehensive understanding of how national economies make the transition to a low emissions future. Given the rapid growth of greenhouse gas emissions globally there is a real need for a greater level of urgency and sophistication around the realities of delivering cost effective strategies, policies and engineering designs to achieve emissions stabilization globally. The *Stern Review* explored in detail the concept of stabilization trajectories and pointed out that there are two distinct phases: 1) global emissions need to stop growing i.e. emissions levels would peak and begin to decline; and 2) there would need to be a sustained reduction of annual greenhouse gas emissions across the entire global economy. The *Stern Review* states that 'The longer action is delayed, the harder it will become. Delaying the peak in global emissions from 2020 to 2030 would almost double the rate of [annual] reduction needed to stabilize at 550ppm CO_2e. A further ten-year delay could make stabilization at 550ppm CO_2e impractical, unless early actions were taken to dramatically slow the growth in emissions prior to the peak.'[17]

16   This material is based on a submission by the author and colleagues of The Natural Edge Project to the Garnaut Climate Change Review initiated by the Australian Federal Government. The full submission can be downloaded at http://www.naturaledge-project.net/Documents/TNEPSubmission.pdf (Accessed: 5 May 2010).

17   Stern, N. 2006. *The Stern Review: The Economics of Climate Change*, Cambridge University Press, Cambridge, Chp 8: The Challenge of Stabilisation, p 10. Available at http://www.sternreview.org.uk/ (Accessed: 5 May 2010).

Figure 1: BAU emissions and stabilization trajectories for 450–550ppm CO₂e

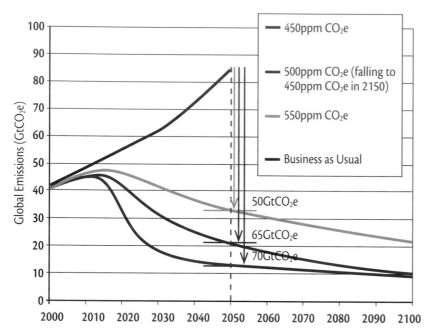

Source: *Stern Review*

The key to the economic impact of an ambitious approach to emissions reduction is to achieve a balance in the timing of the emissions peak and the corresponding requirement for a tailing off of emissions annually. The challenge is the range of combinations of 'peaks' and corresponding 'tails' (i.e. trajectories) that may deliver a given stabilization level, especially when considering that each trajectory will have a different impact on the economy. A late peak will allow short-term reduction levels to be relaxed but will then require a greater level of annual sustained reduction to meet the overall target. An early peak will require a rapid short-term reduction level, but these efforts will be rewarded by a lower level of required sustained annual reductions.

Australian Professor Alan Pears from the Royal Melbourne Institute of Technology explains, '[Greenhouse Gas] Emission reduction sounds like a daunting prospect, and many people imagine that we will have to freeze in the dark, shut down industry, and face misery. But remember, we don't have to slash greenhouse gas emissions in a couple of years – we are expected to phase in savings over decades. This allows us to take advantage of the fact that most energy producing or using equipment, from fridges and computers to cars and power stations, has to be replaced every 5 to 30 years. So we can minimize costs by making sure that, when old equipment is replaced, low greenhouse-impact alternatives are installed. For example, by 2020, most of Australia 's coal-fired power stations will be more than thirty years old, and they will have

to be re-built or replaced; renewable energy, cogeneration and high efficiency energy supply technologies (such as fuel cells) could replace them.'[18]

The risk is that if the peak is too soon it may have significant impacts on our ability to maintain gradual reductions, and if the peak is too late the corresponding annual reductions may be too much for the economy to bear. As the *Stern Review* points out, 'Given that it is likely to be difficult to reduce emissions faster than around 3 per cent per year, this emphasizes the importance of urgent action now to slow the growth of global emissions, and therefore lower the peak.'[19]

The benefit of using stabilization trajectories as the basis for informing a transition in the engineering profession is so we can capitalize on the already abundant opportunities for short-term reductions to achieve the peak, while also building the experience and economies of scale to seriously tackle the issue of sustained reductions. The beauty of the sustained reductions model is that it allows an economy to stage the activities it undertakes to allow for certain industries to be given more time, or 'head room' to respond as the industries that can make short and medium term gains contribute to achieving the average overall reduction, potentially rewarded through an emissions trading scheme or other financial mechanism. When considering each country's role in the global community the situation becomes more complex: efforts across the economy of a country will need to be aggregated to deliver the annual reductions overall; and international efforts need to be aggregated across countries to achieve the global stabilization curve. The *Garnaut Interim Report*, a 2008 economic analysis for Australia, presented a number of country specific trajectory curves based on per capita emissions that could be aggregated to achieve the overall global stabilization trajectory.

It is widely agreed that expecting the rapidly developing countries of China and India to halt their use of fossil fuel consumption is unreasonable considering that the United States, Australia and other developed countries have capitalized on fossil fuels for decades to underpin their development. The strength of the model proposed by Professor Garnaut, and the main reason for our support of it, is that it provides head room for both China and India to develop. Moreover, if all countries follow their per capita curves this may actually make a global transition to stabilization a reality, considering that

18   Smith, M. and Hargroves, K. 2006. *The First Cuts Must be the Deepest*, *CSIRO ECOS*, Issue 128, Dec–Jan. pp. 8–11.

19   Stern, N. 2006. *The Stern Review: The Economics of Climate Change*, Cambridge University Press, Cambridge. Available at http://www.hm-treasury.gov.uk/sternreview_summary.htm (Accessed: 5 May 2010).

Table 1: **Illustrative emissions paths to stabilization**

Stabilisation Level (CO₂e)	Date of peak global emissions	Global emissions reduction rate (% per year)	Percentage reduction in emissions below 2005 values	
			2050	2100
450 ppm	2010	7.0	70	75
	2020	-	-	-
500 ppm (falling to450 ppm in 2150)	2010	3.0	50	75
	2020	4.0 – 6.0	60 – 70	75
	2030	5.0[1] – 5.5[2]	50 – 60	75 – 80
	2040	-	-	-
550 ppm	2015	1.0	25	50
	2020	1.5 – 2.5	25 – 30	50 – 55
	2030	2.5 – 4.0	25 – 30	50 – 55
	2040	3.0 – 4.5[3]	5 - 15	50 – 60

Source: *Stern Review*

already China[20] and India[21] are making increasingly significant commitments to energy efficiency, such as the Chinese 11th five-year plan calling for a 20 per cent fall in energy consumption per unit of gross domestic product (GDP).

Experts predict the global market for climate change solutions will rapidly reach US$1 trillion dollars and will continue to grow. Already many markets for specific low carbon products and services are among the fastest growing in the world. The European Union, Silicon Valley in the United States, China and Japan especially are competing to ensure that their research and development (R&D) bodies and leading businesses innovate the next generation in lighting technologies, energy efficient appliances, renewable energy systems, and fuel efficient cars because these will create multi-billon dollar revenue streams for their businesses over the coming decades. Professor Garnaut summed up the challenge well in February 2008 when launching the *Interim Report*. He stated that, in reaching targets, Australia will have to 'face the reality that this is a hard reform, but get it right and the transition to a low-emissions economy will be manageable ... get it wrong and this is going to be a painful adjustment.'[22]

As Professor Jeffrey Sachs stated at the 2008 Delhi Sustainable Development Summit, 'what is needed is good arithmetic, and good engineering and good economics, all combined... We haven't done the work on that yet. But that is the work that we

Figure 2: **Contraction and convergence for different countries with 'head room' for the rapidly developing economies: a stylised, illustrative scenario.**

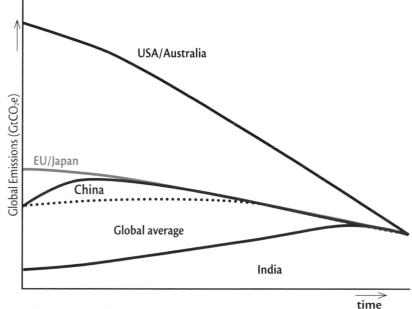

Source: *Garnaut Interim Report* *

20 See China Energy Bulletin at: http://www.energybulletin.net/3566.html (Accessed: 5 May 2010).

21 See India Bureau of Energy Efficiency at: http://www.bee-india.nic.in/ (Accessed: 5 May 2010).

22 Maiden, S. 2008. Garnaut eyes massive carbon reductions, *The Australian*. Available at: http://www.theaustralian.news.com.au/story/0,25197,23251141-11949,00.html (Accessed: 5 May 2010).

* Garnaut Climate Change Review, 2008. *Interim Report to the Commonwealth*, State and Territory Governments of Australia. Available at http://www.garnautreview.org.au/index.htm (Accessed: 5 May 2010).

need to do in the next 2 years in my view – to show a path.'[23] When facing the issues of climate change, it is easy to become hypnotized by the complexity. In order to meet the complexity of the challenges with sophistication and ingenuity of the solutions our professions need to work together to inform on each others' efforts.

The study of economics – if well informed by science – can provide valuable guidance as to the potential impact on an economy from a range of emissions reduction trajectories. A study of science, engineering and design, informed by economics, can provide valuable guidance as to the potential for our industrial economies to achieve such trajectories in light of best practices and balanced by the potential impacts on the environment. Therefore, on its own, a study of economics cannot provide all the answers to our leaders who are seriously considering the trajectories our emissions must follow without being informed by what is physically possible, i.e. by the physical sciences, engineering and design professions. Likewise, a study of science and engineering on its own cannot provide all the answers either without being informed by economics as to the impacts on the economy from a range of potential engineering and design options.

Whether business, government and the community around the world identify and implement the most cost effective greenhouse gas mitigation options depends significantly upon the state of education and training on climate change mitigation solutions. Whether or not decision-makers choose wise policy settings and practice wise adaptive governance on the climate change issues in coming decades, or whether businesses respond well to a carbon price signal depends on their knowledge and skills at being able to identify and implement cost effective mitigation options such as energy efficiency.[24]

The *Stern Review*, having analysed the costs of action and inaction, concluded that costs of action to the global economy would be roughly one per cent of GDP, and stated that 'We estimate the total cost of business as usual climate change to equate to an average reduction in global per capita consumption of 5 per cent at a minimum now and for ever.'[25] The *Stern Review* describes how the cost would increase were the model to take into account additional impacts on environmental and human health, and the effects of positive feedbacks and the disproportionate burden of climate change on the poor and vulnerable globally. It predicts that if fast and dramatic action is not taken on climate change, then climate change could cause an economic recession to rival the great economic recession of the 1930s, concluding, 'If a wider range of risks and impacts is taken into account, the estimates of damage could rise to 20 per cent of GDP or more. The investment that takes place in the next 10–20 years will have a profound effect on the climate in the second half of this century and the next. (Inaction now) and over the coming decades could create risks of major disruption to economic and social activity on a scale similar to those associated with the great wars and the economic depression of the first half of the twentieth century. And it will be difficult or impossible to reverse these changes.'[26]

Developing and meeting greenhouse gas reduction targets is urgent because emissions concentrations are now exceeding environmental thresholds as regards how much the biosphere can accommodate. As Lester Brown writes, the impact of our current form of development means that, 'we are crossing natural thresholds that we cannot see and violating deadlines that we do not recognize. Nature is the time-keeper, but we cannot see the clock. Among other environmental trends undermining our future are shrinking forests, expanding deserts, falling water tables, collapsing fisheries, disappearing species, and rising temperatures. The temperature increases bring crop-withering heat waves, more-destructive storms, more-intense droughts, more forest fires, and of course ice melting.'[27] Scientists like NASA's James Hansen argue that if rapid greenhouse gas reductions do not occur in the next ten years then these ironically termed 'positive feedbacks', once unleashed, will cause a global catastrophe increasing the risk of sea level rises and extreme weather events, and resulting in significant economic and business losses globally.[28] More than ever there is recognition of the need for unprecedented global cooperation to undertake action as rapidly as possible to avoid triggering such feedback effects. Al Gore has called the situation nothing less than a 'planetary emergency', which is surely the most significant future challenge for our current 'young engineers', and which will shape the future of engineering.[29]

23 Sachs, J. 2008. Valedictory Address, delivered to the Delhi Sustainable Development Summit, Delhi (7–9 February 2008).

24 The Natural Edge Project has undertaken a comprehensive national survey of the state of education on energy efficiency in Australian universities funded by the National Framework on Energy Efficiency, and covering 27 of the 33 universities.

25 Stern, N. 2006. *The Stern Review: The Economics of Climate Change, Executive Summary* Cambridge University Press, Cambridge, p 10. Available at: http://www.hm-treasury.gov.uk/media/8AC/F7/Executive_Summary.pdf (Accessed: 29 May 2010).

26 Stern, N. 2006. *Stern Review*.

27 Brown, L. R. 2008. *Plan B 3.0: Mobilizing to Save Civilization*. W.W. Norton & Company, 398 p.

28 Hansen, J. and Sato, J. *et al.* 2007. Climate change and trace gases, *Phil. Trans. Royal Soc*, Vol. 365, pp 1925–1954. Available at http://pubs.giss.nasa.gov/abstracts/2007/Hansen_etal_2.html (Accessed: 5 May 2010).

29 Barringer, F. and Revkin, A.C. 2007. Gore Warns Congress of 'Planetary Emergency', *The New York Times*. Available at http://www.nytimes.com/2007/03/22/washington/22gore.html (Accessed: 5 May 2010).

3.4 The engineering message – getting it across

Philip Greenish and Beverley Parkin

Engineers make a huge contribution across the world but – in the UK at least – their role is generally poorly understood. Public policy benefits from having the engineering dimensions considered early in the policymaking process but – again in the UK – engineers are not always engaged. Engineering solves global problems and increases the health and wealth of nations, so the world needs more engineers to help address the enormous challenges we all face.

These propositions drive the Royal Academy of Engineering's mission to 'put engineering at the heart of society.' This is about helping engineers that need institutional support make their fullest contribution for both the benefit of society and to create recognition of the value of that contribution. The issue also calls for more work to inspire young people with the fascination and excitement of engineering, and to encourage more of them go on to become the next generation of engineers.

Perceptions

So what are the key public perception issues that need to be tackled? In 2007, the UK Royal Academy of Engineering[30] and the UK Engineering and Technology Board commissioned a survey to find answers to this question.[31] The survey verified much of what the engineering community had suspected over many years – that people in the UK have little or no understanding of the nature of engineering, its scope, diversity and impact on society. This limited awareness and understanding of engineering is coupled with a significant lack of confidence in and knowledge of the profession and the work that engineers do. Nearly half of the survey respondents felt they knew 'very little' or 'not very much' about engineering, and six out of ten people thought that 'hardly anyone knows what engineers do.' Younger people in particular were found to have a limited understanding of engineering.

Engineers operate across a broad range of activities and sectors and it may be that this very breadth is, in fact, a barrier to awareness and understanding of what they do. Indeed, the study found that engineering was regarded as difficult to define with eight out of ten respondents agreeing that there are so many types of engineers that it makes 'engineering' a difficult role to grasp. This is not helped when, for example, the media cloaks the specific word 'engineering' under different terms such as 'design', 'science' or 'innovation'. A study of US magazine *Science Times* found that engineers and engineering were explicitly mentioned in only one in five of the stories that were clearly about engineers and engineering.[32] UK broadcast programming and print articles similarly lack content that is actually designated as 'engineering' even when the subject is actually engineering-focused.

Communicating with young people is a particular challenge. In the UK, we need more young people to choose engineering as a career. We must also engage many more young people with the societal impacts of engineering so that they can take part in the debate on the big issues of the day. The essence of engineering can be hard for young people to grasp so conveying an engineering message has to start in school. Entering a career in engineering depends on young people studying the right subjects and having access to effective guidance, communications and role models. Very few young people in the UK can name a famous engineer other than perhaps Brunel, who died in 1859. There is a growing research base that suggests that the key to success in communications with young people is having engineering role models who look and sound like the young people they are talking to. Role model recognition is also a factor. A key concern, therefore, is the under-representation in the profession of women and of people from ethnic backgrounds and some socio-economic groups.

The world is experiencing a time of rapid technological advancement, driven by engineering. Society needs to engage and explore important questions with its engineers. As a profession, engineering needs to work together, nationally and internationally, to ensure that communications challenges are addressed and that engineers have every opportunity to get their important messages across. After all, engineering is for and about people, about making the world a better place. Many of the Academy's own Fellows (elected members) regularly appear in the media and have a high public profile as a result of their work, yet are not necessarily described or recognized as 'engineers'.

The case study in the following box outlines the three workstreams that the Academy has developed in response to these challenges: public affairs and policy, communicating with the public at large, and communicating with young people. Increasingly, the Academy is working in these areas with partners in the professional engineering community to create a unified voice and more visible presence. Although the Academy has a national remit, the achievement of its objectives requires a global outlook and an appreciation of the wider international context of engineering.

---

30   Go to: http://www.raeng.org.uk

31   New survey finds deep misconceptions of engineering among young people that could worsen shortfall in engineers. Available at http://www.raeng.org.uk/news/releases/shownews.htm?NewsID=416 /pa (Accessed: 5 May 2010).

32   Clark, F. and Illman, D.L. 2006. Portrayals of Engineers in Science Times, *Technology and Society Magazine*, IEEE, Vol. 25, No.1, Spring 2006. pp.12–21.

CASE STUDY: The UK Royal Academy of Engineering

Introduction

The Royal Academy of Engineering is the UK's national academy for the engineering profession. Fellows and staff work with a wide range of partner organizations, including the government Office of Science and Innovation, the British Council, the UK research councils, and parliamentary and governmental groups. The Academy is a founding member of both the International Council of Engineering and Technological Sciences (CAETS), the European Council of Applied Sciences and Technologies and Engineering (Euro-CASE); all are important vehicles for influencing international policy. In the UNESCO Commission, an Academy-nominated member of the Natural Sciences Committee helps to ensure that the engineering dimension is represented in debate.

You can view the Academy's website, including links to our recent media coverage at http://www.raeng.org.uk and read our flagship publication at http://www.ingenia.com

Public policy

Society benefits when engineers are involved in public life and public debate. Almost all government policy has an engineering dimension, which is crucial to the successful delivery of its objectives. Policy that has been designed from the outset with an understanding of the engineering dimensions of delivery is more likely to be workable. Equally, the engineering approach to problem-solving can support the formation of policy that is fit for purpose and sustainable. Effective responses to the grand challenges such as climate change, energy security, world poverty, global disease burdens and international terrorism can only be developed with engineering input.

Through its Fellows (elected members), the UK Royal Academy of Engineering is well networked with government and parliament. A programme of public affairs work seeks to build on that network and promote a focused set of messages based on policy in education, engineering and international affairs to target audiences across parliamentary institutions, government and its agencies. We brief all UK Parliamentary parties and their spokespeople on policy interests. Very few UK politicians have an engineering background so the Academy runs a programme of meetings to provide information on the key issues. With so much legislation deriving from the European Union, this work is now extending into EU institutions as well. Finally, because the Academy is independent of government, it is able to provide impartial, expert advice. Almost all government policy has an engineering dimension, which is crucial to the successful delivery of its objectives. Policy that has been designed from the outset with an understanding of the engineering dimensions of delivery is more likely to be workable. Equally, the engineering approach to problem-solving can support the formation of policy that is fit for purpose and sustainable. Effective responses to the grand challenges such as climate change, energy security, world

poverty, global disease burdens and international terrorism can only be developed with engineering input.

Building influence

Over the last year, the Academy has been working with partners across the UK professional engineering community to ensure that government policymakers have access to the engineering expertise across the sectors. This has resulted in government departments enlisting our support and the expertise of our leading engineers for a range of policy areas as climate change and energy, water security and national infrastructure. Furthermore, in order to see the engineering perspective underpinning decision-making across government, the Academy is working to improve engineering capacity and understanding within the civil service (policy staff).

The global economic downturn and some high profile failures in the financial services industry are providing an opportunity to highlight the importance of engineering innovation to support a more resilient future economy and address the huge challenges we face.

Another important element of the Academy's work in national policy is in influencing the education of young people, particularly in encouraging them to study science, technology, engineering and mathematics subjects. The Academy helped to create a vocationally-focused yet academically robust qualification for 14–19 year old students known as the Diploma and advises government on a range of aspects of engineering education.

Fellows and staff work with a wide range of partner organizations to promote the Academy's policy agenda, including the Office of Science and Innovation, the British Council, the UK research councils, the parliamentary committees for Science and Technology and the Foreign and Commonwealth Office's Science and Innovation network. The Academy is a founding member of both the International Council of Academies of Engineering and Technological Sciences (CAETS), the European Council of Applied Sciences and Technologies and Engineering (Euro-CASE); all are important vehicles for influencing international policy. Euro-CASE is already proving its value in drawing the European Commission's attention to such issues as the engineering dimension of renewable energy targets. In the UNESCO Commission, an Academy-nominated member of the Natural Sciences Committee helps ensure that the engineering dimensions is represented in debate.

Media profile

The Academy's communication with the public aims to raise the profile of the organization and the role, contribution, achievements and challenges facing engineers. Communications try to engage people of all ages and from all walks of life in the debate on engineering and its impact on society, the nation and the world. A key means of communications with the public are the media. We set our-

selves the goal of getting a serious engineering story into the national media every week of the year. Our success in this endeavour is due to the Academy's Fellows who regularly appear in the print and broadcast media on a range of topical issues.

Now that the scientific case for climate change has been proven to most people's satisfaction, the media debate in the UK is shifting its focus towards how to adapt and mitigate the risks. The media has developed an appetite for ideas and stories on the new technologies and innovative solutions to mitigate climate change, providing a fruitful opportunity for engineers to showcase their ideas and engage in the debate.

An important part of the strategy is to make the link between engineering technologies and the impact they have or may have on society, devising ways to convey them that are engaging and thought-provoking, and to engage with topical issues. Policy issues such as privacy and surveillance, autonomous vehicles and other systems, synthetic biology and nanotechnology all have powerful implications for society and the Academy's work in these areas has received considerable media interest worldwide.

We also communicate through our publications. *Ingenia*, our quarterly magazine, is mailed out free of charge to over 3,000 UK secondary schools and to 11,000 destinations around the world. The online version has also become a significant engineering resource, with hundreds of thousands of visitors logging on each year. A recent publication *Engineering Change* is a book of essays highlighting the role of engineering in international development, particularly in Africa.*

Public engagement

If public relations are about persuading and inspiring the public with the aim of creating impact and raising profile, public engagement is about helping people debate and reflect on the impact of engineering on the world. The Academy undertakes public engagement through a variety of activities that raise awareness and stimulate nationwide or local debate about engineering, including media coverage, live events, festivals, exhibitions and drama productions. Current issues include developments in electronic patient databases for healthcare research, robotics and artificial intelligence, and synthetic biology.

The Royal Academy of Engineering

---

* Go to: http://www.raeng.org.uk/news/publications/list/reports/ Engineering_Change.pdf (Accessed: 5 May 2010).

3.5 Engineering and technology in the third millennium

Tony Ridley

How will engineering and technology develop in the next thousand years? Nearly forty years ago Toffler (1971)[33] argued that by changing our relationship to the resources that surround us, by violently expanding the scope of change and most crucially, by accelerating its pace, humanity has broken irretrievably with the past. We have cut ourselves off from the old ways of thinking, of feeling, of adapting. We have set the stage for a completely new society and we are now racing towards it.

What we could see only dimly in the 1970s, we now both witness and understand better as the dramatic development of technologies such as computing, global communications, biomedical engineering and nanotechnology (to name a few) have shown us. As an academic coming towards retirement at the end of the twentieth century, I suddenly realized that my career would not end when I reached sixty-five, but until about 2040 when the undergraduates I have been teaching would themselves reach retirement. We have learned that teachers, researchers, government and business need to look far ahead in order to keep up.

Recognition of the *need* for change is a main driving force. The engineering profession will be influenced by wider political, social and economic trends over which it currently has little influence in return. Sustainability has had widespread and far-reaching influence on the profession. The growth of alternative sources of finance (such as public, private partnerships, etc.) demands a far more proactive and commercially oriented approach than we have been used to.

Political changes also offer an opportunity to reassess and re-invent the role of engineering in meeting society's needs.

Building consensus among all interested parties is becoming an increasingly important element of this role. To enhance our value to society, we also have to maintain an involvement in all stages of the life cycle of our products and services. Sustainability, ethics and acceptability are becoming closely interlinked themes within our work. We must therefore take the lead in setting ethical standards in our areas of responsibility.

Creative and successful engineering can be found in the interaction of design and project management. While design must not to be reduced to technical analysis, project management must not be reduced to administrative control. Risk management is becoming a central aspect of developing optimum solutions, not least because of a growing awareness of financial risks.

Engineering activity

What kind of engineering is going to take us forward in the twenty-first century? The Universe of Engineering (RAEng, 2000)[34] takes a comprehensive view of that question, and it is necessary to first consider a number of definitions of related subjects (Box 1).

The title 'Universe of Engineering' was used to describe the range of activities in which engineering is involved. It is much larger than generally supposed. At least half of the companies, other than purely financial companies, quoted daily in the financial pages of the newspapers depend on engineering to be competitive, and so survive and prosper. The so-called 'new economy' was created, and continues to be created through

33 Toffler, A. 1971. *Future Shock*. Pan Books, London.

34 Royal Academy of Engineering. 2000. *The Universe of Engineering – a UK perspective*, London.

Subjects related to engineering

Science: the body of, and quest for, fundamental knowledge and understanding of all things natural and man-made; their structure, properties, and how they behave. *Pure science* is concerned with extending knowledge for its own sake. *Applied science* extends this knowledge for a specific purpose. Science as an activity is not a profession, though strong socially responsible codes of conduct and practices have developed.

Engineering Science: The knowledge required – *know-what* – is the growing body of facts, experience and skills in science, engineering and technology disciplines; coupled to an understanding of the fields of application.

Engineering Design: The process applied – *know-how* – is the creative process that applies knowledge and experience to seek one or more technical solutions to meet a requirement, solve a problem, then exercise informed judgement to implement the one that best meets constraints.

Technology: an *enabling package* or tool formed of knowledge, devices, systems, processes and other technologies created for a specific purpose. The word 'technology' is used colloquially to describe a complete system, a capability or a specific device.

Innovation: the successful introduction of something new. In the context of the economy it relates to something of

practical use that has significant technical content and achieves commercial success. In the context of society it relates to improvements in the quality of life. Innovation may be wholly new, such as the first cellular telephone, or a significantly better version of something that already exists.

The central role of engineering in society and the economy is neither evident to the public at large nor to the media in particular. The popular perception is generally confined to manufacturing and major building works. The engineering profession is considered by many, including unfortunately many young, as a somewhat dull, uncreative activity wholly associated with the 'old economy'.

the process of engineering. Economists have added *technology* to the traditional three prime inputs to all economic activity – *labour, capital* and *materials*. It is the engineering process that creates technology, and which makes technology useful to people.

Engineering community

There is a wider engineering community that describes the very many people, engineers, scientists, metallurgists, programmers and many others who practise engineering in one form or another, to a greater or lesser degree, in the course of their professional activities. It is much larger than generally recognized. For example, there are about two million people in the UK who call themselves engineers, about three-quarters of whom have a professional engineering qualification, and only 160,000 are formally 'registered'. There are no common or reliable figures – or even in some cases measures – to estimate the numbers of people in the wider engineering community who do not call themselves engineers, but who practise engineering in the course of their work.

In 1995 the UK Institution of Civil Engineers suggested that in the field of infrastructure, engineers were responsible for much of the essentials of modern life:

- The muscles and sinews that hold our society together (bridges, roads, railways, dams, airports, docks, tunnels).

- The provision and maintenance of its hearts and lungs (clean water, natural resources in, waste out).

- Transport for safe and effective movement.

- Energy to make it all work (offshore gas and oil, nuclear, hydro, tidal and wind power).

We know that the whole life cycle of an engineering project must be addressed if we are to make wise decisions to proceed with planning, finance, design, procurement, construction, commissioning, operations and maintenance, and decommissioning. In the past there has been a tendency to concentrate on the design stage.

To create successful projects, we need engineers who can command the totality of the physical attributes of a project: operation, communication and human resources, finance and funding, organizational and institutional questions, and environmental impacts. This may be summed up as a pentagon of hardware, software, 'finware', 'orgware' and 'ecoware'. Not only is each element of the pentagon important in its own right in the creation of an engineering project, it is also the interrelationship between them that raises the greatest problems. Nearly all engineering problems, in the design, development and operation of any system, arise at interfaces. At a larger dimension it is at the interfaces between the five elements of the pentagon that the greatest difficulties arise.

Technology is the subject of technique, but it is also about products and processes. Civil engineering, for example, relies on science but specifically on technology-based science. In the late twentieth century and early twenty-first century, biology and chemistry have been increasingly important to the future of civil engineering, as are maths and physics. This reflects the broader, larger view of the profession that is appropriate for the future. The family of civil engineers now includes disciplines not traditionally thought to be part of the profession.

Engineering process

Technological change is a complex process that must be managed all the way from concept to the market place. Technological knowledge is cumulative and grows in path-dependent ways.

Ziman (1995)[35] has pointed out the distinction between technology-based science and science-based technology where novel technologies have developed from basic, discovery-based research. The electrical industry, nuclear engineering and radar are examples of the latter. Conversely, technology-based science has developed out of practical techniques such as mining and metallurgy that have their origins in the mists of antiquity.

In the nineteenth century, a variety of ancient crafts transformed the technology-based science of industrial chemistry, whilst in the twentieth century the practical technical knowledge of the metallurgist has been incorporated in a new science of materials. The same process is to be observed in almost all fields of practical human activity as we seek to explore and understand. Agriculture, civil engineering, food processing, architecture and many other fields have developed their respective sciences to guide further technical progress. In these cases, engineering is not a sub-set of science but has actually created new opportunities for scientific research.

Morita (1992)[36] has said that technology comes from employing and manipulating science into concepts, processes and devices. The true missionaries who can really capture technology and use it to chart the future course of industry are what he called 'technologists', individuals who have a wide understanding of science and engineering, as well as a broad vision and true commitment to the needs of society. It is technology that drives industry and it is the engineer who guides technology.

Krugman (1994)[37] suggests that it often takes a very long time before a new technology begins to make a major impact on productivity and living standards. The reason for these long lags is that technology often does not have its full impact when it is

35   Ziman, J. 1995. *An introduction to science studies – the philosophical and social aspects of science and technology*, Cambridge University Press.

36   Morita, A. 1992. First UK Innovation Lecture, Royal Society, London.

37   Krugman, P. 1994. *Peddling prosperity – economic sense and nonsense in the age of diminished expectations*, Norton, New York and London.

used in isolation. It is only when it becomes broadly applied and interacts with other technologies that its true potential can be exploited. In these circumstances, engineering education must recognize the importance of synthesis and design as well as more conventional analysis. But it must also recognize the importance of the iterative approach (feedback) whether in design, in sustainability or in innovation.

Researchers in technology would be well advised to address customer and societal needs and market requirements and not just research for research or technology's sake. However, industry would be better served if it sought out good and relevant research more positively, and if it developed more industry/academic partnerships. Thereafter industry and academia together should treat the task of taking research into practice as a business process to which the disciplines of good project management can and should be applied.

Thus, a way ahead for both researchers and industrialists might be to ask in each case: What is the societal problem? What is the technological challenge? What is the business driver? How to define the research project? What are the findings (actual or potential)? What are the potential applications? and, What is the mechanism (business process) for advancing research into practice? The process is iterative. The industrialist/businessman defines the problem, the technological challenge sets the research agenda, but the research equally defines the technological possibilities.

If we are to advance research into practice it is not enough for governments, industry or research councils simply to sit in judgement on research proposals. They must actively seek out good researchers and, through mutual discussion, develop programmes that address societal needs. Engineers provide services to meet the needs of society and it is creativity that is our essential contribution. The Latin *ingenerare* means 'to create'.

The engineering community in the third millennium needs to create a new vision, goal and strategy for itself. Though it is impossible to predict what the world will be like even in 2020, that vision should include a genuine improvement in the quality of life for all as well as long-term environmental, social and economic sustainability. The goal of engineering would then be to contribute towards achieving that vision, with its strategy focusing on the development of whatever structures, skills and technologies are needed.

4 An Overview of Engineering

This is one of the main chapters of the Report and presents an overview of engineering around the world. The chapter begins with a review of statistics and indicators on engineering, with reference to the need for and availibility of information on engineering, how engineering and engineers are defined, OECD and UNESCO statistics relating to engineering, engineering education and employment. As noted here and elsewhere in the Report, there is a particular need for better indicators on engineering at the international level. The chapter continues with reviews of the major fields of civil, mechanical, electrical and electronic, chemical, environmental, agricultural and medical engineering to give a flavour of the diverse range of fields in industry, manufacturing, government, research and development, and consulting in which engineers work. Consulting engineering, for example, is a major industry with an annual revenue of around US$490 billion, and helps generate half the world's GDP.

The engineering profession and its organization is then discussed, with reference to the history and development of engineering, national, regional and international cooperation. Reference is also made to leading engineering organizations, including the World Federation of Engineering Organizations (WFEO), the International Council of Academies of Engineering and Technological Sciences (CAETS), the International Federation of Consulting Engineers (FIDIC), the European Federation of National Engineering Associations (FEANI), the Federation of Engineering Institutions of Asia and the Pacific (FEIAP), the Association for Engineering Education in Southeast and East Asia and the Pacific (AEESEAP), the Asian and Pacific Centre for Transfer of Technology (APCTT) and the African Network of Scientific and Technological Institutions (ANSTI). Organizations focused on engineering and technology also make an important contribution to international development, and include Practical Action, Engineers Without Borders, Engineers Against Poverty and Engineers for a Sustainable World.

Compared to science, engineering has lacked a reflective disciplinary focus on social and policy issues. It is good therefore that an international network on engineering studies has recently been developed, which is presented in the following section together with a discussion on engineering, science and technology policy and the transformation of national science and engineering systems, with reference to New Zealand and South Africa. This is followed by a section on engineering ethics and anti-corruption, which includes contributions on engineers against corruption, and business integrity management systems in consulting engineering. The chapter concludes with a section on women and gender issues in engineering, including a case study from Australia.

4.1   Engineering indicators – measurement and metrics

Gunnar Westholm

Section 4.1 summarizes the methods developed and employed (and the problems encountered) by the principal international agencies for the collection, analysis and distribution of internationally comparable data on 'science and technology' personnel in general and, where applicable, on engineers in particular. It outlines some historical issues, the challenges faced in using these methods, and the role of the principle international agencies involved (UNESCO, OECD, Eurostat, ILO etc.).

Specific attention is given to the OECD *Frascati Manual* for the measurement of research and development resources, the OECD/Eurostat *Canberra Manual* for the measurement of stocks and flows of human resources devoted to science and technology, and to the recent OECD/UNESCO/Eurostat project on the careers of doctorate holders. The international education and employment classifications (ISCED, ISCO) are reviewed. A number of statistical tables on engineering education and employment (enrolments, graduates, gender) are also presented and briefly discussed.

This section will explore some historical issues of science and technology (S&T) indicators, their theoretical definitions and practical applications, and make reference to human S&T resources in general and, where applicable, to engineering and engineers in particular. The role of the principal international organizations involved in the development of international classifications and data collection (UNESCO, OECD, Eurostat, ILO, etc.) will be discussed. The experience of a small number of national science and technology policy agencies (notably the United States National Science Foundation) with recognized practice in the field is mentioned to show procedures that may perhaps inspire other countries or institutions.

Some local or regional data are presented in other sections of this Report, so this section attempts to present reasonably comparable statistics currently available at the international level (the bulk of which comes from the databases of the above international agencies, and principally concerning engineering education). Data are more-or-less complete for most industrialized economies (typically full members of the OECD or European Union) but are weaker elsewhere (note that data collection efforts are taking place at the UNESCO Institute for Statistics and the data coverage is rapidly improving, albeit from a low base).

4.1.1 The need for science and technology data and indicators

Capacity and competence are central to proficient science and technology policies where engineering and engineers are of crucial significance. Even if the broad family of engineers is sometimes first associated with 'big science' (high technology, aerospace, nuclear, defence etc.), their presence is more strongly experienced in everyday life by creating, operating, maintaining and improving public and private infrastructure (in areas such as industry, energy, transportation, communications, agriculture, health and utilities) and perhaps also in creating new understanding vital for all aspects of sustainable development for the future of society (such as renewable energy technologies, climate change and environmental issues, and so on).

The lack of qualified engineers and technicians is currently reported to be one of the principal obstacles to economic growth encountered by innovative firms in many industrialized and industrializing countries. The importance of engineering and engineers and the significance of their role can therefore be appreciated, and is highlighted throughout this Report. However quantitative and qualitative data are not always available, known to policy-makers or kept up to date.

Data on scientists and engineers, however defined, have since the early days of statistics been widely assembled within the customary statistical framework of countries such as, for instance, in population, labour force and education surveys or national censuses. Interest in such data for policy reasons (such as in science and technology policy) was recognized much later, as was the inadequacy of existing data to meet the new demands in many cases. A number of initiatives have therefore been taken, at both national and international levels, to gather data to meet these new demands. Policy-makers wanted to address, among other things, worries about the increasing age of the science and technology workforce, the expected general or specific levels of supply and demand for highly-qualified personnel (and hence capacity to adapt and innovate etc.), gender considerations, brain-drain and brain gain (to inform immigration policy, and so on), and the levels of interest in science and technology studies among young people.

4.1.2 The statistical dilemma: What is engineering? Who is an engineer?

Engineering is a multi-dimensional socio-economic activity and there are a multitude of educational and/or functional proposals to identify the engineers' profile, with different approaches to meet national and international needs for comparable data and indicators. There are hence significant differences in the availability of information from one country to the next, and particularly between already industrialized countries and industrializing countries. This, in turn, is due to the fact that there about as many types of organization for the education and training of engineers as there are countries (and certainly more than for the training of scientists).

Furthermore, there are no clear-cut definitions, in particular definitions that might allow international comparisons of what is covered by the concept of 'engineering', or who in the workforce is really an engineer. An engineer may be someone who has graduated, at one level or another, from engineering education (an education and training approach), or they may be registered or working as an engineer (a membership or an occupation approach). The same definition problem also affects technicians. And the analysis of the situation is certainly not helped by the fact that the field of engineering, technology and engineers, from the earliest days of statistics and indicators, has been merged with the field of science (it is common to find data of 'science and technology' or 'scientists and engineers' as statistical measures).

© EWB-UK

⌒ *Good information is important to promote women in engineering.*

> One of the many definitions of engineering and of engineers is that suggested by open collaborative online encyclopaedia 'Wikipedia', in an article which has had many individual contributions and edits:
>
> 'Engineering is the discipline and profession of applying scientific knowledge and utilizing natural laws and physical resources in order to design and implement materials, structures, machines, devices, systems and processes that realize a desired objective and meet specified criteria...
>
> ... One who practices engineering is called an engineer and those licensed to do so may have more formal designations such as Professional Engineer, Chartered Engineer or Incorporated Engineer...
>
> ... The broad discipline of engineering encompasses a range of more specialised sub-disciplines, each with a more specific emphasis on certain fields of application and particular areas of technology...'

4.1.3 The OECD Frascati Manual on the measurement of research and development resources

The basic definitions

The first proposals for guidelines for systematic measurement of national science and technology (S&T) expenditures and workforces were those of the OECD in the early 1960s, resulting in the *Frascati Manual*. Named after meetings held in Frascati, Italy, the manual is currently in its sixth edition issued in 2002.

Even though the very first guidelines in 1962 discussed appraising the total annual resources for S&T in a country, they were soon reduced to the measurement of research and development (R&D) expenditures and personnel only. R&D represents only a very small part of the total science and technology activities within a country (discussed in more detail with UNESCO, below) and the boundaries between R&D and other related activities were hard to define. These boundary issues have, ever since, been more thoroughly discussed in all successive editions of the *Frascati Manual* and concern both financial and human resources in R&D.

The collection of international R&D data was a totally new exercise that called for new concepts, definitions and exploratory guidelines. The *Frascati Manual* defines R&D as:

'Research and experimental development (R&D) comprise creative work undertaken on a systematic basis in order to increase the stock of knowledge, including knowledge of man, culture and society, and the use of this stock of knowledge to devise new applications.'

Paragraph 63 of the 2002 Frascati Manual

The manual defines the basic statistical coverage of R&D personnel as:

'... All persons employed directly on R&D should be counted, as well as those providing direct services such as R&D managers, administrators and clerical staff.'

Paragraph 294 of the 2002 Frascati Manual

The above definition of R&D is very theoretical, and covers 'basic research' or 'fundamental research', 'applied research' and 'experimental development'. However, this definition has never been abandoned, despite numerous debates. Note that the OECD collected data only for natural sciences and engineering using the *Frascati Manual* until, in 1983, the short phrase '...knowledge of man, culture and society' was added with a view to embracing R&D in the social sciences and humanities (in line with UNESCO practice).

Problems of measuring human resources

A specific dilemma emerged regarding the measurement of R&D personnel. R&D is not a full-time activity in many cases, such as in some enterprises or in tertiary education institutions (universities), for example, where it may be more a part-time activity. Therefore, to include every person engaged in R&D in some way in the 'head-count' would grossly inflate the human resource input. Since interest focused at the time on the overall real R&D resource, it was recommended from the start that the head-count data be converted (i.e. reduced) into full-time equivalents (FTE) or 'person-years', for a long time this was the only recommended approach.

Interest in head-counts reappeared only much later, with the intensification of indicator work correlating diverse data sets expressed in numbers of persons (such as engineers as a share of total population, women scientists as a proportion of total scientists, etc.). Therefore, equal significance is now given to both full-time equivalents and to head-counts in the latest version of the *Frascati Manual* (2002).

From research and development statistics to science and technology indicators

At the time, the R&D statistics service at the OECD acted more-or-less like any national central statistical bureau: collecting data (via surveys addressed to the national authorities) and processing and publishing the resulting statistics. Analysis of the information was not yet a main concern.

Gradually, however, the OECD became the prime customer of its own R&D statistics, used for a rising number of policy studies. This analytical drive helped to identify weaknesses in the proposed theoretical guidelines that were then amended in subsequent editions of the *Frascati Manual*. The same work was also the opening of the first OECD R&D/S&T indicators series, largely inspired by the experience of the National Science Foundation (NSF) in the United States.

The principal international standard classifications

All the Frascati Manual recommendations were, from the outset, soundly backed up by references to internationally-adopted standard classifications, including the United Nations Systems of National Accounts (SNA), the International Standard Classification of Education (ISCED), the International Standard Classification of Occupations (ISCO) and the International Standard Classification of All Industrial Activities (ISIC). These classifications have over time been revised on several occasions (further revisions still underway) and, as a consequence, the OECD guidelines also had to follow. This notably affected the R&D human resource series, referenced in terms of education or occupation classifications, or both.

Over the years, the *Frascati Manual* had to respond to new political priorities or the latest S&T policy interests, from the first post-war 'big science' objectives (aerospace, nuclear, defence etc) to more society-directed goals (social policies, environment, health, energy, information and communication technologies, biotechnologies, and so on).

The *Frascati Manual* recommends an institutional breakdown of the national economy into four broad sectors of R&D expenditures and employment (personnel): Business Enterprise; Government; Higher Education; and Private Non-Profit. With the exception of the government sector, additional and more detailed sub-sectors are suggested. For the Business Enterprise sector, this is by detailed industrial branches defined in terms of ISIC. For Higher Education and Private Non-Profit sectors, this is by six broad fields of science and technology drawing on ISCED, namely 'natural sciences', 'medical sciences', 'agricultural sciences', plus the 'social sciences' and 'humanities' and – of specific interest to this Report – 'engineering and technology' (see Box).

It goes without saying that no international engineering data of the very detailed kind above have ever been published; the only (and usually still rather scarce) information available is for R&D expenditures and personnel in the higher education and private non-profit sectors. However, some new fields-of-science aspects are discussed later (referring to a few of the statistical tables of human resources, mainly education statistics, compiled for this Report).

The specific classifications of research and development science and technology personnel

For the analysis of the R&D personnel series (and for other S&T personnel series as well), two parallel approaches are recommended in the *Frascati Manual*. The first is by occupation and the second is by level of formal qualification. These are defined in terms of the 1990 International Standard Classification of Occupation (ISCO) by the International Labour Office (ILO) and the 1997 International Standard Classification of Education (ISCED) by UNESCO.

In the classification by occupation approach, three broad classes of R&D personnel have been defined:

- Researchers: '...professionals engaged in the conception or creation of new knowledge, products, processes, methods and systems and also in the management of the projects concerned.'

- Technicians and equivalent staff: '...persons whose main tasks require technical knowledge and experience in one or more fields of engineering, physical and life sciences or social sciences and humanities. They participate in R&D by performing scientific and technical tasks involving the

application of concepts and operational methods, normally under the supervision of researchers. Equivalent staff perform the corresponding R&D tasks under the supervision of researchers in the social sciences and humanities.'

- Other supporting staff: '...includes skilled and unskilled craftsmen, secretarial and clerical staff participating in R&D projects or directly associated with such projects.'

The 'researchers' category is frequently also referred to as 'scientists and engineers' (RSEs) and is of most specific relevance to this Report.

In classification by level of formal qualification approach, six broad categories are suggested (ISCED 1997) and defined in terms of the level of study (as a rule linked to the duration of study) regardless of the specific field of science and technology in which the highest degrees have been attained:

- ISCED level 6: holders of university degrees at PhD level (with a highest sub-class second stage of tertiary education, leading to an advanced research qualification)

- ISCED level 5A: holders of basic university degrees below the PhD level

- ISCED level 5B: holders of other tertiary diplomas

- ISCED level 4: holders of other post-secondary non-tertiary diplomas

- ISCED level 3: holders of diplomas of secondary education

- Other qualifications

Compared to the previous version of ISCED, dating back to 1976, the current 1997 ISCED constitutes another break in the series of education statistics, specifically in the distribution of levels of formal qualification. The new sub-class of the highest tertiary level, 'leading to an advanced research qualification' (to be understood as preparing for PhD degrees), is an important novelty in the education statistics on enrolments for the recently (2004) initiated OECD/UNESCO/Eurostat study of labour market characteristics, careers and international mobility of doctorate holders.

ISCED is first and foremost a catalogue of education by levels of study, but it also provides a record of very detailed *fields* of study that frequently serves as a proxy list of fields of science and technology for purposes of classification other than just education (such as the classification of institutions, scientific programmes, reports and articles, and so on).

From the international point of view, the education and training of engineers and technologists, however defined, is very country-specific. This is particularly true for the duration of the various intermediate qualification levels (with or without practical train-

---

Engineering and Technology (ISCED 1976 Classification)

1. Civil engineering (architecture engineering, building science and engineering, construction engineering, municipal and structural engineering and other allied subjects).

2. Electrical engineering, electronics (electrical engineering, electronics, communication engineering and systems, computer engineering (hardware only) and other allied subjects).

3. Other engineering sciences (such as chemical, aeronautical and space, mechanical, metallurgical and materials engineering, and their specialised subdivisions: forest products; applied sciences such as geodesy, industrial chemistry, etc.; the science and technology of food production; specialised technologies of interdisciplinary fields, e.g. systems analysis, metallurgy, mining, textile technology and other allied subjects).

The Frascati Manual provides guidelines on the measurement of research and development.

ing or apprenticeships associated with academic study). In some countries, the level of some polytechnic institutions has upgraded over time to university status (this is also true, for instance, for the training of nurses and other medical personnel).

4.1.4 UNESCO statistics and indicators in Science & Technology, Research & Development

Roughly at the same time as the OECD, UNESCO also initiated its first international surveys in science and technology. They were intended to cover all S&T activities in a country but in practice, like those of the OECD, became mainly focused on measurement of R&D only. The provisional UNESCO guidelines for the surveys had to take into account the very diverse political and economic structures of the Organization's Member States, which grouped 'capitalist countries' (many already members of the OECD), 'socialist/communist countries' and 'developing countries'. UNESCO had to develop a particular institutional sector breakdown for the common reporting of S&T and R&D resources that – though both were based on the UN SNA classifications – was very dissimilar from those of the OECD (indeed, only the Higher Education sector breakdowns were identical).

The principal theoretical contribution of UNESCO to the systematic measurement of total S&T expenditures and personnel in the global economy date back to 1978 and its ambitious *Recommendation Concerning the International Standardization for Statistics on Science and Technology* and related practical guidelines.

The Recommendation suggested a complete and detailed inventory of the 'scientific and technological activities' (STA) to be measured:

- Research and Experimental Development (R&D), similar to the OECD *Frascati Manual* definitions.

- Science and Technology Education and Training (STET) at broadly the third level.

- Scientific and Technological Services (STS).

The coverage of the STS group was complete for the mid-1970s but is today outdated and is, accordingly, in serious need of revision. It does not, for instance, take into account recent fields such as space sciences, information and communications services, innovation, biotechnologies or nanotechnologies) and is, accordingly, in serious need of revision.

Comparisons of OECD and UNESCO data were not easy, especially for S&T and R&D expenditures. At the time, OECD was measuring in US dollars for its international assessments of expenditure – a moderately uncomplicated approach given

the relative homogeneity of its Member States. This was however not the case for UNESCO which was reduced to publishing its expenditure data in national currencies and that did not facilitate international analysis. These currency conversion problems have been gradually overcome following the launch of Purchasing Power Parities (PPPs), now systematically used for most international comparisons of financial data.

Given the technical problems with expenditure, one would have expected that personnel data would be easier to handle for international comparisons. Even here, there were setbacks however due to issues such as confusion between occupational and educational criteria in the UNESCO guidelines. Also, and with the effect of making comparisons yet more difficult, UNESCO personnel data were often reported by head-count (whereas the OECD used full-time equivalents) and measured staff in a broad range of S&T activities (whereas OECD data was focused only on staff in R&D activities).

In other words, the UNESCO figures from UNESCO Member States (both expenditure and personnel) were much higher when compared to the corresponding OECD data for OECD Member States. In the days of the Cold War, this manifested in an apparent dominance of socialist/communist countries in S&T resources (resources that were to a high degree associated with the military) and raised concern in the West (where the critical competence in data analysis had perhaps not yet reached its best!).

Statistical work at UNESCO was hampered by drastic budget cuts after the withdrawal of a number of the Organization's member countries (among which its principal economic contributor, the USA) in the middle of the 1980s. It was only in 1999, with the creation of the new independent UNESCO Institute for Statistics (UIS) installed in Montreal, Canada (and replacing the former Division of Statistics), that UNESCO's statistical activities on education and literacy, S&T, and culture and communication recovered. This required intensified in-house work and cooperation on data collection, diffusion and methodological developments with the other international agencies, and more of its own or out-sourced analytical efforts.

4.1.5 The OECD/Eurostat Canberra Manual on the measurement of stocks and flows of S&T personnel

In the late 1980s, serious concern was expressed in a number of Western economies (notably the United States) that crucial mismatches might soon occur on the labour market between the supply and the demand for engineers, scientists and technicians. Of particular concern were the imminent massive departures of people who had begun their S&T careers during the Second World War or during the first post-war big-science period who were about to retire. Other factors reinforced these concerns such as demographic trends, the increasingly technology-intensive nature of national economies (for example the growth in new information and communication technologies) and some disturbing signs of decreasing interest in S&T careers among young people. At the same time, however, there were concerns that other changes such as economic restructuring and the downsizing of defence industries in some countries might in fact lead to a surplus of highly-skilled engineers and technicians.

None of these problems really came about. The enrolments in S&T studies continued to grow in absolute terms (though were decreasing in relative terms) compared to other study opportunities. 'Untapped' labour resources, such as women and minorities, who in the past had acquired S&T competence but may never have taken up jobs in the sector (the 'leaky pipe-line'), integrated into the S&T workforce. The so-called 'brain-gain' continued in several industrialized countries, either by way of immigration of trained specialists or through larger numbers of international students who then stayed in their host country after graduation.

Many of the concerns were without doubt based more on anecdotal evidence than on solid data. No international agency was, at the time, able to provide policy-makers with relevant information and statistics. This drove the OECD, in close cooperation with Eurostat, to develop in 1989 another set of guidelines and indicators to assess the total national stocks and flows of highly qualified persons. The new guidelines were similar to its other manuals on measuring S&T activities but went well beyond the coverage of the *Frascati Manual* for R&D only. In the specifications for the new indicators, it was clearly asserted that no new data surveys should be initiated. Instead, work would only draw on the deployment and scrutiny of already existing data sets (such as education and labour force statistics), though it was recognized from the start that these data had never been intended to serve as a basis for specific S&T analysis. The same approach has been suggested for some of the other subsequent OECD manuals on measuring science and technology activities (see Box).

After several years of intense work and discussions, a new manual was approved at an experts' meeting in Australia in 1994. In recognition of the support of the national authorities, it came to be known as the *Canberra Manual.*

For the purposes of the *Canberra Manual,* a new term 'Human Resources in Science and Technology' (HRST) was coined. Once again, all guidelines proposed were strictly in line with international standards to account for as many aspects as possible of supply (education, in terms of qualifications) and demand (occupation, in terms of jobs or posts) of highly skilled personnel, allowing for possible cross-classifications between the two. It was not possible to give priority to any of the two criteria; both features had to be exploited for the HRST exercise (cross-classifications according to ISCED-1976 and ISCO-1988).

The broad and general definition of the HRST reads as follows:

> 'HRST are people who fulfil one or other of the following conditions: successfully completed education at the third level in an S&T field of study; or not formally qualified as above, but employed in an S&T occupation where the above qualifications are normally required.'

Paragraph 49 of the 1995 Canberra Manual

This description of course is still rather vague and therefore is accompanied by a number of supplementary criteria. 'Stocks' provide a snapshot of the HRST situation at a specific moment in time whereas 'flows' refer to movements in or out of the stock over a given time period (generally a year).

For these variables the *Canberra Manual* suggests the following definitions:

- **HRST stock:** '...the number of people at a particular point in time who fulfil the conditions of the definition of HRST' (paragraph 107 of the 1995 Canberra Manual). For example, the number of PhDs in physics employed in a country and sector on a fixed date.

The 'Frascati Family' of guidelines for the measurement of science and technology activities

- 1990: Proposed Standard Method of Compiling and Interpreting Technology Balance of Payments Data – the TBP Manual (OECD, 1990)

- 1993: Proposed Standard Practice for Surveys of Research and Experimental Development – the Frascati Manual, fifth edition (OECD, 1993)

- 1994: Using Patent Data as Science and Technology Indicators (revision underway 2008) – the Patent Manual (OECD)

- 1995: Proposed Standard Method of Compiling and Interpreting Technology Balance of Payments Data – the TBP Manual (OECD, 1990)

- The Measurement of Human Resources devoted to Science and Technology – the Canberra Manual (OECD/Eurostat 1995)

- 2005: Guidelines for Collecting and Interpreting Innovation Data – the Oslo Manual, third edition (OECD/Eurostat 2005)

- 2005: Using Patent Data as Science and Technology Indicators – Patent Manual (OECD, 1994) (revision underway 2008)

- Measuring Globalisation – OECD Handbook on Economic Globalisation Indicators (OECD, 2005)

- **HRST flows:** '...the number of people who do not fulfil any of the conditions for inclusion in the HRST at the beginning of a time period but gain at least one of them during the period (inflow) as well as the number of people who fulfil one or other of the conditions of the definition of HRST at the beginning of a time period and cease to fulfil them during the period (outflow)' (paragraph 109 of the 1995 Canberra Manual). For example, the number of electronics engineers graduating from a country's universities in a given year would be an inflow.

- **Internal flows:** '...people who are part of the HRST stock, some of whose characteristics change during the time period considered without, however, losing the essential characteristics for inclusion in HRST' (paragraph 112 of the 1995 Canberra Manual). For example, the number of people who change their sector of employment or achieve a qualification at a higher ISCED level.

In its very broadest sense, nearly everybody who has a relevant academic qualification or is employed in some relevant activity may be considered HRST. It is however clear that some qualifications or some occupations are of more specific science and technology policy interest than others. The HRST are therefore split into two major categories: university level HRST and technician level HRST (who, furthermore, may have graduated in a number of different fields of study, not all of which are of equal interest for our analysis of the S&T labour force).

The different diplomas are then broken down into categories, the highest being the 'core coverage' for the top tertiary-level qualifications in the natural sciences, engineering and technology, medical sciences, the agricultural sciences and the social sciences. The other categories ('extended coverage' and 'complete coverage') refer to other fields of study, such as the humanities, or to lower-level training that may be of less relevance.

The *Canberra Manual* also reviews, similarly with the *Frascati Manual*, a number of technical issues, such as: units of classification (the reporting vs. the statistical unit); head-count vs. full-time equivalence; demographics of the HRST labour force (age distribution, gender, national origin, ethnicity); and combined quantitative and qualitative matters including unemployment, training and retraining, salaries, retirement ages, public attitudes to science and technology, and so on.

⟲ *Engineering is fun!*

There is also a commented record of potential international and national data sources for the inventory of HRST stocks and flows, principally the OECD, Eurostat and UNESCO education and R&D statistics, the labour force statistics of the United Nations International Labour Office (ILO) and national population censuses. All the basic data have been provided to these international bodies by national bureaus

of statistics whose databases are by and large more exhaustive than the consolidated data published (the international data issued being for the lowest common denominator). Some smaller industrialized countries (such as Scandinavian countries) also keep detailed national registers of their HRST workforce, as do a number of professional bodies (here, international and national engineering associations are particularly present). Population censuses are undertaken only at intervals of several years (sometimes five to ten years) but their coverage usually surpasses that of more frequent (annual or even quarterly) household or employment/labour force surveys. These are usually based on sampling only, meaning that much of the detailed HRST information requested vanishes (such as the gender dimension of the figures).

As has been already suggested, the *Canberra Manual* is theoretically rigorous but difficult to use in practice for harmonized comparisons, despite several significant methodological and analytical attempts (notably by Eurostat). The problems are essentially due to the inadequacy of the recommended data sources. ISCED was revised in 1997 with a number of breaks in coverage of levels and disciplines (as mentioned earlier) but no revision of the *Canberra Manual* has followed as yet. The *Canberra Manual* HRST concept and definitions are, however, now globally recognized and serve as key references for most analytical studies of the science and technology workforce.

4.1.6 The international study of careers of doctorate holders

The most recent – and certainly most promising – international HRST project underway is on mapping the careers of doctorate holders (CDH) and their mobility, once again involving the OECD, the UNESCO Institute for Statistics and Eurostat. This project has called for additional guidelines, which to a large extent are drawing more from national practice than from the Frascati or the Canberra manuals.

The purpose of the CDH exercise is to collect quantitative and qualitative information on a large number of variables for this important category of S&T personnel, not only absolute or relative numbers (in relation to population, labour force or other denominators) but also, for instance, information on their:

- demographic characteristics (gender, age etc);

- educational characteristics (level of education, year of doctoral degree, age, field of doctoral degree, graduation age, duration of doctoral degree in months, primary sources of doctorate funding);

■ labour market status and characteristics (inactivity and unemployment rates, full-time vs. part-time, type of employment contract), salaries (median annual salaries for persons working as researchers, by gender, sector of employment, and field of employment);

■ national origins, mobility (international, national, job-to-job mobility, mobility intentions);

■ employment satisfaction; and

■ outputs (articles, books, patents, commercialized products or processes etc.).

A first pilot CDH survey embracing just seven volunteering countries (Argentina, Australia, Canada, Germany, Portugal, Switzerland and the United States) was initiated in 2005, and the first preliminary results were issued in 2007. It was followed by a second survey launched later the same year and responses were received by mid-2008 by the OECD from no less than twenty-five countries, of which several were Eastern European states as new members of the European Union.

This wide and rapid survey participation clearly emphasizes the very strong international and national policy interest in the new CDH approach of assessing human resources for S&T and, furthermore, that it is closely linked to public and private innovation concerns, especially in the services sector where R&D investments now grow faster than in manufacturing.

A wealth of statistics on doctorate holders and their working conditions was assembled in the two surveys, though they have not yet been systematically published. For further analytical purposes, a subset of these data – common to all participating countries – was isolated for a target population of persons, under the age of seventy, having earned their diplomas during the time period 1990 to 2006.

The country coverage of the 2005 CDH survey was obviously neither exhaustive nor representative for the global economy and, furthermore, not particularly engineering-oriented (nor was the second survey). The experience of the first exercise however, seems to be confirmed by the results of the second survey and responds to most of the concerns of the S&T community and policy-makers today.

Once further enlarged and refined, these CDH surveys may shed light upon issues related to the stocks and flows of highly-qualified and skilled personnel at the global scale and, hopefully, in the medium and longer terms, the results may be of significance to specific branches of interest as well, such as the engineering profession.

To this end, however, additional resources and supplementary methodological developments are necessary. This is particularly important for the detailed subgroups of the international standard classifications (ISCED, ISCO and ISIC) where it is still difficult to separate out, from S&T more generally, engineering as a field of study, or engineers (and technicians) as a profession. Lobbying will undoubtedly be required to induce these statistical agencies to meet customers' needs for more specific data – but by whom?

Pending a more comprehensive presentation by OECD/UIS/Eurostat of the results of the first two CDH surveys, a few items of interest are commented below. Note that these data are for overall S&T doctorate holders with only some limited linkage to engineering or engineers (and many figures are still to be considered as broad orders of magnitude).

One of the principal indicators is the number of doctorate holders in the population, reported in absolute terms. As a result of massive expansion of higher education both inside and outside the OECD area (for instance in China, India and Brazil), the world stocks of highly skilled personnel are rapidly growing in a context of economic globalization. Whereas in 1998 broadly some 140,000 doctoral degrees were awarded in the OECD area as a whole, around 200,000 were registered in 2006, an increase of more than 40 per cent. There are not yet any estimates for the worldwide stock of doctorate holders in general or engineering doctorates holders in particular but the CDH studies suggest that, for instance, by 2006 some 340,000 (1990–2006) doctoral graduates (all disciplines) were found in the United States and nearly 275,000 in Germany.

The number of doctorate holders were also analysed per 1,000 of the national labour force. In 2002 (first CDH survey) the following ratios were obtained showing quite large variations between countries: Switzerland (27.5), Germany (20.1), United States (10.7), Canada (8.2), Australia (7.8), Portugal (2.6), and Argentina (0.5).

All the European countries covered by the survey show that the natural sciences are the prime (first or second) major field of specialization of their doctorate holders, whereas the weighting of the other main S&T fields of S&T varies considerably. Within the extended European Union, the natural sciences represent, with only one or two exceptions only, at least 20 per cent of doctorate holders with some seven countries in the 30–40 per cent interval.

According to the same series, in about half the European countries, for which data are reported, engineering doctorates account for about 20 per cent of total doctorates but once again there are large variations between countries in comparison with other disciplines. The relative importance of engineering is notable in the East European countries (see below)

© UNESCO

◑ *UNESCO toolkit on Gender Indicators in SET.*

Doctorates in engineering as a percentage of total doctorates in 2006 (rounded figures)

Slovak Republic (27%), Poland (26%), Bulgaria (25%), Romania (23%), Czech Republic (22%), Cyprus (21%), Belgium (20%), Portugal (20%), Lithuania (19%), Latvia (18%), Denmark (16%), Austria (14%), Estonia (9%), Germany (9%), Spain (9%).

whereas, for instance Germany, Estonia and Spain (with around 10 per cent) show other preferences (medical sciences are 30 per cent in Germany and 20 per cent in Spain). The humanities show between 10–15 per cent of total doctorate degrees in a majority of the countries observed. The study estimates the share of engineering science doctorates in the United States as perhaps some 15 per cent.

Whereas the numbers of women are increasingly equalling or surpassing those of men at the lower levels of tertiary education (enrolments, graduates) – of course still with variations between countries and fields of study – they are still under-represented among overall doctorate holders and as science and engineering graduates compared to men. They are also overall less engaged in typical engineering and technician professions and in research occupations. Female 1990–2006 doctorates accounted for between 30–50 per cent of the total; the median of some twenty-two countries (Europe and the United States) being just under 40 per cent in 2006. There are however clear signs that since 1998, the numbers of female doctorates are now increasing faster than those of men, but they still have to catch up in both the science fields (with 38 per cent on average of total doctorates) and notably in engineering where they only represented 21 per cent of the total doctorates in 2006.

Overall unemployment rates for doctorate holders (not exceeding 2–3 per cent in 2006) are currently about half those of graduates with lower level diplomas and still lower than those of the population as a whole, though with variations between countries and fields of training. Women are more likely to be unemployed than men and are also engaged in more unstable positions than men. Unemployment rates are generally higher in the humanities and social sciences (where there is a majority of female doctorates) than in the 'hard sciences' (including engineering) where men still constitute the majority of the workforce. The first CDH survey had shown that in the United States (2003), the unemployment rate for engineering and technology doctorate holders (and also in the natural sciences) was higher than that of any other broad discipline, notably the social sciences and the humanities but, apparently, this situation is slowly becoming more balanced.

The world median age at graduation of doctorate holders in engineering appears to be about 32 years around 2005–2006 (with some fifteen countries in the 30–35 years interval), but this figure reveals considerable differences notably between

Western and Eastern Europe countries – lowest in Belgium and Cyprus (only 28 years) but significantly higher in, for instance Bulgaria (44), Lithuania (42), Romania and the Czech Republic (40). In about half the countries surveyed, women obtained their engineering doctorates faster than their male counterparts (Table 1).

Broadly three-quarters of the overall doctorate holders are working in the higher education sector. The government sector is also an important employer of doctorate holders who are active in research and teaching activities or otherwise working in management and professional positions. Engineering doctorate holders would be expected essentially to work in the enterprise sector but in nine out of the thirteen countries for which such sector of employment data are available, the university sector attracts more engineering doctors than firms. In the other four countries (Austria, Belgium, the Czech Republic and the United States) enterprise is employing something like at least 10 per cent of the engineering doctors population.

Table 1: **Median age at graduation of engineering doctoral graduates 2005–2006**

	Women	Men	Total
Argentina	..	..	33
Australia	31	31	31
Austria	30.9	32.5	32.4
Belgium	29	28	28
Bulgaria	34	45	44
Cyprus	..	28	28
Czech Republic	33.5	40.0	39.5
Denmark	31.7	31	31.2
Estonia	37.0	32.0	34.5
Finland	34	33	33
Japan	33.5	34.0	..
Latvia	32	32	32
Lithuania	31	29	30
Norway	30.7	31.1	31.0
Poland	32	32	32
Portugal	34	36	36
Romania	38	43	40
Slovakia	30	30	30
Spain	31	32	32
Sweden	32	32	32
Switzerland	30	31	31
United States	30.2	31.0	30.8

Source: OECD, UNESCO Institute for Statistics, Eurostat

It is a well known fact that there are significant salary differences between men and women also for doctorate holders across sectors. In the United States women's salaries were overall 25 per cent lower than those of men in 2003, and in Canada 20 per cent lower. Discontent with salaries is a principal cause of employment dissatisfaction and mobility inclination. Dissatisfaction with salaries touched some 20 per cent of the doctorate holders in the United States, 40 per cent in Portugal and 55 per cent in Argentina. The percentages were even higher among women (2003).

Concerning the outputs of doctorate holders working as researchers, the data available are not yet sufficient for overall conclusions, though the United States' data suggest that, in general, men produce more in terms of, for example, articles and publications than women who are 'more comfortable with other means of knowledge diffusion, such as teaching.'

Concerning the measurement of doctorate holders of foreign origin, a noteworthy section of the first CDH survey examines the difference between two basic concepts for the understanding of the results: Are the data for foreign-born people, or are they for people of foreign nationality? The former category reflects the culmination of immigrants over a longer time period, some of whom may eventually have obtained the citizenship of the receiving country, while the second – more or less – presents the circumstances at a given date.

Depending on the approach chosen, the statistical results may differ. The first CDH report indicates that individuals of foreign origin are very present among doctorate holders in Switzerland in terms both of foreign-born at 41 per cent and of foreign nationality at 30 per cent. In Canada and Australia, they are are even higher at 54 per cent and 46 per cent respectively, but those of foreign nationals considerably lower at 18 per cent and 14 per cent. The shares of foreign-born doctorate holders are much larger in Canada and in Australia than in the United States. In absolute terms, there are more foreign-born doctorate holders in Canada than are born in the country. Propensities are high among foreign doctorate holders to acquire citizenship in the settlement countries, notably in Australia, Canada and the United States. On the other hand, international mobility of United States doctorate holder citizens is low.

4.1.7 Statistics and an analysis of engineers in education and employment

Introduction to the statistics

The tables and charts in this section show education and employment statistics for recent years from UNESCO, OECD and Eurostat. They attempt to place engineers in the global context. This education data was initially collected from

Table 2: **The principal OECD methodological manuals**

A. The 'Frascati Family' of Manuals:	
R&D	• The Measurement of Scientific and Technological Activities Series: - "Frascati Manual: Proposed Standard Practice for Surveys of Research and Experimental Development" – 6th Edition (OECD 2002)
	• "R&D Statistics and Output Measurement in the Higher Education Sector" – Frascati Manual Supplement (OECD 1989)
Technology Balance of Payments	• "Manual for the Measurement and Interpretation of Technology Balance of Payments Data –TBP Manual" (OECD 1990) *
Innovation	• "Oslo Manual - Guidelines for Collecting and Interpreting Innovation Data" (3rd Edition, OECD 2005)
Patents	• "OECD Patent Statistics Manual "(OECD 2009)
S&T Personnel	• "The Measurement of Human Resources Devoted to Science and Technology - Canberra Manual" (OECD /Eurostat 1995) *
B. Other Methodological Frameworks for S&T:	
High technology	• "Revision of High-technology Sector and Product Classification" (OECD, STI Working Paper 1997/2)
Bibliometrics	• "Bibliometric Indicators and Analysis of Research Systems: Methods and Examples", by Yoshiko OKUBO (OECD, STI Working Paper 1997/1 (OECD 1997) **
Globalisation	• "Measuring Globalisation – OECD Handbook on Economic Globalisation Indicators" (OECD 2005)
Productivity	• "Measurement of Aggregate and Industry-Level Productivity Growth - OECD Manual" (OECD 2001)
Biotechnology	• "A Framework for Biotechnology Statistics" (OECD 2005)
* Dealing mainly with the classification and interpretation of existing information (not originally collected for the purpose of S&T analysis and policy)	
** Working paper, without recognised manual status	

respective Member States using a common questionnaire, though each agency manages its own database and analysis.

With regard to engineers in particular, the ISCED 1997 classification introduces a new set of ten broad fields of education, one of which is the 'engineering, manufacturing and construction' category with three new sub-categories (different from the ISCED 1976 classification described in section 4.1.3). They are, as much as possible, used for the data presented in the tables and charts.

Tables 1 to 6 show data for the world. Tables 7 to 12 show data for countries in the OECD and the European area, as there are no corresponding worldwide data available. (Go to section 4.1.8 to view the Tables).

Engineering, Manufacturing and Construction (ISCED 1997 Classification)

Engineering and engineering trades: engineering drawing, mechanics, metal work, electricity, electronics, telecommunications, energy and chemical engineering, vehicle maintenance and surveying.

Manufacturing and processing: food and drink processing, textiles, clothes, footwear, leather, materials such as wood, paper, plastic and glass.

Architecture and building: architecture and town planning, structural architecture, landscape architecture, community planning, cartography, building construction and civil engineering.

Notes on the statistics

These macro-statistics should be interpreted with care given that the quality of the data is not always fully satisfactory.

UNESCO data on education is only available for the broad 'engineering, manufacturing and construction' category as a whole, whereas in the case of OECD and Eurostat they issue separate data for its three sub-categories. Therefore, with the worldwide UNESCO data as the lowest common denominator, the tables and charts show the data for the whole category as a priority. Some separate data from OECD and Eurostat are available in the three sub-categories for the new levels introduced for the highest classes of the revised ISCED, notably 6, 5A and 5B (see section 4.1.3 for more detail). The UNESCO data for ISCED categories 5 and 6 have been amalgamated and this again is used as the lowest common denominator for comparison.

Discrepancies in data availability can also be seen in the tables, particularly those between industrialized countries (typically OECD and associated states) where the bulk of the world's engineers are still found, and the emerging economies. Unfortunately, statistical information for the industrializing countries, which are the major regional economies, is also not yet available.

Trends are often more important for policy analysis than examining absolute figures at a given moment in time. Time series are most complete for the industrialized countries, though the situation is steadily improving for a number of the industrializing UNESCO Member States.

Data for tertiary education statistics are collected for students entering education (enrolments), students in the pipeline, and students leaving education with an appropriate qualification (graduates). Enrolment numbers may reflect present interest in specific studies, whereas, several years previously, graduate numbers perhaps reflected more on policy or employment concerns. Gender data are by and large available for both enrolments and graduates.

As a rule, analysing trends is more informative for policy analysis than examining absolute figures at a given moment in time. Time series are still most complete for 'developed' countries though the situation is steadily improving also for a number of industrializing UNESCO Member States.

Given that the quality criteria of the data are not always fully satisfactory, these 'macro' series should be interpreted with care. Furthermore, statistical information is still unfortunately unavailable for some of the principal regional economies in the world (Russian Federation, China, Indonesia, Singapore, Thailand, Egypt, Nigeria and others) though there is hope that the statistical series concerned will already be completed in the rather short term.

As far as 'engineers' are concerned, the 'new' ISCED (1997) introduces a novel set of ten broad groups of fields of education, one of which is 'Engineering, manufacturing and construction' (different from the ISCED-76 version described earlier) with three new subcategories (and programmes):

- Engineering and engineering trades: Engineering drawing, mechanics, metal work, electricity, electronics, telecommunications, energy and chemical engineering, vehicle maintenance, surveying.

- Manufacturing and processing: Food and drink processing, textiles, clothes, footwear, leather, materials (wood, paper, plastic, glass, etc.)

- Architecture and building: Architecture and town planning, structural architecture, landscape architecture, community planning, cartography, building construction, civil engineering.

Whereas the OECD and Eurostat issue separate data for each of the above three sub-categories (where the first one, Engineering and engineering trades, is of particular interest), UNESCO only provides their full subtotal, which – as the smallest common denominator – is presented as priority in the worldwide enrolments and graduates series below. Earlier (see the section 4.1.6 on the careers of doctorate holders) we also discussed the breakdown of new levels of the highest classes of the revised ISCED (notably 6 and 5A and 5B) for which some separate data are available from OECD and Eurostat. However, once again, we shall have to draw on the UNESCO series where the above ISCED categories 5 and 6 have been amalgamated.

Introductory analysis of the statistics on education

What do these statistics tell us concerning the current and near-future supply of engineers? Are the recurring concerns of mismatches between demand and supply justified?

To begin with, engineering studies enrolments have increased in every country in absolute terms over the last decade, with only very few exceptions. The rates of increase, of course, are varied.

However, engineering studies enrolments indicate a decline in most countries in relative terms over the same period – despite their absolute growth – when compared to total enrolments in tertiary education in a country and enrolments in other disciplines. The increases in absolute enrolment numbers are therefore explained, to some extent, by the general overall increases in the numbers entering tertiary education, rather than a move towards engineering studies by young people.

It is also clear that female engineering studies enrolments are increasing more quickly than those of male enrolments, and accordingly also their share in the total student and graduate numbers. The proportions are however still low in most countries, and in some very low. It is not really possible to pinpoint any common trends (increases, stagnation or decreases) between and within the regions of the world (essentially UNESCO groupings). Whereas numbers are reasonably stable over time in the largest countries, more relative year-to-year variations may be observed in smaller countries and, notably, in those of the developing regions for which data is not regularly available.

The overall tendency within the countries covered by the OECD/Eurostat data is slow but steady growth in the numbers of engineering studies enrolments. The principal exceptions to this are Japan, the Netherlands, Norway and Korea where notable decreases of some 5 to 10 per cent have been recorded since the late 1990s. Such declines are taken very seriously by national authorities at a time of stagnating demographics and the retirement of engineers who graduated immediately after the 'baby boom'. In Japan for instance, various measures are taken with a view to reinforcing immigration of qualified scientists and engineers from, or outsourcing R&D to, other countries in the region. Initiatives are also reinforced in a number of countries to stimulate the return home of highly qualified expatriates.

It is worthwhile noting, just as an example, that total engineering studies enrolments in Korea are about one-third higher than those of Japan (according to the UNESCO series).

In Europe and the broader OECD area, which shows a median increase of 10 per cent, enrolments appear to be growing faster in several of the new European Member States, many of which were in earlier times integrated in the Eastern Bloc or part of the former Federation of Yugoslavia. Similar growth is seen in a number of the former Soviet republics in Central Asia.

Considerable and regular progress is noticed in the Mediterranean region, including Turkey (an OECD member) and the countries of North Africa and, with the perceptible exception of Saudi Arabia, in the Arab countries in general.

In the South and West Asian region, enrolments in engineering studies have risen five-fold in Bangladesh since the start of the century and by around half in India, Iran and Pakistan. In the first three of these countries, the numbers of female students are also increasing at high rates but are decreasing in Pakistan.

In the sub-Saharan region of Africa, there are still many countries not yet reporting to UNESCO despite the UIS's steadily intensified capacity-building efforts. South Africa appears to be the leading country in the region for engineering studies enrolments in absolute terms with a 60 per cent increase between 2000 and 2006. All reporting African countries (with only one or two exceptions) saw average growth well above that of Europe for instance; the growth is however starting from a lower base. Here again, much of the progress is due to increased female participation. For example, Ethiopia appears to have the second highest growth rates in this vast region, and it nearly tripled its numbers over the five years to 2005 (though followed by a dramatic drop in 2006). The increases included the quadrupling of female engineering students.

UNESCO Member States in East Asia, the Pacific and the Caribbean include a large number of smaller states for which no data are reported.

No common picture may be drawn for Latin America where enrolments in engineering studies are increasing in Columbia, Mexico and Brazil but are decreasing in Argentina and Chile. The situation again varies in the smaller countries in the continent, perhaps with a slight tendency though towards slow growth or levelling-off.

4.1.8   Engineering indicators – Tables

Table 1: Students Enrolled in Tertiary-Level "Engineering"* Education, 1999-2006, Total (persons) - World

	1999	2000	2001	2002	2003	2004	2005	2006
Europe (OECD/Eurostat)								
Austria	...	40,448	...	...	31,158	30,004	29,674	29,890
Belgium	...	41,903	40,886	41,513	39,729	44,270	40,451	41,670
Bulgaria	49,639	52,426	52,777	51,941	50,948	50,463	50,504	51,083
Croatia	18,941	...	19,916	20,920	20,722	...	21,891	22,283
Cyprus	886	670	550	522	637	843	1,009	1,262
Czech Republic	51,105	40,800	41,536	58,958	58,661	65,655	66,248	...
Denmark	17,481	18,982	19,720	19,406	21,771	22,501	24,005	23,077
Estonia	7,517	7,420	7,320	7,107	7,357	7,859	8,269	8,412
Finland	64,738	69,230	72,303	73,363	77,596	80,167	80,827	80,153
France	...	...	...	...	...	...	...	252,882
Germany	338,901	325,667	323,953	332,161	341,652	360,034	...	360,394
Greece	...	...	...	72,813	...	90,404	106,528	93,626
Hungary	51,295	54,389	51,256	46,064	55,476	54,406	53,965	54,569
Iceland	483	556	606	693	870	980	1,022	1,149
Ireland	17,967	18,241	19,343	19,971	20,310	20,790	19,233	19,420
Israel	41,015	39,138	52,987	60,116	57,929	58,661	56,812	55,537
Italy	306,157	297,928	299,778	303,435	312,170	319,739	320,343	316,135
Latvia	13,215	9,300	10,128	11,320	11,764	12,280	12,352	13,159
Lithuania	24,122	27,275	29,419	30,059	33,099	35,578	36,376	35,775
Luxembourg	...	...	...	...	...	...	...	405
Malta	431	411	459	525	674	698	737	...
Netherlands	51,008	52,218	53,641	54,219	53,084	44,576	44,475	47,292
Norway	15,733	12,953	12,386	12,598	13,395	13,874	14,726	...
Poland	203,095	213,125	234,638	258,483	269,726	272,641	248,542	269,810
Portugal	...	67,007	...	81,648	84,526	85,414	83,079	80,597
Romania	91,450	98,964	108,672	117,244	138,909	145,106	150,203	152,176
Russian Federation	...	...	...	...	...	...	...	...
Slovakia	26,152	28,210	29,637	29,069	28,279	28,621	31,521	32,439
Slovenia	14,980	15,450	16,026	16,530	17,456	17,508	17,753	17,962
Spain	281,760	295,266	303,122	314,066	322,932	324,936	319,340	318,881
Sweden	64,634	66,287	68,206	69,410	71,736	71,949	70,089	68,846
Switzerland	24,638	23,305	23,293	24,255	25,384	26,622	26,376	27,418
Turkey	...	...	211,449	220,243	259,069	281,986	292,623	312,420
United Kingdom	182,761	178,410	217,529	225,784	177,164	180,656	185,283	191,182
Other OECD (outside Europe)								
Australia	98,305	97,686	99,662	108,113	110,171	108,488	108,319	108,319
New Zealand	10,568	11,586	11,607	10,793	13,975	14,839	15,124	15,788
Canada	122,974	...	...	128,337	...	...	...	...
Mexico	310,974	332,646	358,543	391,952	415,429	476,228	437,442	454,399

	1999	2000	2001	2002	2003	2004	2005	2006
United States	…	…	…	…	…	…	1154,971	1166,545
Japan	718,782	706,998	701,698	694,580	685,063	677,544	668,526	655,851
Rep. of Korea	1019,703	1096,304	1046,279	1079,584	1036,741	993,934	1022,845	971,722

Western Europe n.e.c

	1999	2000	2001	2002	2003	2004	2005	2006
Andorra	…	…	…	-	-	-	-	-
Gibralter	…	…	…	…	…	…	…	…
Holy See	-	-	-	…	…	…	…	…
Liechtenstein	…	…	…	…	111	149	135	…
Monaco	.	.	.	.	.	.	…	…
San Marino	.	141	…	…	…	…	…	…

Central and Eastern Europe n.e.c.

	1999	2000	2001	2002	2003	2004	2005	2006
Albania	…	2,599	2,708	…	3,738	4,243	…	…
Belarus	…	…	…	…	…	…	132,527	138,417
Bosnia and Herzegovina	…	…	…	…	…	…	…	…
Montenegro	…	…	…	…	…	…	…	…
Rep. of Moldova	…	…	…	…	…	…	…	…
Serbia	…	…	…	…	…	…	…	
Rep. of Macedonia	6,558	7,793	7,709	9,152	9,035	8,376	8,936	…
Ukraine	494,995	…	456,901	487,137	513,638	545,764	581,761	606,853

Arab States

	1999	2000	2001	2002	2003	2004	2005	2006
Algeria	…	…	…	…	…	71,445	78,175	80,826
Bahrain	…	…	…	…	2,080	…	1,589	1,581
Djibouti	…	…	13	…	…	28	…	114
Egypt	…	…	…	…	…	…	…	…
Iraq	…	28,857	…	…	…	78,227	…	…
Jordan	…	…	…	…	22,636	22,636	25,087	27,601
Kuwait	…	…	…	…	…	…	…	…
Lebanon	…	13,851	15,166	16,492	16,608	15,552	19,276	20,067
Libyan Arab Jamahiriya	…	59,645	…	…	…	…	…	…
Mauritania	…	…	…	…	-	…	-	…
Morocco	5,350	7,170	16,517	…	13,570	13,221	16,790	21,392
Oman	…	…	…	…	…	…	4,488	…
Palestinian Aut. Terr.	4,781	4,201	4,168	5,967	8,074	8,688	…	11,149
Qatar	…	…	289	276	312	432	…	…
Saudi Arabia	…	32,865	…	…	44,233	15,721	19,780	…
Sudan	…	…	…	…	…	…	…	…
Syrian Arab Rep.	…	…	…	…	…	…	…	…
Tunisia	…	…	…	…	23,697	…	…	34,802
United Arab Emirates	…	…	…	…	…	…	…	…
Yemen	…	…	…	…	…	…	…	…

	1999	2000	2001	2002	2003	2004	2005	2006
Central Asia								
Armenia	...	...	4,725	...	4,632	4,921	5,841	6,169
Azerbaijan	...	...	...	...	...	...	...	...
Georgia	21,505	23,282	27,734	31,251	36,344	35,657	31,812	10,678
Kazakhstan	...	...	...	...	...	...	...	...
Kyrgyzstan	...	...	21,363	34,582	19,949	14,202	21,061	22,633
Mongolia	11,124	12,993	14,649	16,059	18,316	18,545	20,117	22,478
Tajikistan	...	3,912	5,967	6,397	5,449	6,863	15,488	19,189
Turkmenistan	...	...	...	...	...	...	...	...
Uzbekistan	...	...	...	...	...	...	...	43,065
East Asia and the Pacific n.e.c.								
Brunei Darussalam	108	153	228	...	202	170	218	334
Cambodia	...	...	722	803	...	1,066	...	2,740
China	...	...	...	...	...	...	...	...
Cook Islands	...	...	...	.	...	...	...	...
Dem. P. Rep. of Korea	...	...	...	...	...	...	...	...
Fiji	...	...	...	...	...	...	...	...
Hong Kong (China)	...	...	...	...	25,302	24,990	24,466	24,379
Indonesia	...	...	...	...	...	...	...	...
Kiribati	...	...	...	...	...	...	...	...
Lao P. Dem. Rep.	...	1,393	1,656	...	1,922	3,560	2,337	4,382
Macao, China	...	...	...	316	413	...	505	501
Malaysia	...	...	...	150,285	...	156,286	128,376	...
Marshall Islands	...	...	...	...	...	...	...	...
Micronesia (Fed. St. of)	...	...	...	...	...	...	...	...
Myanmar	...	...	29,957	...	...	...	...	...
Nauru	...	...	...	...	...	...	...	...
Niue	...	...	...	...	...	...	...	...
Palau	...	...	...	...	...	...	...	...
Papua New Guinea	...	...	...	...	...	...	...	...
Philippines	...	...	...	...	299,831	376,224	...	...
Samoa	...	57	...	...	...	...	...	...
Singapore	...	...	...	...	...	...	...	...
Solomon Islands	...	...	...	...	...	...	...	...
Thailand	...	...	...	...	...	...	...	...
Timor-Leste	...	...	...	...	...	...	...	...
Tokelau	...	...	...	...	...	...	...	...
Tonga	...	...	...	...	...	...	...	...
Tuvalu	...	...	...	...	...	...	...	...
Vanuatu	...	...	...	...	...	...	...	...
Viet Nam	141,930	132,569	...	154,846	164,141	...	...	...

	1999	2000	2001	2002	2003	2004	2005	2006
South and West Asia								
Afghanistan	...	...	...	...	...	...	...	...
Bangladesh	...	8,845	11,903	12,935	14,049	27,349	45,482	...
Bhutan	...	...	...	...	...	...	...	,597
India	...	...	418,193	526,476	...	...	696,609	...
Iran, Islamic Rep. of	...	...	...	...	...	451,768	578,053	727,116
Maldives	...	...	.	.	.	...	...	...
Nepal	...	...	...	...	...	...	...	...
Pakistan	...	...	...	...	...	...	31,240	46,090
Sri Lanka	...	...	...	...	...	...	...	...
Latin America and the Caribbean								
Anguilla	...	...	...	.	.	...	.	.
Antigua and Barbuda	...	.	...	.	...	...	...	...
Argentina	...	...	...	...	177,475	...	168,914	...
Aruba	...	423	391	383	438	399	...	408
Bahamas	...	...	...	...	...	...	...	...
Barbados	...	...	...	...	...	...	...	...
Belize	...	...	...	...	...	1	...	...
Bermuda	...	...	...	...	...	...	89	...
Bolivia	...	...	...	...	...	...	...	...
Brazil	...	...	...	279,716	301,158	319,175	344,714	...
British Virgin Islands	...	...	...	...	...	...	...	...
Cayman Islands	...	...	...	...	...	...	...	.
Chile	...	...	...	163,834	169,310	99,755	120,942	122,447
Colombia	...	...	283,661	...	...	319,910	364,589	424,362
Costa Rica	...	...	9,979	11,080	...	16,157	...	...
Cuba	...	...	...	...	...	...	...	14,393
Dominica	...	...	...	...	...	...	...	...
Dominican Republic	...	...	...	...	...	...	...	...
Ecuador	...	...	...	...	...	...	...	...
El Salvador	...	...	...	13,870	15,477	...	14,898	14,905
Grenada	...	...	...	...	...	...	...	...
Guatemala	...	...	...	19,092	...	...	...	20,824
Guyana	...	...	...	...	...	447	446	477
Haiti	...	...	...	...	...	...	...	...
Honduras	...	...	...	...	21,533	...	...	...
Jamaica	...	...	...	...	...	...	...	...
Montserrat	...	...	...	...	...	...	...	.
Netherlands Antilles	...	864	783	...	...	...	...	...
Nicaragua	...	...	...	...	...	...	...	...
Panama	...	...	...	21,241	18,585	15,251	14,616	14,664

	1999	2000	2001	2002	2003	2004	2005	2006
Paraguay	...	...	...	...	...	...	...	...
Peru	...	...	...	...	...	...	...	5,286
St. Kitts and Nevis	...	...	...	...	...	...	...	...
St.Lucia	...	...	...	...	...	...	...	.
St. Vincent & the Grenadines	...	...	...	...	...	...	...	...
Suriname	...	...	...	526	...	...	...	...
Trinidad and Tobago	...	1,300	1,399	...	...	3,788	...	...
Turks and Caicos Islands	...	...	...	...	.	.	...	...
Uruguay	...	...	...	...	...	...	12,321	...
Venezuela	...	...	...	...	...	...	...	...

Sub-Saharan Africa

	1999	2000	2001	2002	2003	2004	2005	2006
Angola	674	...	...	1079	...	...	...	...
Benin	...	...	...	...	...	...	...	...
Botswana	...	...	352	353	...	534	603	...
Burkina Faso	...	...	...	...	...	...	...	1,721
Burundi	...	...	...	500	...	...	...	...
Cameroon	...	...	...	...	...	2,170	...	5,906
Cape Verde	...	...	...	...	...	...	...	...
Central African Rep.	...	...	...	...	...	...	...	...
Chad	...	...	...	...	...	...	...	...
Comoros	...	...	...	...	.	...	...	...
Congo	...	...	.	116	...	...	...	...
Côte d'Ivoire	...	...	...	...	...	...	...	...
Dem. Rep. of Congo	...	...	...	...	...	...	...	...
Equatorial Guinea	...	...	...	...	...	...	...	...
Eritrea	174	372	451	-	...	1,286	...	...
Ethiopia	5,918	5,892	11,421	9,383	13,625	17,347	16,972	12,967
Gabon	...	...	...	...	...	...	...	...
Gambia	...	...	...	...	...	.	...	...
Ghana	...	8,050	8,972	9,438	...	8,115	...	...
Guinea	...	...	...	...	...	2,060	...	1,672
Guinea-Bissau	...	...	...	...	...	...	...	...
Kenya	...	16,435	17,652	...	...	...	...	...
Lesotho	-	...	...	...	-	...	52	-
Liberia	...	2,013	...	...	...	...	...	...
Madagascar	...	...	...	...	...	...	2,295	2,976
Malawi	1,041	...	...	...	...	...	...	...
Mali	...	...	...	...	...	...	...	...
Mauritius	1,909	1,833	1,978	1,847	2,169	2,482	2,971	2,585
Mozambique	...	...	...	...	...	2,424	2,788	...

	1999	2000	2001	2002	2003	2004	2005	2006
Namibia	305	...	475	...	539	...	...	...
Niger	...	...	...	...	...	...	...	...
Nigeria	...	...	...	...	...	...	187	...
Rwanda	...	...	...	...	...	...	...	...
Sao Tome and Principe	.	.	.	.	.	.	.	...
Senegal	...	...	...	...	...	...	...	...
Seychelles	.	.	.	.	.	.	.	.
Sierra Leone	...	49	80	...	...	...	...	...
Somalia	...	...	...	...	...	...	...	...
South Africa	...	43,354	...	...	54,038	62,013	69,028	70,339
Swaziland	361	327	268	...	...	305	225	174
Togo	...	256	...	...	...	...	...	...
Uganda	4,356	2,095	3,366	...	...	6,332	...	...
United Rep. of Tanzania	3,406	...	...	...	...	...	4,589	...
Zambia	...	...	...	...	...	...	...	...
Zimbabwe	...	...	...	...	...	...	...	...

Source: UNESCO

* Sub-total for "Engineering" (no separate breakdown available for the subclasses of ISCED - 97 Group "Engineering, Manufacturing and Construction")

Table 2: Female Students Enrolled in Tertiary-Level "Engineering"* Education, 1999-2006, Total (persons) - World

	1999	2000	2001	2002	2003	2004	2005	2006
Europe (OECD/Eurostat)								
Austria	...	7,526	...	...	6,169	6,170	6,149	6,366
Belgium	...	7,712	7,561	8,519	8,006	10,106	8,498	10,075
Bulgaria	19,908	20,201	19,482	17,972	17,256	16,263	16,170	16,259
Croatia	5,163	...	4,957	5,385	5,165	...	5,400	5,651
Cyprus	201	74	43	39	49	85	130	177
Czech Republic	9,976	10,551	10,709	12,359	12,154	13,348	14,061	...
Denmark	5,103	5,308	5,175	5,989	7,130	7,555	7,951	7,596
Estonia	2,005	1,987	2,055	2,061	2,044	2,111	2,270	2,292
Finland	11,252	12,306	13,163	13,797	14,457	14,841	15,082	15,077
France	...	...	...	...	...	...	...	59,215
Germany	60,653	60,054	60,847	62,636	64,661	68,152	...	65,693
Greece	...	...	...	19,629	...	25,431	29,547	22,066
Hungary	10,625	...	10,295	9,884	11,195	10,142	10,285	10,179
Iceland	103	126	156	182	244	305	320	368
Ireland	3,105	3,247	3,613	3,577	3,645	3,468	3,142	3,177
Israel	10,902	9,584	14,230	17,467	13,103	15,904	15,216	15,109
Italy	78,998	78,381	79,478	80,140	83,367	86,809	88,784	89,599
Latvia	3,192	2,480	2,520	2,582	2,531	2,570	2,648	2,735
Lithuania	7,855	8,540	9,013	8,796	9,292	9,896	9,446	9,000
Luxembourg	...	...	...	...	...	...	...	...
Malta	97	95	107	145	186	188	209	...
Netherlands	6,267	6,306	6,408	6,448	6,230	6,009	5,991	7,107
Norway	3,975	3,231	2,974	2,973	3,230	3,305	3,550	...
Poland	41,910	44,274	50,907	57,491	59,657	61,478	63,715	73,133
Portugal	...	19,745	...	22,118	22,658	22,785	21,599	20,720
Romania	22,141	25,100	28,876	32,608	40,704	43,752	44,003	45,247
Russian Federation	...	...	...	...	...	...	...	...
Slovakia	7,287	7,378	8,022	8,315	8,081	8,207	8,821	9,247
Slovenia	3,667	3,869	3,960	4,056	4,056	4,143	4,287	4,335
Spain	71,211	75,065	77,229	83,606	88,124	89,946	88,796	89,280
Sweden	17,536	18,789	19,967	20,270	20,628	20,260	19,611	19,116
Switzerland	2,631	2,722	2,954	3,176	3,435	3,708	3,746	3,984
Turkey	...	...	45,960	47,708	48,258	53,182	53,253	58,147
United Kingdom	31,548	31,550	36,088	35,980	32,921	34,105	35,448	37,881
Other OECD (outside Europe)								
Australia	17,481	17,946	18,562	21,475	22,170	22,480	22,643	22,782
New Zealand	3,000	3,422	3,083	3,452	3,953	3,390	3,518	3,977
Canada	25,014	...	...	26,843	...	...	...	...
Mexico	67,007	73,806	79,806	91,200	99,133	128,011	107,270	111,726

	1999	2000	2001	2002	2003	2004	2005	2006
United States	...	...	...	...	...	...	186,682	189,427
Japan	77,278	77,674	79,201	80,825	81,260	80,682	79,468	76,922
Rep. of Korea	185,728	195,251	175,300	188,797	189,299	160,346	165,982	156,216

Western Europe n.e.c

	1999	2000	2001	2002	2003	2004	2005	2006
Andorra	...	...	...	-	-	-	-	-
Gibralter	...	...	...	...	...	...	...	...
Holy See	-	-	-	...	...	...	...	...
Liechtenstein	...	...	...	...	32	43	42	...
Monaco	.	.	.	.	.	.	...	...
San Marino	.	36	...	...	...	...	...	...

Central and Eastern Europe n.e.c.

	1999	2000	2001	2002	2003	2004	2005	2006
Albania	...	601	650	...	955	1,115	...	...
Belarus	...	...	...	...	...	...	38,319	40,440
Bosnia and Herzegovina	...	...	...	...	...	...	...	...
Montenegro	...	...	...	...	...	...	...	...
Rep. of Moldova	...	...	...	...	...	...	...	...
Serbia	...	...	...	...	...	...	...	...
Rep. of Macedonia	1,833	2,196	2,194	2,580	2,619	2,646	2,835	...
Ukraine	...	...	...	...	...	...	...	...

Arab States

	1999	2000	2001	2002	2003	2004	2005	2006
Algeria	...	...	...	...	...	22,080	24,288	25,334
Bahrain	...	...	...	...	509	...	359	333
Djibouti	...	...	...	...	...	7	...	24
Egypt	...	...	...	...	...	...	...	...
Iraq	...	6,416	...	...	...	14,707	...	...
Jordan	...	...	...	...	6,858	6,858	6,149	7,326
Kuwait	...	...	...	...	...	...	...	...
Lebanon	...	3,155	3,030	3,364	3,561	3,496	3,769	4,137
Libyan Arab Jamahiriya	...	...	...	...	...	...	...	...
Mauritania	...	...	...	...	...	...	...	...
Morocco	1,267	1,628	5,686	...	3,024	3,091	4,018	5,804
Oman	...	...	...	...	...	...	904	...
Palestinian Aut.. Terr.	1,212	1,002	1,060	1,804	2,866	2,727	...	3,090
Qatar	...	...	...	...	50	68	...	...
Saudi Arabia	...	204	...	...	345	2,841	3,022	...
Sudan	...	...	...	...	...	...	...	...
Syrian Arab Rep.	...	...	...	...	...	...	...	...
Tunisia	...	...	...	...	...	...	...	...
United Arab Emirates	...	...	...	...	...	...	...	...
Yemen	...	...	...	...	...	...	...	...

	1999	2000	2001	2002	2003	2004	2005	2006
Central Asia								
Armenia	...	...	1,256	...	1,252	1,330	1,528	1,825
Azerbaijan	...	...	...	...	...	...	...	...
Georgia	5,400	5,168	7,308	8,803	11,384	11,236	10,512	2,948
Kazakhstan	...	...	...	...	...	...	...	...
Kyrgyzstan	...	...	6,143	14,954	6,091	3,240	6,161	6,649
Mongolia	5,311	6,095	6,960	7,914	8,775	8,058	8,253	8,674
Tajikistan	...	...	679	...	...	...	...	...
Turkmenistan	...	...	...	...	...	...	...	...
Uzbekistan	...	...	...	...	...	...	...	5,175
East Asia and the Pacific n.e.c.								
Brunei Darussalam	33	54	93	...	76	65	84	122
Cambodia	...	...	40	33	...	45	...	172
China	...	...	...	...	...	...	...	...
Cook Islands	...	...	...	...	...	...	...	...
Dem. P. Rep. of Korea	...	...	...	...	...	...	...	...
Fiji	...	...	...	...	...	...	...	...
Hong Kong (China)	...	...	...	...	4,819	5,012	5,100	5,149
Indonesia	...	...	...	...	...	...	...	...
Kiribati	...	...	...	...	...	...	...	...
Lao P. Dem. Rep.	...	169	190	...	184	397	347	481
Macao, China	...	...	...	...	...	...	63	70
Malaysia	...	...	...	46,037	...	57,921	50,240	...
Marshall Islands	...	...	...	...	...	...	...	...
Micronesia (Fed. St. of)	...	...	...	...	...	...	...	...
Myanmar	...	...	...	...	...	...	...	...
Nauru	...	...	...	...	...	...	...	...
Niue	...	...	...	...	...	...	...	...
Palau	...	...	...	...	...	...	...	...
Papua New Guinea	...	...	...	...	...	...	...	...
Philippines	...	...	...	...	90,816	...	...	...
Samoa	...	2	...	...	...	...	...	...
Singapore	...	...	...	...	...	...	...	...
Solomon Islands	...	...	...	...	...	...	...	...
Thailand	...	...	...	...	...	...	...	...
Timor-Leste	...	...	...	...	...	...	...	...
Tokelau	...	...	...	...	...	...	...	...
Tonga	...	...	...	...	...	...	...	...
Tuvalu	...	...	...	...	...	...	...	...
Vanuatu	...	...	...	...	...	...	...	...
Viet Nam	14,936	15,619	...	22,355	23,576	...	...	...

	1999	2000	2001	2002	2003	2004	2005	2006
South and West Asia								
Afghanistan	...	...	...	...	...	...	...	...
Bangladesh	...	1,185	1,188	1,366	1,531	3,521	6,779	...
Bhutan	...	...	...	...	...	...	...	117
India	...	...	93,279	130,832	...	...	165,402	...
Iran, Islamic Rep. of	...	...	...	...	...	78,101	119,744	189,291
Maldives	...	...	.	.	.	...	...	...
Nepal	...	...	...	...	...	...	...	...
Pakistan	...	...	...	...	...	...	13,341	6,882
Sri Lanka	...	...	...	...	...	...	...	...
Latin America and the Caribbean								
Anguilla	...	...	...	.	.	...	.	.
Antigua and Barbuda	...	.	...	.	...	...	...	...
Argentina	...	...	...	...	...	...	51,796	...
Aruba	...	51	42	43	60	50	...	47
Bahamas	...	...	...	...	...	...	...	...
Barbados	...	...	...	...	...	...	...	...
Belize	...	...	...	...	...	-	...	...
Bermuda	...	...	...	...	...	...	2	...
Bolivia	...	...	...	...	...	...	...	...
Brazil	...	...	...	75,512	79,351	84,177	90,064	...
British Virgin Islands	...	...	...	...	...	...	...	...
Cayman Islands	...	...	...	...	...	...	...	.
Chile	...	...	...	40,565	37,050	21,171	25,915	29,137
Colombia	...	...	94,787	...	...	102,624	115,575	155,073
Costa Rica	...	...	2,959	2,716	...	4,626	...	...
Cuba	...	...	...	...	...	...	...	3,570
Dominica	...	...	...	...	...	...	...	...
Dominican Republic	...	...	...	...	...	...	...	...
Ecuador	...	...	...	...	...	...	...	...
El Salvador	...	...	...	3,485	4,030	...	3,765	3,722
Grenada	...	...	...	...	...	...	...	...
Guatemala	...	...	...	3,580	...	...	...	5,244
Guyana	...	...	...	...	...	58	52	74
Haiti	...	...	...	...	...	...	...	...
Honduras	...	...	...	...	7,266	...	...	...
Jamaica	...	...	...	...	...	...	...	...
Montserrat	...	...	...	...	...	...	...	.
Netherlands Antilles	...	112	115	...	...	...	...	...
Nicaragua	...	...	...	...	...	...	...	...
Panama	...	...	...	6,221	5,540	4,274	4,537	4,473

	1999	2000	2001	2002	2003	2004	2005	2006
Paraguay	...	...	...	...	...	...	...	...
Peru	...	...	...	...	...	...	...	1,027
St. Kitts and Nevis	...	...	...	...	...	...	...	...
St. Lucia	...	...	...	...	...	...	...	.
St. Vincent & the Grenadines	...	...	...	...	...	...	...	...
Suriname	...	...	...	174	...	...	...	...
Trinidad and Tobago	...	317	379	...	...	803	...	...
Turks and Caicos Islands	...	...	...	...	.	.	...	...
Uruguay	...	...	...	...	...	...	4,440	...
Venezuela	...	...	...	...	...	...	...	...

Sub-Saharan Africa

	1999	2000	2001	2002	2003	2004	2005	2006
Angola	138	...	...	...	...	...	...	...
Benin	...	...	...	...	...	...	...	...
Botswana	...	...	78	58	...	62	74	...
Burkina Faso	...	...	...	...	...	...	...	733
Burundi	...	...	...	43	...	...	...	...
Cameroon	...	...	...	...	...	...	...	...
Cape Verde	...	...	...	...	...	...	...	...
Central African Rep.	...	...	...	...	...	...	...	...
Chad	...	...	...	...	...	...	...	...
Comoros	...	...	...	...	.	...	...	...
Congo	...	...	.	12	...	...	...	...
Côte d'Ivoire	...	...	...	...	...	...	...	...
Dem. Rep. of Congo	...	...	...	...	...	...	...	...
Equatorial Guinea	...	...	...	...	...	...	...	...
Eritrea	7	17	22	-	...	123	...	...
Ethiopia	516	454	991	765	1,077	1,932	2,433	2,134
Gabon	...	...	...	...	...	...	...	...
Gambia	...	...	...	...	...	.	...	...
Ghana	...	881	962	781	...	632	...	...
Guinea	...	...	...	...	...	141	...	201
Guinea-Bissau	...	...	...	...	...	...	...	...
Kenya	...	2,168	2,229	...	...	...	...	...
Lesotho	-	.	...	...	-	...	19	...
Liberia	...	499	...	...	...	...	...	...
Madagascar	...	...	...	...	...	...	424	537
Malawi	174	...	...	...	...	...	...	...
Mali	...	...	...	...	...	...	...	...
Mauritius	433	338	398	390	487	662	841	708
Mozambique	...	...	...	...	...	245	278	...

	1999	2000	2001	2002	2003	2004	2005	2006
Namibia	35	...	78	...	97	...	...	...
Niger	...	...	...	...	...	...	...	...
Nigeria	...	...	...	...	...	...	21	...
Rwanda	...	...		...	...	...	...	...
Sao Tome and Principe	.	.	.	.	.	.	.	...
Senegal	...	...	...	...	...	...	...	...
Seychelles	.	.	.	.	.	.	.	.
Sierra Leone	...	14	20	...	...	...	...	...
Somalia	...	...	...	...	...	...	...	...
South Africa	...	7,190	...	...	13,125	15,756	16,847	18,231
Swaziland	25	19	41	...	...	48	24	15
Togo	...	16	...	...	...	...	...	...
Uganda	741	561	596	...	...	1,196	...	...
United Rep. of Tanzania	294	...	...	...	...	...	468	...
Zambia	...	...	...	...	...	...	...	...
Zimbabwe	...	...	...	...	...	...	...	...

Source: UNESCO

* Sub total for "Engineering" (no separate breakdown available for the subclasses of ISCED - 97 Group "Engineering, Manufacturing and Construction")

Table 3: **Students Enrolled in Tertiary-Level "Engineering"* Education, 1999-2006, as a % of All Students - World**

	1999	2000	2001	2002	2003	2004	2005	2006
Europe (OECD/Eurostat)								
Austria	...	12,9	...	...	13,6	12,6	12,1	11,8
Belgium	...	11,8	11,4	11,3	10,6	11,5	10,4	10,6
Bulgaria	18,4	20,1	21,4	22,7	22,1	22,1	21,2	21,0
Croatia	19,8	...	19,1	18,6	17,0	...	16,3	16,3
Cyprus	8,2	6,4	4,6	3,7	3,5	4,0	5,0	6,1
Czech Republic	22,1	16,1	16,0	20,7	20,4	20,6	19,7	...
Denmark	9,2	10,0	10,3	9,9	10,8	10,4	10,3	10,1
Estonia	15,4	13,8	12,7	11,7	11,6	12,0	12,2	12,3
Finland	24,6	25,6	25,9	25,8	26,6	26,7	26,4	25,9
France	...	...	...	...	...	...	...	11,5
Germany	16,2	15,8	15,5	15,4	15,2	15,4	...	15,7
Greece	...	...	...	13,8	...	15,1	16,5	14,3
Hungary	18,4	17,7	15,5	13,0	14,2	12,9	12,4	12,4
Iceland	5,7	5,8	6,0	6,0	6,5	6,7	6,7	7,3
Ireland	11,9	11,4	11,6	11,3	11,2	11,0	10,3	10,4
Israel	16,6	15,3	19,6	20,1	19,2	19,5	18,3	17,9
Italy	17,0	16,8	16,5	16,4	16,3	16,1	15,9	15,6
Latvia	16,1	10,2	9,9	10,2	9,9	9,6	9,5	10,0
Lithuania	22,5	22,4	21,6	20,2	19,7	19,5	18,6	18,0
Luxembourg	...	...	...	...	...	...	...	15,0
Malta	7,5	6,5	6,2	7,2	7,5	8,9	7,8	...
Netherlands	10,9	10,7	10,6	10,5	10,1	8,2	7,9	8,2
Norway	8,4	6,8	6,5	6,4	6,3	6,5	6,9	...
Poland	14,5	13,5	13,2	13,6	13,6	13,3	11,7	12,6
Portugal	...	17,9	...	20,7	21,1	21,6	21,8	21,9
Romania	22,4	21,9	20,4	20,1	21,6	21,2	20,3	18,2
Russian Federation	...	...	...	...	...	...	...	...
Slovakia	21,3	20,8	20,6	19,1	17,9	17,4	17,4	16,4
Slovenia	18,9	18,4	17,5	16,7	17,2	16,8	15,8	15,6
Spain	15,8	16,1	16,5	17,1	17,5	17,7	17,6	17,8
Sweden	19,3	19,1	19,1	18,1	17,3	16,7	16,4	16,3
Switzerland	15,8	14,9	14,3	14,3	13,6	13,6	13,2	13,4
Turkey	...	...	13,2	13,1	13,5	14,3	13,9	13,3
United Kingdom	8,8	8,8	10,5	10,1	7,7	8,0	8,1	8,2
Other OECD (outside Europe)								
Australia	11,6	11,6	11,5	10,7	11,0	10,8	10,6	10,4
New Zealand	6,3	6,7	6,5	5,8	7,1	6,1	6,3	6,6
Canada	10,1	...	...	10,2	...	...	...	...
Mexico	16,9	16,9	17,5	18,3	18,6	20,5	18,3	18,6

	1999	2000	2001	2002	2003	2004	2005	2006
United States	...	...	...	...	...	...	6,7	6,7
Japan	18,2	17,8	17,7	17,5	17,2	16,8	16,6	16,1
Rep. of Korea	38,7	38,6	34,8	34,5	32,3	30,8	31,7	30,3

Western Europe n.e.c

	1999	2000	2001	2002	2003	2004	2005	2006
Andorra	...	...	...	...	...	...	...	...
Gibralter	...	...	...	...	...	...	...	...
Holy See	...	...	...	...	...	...	...	...
Liechtenstein	...	...	...	...	25,2	28,0	25,6	...
Monaco	...	...	...	...	...	...	...	...
San Marino	...	15,0	...	...	...	...	...	...

Central and Eastern Europe n.e.c.

	1999	2000	2001	2002	2003	2004	2005	2006
Albania	...	6,5	6,6	...	8,6	8,0	...	...
Belarus	...	...	...	...	...	...	25,1	25,4
Bosnia and Herzegovina	...	...	...	...	...	...	...	...
Montenegro	...	...	...	...	...	...	...	...
Rep. of Moldova	...	...	...	...	...	...	...	...
Serbia	...	...	...	...	...	...	...	...
Rep. of Macedonia	18,7	21,1	19,2	20,5	19,8	18,0	18,1	...
Ukraine	28,5	...	23,4	22,8	22,4	22,1	22,3	22,1

Arab States

	1999	2000	2001	2002	2003	2004	2005	2006
Algeria	...	...	...	...	...	10,0	9,9	9,9
Bahrain	...	...	...	...	10,9	...	8,4	8,6
Djibouti	...	...	2,6	...	...	2,5	...	5,9
Egypt	...	...	...	...	...	...	...	...
Iraq	...	10,0	...	...	...	19,0	...	...
Jordan	...	...	...	...	12,2	10,6	11,5	12,5
Kuwait	...	...	...	...	...	...	...	...
Lebanon	...	11,9	11,3	11,5	11,5	10,1	11,6	11,6
Libyan Arab Jamahiriya	...	20,6	...	...	...	...	...	...
Mauritania	...	...	...	...	...	...	...	...
Morocco	2,0	2,6	5,3	...	4,0	3,8	4,6	5,6
Oman	...	...	...	...	...	...	9,3	...
Palestinian Aut. Terr.	7,2	5,9	5,2	6,7	7,7	7,1	...	6,6
Qatar	...	...	3,7	3,5	4,0	4,7	...	...
Saudi Arabia	...	8,1	...	...	8,4	2,7	3,3	...
Sudan	...	...	...	...	...	...	...	...
Syrian Arab Rep.	...	...	...	...	...	...	...	...
Tunisia	...	...	...	...	9,0	...	...	10,7
United Arab Emirates	...	...	...	...	...	...	...	...
Yemen	...	...	...	...	...	...	...	...

	1999	2000	2001	2002	2003	2004	2005	2006
Central Asia								
Armenia	...	...	6,9	...	6,3	6,2	6,7	6,2
Azerbaijan	...	...	...	...	...	...	...	...
Georgia	16,5	17,0	19,7	21,0	23,4	23,0	18,3	7,4
Kazakhstan	...	...	...	...	...	...	...	...
Kyrgyzstan	...	...	11,2	16,5	9,9	6,9	9,6	9,7
Mongolia	17,0	17,6	17,2	17,8	18,7	17,1	16,2	16,3
Tajikistan	...	4,9	7,6	7,5	5,6	6,3	13,0	14,4
Turkmenistan	...	...	...	...	...	...	...	...
Uzbekistan	...	...	...	...	...	...	...	15,3
East Asia and the Pacific n.e.c.								
Brunei Darussalam	2,9	3,8	5,1	...	4,4	3,5	4,3	6,6
Cambodia	...	...	2,8	2,5	...	2,3	...	3,6
China	...	...	...	...	...	...	...	...
Cook Islands	...	...	...	...	...	...	...	...
Dem. P. Rep. of Korea	...	...	...	...	...	...	...	...
Fiji	...	...	...	...	...	...	...	...
Hong Kong (China)	...	...	...	...	17,3	16,9	16,1	15,7
Indonesia	...	...	...	...	...	...	...	...
Kiribati	...	...	...	...	...	...	...	...
Lao P. Dem. Rep.	...	9,8	9,9	...	6,8	10,5	4,9	7,7
Macao, China	...	...	...	1,5	1,6	...	2,2	2,2
Malaysia	...	...	...	23,8	...	21,4	18,4	...
Marshall Islands	...	...	...	...	...	...	...	...
Micronesia (Fed. St. of)	...	...	...	...	...	...	...	...
Myanmar	...	...	5,4	...	...	...	...	...
Nauru	...	...	...	...	...	...	...	...
Niue	...	...	...	...	...	...	...	...
Palau	...	...	...	...	...	...	...	...
Papua New Guinea	...	...	...	...	...	...	...	...
Philippines	...	...	...	...	12,4	15,5	...	...
Samoa	...	4,8	...	...	...	...	...	...
Singapore	...	...	...	...	...	...	...	...
Solomon Islands	...	...	...	...	...	...	...	...
Thailand	...	...	...	...	...	...	...	...
Timor-Leste	...	...	...	...	...	...	...	...
Tokelau	...	...	...	...	...	...	...	...
Tonga	...	...	...	...	...	...	...	...
Tuvalu	...	...	...	...	...	...	...	...
Vanuatu	...	...	...	...	...	...	...	...
Viet Nam	17,5	18,1	...	19,7	19,8	...	...	...

	1999	2000	2001	2002	2003	2004	2005	2006
South and West Asia								
Afghanistan	...	...	...	...	...	...	...	...
Bangladesh	...	1,2	1,4	1,5	1,6	3,3	5,0	...
Bhutan	...	...	...	...	...	...	...	14,4
India	...	...	4,3	5,0	...	...	5,9	...
Iran, Islamic Rep. of	...	...	...	...	...	23,1	27,2	30,3
Maldives	...	...	...	...	...	...	...	...
Nepal	...	...	...	...	...	...	...	...
Pakistan	...	...	...	...	...	...	4,0	5,6
Sri Lanka	...	...	...	...	...	...	...	...
Latin America and the Caribbean								
Anguilla	...	...	...	...	...	...	...	...
Antigua and Barbuda	...	...	...	...	...	...	...	...
Argentina	...	...	...	...	8,4	...	8,1	...
Aruba	...	26,8	24,0	24,1	26,2	23,4	...	19,5
Bahamas	...	...	...	...	...	...	...	...
Barbados	...	...	...	...	...	...	...	...
Belize	...	...	...	...	...	0,1	...	...
Bermuda	...	...	...	...	...	...	13,9	...
Bolivia	...	...	...	...	...	...	...	...
Brazil	...	...	...	7,8	7,5	7,5	7,5	...
British Virgin Islands	...	...	...	...	...	...	...	...
Cayman Islands	...	...	...	...	...	...	...	...
Chile	...	...	...	31,4	29,9	17,2	18,2	18,5
Colombia	...	...	29,0	...	...	28,8	29,8	32,3
Costa Rica	...	...	12,6	14,3	...	14,9	...	...
Cuba	...	...	...	...	...	...	...	2,1
Dominica	...	...	...	...	...	...	...	...
Dominican Republic	...	...	...	...	...	...	...	...
Ecuador	...	...	...	...	...	...	...	...
El Salvador	...	...	...	12,2	13,3	...	12,2	11,9
Grenada	...	...	...	...	...	...	...	...
Guatemala	...	...	...	17,1	...	...	...	18,6
Guyana	...	...	...	...	...	6,4	6,1	6,5
Haiti	...	...	...	...	...	...	...	...
Honduras	...	...	...	...	18,0	...	...	...
Jamaica	...	...	...	...	...	...	...	...
Montserrat	...	...	...	...	...	...	...	...
Netherlands Antilles	...	33,7	32,2	...	...	...	...	...
Nicaragua	...	...	...	...	...	...	...	...
Panama	...	...	...	18,1	14,3	11,9	11,6	11,2

	1999	2000	2001	2002	2003	2004	2005	2006
Paraguay	...	...	...	...	...	...	...	...
Peru	...	...	...	...	...	...	...	0,6
St. Kitts and Nevis	...	...	...	...	...	...	...	...
St. Lucia	...	...	...	...	...	...	...	...
St. Vincent & the Grenadines	...	...	...	...	...	...	...	...
Suriname	...	...	...	10,1	...	...	...	...
Trinidad and Tobago	...	16,8	16,2	...	...	22,6	...	...
Turks and Caicos Islands	...	...	...	...	...	...	...	...
Uruguay	...	...	...	...	...	...	11,1	...
Venezuela	...	...	...	...	...	...	...	...

Sub-Saharan Africa

	1999	2000	2001	2002	2003	2004	2005	2006
Angola	8,6	...	...	8,6	...	...	...	...
Benin	...	...	...	...	...	...	...	...
Botswana	...	...	4,7	4,2	...	5,2	5,5	...
Burkina Faso	...	...	...	...	...	...	...	5,6
Burundi	...	...	...	4,7	...	...	...	...
Cameroon	...	...	...	...	...	2,6	...	4,9
Cape Verde	...	...	...	...	...	...	...	...
Central African Rep.	...	...	...	...	...	...	...	...
Chad	...	...	...	...	...	...	...	...
Comoros	...	...	...	...	...	...	...	...
Congo	...	...	...	1,0	...	...	...	...
Côte d'Ivoire	...	...	...	...	...	...	...	...
Dem. Rep. of Congo	...	...	...	...	...	...	...	...
Equatorial Guinea	...	...	...	...	...	...	...	...
Eritrea	4,4	9,0	8,2	...	...	27,9	...	...
Ethiopia	11,3	8,7	13,1	9,2	9,2	10,1	8,9	7,2
Gabon	...	...	...	...	...	...	...	...
Gambia	...	...	...	...	...	...	...	...
Ghana	...	14,7	14,0	13,8	...	11,6	...	...
Guinea	...	...	...	...	...	12,0	...	3,9
Guinea-Bissau	...	...	...	...	...	...	...	...
Kenya	...	18,5	18,7	...	...	...	...	...
Lesotho	...	...	...	...	...	...	0,7	...
Liberia	...	3,9	...	...	...	...	...	...
Madagascar	...	...	...	...	...	...	5,1	6,0
Malawi	32,7	...	...	...	...	...	...	...
Mali	...	...	...	...	...	...	...	...
Mauritius	25,3	22,2	15,9	14,7	12,9	14,0	17,6	15,4
Mozambique	...	...	...	...	...	10,9	9,9	...

	1999	2000	2001	2002	2003	2004	2005	2006
Namibia	3,2	...	3,6	...	4,6	...	...	...
Niger	...	...	...	...	...	...	...	...
Nigeria	...	...	...	...	...	...	0,0	...
Rwanda	...	...	...	...	...	...	...	...
Sao Tome and Principe	...	...	...	...	...	...	...	...
Senegal	...	...	...	...	...	...	...	...
Seychelles	...	...	...	...	...	...	...	...
Sierra Leone	...	0,7	0,9	...	...	...	...	...
Somalia	...	...	...	...	...	...	...	...
South Africa	...	6,7	...	...	7,5	8,3	9,4	9,5
Swaziland	7,4	6,9	5,6	...	...	4,6	3,8	3,1
Togo	...	1,7	...	...	...	...	...	...
Uganda	10,7	3,8	5,4	...	...	7,2	...	...
United Rep. of Tanzania	18,1	...	...	...	...	...	9,0	...
Zambia	...	...	...	...	...	...	...	...
Zimbabwe	...	...	...	...	...	...	...	...

Source: UNESCO

* Sub-total for "Engineering" (no separate breakdown available for the subclasses of ISCED - 97 Group "Engineering, Manufacturing and Construction"

Table 4: **Female Students as a % of All Enrolled Students in Tertiary-Level "Engineering"* Education, 1999-2006 - World**

	1999	2000	2001	2002	2003	2004	2005	2006
Europe (OECD/Eurostat)								
Austria	...	18,6	...	...	19,8	20,6	20,7	21,3
Belgium	...	18,4	18,5	20,5	20,2	22,8	21,0	24,2
Bulgaria	40,1	38,5	36,9	34,6	33,9	32,2	32,0	31,8
Croatia	27,3	...	24,9	25,7	24,9	...	24,7	25,4
Cyprus	22,7	11,0	7,8	7,5	7,7	10,1	12,9	14,0
Czech Republic	19,5	25,9	25,8	21,0	20,7	20,3	21,2	...
Denmark	29,2	28,0	26,2	30,9	32,7	33,6	33,1	32,9
Estonia	26,7	26,8	28,1	29,0	27,8	26,9	27,5	27,2
Finland	17,4	17,8	18,2	18,8	18,6	18,5	18,7	18,8
France	...	...	...	...	...	...	...	23,4
Germany	17,9	18,4	18,8	18,9	18,9	18,9	...	18,2
Greece	...	...	...	27,0	...	28,1	27,7	23,6
Hungary	20,7	...	20,1	21,5	20,2	18,6	19,1	18,7
Iceland	21,3	22,7	25,7	26,3	28,0	31,1	31,3	32,0
Ireland	17,3	17,8	18,7	17,9	17,9	16,7	16,3	16,4
Israel	26,6	24,5	26,9	29,1	22,6	27,1	26,8	27,2
Italy	25,8	26,3	26,5	26,4	26,7	27,1	27,7	28,3
Latvia	24,2	26,7	24,9	22,8	21,5	20,9	21,4	20,8
Lithuania	32,6	31,3	30,6	29,3	28,1	27,8	26,0	25,2
Luxembourg	...	...	...	...	...	...	...	...
Malta	22,5	23,1	23,3	27,6	27,6	26,9	28,4	...
Netherlands	12,3	12,1	11,9	11,9	11,7	13,5	13,5	15,0
Norway	25,3	24,9	24,0	23,6	24,1	23,8	24,1	...
Poland	20,6	20,8	21,7	22,2	22,1	22,5	25,6	27,1
Portugal	...	29,5	...	27,1	26,8	26,7	26,0	25,7
Romania	24,2	25,4	26,6	27,8	29,3	30,2	29,3	29,7
Russian Federation	...	...	...	...	...	...	...	...
Slovakia	27,9	26,2	27,1	28,6	28,6	28,7	28,0	28,5
Slovenia	24,5	25,0	24,7	24,5	23,2	23,7	24,1	24,1
Spain	25,3	25,4	25,5	26,6	27,3	27,7	27,8	28,0
Sweden	27,1	28,3	29,3	29,2	28,8	28,2	28,0	27,8
Switzerland	10,7	11,7	12,7	13,1	13,5	13,9	14,2	14,5
Turkey	...	...	21,7	21,7	18,6	18,9	18,2	18,6
United Kingdom	17,3	17,7	16,6	15,9	18,6	18,9	19,1	19,8
Other OECD (outside Europe)								
Australia	17,8	18,4	18,6	19,9	20,1	20,7	20,9	21,0
New Zealand	28,4	29,5	26,6	32,0	28,3	22,8	23,3	25,2
Canada	20,3	...	...	20,9	...	...	...	...
Mexico	21,5	22,2	22,3	23,3	23,9	26,9	24,5	24,6

	1999	2000	2001	2002	2003	2004	2005	2006
United States	…	…	…	…	…	…	16,2	16,2
Japan	10,8	11,0	11,3	11,6	11,9	11,9	11,9	11,7
Rep. of Korea	18,2	17,8	16,8	17,5	18,3	16,1	16,2	16,1

Western Europe n.e.c

	1999	2000	2001	2002	2003	2004	2005	2006
Andorra	…	…	…	…	…	…	…	…
Gibralter	…	…	…	…	…	…	…	…
Holy See	…	…	…	…	…	…	…	…
Liechtenstein	…	…	…	…	28,8	28,9	31,1	…
Monaco	…	…	…	…	…	…	…	…
San Marino	…	25,5	…	…	…	…	…	…

Central and Eastern Europe n.e.c.

	1999	2000	2001	2002	2003	2004	2005	2006
Albania	…	23,1	24,0	…	25,5	26,3	…	…
Belarus	…	…	…	…	…	…	28,9	29,2
Bosnia and Herzegovina	…	…	…	…	…	…	…	…
Montenegro	…	…	…	…	…	…	…	…
Rep. of Moldova	…	…	…	…	…	…	…	…
Serbia	…	…	…	…	…	…	…	…
Rep. of Macedonia	28,0	28,2	28,5	28,2	29,0	31,6	31,7	…
Ukraine	…	…	…	…	…	…	…	…

Arab States

	1999	2000	2001	2002	2003	2004	2005	2006
Algeria	…	…	…	…	…	30,9	31,1	31,3
Bahrain	…	…	…	…	24,5	…	22,6	21,1
Djibouti	…	…	…	…	…	25,0	…	21,1
Egypt	…	…	…	…	…	…	…	…
Iraq	…	22,2	…	…	…	18,8	…	…
Jordan	…	…	…	…	30,3	30,3	24,5	26,5
Kuwait	…	…	…	…	…	…	…	…
Lebanon	…	22,8	20,0	20,4	21,4	22,5	19,6	20,6
Libyan Arab Jamahiriya	…	…	…	…	…	…	…	…
Mauritania	…	…	…	…	…	…	…	…
Morocco	23,7	22,7	34,4	…	22,3	23,4	23,9	27,1
Oman	…	…	…	…	…	…	20,1	…
Palestinian Aut. Terr.	25,4	23,9	25,4	30,2	35,5	31,4	…	27,7
Qatar	…	…	…	…	16,0	15,7	…	…
Saudi Arabia	…	0,6	…	…	0,8	18,1	15,3	…
Sudan	…	…	…	…	…	…	…	…
Syrian Arab Rep.	…	…	…	…	…	…	…	…
Tunisia	…	…	…	…	…	…	…	…
United Arab Emirates	…	…	…	…	…	…	…	…
Yemen	…	…	…	…	…	…	…	…

	1999	2000	2001	2002	2003	2004	2005	2006
Central Asia	...	...	...	...	...	...	...	...
Armenia	...	...	26,6	...	27,0	27,0	26,2	29,6
Azerbaijan	...	...	...	...	...	...	...	...
Georgia	25,1	22,2	26,4	28,2	31,3	31,5	33,0	27,6
Kazakhstan	...	...	...	...	...	...	...	...
Kyrgyzstan	...	...	28,8	43,2	30,5	22,8	29,3	29,4
Mongolia	47,7	46,9	47,5	49,3	47,9	43,5	41,0	38,6
Tajikistan	...	...	11,4	...	...	...	...	...
Turkmenistan	...	...	...	...	...	...	...	...
Uzbekistan	...	...	...	...	...	...	...	12,0
East Asia and the Pacific n.e.c.								
Brunei Darussalam	30,6	35,3	40,8	...	37,6	38,2	38,5	36,5
Cambodia	...	...	5,5	4,1	...	4,2	...	6,3
China	...	...	...	...	...	...	...	...
Cook Islands	...	...	...	...	...	...	...	...
Dem. P. Rep. of Korea	...	...	...	...	...	...	...	...
Fiji	...	...	...	...	...	...	...	...
Hong Kong (China)	...	...	...	...	19,0	20,1	20,8	21,1
Indonesia	...	...	...	...	...	...	...	...
Kiribati	...	...	...	...	...	...	...	...
Lao P. Dem. Rep.	...	12,1	11,5	...	9,6	11,2	14,8	11,0
Macao, China	...	...	...	...	...	...	12,5	14,0
Malaysia	...	...	...	30,6	...	37,1	39,1	...
Marshall Islands	...	...	...	...	...	...	...	...
Micronesia (Fed. St. of)	...	...	...	...	...	...	...	...
Myanmar	...	...	...	...	...	...	...	...
Nauru	...	...	...	...	...	...	...	...
Niue	...	...	...	...	...	...	...	...
Palau	...	...	...	...	...	...	...	...
Papua New Guinea	...	...	...	...	...	...	...	...
Philippines	...	...	...	...	30,3	...	...	...
Samoa	...	3,5	...	...	...	...	...	...
Singapore	...	...	...	...	...	...	...	...
Solomon Islands	...	...	...	...	...	...	...	...
Thailand	...	...	...	...	...	...	...	...
Timor-Leste	...	...	...	...	...	...	...	...
Tokelau	...	...	...	...	...	...	...	...
Tonga	...	...	...	...	...	...	...	...
Tuvalu	...	...	...	...	...	...	...	...
Vanuatu	...	...	...	...	...	...	...	...
Viet Nam	10,5	11,8	...	14,4	14,4	...	...	...

	1999	2000	2001	2002	2003	2004	2005	2006
South and West Asia								
Afghanistan	...	...	...	...	...	...	...	...
Bangladesh	...	13,4	10,0	10,6	10,9	12,9	14,9	...
Bhutan	...	...	...	...	...	...	...	19,6
India	...	...	22,3	24,9	...	...	23,7	...
Iran, Islamic Rep. of	...	...	...	...	...	17,3	20,7	26,0
Maldives	...	...	...	...	...	...	...	...
Nepal	...	...	...	...	...	...	...	...
Pakistan	...	...	...	...	...	...	42,7	14,9
Sri Lanka	...	...	...	...	...	...	...	...
Latin America and the Caribbean								
Anguilla	...	...	...	...	...	...	...	...
Antigua and Barbuda	...	...	...	...	...	...	...	...
Argentina	...	...	...	...	...	...	30,7	...
Aruba	...	12,1	10,7	11,2	13,7	12,5	...	11,5
Bahamas	...	...	...	...	...	...	...	...
Barbados	...	...	...	...	...	...	...	...
Belize	...	...	...	...	...	...	...	...
Bermuda	...	...	...	...	...	...	2,2	...
Bolivia	...	...	...	...	...	...	...	...
Brazil	...	...	...	27,0	26,3	26,4	26,1	...
British Virgin Islands	...	...	...	...	...	...	...	...
Cayman Islands	...	...	...	...	...	...	...	...
Chile	...	...	...	24,8	21,9	21,2	21,4	23,8
Colombia	...	...	33,4	...	...	32,1	31,7	36,5
Costa Rica	...	...	29,7	24,5	...	28,6	...	...
Cuba	...	...	...	...	...	...	...	24,8
Dominica	...	...	...	...	...	...	...	...
Dominican Republic	...	...	...	...	...	...	...	...
Ecuador	...	...	...	...	...	...	...	...
El Salvador	...	...	...	25,1	26,0	...	25,3	25,0
Grenada	...	...	...	...	...	...	...	...
Guatemala	...	...	...	18,8	...	...	...	25,2
Guyana	...	...	...	...	...	13,0	11,7	15,5
Haiti	...	...	...	...	...	...	...	...
Honduras	...	...	...	...	33,7	...	...	...
Jamaica	...	...	...	...	...	...	...	...
Montserrat	...	...	...	...	...	...	...	...
Netherlands Antilles	...	13,0	14,7	...	...	...	...	...
Nicaragua	...	...	...	...	...	...	...	...
Panama	...	...	...	29,3	29,8	28,0	31,0	30,5

	1999	2000	2001	2002	2003	2004	2005	2006
Paraguay	...	...	...	...	...	...	...	...
Peru	...	...	...	...	...	...	...	19,4
St. Kitts and Nevis	...	...	...	...	...	...	...	...
St. Lucia	...	...	...	...	...	...	...	...
St. Vincent & the Grenadines	...	...	...	...	...	...	...	...
Suriname	...	...	...	33,1	...	...	...	...
Trinidad and Tobago	...	24,4	27,1	...	...	21,2	...	...
Turks and Caicos Islands	...	...	...	...	...	...	...	...
Uruguay	...	...	...	...	...	...	36,0	...
Venezuela	...	...	...	...	...	...	...	...

Sub-Saharan Africa

	1999	2000	2001	2002	2003	2004	2005	2006
Angola	20,5	...	...	...	...	...	...	...
Benin	...	...	...	...	...	...	...	...
Botswana	...	...	22,2	16,4	...	11,6	12,3	...
Burkina Faso	...	...	...	...	...	...	...	42,6
Burundi	...	...	...	8,6	...	...	...	...
Cameroon	...	...	...	...	...	...	...	...
Cape Verde	...	...	...	...	...	...	...	...
Central African Rep.	...	...	...	...	...	...	...	...
Chad	...	...	...	...	...	...	...	...
Comoros	...	...	...	...	...	...	...	...
Congo	...	...	...	10,3	...	...	...	...
Côte d'Ivoire	...	...	...	...	...	...	...	...
Dem. Rep. of Congo	...	...	...	...	...	...	...	...
Equatorial Guinea	...	...	...	...	...	...	...	...
Eritrea	4,0	4,6	4,9	...	...	9,6	...	...
Ethiopia	8,7	7,7	8,7	8,2	7,9	11,1	14,3	16,5
Gabon	...	...	...	...	...	...	...	...
Gambia	...	...	...	...	...	...	...	...
Ghana	...	10,9	10,7	8,3	...	7,8	...	...
Guinea	...	...	...	...	...	6,8	...	12,0
Guinea-Bissau	...	...	...	...	...	...	...	...
Kenya	...	13,2	12,6	...	...	...	...	...
Lesotho	...	...	...	...	...	...	36,5	...
Liberia	...	24,8	...	...	...	...	...	...
Madagascar	...	...	...	...	...	...	18,5	18,0
Malawi	16,7	...	...	...	...	...	...	...
Mali	...	...	...	...	...	...	...	...
Mauritius	22,7	18,4	20,1	21,1	22,5	26,7	28,3	27,4
Mozambique	...	...	...	...	...	10,1	10,0	...

	1999	2000	2001	2002	2003	2004	2005	2006
Namibia	11,5	...	16,4	...	18,0	...	...	...
Niger	...	...	...	...	...	...	...	...
Nigeria	...	...	...	...	...	...	11,2	...
Rwanda	...	...	...	...	...	...	...	...
Sao Tome and Principe	...	...	...	...	...	...	...	...
Senegal	...	...	...	...	...	...	...	...
Seychelles	...	...	...	...	...	...	...	...
Sierra Leone	...	28,6	25,0	...	...	...	...	...
Somalia	...	...	...	...	...	...	...	...
South Africa	...	16,6	...	...	24,3	25,4	24,4	25,9
Swaziland	6,9	5,8	15,3	...	...	15,7	10,7	8,6
Togo	...	6,3	...	...	...	...	...	...
Uganda	17,0	26,8	17,7	...	...	18,9	...	...
United Rep. of Tanzania	8,6	...	...	...	...	...	10,2	...
Zambia	...	...	...	...	...	...	...	...
Zimbabwe	...	...	...	...	...	...	...	...

Source. UNESCO

* Sub-total for "Engineering" (no separate breakdown available for the subclasses of ISCED - 97 Group "Engineering, Manufacturing and Construction"

Table 5: **Students Graduating in Tertiary-Level "Engineering"* Education, 1999-2007, Total (persons) - World**

	1999	2000	2001	2002	2003	2004	2005	2006	2007
Europe (OECD/Eurostat)									
Austria	...	5,642	5,583	...	6,246	6,281	6,704	...	...
Belgium	...	7,906	7,535	7,689	...	4,976	...	7,587	...
Bulgaria	6,503	6,319	7,128	10,654	7,432	7,418	7,429	...	...
Croatia	2,657	2,719	2,517	2,272	2,229	...	2,319	2,388	...
Cyprus	185	...	...	160	188	119	...	...	...
Czech Republic	5,988	5,159	5,017	5,196	7,244	8,018	8,728	10,377	...
Denmark	3,773	3,579	5,293	5,126	4,800	5,692	5,221	5,176	...
Estonia	905	926	923	781	914	854	1,133	1,148	...
Finland	8,674	7,376	8,195	8,240	8,005	8,189	...	...	...
France	82,407	75,387	...	87,943	95,481	97,509	94,737	...	...
Germany	56,199	52,174	50,157	49,567	51,718	53,725	55,998	...	...
Greece	...	...	...	...	...	4,864	7,374	9,137	...
Hungary	6,720	5,820	4,363	5,821	5,772	5,301	5,124	4,669	...
Iceland	82	110	113	98	139	145	168	219	...
Ireland	5,173	5,415	5,331	4,754	6,281	7,061	7,157	...	...
Israel	...	14,605	3,849	4,540	...	...	...	...	...
Italy	29,689	31,013	32,144	37,846	45,300	49,744	56,428	...	...
Latvia	1,255	1,438	1,441	1,460	1,484	1,845	...	1,794	...
Lithuania	4,742	5,340	5,673	5,571	5,983	6,489	6,890	6,892	...
Luxembourg	...	...	...	...	...	...	...	...	...
Malta	38	122	103	82	98	112	101	...	...
Netherlands	8,661	8,254	8,385	8,958	9,590	8,693	8,940	9,691	...
Norway	2,512	2,351	2,486	2,150	2,540	2,559	2,449	...	...
Poland	...	...	29,831	33,105	36,110	34,144	37,304	42,564	...
Portugal	...	7,148	...	8,239	8,926	10,008	10,585	...	...
Romania	11,787	12,866	14,032	15,392	24,912	26,015	27,501	27,653	...
Russian Federation	...	...	...	...	...	335,655	360,535	417,343	...
Slovakia	2,889	3,317	4,450	4,680	4,870	5,220	6,085	6,018	...
Slovenia	2,037	...	1,995	2,295	2,120	2,219	2,259	2,168	...
Spain	37,855	38,584	45,112	48,185	50,663	50,368	...	47,181	...
Sweden	7,788	8,824	9,373	9,970	10,319	11,945	...	...	...
Switzerland	8,146	7,871	7,300	7,353	6,811	7,214	8,639	...	...
Turkey	...	...	41,506	43,873	46,331	49,910	51,145	53,311	...
United Kingdom	56,069	49,198	57,969	56,315	52,729	48,284	50,704	52,798	...
Other OECD (outside Europe)									
Australia	11,957	12,520	18,083	18,860	19,578	...	21,314	22,499	...
New Zealand	2,191	2,143	2,174	2,311	2,173	2,724	2,870	3,061	...
Canada	24,614	...	...	25,722	...	...	...	...	...
Mexico	37,716	44,606	46,424	50,812	59,303	...	59,117	...	...

	1999	2000	2001	2002	2003	2004	2005	2006	2007
United States	176,430	179,276	179,965	179,002	184,740	189,402	189,938	189,532	...
Japan	212,706	209,938	204,502	203,151	199,405	195,241	195,670	...	...
Rep. of Korea	167,655	174,299	168,296	180,233	173,614	172,703	165,812	179,143	169,831

Western Europe n.e.c

	1999	2000	2001	2002	2003	2004	2005	2006	2007
Andorra	...	...	...	-	-	-	-	-	...
Gibralter	.	.	.	.	.	...	...	...	...
Holy See	-	...	...	...	...	...	...	...	...
Liechtenstein	...	...	...	...	14	4	...	46	...
Monaco	.	.	.	.	.	.	...	...	...
San Marino	...	...	...	...	...	...	...	...	...

Central and Eastern Europe n.e.c.

	1999	2000	2001	2002	2003	2004	2005	2006	2007
Albania	...	243	178	...	218	...	...	...	...
Belarus	...	...	...	...	...	22,725	23,906	24,871	...
Bosnia and Herzegovina	...	...	...	...	...	...	...	...	...
Montenegro	...	...	...	...	...	...	...	...	...
Rep. of Moldova	...	...	...	...	...	...	...	...	...
Serbia	...	...	...	...	...	...	...	...	...
Rep. of Macedonia	732	882	602	649	730	793	802	...	...
Ukraine	119,886	...	111,563	112,693	112,390	121,394	99,293	107,112	...

Arab States

	1999	2000	2001	2002	2003	2004	2005	2006	2007
Algeria	...	...	...	...	...	10,842	...	12,156	...
Bahrain	...	...	...	...	255	...	326	296	...
Djibouti	.	...	...	...	...	...	.	...	...
Egypt	...	...	...	...	...	...	...	...	...
Iraq	...	5,646	...	...	...	22,565	...	...	...
Jordan	...	...	...	...	...	3,797	3,755	...	...
Kuwait	...	...	...	...	...	...	...	...	...
Lebanon	...	1,797	2,335	2,276	...	2,487	3,294	3,497	...
Libyan Arab Jamahiriya	...	...	...	...	...	...	...	...	...
Mauritania	...	...	...	...	...	...	-	-	...
Morocco	...	721	...	...	1,243	1,099	2,829	3,550	...
Oman	...	...	...	...	...	...	...	260	...
Palestinian Aut. Terr.	...	575	810	...	1,178	1,181	...	1,592	...
Qatar	...	...	68	62	76	...	...	...	...
Saudi Arabia	...	...	...	...	...	1,145	2,110	...	...
Sudan	...	...	...	...	...	...	...	...	...
Syrian Arab Rep.	...	...	...	...	...	...	...	...	...
Tunisia	...	...	...	...	...	...	...	...	...
United Arab Emirates	...	...	...	...	...	...	...	...	...
Yemen	...	...	...	...	...	...	...	...	...

	1999	2000	2001	2002	2003	2004	2005	2006	2007
Central Asia									
Armenia	...	...	1,174	846	...	827	...	723	...
Azerbaijan	...	...	...	...	...	...	...	...	...
Georgia	4,060	3,402	3,164	3,473	4,272	4,307	...	4,514	...
Kazakhstan	...	...	...	...	...	...	...	...	...
Kyrgyzstan	1,660	...	2,167	1,835	2,868	2,038	2,224	2,299	...
Mongolia	1,587	1,815	2,203	2,401	2,541	2,354	2,653	2,946	...
Tajikistan	...	1,079	1,466	1,201	722	842	915	1,296	...
Turkmenistan	...	...	...	...	...	...	...	...	...
Uzbekistan	...	...	...	...	...	...	...	9054	...
East Asia and the Pacific n.e.c.									
Brunei Darussalam	13	67	80	...	72	91	96	89	...
Cambodia	...	65	78	74	...	178	...	518	...
China	...	...	...	...	...	...	...	...	...
Cook Islands	.	.	.	.	.	.	...	...	...
Dem. P. Rep. of Korea	...	...	...	...	...	...	...	...	...
Fiji	...	...	...	...	...	...	...	...	...
Hong Kong (China)	...	...	...	...	8,955	8,299	8,267	8,023	...
Indonesia	...	...	...	...	...	...	...	...	...
Kiribati	...	...	...	...	...	...	...	...	...
Lao P. Dem. Rep.	...	335	330	...	408	237	737	852	...
Macao, China	...	...	53	49	63	...	73	90	...
Malaysia	...	...	...	...	...	47,620	...	...	...
Marshall Islands	...	...	...	...	...	...	...	...	...
Micronesia (Fed. St. of)	3	...	...	...	...	...	...	...	...
Myanmar	...	...	...	...	...	...	...	...	...
Nauru	.	.	.	.	.	.	...	...	...
Niue	.	.	.	.	.	.	...	...	...
Palau	...	...	...	...	...	...	...	...	...
Papua New Guinea	...	...	...	...	...	...	...	...	...
Philippines	...	...	...	...	39,518	56,628	...	...	...
Samoa	103	23	...	...	...	...	...	...	...
Singapore	...	...	...	...	...	...	...	...	...
Solomon Islands	...	...	...	...	...	...	...	...	...
Thailand	...	...	...	...	...	...	...	...	...
Timor-Leste	...	...	...	...	...	...	...	...	...
Tokelau	.	.	.	.	.	.	...	...	...
Tonga	...	...	...	...	...	...	...	...	...
Tuvalu	.	.	.	.	.	.	...	...	...
Vanuatu	...	...	...	...	...	...	...	...	...
Viet Nam	...	...	...	...	...	...	38,786	...	...

	1999	2000	2001	2002	2003	2004	2005	2006	2007
South and West Asia									
Afghanistan	...	...	...	...	...	...	...	...	...
Bangladesh	...	845	...	826	870	...	...	...	...
Bhutan	...	...	...	...	...	...	...	...	...
India	...	...	...	...	...	...	...	...	...
Iran, Islamic Rep. of	...	...	...	...	...	67,978	86,373	94,218	...
Maldives	.	.	.	.	.	...	...	...	...
Nepal	...	...	...	...	...	...	...	...	...
Pakistan	...	...	...	...	...	...	...	...	...
Sri Lanka	...	...	...	...	...	...	...	...	...
Latin America and the Caribbean									
Anguilla	...	.	.	.	.	...	...	.	...
Antigua and Barbuda	.	.	.	.	...	...	...	...	...
Argentina	...	...	...	...	...	...	...	...	...
Aruba	67	61	74	62	49	33	...	34	...
Bahamas	...	...	...	...	...	...	...	...	...
Barbados	...	...	...	...	...	...	...	...	...
Belize	...	...	...	...	...	-	...	...	...
Bermuda	...	...	10	...	...	...	...	...	26
Bolivia	...	2,233	...	...	...	...	...	...	...
Brazil	...	...	25,310	28,024	30,456	33,148	36,918	...	...
British Virgin Islands	...	...	...	...	...	...	...	...	...
Cayman Islands	...	...	...	...	...	...	...	.	...
Chile	...	...	...	...	16,297	17,365	...	12,495	...
Colombia	...	...	...	14,744	...	...	30,824	29,231	...
Costa Rica	...	692	2079	1579	...	...	...	974	...
Cuba	...	...	...	...	...	...	...	1,755	...
Dominica	...	...	...	...	...	...	...	...	...
Dominican Republic	...	...	...	...	...	...	...	...	...
Ecuador	...	...	...	...	...	...	...	...	...
El Salvador	...	...	...	1,412	2,017	...	1,782	1,630	...
Grenada	...	...	...	...	...	...	...	...	...
Guatemala	...	...	...	435	...	...	...	833	...
Guyana	...	...	...	...	...	101	...	108	...
Haiti	...	...	...	...	...	...	...	...	...
Honduras	...	...	...	...	808	...	...	...	...
Jamaica	...	...	...	...	...	...	...	...	...
Montserrat	...	...	...	...	...	...	...	.	...
Netherlands Antilles	...	114	...	...	...	...	...	...	...
Nicaragua	...	...	...	...	...	...	...	...	...
Panama	...	...	...	2,523	3,100	1,478	1,957	2,178	...

	1999	2000	2001	2002	2003	2004	2005	2006	2007
Paraguay	...	...	...	...	...	...	...	...	...
Peru	...	...	...	...	...	...	...	...	...
St. Kitts and Nevis	...	...	.	.	...	...	...	...	...
S.t Lucia	...	...	...	...	...	...	...	...	...
St. Vincent & the Grenadines	...	...	...	...	...	...	...	...	...
Suriname	...	...	...	...	...	...	...	...	...
Trinidad and Tobago	274	279	296	269	...	611	...	...	...
Turks and Caicos Islands	...	...	...	...	.	.	...	...	...
Uruguay	...	...	...	...	...	...	680	556	...
Venezuela	...	11,871	...	...	...	...	...	...	...

Sub-Saharan Africa

	1999	2000	2001	2002	2003	2004	2005	2006	2007
Angola	16	...	...	15	...	...	...	...	...
Benin	140	...	...	...	...	...	...	...	...
Botswana	54	...	38	...	...	...	...	...	...
Burkina Faso	...	...	...	...	...	...	...	...	...
Burundi	...	...	34	...	...	148	...	...	...
Cameroon	...	...	...	...	...	...	...	1619	...
Cape Verde	...	...	...	...	...	...	...	...	...
Central African Rep.	...	...	...	...	...	...	...	...	...
Chad	...	.	...	...	...	...	...	...	...
Comoros	.	.	...	...	...	...	...	...	...
Congo	...	...	...	...	...	...	...	...	...
Côte d'Ivoire	...	...	...	...	...	...	...	...	...
Dem. Rep. of Congo	...	...	...	...	...	...	...	...	...
Equatorial Guinea	...	...	...	...	...	...	...	...	...
Eritrea	...	...	159	65	185	82	...	...	...
Ethiopia	661	704	...	1,259	2,197	2,511	2,396	2,235	2,813
Gabon	...	...	...	...	...	...	...	...	...
Gambia	...	373	...	...	...	.	...	...	...
Ghana	...	2,124	...	...	...	...	...	...	...
Guinea	...	...	...	...	...	...	...	...	...
Guinea-Bissau	...	...	...	...	...	...	...	...	...
Kenya	...	4,975	...	...	...	...	...	...	...
Lesotho	-	.	.	-	-	...	...	...	...
Liberia	...	638	...	...	...	...	...	...	...
Madagascar	...	...	306	102	...	...	632	441	...
Malawi	...	...	...	...	...	...	...	...	...
Mali	...	...	...	...	...	...	...	...	...
Mauritius	...	...	387	329	294	734	743	729	...
Mozambique	...	...	...	...	...	105	162	...	...

	1999	2000	2001	2002	2003	2004	2005	2006	2007
Namibia	...	...	10	...	38	...	...	...	...
Niger	...	...	...	...	...	...	...	...	...
Nigeria	...	...	...	...	...	...	...	...	...
Rwanda	...	...	...	...	...	...	...	...	...
Sao Tome and Principe	.	.	.	.	.	.	.	...	...
Senegal	...	...	...	...	...	...	...	...	...
Seychelles	.	.	.	.	.	.	.	.	...
Sierra Leone	...	40	...	...	...	...	...	...	...
Somalia	...	...	...	...	...	...	...	...	...
South Africa	...	5,360	...	7,079	7,364	8,358	9,003	10,387	...
Swaziland	...	3	-	8	...	5	36	6	...
Togo	...	164	...	...	...	...	...	...	...
Uganda	519	1,077	...	...	...	1,354	...	...	...
United Rep. of Tanzania	957	...	...	...	...	727	...	...	...
Zambia	...	...	...	...	...	...	...	...	...
Zimbabwe	...	...	...	...	...	...	...	...	...

Source: UNESCO

* Sub-total for "Engineering" (no separate breakdown available for the subclasses of ISCED - 97 Group "Engineering, Manufacturing and Construction"

Table 6: **Students Graduating in Tertiary-Level "Engineering"* Education as a % of All Graduates, 1999 - World**

	1999	2000	2001	2002	2003	2004	2005	2006	2007
Europe (OECD/Eurostat)									
Austria	...	22,6	20,6	...	21,4	20,4	20,4	...	...
Belgium	...	11,6	10,7	10,5	...	11,1	...	9,3	...
Bulgaria	14,5	13,5	15,0	21,1	15,7	16,1	16,1	...	...
Croatia	18,8	19,0	17,4	15,4	14,0	...	11,9	11,5	...
Cyprus	7,1	...	...	5,6	6,0	3,4	...	...	...
Czech Republic	17,2	13,4	11,5	11,9	15,4	14,8	15,9	15,0	...
Denmark	12,2	10,8	13,6	13,0	11,3	9,0	10,5	10,9	...
Estonia	14,1	13,1	12,1	10,1	9,3	8,3	9,6	9,9	...
Finland	22,8	20,4	22,2	21,3	20,7	21,2	...	...	...
France	16,6	15,1	...	16,5	16,3	14,7	14,7	...	...
Germany	17,8	17,3	16,9	16,9	17,0	16,8	16,3	...	...
Greece	...	...	...	...	...	10,1	12,3	...	...
Hungary	14,0	9,7	7,5	9,3	8,5	7,8	6,9	6,5	...
Iceland	5,0	6,2	5,5	4,5	5,5	5,1	5,8	6,4	...
Ireland	12,1	12,9	11,6	10,6	11,7	12,6	12,0	...	...
Israel	...	23,4	5,7	6,3	...	...	...	...	...
Italy	15,6	15,3	14,7	15,2	15,6	15,3	14,9	...	...
Latvia	10,0	9,4	7,1	7,7	7,1	7,7	...	6,8	...
Lithuania	21,7	21,2	20,7	18,7	17,4	17,0	16,6	15,9	...
Luxembourg	...	...	...	...	...	...	...	...	...
Malta	2,8	6,2	5,1	4,4	4,8	5,2	3,7	...	...
Netherlands	11,2	10,4	10,3	10,4	10,7	9,0	8,4	8,3	...
Norway	8,8	7,9	7,7	7,3	8,4	8,0	7,7	...	...
Poland	...	...	6,9	7,2	7,6	7,0	7,4	8,4	...
Portugal	...	12,2	...	12,9	13,0	14,6	15,1	...	...
Romania	18,5	18,9	18,4	16,5	18,1	17,6	17,6	15,8	...
Russian Federation	...	...	...	...	...	19,7	19,9	22,3	...
Slovakia	13,6	14,6	16,9	16,6	15,3	14,8	16,7	15,0	...
Slovenia	19,3	...	16,6	16,1	15,2	14,9	14,3	12,6	...
Spain	14,2	14,8	16,2	16,5	16,9	16,9	...	16,5	...
Sweden	20,0	20,8	21,9	21,9	20,9	20,1	...	...	...
Switzerland	15,1	14,1	13,0	12,7	11,8	12,0	13,6	...	...
Turkey	...	...	17,2	15,3	14,9	19,3	18,8	14,3	...
United Kingdom	11,8	9,8	10,5	10,0	8,8	8,1	8,0	8,2	...
Other OECD (outside Europe)									
Australia	7,9	7,4	8,3	7,9	7,8	...	7,9	7,9	...
New Zealand	5,8	5,0	4,9	5,2	4,6	5,2	5,3	5,2	...
Canada	10,9	...	...	10,4	...	...	...	...	...
Mexico	13,7	14,9	14,9	15,0	17,5	...	15,5	...	...

	1999	2000	2001	2002	2003	2004	2005	2006	2007
United States	8,5	8,3	8,3	8,0	7,8	7,7	7,4	7,2	...
Japan	19,1	19,4	19,2	19,4	19,2	18,6	18,5	...	...
Rep. of Korea	36,4	35,4	32,4	32,0	30,0	28,4	27,5	29,5	28,1

Western Europe n.e.c

	1999	2000	2001	2002	2003	2004	2005	2006	2007
Andorra	...	...	...	...	...	...	...	...	...
Gibralter	...	...	...	...	...	...	...	...	...
Holy See	...	...	...	...	...	...	...	...	...
Liechtenstein	...	...	...	...	23,0	5,5	...	34,8	...
Monaco	...	...	...	...	...	...	...	...	...
San Marino	...	...	...	...	...	...	...	...	...

Central and Eastern Europe n.e.c.

	1999	2000	2001	2002	2003	2004	2005	2006	2007
Albania	...	5,1	3,9	...	4,2	...	...	...	...
Belarus	...	...	...	...	...	22,6	23,4	23,6	...
Bosnia and Herzegovina	...	...	...	...	...	...	...	...	...
Montenegro	...	...	...	...	...	...	...	...	...
Rep. of Moldova	...	...	...	...	...	...	...	...	...
Serbia	...	...	...	...	...	...	...	...	...
Rep. of Macedonia	23,4	22,8	16,3	17,2	16,1	15,3	14,1	...	...
Ukraine	31,9	...	26,3	24,2	21,9	20,9	21,1	20,5	...

Arab States

	1999	2000	2001	2002	2003	2004	2005	2006	2007
Algeria	...	...	...	...	...	11,8	...	11,3	...
Bahrain	...	...	...	...	10,0	...	10,2	10,3	...
Djibouti	...	...	...	...	...	...	...	...	...
Egypt	...	...	...	...	...	...	...	...	...
Iraq	...	10,3	...	...	...	25,7	...	...	...
Jordan	...	...	...	...	...	10,0	8,9	...	...
Kuwait	...	...	...	...	...	...	...	...	...
Lebanon	...	12,5	14,2	13,1	...	10,5	12,8	11,5	...
Libyan Arab Jamahiriya	...	...	...	...	...	...	...	...	...
Mauritania	...	...	...	...	...	...	...	...	...
Morocco	...	2,6	...	...	5,0	4,1	5,9	6,5	...
Oman	...	...	...	...	...	...	...	2,6	...
Palestinian Aut. Terr.	...	5,7	7,0	...	9,2	9,4	...	7,3	...
Qatar	...	...	5,2	5,1	5,5	...	...	...	...
Saudi Arabia	...	...	...	...	...	1,4	2,6	...	...
Sudan	...	...	...	...	...	...	...	...	...
Syrian Arab Rep.	...	...	...	...	...	...	...	...	...
Tunisia	...	...	...	...	...	...	...	...	...
United Arab Emirates	...	...	...	...	...	...	...	...	...
Yemen	...	...	...	...	...	...	...	...	...

	1999	2000	2001	2002	2003	2004	2005	2006	2007
Central Asia									
Armenia	...	...	10,6	7,2	...	6,9	...	5,3	...
Azerbaijan	...	...	...	...	...	...	...	...	...
Georgia	18,2	15,9	15,5	15,6	17,7	17,9	...	15,7	...
Kazakhstan	...	...	...	...	...	...	...	...	...
Kyrgyzstan	12,8	...	11,8	8,0	10,8	6,5	6,7	7,1	...
Mongolia	16,1	17,6	14,8	13,6	13,9	11,2	11,8	12,5	...
Tajikistan	...	8,1	10,6	9,8	6,1	6,2	6,3	8,8	...
Turkmenistan	...	...	...	...	...	...	...	...	...
Uzbekistan	...	...	...	...	...	...	...	15,4	...
East Asia and the Pacific n.e.c.									
Brunei Darussalam	1,9	5,9	7,4	...	4,6	6,6	5,7	5,2	...
Cambodia	...	2,5	2,7	2,4	...	2,0	...	6,2	...
China	...	...	...	...	...	...	...	...	...
Cook Islands	...	...	...	...	...	...	...	...	...
Dem. P. Rep. of Korea	...	...	...	...	...	...	...	...	...
Fiji	...	...	...	...	...	...	...	...	...
Hong Kong (China)	...	...	...	...	22,2	19,5	19,9	19,5	...
Indonesia	...	...	...	...	...	...	...	...	...
Kiribati	...	...	...	...	...	...	...	...	...
Lao P. Dem. Rep.	...	17,1	11,3	...	7,9	5,5	14,1	11,6	...
Macao, China	...	...	1,1	1,0	0,8	...	1,2	1,5	...
Malaysia	...	...	...	...	...	23,5	...	...	...
Marshall Islands	...	...	...	...	...	...	...	...	...
Micronesia (Fed. St. of)	2,2	...	...	...	...	...	...	...	...
Myanmar	...	...	...	...	...	...	...	...	...
Nauru	...	...	...	...	...	...	...	...	...
Niue	...	...	...	...	...	...	...	...	...
Palau	...	...	...	...	...	...	...	...	...
Papua New Guinea	...	...	...	...	...	...	...	...	...
Philippines	...	...	...	...	10,3	14,1	...	...	...
Samoa	18,9	5,7	...	...	...	...	...	...	...
Singapore	...	...	...	...	...	...	...	...	...
Solomon Islands	...	...	...	...	...	...	...	...	...
Thailand	...	...	...	...	...	...	...	...	...
Timor-Leste	...	...	...	...	...	...	...	...	...
Tokelau	...	...	...	...	...	...	...	...	...
Tonga	...	...	...	...	...	...	...	...	...
Tuvalu	...	...	...	...	...	...	...	...	...
Vanuatu	...	...	...	...	...	...	...	...	...
Viet Nam	...	...	...	...	...	...	21,3	...	...

	1999	2000	2001	2002	2003	2004	2005	2006	2007
South and West Asia									
Afghanistan	...	...	...	...	...	...	...	...	...
Bangladesh	...	0,6	...	0,4	0,5	...	...	...	...
Bhutan	...	...	...	...	...	...	...	...	...
India	...	...	...	...	...	...	...	...	...
Iran, Islamic Rep. of	...	...	...	...	...	24,0	23,6	26,4	...
Maldives	...	...	...	...	...	...	...	...	...
Nepal	...	...	...	...	...	...	...	...	...
Pakistan	...	...	...	...	...	...	...	...	...
Sri Lanka	...	...	...	...	...	...	...	...	...
Latin America and the Caribbean									
Anguilla	...	...	...	...	...	...	...	...	...
Antigua and Barbuda	...	...	...	...	...	...	...	...	...
Argentina	...	...	...	...	...	...	...	...	...
Aruba	34,5	22,3	25,7	24,1	13,9	15,0	...	12,6	...
Bahamas	...	...	...	...	...	...	...	...	...
Barbados	...	...	...	...	...	...	...	...	...
Belize	...	...	...	...	...	...	...	...	...
Bermuda	...	...	10,1	...	...	...	...	...	15,6
Bolivia	...	10,8	...	...	...	...	...	...	...
Brazil	...	...	6,0	5,6	5,4	5,0	4,9	...	...
British Virgin Islands	...	...	...	...	...	...	...	...	...
Cayman Islands	...	...	...	...	...	...	...	...	...
Chile	...	...	...	...	25,3	16,3	...	17,1	...
Colombia	...	...	...	22,4	...	...	23,4	25,3	...
Costa Rica	...	7,2	8,9	6,0	...	...	...	9,0	...
Cuba	...	...	...	...	...	...	...	1,7	...
Dominica	...	...	...	...	...	...	...	...	...
Dominican Republic	...	...	...	...	...	...	...	...	...
Ecuador	...	...	...	...	...	...	...	...	...
El Salvador	...	...	...	13,9	16,1	...	12,8	11,9	...
Grenada	...	...	...	...	...	...	...	...	...
Guatemala	...	...	...	10,6	...	...	...	13,7	...
Guyana	...	...	...	...	...	9,0	...	7,6	...
Haiti	...	...	...	...	...	...	...	...	...
Honduras	...	...	...	...	10,8	...	...	...	...
Jamaica	...	...	...	...	...	...	...	...	...
Montserrat	...	...	...	...	...	...	...	...	...
Netherlands Antilles	...	20,0	...	...	...	...	...	...	...
Nicaragua	...	...	...	...	...	...	...	...	...
Panama	...	...	...	15,1	16,4	7,9	11,2	11,1	...

	1999	2000	2001	2002	2003	2004	2005	2006	2007
Paraguay	...	...	...	...	...	...	...	...	...
Peru	...	...	...	...	...	...	...	...	...
St. Kitts and Nevis	...	...	...	...	...	...	...	...	...
St. Lucia	...	...	...	...	...	...	...	...	...
St. Vincent & the Grenadines	...	...	...	...	...	...	...	...	...
Suriname	...	...	...	...	...	...	...	...	...
Trinidad and Tobago	15,3	14,3	12,9	11,3	...	19,2	...	...	...
Turks and Caicos Islands	...	...	...	...	...	...	...	...	...
Uruguay	...	...	...	...	...	...	8,6	6,6	...
Venezuela	...	19,5	...	...	...	...	...	...	...

Sub-Saharan Africa

	1999	2000	2001	2002	2003	2004	2005	2006	2007
Angola	5,7	...	...	8,7	...	...	...	...	...
Benin	14,0	...	...	...	...	...	...	...	...
Botswana	4,0	...	#VALEUR!	...	...	...	...	...	...
Burkina Faso	...	...	...	...	...	...	...	...	...
Burundi	...	...	4,5	...	...	8,5	...	...	...
Cameroon	...	...	...	...	...	...	...	5,8	...
Cape Verde	...	...	...	...	...	...	...	...	...
Central African Rep.	...	...	...	...	...	...	...	...	...
Chad	...	...	...	...	...	...	...	...	...
Comoros	...	...	...	...	...	...	...	...	...
Congo	...	...	...	...	...	...	...	...	...
Côte d'Ivoire	...	...	...	...	...	...	...	...	...
Dem. Rep. of Congo	...	...	...	...	...	...	...	...	...
Equatorial Guinea	...	...	...	...	...	...	...	...	...
Eritrea	...	...	17,6	6,0	16,5	6,5	...	...	...
Ethiopia	7,7	6,1	...	6,9	7,7	6,1	8,1	8,3	8,7
Gabon	...	...	...	...	...	...	...	...	...
Gambia	...	36,9	...	...	...	...	...	...	...
Ghana	...	18,4	...	...	...	...	...	...	...
Guinea	...	...	...	...	...	...	...	...	...
Guinea-Bissau	...	...	...	...	...	...	...	...	...
Kenya	...	17,9	...	...	...	...	...	...	...
Lesotho	...	...	...	...	...	...	...	...	...
Liberia	...	9,1	...	...	...	...	...	...	...
Madagascar	...	...	4,5	1,6	...	...	6,0	4,4	...
Malawi	...	...	...	...	...	...	...	...	...
Mali	...	...	...	...	...	...	...	...	...
Mauritius	...	...	17,7	15,1	10,3	17,7	11,7	11,9	...
Mozambique	...	...	...	...	...	3,6	4,5	...	...
Namibia	...	...	0,3	...	1,9	...	...	...	...

	1999	2000	2001	2002	2003	2004	2005	2006	2007
Niger	...	...	...	...	...	...	...	...	...
Nigeria	...	...	...	...	...	...	...	...	...
Rwanda	...	...	...	...	...	...	...	...	...
Sao Tome and Principe	...	...	...	...	...	...	...	...	...
Senegal	...	...	...	...	...	...	...	...	...
Seychelles	...	...	...	...	...	...	...	...	...
Sierra Leone	...	0,6	...	...	...	...	...	...	...
Somalia	...	...	...	...	...	...	...	...	...
South Africa	...	5,2	...	7,0	6,7	7,2	7,5	8,3	...
Swaziland	...	0,3	...	0,7	...	0,5	3,5	0,3	...
Togo	...	2,8	...	...	...	...	...	...	...
Uganda	5,0	7,4	...	...	...	6,4	...	...	...
United Rep. of Tanzania	24,3	...	...	...	...	18,0	...	...	...
Zambia	...	...	...	...	...	...	...	...	...
Zimbabwe	...	...	...	...	...	...	...	...	...

Source: UNESCO

* Sub-total for "Engineering" (no separate breakdown available for the subclasses of ISCED - 97 Group "Engineering, Manufacturing and Construction"

Table 7: **Percentage Distribution of Tertiary-Level Enrolled Students, by Engineering Subfield, 1998 and 2005 - Europe/OECD - Selected Countries**

	1998				2005			
	Total	Engineering & Eng. Trades	Manufacturing & Processing	Architecture & Building	Total	Engineering & Eng. Trades	Manufacturing & Processing	Architecture & Building
Albania	...	...	...	...	...	...	...	...
Austria	...	...	...	...	100,0	55,0	10,4	34,6
Belgium	...	...	...	...	100,0	62,1	1,1	36,8
Bulgaria	100,0	88,6	8,8	2,6	100,0	79,7	8,9	11,4
Croatia	...	...	...	...	100,0	58,3	17,2	24,6
Cyprus	...	...	...	...	100,0	74,6	0,0	25,4
Czech Republic	100,0	60,4	15,4	24,2	100,0	63,8	11,1	25,2
Denmark	100,0	42,0	9,9	48,2	100,0	59,8	6,3	33,9
Estonia	100,0	52,6	24,4	23,0	100,0	49,1	17,3	33,6
Finland	98,7	76,1	8,1	14,5	98,6	81,6	5,3	11,7
France	...	...	...	...	...	...	...	...
Germany	100,0	57,9	3,4	38,8	100,0	67,9	5,1	26,9
Greece	...	...	...	...	100,0	31,7	47,3	21,0
Hungary	100,0	75,0	8,3	16,7	100,0	69,1	10,4	20,4
Iceland	96,6	57,3	15,1	24,1	100,0	61,4	3,3	35,2
Ireland	100,0	54,4	15,9	29,6	100,0	48,0	7,6	44,3
Italy	100,0	69,9	2,6	27,5	100,0	59,3	4,4	36,2
Latvia	100,0	93,4	4,0	2,6	100,0	55,7	11,4	32,9
Liechtenstein	...	...	...	...	100,0	0,0	0,0	100,0
Lithuania	100,0	59,2	18,5	22,3	100,0	65,3	10,9	23,8
Luxembourg (Grand-Duché)	100,0	55,8	0,0	44,2	...	...	...	...
Macedonia	...	...	...	...	100,0	58,6	23,1	18,3
Malta	...	...	...	...	100,0	54,0	0,0	46,0
Netherlands	100,0	61,2	5,5	33,3	100,0	55,4	4,7	39,9
Norway	100,0	76,0	4,6	19,3	98,4	66,6	4,9	27,0
Poland	98,2	68,8	12,0	17,4	97,4	63,6	11,2	22,5
Portugal	100,0	60,4	7,5	32,1	100,0	59,5	5,4	35,1
Romania	100,0	57,8	39,5	2,6	100,0	72,8	21,8	5,3
Slovakia	100,0	63,2	13,7	23,1	100,0	66,3	9,6	24,2
Slovenia	100,0	63,8	14,5	21,8	100,0	51,8	23,3	24,9
Spain	100,0	65,8	4,2	30,0	100,0	66,3	5,0	28,7
Sweden	100,0	100,0	0,0	0,0	100,0	81,0	2,9	16,1
Switzerland	...	...	...	...	100,0	66,3	3,3	30,4
Turkey	...	...	...	...	100,0	63,6	20,5	16,0
United Kingdom	...	...	...	26,0	100,0	56,2	9,2	34,6
United States	...	...	...	...	100,0	70,3	20,4	9,3
Japan	...	...	...	...	...	...	...	...

Source: Eurostat

Table 8: **Percentage Distribution of Tertiary-Level Graduates, by Engineering Subfield, 1998 and 2005 - Europe/OECD - Selected Countries**

	1998				2005			
	Total	Engineering & Eng. Trades	Manufacturing & Processing	Architecture & Building	Total	Engineering & Eng. Trades	Manufacturing & Processing	Architecture & Building
Albania	...	...	...	...	...	...	...	...
Austria	62,6	34,7	15,3	12,5	100,0	62,5	12,6	24,9
Belgium	...	...	...	...	100,0	67,0	2,8	30,3
Bulgaria	100,0	84,4	7,0	8,6	100,0	82,3	9,7	8,0
Croatia	...	...	...	...	100,0	59,2	15,7	25,0
Cyprus	...	...	...	...	100,0	75,8	3,0	21,2
Czech Republic	100,0	60,8	14,4	24,8	100,0	66,0	11,7	22,4
Denmark	100,0	61,4	6,2	32,3	100,0	54,3	10,6	35,2
Estonia	100,0	58,5	17,4	24,1	100,0	56,1	21,4	22,4
Finland	100,0	72,2	8,8	19,0	98,4	82,1	5,4	10,9
France	...	...	1,3	0,2	89,6	67,7	8,4	13,5
Germany	100,0	62,4	6,4	31,3	100,0	64,5	6,3	29,2
Greece	...	...	...	...	100,0	58,9	8,5	32,6
Hungary	100,0	65,1	13,1	21,8	100,0	61,1	18,1	20,9
Iceland	97,5	45,7	17,3	34,6	100,0	61,9	3,0	35,1
Ireland	100,0	47,3	13,3	39,4	100,0	56,1	7,1	36,9
Italy	100,0	66,1	2,5	31,4	100,0	66,7	4,5	28,8
Latvia	100,0	89,3	7,5	3,2	100,0	60,9	10,9	28,2
Liechtenstein	...	...	...	...	100,0	0,0	0,0	100,0
Lithuania	100,0	57,1	22,4	20,5	100,0	59,3	14,9	25,8
Luxembourg (Grand-Duché)	100,0	61,1	...	38,9	...	...	...	...
Macedonia	100,0	63,2	19,8	17,0	100,0	58,6	25,3	16,1
Malta	100,0	100,0	0,0	0,0	100,0	90,1	0,0	9,9
Netherlands	100,0	66,8	5,9	27,3	93,8	51,6	4,4	37,9
Norway	100,0	78,4	4,5	17,1	100,0	61,5	3,2	35,3
Poland	97,1	68,5	13,9	14,8	97,5	64,1	12,0	21,4
Portugal	100,0	61,8	5,4	32,8	100,0	56,4	10,4	33,4
Romania	100,0	54,8	42,6	2,6	100,0	73,7	18,5	7,8
Slovakia	100,0	57,1	17,0	25,9	100,0	65,8	8,8	25,4
Slovenia	100,0	78,4	9,3	12,3	100,0	56,9	21,1	22,0
Spain	100,0	67,9	4,7	27,4	100,0	71,1	6,3	22,5
Sweden	100,0	100,0	0,0	0,0	100,0	81,6	3,8	14,6
Switzerland	...	...	...	...	100,0	56,8	25,7	17,5
Turkey	...	...	...	...	100,0	63,3	21,5	15,2
United Kingdom	...	...	...	...	100,0	54,9	8,9	36,2
United States	100,0	86,0	7,0	6,9	100,0	66,6	14,9	18,5
Japan	...	...	...	...	...	...	...	...

Source: Eurostat

Table 9: **Women as % of Total Enrolled Tertiary-Level Students, by Engineering Subfield, 1998 and 2005 - Europe/OECD - Selected Countries**

	1998				2005			
	Total	Engineering & Eng. Trades	Manufacturing & Processing	Architecture & Building	Total	Engineering & Eng. Trades	Manufacturing & Processing	Architecture & Building
Albania	...	...	...	...	...	...	...	...
Austria	16,7	...	...	...	20,7	12,4	32,0	30,5
Belgium	...	...	...	...	21,0	13,0	46,3	33,8
Bulgaria	39,6	38,2	51,5	44,2	32,0	28,8	49,9	40,9
Croatia	...	...	...	...	24,7	13,6	53,5	30,8
Cyprus	...	...	...	...	12,9	6,1	...	32,8
Czech Republic	20,1	13,4	39,5	24,3	21,2	11,7	58,5	29,1
Denmark	35,4	33,0	64,9	31,5	33,1	26,2	85,2	35,5
Estonia	27,1	12,5	62,9	22,3	27,5	17,8	50,7	29,6
Finland	16,6	11,6	46,4	25,1	18,7	15,9	42,7	25,1
France	...	...	...	...	...	...	...	...
Germany	16,6	6,4	25,9	30,9	18,4	10,1	37,3	35,8
Greece	...	...	...	...	27,7	26,5	18,2	51,1
Hungary	20,9	14,7	51,7	33,5	19,1	9,3	51,9	35,3
Iceland	20,6	10,0	65,2	18,1	31,3	22,9	73,5	41,9
Ireland	15,7	15,8	17,0	14,8	16,3	12,3	33,1	17,8
Italy	25,3	15,3	55,6	47,9	27,7	17,1	48,7	42,6
Latvia	24,9	23,8	25,2	61,8	21,4	14,2	51,1	23,5
Liechtenstein	...	...	...	...	31,1	...	...	31,1
Lithuania	33,0	20,1	70,0	36,2	26,0	16,4	71,8	31,3
Luxembourg (Grand-Duché)	5,3	0,8	...	11,0	...	...	...	...
Macedonia	...	...	...	...	31,7	19,5	53,2	43,9
Malta	...	...	...	...	28,4	19,3	...	38,9
Netherlands	12,4	5,4	52,9	18,8	13,5	5,5	73,1	17,6
Norway	24,6	22,2	47,3	28,8	24,1	18,5	46,7	33,9
Poland	20,9	15,2	45,1	25,5	25,6	17,8	47,5	36,5
Portugal	28,8	22,2	55,3	35,2	26,0	17,7	58,2	35,2
Romania	23,1	24,6	19,8	41,7	29,3	28,7	26,1	49,8
Slovakia	28,1	23,4	43,9	31,5	28,0	23,3	49,0	32,6
Slovenia	23,9	12,1	60,8	33,8	24,1	6,6	51,7	34,9
Spain	25,1	20,3	34,2	34,3	27,8	22,2	49,2	37,1
Sweden	24,9	24,9	...	...	28,0	24,6	44,4	41,9
Switzerland	...	...	...	...	14,2	8,3	35,8	24,7
Turkey	...	...	...	...	18,2	6,9	44,1	30,2
United Kingdom	15,9	...	...	24,5	19,1	12,4	29,0	27,5
United States	...	...	...	...	16,2	15,5	7,0	41,4
Japan	10,4	...	...	...	11,9	...	...	...

Source: Eurostat

Table 10: **Total Persons, 2003-2006, with Tertiary-Level Engineering Qualifications in the Labour Force (aged 15-74) - thousands - Europe/OECD - Selected Countries**

	Total				Male				Female			
	2003	2004	2005 *	2006*	2003	2004	2005*	2006*	2003	2004	2005*	2006*
European Union (27 countries)	8,118	11,056	10,963	12,778	6,970	9,419	9,250	10,837	1,148	1,637	1,713	1,941
European Economic Area (EEA)**	8,173	11,109	11,021	12,783	7,020	9,468	9,302	10,841	1,153	1,641	1,719	1,942
Austria	...	270	254	253	...	243	228	226	...	27	26	28
Belgium	...	270	269	282	...	227	233	240	...	43	36	42
Bulgaria	243	260	254	252	162	169	160	162	81	91	94	90
Cyprus	18	17	17	19	15	14	15	15	4	3	3	4
Czech Republic	209	...	...	228	173	...	...	190	36	...	...	38
Denmark	187	179	192	200	141	143	151	159	46	36	41	42
Estonia	77	72	82	79	47	45	52	51	30	27	30	28
Finland	232	242	241	242	205	211	208	215	26	31	33	27
France	1,200	1,292	1,443	1,548	1,035	1,093	1,205	1,332	165	199	238	216
Germany	3,170	3,227	3,658	3,489	2,812	2,833	3,232	3,086	358	394	426	403
Greece	184	199	202	227	146	157	157	177	37	42	45	50
Hungary	200	213	220	221	162	172	176	176	38	41	43	45
Iceland	5	5	6	4	4	4	5	4	...	...	...	...
Ireland	...	83	88	...	...	76	80	...	...	7	8	...
Italy	531	535	574	662	414	428	462	502	117	108	113	160
Latvia	63	66	68	38	39	41	45	26	24	24	23	12
Lithuania	...	150	150	144	...	105	108	101	...	45	42	43
Luxembourg	6	10	11	10	5	9	10	9	1	1	2	1
Malta	...	2	3	3	...	2	3	2	...	...	...	...
Netherlands	310	334	312	288	284	307	284	267	25	27	29	21
Norway	50	48	53	...	45	45	47	...	...	...	6	...
Poland	...	42	570	609	...	36	474	484	...	6	96	125
Portugal	...	108	128	134	...	87	95	100	...	22	33	34
Romania	...	363	378	403	...	247	256	276	...	116	122	127
Slovakia	89	104	117	120	71	76	89	97	17	29	28	23
Slovenia	39	44	50	52	31	36	41	43	8	9	9	9
Spain	1,360	1,399	...	1,586	1,226	1,256	...	1,416	134	143	...	170
Sweden	...	212	235	251	...	166	182	196	...	46	53	55
Switzerland	112	185	230	288	100	168	210	262	12	17	20	25
Turkey	...	...	...	649	...	...	...	497	...	...	...	152
United Kingdom	...	1,360	1,447	1,437	...	1,242	1,305	1,290	...	118	141	147

Source: Eurostat

* For most countries there is a break in series between 2005 and 2006

** EU-27 plus Iceland, Lithuania and Norway

Table 11: **Women as % of Total Qualified Engineers in the Labour Force, 2003-2006 (aged 15 to 74) - Europe/OECD - Selected Countries**

	2003	2004	2005*	2006*
European Union (27 countries)	14,1	14,8	15,6	15,2
European Economic Area (EEA)**	14,1	14,8	15,6	15,2
Austria	..	10,0	10,2	11,1
Belgium	..	15,9	13,4	14,9
Bulgaria	33,3	35,0	37,0	35,7
Cyprus	22,2	17,6	17,6	21,1
Czech Republic	17,2	..	..	16,7
Denmark	24,6	20,1	21,4	21,0
Estonia	39,0	37,5	36,6	35,4
Finland	11,2	12,8	13,7	11,2
France	13,8	15,4	16,5	14,0
Germany	11,3	12,2	11,6	11,6
Greece	20,1	21,1	22,3	22,0
Hungary	19,0	19,2	19,5	20,4
Iceland	..	..	..	..
Ireland	..	8,4	9,1	..
Italy	22,0	20,2	19,7	24,2
Latvia	38,1	36,4	33,8	31,6
Lithuania	..	30,0	28,0	29,9
Luxembourg	16,7	10,0	18,2	10,0
Malta	..	..	..	..
Netherlands	8,1	8,1	9,3	7,3
Norway	..	..	11,3	..
Poland	..	14,3	16,8	20,5
Portugal	..	20,4	25,8	25,4
Romania	..	32,0	32,3	31,5
Slovakia	19,1	27,9	23,9	19,2
Slovenia	20,5	20,5	18,0	17,3
Spain	9,9	10,2	..	10,7
Sweden	..	21,7	22,6	21,9
Switzerland	10,7	9,2	8,7	8,7
Turkey	..	..	..	23,4
United Kingdom	..	8,7	9,7	10,2

Source: Eurostat

* For most countries there is a break in series between 2005 and 2006

** EU-27 plus Iceland, Lithuania and Norway

Table 12: Total, Male and Female Engineering Qualifications as % of All Qualifications in the Labour Force, 2003-2006 (aged 15-74) - Europe/OECD - Selected Countries

	Total				Male				Female			
	2003	2004	2005 *	2006*	2003	2004	2005*	2006*	2003	2004	2005*	2006*
European Union (27 countries)	20,3	19,1	19,1	18,8	33,4	31,9	31,8	31,7	6,0	5,8	6,1	5,7
European Economic Area (EEA)**	20,0	18,9	18,9	18,8	32,9	31,6	31,5	31,7	5,9	5,7	6,0	5,7
Austria	..	28,6	28,1	28,1	..	42,8	42,9	42,7	..	7,2	7,0	7,6
Belgium	..	14,0	13,6	13,8	..	24,0	24,4	24,2	..	4,3	3,5	4,0
Bulgaria	23,8	25,2	24,5	23,7	39,6	40,6	38,5	38,4	13,2	14,7	15,2	14,0
Cyprus	14,6	13,6	13,5	13,3	23,8	22,2	24,2	22,4	6,7	4,8	4,6	5,3
Czech Republic	26,8	..	..	25,2	39,1	..	..	38,3	10,7	..	..	9,3
Denmark	18,0	16,9	17,8	17,6	28,3	28,0	29,2	29,4	8,5	6,6	7,3	7,1
Estonia	30,4	27,0	28,8	27,7	51,1	46,9	50,5	47,7	18,6	15,8	16,5	15,7
Finland	23,0	23,1	22,6	22,2	45,6	45,1	44,2	45,1	4,7	5,4	5,5	4,4
France	14,2	14,8	15,3	15,6	25,8	26,4	27,2	28,3	3,7	4,3	4,8	4,1
Germany	30,3	29,7	29,6	28,7	44,0	43,2	43,3	42,5	8,8	9,2	8,7	8,3
Greece	15,6	14,9	15,2	16,0	23,4	22,2	22,5	24,1	6,6	6,7	7,1	7,3
Hungary	20,9	20,3	20,5	19,7	35,4	35,0	35,6	34,4	7,6	7,4	7,4	7,4
Iceland	11,6	12,2	13,0	11,4	19,0	20,0	23,8	25,0	..	..	..	..
Ireland	..	12,0	12,1	..	..	23,1	23,6	..	..	1,9	2,1	..
Italy	14,1	13,4	13,6	14,2	21,9	22,1	22,6	22,8	6,3	5,3	5,2	6,5
Latvia	23,7	23,5	21,7	13,5	36,8	37,6	36,6	26,3	15,0	13,9	12,1	6,6
Lithuania	..	29,5	27,5	26,0	..	48,8	46,0	45,5	..	15,3	13,5	13,0
Luxembourg	15,4	15,4	14,9	14,9	21,7	23,7	24,4	24,3	6,3	3,7	6,1	3,2
Malta	..	7,1	10,0	9,1	..	13,3	17,6	12,5	..	..	..	..
Netherlands	11,4	11,4	10,6	9,6	18,9	19,1	17,7	16,6	2,1	2,1	2,2	1,5
Norway	5,8	5,5	5,9	..	10,9	10,7	11,0	..	..	..	1,3	..
Poland	..	13,2	16,1	15,6	..	31,6	31,1	29,2	..	2,9	4,8	5,5
Portugal	..	13,3	15,7	15,3	..	26,8	29,3	28,2	..	4,5	6,7	6,6
Romania	..	26,4	26,3	26,3	..	34,6	34,4	35,3	..	17,6	17,7	17,0
Slovakia	24,1	25,1	25,7	24,5	38,8	37,4	38,2	38,2	9,1	13,8	12,6	9,8
Slovenia	17,9	18,4	19,4	18,9	32,0	33,3	35,7	35,0	6,6	6,9	6,3	5,9
Spain	20,2	19,5	..	18,7	36,0	35,1	..	33,5	4,0	4,0	..	4,0
Sweden	..	14,1	14,7	15,1	..	25,8	26,5	27,1	..	5,3	5,8	5,8
Switzerland	24,6	25,5	23,9	24,6	34,0	35,4	33,4	34,3	7,5	6,8	6,0	6,1
Turkey	..	..	..	16,8	..	..	..	21,0	..	..	..	10,1
United Kingdom	..	15,0	15,0	14,3	..	26,6	26,5	25,5	..	2,7	3,0	3,0

Source: Eurostat

* For most countries there is a break in series between 2005 and 2006

** EU-27 plus Iceland, Lithuania and Norway

4.2 Fields of engineering

4.2.1 Civil engineering

Jose Medem Sanjuan

Introduction

Civil engineers bring unique services to society – services that involve creative skills and personal decisions that carry substantial responsibility. Their skills and decisions touch the lives of people around the world in their role as professionals managing the built environment. Indeed, human life for the most part depends on these services, which have to be reliable, safe and of high quality to ensure a high standard of living. If the services of the civil engineer are flawed then disruption and other grave consequences may result including sickness, injury and death to, potentially, a large number of people. Consequently, civil engineering is often better known for its rare failures than for its constant successes.

The challenge of sustainable development requires ethical and technical commitment from the civil engineering community around the world. Professional ethics are important in order to reduce corruption in the industry and to adopt a zero-tolerance approach to bribery, fraud, deception and corruption in any form; with annual global expenditure in the construction industry in 2004 at around US$3.9 trillion, Transparency International estimates that 10 per cent is lost through corrupt practices. Many, many more roads, water systems and jobs could be created with that money.

Civil engineers make up a significant proportion, about 50 per cent, of all engineers, and many are members of national, regional and international engineering organizations. Solidarity between those in developed and developing countries requires the full commitment of the civil engineering profession in order to help developing countries raise the standard of civil engineering services in their own contexts.

The profession faces significant and rapid changes. Challenges to public safety, health and welfare are becoming more demanding. It is therefore critical to promote high technical standards of civil engineering through, for example, the assurance of mobility of our professionals to enable the sharing of knowledge and access to technology. Out of these beliefs and concerns, and in order to address the global problems specific to civil engineers and civil engi-

⌒ Blackfriars Bridge, London, under construction.

neering, the World Council of Civil Engineers (WCCE)[1] was created in July 2006.[2]

Some concerns of civil engineering

WCCE members from different parts of the world briefly discuss below some key questions of concern such as mobility, the decline in civil engineering students, corruption in civil engineering and the importance of potable water and sanitation in developing countries.

Mobility

Professional recognition of civil engineering qualifications is generally straightforward at a national level, however across a border it can become a serious problem and, indeed, civil engineering is not a regulated profession in some countries. Hence mobility continues to be a very difficult issue, despite international accreditation agreements and accords.

There are many differences within the profession worldwide brought on by geography, climate, resources, people, history, culture, traditions, idiosyncrasy and language. These can vary substantially even within nations. Also, and more practically, modernization of technology and techniques have been conducted in different ways according to economic and industrial development. There are differences too in the content and duration of civil engineering studies, some demanded by local context but also because courses are, necessarily, continuously changing.

Decline in numbers of civil engineering students

In many countries, the number of students that choose a civil engineering career is in decline. Success patterns in society have changed and many prospective students believe that an engineering career is a more difficult route to success than others. This perception may be due to obsolete study plans, perceived high work commitment, perceived low salaries, a lack of research careers, or a view that civil engineers are technicians that do not get to the 'top' compared to, say, business or management graduates. But it is also because civil engineering has not recently been explained well to society,

---

1   The work of the World Council Civil Engineers (WCCE) focuses on civil engineers and their representation and concerns. A unique feature of WCCE is that individual civil engineers can become members, not just national and regional organizations and businesses. It will facilitate a global platform where all the members are equal, regardless of their nationality. WCCE's work will reflect core values such as collaboration, honesty, integrity, ethical practice, high standards, and total opposition to corruption. For more information: http://www.wcce.net/

2   WCCE has celebrated two General Assemblies, the first in July 2006 in Mexico, which was also the official founding event followed by a regional Congress on Urban Development, and the second in May 2007 in Zimbabwe followed by a regional Congress on Education and Capacity Building.

compared to science or other branches of engineering and technology such as ICT.

Other reasons for such perceptions are:

- The study of civil engineering is hard with a high mathematical component compared to other study programmes such as the social sciences, and the entrance salary is low compared to other professions; and the new Bachelor degrees in civil engineering may make this even worse.

- Civil engineering companies and other professions within the built environment do not encourage continuous professional development; they employ engineers when there is work and drop them when the contract terminates.

- In the hierarchy of building companies, civil engineers are often regarded as expendable, less important than other professionals when in fact they are the resources upon which such companies are based.

- Time and working pressure is extremely high during the 'hot' phases of construction and supervision at building sites, which are usually away from the company office and demands additional time for travelling or working away from home.

Fight against corruption in civil engineering

The infrastructure construction sector faces the greatest challenges of corruption in both developed and developing countries. Corruption has a human cost; it damages economies, projects and careers. Unfortunately, many societies have to tolerate a certain level of corruption as routine. Corruption can occur in both the public and private sectors, in the procurement phase as well as during the design and construction phase of a project, and among both employers and employees. Furthermore, companies that refuse to pay bribes may be denied contract awards, certificates, payments and permits.

Corruption is a complex problem and there is no single or simple method to prevent it, but laws against corrupt practices are not enough. As part of the solution it is vital that civil engineering societies and institutions adopt and publish transparent and enforceable guidelines for ethical professional conduct. Universities should teach compulsory courses in ethical professional conduct and raise the awareness of future civil engineers in how to recognize and fight corruption. On construction projects, corruption should be addressed as part of safety and quality control using a comprehensive and systematic approach. In this respect it is important to highlight the activity of Transparency International and their *Anti-Corruption Training Manual* for infrastructure, construction and engineering sections (discussed elsewhere), which is a very important tool that provides an easy read overview of what constitutes corruption.

The importance of clean drinking water and sanitation

Many people believe that improved medicines are the basis of a more healthy society. Fewer realize that civil engineering works are the first line of defence in public health. Potable water and improved sanitation are the most effective means of improving health whether for a person, a community or an entire society.

Many waterborne diseases are preventable by treating drinking water to potable standards, and delivery of water to the home frees up time for family, education and livelihoods. Implementing a wide range of sanitation schemes will to help control liquid and solid wastes. Proper treatment and disposal of human and animal waste will reduce the opportunities for infection, take the strain off medical facilities and improve the aesthetics of a place through adequate control of odours and insects. Such solutions bring communities together to establish organizations and governance for their shared resource, and hence they reduce conflict. Furthermore, initial implementation at the school and village level reaches larger populations. The development and implementation of such actions is primarily the responsibility of the civil engineer.

The provision of potable water may be on an individual or community-based system. Thus, the civil engineer can support the development of the entire society while improving the health of its people.

4.2.2 Mechanical engineering

Tony Marjoram, in consultation with various national and international institutions and organizations in mechanical engineering

Mechanical engineering is one of the oldest and most diverse branches of engineering covering the design, production and use of tools, machines and engines, and can therefore be considered a central feature of the transition from ape to tool-designing and tool-using human. Mechanical engineering includes the use of mechanics, materials, heat, fluids and energy, and combines the applications and understanding of associated underlying principles and science in static and dynamic mechanics, structures, kinematics, materials science, thermodynamics, heat transfer, fluid mechanics, energy systems and conversion. Mechanical engineers not only apply but also generate underlying science in such areas as finite element analysis (a numerical method for solving partial differential equations in the analysis of complex systems such as mechanical simulations and weather modeling), computational fluid dynamics, and computer-aided design and manufacturing (CAD-CAM). Mechanical engineering underpins industrial development in such areas as manufacturing and production, energy generation and conversion, transportation, automation and robotics.

Concorde.

© Wikimedia - Arpingstone

◯ *Water filter, West Bengal.*

From the development of early tools and machines, many of which had military applications as 'engines' of war and were therefore used to destroy the creations of civil engineering, mechanical engineering developed around the world, the results of which were quite often unknown elsewhere until much later. Mechanical devices, including clocks, vehicles, drive system cranks, gears, camshafts and chains were developed by the ancient Greeks, Egyptians, Chinese and Arabs. Leonardo da Vinci was the first famous mechanical engineer, although he is most commonly regarded today as an artist. Other famous mechanical engineers and their contributions to social and economic development include Archimedes (screw pump), Charles Babbage ('Difference Engine' – the first mechanical computer), Karl Benz and Gottlieb Daimler, Henry Bessemer (steel), Louis Blériot, Isambard Kingdom Brunel, Nicolas Léonard Sadi Carnot (thermodynamics – Carnot cycle), Rudolf Diesel, Henry Ford, Yuan-Cheng Fung (biomechanics), Henry Laurence Gantt (Gannt chart), Hero of Alexandria (the windwheel and first steam turbine), Joseph Marie Jacquard (Jacquard loom – a forerunner of the computer), Henry Maudslay (machine tools), Thomas Newcomen (first steam engine), Nicolaus Otto (four-stroke engine), Charles Parsons (steam turbine), William Rankine (thermodynamics), Osbourne Reynolds (fluid dynamics – Reynolds Number), Igor Sikorsky (helicopter), Ernst Werner von Siemens and Sir William Siemens, Nikola Tesla (physicist, electrical and mechanical engineer – AC power systems), George Stephenson, Robert Stephenson, Richard Trevithick (steam power), James Watt (steam engine), Frank Whittle (jet engine), Joseph Whitworth (threads and precision machining), Felix Wankel (rotary engine), Zhang Heng (spherical astrolabe and seismometer).

Mechanical engineering underpinned and was in turn driven forward by the successive waves of innovation and Industrial Revolution. The first wave of Industrial Revolution focused on the textile industry from 1750–1850; the second wave focused on steam and the railways from 1850–1900; the third wave was based on steel, machine tools, electricity and heavy engineering from 1875–1925; and the fourth wave based on oil, the automobile and mass production from 1900 onwards, all of which were based on mechanical engineering. The fifth wave, based on information and telecommunications from 1950, is related to electrical and mechanical engineering, as is the sixth wave, beginning around 1980, based on new knowledge production and application in such fields as IT, biotechnology and materials. The seventh wave, beginning around 2005, based on sustainable 'green' engineering and technology to promote sustainable development, climate change mitigation and adaptation, will once again be focused particularly on a core of mechanical engineering.

Mechanical engineering institutions, education and accreditation

The first professional institution of mechanical engineers (IMechE) was founded in the UK in 1847, thirty years after the creation of the Institution of Civil Engineers, partly as a breakaway from the ICE by George Stephenson (the 'Father of Railways' and creator of the 'Rocket') and others on the mechanical side of engineering, which was at the time part of the ICE. Institutions of mechanical engineering then arose in continental Europe, the United States and elsewhere. This wave of institutional development occurred around the same time as the establishment of departments of engineering focusing on mechanical engineering in major universities around the world. The approach to engineering education coursework and pedagogy was based on the 'Humboldtian' model building on a 'fundamentals' approach to education with a foundation in mathematics and the engineering 'science', as discussed elsewhere. Largely unchanged in 150 years, it is one of the factors responsible for the decline of contemporary interest of young people in engineering education. These days, of course, there is more mathematics, building upon finite element analysis and related tools, and more core subjects than the statics and dynamics, strengths of materials, thermodynamics, fluids, control theory, machine tools, materials science, computing, engineering drawing and design subjects that comprised the typical mechanical engineering degree course a generation ago. Nowadays students will also encounter computational fluid dynamics, CAD and computer modeling, mechatronics, robotics, biomechanics and nanotechnology.

Even before they graduate, young mechanical engineers also encounter a changing world in terms of accreditation and possible mobility. The move to a competence-based approach and systems of recognition and accreditation of engineering and associated curricula has been driven by various international groups, particularly the Washington Accord, signed in 1989 as an international agreement among national bodies responsible for accrediting engineering degree programs (and the recognition of substantial equivalence in the accreditation of qualifications in professional engineering). The six international agreements governing mutual recognition of engineering qualifications and professional competence also include the associated Sydney Accord for Engineering Technologists or Incorporated Engineers and the Dublin Accord for the international recognition of Engineering Technician qualifications. The Washington Accord group includes Australia, Canada, Chinese Taipei, Hong Kong China, Ireland, Japan, Korea, Malaysia, New Zealand, Singapore, South Africa, United Kingdom and the United States; provisional members include Germany, India, Russia and Sri Lanka.

Applications and development

When they graduate from the increasing diverse branches of mechanical engineering, young engineers are faced with a diversity of possible careers in established and emerging fields of engineering and engineering applications. Many young engineers are concerned about the role of engineering in addressing the issues and challenges of development, and see opportunities for involvement with such groups as Engineers Without Borders and Engineers Against Poverty, based at IMechE in the UK. Many other mechanical engineers are also concerned about the social responsibility of engineers and engineering organizations, and the need to engage more effectively with development issues in such fields as:

- water supply and sanitation;

- cleaner production and recycling;

- energy efficiency and conservation, renewable energy and clean coal technology;

- emergencies and disaster preparedness and response including urban security;

- post disaster and conflict restoration, rehabilitation and reconstruction; and

- engaging engineers in decision-making, policy-making and planning.

Mechanical and related national and international engineering organizations have a responsibility to assist engineers engaged in such activities through enhanced international cooperation, staff and student exchange.

4.2.3 Electrical and Electronic engineering

Tony Marjoram, in consultation with Andrew Lamb and various national and international institutions and organizations in electrical and electronics engineering

Electrical and electronics engineering is the field of engineering that focuses on the study and application of electricity, electromagnetism and, since the Second World War, the development and application of electronics and electronics engineering in the later 1950s, from what was previously referred to as 'radio engineering'. Due to the rapid pace of change since 1945, electrical and electronics engineering include an increasingly diverse of topics, from the more traditional electrical engineering subjects of power generation and distribution, electric circuits, transformers, motors, electromagnetic and associated devices, to the development of electronic engineering from telephone, radio, television and telecommunications, through the dramatic development of electronic technologies such as radar, sonar and weapons systems in the Second World

War, to more recent electronic materials, devices and circuits, integrated circuits and computer systems, microwave systems, mobile telephony, computer networking, increasingly sophisticated information and communication technologies, optical fibres and optoelectronic devices, photonics and nanotechnologies.

Broadly speaking, electrical engineering deals with larger scale systems of electricity, power transmission and energy, while electronics engineering deals with smaller systems of electricity, electronics and information transmission. Such systems operate on an increasing micro-scale such that the term 'microelectronics' is now common. Indeed, 'Moore's law', named after Gordon Moore, co-founder of Intel, describes the trend in computing hardware as the surface density of transistors in an integrated circuit that doubles almost every two years.

The study of electricity effectively began in the seventeenth century with the study of static electricity by William Gilbert – credited as the father of electrical engineering – who coined the term 'electricity' from the Greek *elektron* for amber (used in his experiments), and who distinguished between electricity and magnetism. Lightning was another natural electrical phenomena that attracted interest, and Benjamin Franklin, a polymath with a particular interest in electricity, proposed flying a kite in a storm in 1750 to illustrate that lightning is electricity. While it is not known if he conducted the experiment, the course of history may well have been different had he been holding the string as he went on to be the United States ambassador to France and was instrumental in drafting the Treaty of Paris in 1783 to mark the end of the American War of Independence.

In 1775 Alessandro Volta developed a machine to produce statice electricity, and the voltaic pile in 1800, a precursor to the electric battery, to store it. Interest increased into the nineteenth century, with Ohm's work on current and potential difference, Michael Faraday's discovery of electromagnetic induction in 1831 and James Clerk Maxwell theoretical link between electricity and magnetism in 1873. Based on this work, and the invention of the light bulb, Thomas Edison built the first (direct current) electricity supply system in Manhattan in 1882. At the same time, Nikola Tesla was developing the theory of alternating current power generation and distribution that was promoted by Westinghouse, which lead to a 'War of Currents' with the Edison Illuminating Company. AC gradually displaced DC on grounds of range, efficiency and safety, with Edison regretting not adopting AC. Tesla developed induction motors and polyphase systems, Edison developed telegraphy and the Edison Illuminating Company became General Electric. The development of radio at the end of the century lead to the cathode ray tube, diode, amplifying triode and magnetron as enabling technologies for the oscillo-

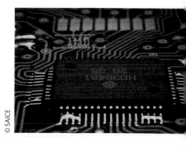

() *Computer chip.*

© SAICE

scope, television, microwave and computing, furthered by the transistor in 1947, integrated circuits in 1958 and the microprocessor in 1968.

Electrical and electronics engineering institutions, education and applications

In the early years the study of electricity, with few applications, was essentially part of physics. With increasing interest in the commercialization of electrical power supply and the electric telegraph, electrical engineering began to develop in the late nineteenth century and professional bodies began to appear while university departments of electrical engineering began to offer degree courses in the later 1800s. Building on earlier curricula, electrical and electronics engineering degrees cover a range of subjects and may including power, control systems, nonlinear systems, microelectronics, computer engineering, systems analysis, information theory, signal processing, mechatronics, robotics, telecommunications, data communications, communication systems and nanotechnology.

Professional bodies for electrical and electronics engineers include, in particular, the Institute of Electrical and Electronics Engineers (IEEE) based in the United States and the Institution of Engineering and Technology (IET) based in the UK. The IEEE has the largest worldwide membership, number of publications, conferences and related events. While such mega engineering organizations may be good at communications and facilitating continuous professional development, which is especially useful in a rapidly changing field, they may also however undermine professional development and applications at the local level, especially in developing countries.

Power engineers are responsible for the design and maintenance of power grids and power systems connecting to the grid. On-grid power systems may also feed power into the grid, as with the increasing interest in microgeneration. There is also increasing interest in power system control, including satellite control systems, to reduce the risk of blackouts and surges. Control systems engineering monitors and models control and other systems as well as designs system controllers using signal processors and programmable logic controllers (PLCs). Control engineering applications include industrial automation, aircraft and automobile control systems and battery charge regulating technology for solar photovoltaic systems.

The design and testing of electronic circuits is a significant part of electronic engineering and involves the properties of individual components: resistors, capacitors, inductors, diodes and transistors, for particular purposes. Microelectronics and integrated circuits allow this at the micro- and nano-electric scale, enabling modern microelectronic devices. Microelectronics is at the microscopic scale and requires knowledge of chemistry, materials science and quantum mechanics. Signal processing relates increasingly to digital systems and is rapidly

expanding to include applications in most areas of electrical engineering and electronics – in communications, control, power systems and biomedical engineering. Integrated circuits are now found in almost all electronic systems and devices, including radio, audio and TV systems, mobile communication, recording and playback devices, automobile control systems, weapons systems and all types of information processing systems. Signal processing is also related to instrumentation and control engineering.

One of the greatest areas of potential for electrical engineering and electronics is in combination with other areas of engineering, especially mechanical engineering, in mechatronics where electromechanical systems have increasingly diverse applications in such areas as robotics and automation, heating and cooling systems, aircraft, automobile and similar control systems. Such systems are working on an increasingly miniature scale, such as the microelectromechanical systems (MEMS) that control vehicle airbags, photocopiers and printers. In biomedical engineering, for example, mechatronics is enabling the development of better and more mobile medical technology, and MEMS, the development of implantable medical devices such as cochlear implants, pacemakers and artificial hearts. Electrical engineering and electronics is of obvious importance in the development context but is challenged by the increasing level of support knowledge and technology that may be required, as is the case with modern automobile diagnostic devices, for example.

4.2.4 Chemical engineering

Jean-Claude Charpentier

The state of modern chemical engineering

Chemical engineering involves the application of scientific and technological knowledge to create physical, chemical and biological transformations of raw materials and energy into targeted products. This involves the synthesis and optimization of the design, materials, manufacturing and control of industrial processes. It involves physical-biological-chemical separations (using processes such as distillation, drying, absorption, agitation, precipitation, filtration, crystallization, emulsification, and so on), and chemical, catalytic, biochemical, electrochemical, photochemical and agrochemical reactions.

Customers require increasingly specialized materials, active compounds and 'special effects chemicals' that are much more complex than traditional high-volume bulk chemicals. Indeed, many chemical products now rely on their specialized microstructures as well as their chemical composition to achieve their purpose; think ice-cream, paint, shoe polish, and so on.

Figure 1: **Biochemistry and biochemical engineering**

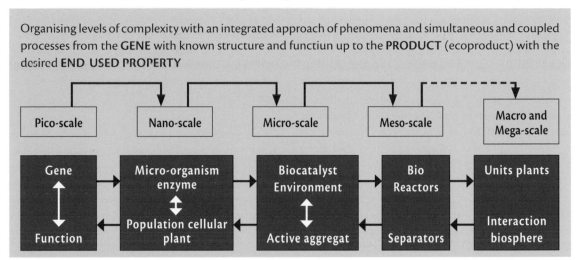

Chemical engineering already plays an essential role in attempts to feed the population of the planet, to tap new sources of energy, to clothe and house humankind, to improve health and eliminate sickness, to provide substitutes for rare raw materials, to design sophisticated materials for ever evolving information and communication devices, and to monitor and to protect our environment, among other things.

Chemical engineers involved in the production of structured materials face many challenges in fundamentals, product design, process integration and in process control. Organizing scales and complexity is necessary to understand and describe the events at the nano- and micro-scales, and to better convert molecules into useful products at the process scale. This leads chemical engineers to translate molecular processes into phenomenological macroscopic laws that create and control the required end-use properties and functionality of products. Essentially, to transform molecules into money.

The work of today's chemical engineers involves strong multi-disciplinary collaboration with physicists, chemists, biologists, mathematicians, instrumentation specialists and business people. Biology is now included as a foundation science in the education of chemical engineers (along with physics and chemistry) in order to address genetics, biochemistry and molecular cell biology. Developing new concepts within the framework of what could be called 'physical-biological-chemical engineering' justifies the qualification of 'process engineering' as an extension of chemical engineering.

Chemical and process engineers are one of the few groups of engineers who work in the natural sciences, technology and economics. Chemical engineers need to be good problem solvers, creative, pragmatic, innovative and have the skills for technical rigour, systems thinking and multidisciplinary tasks. The business of chemical engineers is to imagine and invent

reactions that will convert the chemical substances we find around us into substances or products that meet a need, and to address the problems and challenges posed by chemical and process industries.

Figure 2: **Biochemistry and biochemical engineering**

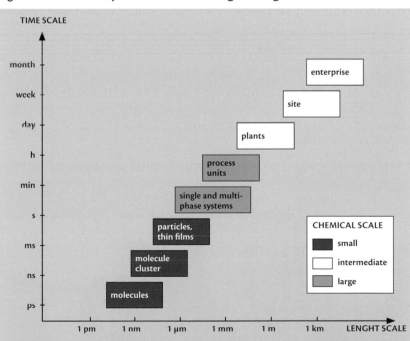

Chemical and Process Engineering is now concerned with the understanding and development of systematic procedures for the design and operation of chemical process systems, ranging:
FROM nano and microsystems scales where chemicals have to be synthesize and charachterize at the molecular-level
TO industrial-scale continuous and batch processes

The chemical and process industries – the heart of the challenges

Today, the chemical and related industries – including oil and gas, oil shale, petrochemicals, pharmaceuticals and health, agriculture and food, environment, pulp and paper, textile and leather, iron and steel, bitumen, building materials, glass, surfactants, cosmetics and perfume, and electronics, and so on – are evolving rapidly. This is due to unprecedented demands and constraints, stemming not least from public concern over environmental and safety issues. Only 25 per cent by weight of extracted resources is used for the production of goods and services; the other 75 per cent is lost to pollution, waste and environment disturbances.

Chemical knowledge is also growing rapidly and the rate of discovery increases every day. More than fourteen million different molecular compounds could be synthesized in 2005. About 100,000 can regularly be found on the market, but only a small fraction of them can be found in nature. Most of them are deliberately conceived, designed, synthesized and manufactured to meet a human need, to test an idea or to satisfy our quest for knowledge. The development of combined chemical synthesis with nanotechnology is a current example.

There are two major demands associated with the challenge to assure development, competitiveness, sustainability and employment in chemical industries. The first is how to compete in the global economy where the key factors are globalization, partnership and innovation (which mainly involves the acceleration of innovation as a process of discovery and development). For example, in the fast-moving consumer goods business, time to market has decreased from about ten years in 1970 to an estimated 2–3 years in the year 2000. Now, even one year is often considered long. The second major demand is to respond to market demands. This actually presents a double challenge. In industrializing countries, labour costs are low and there are fewer regulations. In industrialized countries, there is rapid growth in consumer demand for specific end-use properties and significant concern for the environment and safety.

The chemical engineering profession is already responding to these demands and the necessity for more sustainable products and processes. It will increasingly research innovative processes for production to transition, from the now traditional high-bulk chemistry, into new industries of specialized and active material chemistry.

For example, in the production of commodity and intermediate products (ammonia, calcium carbonate, sulphuric acid, ethylene, methanol, ethanol and so on representing 40 per cent of the market), patents usually do not apply to the product but rather to the process, and the process can no longer be determined by economic considerations alone. The need is to produce large quantities at the lowest possible price, but the economic constraints will no longer be defined as 'sale price, minus capital, plus operating, plus raw material, plus energy cost'. Increased selectivity and the savings linked to the process itself must be considered, which needs further research. Furthermore, it has to be added that the trend towards global-scale facilities may soon require a change of technology, with the current technology no longer capable of being built 'just a bit bigger'. This may involve an integrated multi-scale chemical process design. It may mean that large-scale production units are created by the integration and interconnection of diverse, smaller-scale elements.

For high-margin products that involve customer-designed or perceived formulations, chemical engineers need to design new plants that are no longer optimized to produce one product at high quality and low cost. The need is for multi-purpose systems and generic equipment that can be easily switched over to other recipes; systems like flexible production, small batches, modular set-ups, and so on.

Chemical and process engineering in the future

Briefly, the years to come seem to be characterized by four main parallel and simultaneous changes:

1. Total multi-scale control: process to increase selectivity and productivity.

2. Process intensification: including the design of novel equipment, new operating modes and new methods of production (Figure 3).

Figure 3: **A plant of the future**

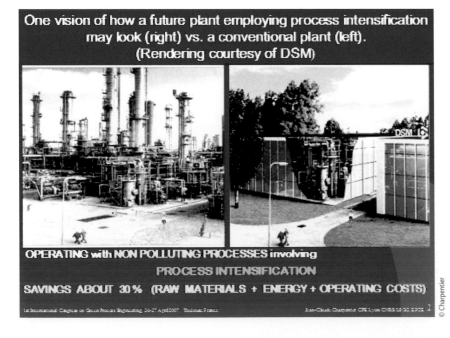

© Charpentier

3. Manufacturing end-use properties: product design and engineering.

4. Application of multi-scale and multi-disciplinary computational modeling: for example from the molecular-scale, to the overall complex production scale, to the entire production site, and involving process control and safety.

With these changes in mind, modern chemical engineering can be seen as a tool for driving sustainable social and economic development in the contexts of 'society and market demands versus technology offers' and the concept of transforming molecules into money.

Clearly, the chemical industries are confronted with a great number of challenges, all within a framework of globalization, competition and sustainability. To satisfy these consumer needs and market trends, chemical and process engineers must develop innovative technologies and take a multi-disciplinary, multi-scale and integrated approach. Moreover, they can use this approach to respond to increasing environmental, societal and economic requirements, and to smooth the transition towards sustainability whatever their particular industry may be.

Chemical engineering today drives economic development and is fundamental to wealth creation in the framework of globalization and sustainability. Engineers must constantly adapt to new trends, and the education of the next generation of students must arm them with the tools needed for the world as it will be, and not only as it is today, as well as prepare them for the technology-driven world of the future.

4.2.5 Environmental engineering

Cheryl Desha and Charlie Hargroves

Since the start of the Industrial Revolution engineers have made significant advances in delivering a range of crucial solutions and services to the world's growing communities. However, until the latter part of the twentieth century, engineers gave little consideration to broader environmental impacts, in part due to a lack of scientific understanding of the world's natural systems and their limited resilience. As scientific knowledge increased, the field of environmental science emerged and expertise developed around better understanding of the impacts of development on the environment. Efforts were made to incorporate key components of this new knowledge across the engineering disciplines. However, the most visible action was in developing a new discipline to focus on the interface of engineering and environmental issues, in the form of 'environmental engineering'.

The emergence of environmental engineering as a distinct discipline in the USA
James R. Mihelcic

Over the past several decades, environmental engineering has emerged as a distinct engineering discipline around the world. Taking just a few examples from the United States:

- The Accreditation Board for Engineering and Technology (ABET) now accredits more than fifty environmental engineering programmes.

- Environmental engineering has become a recognized specialization on professional engineering licensing exams.[a]

- As of May 2005, the US Bureau of Labor Statistics (BLS)[b] counted over 50,000 environmental engineers. A wider estimate shows that this may be as high as 100,000.[c]

- As a profession, environmental engineering is now larger than biomedical, materials and chemical engineering (which in 2002 had 8,000, 33,000 and 25,000 members, respectively) and trends show that it is growing more quickly.

- The predicted 30 per cent growth in the number of environmental engineers to 65,000 by 2012 will account for 5 per cent of all engineering jobs created over the decade ending in 2012. For comparison, 11 per cent will be in civil engineering, 14 per cent in mechanical engineering, 1 per cent in biomedical engineering, 2 per cent in chemical engineering, and 4 per cent in aerospace engineering.[d]

---

a   Final Report of the Joint Task Force for the Establishment of a Professional Society for Environmental Engineers of the American Academy of Environmental Engineers (AAEE) and the Association of Environmental Engineering and Science Professors (AEESP), September 2006.

b   United States Bureau of Labor Statistics website: http://www.bls.gov/oco/ocos027.htm

c   This higher estimate is based on the fact is that 34.5 per cent of the members of the American Society of Civil Engineers (ASCE) now classify themselves as environmental engineers and, depending on who counts them, there are 228,000 to 330,000 civil engineers in the U.S. (based on 2002 U.S. government estimate and 2000 U.S. National Science Foundation estimate, respectively).

d   S. Jones et al. 2005. An Initial Effort to Count Environmental Engineers in the USA. *Environmental Engineering Science*, Vol. 22, No. 6, pp. 772–787.

As knowledge about the extent and complexity of the environmental challenge has grown, it has become clear that expertise developed as part of the environmental engineering discipline over the last two decades will be increasingly important. However, the challenge is far too great, and the time to respond too short to expect environmental engineers to take care of all the environmental issues for the entire profession; environmental engineering is not a substitute for sustainable engineering. Rather, critical knowledge and skills in environmental science, previously only taught in environmental engineering, must be quickly and effectively integrated across all engineering disciplines. Meanwhile, the environmental engineering discipline itself must continue to evolve as an advanced and specialist field, for example in such areas as modeling, monitoring, impact assessment, pollution control, evaluation and collaborative design.

'Our discipline has at times struggled to understand its place – environmental engineering must move on from simply being a practice area that cleans up the output of other engineering disciplines. It must embrace a deeper understanding of the systems of the earth and the interaction of those systems with the manufactured or built form. Only then can it build a respected body of knowledge and become a practice area truly independent of other engineering disciplines.'[3]

Adjunct Professor David Hood, the Institution of Engineers Australia's College of Environmental Engineers, 2009 Chairman.

With this in mind, as the education sector mobilizes to prepare all engineering graduates for sustainable engineering, environmental engineering can play a key role in the transition and thereafter. As one of the newer disciplines, it will be increasingly called upon to assist all other engineering disciplines to understand how to deliver sustainable engineering solutions.

4.2.6 Agricultural engineering

Irenilza de Alencar Nääs and
Takaaki Maekawa

Agriculture has a very long history. Evidence of agricultural engineering can be found in ancient civilizations with tools and technologies such as ploughs, grain storage and irrigation. Modern agricultural engineering, as we know it today, began to grow after the 1930s. At the time, it played only a marginal role in Europe though with variations from country to country. Various machines had been developed and improved for agricultural use in the course of the proceeding century – feeding the growth of urban populations. However, despite the importance of agricultural engineering for this primary sector, development of the profession was still slow and limited in scope. The design of agricultural machines and buildings was based on skills and accumulated experience rather than coordinated scientific research. The same applies to post-harvesting technologies and greenhouses as well as ergonomics, safety and labour organization. Environmental protection and sustainable landuse did not become subjects of scientific research until much later.

To address these issues and to foster international cooperation of researchers and combine cooperation with a concern for improved working conditions in farming and rural activities, the International Commission of Agricultural Engineering (CIGR) was founded in 1930.[4] The technical problems in the

The International Commission of Agricultural Engineering (*Commission Internationale du Génie Rural - CIGR*)

CIGR technical sections

Section 1. Land and water engineering: engineering applied to the science of soil and water management.

Section 2. Farm buildings, equipment, structures and environment: optimization and design of animals, crops and horticultural buildings and related equipment, climate control and environmental protection, farm planning and waste management.

Section 3. Equipment engineering for plants: farm machinery and mechanization, forestry mechanization, sensing and artificial intelligence, modeling and information systems and the application of advanced physics.

Section 4. Rural electricity and other energy sources: application of electricity and electro technology to agriculture, the rationalization of energy consumption, use of renewable energy sources and related technologies, and automation and control systems.

Section 5. Management, ergonomics and systems engineering: farm management, working methods and systems, labour and work planning, optimization, human health, ergonomics and safety of workers, rural sociology and systems engineering.

Section 6. Post-harvest technology and process engineering: physical properties of raw (food and non-food) materials, quality of final products, processing technologies, and processing management and engineering.

Section 7. Information systems: the mission of this section is to advance the use of information and communication systems in agriculture.

CIGR Working Groups

1. Earth Observation for Land and Water Engineering Working Group.
2. Animal Housing in Hot Climates Working Group.
3. Rural Development and the Preservation of Cultural Heritages Working Group.
4. Cattle Housing Working Group.
5. Water Management & Information Systems Working Group .
6. Agricultural Engineering University Curricula Harmonization Working Group.
7. Image Analyses for Advanced Grading and Monitoring in Agricultural Processes.
8. Rural Landscape Protection and Valorization.

realm of agricultural engineering were few and relatively simple, and research was focus on agricultural tools. Over time, farm machinery, adapted mechanics, machine testing and

---

3 Hood, D. Personal communication with the authors, 16 February 2009.

4 CIGR was founded in 1930 at Liège in Belgium at the first International Congress of Agricultural Engineering. It is a worldwide network involving regional and multinational associations, societies, corporations and individuals working in science and technology and contributing to the different fields of agricultural engineering. It supports numerous free activities carried out by management and individual specialist

groups, agricultural societies and union bodies in each country. CIGR is allied with international bodies such as the Food and Agriculture Organization (FAO), the International Organization for Standardization (ISO) and the United Nations Industrial Development Organization (UNIDO).

For more information, go to: http:// www.cigr.org.

© CIGR

⟳ *Participants of CIGR World Congress 2006 in front of the University of Bonn building.*

standardization became major subjects while scientific labour organization strongly accentuated attitude, living and health conditions in all human work.

After the catastrophe of the Second World War, agriculture was one area in which an immense rebuilding effort was necessary. Demography was seriously affected, distorted economies had to be re orientated and societies had to sprout again Farm materials and equipment had to be rebuilt, renewed or even created. It was necessary to provide for the populations needs as fast as possible and agricultural engineering enabled agriculture – the bedrock of the recovering economies. From the end of the 1950s, once the problems of the post-war period had concluded, the profession experienced considerable and unexpected growth.

The main concerns of today's agricultural engineers are best understood by looking at the technical sections and current working groups of the CIGR. In terms of education, the scope of agricultural engineering means that it is now, in many cases, taught under the headings of the other branches of engineering – notably environmental engineering.

Looking into the future, the human race is confronted by many problems as a result of its own activity, such as the disturbance of ecosystems, population growth, the depletion of resources and environmental decay. Our challenge is to use our knowledge and innovation to overcome these problems in the context of a changing climate and environment in order to meet some of the fundamental needs of life: enough food to eat and enough water to drink for everyone.

Overview of CIGR

The International Commission of Agricultural Engineering (CIGR) brings together specialists to contribute to the progress of the human race and the efficient use of resources through the formation of systems for sustainability, land management, farming, food production and similar.

4.2.7   Medical Engineering

J. P. Woodcock

The purpose of medical technology is to provide accurate diagnoses and treatment and, in the case of rehabilitation, to help individuals achieve ordinary day-to-day tasks so that they can play a full role in society.

Medical technology in developing countries

According to a report from the World Health Organization (WHO), around 95 per cent of medical technology in developing countries is imported and 50 per cent of the equipment is not in use. The main reasons for this are lack of maintenance due to the lack of suitable training on the use of the equipment and the fact that much of the equipment is too sophisticated for the real needs of the population[1]. Bearing in mind these drawbacks to the delivery of healthcare to developing countries, the potential role of information and communication technologies holds promise for the provision of adequate support and training. However, underlying all of this is the fact that, whereas the United States spends US$5,274 per capita on healthcare, most developing countries are only able to spend less than US$100.[5]

Major problems for developing countries lie in the high initial and running costs, the remoteness of the manufacturers, the fact that much of the latest equipment is controlled by microprocessors and that the equipment is not designed to operate under a wide range of climatic conditions.[6]

Much of the technology made available involves disposable items such as special gels for electrodes and ultrasound gel to achieve proper contact with the skin during ultrasound examinations. These are initially sterile, but quickly become

5   Nkuma-Udah K.I., and Mazi E.A. 2007. Developing Biomedical Engineering in Africa: A Case for Nigeria, *IFMBE Proceedings*, 14 June 2007, International Federation for Medical and Biological Engineering.

6   Rabbani, K.S. 1995. Local Development of Bio-Medical Technology – a Must for the Third World. *Proceedings of RC IEEE-EMBS & 14th BMESI*, 1.31–1.32.

contaminated unless correctly stored. These items are usually imported at a high cost to the importer. More sophisticated modern equipment is often not needed and a basic item is of greater use, but the sophisticated system may have to be bought at a high price because of the lack of choice. Repair facilities and spare parts are often unavailable, and the equipment has to be returned to the manufacturer, or specialized technicians have to be brought in at great cost.

A problem particularly relevant to developing countries is the donation of equipment, which is surplus to requirements or outdated. Many countries depend on the donation of medical equipment but often there is no funding for the transportation of equipment, installation, maintenance and training.[7]

Personnel and training

In developing countries there is a shortage of properly trained medical engineering professionals, with very few engineers – most being technicians – and very few training institutes.[8] If equipment is to perform optimally, and have a long service life, then the engineering staff are as important as the medical staff in the delivery of healthcare. These skilled staff must have appropriate training so that they can carry out the work effectively. They must also be conversant with the appropriate standards and regulatory bodies.

It is important to build up the knowledge and expertise available in developing nations. This will require training programmes and courses at undergraduate and postgraduate levels, but to achieve this, support is needed from international bodies such as the International Federation for Medical and Biological Engineering (IFMBE), the International Union for Physical and Engineering Sciences in Medicine (IUPESM), the World Health Organization and UNESCO.

It is also important to arrange 'training' facilities between universities from both the developing world and richer countries, as well as benefitting from distance learning Master degrees (such as the MSc in Clinical Engineering offered at Cardiff University, UK). This high-level cooperation will involve organizations within the developing countries: for example, the Nigerian Institute for Biomedical Engineering (NIBE) was set up in 1999 and has held six national biomedical engineering conferences and four national professional development courses in Nigeria. NIBE's professional journal, the Nigerian Journal of Biomedical Engineering, was first published in 2001.

The African Union of Biomedical Engineering and Sciences (AUBES) was set up in 2003. The aim of AUBES is to foster cooperation between biomedical engineering professionals across Africa.[9] A similar success story is reported from Bangladesh.

The future

Information and communication technologies (ICTs) have the potential to transform the delivery of healthcare and to address future health challenges.[10] The Royal Society report *Digital Healthcare* identifies three broad areas where ICTs will make a significant contribution to medical practice: Home Care Technologies, Primary Care Technologies and Secondary and Tertiary Care Technologies.

Home Care Technologies could be used by healthcare professionals or the patients themselves for 'treating known medical conditions, self care, detecting and identifying new conditions and/or monitoring/maintaining health.'[11] Primary Care Technologies would be used by general practitioners, public health specialists, community nurses, health centre staff and community hospitals. Areas such as prevention and control of common health problems, hygiene, and education, and the diagnoses of common diseases/injuries and provision of essential medicine would benefit. Secondary and Tertiary Care technologies would be used in hospitals for diagnosis and treatment of medical conditions that need specialized facilities.

Sensor technologies could be used to monitor individuals more effectively within the home and workplace environments. Sensors are being developed based on low-cost computer technology bought over the counter or the Internet.[12] Instrumentation such as thermometers, measuring scales, heart rate and blood pressure monitors, blood sugar and body fat monitors could send information to personal computers or even mobile phones. This information could then be assessed by the individual concerned as well as their healthcare support team resulting in immediate support for the patient concerned.

At present most developing countries do not have the necessary infrastructure to contribute as equal partners in the area of knowledge production and dissemination. The numbers of computer terminals, networks, communications channels with bandwidth and so on are limited. However, an investment in this infrastructure would markedly improve all aspects of instrumentation and training problems[13] and open up the emerging opportunities in the above three areas.

---

7   *Digital Healthcare: the impact of information and communication technologies on health and healthcare.* The Royal Society, Document 37/06, 2006.

8   Ibid. 105.

9   Ibid. 105.

10   Ibid. 107.

11   Ibid. 107.

12   Ibid. 107.

13   Srinivasan, S., Mital, D.P., and Haque, S. 2008. Biomedical informatics education for capacity building in developing countries. *Int. J. Medical Engineering and Informatics*, Vol.1, No.1, pp.39–49.

Biomedical informatics provides the potential to lessen poverty and the disease burden in developing countries. Again, infrastructure is the key, for example India has initiated an ambitious national development programme. The Asia-Pacific region is also investing in biomedical informatics, and progress in Africa can be seen in South Africa, Kenya, Nigeria and Ghana.[14]

Consideration might also be given to local fabrication of instrumentation[15] such as ECG monitors, digital thermometers, weighing scales and blood-glucose monitors. Potential benefits of such investment would be in the lower cost of fabrication and the local availability of expertise and spares.

---

14   Ibid. 113.

15   Ibid. 106.

This will also improve response times and a decrease in the downtime of vital equipment. The equipment would also be developed to operate under local climate conditions, and may result in the elimination of expensive air conditioning and dehumidifiers. The building of local expertise would result in increasing confidence, and will have positive feedback in the training of engineers and technicians.

The future of medical engineering and technology in developing countries can be positive if these types of investment can be made. The power of modern communication systems, their decreasing costs and new learning methods can deliver a better standard of healthcare in the medium term. When this is combined with local fabrication, medical engineers will become more self-reliant and will better support the delivery of basic healthcare, at a more acceptable cost, in places where it is desperately needed.

4.3   The engineering profession and its organization

4.3.1   An introduction to the organization of the profession

Tony Marjoram

As discussed elsewhere, human beings are defined for their tool-making, designing and engineering skills as well as the socialization and communication that also developed with this inventive, innovative activity – as can be closely connected to the development and transfer of technology still seen today. The history of engineering as a profession, where payment is made for services, began with tool- and weapon-making over 150,000 years ago, making engineering one of the oldest professions. An 'engineer' was first used to describe a person who operated a military engine or machine; 'engine' derives from the Latin *ingenium* for ingenuity or cleverness and invention.

The professionalization of engineering continued with the development of crafts and guilds, and the formalization of associated knowledge and education. Simple patriarchal forms of engineering education in ancient societies developed into vocational technical schools of different types in the Middle Ages, the Renaissance and the Scientific Revolution of the sixteenth and seventeenth centuries, when Leonardo was the *Ingegnere Generale*. The most crucial period in the development of engineering was the eighteenth and nineteenth centuries, particularly the Iron Age and Steam Age of the second phase of Industrial Revolutions. In Britain, where the industrial revolution began, many engineers had little formal or theoretical training. With practical activity preceding scientific

understanding, engineering education was initially based on a system of apprenticeship with a working engineer, artisanal empiricism and laissez-faire professional development. Britain tried to retain this lead by prohibiting the export of engineering goods and services in the early 1800s, and countries in continental Europe developed their own engineering education systems based on French and German models, with a foundation in science and mathematics rather than the British model. France developed the system of formal schooling in engineering after the Revolution under Napoleon's influence, and engineering education in France has retained a strong theoretical character. The French model influenced the development of polytechnic engineering education institutions around the world at the beginning of the nineteenth century, especially in Germany where early interest in the development of engineering education took place in the mining industry.

By the end of the nineteenth century, most of the now industrialized countries had established their own engineering education systems based on the French and German 'Humboldtian' model. In the twentieth century, the professionalization of engineering continued with the development of professional societies, journals, meetings, conferences, and the professional accreditation of exams, qualifications and universities, which facilitated education, the flow of information and continued professional development. Through the nineteenth and into the twentieth century, partly due to fears that Britain was lagging behind the European model in terms of international competition, engineering education in Britain also changed toward a science and university based system and the rise of the 'engi-

⊃ *Engineering School in Peshawar, Pakistan, in the 1960s.*

© Ch. Hills/UNESCO

practical, problem-solving methodology and approach that includes soft social as well and technical skills. These include motivation, the ability to perform for rapid understanding, communication and leadership under pressure, and social-technical skills in training and mentoring. Engineering encompasses a diverse and increasing range of areas, fields, disciplines, branches or specialities. These have developed from civil, mechanical, chemical, electrical and electronic engineering, as knowledge developed and differentiated, as subjects subdivided and merged or new subjects arose. The emergence of new branches of engineering are usually indicated by the establishment of new university departments, sections in existing or new professional engineering organizations.

neering sciences' – partly in recognition of the increasingly close connection between engineering, science and mathematics. The engineering profession, as other professions, is a vocation or occupation based upon specialized education and training, as providers of professional advice and services. Other features that define occupations as professions are the establishment of training and university schools and departments, national and international organizations, accreditation and licensing, ethics and codes of professional practice. While engineering is one of the oldest professions, along with divinity, medicine and law, a perception has arisen of engineers as applied scientists, reflecting the 'linear model' that pure science leads to applied engineering. As indicated elsewhere, this is a misleading distortion of reality, diverting attention away from the need for a better public and policy understanding of the role of engineering and science in knowledge societies and economy.

People who are qualified in or practice engineering are described as engineers, and may be licensed and formally designated as professional, chartered or incorporated engineers. As noted above, the broad discipline of engineering includes a range of specialized disciplines or fields of application and particular areas of technology. Engineering itself is also differentiated into engineering science and different areas of professional practice and levels of activity. The process of professionalization continued with the development of international agreements relating to accreditation and the mutual recognition of engineering qualifications and professional competence, which include the Washington Accord (1989), the Sydney Accord (2001), the Dublin Accord (2002), the APEC Engineer (1999), the Engineers Mobility Forum (2001) and the Engineering Technologist Mobility Forum (2003), and the 1999 Bologna Declaration relating to quality assurance and accreditation of bachelor and master programmes in Europe.

Apart from a degree or related qualification in one of the engineering disciplines and associated skillsets, which includes design and drawing skills – now usually in computer-aided design (CAD) and continued professional development (CPD) – and awareness of new techniques and technologies, engineering education also seeks to develop a logical,

The engineering profession now consists of the diversity of types and levels of engineer, working in an expanding range of increasingly overlapping fields in various modes of employment, who may or may not be members of different professional organizations, who read a variety of professional journals and magazines, attend and participate in a mixture of continuous professional development (CPD) training courses, workshops and conferences. Publications and conferences are now big business for engineering organizations with many earning their largest income from such sources.

Professional engineers work in industry, government, consulting and academia. Professional engineering institutions and organizations operate at the national, regional and international level, similar to professional scientific organizations. Larger countries and economies usually have separate organizations dedicated to the specific fields of engineering, linked by overall 'umbrella' organizations such as the American Association of Engineering Societies (AAES) or the Engineering Council in the UK (ECUK). There may be advantages and disadvantages of having specific or collective national organizations (as in Australia and Canada, for example) from the point of view of advocacy, interdisciplinarity, coordination and so on, as umbrella organizations are inevitably far smaller than their members. National organizations are mainly linked at the international level by the World Federation of Engineering Organizations (WFEO). WFEO has over 100 national and international member organizations representing fifteen million engineers around the world. Larger countries often have academies of engineering, and the International Council of Academies of Engineering and Technological Sciences (CAETS) now has twenty-six members.

There are around 5,000 universities with accredited faculties, schools or divisions of engineering around the world (according to the International Association of Universities), and hundreds of journals and magazines on engineering. International accreditation bodies are mentioned above, and these link with national bodies in most large countries. There are also hundreds of national and international conferences on engineering around the world every year, and every four years there is the World Engineers' Convention (most recently WEC2008 in Brasília, and WEC2011 in Geneva). Because of the diverse nature of engineering, various international organizations have interests in the subject, although UNESCO is the only international organization with a specific mandate for science and engineering. WFEO was itself established at UNESCO in Paris in 1968 in response to calls for such an international organization to represent the engineering community around the world. WFEO, CAETS and the International Federation of Consulting Engineers (FIDIC) are presented in this Report, as are the European Federation of National Engineering Associations (FEANI), the Federation of Engineering Institutions of Asia and the Pacific (FEIAP, formerly FEISEAP), the Association for Engineering Education in Southeast and East Asia and the Pacific (AEESEAP), the Asian and Pacific Centre for Transfer of Technology (APCTT), the African Network of Scientific and Technological Institutions (ANSTI), the African Engineers Forum (AEF) and the International Federation of Engineering Societies (IFEES). International development organizations with a focus on engineering are also presented and these include Practical Action (formerly the Intermediate Technology Development Group), Engineers Without Borders (with increasing numbers of groups in an increasing number of countries), Engineers Against Poverty (UK) and Engineers for a Sustainable World (USA).

4.3.2 International cooperation

Tony Ridley

The twentieth century was a time of increasing interdependence. Engineers work in their own country to assist their development, but engineers have been travelling to other countries for many years, particularly during the colonial era. Today, engineers work in a more collaborative, cooperative way.

One of the major developments in engineering at the global level during the last twenty years has involved concern for the environment. Following the 1992 Earth Summit in Rio de Janeiro, the United Nations Commission on Sustainable Development (CSD) was established by the United Nations General Assembly in December 1992. Since the outset its meetings have involved participation by members of civil society. Surprisingly, engineers were not included among those initially invited; notwithstanding the crucial role they play in the delivery of development, while protecting the environment in every country in the world.

Following representations made by WFEO, engineers were at last invited, together with scientists through the International Council of Scientific Unions (ICSU), to attend CSD-9 in 2001.

They have been involved ever since with increasing influence, together with other representatives of civil society: women, children and youth, indigenous peoples, NGOs, local authorities, workers and trade unions, business, industry and farmers. This was followed by participation in the World Summit for Sustainable Development (WSSD) in Johannesburg in 2002 and then the United Nations Millennium Project.

The Millennium Development Goals (MDGs), adopted by the United Nations in 2000, are the world's targets for reducing extreme poverty in its many dimensions: income poverty, hunger, disease, lack of infrastructure and shelter, while promoting gender equality, education, health and environmental sustainability. The UN Millennium Project was commissioned by the then Secretary-General, Kofi Annan, to develop a practical plan of action to meet the targets.

The core of the work of the Millennium Project was carried out by ten thematic task forces. Task Force 10 included a number of engineers. Its report *Innovation: Applying Knowledge in Development* argued that meeting the MDGs would require a substantial reorientation of development policies so as to focus on economic growth, particularly the use of scientific and technological knowledge and related institutional adjustments. It outlined key areas for policy action focusing on platform or generic technologies, defining infrastructure services as a foundation for technology, improving higher education in science and placing universities at the centre of local development, spurring entrepreneurial activities, improving the policy environment, and focusing on areas of underfunded research for development. A key point – after all the excellent work done in policy planning – was the recognition that engineers were needed to turn the policies into reality and hence should be involved in the planning.

Out of Task Force 10 developed 'Infrastructure, Innovation and Development' (Ridley *et al.*, 2006),[16] which argued that the absence of adequate infrastructure services is one of the main problems hindering efforts to develop Africa. Technology and innovation are the engines of economic growth. With the globalization of trade and investment, technological capabilities are a source of competitive advantage. While infrastructure development and technological development are two of the most important areas of development policy, practitioners and policy-makers alike tend to consider them as separate issues. The focus of infrastructure development in recent years has shifted from the mere construction of physical facilities to the appropriate provision of services. Environmental and social factors have become part of infrastructure development and planning, yet most infrastructure projects are not explicitly linked to technological development efforts.

President Lula at the 2008 World Engineers' Convention.

16 Ridley, T. M, Y-C. Lee and C. Juma, Infrastructure, innovation and development, *Int J. Technology and Globalization*, Vol.2, No.3/4, pp.268–278.

4.3.3 The World Federation of Engineering Organizations (WFEO)

Barry Grear

Engineering is a profession that is truly international. An idea for a structure, project or product may be conceived by an engineer in one country, it may be designed in one or more countries, constructed or produced with components from many countries, operated and maintained where used and disposed of with international support. In this era, the concept of an engineer belonging to a country is challenged and may even be considered obsolete. It is however important for all engineering associations, governments and firms to have confidence in the abilities, standards and experience of engineers working across international boundaries. The World Federation of Engineering Organizations (WFEO) therefore has several important roles as the international body representing the engineering profession worldwide. The national professional institutions that constitute WFEO have ten million engineers worldwide in their registered memberships. WFEO therefore aims to be the internationally recognized and chosen leader of the engineering profession, and it cooperates with other national and international professional engineering organizations such as FIDIC and CAETS. WFEO's mission is to:

- represent the engineering profession internationally, providing the collective wisdom and leadership of the profession to assist national agencies choose appropriate policy options that address the most critical issues facing the world;

- enhance the practice of engineering;

- make information on engineering available to all countries of the world and to facilitate communication of best practice between its members;

- foster socio-economic security, sustainable development and poverty alleviation among all countries of the world, through the proper application of technology; and

- serve society and to be recognized by national and international organizations and the public as a respected and valuable source of advice and guidance on the policies, interests and concerns that relate engineering and technology to the human and natural environment.

WFEO has eight Standing Committees that are each convened with international membership:

- *The Committee on Engineering and the Environment*
  Responsible for issues relating to engineering, the environment and sustainable development, climate change mitiga-tion and adaptation and associated infrastructure, advising various bodies including the United Nations Commission on Sustainable Development.

- *The Committee on Information and Communication*
  Responsible for engineering and information and communication technologies, including advice regarding the introduction and application of ICTs for development, and reduction of the information divide.

- *The Committee on Education and Training*
  Responsible for matters relating to engineering education and training, and providing advice and assistance in setting international standards, including the mobility of graduate and experienced engineers.

- *The Committee on Technology*
  Works on a wide range of projects relating to appropriate technologies, including the provision of advice regarding the development of building code and urban infrastructure in developing countries.

- *The Committee on Capacity Building*
  Responsible for issues relating to capacity-building in engineering, including the provision of advice and assistance to communities in sub-Saharan Africa, Latin America and the Caribbean, and the development of a model to ensure the transfer of technology when development projects are undertaken.

- *The Committee on Energy*
  Working in all areas related to engineering and energy, including the development of reports on the feasibility conditions of different energy technologies, with publications on wind energy and nuclear power energy, and current preparation of reports on solar energy and bio energy.

- *The Committee on Anti-Corruption*
  Focal point for the provision of advice to WFEO members and linkage with related organizations such as UNESCO, the World Bank and Transparency International to develop activities to minimize corruption that reduce the effectiveness of development assistance.

- *The Committee on Women in Engineering*
  Responsible for activities relating to women and gender issues in engineering, including the development of a program to empower women in engineering and technology by networking and developing leadership skills, utilizing the experience of long established women's groups and providing assistance in strengthening new initiatives.

Economic efficiency requires a country to rapidly deploy new technologies from elsewhere, and to attract capital to purchase those technologies. Many developing countries do not have sufficient capital of their own and therefore need to attract foreign direct investment (FDI). This in turn requires adherence to intellectual property laws, but also low levels of corruption and fair taxation and/or tariffs. Political instability and access to finance are important factors but electricity supply and adequate roads are also rated as significant obstacles by the World Development Bank. Worldwide, engineering qualifications have become highly regarded by employers because of their emphasis on risk management, ethical practice and sustainable outcomes. In this way, graduates from engineering courses have become a new source of managers and leaders for many organizations and professions. Whenever capital is made available it is vital that the nation has the technical capability to make good technology decisions.

The WFEO has been able to vigorously represent the engineering profession in global policy settings, especially with regard to issues of sustainable development and human welfare. This means interacting visibly and effectively with the United Nations and its specialized agencies such as UNESCO and the World Bank, as well as the international and regional development banks and financing agencies. With the whole-hearted endorsement and support of WFEO members, there has been significant achievement. For example, the UN Millennium Development Goals Task Force on Science, Technology and Innovation was co-chaired by WFEO.

Sadly there are still too many people who have never turned on a light switch, never walked on a built roadway, let alone ridden on one. This leads on to a final point regarding the poor condition of infrastructure worldwide. An ever-increasing global population that continues to shift to urban areas requires widespread adoption of sustainability. Demands for energy, drinking water, clean air, safe waste disposal, and transportation will drive environmental protection and infrastructure development. Society will face increased threats from natural events, accidents, and perhaps other causes such as terrorism. The public is becoming increasingly aware that development need not come at the price of a compromised and depleted environment for them and their children, and has begun to see sustainability, not as an unattainable ideal, but as a practical goal. To answer that call, engineers associated with WFEO increasingly transform themselves from designers and builders to lifecycle project 'sustainers'.

On the demographic front, the world is well on its way to a population exceeding ten billion people in 2050. Today, people occupy more space on the planet than they did thirty years ago, and they are straining the earth's environment, particularly the requirements for energy, fresh water, clean air, and safe waste disposal. Over the past thirty years, gradual global warming has profoundly impacted on more than half of the world's population living within fifty miles of coastal areas.

These areas have become much harsher places to live because of sea level rise, increased storm activity, and greater susceptibility to flooding. Growing population, shrinking resources and climate change have put us on the path to sustainability, and have put sustainability at the forefront of issues requiring global attention. WFEO and its members continue to strive to understand the aspirational role that they will play in that radically transformed world.

4.3.4 International Council of Academies of Engineering and Technological Sciences (CAETS)

William Salmon

The International Council of Academies of Engineering and Technological Sciences (CAETS) consists of national academies of engineering and technological sciences from different countries. CAETS was established in 1978 with five founding academies and held its first Convocation that year in Washington DC at the invitation of the US National Academy of Engineering (NAE). Each CAETS member academy consists of peer-elected members representing the highest standard of excellence and achievement in their profession for that nation. With a well-established program of service on important national and international issues with significant engineering and technological content, many of these national academies are called upon by their governments to provide authoritative, objective advice on technological issues of national importance. Working together in CAETS, the academies form a worldwide engineering resource that can address with the highest skills and capabilities major global issues that require the considered judgement of the world's most outstanding engineering talent. CAETS was created with a vision that national and international decision-making on economic, social and environmental issues is properly informed by relevant scientific, technological and engineering considerations so that all people can fully benefit from the capabilities of science, technology and engineering.

Objectives

Consistent with its Articles of Incorporation and in support of its mission, CAETS:

- provides an independent non-political and non-governmental international organization of engineering and technological sciences academies prepared to advise governments and international organizations on technical and policy issues related to its areas of expertise;

- contributes to the strengthening of engineering and technological activities in order to promote sustainable economic growth and social welfare throughout the world;

- fosters a balanced understanding of the applications of engineering and technology by the public;

- provides an international forum for discussion and communication of engineering and technological issues of common concern;

- fosters cooperative international engineering and technological efforts through meaningful contacts for the development of programs of bilateral and multilateral interest;

- encourages improvement of engineering education and practice internationally;

- fosters establishment of additional engineering academies in countries where none exist; and

- undertakes other projects, programs and activities.

Mission

The CAETS mission is to foster effective engineering and technological progress for the benefit of societies of all countries. Specifically, CAETS provides the mechanism through which the engineering and applied science academies of the world work together on internationally important issues. Member academies each have a well-established programme of service on important national and international issues with significant engineering and technological content, and many are called upon by their governments to provide authoritative, objective advice on technological issues of national importance. CAETS enables each academy to draw on the total global experience and expertise of all member academies when addressing issues at their own national level. It also ensures that the best technological and engineering expertise is made available and used to best advantage by key international and inter-governmental institutions and organizations.

Governance

The administrative and policy body of CAETS, on which each academy has one representative, is the Council which elects the Officers (President, President-elect, Past President and Secretary/Treasurer) and the Board of Directors, which consists of the Officers (the Executive Committee) and four other members each serving, except for the Secretary/Treasurer, for one year terms. The major CAETS events are its annual Council meetings, its biennial Convocations and its host-academy sponsored symposia in alternate non-Convocation years. Past Convocations have focused on 'Engineering, Innovation and Society', 'Technology and Health', 'World Forests and Technology', 'Entertaining Bytes', 'Oceans and

the World's Future', 'Hydrogen Economy: Clean Energy for this Century' and 'Environment and Sustainable Growth'.

Strategy

CAETS priorities include engagement with the United Nations specialized agencies and related international organizations, fostering and strengthening national academies of engineering and technological sciences, convocations, symposia and reports, support for member academy initiatives, and addressing issues of common concern of the member academies.

With respect to its first priority listed above, CAETS participates in an ongoing advisory/consultative role with the relevant scientific/technological organizations of the United Nations (UN) System, and it has established working relations with WFEO, IAC, ICSU and other relevant non-governmental bodies in respect of CAETS linkages with the UN.

The CAETS website (http://www.caets.org) includes information on all aspects of CAETS activities, and mailing addresses of and links to the websites of its member academies. CAETS is incorporated in the District of Columbia, USA, June 30 2000 and is an IRS 510(c)(3) tax-exempt, charitable organization.

4.3.5   International Federation of Consulting Engineers (FIDIC)

Peter Boswell

The International Federation of Consulting Engineers (FIDIC) represents the consulting engineering industry at the international level. A macroeconomic analysis confirms the industry's significance and importance. The consulting engineering industry, which comprises independent private consulting firms supplying services on a fee-for-service basis, is a major industry worldwide. It has an annual revenue of some US$490 billion, and is heavily involved with the construction, management and industrial sectors that generate one-half of the world's GDP. Any industry sector, especially one that makes major contributions to conceiving, designing, delivering and maintaining the world's infrastructure, aims to be able to quantify the scope and importance of its activities. However, unlike the manufacturing sector, the services sector, of which the consulting engineering industry forms a part, does not lend itself to a straightforward analysis. Data is lacking and the classification of activities often prevents a rigorous analysis.

Most recent discussions of the industry's activities have taken place within the context of the World Trade Organization's trade in service negotiations and the harmonization of national statistics. These two approaches have converged on a reasonably robust classification of the consulting engineering industry's activities that span both architectural and civil engineering services in the broadest sense, as well as industrial consultancy. Given this perspective, and faced with the need to quantify in detail industry activity at the national level to sum up the global demand for consulting engineering services, FIDIC has developed a top-down macroeconomic approach based on investments to estimate the global demand. This is of sufficient importance to discuss in more detail.

FIDIC's role in quantifying the consultancy industry

The WTO GATS classification: Bottom-up industry data

Consulting engineers are generally recognized as supplying technology based intellectual services for two broad market sectors: the built environment (comprising buildings, infrastructure and the environment), and industry (involving manufacturing, equipment and process plant). Since industry also involves the built environment it is convenient to distinguish consulting engineering in terms of architectural and engineering (A&E) services and product engineering (or industrial consultancy).

These services may be supplied a) internally by organizations responsible for a project or for supplying plant and equipment to a project, or b) externally by both specialized and multidisciplinary firms coming from consulting engineering and other industries. The General Agreement on Trade in Services (GATS) is a treaty of the World Trade Organization (WTO) that has been the focus of most recent discussion on quantifying the industry's importance. The GATS Services Sectoral Classification List MTN.GNS/W/120 spreads engineering services over only two categories:

- Professional Services, namely Architectural, Engineering, Integrated Engineering and Urban and Landscaping Services (collectively called 'A&E Services') provided by qualified architects and engineers.

- Construction and Related Engineering Services, which refer to physical construction and related engineering works and are classified as Construction Services.

Numerous commentators have pointed out that:

a) Construction Services involve Professional Services, and vice versa.

b) Some A&E Services are not included, such as services provided by surveyors, topographical engineers, construction economists and quantity surveyors.

c) Engineering services are required in other services sectors – including under the W/120 Environmental Services category and Professional Services classified under the Computer and Related Services category as well as under Other Business Services (mining, manufacturing, fisheries, agriculture, testing, energy distribution, security

equipment maintenance, building services; management consulting) – all of which are very much the domain of consulting engineers.

d) Industrial consultancy services for engineered machinery (Standard Industrial Classification SIC 353-9; SIC 361-6) are a major category in some countries' national statistics but have no W/120 equivalent here.

Given the evident confusion, the question therefore is whether existing statistical databases can give a reasonably accurate picture of consulting engineering that does justice to the industry's importance.

National sector statistics: A&E Professional Services

Regarding W/120 A&E Professional Services, it has been noted that International Standard Industrial Classification of all Economic Activities (ISIC) categories for Professional and Other Business Services (ISIC 882 Architectural, engineering and other technical activities), upon which many national statistics are based, correspond to the W/120 A&E Services (CPC Codes 8671-4). In turn, the W/120 A&E Professional Services (CPC Codes 8671-4) correspond to the International Labour Organization's International Standard Classification of Occupation ISCO-88: 214. Thus, there is a possibility that national statistics based on engineering disciplines are in some cases sufficiently disaggregated to be able to measure W/120 A&E Professional Services.

National sector statistics: Construction and related engineering services

Regarding W/120 Construction and Related Engineering Services (CPC 512-7), it is also noted that they correspond to ISIC Construction and Engineering-Related Services (ISIC 501-5), which form the basis for many national statistics. UNCTAD has separated Construction and Related Engineering Services into 'Construction and Related Engineering Services for A&E Design' and 'Construction and Related Engineering Service for Physical Construction'. The latter is accurately reflected in:

- ISIC Revision 3 Construction (ISIC 451-5) covering all aspects of physical construction of a building (site preparation; building of complete constructions or parts thereof; civil engineering; building installation; building completion; renting of construction or demolition equipment with operator).

- Extended Balance of Payments Services (EBOPS) 249 covering site preparation and general construction for buildings and other structures, construction work for civil engineering, as well as installation and assembly work. It also includes repairs, renting services of construction or demolition equipment with operator, and exterior cleaning work of buildings.

- Foreign Affiliates Trade in Services (FATS) statistics recorded in the OECD Globalisation Indicators database.

EBOPS249 helps overcome the traditional approach to separate 'construction' (mainly infrastructure development) from 'building' involving residential and non-residential structures, where infrastructure, as a public good, is provided by the public sector, and the building industry is dominated by the private sector. The increasing tendency for governments to outsource construction and to partner with the private sector has rendered the traditional approach misleading.

National sector statistics: Industrial consultancy

Industrial consultancy services for engineered machinery are covered in many national statistical databases under categories equivalent to the American Industry Classification System NAICS and can in principle be readily identified. For instance, concordance tables exist between NAICS Canada, ISIC Revison 3.1 and the Statistical Classification of Economic Activities in the European Community (NACE). Revision 1.1. NAICS codes are commonly used to standardize the definitions of services industries between different countries.

National sector statistics: Conclusion

The conclusion is that by considering:

- A&E services;

- W/120 A&E Professional Services;

- W/120 Construction and Related Engineering Services for A&E Design;

- W/120 Construction and Related Engineering Services for Physical Construction;

- W/120 Environmental Services and W/120 engineering Professional Services used in other W/120 sectors, and some relatively small sectors not covered by W/120;

- industrial consultancy; and

- engineering for engineered machinery (CPC 353-9; CPC 361-6),

it should be possible to generate national data for the consulting engineering industry. Indeed, France has undertaken a rigorous analysis that simplifies the industry's activities to:

- A&E services.

- Construction (infrastructure, buildings, industrial).

- Management (territorial; organization).

- Industrial consultancy.

- Production and development of goods (physical, immaterial).

Table 1 shows how this may be facilitated by specifying the type of services for the various activities.

Here, the 'X' indicates the services that are common and easily identified. In 2007 in France, A&E Services accounted for 72 per cent of industry turnover (of which 21 per cent was for turnkey projects) and 28 per cent for Industrial Consultancy. In Sweden, the percentages were 65 per cent and 37 per cent. For South Africa in 2005, Industrial Consultancy amounted to some 20 per cent of Construction. The most important activ-

Table 1: **Types of activities for consultancy services**

		Types of services					
		Pre-decision consulting	Design	Project Management	Control	Technical Assistance	Turnkey Projects
A&E	Construction	X	X	X	X	X	X
	Management; Solution integration; Special studies	X	X				
Industrial	Production; Process development; Product development	X	X				

ity in all countries remains activities in Construction, a sector that has a major social and economic role. In general, organizations representing the consulting engineering industry rarely cover industrial consultancy, so data leading to adequate understanding of the industry's role is often lacking. Developing a global view of the industry based on national statistics has not been attempted.

Quantifying the consultancy industry: Top-down macroeconomic data

A&E and industrial GFCF

Given the difficulty in estimating the consulting engineering industry revenue and market size using industry statistics it is useful to turn to output data for different countries. Both GDP (Gross Domestic Product) and Gross Fixed Capital Formation (GFCF) have become standardized in the 1993 System of National Accounts (SNA). The system consists of several consolidated accounts for an economy as a whole, of which the Capital Account shows how gross savings have been spent on GFCF and changes in inventories, resulting in net lending/net borrowing.

Capital formation takes place in a country's production units. It consists of change in inventories minus disposals, and additions to fixed assets, called Fixed Capital Formation produced as outputs from production processes that are themselves used repeatedly or continuously in other processes of production for more than one year. A country's GDP expenditure should by definition only include newly produced fixed assets. GFCF is one of the principal components of GDP, typically accounting for around 20 per cent.

The extent of loss of GFCF's productive potential is known as the Consumption of Fixed Capital (CFC), which is to be compensated by the acquisition of an equal amount of fixed capital. GFCF is Fixed Capital Formation (FCF) computed without deducting CFC. It is GFCF less inventories. Statistically, GFCF measures the value of additions to fixed assets purchased by business, government and households, minus disposals of fixed assets sold off or scrapped. So it is a measure of the net new investment in the domestic economy in fixed capital assets. While GFCF is called 'gross', because it does not include the depreciation of assets, this terminology is confusing because the aim is to measure the value of the net additions to the fixed capital stock.

Estimates of capital formation are prepared by three methods: flow of funds (the sum of saving and net capital inflow from abroad); commodity flow (by type of assets and change in stock by industry of use); and expenditure (by adding GFCF by industry of use).

Under SNA, GFCF is categorized as Tangible Produced Fixed Asset comprising construction (dwellings, other buildings and structures, non-residential buildings, other structures); plant, machinery and equipment; and other assets (land improvements, fences, ditches, drains, and so on). As an illustration, GFCF in plant, machinery and equipment by producers consists of the value of their acquisitions of new and existing machinery and equipment minus the value of their disposals of their existing machinery and equipment. It covers transport equipment and other machinery and equipment, including office equipment, furniture, and so on.

Consulting engineers now routinely provide services classified under business services (such as were permitted) so these should be included. There has also been much debate recently about separating out information technology and computing, and introducing research and development. Inevitably, there is considerable overlap so first-order estimates based on the traditional GFCF categories are adequate for market analysis. Table 2 illustrates that the traditional GFCF categories can be matched to the WTO categories.

Table 2: **Matching traditional GFCF categories to WTO categories**

	WTO	GFCF	Types of Services					
			Pre-decision consulting	Design	Project Management	Control	Technical Assistance	Turnkey Projects
A&E	Construction	Construction	X	X	X	X	X	X
	Management; Solution integration; Special studies	Other Assets	X	X				
Industrial	Production; Process development; Product development	Plant, Machinery and Equipment	X	X				

The Other Assets GFCF represents at most a few per cent of total GFCF. Like Construction, it generally involves activities that require technology-based intellectual services, so for the purposes of estimating the potential demand for these services, it can be combined with Construction GFCF leaving only two categories: A&E and Industrial.

World GFCF in 2007 was US$9,271 billion for a GDP of US$54,747 billion. National statistics also give accurate estimates of A&E and Industrial GFCF (e.g. European Union 2007: 54 per cent and 46 per cent, respectively). GFCF is considered to be a better indicator than CFC for monitoring trends as changes in inventories are subject to large fluctuations. Thus, GFCF fluctuations often reflect future business activity and the pattern of economic growth.

The consulting engineering industry

Given the extent and depth of GFCF data, and the fact that the data mirror the categories that would be used in a bottom-up approach to measuring the demand for consulting engineering services, it is clearly attractive to use GFC for industry sector statistics. The only reported examples of this approach are for the UK construction industry and for the European Union transport sectors.

For construction and plant, GFCF includes new build structures and new plant, but depreciation and repair and maintenance are not taken into account. The durability of buildings and some plant means that repair and maintenance, which is almost half of construction output and a significant part of manufacturing output, is largely ignored. This is consistent with omitting depreciation from GFCF as the repair and maintenance accounts for capital consumption (GFCF is a measure of net new investments in fixed capital in the domestic economy).

Allowances for repair and maintenance can be estimated by noting that the construction industry typically reports that 7 per cent of its turnover is spent doing repair and maintenance. The figure for plant and equipment will be less owing to the much shorter lifetime, say 3 per cent. As a first-order approximation, A&E and Industrial GFCF should be multiplied by factors of 1.07 and 1.03, respectively. Making these allowances, worldwide A&E GCF is 52 per cent of total GFCF of US$9,693 billion and Industrial is 48 per cent.

As mentioned above, it is assumed that all construction GFCF requires technology-based intellectual services of the types supplied by a consulting service. However, only a percentage of Industrial GFCF will require these services. In principle, it is possible to sum up the value of technology-based intellectual services supplied in each of the product categories that make up Industrial GFCF. Some categories will require a considerable amount of, say, engineering design service (e.g. engines, non-electrical machinery, electric generators, motors, electri-

cal machinery, and communications equipment) in all phases of their production, installation and maintenance. Others will require much less. Overall, preliminary estimates indicate that 54 per cent of worldwide Industry GFCF requires technology-based intellectual services, so the total of investments in fixed assets that require these services is US$7,553 billion in 2007.

The final stage of the analysis is probably the most difficult. What is needed is an estimate of the percentage of the US$7,553 billion in investments that is spent on technology-based intellectual services. Only a few attempts have been made to estimate the demand for technology-based intellectual services for the A&E and Industrial sectors. For instance, the value added by a sector (that measures the activity in the sector and provides the level of demand for services in the sector), the breakdown between asset types (from GFCF data) and the skills profiles of staff working in the sector, gives the skills required and thus an estimate of the number of jobs. Such an exercise has been carried out for the South African construction sector. Similarly, a European Union study used a so-called marginal labour-to-capital ratio method to quantify the number of jobs created by an injection of a given GFCF into the A&E and Industrial sectors. Given the numbers of jobs and the salary levels for the various skill levels, one can estimate fee revenues for technology-based intellectual services.

The usual approach, however, is to use national statistical data for product categories in order to estimate the volume of technology-based intellectual services. Samples taken from a selection of countries indicate that the average for the A&E and Industrial sectors combined is 8.3 per cent or US$627 billion. This represents the potential worldwide demand for technology-based intellectual services. As mentioned above, some of the demand (estimated to be 42 per cent worldwide) will be supplied internally by organizations responsible for a project or for supplying plant and equipment to a project. The remainder (78 per cent) will be supplied externally by both specialized and multidisciplinary firms whose principle activity (more than one-half of firm revenue) is to meet this demand. It is these firms that make up the consulting engineering industry with a worldwide turnover of US$490 billion.

4.3.6 European Federation of National Engineering Associations (FEANI)

Willi Fuchs and Philippe Wauters

It was the conviction that the engineering community in Europe could and should contribute to peaceful development in a continent so deeply devastated by the Second World War, that lead in 1951 to the creation of the 'International Federation of National Engineers Associations' by engineering organizations from seven European countries. In 1956 it was renamed 'European Federation of National Engineering Associations' (FEANI) so as to focus on the European character of the Federation. The means to realize the contribution of the engineer was discussed at a congress on 'The Role of the Engineer in Modern Society' and a goal was set to strengthen the presence of engineers in every national and international movement of economic and social importance.

Now, more than fifty years later, what has happened within FEANI? First of all, there has been a remarkable growth in the number of National Engineering Associations that have joined FEANI and consequently in the number of European countries represented within it. Indeed, from FEANI's initial seven member countries, thirty European countries are now represented by their national engineering aassociations. These include many European countries, all Member States of the European Union (except two Baltic states) as well as other European countries such as Norway, Iceland, Switzerland, Serbia and Russia (as a Provisional Member, on the way to full membership). This makes FEANI by far the largest European multi-discipline engineering organization, representing engineers who have successfully completed either short or long cycle academic education. FEANI will most probably grow further since engineering associations from other European countries have, or are on their way to, applying for membership.

To cope with this growth, FEANI has developed a modern organization and has defined rules, agreed upon by its members, and described in its Statutes and Bylaws, which conform to the Belgian legislation on AISBL (non-profit organizations). The headquarters of FEANI, the Secretariat General, is located in Brussels. The Statutes stipulate that countries seeking to become members of FEANI first have to nominate one FEANI National Member body to officially represent their various national associations. There can only be one FEANI National Member per country. FEANI today is thus composed of its Secretariat, thirty national members and, through them, a network of more than 350 national engineering organizations representing about 3.5 million engineers. The FEANI organization is governed by a General Assembly (GA), the decision making body, at which all National Members are present. An elected Executive Board is responsible for implementing the decisions taken by the General Assembly, and the Secretariat General is in charge of the day-to-day business. In addition, the Executive Board may from time-to-time establish Committees and ad hoc Working Groups to deal with issues of common interest.

Is the initial objective of FEANI, namely to contribute to peace in Europe, still valid? Fortunately, Europe is enjoying one of the longest periods of peace in its history so its found-

ing objective, which remains valid, can be seen today as the basis for developing the benefits of more concrete and technical issues to support individual engineers. Among these issues is the need to ensure excellence in education for European engineers and to support the recognition of their professional qualifications. These, in turn, support the mobility of European engineers both within Europe and the rest of the world. Three examples of FEANI projects are:

EUR-ACE

Together with other stakeholders such as universities, accreditation agencies, professional engineering bodies and trade unions, FEANI has recently started the Accreditation of European Engineering Programmes (EUR-ACE) project. The project is financed by the EU Commission and has developed an accreditation system based on output criteria covering the first and the second cycle of engineering education as defined in the Bologna Declaration. The EUR-ACE Standards and Procedures are now being implemented by six accreditation agencies that have been authorized to deliver the EUR-ACE label. The EUR-ACE system is 'complementary' to the FEANI system, and programmes with a EUR-ACE label are now being included in the FEANI INDEX.

EUR-ING

FEANI has defined a quality professional title 'European Engineer' (EUR ING) for professional engineers based on a sound education (programmes listed in the INDEX or equivalent) and assessed professional experience. This FEANI proprietary professional title is a de facto quality standard recognized in Europe and worldwide, and particularly in those countries that do not regulate the profession.

European Professional Card Feasibility Study

The recognition of professional qualifications is a major concern for the EU institutions involved in developing solutions to implement the full content of the EU Treaty, as far as the three liberties are concerned. In particular, the liberty on the right to pursue a profession in an EU Member State, other than the one in which the professional qualifications have been obtained. With this aim, the European Union Directive on Recognition of Professional Qualifications (2005/36/EC) states that Member States should encourage professional organizations to introduce a so-called 'professional card' to facilitate the recognition of the qualification and the mobility of professionals. The card could contain information on the professional's qualifications (university or institution attended, qualifications obtained, professional experience), employment experience, legal establishment, professional penalties received relating to his profession and the details of the relevant competent authority. At the request of the European Commission, FEANI has undertaken a feasibility study into the concept. A professional card should provide for its owner recognition of his/her professional qualifications, both in Europe and worldwide, as an independent body would validate all the data.

In addition to these major activities, FEANI also produces position papers on subjects of important interest to society; it has developed a framework for a European Code of Conduct for Engineers, adopted in 2006 by all National Members; is involved in CPD (Continuous Professional Development) activities; issues regularly the *FEANI News* and maintains a website (www.feani.org), which is the basis of its communication system and regularly updated.

4.3.7 Federation of Engineering Institutions of Asia and the Pacific (FEIAP)

Tan Seng Chuan

The Federation of Engineering Institutions of Southeast Asia and the Pacific (FEISEAP) was founded on 6 July 1978. Its establishment followed an exploratory meeting convened and organized by the Engineering Institute of Thailand under the King's patronage with the support of UNESCO. It was created as an umbrella organization for engineering institutions, and had the following objectives:

- to foster cooperation and exchange of information between its members;

- to encourage the application of technical progress to economic and social advancement in the region;

- to collaborate with international, regional and national governmental and non-governmental organizations; and

- to encourage engineers in the region to contribute to the engineering community.

It is an international member of the World Federation of Engineering Organizations (WFEO).

The Change to FEAIP

At its 14th General Assembly held in Cebu, Philippines, on 26 November 2007, the question of the continuation of FEISEAP was discussed. It was unanimously agreed to review FEISEAP's constitution to define its objectives more clearly and to broaden the scope of its membership to include more member economies. The revised constitution was discussed and adopted at the 15th General Assembly. The constitution incorporated a change of name to the 'Federation of Engineering Institutions of Asia and the Pacific' (FEIAP).

Along with the change of name and constitution, three new working groups were formed to collaboratively achieve FEIAP's aims and objectives. They are, namely, the Environmental Working Group, the Engineering Education Working Group and the Professional Ethics Working Group.

The Environmental Working Group aims to promote environmental activities within regional economies, increase collaboration among member economies, and provide support to the Engineering Education Work Group on environmental engineering related activities. The Working Group published a publication themed 'Environmental Sustainability' in 2008. The Engineering Education Working Group is working towards the collaboration and promotion of engineering education among member economies within the region, and the formulation of benchmarks and best practice guidelines to assist member economies on the international engineering accreditation programmes. The Professional Ethics Working Group will be providing a set of ethical guidelines for engineers in their decision-making processes, especially during the design stage, with a long-term view towards sustainable development.

Besides the formation of the three working groups, FEIAP also re-launched its website and replaced its logo to reflect a more dynamic and vibrant organization. The website will be the key platform to leverage the latest technology, facilitating greater interaction and sharing of information among member economies within the region. Another initiative is the 'FEIAP Engineer of the Year' Award, which aims to recognize and encourage engineers on their contributions and achievements in the field of engineering among member economies. The award will also serve as a source of motivation for the recipients and one which all engineers aspire to achieve.

The Challenge

Thirty years is indeed a milestone and a great achievement for FEIAP. It is expected that the coming years will continue to be challenging for the Federation due to the manifold challenges of the effects of globalization, offshore outsourcing, climate change, and the increasing demand for innovation and expertise to remain competitive and sustainable in the market place are becoming more pronounced. One of the greatest challenges today is the diversification of culture in the Asia and Pacific region. Thus the building and strengthening of FEIAP's networks is a crucial item in the agenda of the Federation. To rise to this challenge, FEIAP aims to promote the exchange of experience and information related to science and technology for the advancement of the engineering profession, especially with regard to the national and regional economic and social developments in the years ahead. The FEAIP website is a key platform to leverage the latest technology, and thus facilitate greater interaction and information-sharing among member economies within the region. Another new initiative is the 'FEIAP Engineer of the Year' award, which recognizes and encourages engineers in their contributions and achievements among member economies.

Another critical challenge is ensuring the high quality of engineering education in the region. It is recognized that national engineering institutions have an important role in determining and accrediting the quality of their national engineering education systems. Thus it is important for the Federation to leverage its resources within the region to share experience and assist the developing economies in adapting accreditation processes internationally. This also implies the benchmarking of the engineering education system against an international accreditation system, for instance, under the Washington Accord.

Climate change is another challenge for the engineers regionally and globally. There is increasingly clear evidence that global warming and several natural disasters is the result of climate change. Engineers, well known for their ingenuity towards solving problems systematically, will be able to address the issue of climate change – one of the major environmental challenges of our time. To this end, FEIAP will be taking the initiative to identify opportunities for collaboration in terms of research and development for critical issues affecting mankind among the member economies. As a regional organization, FEIAP plays an important role in creating opportunities for engineers across geographical boundaries to meet and share their experiences. FEIAP will also be the conduit in the facilitation of dialogue with relevant governmental and non-governmental organizations in order to provide possible solutions to the challenges we face now and in the future.

Conclusion

With the recent changes in FEIAP's name, logo and constitution, FEIAP is seeking to be a more inclusive organization focused on its objectives to foster greater collaboration and sharing of information among member economies and participation in international initiatives. FEIAP is set to stay relevant in the new economy and to be a driving force for the engineering profession in Asia and the Pacific regions.

4.3.8 Association for Engineering Education in Southeast and East Asia and the Pacific (AEESEAP)

R. M. (Bob) Hodgson

The foundation of AEESEAP was the outcome of a UNESCO regional seminar on 'New Approaches to Engineering Education in Asia' held in Kuala Lumpur in 1973. During the seminar

it was recommended that a permanent organization for engineering education for the South-East Asian region be formed. Subsequent action by UNESCO and the World Federation of Engineering Organizations (WFEO) led to the formation of AEESEA, the Association for Engineering Education in South-East Asia. In 1989 this organization changed its name to the Association for Engineering Education in Southeast and East Asia and the Pacific with the acronym AEESEAP, to better represent the region occupied by the member countries.

The aims and goals of AEESEAP

These are to assist in the development and enhancement of technology and engineering capabilities within South-East Asia, East Asia and the Pacific by improving the quality of the education of engineers and technologists. The association seeks to facilitate networking and cooperation between institutions engaged in engineering education, industry and other relevant organizations in the region, and to promote the development of systems and standards for engineering and technology education. These goals are seen as important contributions to economic development and the advancement of the welfare of the people of the region.

The aims of AEESEAP are as follows:

- to promote an awareness of the role of engineering in the creation of wealth and the enhancement of national health and well-being;

- to promote the development and delivery of high quality curricula for engineering and technology;

- to facilitate and stimulate regional cooperation in the education and training of engineers and technologists;

- to facilitate participation in international assistance programmes for engineering education as donors and recipients as appropriate;

- to be proactive in the identification of problems in engineering education and training, and in finding solutions to them through the exchange of information and personnel;

- to provide services and advice on the quality improvement of engineering education programmes;

- to provide advice on the establishment of new facilities and institutions for the delivery of education and training in engineering and technology;

- to promote continuing education and professional development of engineers, technologists and educators;

■ to promote cooperation between industry and educators on a national and international basis;

■ to assist existing national societies of engineers and engineering technicians and groups of educators of engineers and engineering technicians in their efforts to improve engineering education; and

■ to assist in the establishment of societies or groups of engineering technicians for this purpose where they do not already exist.

The membership of AEESEAP

AEESEAP has a comprehensive range of membership classes. These are as follows: Voting Members, Ordinary Members, Individual Members, Supporting Members, Correspondent Members, Honorary Members and Subscribing Library Members. Voting members are key to the operation of the Association as the representatives of the voting members also form the AEESEAP Executive Committee and thus act as the board of the Association. The voting members are drawn from fifteen countries in the region. Sadly, some of the voting members have not been in active membership for some time and are in arrears with their subscriptions. A continuing problem in this context is that the individuals who are the nominated representatives of the voting members often change and it has proved difficult to contact the responsible persons, noting that the voting members are institutions or agencies and not individuals. A determined effort is now underway to overcome this problem and to restore the membership base such that an emphasis will be placed on rebuilding the base of committed voting members as national representatives.

Recent activities

The AEESEAP secretariat and presidency is rotated between fifteen member countries at three-year intervals and is currently located in New Zealand, the last handover having taken place early this year in February 2007. Prior locations were the Philippines followed by Indonesia and then Malaysia. The most recent handover took place in Kuala Lumpur in February in association with an AEESEAP Regional Symposium on Engineering Education with the theme 'New Strategies in Engineering Education'. Over fifty papers were presented at the symposium with two thirds on matters of curriculum design and delivery and one third on technological themes. In addition to the curriculum and technical papers, the traditional country reports on the state of engineering education in the countries of the voting members were presented.

Consideration of the patterns that have been emerging for some time and the events briefly detailed above led to the conclusion that the presence of the AEESEAP secretariat typically leads to activities appropriate to a national or local regional association where one does not exist or is inactive. Here it

must be made very clear that in presenting this analysis, no criticism is implied or intended of the recent AEESEAP office bearers from Malaysia or before them, Indonesia. What has become clear is that although the aims and goals of AEESEAP remain relevant to the region, the activities that gain support in pursuit of these goals have changed.

Thirty-five years of dynamic change in the region

As the economies of the nations in the region served by AEESEAP change from underdeveloped to developing and then to developed or mature, a corresponding change occurs in engineering education and accreditation systems – though this is observed to be somewhat ad hoc. Since AEESEAP was established, international engineering accreditation systems have also been developed. Such systems are most fully developed and applied at the level of professional degrees, usually four year, accredited through for example the Washington Accord. This accord was established in 1983 with AEESEAP nations Australia and New Zealand as two of the original signatories. Currently, of AEESEAP members, Australia, New Zealand, Japan, Korea and Singapore are full signatories of the Washington Accord, with Malaysia a provisional member and several nations in the region currently working towards provisional membership as a step towards full membership. The Washington Accord is essentially a system for accrediting national accreditation systems and subsequently for mutual recognition of accreditation decisions made by the national bodies at the institution, usually university and degree major level. In recent years, similar systems have been developed for engineering technician degrees through the Sydney Accord, and for technician diplomas through the Dublin Accord. Once nations have achieved membership of these accords, many of the aims of AEESEAP are seen to have been achieved, at least on a national basis.

Future directions for AEESEAP

For AEESEAP to survive and to play a useful role in the region, consideration must be given to the factors discussed above which are: the rapid industrialization and surge to prosperity of several AEESEAP nations, the development of national societies devoted to engineering education, the increasing involvement of the AEESEAP Members and Potential Members in international accreditation agreements and, not discussed but of importance here, the increasing internationalization in scope and view of trans-global learned societies including IEEE and IET (formally IEE). Consideration of these factors leads to the suggestion that the future role of AEESEAP may be to act as a regional forum for national engineering societies and as a source of advice and expertise to nations as they seek to develop engineering education and the related accreditation systems.

Conclusions

In the thirty-five years of its existence, AEESEAP has played a useful role in the region served through both the development of international personal networks and the provision of conferences. These conferences have been valuable as a forum for the sharing of best and evolving practice. At the present time the future of AEESEAP is under discussion because a number of the Voting Members have ceased to be active in the association and the AEESEAP conferences have developed a local rather than international emphasis. The key factors leading to these changes have been identified and two key and related roles for AEESEAP have been proposed and are under discussion. The future role of AEESEAP may be to act as a regional forum for national engineering societies and as a source of advice and expertise to nations as they seek to develop their engineering education and the related accreditation systems.

4.3.9 Asian and Pacific Centre for Transfer of Technology (APCTT)

Krishnamurthy Ramanathan

Interest in setting up an Asia-Pacific mechanism to foster technology transfer was expressed as early as 1965 at the first Asian Congress on Industrialization in Manila. Subsequently, through resolutions passed at the Commission Sessions of the United Nations Economic and Social Commission for Asia and the Pacific (UNESCAP), the Regional Centre for Technology Transfer (RCTT) was established in Bangalore in India on 16 July 1977 with the Government of India offering host facilities for the Centre. In 1985, the Centre was renamed the Asian and Pacific Centre for Transfer of Technology (APCTT). APCTT was relocated from Bangalore to New Delhi, with the support of the Government of India on 1 July 1993. APCTT has the status of a subsidiary body of UNESCAP and its membership is identical to the membership of UNESCAP.

APCTT is widely regarded as the first technology and engineering body for technology capacity-building in the Asia-Pacific region. Its objectives are to assist the members and associate members of UNESCAP by: strengthening their capabilities to develop and manage national innovation systems; develop, transfer, adapt and apply technology; improve the terms of transfer of technology; and identify and promote the development and transfer of technologies relevant to the region. During its initial phase (1977–1984) of operation, APCTT functioned as a Technology Information Centre. From 1985 to 1989, the Centre broadened the scope of its technology transfer activities to other areas such as technology utilization and technology management.

In an effort to create awareness among policy-makers in the developing countries on the importance of technology in national development, APCTT published books and monographs on the management of technology transfer, technology development, industrial research, and similar. For example, in 1985, with financial assistance from UNDP, APCTT prepared a series of country studies and a regional report on technology policies and planning in selected countries. The common issues thus identified were then summarized in another publication, *Technology Policy and Planning – Regional Report*, which provided cross-country analysis and the policy-related implications thereof for the different countries of the region. On the basis of the lessons and experiences gained from the activities outlined above, APCTT prepared a *Reference Manual on Technology Policies* that provided the general framework and setting for technology policy formulation. Another example, the Technology Atlas Project of 1986–1989, funded by the Government of Japan, was to help technology planners avoid the pitfalls of a fragmented and uncoordinated approach to technology-based development.

APCTT's technology utilization programme was aimed at linking potential users to the suppliers of relevant technologies through technology expositions, missions, workshops and individual syndication. The emphasis was on the promotion, transfer and utilization of selected, commercially viable technologies in identified priority sectors such as agro-based industries, low-cost construction, renewable energy, energy conservation, biotechnology and microelectronics. These technology transfer activities were refined during 1989 to focus increasingly on technology capacity-building at institutional and enterprise levels. In the 1990s, APCTT's programme was directed at small and medium scale enterprises (SMEs) and the promotion of environmentally sound technologies. Emphasis was placed on more effective and efficient access to information on technology transfer and its dissemination through linkages and networking. With the support from the Government of Germany through GTZ (1993–2002), the Centre focused increasingly on technological upgradation of SMEs and the promotion of R&D and enterprises cooperation. In this context, as an example, the Technology Bureau for Small Enterprises (TBSE) evolved as a joint venture between APCTT with the Small Industries Development Bank of India (SIDBI) to assist SMEs in finance and technology syndication.

APCTT started deploying web-based tools to strengthen its technology transfer services in cooperation with other partner institutions in the region such as the twin websites http://www.technology4sme.net and http://www.business-asia.net in cooperation with other partner institutions in the region as a comprehensive, online and free technology market business service for SMEs. The http://www.technology4sme.net website, with its database of technology offers and requests, facilitates effective communication and interaction among buyers and sellers of technology. Both websites contain a wide range of information for use by entrepreneurs, investors, technologists, business development experts and policy-makers. Over fourteen countries in the region are at various stages of duplicating this type of technology transfer platform, specific to their own contexts. APCTT has also designed the APTITUDE Search Engine to help seekers of technology simultaneously search several technology databases that are in the public domain.

To ensure that a holistic approach is taken in the planning and management of technology transfer, APCTT is currently promoting a 'National Innovation Systems' approach in countries of the Asia-Pacific region. The aim is to influence policy-makers so that they appreciate the relevance and importance of the NIS approach, and to develop policy frameworks that ensure the effective development and transfer of innovations in industry, research and development institutions, and in universities. APCTT is also implementing a project on Grass-roots Innovation to help member countries scout, document and eventually commercialize such innovations with a view towards promoting inclusive development and social entre-preneurship.

4.3.10 The African Network of Scientific and Technological Institutions (ANSTI)

Jacques Moulot

In Africa, engineers and scientists have traditionally organized themselves in networks based around disciplines. Such networks are often professional associations with political or administrative purposes aimed at addressing gaps affecting the profession and careers of engineers and scientists. Networks aimed at human resource capacity-building are less common. According to Massaquoi and Savage[17] there are mainly two types of such capacity-building networks at regional level in Africa: regional centres of excellence for training and research and regional institutional networks.

The African Network of Scientific and Technological Institutions (ANSTI) is an example of the latter. Established in 1980 by UNESCO, ANSTI is arguably one of the oldest alliances dealing with science in Africa. It draws its political mandate from the first Conference of Ministers Responsible for the Application of Science and Technology to Development in Africa organized in 1974 and its operational mandate from its members and partners.

The membership of ANSTI currently comprises 174 university departments and research centres, following a 77 per cent increase since 1999. The members are located in 35 sub-

Saharan African countries. An estimated one-third of the members provide engineering degrees in various disciplines of engineering. The network functions with a light and cost effective structure composed of a secretariat in charge of the daily operation and implementation of the activities of the network, and a Governing Council that meets once a year to approve the budget and provide policy guidelines for the network.

ANSTI provides capacity-building services and opportunities to scientists and engineers at its member institutions. These include awards and fellowships for postgraduate training, grants for travel to and for the organization of conferences, and funds for visiting professorships. As in any network, information exchange is emphasized. ANSTI pools the resources of its members and seeks partnerships and support from donors to attain its specific objectives (highlighted in the Box). Up to 2008, among other activities, it had provided different types of grants to more than 300 staff of member institutions; facilitated more than 50 staff exchange visits; granted over eighty-five postgraduate fellowships for training of which 35 per cent in the fields of engineering, and provided more than ninety grants to scientists and engineers to attend conferences.

The main objectives of ANSTI

The objectives of ANSTI, as detailed in its 2007–2011 strategic plan are:

- To strengthen the staff of science and engineering training institutions.

- To facilitate the use of African scientists in the diaspora to strengthen teaching and research in science and engineering in universities.

- To promote the use of Information and Communication Technology (ICT) in the delivery of science and engineering education.

- To facilitate the sharing of scientific information and strengthen the coordinating mechanism of the network.

- To strengthen research activities in relevant areas of Science & Technology.

- To provide a forum for the discussion of strategic issues in science and engineering education (including issues of quality and relevance).

Excerpt from ANSTI Strategic Plan 2007–2011

One of the important activities of any capacity-building pro-gramme is the identification and discussion of strategic issues involved in the relevant fields of education. ANSTI, through the meetings of deans and other expert groups, has in the past identified several issues that affect science and technology education in Africa. The network has established a biennial

---

17 Massaquoi, J.G.M. and Savage, Mike (2002) Regional Cooperation for capacity build-ing in science and technology. Popularisation of science and technology education: Some Case Studies for Africa. By Mike Savage and Prem Naido (Eds). Commonwealth Secretariat

forum, the Conference of Vice-Chancellors, Deans of Science, Engineering and Technology (COVIDSET), which brings together university leaders responsible for science and technology to deliberate on strategic issues in higher education relevant to their disciplines. Considering the small amount of funds used to establish the network and the limited resources at the disposal of the small network secretariat, it can be seen that institutional networks effectively contribute to human resource development on a large scale.[18]

---

18 J. Massaquoi. 2008. University as Centres of Research and Knowledge Creation: An Endangered Species? H. Vessuri and U. Teichler (eds.), pp.59–70, Rotterdam, Sense publishers.

4.3.11 The Africa Engineers Forum and AEF Protocol of Understanding

Dawie Botha

The Africa Engineers Forum (AEF) was established in 2000 to build upon the earlier initiative to facilitate more inclusive and broader cooperation of African engineers in order to promote and foster sustainable development within an African context. At the World Summit for Sustainable Development in Johannesburg South Africa in 2001, the World Federation of Engineering Organizations (WFEO) co-hosted an event at which several African engineering initiatives and philosophies, including the AEF protocol, were presented. This resulted in an invitation to AEF participants by WFEO, to attend their 2003 Congress in Tunis as well as to participate in an African Engineers Day event.

The Africa Engineers Forum network of engineering organizations subscribes to shared values in support of viable and appropriate engineering capacity in Africa. Thirteen national engineering professional bodies are currently signatories. AEF strives to ensure an appropriate level of efficient human resource capacity in the built environment professions, but particularly in engineering, to enable Africa to ultimately achieve sustainable development for all the people of Africa. It contributes resources and expertise in partnership with key stakeholders to accomplish the transfer and assimilation of the value of the best practice principles of sustainable development to identified communities at all levels.

The Africa Engineers Forum consists of national volunteer associations of engineering professionals that provide technical leadership in support and enhancement of the principles of:

- wealth creation;
- sustainable engineering as a prerequisite for development;
- quality of life; and
- holistic education and training for capacity-building.

The vision of the AEF is to strive to ensure an appropriate level of efficient human resource capacity in the built environment professions, but particularly in engineering, to enable Africa to ultimately achieve sustainable development for all the people of Africa.

Goals of AEF

The AEF is committed to pursue the goals set out in the Protocol of Understanding and Cooperation in order to achieve its objectives, which are aimed at achieving the following outcomes:

- Excellence in engineering technology in Africa.

- Informed and intelligent decision-making about built environment infrastructure by all government structures and private sector entities by utilizing human capacity-building orientation programmes and projects.

- A sufficient pool of competent professionals by and through:

  – offering and pursuing awareness and orientation programmes, projects and activities regarding the role of Engineering and Technology;

– promotion of interest in mathematics and science at higher grades in primary and secondary schools;

– offering career guidance programmes and activities;

– promoting consistent investment mechanisms for infrastructure and promoting fair and reasonable remuneration for all engineering practitioners;

– facilitating mentorship; and

– offering continued professional development opportunities.

- Sustainable professional frameworks and organizational structures in Africa by:

– creating permanent facilities and administrative mechanisms to support the built environment profession's activities and programmes.

- An awareness relating to AEF activities in order to prepare the countries, its people and its decision-makers for the challenges of the future by:

– utilizing the opportunities offered to enhance the image and raise public awareness about the role and value of engineering and industry in particular, and engineering and the built environment in general.

- Support the development of entrepreneurship in the engineering environment.

The Africa Engineers Protocol

The Africa Engineers Protocol of Understanding and Cooperation was developed by the AEF to cover the essential components of what is seen as 'sustainable engineering', which is a prerequisite for sustainability. The AEF protocol contains the following items:

- Develop and uphold the AEF concepts about sustainable development.

- Communicate at a technical level amongst all engineering professionals, resident within and outside Africa.

- Develop and implement alliance and integration models for AEF interaction and networking with other continental and international engineering and other built environment organizations.

- Promote and accept internationally accepted norms in terms of conduct, integrity, ethics, engineering standards and care for our people and our environment.

- Develop and maintain acceptable and appropriate frameworks to accredit and recognize educational qualifications and professional standards to facilitate reciprocity and equity.

- Encourage and facilitate ongoing learning and professional development for engineering professionals.

- Set up and maintain an African electronic database for technical information linked to the websites of the AEF signatories and other partners of strategic importance and relevance.

- Exchange information and sharing of experiences regarding engineering practice.

- Disseminate relevant published technical papers, articles and editorials.

- Exchange and provide access to technical journals and magazines for reference purposes.

- Arrange professional and technical networking opportunities and events within the influence sphere of participating organizations in cooperation with the other participants in AEF, and make use of the potential contribution and assistance of the African diaspora engineers.

- Set up, maintain and manage an events database concerning annual programmes of events, including those relating to continuous professional development, for the purpose of forward planning and coordination.

- Communicate, accept and implement best practice in terms of desirable and appropriate local and internationally recognized engineering standards, processes, procedures, methods or systems in relation to the delivery processes and the life cycle of products and assets.

- Facilitate the harmonization of standards, documentation, methods and procedures as appropriate.

- Promote the use of procurement as an instrument for development and capacity-building.

- Promote and facilitate entry to and equality for all demographic and gender groups in the engineering profession.

- Provide a platform for influential African engineering professionals who can influence best policy practices at all levels of decision-making in government and the private sector.

- Facilitate and promote networking amongst African tertiary educational institutions involved in engineering related education.

- Facilitate and promote appropriate education and training for engineering professionals dealing with the challenges of rural development.

- Facilitate and offer public awareness programmes in order to enhance the visibility and recognition of the role of the engineering profession in African civil society.

- Promote and support pertinent science and technology policy including the extension of research and development initiatives by governments in Africa.

- Develop and offer capacity-building programmes in order to develop a pool of knowledgeable decision-makers, clients and users of engineering infrastructure and services.

- Invite and facilitate government and private sector participation in engineering practice and related matters.

- Develop, promote, facilitate and lobby for the acceptance of best practice policies relating to foreign investment and donor involvement and influence in Africa.

- Promote appropriate curricula at schools to prepare and enable learners to enter into the field of engineering.

- Develop and provide outreach and career guidance programmes for all school learners.

4.3.12 International Federation of Engineering Education Societies (IFEES)

Hans J. Hoyer with Lueny Morell, Claudio Borri, Sarah Rajala, Seeram Ramakrishna, Xavier Fouger, Bruno Laporte, José Carlos Quadrado, Maria Larrondo Petrie and Duncan Fraser

Introduction

Engineering and technology play a key role in globalization as both developed and developing countries design and implement effective and efficient strategies that advance their economies and social development. Science and engineering education needs to be continuously evolving in order to assist all countries to reduce poverty, boost socio-economic development and make the right decisions for sustainable and environmentally compatible development.

A global approach is needed to effectively innovate in engineering education. The world needs to establish effective engineering education processes of high quality to assure a global supply of well-prepared engineering graduates; engineers who can act locally but think globally. It is imperative that technical know-how be supplemented with professional skills to develop a generation of 'adaptive engineering leaders' capable of addressing the multiple challenges of an ever-changing world – these are the engineering professionals that a globalized world needs.

The role of engineering education in growing knowledge-based economies

Knowledge and innovation have always played a key role in development. Fifty years ago, competitiveness and growth were driven by access to natural resources and labour. With globalization and the technological revolution of the last decades, knowledge has clearly become a key driver of competitiveness. A knowledge economy now is one that utilizes knowledge as the key engine of competitive growth. It is an economy where knowledge is acquired, created, disseminated and used effectively to enhance economic development. Transitioning from a traditional economy to a knowledge economy requires long-term investments in education, innovation and ICT, in addition to an appropriate economic and institutional regime that allows for efficient mobilization and allocation of resources. Innovation in technology, as well as products and business processes, boosts productivity. Today, the prosperity of nations depends on how effectively organizations use their human resources to raise productivity and nurture innovation.

While education has always been a key component of innovation and technological advance, the complexity and speed of the interplay between education, knowledge, technology and skills require far-reaching adjustments of education systems. Knowledge-enabled economies are able to constantly modernize their education systems in line with changes in economic policies. These changes have been both systemic and deep, affecting the nature of teaching and learning. Most OECD countries have increased their public expenditures on education over the last few decades. Developing countries also have made significant investments in education. However, talent and skills have become the world's most sought-after commodity. As economies increasingly shift towards knowledge-intensive directions, the demand for skills and competencies increases significantly.

Performance in the marketplace is driven by the quality, skills and flexibility of labour and management. In addition to traditional 'hard' skills and ICT competencies, knowledge economies require a new set of 'soft' skills such as a spirit of enquiry, adaptability, problem-solving, communications skills, self-learning knowledge discovery, cultural sensitivity, social empathy, and motivation for work. Countries need to develop teaching and learning environments that nurture these skills.

International Federation of Engineering Education Societies

Launched in 2006, the International Federation of Engineering Education Societies (IFEES) aims to create a worldwide network of engineering educators and engineering education stakeholders. Through the collaboration of its member organizations, IFEES's mission is to establish effective and high-quality engineering education processes to assure a global supply of well-prepared engineering graduates. IFEES strives to strengthen its member organizations and their capacity to support faculty and students, attract corporate participation and enhance the ability of engineering faculty, students and practitioners to understand and work in the varied cultures of the world.

To do this, IFEES focuses on four strategic areas: engineering education infrastructure; research, development and entrepreneurship; student recruitment; and success and lifelong learning. It will promote and support activities and initiatives that: promote engineering education; promote access to engineering education; enhance quality; gear engineering education to the needs of society; share teaching methods and curriculum plans; increase transparency and recognition of titles; foster and favour mobility of students and professionals; promote ethics and gender issues; increase awareness of sustainable development; improve humanistic skills and cultural awareness; and foster imagination and innovative thinking in new generations of engineers.

Global Engineering Deans Council

Stakeholders are increasingly expecting engineering colleges to act as leaders in innovation and to provide solutions to society's challenges. The Global Engineering Deans Council (GEDC) is a new initiative of IFEES that brings together deans and heads of engineering education institutions to ensure their schools deliver locally-relevant and globally-relevant courses, and to make engineering more attractive to top candidates and future generations of students.

Student Platform for Engineering Education Development

A new worldwide student initiative is starting to take shape under the title Student Platform for Engineering Education Development (SPEED). SPEED aspires to connect different stakeholders of education, provide input and create a change in the field of engineering education. SPEED offers a platform for student leaders, to facilitate their engagement into cooperation and research on engineering education matters and connect them with representatives from businesses, academia, civil society and politics.

Board of European Students of Technology

In addressing engineering education on a global scale, students should be involved and their input considered. Board of European Students of Technology (BEST) has been providing input into engineering education policies at the European level and beyond since 1995. With the mission to provide services to students, BEST focuses in providing complementary education, educational involvement and career support to European students. BEST is active in thirty countries with 2,000 members and reaching 900,000 students.

4.4 Engineering International Development Organizations

4.4.1 Practical Action - and the changing face of technology in international development

Andrew Scott

Introduction

Over the years, the ways of working of the Intermediate Technology Development Group (ITDG) – now Practical Action – have evolved, as one would expect, through experience, new thinking and through dialogue with others. Our approach to technology, development and change, which is at the core of our work, has itself evolved. This is achieved by tracing the evolution of our approach to technology and relating this to wider trends in thinking about international development, discussed below. It is important to explain why, still in the twenty-first century, organizations like Practical Action, involved with appropriate technology, continue to play such a vital role in development.

The evolution of our approach to technology and poverty reduction can roughly be divided into four phases. These phases do not correspond exactly to the four decades of the organization's existence but by coincidence they are not far off it; they do not have a clear start or end, and they overlap to some extent. They are simply a way to trace changes in our approach to technology through shifts in thinking, each phase marking a period where one set of ideas was predominant. It is a subjective view, perhaps, but serves the purpose.

The first phase concerns the period when the main approach relates to the transfer of technology to developing countries. This evolved during the 1970s when the main questions were related to scale and technology choice, with technology development to make small-scale options available. Then came a focus on the development of technologies specifically for poor people within developing countries – what became known as 'appropriate technologies'. In the late 1980s, when participation became the watchword for all poverty reduction initiatives, Participatory Technology Development (PTD) dominated thinking in the appropriate technology world. More recently, the approach has been to focus on the development of what can be described as people's technological capabilities, which reflects a focus on people and their situations. This evolution of thinking will be explained in more detail using some examples.

From technology transfer to technology development

ITDG began life as an organization providing information and advice about technology to others. Part of the work at the start was promoting the concept of Intermediate or Appropriate Technology, spreading the message, and part was helping people to put it into practice. One of the first activities conducted under ITDG's name was the production and publishing of *Tools for Progress*, a catalogue of technologies for farmers and small-enterprises in developing countries. And quite early on, a Technical Enquiry Service was established that is still going strong.

ITDG relied on a number of panels of voluntary experts to provide this advice. These panel members – at one stage there were over 300 involved – were almost all technical people, with science and engineering backgrounds, and most were in the UK. They sought out technological knowledge and information from companies and researchers in the country, mainly with the intention of transferring this to developing countries.

With the experience of a number of field projects and increased contact with practitioners on the ground, and with the realization too that at times there was no appropriate technology available to transfer, the emphasis moved to the question of technology choice and technology development. This resulted in a concentration on scale. Small was beautiful, and what was needed was small-scale technology for small-scale farmers and small-scale enterprises. ITDG at this time (in the 1970s and 1980s) devoted a lot of its effort to the development in India of small-scale plants for the manufacture of cement, sugar and cotton yarn, with varying success. The work in the case of cement set about reviving a production technique that in Europe had been abandoned in the nineteenth century in favour of a larger-scale processing technology. In the case of small-scale sugar, the development work involved bringing together traditional processing with more recent scientific knowledge; while in the case of cotton it entailed scaling down the size of the machinery and plant.

Cement

Small-scale cement production was one of three manufacturing technologies that ITDG began working on in the 1970s with an Indian partner, ATDA (Appropriate Technology Development Association). The technology was based on the batch processing of limestone using a vertical shaft kiln to produce cement. The ATDA units had a capacity of around fifty tonnes per day, compared with the 2,000 to 3,000 tonnes per day that might be found in conventional, large-scale rotary kilns. The small-scale vertical shaft kiln was developed partly as a response to a national cement shortage. Though the yields were lower and they produced cement of more variable quality, they had the advantage of reduced transport costs, being closer to both raw materials and markets.

The first commercial small-scale cement plant developed by AIDA went into production in 1981. Within four years, there were nineteen units in operation in India, the world's second largest cement producer, and there are now 300 mini-cement plants with a total installed capacity of around 11 million tonnes a year. The largest cement producer, China, has 50,000 mini-cement plants.

Sugar

Turning briefly to sugar processing by the late 1970s, when ITDG first started work on sugar technology, there were several thousand small-scale Open Pan Sulphitation (OPS) plants in India. These OPS units had a capacity of between 100 tonnes and 200 tonnes of cane per day, compared with large-scale mills based on vacuum pan processing with capacities higher than 1,000 tonnes a day, and can reach 20,000 tonnes. The OPS processing technique had developed in India in the 1950s and together with ATDA, ITDG sought to improve the technical efficiencies and to transfer the technology to other countries.

There are four mains steps in the manufacture of sugar: crushing, clarifying, boiling and recovery (crystallization and separation). Over a period of ten years, ITDG and ATDA developed and introduced two main technical improvements: screw expellers to increase the yield at crushing, and shell furnaces, which improved boiling rates and allowed the use of wet bagasse (crushed cane) for fuel. The technology was successfully transferred to Kenya and Tanzania, though the number of OPS plants was fewer than had been hoped.

One reason for the limited spread of OPS plants was the regulated nature of the sugar market, both nationally and internationally. In India price controls sometimes meant that the by-products were worth more than the sugar, while elsewhere there were investment incentives available only for large-scale processors. Sugar continues to generate a lot of debate in discussions of trade regulations.

Cotton

Small-scale cement and small-scale sugar achieved some success; the technology worked – technically speaking – and was financially viable. With cotton, the third processing technology that ITDG devoted a lot of time and effort on, the story is less rosy. In 1986 a review of the textile programme concluded 'It is unfortunate that... little lasting achievement can be credited to the programme.' Why was this? What went wrong?

The cotton story began in India in 1975, when an initial study – as studies often do – recommended further research and the testing of small-scale yarn production. The context is quite important to understand why this was pursued. At this time, the textile industry in India accounted for 15 per cent of industrial employment and, in the decentralized informal sector, was second only to agriculture as a source of employment. It also has to be remembered that because of Gandhi's espousal of cotton spinning as an integral element of traditional Indian way of life, manual technologies for cotton processing held great symbolic meaning to many people. The idea therefore of showing that manual cotton spinning to supply yarn to handloom weavers could work, held great appeal.

In 1978, a pilot project was initiated by ATDA to demonstrate the technical feasibility of cottage spinning and to test its economic viability. Christian Aid supported the project and ITDG provided a technical consultant from the Shirley Institute, the UK's principal textile technology research centre. Technological development focused on improving the performance of the charkhas (the spinning machines) and on cotton pre-processing, i.e. the preparation of raw cotton for use by the spinners.

Over time it was established that a hand-driven charkha would not be practicable with more than six spindles. A 12-spindle pedal-driven charkha was developed, followed by a 24-spindle motor driven charkha. The latter could produce two-and-a-half times the yarn of the 12-spindle charkha without the

⤸ The Monitor Merrimac Memorial Bridge Tunnel, USA.

hard labour, but this was getting away from the Ghandian model. Financially it was eventually shown that the 12-spindle pedal *charkha* could only be viable within the subsidized khadi sector, but the 24-spindle motorized *charkha* could be viable, though would find it hard to compete with mill yarn on grounds of quality.

As far as the cotton pre-processing technology was concerned, the review in 1986 concluded, 'Unfortunately the machine production achieved little other than the production of scaled-down versions of a card and drawframe to high standards of engineering along with a poorly manufactured blowroom.' It did not work. The review concluded, 'the Textile Programme appears to have fallen into a "widget trap" – "widgets" were sought as solutions for problems before the search for a technological "fix" was adequately justified.'

Overall comments

Although small, these three small-scale manufacturing technologies each still required a substantial investment, which was beyond the scope of an individual living on around two dollars a day. They might be small-scale in relation to conventional plant, but not relative to the assets of micro-enterprises or smallholder farmers. Though cooperative ownership was an option – and many OPS sugar plants in India started as cooperatives – for the impoverished, such factories could only mean either wage employment or a market for their agricultural produce.

Attention shifted therefore as ITDG paid greater attention to socio-economic factors, redressing previous neglect of the social, institutional and economic context; attention shifted to technology development for micro- and small enterprises. Here there were some successes, for instance the tray drier and fibre cement roofing tiles. The latter are now in widespread use in much of the developing world. Moreoever, tray driers were successfully developed in Peru by a small enterprise, and transferred to other countries.

Participatory Technology Development

The next phase in ITDG's approach to technology and poverty reduction saw a focus on Participatory Technology Development (PTD). PTD is now a well-established practice in the field of agriculture and can trace its origins back to trials in farmers' fields by agricultural research stations with a shift, though not everywhere, towards more and more of the experimentation into the hands of the farmers themselves. But the concept of PTD applies also to other sectors; and arguably the beta testing of software by IT companies is a form of PTD.

This change during the 1980s – particularly the late 1980s – towards technology users being directly involved in technology development rather than recipients of products, was assisted by two trends in thinking. First, there was greater

understanding of the process of innovation that takes place by small-scale farmers and within small enterprises; how they learn and apply new knowledge. It was recognized that technical change is generally evolutionary and incremental. Radical invention is the exception rather than the rule. Technical change, by and large, consists of very small, minor adjustments to the way people do things based on 'what people are doing', on the knowledge and experience that they have, and the skills they possess to carry them out.

The second change in thinking was a great move towards participatory approaches in the practice of international development. Participatory techniques (such as PRA, RRA or PLA) that recognize the value of existing knowledge and skills became acceptable methods for all kinds of planning and field work, and quite quickly became almost a discipline in themselves. The idea of involving people in the development or adaptation of the technologies they use fitted into this very well. A good example of PTD, featured in ITDG appeal literature for some time with some success, was the donkey ploughs in Sudan.

Ploughs in Sudan

In the conflict in Darfur, large numbers of people have moved to refugee camps – the so-called 'internally displaced people' (IDPs). This has always been a harsh environment to live in, but ITDG has been working in North Darfur for almost two decades – for half of our forty years – where we have been supporting the development of technologies used by small-scale farmers. From the beginning, our approach has been to work with the farmers, enabling them to acquire new knowledge about alternative agricultural techniques, such as soil and water conservation or pest management, and to try and get them to test these new ideas for themselves.

ITDG began working with small-scale farmers in Kebkabiya, North Darfur, in 1987 in collaboration with Oxfam. An initial review of local tools and farmers' needs prompted work on a prototype donkey-drawn plough. While the introduction of animal-drawn ploughs in the region goes back to the 1960s, the models available were too expensive for the great majority of farmers.

Actual plough designs were borrowed from existing designs, from two designs in particular: a wooden ard (scratch *plough* – a type of simple *plough*) and a steel mouldboard plough, which was a scaled-down version of a standard ox-plough, made suitable for donkeys. In Kebkabiya, the approach focused on getting ploughs to farmers and letting them do the real experimentation, rather than on the finer details of technical specification. This approach, or rather the plough design that emerged from it, has generated some criticism from professional agricultural engineers; but the farmers who carried out the trials seemed satisfied. The approach meant that farmers were able to assess the overall value of the 'product', including the qualitative matters such as convenience and drudgery.

The manufacturers of the plough were the local blacksmiths. A total of 120 blacksmiths were trained in making ploughs, and they were able to fine tune basic designs in line with their own skills and resources and take into account of feedback from farmers about the plough's performance and their preferences.

The donkey-drawn plough resulted in considerable savings in time and labour for the 80 per cent of farmers in the district who had access to it. Average yields increased to 682 kg/ha as a result of increased water absorption and the area under cultivation increased. Over 2,800 ploughs have been produced and sold, and more farmers each year adopt the plough.

Technological capabilities

The work of ITDG (and other AT organizations) is now less about identifying or developing specific technological options (hardware) for specific locations at a particular time, and is more about enabling resource-poor women and men to identify and develop technologies to address their needs as these needs change over time. The technology choice focus of the early AT movement – the 1970s and early 1980s – was a static approach that took little account of the ever-changing world that people live in. But there has been a move by AT organizations in recent years towards describing their work in terms of the technological capabilities of people, i.e. people's ability to use, develop and adapt technologies in, and in response to, a changing environment rather than in terms of the characteristics of technologies, as before. The need is to develop local systems that will support or strengthen technological capabilities. One way to do this is through community-based extension workers.

Kamayoqs

Practical Action has several experiences of community-based extension. One of these, in Peru, has recently been recognized as an example of good practice by the UN Food and Agriculture Organization. At the centre of this initiative is the training of farmer-to-farmer extension agents known as Kamayoq. In the sixteenth century Kamayoq was the term used to describe special advisers on agriculture and climate in the Inca Empire. They were trained to anticipate weather patterns and were responsible for advising on key agricultural practices such as optimal sowing dates.

The approach was piloted in the early 1990s in the Vilcanota valley where the farming communities are over 3,500 metres above sea level. Farm households here have one or two head of cattle, some sheep and a number of guinea pigs. The most common crops are maize, potatoes and beans.

In 1996, Practical Action established a Kamayoq School in the town of Sicuani, supported by the local authority, and to date over 140 Kamayoq have been trained of whom 20 per cent are women.

- Trainees come from and are selected by the communities.

- Training is provided in Quechua, the local language.

- The course lasts eight months and involves attendance for one day per week.

- The course focuses on local farmers' veterinary and agricultural needs.

After their training, the Kamayoq are able to address the veterinary and agricultural needs of local smallholder farmers. Farmers pay the Kamayoq for their services in cash or in kind. They are able and willing to do so because the advice and technical assistance they receive can lead to an increase in family income of 10–40 per cent through increased production and sales of animals and crops. The most sought-after service is the diagnosis and treatment of animal diseases. In each of the thirty-three communities where the Kamayoq are active, mortality rates among cattle have fallen dramatically. A recent evaluation found that 89 per cent of farmers reported that mastitis is effectively controlled; milk yields increased from 6.26 to 8.68 litres and sales increased by 39 per cent. In one community, Huiscachani income from crop production increased 73 per cent after receiving technical advice in 2005.

An example of Participatory Technology Development facilitated by Kamayoqs has been the discovery of a natural medicine to treat the parasitic disease on *Fasciola hepatica*. Over a three-year period, the Kamayoq and local villagers experimented with a range of natural medicines until they discovered a particularly effective treatment that is also cheaper than conventional medicines. Other examples of Participatory Technology Development include the treatment of a fungal disease of maize and the control of mildew on onions.

Where are we today?

So where do we stand today? Well, 1.1 billion people do not have access to clean water, 2.4 billion have no sanitation, 2 billion people have no access to modern energy services, 1.5 billion have inadequate shelter and 800 million are underfed. Though for millions the standard of living has improved, millions more remain in absolute poverty. We know technology change can help to change their lives, but access to even low-cost, simple technologies is prevented by their poverty.

At the same time, technology is being looked to as the solution to the world's problems. The Africa Commission concluded in 2005 that strengthening the scientific and technological capac-

⌂ *The One Laptop per Child OLPC $100 computer – small is beautiful?*

157

ity of Africa was an imperative, and favoured the development of centres of excellence. The Commission recommended that donor countries provide US$500 million a year for ten years to African universities. Also in 2005, the Sachs Millennium Project Report for the UN made similar recommendations. Furthermore, the US and others are now looking to technology to overcome the challenge of climate change.

But people are still falling into widget traps. The same mistakes are being made now as were being made twenty, thirty and forty years ago. The lessons that ITDG – Practical Action – has learnt, the lessons that others have learned, the combined experience of decades' work in promoting technology for poverty reduction, are often being ignored in the excitement about the potential of modern, science-based technologies. For example, the US$100 laptop promoted by the US not-for-profit One Laptop per Child (OLPC), an offshoot from MIT's Media Labs, has drawn such criticism. It should be noted however that one modern ICT in particular has made a huge difference to the lives of people throughout the developing world: the mobile phone. Access for many has been made possible not just because of the physical infrastructure of the networks – the widgets – but also the financing and tariff systems. Mobile phones are quite clearly an Appropriate Technology for impoverished communities.

In short, though we might think the concept of appropriate technology is now widely established as part of the received wisdom of international development, this is clearly not reflected in practice. Practical Action will have to continue to persuade people of the basic principles of how technology can be used to reduce poverty.

In his last lecture, Schumacher suggested that when technologies are being assessed for their appropriateness for poverty reduction, one of the questions should be: Is it an appropriate technology from a democratic point of view? An intermediate technology approach, he said, 'is also the democratic way that gives the little people some independence and what the young call "doing one's own thing"'. An essential dimension to AT, and indeed an often-mentioned aspect of Practical Action's approach, is the democratic idea of increasing control over one's own life. This is another way of expressing Amartya Sen's idea of development being the freedom to make decisions about one's own life and livelihood.

Technology Democracy

People are increasingly alienated from the decision-making that affects them in all walks of life, including the use and development of technology. Enabling more democratic technology choice is partly about widening the range of options, including making more productive technologies available, and partly about providing an environment (institutional, financial, social, political) that supports access to technology

options and the freedom to choose by resource-poor people. While much of the effort of the development community is in fact geared to providing a supportive environment, it is often assumed that, once this is in place, appropriate technology decisions will be taken. However, the needs and circumstances of different social groups need to be explicitly addressed and their technology needs must also be explicitly addressed.

Seen holistically, in the complexity of a dynamic social, economic, cultural, and political context, the effective management of technology change is a question of capabilities. The poor must be enabled or empowered to access improved technologies, and to make their own technical choices through the development of their capability. This will enable them to respond to changing needs and opportunities as they arise, and lead to sustainable development.

Much of Practical Action's work is now concerned with strengthening people's technological capabilities so that they can make their own decisions about the technologies that they use. Our projects demonstrating the effectiveness of community extension workers, supporting Participatory Technology Development by farmers, and developing skills in micro-enterprises, are all about strengthening people's capabilities.

For Practical Action, our work will therefore continue to include innovating and demonstrating ways of directly involving women and men in the process of technology development, and involving them in decision-making on the technologies that affect their lives. This is what we have been doing for a number of years, and this what we will continue to do. But we must also seek and promote change in the policy and institutional environment that governs decision-making about technology.

We need to advocate for institutional and policy frameworks that enable, rather than constrain, poor people to make effective choices about the technologies they want to use. This includes making public sector organizations and private sector corporations properly accountable for their environmental and social impact. It includes mechanisms to ensure that scientific research and technological innovation is in the public interest rather than to the advantage of the vested interests of the rich and powerful. It includes making information about technologies and technical knowledge accessible to the people who need it, and includes building the capacity of developing countries to assess for themselves the possible impacts of new technologies on their societies, the livelihoods of their people and their natural environment.

4.4.2 Engineers Without Borders

Andrew Lamb

Background

From chairs and doors to laptops and spacecraft, technology gives people capabilities that extend and enhance their own. For centuries, engineers have developed technology to advance people's capabilities and have used technology to lift the human condition, enrich human endeavours and raise the human spirit. But for all this success, the work is not yet complete. Many engineers feel and know that, in the race for technological advancement, too many people have been left behind. Many engineers see technological development simply happening for its own sake in a world where extreme profligacy and extreme poverty can be contemporaries, with skyscrapers next to slums. Many engineers fear that their work is being motivated only by the drive for economic advancement, which seems increasingly disconnected from the premise of the meeting of basic needs that once formed the very purpose of their profession.

Many engineers, given the apparent absence of alternatives, are increasingly finding their own ways to meet some of the greatest challenges the human race has ever faced. Engineers Without Borders (EWB) groups are part of this movement, and in many ways they have become a movement themselves. They are a reaction to the failure of many governments, engineering companies and engineering institutions to mobilize and use technology and infrastructure to fight poverty and suffering around the world.

Introduction to Engineers Without Borders

Engineers Without Borders groups draw on the expertise of engineers to meet basic needs and provide water, food, shelter, energy, communications, transport, education, training and healthcare – and indeed dignity – to people living in poverty. They focus their work on the poorest nations and, in their own countries, have become voices of awareness, understanding and advocacy on the role of technology in international development. Several EWB groups have become well-established international development organizations in their own right, gaining significant support from the engineering community, engineering firms and other aid organizations. A few EWB organizations focus some of their work on humanitarian relief or on key environmental concerns and sustainability issues. Although most of the leading EWB organizations are in developed nations, there are – excitingly – a growing number of EWB groups in developing countries.

The name Engineers Without Borders is an evocative and powerful one, which has itself contributed to the growth of the movement. It refers to the concept of capabilities and development as freedom, where barriers to development are removed and where people can take their own path out of poverty. It can also refer to the idea that the engineers are working in places 'where there is no engineer', in countries that lack sufficient domestic engineering capacity (which perhaps could be called 'borders without engineers') or where that capacity is being misdirected. Indeed, this is perhaps closer to the meaning of 'Without Borders' as it is used by humanitarian and relief organizations such as *Médecins Sans Frontières* or Reporters Without Borders, where political boundaries are secondary to the humanitarian imperative or universal human rights. Other interpretations of the name include the idea of solidarity with others and it emphasizes that the work is international, charitable/voluntary and inter-disciplinary in nature (i.e. there is no 'Civil Engineers Without Borders' or 'Electrical Engineers Without Borders'). It is worth noting that most EWB groups do not limit participation only to engineers, though the work itself does mainly focus on technology. Some of the names used by EWB groups could translate more accurately into English as 'Engineering Without Borders' or as 'Engineers Without Frontiers', but the ideas behind these names are similar.

History of Engineers Without Borders

The first organization to carry the name Engineers Without Borders started in France. *Ingénieurs sans Frontières* (ISF) was established in 1982 as an association for French international solidarity, created to provide technical assistance to development projects in underprivileged communities in developing countries and to educate the engineering community on the problems in those areas. In the mid-1980s, ISF Belgium was established and it later merged with *Ingénieurs Assistance International* (established in the mid-1990s by a national civil engineering professional body) to form the ISF Belgium of today. *Ingeniería Sin Fronteras* was established in Spain in 1990 and is now the largest EWB organization in the world. These organizations were founded by students at their universities and later grew to form national federations, characteristic of many of the EWB organizations that followed.

⟳ *Working with local people to mix concrete for a bridge anchor in Kibera, Kenya.*

© Joe Mulligan, EWB-UK

Then, after the millennium, a new wave of EWB organizations formed in countries including Denmark, Sweden, Canada, USA, UK, Australia, Greece, Italy, Ecuador, India, Nepal, Germany, Egypt and, later on, Kosovo, Mexico, Palestine, Portugal, Rwanda, South Africa and many others. Several of these EWB groups were inspired by EWB organizations that were forming in other countries, for example EWB Canada helped EWB-UK to begin in 2001, and EWB-USA helped EWB India to begin in 2005. There are now about sixty countries or territories that have independent organizations or groups using the name 'Engineers Without Borders'.

Surprisingly, many of these EWB organizations grew independently and have therefore adopted slightly different approaches and characteristics as a result. Many of these EWB groups began as student groups at universities, which then went on to form a national body built on these local 'branches' or 'chapters'. Some national groups adopted the approach of a strong national organization whereas others adopted an approach of national dialogue and coordination with no strong centre (both approaches have been found to have their challenges). Also, a few EWB groups were set up by professional engineers, for example, EWB Greece was set up by a group of engineers who worked together after the Athens earthquake in 1999. It has undertaken major engineering projects, such as a dam in Ethiopia and a maternity home in Pakistan, that are much larger than projects by other EWB groups. Another example

is EWB Denmark, which was established to work in disaster areas, setting up a roster of experienced engineers who could be recruited by humanitarian agencies (similar to RedR see section 6.1.10). EWB Denmark has more recently started supporting branches at universities.

The different approaches taken by national EWB groups, and perhaps even when and whether an EWB group emerges in a country at all, seems to relate more to national culture rather than, say, geographic or economic considerations. At the international level, the problems of international relations between EWB groups can at times reflect the problems of international relations between national governments, with stereotypes of national characteristics being played out in microcosm! Attempts at international associations (whether regional or global) of EWB groups have struggled to find consensus between the diversity of approaches employed. This is certainly not helped by the lack of resources and capacity for national EWB groups to represent themselves properly at the international level, despite the support and encouragement received from bodies such as UNESCO and others. It is clear that for every EWB group in every country the challenges of international associations are – quite correctly – of a lower priority than their own missions, projects and challenges. There is little doubt however that over time, as the many new EWB groups that have emerged in the last decade grow and become more established, a fully representational international asso-

↺ A small-scale wind turbine in the Philippines provides power and job opportunities.

ciation will almost certainly be formed that will live up to the 'Without Borders' name.

EWB in the context of international development

'No other issue suffers such disparity between human importance and its political priority' is how former UN Secretary General Kofi Annan described the position of water and sanitation in public policy. Water and sanitation is arguably the most vital and most urgent area of attention in international development for engineers. EWB groups are very active in this area. Yet, in this, as in other areas, groups are discovering a fundamental limitation: there is a disparity between the importance of engineering and its place in the priorities of the international development sector.

In the 1960s and 1970s, international development donors placed greatest emphasis on big infrastructure projects. The mistakes made in such projects then led to a focus on small, intermediate technologies in the 1970s and 1980s. When the perception became that 'Africa is littered with wells and pumps that don't work', the focus in the 1980s and 1990s moved more to the social dimensions of technology. International development thinking moved on to a 'rights-based' approach in the 1990s, which led to a focus on the Millennium Development Goals, good governance and international partnerships in the last ten years. Many of the managers and policy-makers in the international development sector today were educated at a time when engineering was 'out of fashion'. Engineering and engineers have therefore been sidelined in many organizations and projects.

It is in this context that engineers began to establish their own international development organizations. EWB groups have been effective at alerting the engineering profession to the challenge of international development. More recently, several EWB groups are showing success at alerting the international development community to the importance of engineering once again. There are early signs that EWB groups are beginning to influence how the rest of the international development sector thinks and works. Part of the problem has been the general lack of public understanding of what the engineer does, and what can be offered by different types of engineer. Understanding continues to improve as EWB groups now engage with aid agencies. But a key problem has been the skill set of the engineer themselves; they have been regarded as offering technical skills only. EWB members who interact with aid agencies are demonstrating that a new generation of engineers is emerging – engineers who understand the social, political, economic and environmental dimensions of their work, who can engage in participatory processes and who design for capabilities (i.e. designing for what is to be achieved, rather than how it is achieved). The problems of, for example, aid agencies building schools without an engineer being involved, and the possible consequences of unsafe structures, will slowly be addressed as understanding and cooperation improve.

It is worth noting that each EWB group can take a different approach to their development work. This is seen most significantly, and not surprisingly, in the different approaches of EWB groups in developed countries and those in developing countries. The common ground, however, is that each EWB group has established some way to address the problems of the capacity of communities to absorb engineering assistance. For example, EWB-USA projects partner with community organizations over many years; EWB Spain and EWB Canada employ expatriate staff in the countries where they work; and EWB Australia works through local partner organizations identified during country programme planning. By providing a forum for engineers to learn about international development, as well as by learning from their own mistakes, EWB groups are improving the way that international development is done overall, and there is huge potential for enhanced cooperation in the future.

EWB in the context of the engineering profession

EWB groups occupy a surprising space in the engineering profession. They do not suffer from the same issues and challenges that face engineering. EWB groups are growing, and growing fast, attracting many young people and significant (or even equal) proportions of women to their memberships. Many EWB members are engineering evangelists who are passionate about their profession and who become role models for their peers, their juniors and their elders; they are also able to communicate engineering very effectively to the public. Despite the huge number of engineering organizations, the institutional frameworks that guide the engineering profession are not set up to respond adequately to multi-disciplinary issues or inter-disciplinary operations, let alone global challenges. For EWB groups, however, these challenges are their reason for being, and they are able to work in a modern, inter-disciplinary manner with ease.

EWB members often have a strong iconoclastic attitude, but find welcoming and supportive homes in engineering professional institutions. Engineering institutions frequently look to EWB groups for their energy and enthusiasm, and provide tremendous support in terms of 'voice' and credibility in particular; they are able to offer strong platforms for advocacy inside and outside the engineering community. It is a very positive sign that traditional engineering institutions want to embrace EWB groups and their ideas. Yet, EWB groups must be careful that they do not become fig leaves for broader change; most EWB groups would not need to exist if established engineering institutions were responding meaningfully – or indeed at all – to poverty and suffering.

Whilst many countries report declines in their numbers of engineers, membership of EWB groups has grown very rapidly.

🎧 *Engineering can reduce the hard work of carrying water for many women and children.*

This is of course partly because they are starting from a low base. Still, several EWB groups around the world have memberships of well over 3,000 fee-paying members, which represent a good proportion of the total number of engineers in their countries.

Women can face particular difficulties when working in engineering. In EWB groups, however, gender issues in their own memberships rarely need to be considered; they effortlessly attract and retain many women engineers. Engineers Without Borders UK, for example, estimates that about 45 per cent of its members are women, which is much higher than in most British university engineering classes and higher than the national figures for new professional engineer registrations (9.8 per cent were women in 2007). In 2009, all six of EWB-UK's main programme areas were led by women, whilst its nine support and community functions were led by a fair mix of men and women. Examples such as these are the norm for EWB groups.

International development and poverty reduction offer a profound motivation for people to get involved and stay involved in engineering. Stories of engineers – of the engineer sat next to you in the office or sat next to you in the lecture hall – working on projects to provide water and lift people out of poverty are very powerful. They clearly depict the true nature of engineering's relationship with society. They demonstrate that engineers make a difference, not by providing a cure but by providing a capability. In many ways, such stories show the human face of engineering. For children and young people, stories from young engineers about their projects in poor communities can touch hearts and minds in a way that the biggest bridge or the longest tunnel never can. They offer people-sized engineering, where projects are at a scale that they can identify themselves with – projects that they can see themselves doing in the future.

The way that EWB groups organize their work is strikingly different to that of the conventional engineering profession. The engineering profession organizes its work around historic and intellectual divisions: civil engineering, mechanical engineering, electrical engineering or structural engineering to name but a few. What does that mean to 'real people'? How many non-engineers know what a 'civil engineer' does? How many non-engineers can explain the difference between an electrician and an electrical engineer, or a mechanic and a mechanical engineer? EWB groups organize their work around the purpose of their projects, around themes that mean something to people: water, sanitation, shelter, energy, food, transport, communications and so on. Most groups have not planned this specifically, but rather it just happened naturally and is unrelated to the type of engineering education of the people involved. For this reason, EWB members are exceptionally good at working in a multi-disciplinary and inter-disciplinary

manner. A wind turbine project might require a mechanical engineer, electrical engineer, structural engineer, aeronautical engineer, electronic engineer, civil engineer and materials engineer to work together. Or it might be done by a member of Engineers Without Borders.

EWB in the context of engineering education

The changes in engineering education over the past ten or fifteen years have created the breeding ground for new EWB groups. As part of their degree courses, undergraduate engineers now have to learn about sustainability, ethics, management, public speaking, basic economics, teamwork and even foreign languages. Many undergraduate engineers have the opportunity to take classes in other areas such as science, business, architecture or even art. Modern engineering education is responding to the demands of *industry* in the twenty-first century. But engineering education is not responding to the demands of *people* in the twenty-first century.

Global problems, and poverty in particular, are not given adequate attention. The technologies being taught in universities – steel and silicon, concrete and combustion – are the technologies that are causing global problems such as climate change, and are taught without giving adequate attention to alternatives. Perhaps the people that engineering education is responding to least effectively are the students themselves. Many young people take engineering at university because they want to make a difference, and to be able to do or to build something. But for the first years of their courses, many students do little else but study mathematics. In this void, EWB groups have thrived. They have offered hands-on learning through practical training courses and real engineering projects in which students can play a key role.

Members of Engineers Without Borders groups are not simply the 'hippies' or the 'bleeding hearts' of the engineering community. Compassion is certainly a characteristic of EWB members, but so too is engineering rigour. EWB groups tend to attract the best and the brightest engineering students who, despite long hours volunteering, frequently achieve higher than average grades. Many of the young graduate engineers who receive professional awards for exceptional engineering work with their companies are EWB members, who volunteer in their spare time. EWB members are highly sought after when they graduate from university, particularly amongst leading engineering consultancies. Despite this evidence that EWB groups attract 'hard-core' engineers, there still remains a challenge to persuade many academics that 'development engineering' and appropriate technologies are academically rigorous subjects and not 'soft options'. This is a challenge when trying to introduce such topics to the curriculum, but attitudes are changing and EWB groups are working hard in this area. For example, EWB Spain helped to establish an entire Master degree course entitled 'Engineering for Development

Cooperation' at the Open University of Catalonia in Barcelona – a course that the university has now taken on itself. The University of Colorado at Boulder has recently established the Mortenson Centre in Engineering for Developing Communities, with the founder of EWB-USA as its director.

EWB in the context of society

It is interesting to reflect on the growth spurt in the Engineers Without Borders movement. Since the year 2000, more than fifty EWB groups have been established. In many developed countries, EWB groups were set up by university engineering students who were perhaps influenced by fundamental shifts in their societies. This new generation of engineers grew up hearing about famine in Ethiopia, Live Aid, the hole in the Ozone Layer, acid rain, the Rio de Janeiro Earth summit, the Rwandan Genocide, global warming, the Jubilee Debt campaign, the Millennium Development Goals, the rise of Fair Trade, climate change, the Indian Ocean Tsunami and the Make Poverty History campaign. They started university at the start of a new millennium. They never knew a world without the Internet, fast and affordable international travel and mobile communications. Their social networks spanned the globe. They might well have travelled to different continents and seen and experienced how difficult cultures live. They had, arguably, a much more global worldview than the generations of engineers who came before them, and they were very concerned about global issues. Their new perspective demanded a new engineering expression, and many chose EWB.

With privatization and liberalization, engineering had become less focused on the public good and more focused on private profit. Governments and engineering firms seemed not to be addressing human development for all, and focused more on economic or commercial development. Aid agencies did not want 'enthusiastic amateurs' and – not recognizing the potential in this new generation – were slow to engage meaningfully with university-level volunteers. So where did these young engineers turn to if they wanted to get involved in global issues? They chose EWB.

Graduate and young professional engineers wanted jobs that not only paid well but that were intellectually stimulating and personally fulfilling as well. When they could not find ways to help people as part of their day job, they turned increasingly to the voluntary sector and to EWB groups in particular. Where an EWB group did not exist, these professional engineers set one up. Certainly, voluntary groups cannot work on the scale of companies – the scale that is required to meaningfully meet global challenges. But, one project at a time, EWB members realized that they could make a difference. It seems bizarre that so many engineers put their hopes and dreams into such tiny organizations as EWB groups when, for most of their professional lives, they would work in large firms that have far more scope and capacity to drive change. But they chose EWB.

Conclusion

Engineers Without Borders represents a new renaissance in the engineering community. With a global agenda and an appetite for change, EWB groups could not come at a better time. The present role of engineering in development policy seems to be of economic importance only, and that it is a key path of innovation and therefore economic growth. The economic imperative of engineering is sound, but international development efforts – in good governance, transparency, anti-corruption, health treatments and primary education – are frequently crippled because basic needs are not being met by engineers. What is needed is a new 'development decade' where a new generation of engineers who understand global issues and social dimensions, play an active role. The signs are that EWB groups are helping to bring about this change in understanding.

For the engineering profession, EWB groups offer ideas and concerns that are profoundly motivating for young engineers, professional engineers and school children alike. The idea of helping people, the joy of hands-on engineering, the ability to see clearly the difference that an engineer can make, the adventure of helping solving global problems. EWB groups embody the very purpose of the engineering profession and will, for many, come to define the engineering profession.

The EWB movement was started by students in universities and, as such, has had a very close association with the problems and potential of engineering education. As EWB groups begin to demonstrate the value of studying technology in development, perhaps in the future their role will change. Many countries suffer from an extreme shortage of engineers.

() *Bamboo wall reinforcement reduces the risk of collapse in earthquakes and saves lives.*

© Stephen Jones, EWB-UK

Yet how is a country supposed to develop without engineers? This lack of capacity is arguably the single biggest barrier to development faced by many developing countries as it lies at the very root of how progress is made. EWB members are already role models for their peers and the next generation in their own countries, so perhaps by extension they will become more involved in engineering education in the countries that need engineers the most – to help inspire more and more young people into engineering in the future and to help build a better world.

Young engineers are attracted to EWB groups as a means of tackling the global problems that they have heard about as they have grown up. A key decision remains, however, after graduation. As new graduate engineers and active EWB members they face a dilemma: should they work for an engineering company and become 'an engineer' or should they work for a charity and practice engineering to help lift people out of poverty? This should be a false choice. It is no longer plausible for engineers working in huge companies to come to tiny organizations such as EWB groups to find a way to 'save the world'. Companies and governments will have to change their modus operandi and find ways to fight poverty, or they risk losing leading engineering talent.

Finally, a key challenge for Engineers Without Borders groups themselves remains. EWB groups and their members are frequently described as having 'huge potential'. Their challenge over the next decade is to realize that potential. They need to

change the game in international development, in the engineering profession, in engineering education and in society at large. They have had a good start, but more remains to be done.

4.4.3 Engineers Against Poverty

Douglas Oakervee

The United Nations Conference on Environment and Development held in Rio de Janeiro in 1992 marked a turning point in public expectations of the private sector. Companies had always contributed to development through promoting growth, creating jobs, supporting enterprise development, transferring technology and paying taxes, but participants at the Rio 'Earth Summit' recognized that 'business as usual' was a wholly inadequate response to the enormous global challenges that we faced. Business, it was agreed, could and should do more.

It was against this background that independent non-governmental organization Engineers Against Poverty (EAP) was established a few years later. Its name captures the desire amongst many in the profession to place science, engineering and technology at the forefront of efforts to fight poverty and promote sustainable development. Supported by the UK Department for International Development and some of the UK's leading engineering services companies, we began to

↻ Schoolchildren celebrate a new bridge in Soweto East, Kenya, avoiding the open sewer below.

© Joe Mulligan, EWB-UK

build a programme of work aimed at delivering practical solutions that would help transform the lives of poor people.

Building a new NGO from scratch is time consuming and difficult. Forging relationships, establishing credibility and developing a coherent programme takes time and this has to be balanced against the understandable impatience of supporters to see tangible results. Ten years on and we have created a highly innovative programme of work across the extractive industries, public sector infrastructure and engineering education, which is delivering a development impact beyond what would usually be expected of a small organization with modest operating costs. We have also learned four key lessons that we believe serve as a template for mobilizing the engineering industry in the fight against global poverty.

Firstly, solutions are needed that can rapidly go to scale. Poverty is a tragedy in progress for the estimated 40,000 people who die each day of poverty related illness. Aid and debt reduction are important in averting this tragedy, but extreme poverty can only be eliminated through sustainable economic growth and the creation of millions of decent jobs. The impact of corporate philanthropy is negligible. It is the enterprise, skills and core business activities of engineering services companies and their clients where there is most potential. Consider for example that oil and gas majors spend approximately US$500 through their supply chains for every US$1 spent on community investment. Innovative business models are needed that harness this economic power and the core competencies of industry to rapidly scale-up business solutions to poverty.

Secondly, whilst it inevitable that tensions will sometimes exist between business and society, strategies for development must focus on their interdependence. In practice this means developing mechanisms that align the commercial drivers of companies with the development priorities of the countries where they work to create 'shared value'. EAP's work in the extractive industries for example, has shown that contractors who invest in developing suppliers from low-income communities secure cost efficiencies for themselves, whilst creating jobs and drawing local companies into the formal economy. The principle of creating shared value could form the basis for a new contract between business and society.

Thirdly, for most companies, the successful alignment of commercial and social priorities and the creation of shared value on a large scale will require a fundamental reappraisal of their business systems and procedures. This includes, importantly, the incorporation of a social dimension into business development, risk management and supply chain development. The management of social issues cannot be delegated to the public affairs or corporate responsibility teams. They are issues that go to the heart of the business

model and challenge the conventional wisdom of corporate strategy. Partnerships with NGOs can be very effective in helping companies to think through these opportunities and identify the most appropriate development challenges for them to take on, and from which they can derive most commercial benefit.

Finally, companies should position themselves to shape the environment needed for good governance and private sector development. There are a growing number of examples of companies working together to tackle development challenges that no single company can resolve alone. The UK Anti-Corruption Forum (UKACF) for example brings together many of the UK's leading engineering services companies and professional bodies to develop industry led actions to fight corruption in the infrastructure, construction and engineering sectors. It represents over 1,000 companies and 300,000 professionals, and demonstrates how the engineering industry can organize itself to articulate an informed and responsible voice in governance debates. An international network of similar initiatives could provide a significant boost to efforts in fighting corruption in the construction industry.

These lessons and our practical experience provide us with an opportunity to provide high-level strategic advice to our partners. We are, for example, a key policy adviser to Price WaterhouseCoopers who run the Secretariat of the Construction Sector Transparency (CoST) initiative for the Department for International Development.[19] We are also working with the UK Institution of Civil Engineers to modify procurement procedures in public sector infrastructure.[20] And we are collaborating with engineering consultancy Arup to develop ASPIRE – a sophisticated software tool for maximizing the sustainability and poverty-reduction impact of investments in infrastructure.[21] This is how we achieve our developmental impact. We reduce our overheads to a bare minimum and focus on strategic interventions with key partners in government and industry that deliver practical solutions.

It was recognized in the Rio 'Earth Summit' that the principal responsibility for eliminating poverty rests with government, but that business had an increasingly critical role to play. Our partnerships demonstrate how it can fulfil this role and simultaneously strengthen its competitive position. Our efforts form part of a broader effort to mobilize engineering and technology to help build a more stable, civilized and prosperous global environment for all people.

Women carrying stones, India.

---

19 See http://www.constructiontransparency.org

20 Wells, J. *et al* (2006) Modifying infrastructure procurement to enhance social development, EAP & ICE, London.

21 For more information: http://www.inesweb.org

4.4.4 Engineers for a Sustainable World

Regina Clewlow

Engineers for a Sustainable World (ESW) is a non-profit engineering association committed to building a better future for all of the world's people. Established in 2002, ESW has grown rapidly and now includes thousands of members across the globe and collegiate chapters at leading engineering institutions. Founded by Regina Clewlow (then a student at Cornell University) and Krishna S. Athreya (then director of women and minority programmes at Cornell), ESW is attracting new and diverse populations into engineering and mobilizing them to develop practical and innovative solutions to address the world's most critical challenges.

ESW's vision is a world in which all people enjoy the basic resources to pursue healthy, productive lives, in harmony with each other and with our Earth. In pursuit of this vision, ESW mobilizes engineers through education, training and practical action, building collaborative partnerships to meet the needs of current and future generations.

ESW's primary goals are to:

- Stimulate and foster an increased and more diverse community of engineers.

- Infuse sustainability into the practice and studies of every engineer.

A growing network

ESW collegiate chapters raise awareness in universities and local communities about critical global issues and the role of engineering and technological solutions. They mobilize the engineering community to participate in broader community events (such as Earth Day and World Environment Day) showcasing engineering solutions that are creating a sustainable future. ESW chapters also coordinate general outreach programmes designed to increase interaction between engineering college students and school students, focused on the theme of sustainability.

Within the engineering community, ESW chapter programmes on campuses aim to increase engineers' understanding of broader societal challenges, and organize them to take action. ESW chapters host speakers through lectures and seminars on topics such as climate change and global poverty. Each year, ESW has an annual conference bringing together hundreds of engineering students, faculty, and industry professionals for a dialogue on global sustainability and the critical role of engineering solutions. Across the United States, ESW chapters play an active role in 'greening' their campuses by initiating pro-

grammes to reduce energy and water consumption in college dormitories and off-campus student housing, coordinating food waste composting from dining facilities, and converting university-based transportation fleets to alternative fuel sources. ESW chapters also play a key role in initiating courses through which students gain hands-on, real-world engineering experience on how to increase access to clean water, sanitation and energy in the world's poorest nations.

Educating the next generation of engineers

Since its inception, ESW has focused on initiating and disseminating transformative engineering curricula that integrates sustainability and sustainable development. More than twenty sustainable engineering courses have been started by ESW faculty and student members at leading engineering institutions. In addition, ESW collegiate chapters are now beginning to establish sustainable engineering certificates and minor and Master degree programmes at their institutions. However, such courses are still not seen as 'mainstream', so ESW continues to focus on developing, improving and disseminating educational materials in order to promote transformational change in the engineering community.

With the support UNESCO and the National Science Foundation, ESW has hosted national and international workshops on engineering education for sustainable development. In 2005, ESW hosted a workshop held in conjunction with its Annual Conference at UT Austin, and in 2006, ESW hosted a workshop at UNESCO headquarters in Paris, France. Both events aimed to facilitate a global dialogue, to exchange experiences and best practices, and to mobilize engineers to address lack of access to clean water, sanitation and energy in developing nations.

In February 2007, ESW co-hosted a National Science Foundation (NSF) planning workshop to support and encourage academic institutions to build effective multidisciplinary programs that integrate business, engineering and sustainability. As the lead engineering institution on the workshop planning committee, ESW identified and reported key sustainability-oriented research and educational initiatives within engineering.

Although through ESW and its collegiate chapters significant progress to integrate sustainability and sustainable development into engineering curricula has been made, these programs have not made it into the mainstream of engineering education. ESW continues to focus on developing, improving and disseminating such educational materials in order to facilitate transformational change in the engineering community.

Meeting the needs of the world's poorest billion

Since the organization was founded, ESW has coordinated the Summer Engineering Experience in Development (SEED)

Program. Through the SEED Program, teams of students and professionals spend between two and three months working on projects that increase access to technology for the world's poorest.

An important characteristic of ESW SEED projects is the collaboration with local technical partner organizations to facilitate knowledge transfer, development of locally-appropriate solutions, and project sustainability. ESW seeks locally-appropriate solutions and ensures project sustainability – transcending failed models of international development where engineering projects typically relied on imported materials and expertise – by partnering with local agencies that have basic technical knowledge.

ESW's SEED Program has resulted in life-changing experiences for its participants. More than half of the volunteers who have participated in ESW's SEED program abroad describe the experience as overwhelmingly positive, with comments such as 'I felt for the first time that I had applied myself completely to solving a real world problem. I was thrilled to apply my engineering education to the immediate improvement of living standards' and 'this was the best experience of my life, not only personally but academically' and 'this experience will no doubt influence my living and working decisions for the rest of my life.'

Students who participate in SEED return to their colleges with a renewed sense of passion and energy for the engineering profession, and their career destinations after university testify to this.

© UNESCO/ F. Pinzon Gil

⋒ *Tents housing schools, Kashmir.*

4.5 Engineering studies, science and technology and public policy

4.5.1 Engineering studies

Gary Lee Downey

What has it meant to be an engineer working in international development, across different territories, at different periods in time, and in association with different kinds of organizations? How have visions of development and progress contributed to the formation of engineers? How have engineers come to see themselves as engaged in projects of societal service that extend beyond their countries into territories and communities often alien to them? Who has tended to make such moves and who has not? Where and for whom have engineers worked? What has that work comprised, and who has benefited? How, in particular, have engineers come to claim jurisdiction over technological developments, and how have these claims varied across time and territory?

At the same time, what has led engineers to be relatively invisible in activities of international development compared with scientists and economists, given that the numbers of participating engineers far exceed the numbers from both other groups? When have engineers achieved great visibility in development projects, and under what conditions? What are likely future trajectories for engineering education and engineering work, both within and beyond projects of development and progress?

These are the types of questions related to development that are of interest to researchers in Engineering Studies. Asking these questions is important because they call attention to the dimensions of international development work that extend beyond technical problem-solving. Engineers involved in development projects must always deal with both the technical and non-technical dimensions of such work. Yet the focus

on technical problem-solving in engineering education may not prepare them to do so well. Indeed, it may actively dissuade engineers from considering anything beyond technical problem-solving to be important.

Research and teaching in engineering studies can help. Its key contribution to engineers involved in international development is to help them see and understand that technical problem-solving always has non-technical dimensions. It matters, for example, who is involved in decision-making, as well as who benefits from the engineers' contributions to development work, or who does not. It also matters how engineers carry their forms of knowledge with them into engagements with co-workers, including both engineers and non-engineers, within and beyond project organizations.

Engineering studies is a diverse, interdisciplinary arena of scholarly research and teaching built around a central question: What are the relationships among the technical and the non-technical dimensions of engineering practices, and how have these relationships evolved over time? Addressing and responding to this question can sometimes involve researchers as critical participants in the practices they study, including, for example, engineering formation, engineering work, engineering design, equity in engineering (gender, racial, ethnic, class, geopolitical), and engineering service to society.

The lead organization for engineering studies research and teaching is the International Network for Engineering Studies (INES).[22] INES was formed in Paris in 2004. Its mission is threefold:

22 Go to: http://www.inesweb.org

1. To advance research and teaching in historical, social, cultural, political, philosophical, rhetorical, and organizational studies of engineers and engineering.

2. To help build and serve diverse communities of researchers interested in engineering studies.

3. To link scholarly work in engineering studies to broader discussions and debates about engineering education, research, practice, policy, and representation.

The lead research journal in the field is *Engineering Studies: Journal of the International Network for Engineering Studies.*[23] published three times yearly.

Researchers and teachers in engineering studies are sometimes engineers with advanced degrees in the social sciences and humanities. Sometimes they are social researchers and teachers interested in engineering education and practice. Sometimes they are practicing engineers interested in the non-technical dimensions of engineering work. The work of engineering studies researchers can be found most frequently at the annual meetings and publications of the Society for Social Studies of Science, Society for History of Technology, and other outlets for interdisciplinary science and technology studies.

One reason the practices of engineers are important to study is because they constitute examples of knowledge put in service to society. Studying how, when, where, and for whom engineers serve is crucial to understanding how engineering work has contributed to the emergence of key dimensions of contemporary life. To what extent, for example, has engineering education and work been focused on developing, maintaining, and extending the territorial boundaries of countries? Furthermore, studying the formation, everyday work, and career trajectories of engineers in the context of broader societal visions and initiatives offers insights into how evolving forms of engineering knowledge have become linked to varying forms of service. The participation of engineers in development work constitutes a case in point.

Over the past half-century, the participation of engineers in international development has expanded dramatically.[24] Engineers have participated in the full range of development activities, including large infrastructure development and small-scale community development, state-led development and non-governmental humanitarian work, and, most recently, emergent forms of sustainable development. How have engineering practices working within visions of devel-

opment contributed to transformations in communities, societies, and landscapes? What are the implications of such transformations? To what extent, for example, has engineering development work achieved development?

Publication of this volume as the first ever international engineering report is stark testimony of the fact that millions of engineers working in the world today serve in relative obscurity. This is true not only for arenas of international development but for all areas of engineering work. Science has long been understood in popular thinking as the key site of knowledge creation, with technology the product of its application. In this way of thinking, engineers have been located downstream of scientists, between science and technology. Engineering is the product of applied science.

In the case of development work, engineers have often appeared to be mere technicians of larger intellectual and societal projects imagined and run by others. The relative obscurity of engineers is especially pronounced as political leaders have often defined the goals of development projects while scientists have gained responsibility for defining their means and economists their metrics, leaving engineers to implement what others have conceived. The absence of engineers is striking, for example, at the Science and Development Network.[25] One of the largest online resources on development work, the Network 'aims to provide reliable and authoritative information about science and technology for the developing world.' Engineering, although a key dimension of every topic covered by the network, is rarely discernible. The relative invisibility of engineering in development vis-à-vis science perhaps reached a new low in 2007 when a science magazine editorial announced that, in October 2007, 'more than 200 science journals throughout the world will simultaneously publish papers on global poverty and human development—a collaborative effort to increase awareness, interest, and research about these important issues of our time.'[26] The editorial did not mention engineers or engineering. No such effort has been attempted by engineering publications.

Yet engineering work is not captured by the image of applied science. Engineers make only selective use of findings from the so-called basic sciences. The engineering sciences differ from the basic sciences by actively seeking demonstrable gain. Once one begins to think about how engineers use the sciences along with other tools, it no longer makes sense to devalue or ignore the actions and agencies of engineers, not only in development work but also technological developments in general.

23   Go to: http://www.informaworld.com/engineeringstudies

24   For an overview, see Lucena, Juan C. and Jen Schneider, 2008, Engineers, Development, and Engineering Education: From National to Sustainable Community Development, *European Journal of Engineering Education*. Vol. 33, No.3 June 2008, pp. 247–257.

25   For more information: http://www.scidev.net

26   Borlaug, Norman E. 2007.Feeding a Hungry World, *Science*, Vol. 318, No. 5849, pp. 359.

◌ *Hoover Dam, USA.*

Furthermore, an increasing number of academic fields are now claiming jurisdiction over technological developments. Consider, for example, all the scientific fields involved in water treatment. Yet few scientific fields frame their contributions explicitly within larger projects of service to society, as engineers have long done. Engineers are playing crucial roles, yet these are frequently hidden.

Judgements about the value of specific engineering projects to the welfare of diverse stakeholders or the health of ecosystems span a broad spectrum. Conflict and disagreement are perhaps more the rule than the exception. Precisely for this reason, it is both important and revealing to investigate the conditions of service under which engineers have contributed to development visions and projects in the past, are contributing in the present, and will likely contribute in the future. Have engineers contributed to their own relative obscurity, for example, when they attempt to enforce boundaries between the technical and non-technical dimensions of the problems they encounter, claiming exclusive jurisdiction over the former while leaving the latter to others? To what extent have engineers understood their service as blind technical support that assigns larger societal and political responsibilities to others? At the same time, what have been the specific circumstances and conditions through which engineers have successfully achieved great visibility in development work? How have such

people understood the connections, or tensions, between the technical and non-technical dimensions of their identities?

Examining the intellectual and social contents of engineering service as well as the concrete conditions under which engineers have actually worked can also provide crucial insights into how development projects have emerged, including how and why particular forms of engineering design, analysis, and construction have succeeded or failed in specific cases, and from whose points of view. It can be worthwhile, for example, to examine specific efforts such as those by the 1960s group Volunteers in Technical Assistance (VITA). In what ways and to what extent might VITA engineers have brought to international development efforts specific expectations drawn from their education in new science-based curricula and/or employment in newly emerging defense industries? [27]

Engineering studies researchers tend to ask difficult historical, philosophical, social, cultural, political, rhetorical and organizational questions. Consider, for example, the construction of a hydroelectric dam, a typical project in the early history of development. Engineering studies researchers are interested

27 Pursell, Carroll. 2001. Appropriate Technology, Modernity and U.S. Foreign Aid. In: *Proceedings of the XXIst International Congress of History of Science*, Mexico City, 7–14 July, pp. 175–187.

in the specific historical convergences that brought engineers together with other practitioners and stakeholders and put their various forms of knowledge into contact with one another. How did these projects emerge and what contributed to their broader significance? Who had stakes in their development and outcomes? What were the outcomes, and for whom?

It makes a difference to the status of engineering work that many hydroelectric dams in the United States were built during the New Deal as means to revitalize economic growth and employment while many hydroelectric dams in what has been called the 'developing world' were built during the geopolitical competitions of the Cold War. In the first case, the focus was on using engineers within the home country to facilitate recovery from the Depression, positioning the engineers as agents of collective welfare, sometimes even granting them heroic status (e.g. Hoover Dam).[28] In the second, the project was often an explicit negotiation between political and economic leaders in two different countries, one agreeing to accept technological assistance in exchange for political and economic commitments, and the other using engineering to extend and maintain political and economic influence through assistance. In this latter case, the meaning of engineering work was frequently more ambiguous, depending upon who was making the judgement. Yet even in the first case, the dominant accounts of collective benefit and heroic achievement do not take account of the perspectives of those for whom hydroelectric power counted as a loss rather than a gain. It is probably safe to say no development project exists in which every stakeholder wins or finds their interests and identities affirmed. For those who do not benefit or who contest its larger societal missions, the image of development can be a distinctly negative one.

Another type of question is philosophical. How do engineers involved in development projects define and understand the engineering content of their work, whether explicitly or implicitly? And how and why does that matter? For example, the achievement of effective low-cost, low-tech solutions for the removal of arsenic – a more recent type of development project – may be the product of engineers actively exchanging knowledge with members of local communities, non-governmental organizations, and other fields of technical expertise, e.g. chemistry. Might engineers who are trained to see themselves primarily as technical problem solvers find themselves at a disadvantage in effectively engaging groups who understand and define problems differently than they do? Might they be reluctant, if not actively resistant, to critically engaging the larger contexts within which they undertake development work? Would it make a difference if engineers emerged from degree programs and other mechanisms of formation expecting to work with people who define problems differently than they do, including both engineers and non-engineers? Would it make a difference if they emerged with a commitment to engage in collaborative activities of problem definition and solution?[29]

Social, cultural, and political questions about engineers and engineering often blend together, with different researchers calling attention to distinct dimensions. One common interest is in engineering identities, i.e. how participating in engineering projects contributes to reorganizing and restructuring the identities of engineers. Continuing our examples, one might ask: how did construction of the Aswan High Dam contribute to furthering or transforming the identities of both Soviet and Egyptian engineers? Did the Soviet engineers understand their work as action in the service of socialism, sharpening a focus on successful completion of the dam itself? Did completion of the dam enhance a sense of nationalism among Egyptian engineers, stimulating further interest in engineers and engineering education across Egypt?[30] Or for engineers involved in the El Cajón Dam in Honduras, how might actively engaging members of local communities and possibly selecting European components and expertise have affected the standing and career aspirations of participating Honduran engineers? To what extent did they understand themselves in relation to other engineers, other technical experts, and members of the local communities they were developing their technology to serve?[31] In general, engineering studies researchers are interested both in what is included in development projects and what is left out, in whose perspectives gain authority and whose do not, and in what is ultimately emphasized and what remains relatively hidden.

In coming years, a key reason for the relative invisibility of engineers, their location and work as technical mediators, could become a crucial site for the examination of engineering work.[32] The work of mediation between science and technology has long been dismissed as a relatively unimportant

28   Billington, David P. 2006. *Big Dams of the New Deal Era: a confluence of engineering and politics.* Norman: University of Oklahoma Press.

29   For accounts of two educational efforts in this direction, see Downey, Gary Lee, Juan C. Lucena, Barbara M. Moskal, Thomas Bigley, Chris Hays, Brent K. Jesiek, Liam Kelly, Jane L. Lehr, Jonson Miller, Amy Nichols-Belo, Sharon Ruff, and Rosamond Parkhurst. 2006. The Globally Competent Engineer: Working Effectively with People Who Define Problems Differently, *Journal of Engineering Education,* Vol. 95, No. 2, pp.107–122; Downey, Gary Lee. 2008. The Engineering Cultures Syllabus as Formation Narrative: Conceptualising and Scaling Up Problem Definition in Engineering Education. *University of St. Thomas Law Journal* (special symposium issue on professional identity in law, medicine, and engineering) Vol. 5, No. 2, pp. 101–1130; and Schneider, Jen, Jon A. Leydens, Juan C. Lucena. 2008. Where is 'Community'?: Engineering Education and Sustainable Community Development," *European Journal of Engineering Education,* Vol.33, No.3, pp. 307–319.

30   Moore, Clement Henry. 1994. *Images of Development: Egyptian Engineers in Search of Industry.* Cairo: The American University of Cairo Press.

31   Jackson, Jeffery. 2007. *The Globalizers: Development Workers in Action.* Baltimore: John Hopkins University Press.

32   Downey, Gary Lee. 2005. Keynote Address: Are Engineers Losing Control of Technology? From 'Problem Solving' to 'Problem Definition and Solution' in Engineering Education, *Chemical Engineering Research and Design,* Vol. 83. No.A8, pp.1–12.

process of diffusion or circulation. But if mediation includes translation from isolated worlds of researchers into terms and means of implementation that must fit the conditions of affected communities and lives of diverse stakeholders, such work is a crucial site of creative contribution. In recent years, engineers engaged in sustainable community development have found themselves mediating the perspectives and forms of knowledge of local communities, municipal governments, national government agencies, and international organizations. Is such work external to engineering practice or an integral component?

Engineering Studies researchers thus call direct attention to the existence and presence of engineers, as well as to the technical and non-technical contents of engineering work. They seek to increase the visible presence of engineers and engineering work and to contribute to improving the abilities of engineers to both serve and critically analyse the projects they engage. Built into engineering knowledge and engineering work is a sense of altruism that has received relatively little critical analysis or attention. Preserving the work of putting engineering knowledge into service, making more visible what is both included and excluded from that service work, and enhancing the extent to which engineering service benefits widely distributed populations, including those at low-income levels, all depends upon both understanding and critically engaging what engineering is, who engineers are, and what engineers do. Engineering studies researchers aspire to such contributions, in order both to understand and to help.

Acknowledgements

The authors thank Saul Hafon, Olga Pierrakos and Matthew Wisnioski for their helpful comments on earlier drafts. Gary Downey acknowledges support from the U.S. National Science Foundation through Grant #EEC-0632839: Engineering Leadership through Problem Definition and Solution. Juan Lucena acknowledges support from the U.S. National Science Foundation through Grant # EEC-0529777: Enhancing Engineering Responsibility with Humanitarian Ethics: Theory and Practice of Humanitarian Ethics in Graduate Engineering Education.

4.5.2 Engineering, science and technology policy

Tony Marjoram

Introduction

Engineering and technology policy consists of background information, discussions and debates, policy papers, plans, regulatory frameworks, legislation and laws underpinning actions, funding prioritization and decision-making of government, governmental entities and agencies, non-governmental organizations and the private sector. Policy perspectives are particularly represented and reflected in legislation and budgetary priorities. Engineering and technology policy includes the process relating to the need for, development of and decisions relating to policy issues being considered and implemented. This process includes various power interests, actors and lobbies in government, industry and the private sector, professional organizations, universities and academia; policy research, institutes, journals and reports are an important input into the policy process, particularly in developed countries. Various models of decision-making may be used to analyse policy issues and formation, these include rational-, political- and organizational-actor models, although one person making an influential presentation to a relevant government minister can also make a difference – for example, to make reference to engineering in a national Poverty Reduction Strategy Paper. Engineers can make a difference at the personal, political and policy levels, and need to develop and share skills and experience in these areas.

Policies include political, managerial, financial, and administrative guidelines for action to achieve general or specific goals in the public and private sectors, at institutional, divisional and personal levels. Policies may be broadly distributive (e.g. public welfare, education) or constituent (executive or legislative), and more specifically regulatory or sectoral; most policies, like development plans, are sectoral in nature. Policy is usually produced as part of a 'policy cycle', which includes the following phases and processes:

- Issue presentation, identification of scope, applicability, responsibilities.

- Policy analysis, consultation, dialogue.

- Policy formulation, coordination, instrument development.

- Policy decision, adoption.

- Policy implementation.

- Policy monitoring, evaluation, review, reformulation.

While policies are goal-oriented, there may be policy 'interference' and counterintuitive, unexpected and unintended effects and impacts, hence the need for policy coherence, review and possible reformulation. Governments may have policies to promote renewable energy for example, and at the same time have high tax/import duties on solar panels. At the organizational level, executive decisions may similarly promote renewable energy but make cuts in the engineering programmes necessary to support such activities. Policies and policy frameworks are usually explicit, in the form of papers, instruments and processes, but may also be implicit; the absence of policy statements does not infer the absence of policy preferences, as illustrated by the discussion of the linear model of innovation and the basic sciences below. And while it is important to get engineering issues into policy documents and to have policies for engineering in terms of education, capacity-building and applications, such as poverty reduction, these policy statements then have to be implemented rather than left on bookshelves.

Policies and policy statements usually include reference to background, definitions, purpose, reason for the policy and intended results, scope and applicability, identification of policy actors, their roles and responsibilities, duration and modes of implementation, monitoring and response. Policies may appear as presidential orders and decrees, executive statements, or more often as 'white papers', which may follow the production of a 'green paper' for discussion and consultation. Policies need to be dynamic, monitoring results to see if intended outcome are being achieved and changing if necessary.

Engineering policy is mainly a sectoral policy, distinct from but part of the larger context of science or science and technology policy, although this may often be overlooked (as is engineering as part of the broader domain of science). At the same time, engineering policy, similar to science policy, is also part of other sectoral and broader categories such as education, research, defence, international development, industry, human resource and infrastructure policy, all of which relate importantly to engineering, as an underpinning, enabling component of the knowledge economy. This present discussion will mainly focus on engineering policy as part of science and technology policy, which is where it is mostly mentioned, with reference to broader policy contexts.

Background and history

Although there was preceding interest, the focus of attention on science policy and planning increased, particularly in the later 1940s and 1950s after the Second World War. The role of science and knowledge applications in the war – as in wars past – was emphatically apparent in such areas as electronics, materials and nuclear science, and also in new methods of design, manufacture and production, for example operations research, which later became systems analysis and then management science. Post-war reconstruction in Europe was based on industrial development and the Marshall Plan coordinated by the Organisation for European Economic Co-operation, which later became the Organisation for Economic Co-operation and Development (OECD) and has retained a focus on science-based industrial modernization and, subsequently, innovation. Interest in science, technology, industrialization and development was also reflected in the establishment of UNESCO in 1946 and UNIDO in 1966. The interest in science and technology policy and planning was spurred by the developing Cold War and hi-tech space race into the 1980s. Into

the 1980s interest in smaller government, the free-market and structural adjustment also increased however, and with it a decline in state-supported S&T policy. Interest in S&T policy developed into the 1990s and 2000s with an increasing focus on innovation. Science and technology policies have tended to be descriptive rather than prescriptive.

Reflecting governmental interest, departments of science and technology studies and policy were established in the 1960s at several universities around the world, especially in the UK and US, at the same time as increasing interest in business schools and MBAs. Most focused on science and technology studies, policy and planning, with little reference to engineering. While science and technology policy received a boost with this interest and support, the study of engineering and engineering policy remained a rather neglected area of interest and emphasis, for example, it took until 2004 for the International Network of Engineering Studies (INES) to be founded at a conference in Paris (for INES see section 4.5.1). Why this should be so is discussed elsewhere, and reflects the general public and policy awareness and perception of engineering. There are of course exceptions reflecting common usage; there are several university departments focused on science, engineering and technology policy in the US. In the UK the Policy Research in Engineering, Science and Technology (PREST) centre was established at the University of Manchester in 1977 in the Department of Science and Technology Policy, formerly the Department of Liberal Studies in Science established in 1966. In 2007 PREST merged with the Centre Research in Innovation and Competition and became the Manchester Institute of Innovation Research (MIoIR).

One of the reasons that science and technology policy has a focus on basic science rather than engineering is that it developed partly at the junction of public policy and research policy. Research policy developed in the UK from the so-called 1904 'Haldane Principle'; that decisions regarding the allocation of research funds should be made by researchers rather than politicians. R. B. Haldane later chaired a committee that became the University Grants Committee, then the Higher Education Funding Council. In 1918 the Haldane Report recommended that government-supported research be divided into specific departmental research, and more general scientific research administered by autonomous Research Councils. The 'Haldane Principle' regarding the political independence of research funding became a touchstone of research policy around the world and critique, for example J. D. Bernal argued in *The Social Function of Science* in 1939 that scientific research should be for the social good. In 1971, Solly Zuckerman (UK Chief Scientific Advisor) criticized the artificial separation of basic and applied sciences reflected in the Haldane Principle and the undue emphasis on basic science.

Another reason for the emphasis on science and research, rather than engineering and technology in science policy, relates to the fact that, in classical political science and economics, technology is regarded as residual to the main three factors of production: land, labour and capital. Science policy has been based particularly on the so-called 'linear model' of innovation; that research in the basic sciences leads, through applied research and development in engineering, to technological application, innovation and diffusion. As discussed elsewhere in this Report, this model is of unclear origin but was promoted in *Science: the Endless Frontier*, one of the first and most enduring manifestos for scientific research published in 1945 by Vannevar Bush, an electrical engineer who helped develop the atomic bomb and was responsible for the Manhattan Project. This linear thinking was reinforced by the work of Thomas Kuhn on the structure of scientific revolutions. While this conceptualization has endured with scientists and policy-makers on grounds of simplicity and funding success, many science and technology policy specialists regard the 'linear model' as descriptively inaccurate and normatively undesirable, partly because many innovations were neither based on nor the result of basic science research.

Many innovations in fact derive from engineers and engineering, and it is to the detriment of engineering that this 'appliance of science' model persists, when there is an awareness of the descriptive inaccuracies of the linear model and the fact that 'rocket science' is more about engineering than science. The model is normatively undesirable with regard to engineering because the word 'engineering' does not usually feature in discussions on 'science and technology' policy in many countries (the United States is an interesting exception, where the term 'science and engineering' is more commonly used). The notion that science leads to technology is further reinforced by the fact that the study of science and technology and associated policy is relatively recent, and the implicit assumption that the development of science is non-problematic, with little critical review of how science is created, by who, and how. The study of engineering is even more recent, and even more urgent.

Science and technology policy and international development

Interest in science and technology policy and international development began towards the end of the colonial period in the 1960s, along with the growth of institutions of higher education in developing countries, and the take-off of science and technology policy and development studies itself. This was indicated by the establishment of the Science Policy Research Unit (SPRU) and the Institute for Development Studies (IDS) at the University of Sussex in the UK in 1966, and the subsequent publication of *The Sussex Manifesto: Science and Technology to Developing Countries during the Second Development Decade* in 1970. One of the pioneers of science and technology for development was Charles Cooper who joined SPRU

and IDS in 1969 to build the new programme and produced the seminal *Science, technology and development: the political economy of technical advance in underdeveloped countries* in 1973 (Cooper, 1973),[33] and was later the founding director of UN University Institute for New Technologies at Maastricht from 1990 to 2000.

In 1963, UNESCO began to organize of a series of Regional Ministerial Conferences on the Application of Science and Technology (CAST) to Development and Conferences of Ministers of European Member States responsible for Science Policy (MINESPOLs). The first to be held was CASTALA for Latin America, held in Santiago de Chile in 1965, followed by CASTAsia in New Delhi in 1968, MINESPOL in Paris in 1970, CASTAfrica in Dakar in 1974 and CASTArab in Rabat in 1976. A second round of conferences took place from 1978, with MINESPOL II in Belgrade in 1978, CASTAsia II in Manila in 1982, CASTALAC II in Brasìlia in 1985 and CASTAfrica II in Arusha in 1987.

It was generally considered that the first round of CAST conferences from 1965–1976 addressed the goal of raising awareness of the importance of national efforts to apply science and technology to social and economic development, resulting in the strengthening and development of national science and technology policies and planning.

The second round of CAST conferences and two MINESPOL conferences appear to have had less tangible results in terms of national S&T activities. It was apparent that such meetings benefit from preparation, focus on needs, opportunities and practical actions and implementation at the national level (Mullin, J., IDRC, 1987).[34] This may relate to the fact that the two rounds of CAST conferences were interposed by the United Nations Conference on Science and Technology for Development (UNCSTD), held in Vienna in 1979, which concluded in compromise rather than confrontation after the threat of a G77 walkout. UNCSTD was the last of the large UN conferences of the 1970s, and although awareness was certainly raised regarding the issues of science, technology and development, the Conference had a focus more on funding and institutional arrangements than science, technology or development and the particularities of science policy and technology transfer. On the positive side, UNCSTD lead to the foundation of the African Network of Scientific and Technological Institutions (ANSTI) in 1980, the creation of the Eastern Africa and Southern African Technology Policy Studies Network (EATPS) and the Western Africa Technology Policy Studies Network (WATPS) in the 1980s, which merged into the African Technology Policy Studies Network (ATPS) in 1994.

---

33   Cooper, Charles. 1973. *Science, technology and development: the political economy of technical advance in underdeveloped countries*, Frank Cass, London.

34   Mullin, J., IDRC. 1987. *Evaluation of UNESCO's Regional Ministerial Conferences on the Application of Science and Technology to Development*, IDRC, Ottawa, Canada.

The CASTAsia conferences and associated networking and activities certainly also appear to have played a part in the Asia-Pacific region, especially in the rise of the knowledge-based 'tiger' economies, and also in Latin America. In addition to the above, networks established by UNESCO include the Science and Technology Policy Asian Network STEPAN (established in 1988), the Network for the Popularization of Science and Technology in Latin America and the Caribbean (Red-POP, 1990), and the Science and Technology Management Arab Regional Network (STEMARN, 1994). More recent activities include the Red-CienciA network of research and development for postgraduates in science in Central America, launched in 1998, and the Cariscience network of R&D and Postgraduate Programmes in the Basic Sciences in the Caribbean, launched in 1999. An increased focus on science policy and the basic sciences was emphasized at the World Conference on Science in 1999.

The importance of technology appropriate to local conditions of affordability, labour availability and skills, using locally available materials and energy at the smaller scale has been discussed elsewhere. Putting such 'small is beautiful' ideas into practice has been limited by policy at the macro level that favours the choice of 'conventional' but often inappropriate technologies, and ignores micro-level solutions to the problems of poverty that many people face in developing countries. Technology choice and decision-making is a vital component and consideration of science and technology policy, and in this context policies are required at macro level that promote appropriate R&D, innovation, technical support, finance and credit at the micro-level. These issues were the subject of, *The Other Policy: The influence of policies on technology choice and small enterprise development* published in 1990 (Stewart *et al.*, 1990).[35] A study of development bank lending in the Pacific Islands also indicated that most small loans (less than US$5,000) were for technologies around which many small businesses are based (Marjoram, 1985).[36] Since the 1990s, interest in micro-finance and micro-credit has certainly taken off, as evidenced by the work of the Grameen Bank and others. This interest is also reflected in the work of the Development Alternatives Group established in 1983 to promote sustainable livelihoods, and publications such as, *The Slow Race: Making technology work for the poor* (Leach and Scoones, 2006).[37] The development of policies that encourage appropriate R&D, innovation and associated technical support have been less evident however, and require continued promotion and support.

Science and technology policy in practice

As noted above, science and technology policy studies began in the 1960s with a focus on what are now the industrialized OECD countries, but not exclusively so. Various countries were stimulated to undertake S&T policy reviews at the time of the CAST conferences in the 1960s–1970s. After a lull in the 1980s, interest in S&T policy studies increased again in the 1990s and 2000s with increasing emphasis on innovation and the commercialization of R&D. Since 2000 and the Millennium Summit, interest has also increased in the role of science, technology and innovation for development, and addressing the Millennium Development Goals, especially in the context of poverty reduction and sustainable development, and most recently on climate change mitigation and adaptation (see for example the 2005 report of the UN Millennium Project Task Force on Science, Technology and Innovation).[38]

When looking at S&T policy documents from the 1960s to the present, it is apparent that a fairly similar format is used for almost all countries. This usually follows the 'Frascati Family' of manuals produced by the National Experts on Science and Technology Indicators (NESTI) group of the OECD Committee for Scientific and Technological Policy over the past forty years. These focus on R&D (the Frascati Manual, officially known as *The Proposed Standard Practice for Surveys of Research and Experimental Development* was first published in 1963, with a 6th edition in 2002), innovation (*Oslo Manual*, 3rd edition 2005), human resources in S&T (*Canberra Manual*, 1995), data on enrolment and graduation in higher education, technological balance of payments and patents. As discussed elsewhere in this Report, this approach aggregates 'scientists and engineers' and emphasizes R&D and patents as indicators of science and technology. This gives a slightly distorted view of science and engineering in developed countries, where many engineers are not involved in R&D and patenting activity, and especially in developing and least developed countries. This has serious implications for science, engineering and technology, let alone associated policy, planning and management. These issues have been recognized, and the development of appropriate indicators of science, engineering, technology and innovation is an important challenge for developing and least developed countries – where, for example, the conditions for innovation are different in terms of firms and firm sizes, S&T institutions, technological capability and absorptive capacity. Attempts to address these issues include the production of the *Bogota Manual* on the 'Standardization of Indicators of Technological Innovation in Latin American and Caribbean Countries' in 2001.

The most recent examples of science, engineering and technology policy and international development, albeit more at the

---

35   Frances Stewart, Henk Thomas and Ton de Wilde. 1990. *The Other Policy: The influence of policies on technology choice and small enterprise development*, ITDG and ATI.

36   Tony Marjoram. 1985. *Study of small development bank loans for technology in the Pacific Islands*, Institute of Rural Development, University of the South Pacific.

37   Melissa Leach and Ian Scoones. 2006. *The Slow Race: Making technology work for the poor*, Demos, London.

38   Task Force on Science, Technology and Innovation, UN Millennium Project, Lead Authors: Calestous Juma and Lee Yee-Cheong. *Innovation: Applying Knowledge in Development*. London and Sterling, Va.: Report for Earthscan Publishing, 01 2005.

implicit level, relate to the production of Poverty Reduction Strategy Papers (PRSPs), which are documents conforming to the economic prescriptions of the World Bank and IMF (Washington Consensus) prepared for the Heavily Indebted Poor Countries (HIPC) programme by the forty poorest developing countries so that they may be considered for debt relief. PRSPs are a replacement of the Structural Adjustment Programmes of the 1980s and 1990s, and partner to the national development plans produced by many developing countries since the 1960s as preconditions for overseas aid; like 'shopping lists' of possible projects for donors. PRSPs, like most national development plans, are generally prepared by economic planners and use a sectoral approach, which tend to focus on sectors and themes to the detriment of core cross-cutting considerations such as engineering. This, together with the disregard of classical economics, meant that there was little mention of science, engineering and technology in the first round of PRSPs (2000–2005), with some exceptions. This formed part of the critique of the first PRSPs, together with the broader need for enhanced national input, and a move from 'donorship to ownership'.

While many developing countries and donors recognize the importance of science, and especially engineering and technology in national development and poverty reduction, many fail to put policies that promote the development and application of science and engineering and technological innovation at the centre of systematic strategies to address such issues. Instead, there is often a focus on education, capacity-building and infrastructure which, while important, do not tackle the main problem (UNCTAD, 2007).[39] In Africa, in particular, there is a vital need for cooperation with the African Union, the New Partnership for Africa's Development (NEPAD) and the *African Ministerial Council on Science and Technology (AMCOST)* in developing and implementing Africa's Science and Technology Consolidated Plan of Action, 2006–2010.

Concluding comments

We need to develop a more holistic view of science and technology, better integrating engineering into the rather narrow, linear model focusing on the basic sciences, research and development. To do this, we need to emphasize the way engineering, science and technology contributes to social and economic development, promotes sustainable livelihoods, and helps mitigate and adapt to climate change. We also need a better integration of engineering issues into science and technology policy and planning, and of engineering, science and technology considerations into development policy and planning, PRSPs and the PRSP process in order to provide a more useful, beneficial and accurate reflection of reality.

This apparently difficult task might best be achieved by taking a more cross-cutting and holistic approach, with greater reference to the important role of engineering, science, technology and innovation in economic and social development and in poverty reduction. As the core drivers of development and as essential elements of poverty reduction and engineering, science and technology needs to be placed at the core of policies that address these issues, with particular reference to the development and application of engineering, science and technology at the national level. Development policy and PRSP documents would also benefit from a broader approach and 'evidence-based' analysis of the way engineering and science and technology drives development and reduces poverty – as the adage goes, without data there is no *visibility, and without visibility* there is *no* priority. International organizations such as UNESCO should play a more active role in the development and dissemination of such a cross-cutting and holistic approach to these issues.

4.5.3 Engineers in government and public policy

Patricia D. Galloway

Introduction

The roles that engineers have taken on go far beyond the realm of knowledge and technology. Engineering impacts the health and vitality of a nation as no other profession does. The business competitiveness, health and standard of living of a nation are intimately connected to engineering. As technology becomes increasingly engrained into every facet of our lives, the convergence between engineering and public policy will also increase. This will require that engineers develop a stronger sense of how technology and public policy interact.[40] The public is playing a much more active role in private and public projects alike, through more open planning processes, environmental regulations and elevated expectations that place greater responsibility on those executing projects.[41]

While engineers have indirectly pursued connections to public policy through lobbying organizations and their own professional engineering societies, the engagement of engineers in public policy issues has been haphazard at best. It is both the responsibility of the engineer and central to the image of the engineering profession that engineers make a better connec-

---

39 UNCTAD. 2007. Alex Warren-Rodriguez, *Science & Technology and the PRSP Process: A Survey of Recent Country Experiences*, Background Paper No. 8 to the UNCTAD Least Developed Countries Report, School of Oriental and African Studies (SOAS).

40 National Academy of Engineering. 2004. *The Engineer of 2020*, The National Academies Press, 500 Fifth Street, N.W., Washington, D.C., 20055.

41 ASCE. 2004. *Civil Engineering Body of Knowledge for the 21st Century*, American Society of Civil Engineers, 1801 Alexander Bell Drive, Reston, Virginia, 2191-4400, USA, 2004, pp. 14.

tion with public policy in the future.[42] The engineer of the twenty-first century will need to assume leadership positions from which they can serve as a positive influence in the making of public policy and in the administration of government and industry.[43] Essential public policy and administration fundamentals include the political process, public policy, laws and regulations, funding mechanisms, public education and engagement, government-business interaction and the public service responsibility of professionals.[44]

The issue

Engineers have had little to say about the strategies that are driving some of the most important initiatives introduced over the past decade, which are those aimed at maintaining a livable world. Instead, to their credit, public policy experts, economists, lawyers and environmental group leaders have led efforts to identify solutions to myriad problems, even though science and technology are at the centre of those solutions. The issues are big and global in nature and include conserving water, energy, food and habitat while fulfilling the rights and meeting the needs and desires of a growing world population. Why haven't the engineers most able to innovate and design those solutions been part of the movement from the start? What are the weaknesses and, eventually, the cost of developing public policies and designing action strategies for reform without the influence of those who are best able to develop innovative solutions and technology? To a large extent, engineers are at fault for their lack of influence. Engineers simply have not, as individual leaders or as parts of national professional groups, stepped up and actively and publicly participated in the movements that are, rightly, calling attention to the need for reform in how we use resources. Engineers have ceded the leadership roles in public forums that advocate for new policies, and seem satisfied to play a secondary role to help others carry out their ideas. While others design the strategy for reform and determine the routes nations will take, engineers seem content to build the locomotives and put down the rails. The problem of engineers being second-and third-stage implementers rather than first-stage innovators is that there can be a cost, either in too many dollars being spent on a solution or a solution that cannot deliver on the expectation when public policy is designed without adequate recognition for the technical requirements necessary for success.

The reason engineers are not known to the public partially lies in the lack of involvement of civil engineers in the public policy process. Over the years, engineers have simply not recognized

the direct link of the public policy process to their ethical and moral role, and responsibility to protect the health, safety and welfare of the public. There is often a misunderstanding and perception that, as non-profit organizations, our professional engineering societies cannot lobby or speak for the profession. There is a misconception that engineers and members of professional engineering organizations should not hold office or assist in political campaigns. Engineers have simply taken a back seat to politics and have chosen not to get caught up in the perceived 'corrupt' and 'political' process, and thus have viewed public policy as a frustrating foe.[45] However, as Pericles observed in 430 BC, 'Just because you do not take an interest in politics doesn't mean politics won't take an interest in you.'

One of the key ingredients of engineering leadership is the understanding of public policy. How many engineers realize that policies prepared by professional engineering organizations assist legislation and the lawmakers who vote on that legislation? How many realize that these engineering policies prepared by engineers behind the scenes are actually used by regulators in determining what happens to infrastructure? How many engineers recognize that it is these policies upon which codes and standards are developed and promoted for projects around the world? Public policy is not just a professional engineering organization national programme, it goes to the heart of the engineering profession and requires the energy and volunteerism at all levels of government.

Two major barriers holding back engineers in the public policy area are the lack of understanding of what their professional engineering organization can and cannot do, and the uncomfortable feeling, for many engineers, to stand up and speak out on public policy issues. In turn, public policy has not been a priority with engineers, resulting in little funding to tackle the one area that affects all engineers as well as the public: quality of life. Consequently, engineers hold fewer leadership positions and have a reduced voice with key decision-makers on critical engineering issues. Politicians therefore struggle with an overwhelming number of decisions and need sound, practical advice. If unavailable, decisions are too often made without it.[46]

The reasons why engineers are ideally suited to public policy

Engineers are trained to analyse problems and find solutions in a rational, systematic way. The entire engineering mindset is to define a problem, identify alternatives, select the best solution, and then implement it. Engineers are knowledgeable about an array of subjects including business and public

42 National Academy of Engineering. 2004. *The Engineer of 2020*, The National Academies Press, 500 Fifth Street, N.W., Washington, D.C., 20055, 2004 38.

43 National Academy of Engineering. 2004. *The Engineer of 2020*, The National Academies Press, 500 Fifth Street, N.W., Washington, D.C., 20055, 2004.

44 ASCE. 2004. *Civil Engineering Body of Knowledge for the 21st Century*, American Society of Civil Engineers, 1801Alexander Bell Drive, Reston, Virginia, 2191-4400, USA, 2004, pp. 29.

45 Galloway, P. 2004. Public Policy-Friend or Foe in Advancing the Engineering Profession, *ASCE NEWS*, January 2004.

46 Wiewiora, J. 2005. Involvement of Civil Engineers in Politics, *The American Society of Civil Engineers Journal of Professional Issues in Engineering Education and Practice*, April 2005, Vol.131.

health as well as technology. They are also people just like the rest of the population! These attributes make engineers ideally suited to advocate feasible solutions to problems faced by society. If engineers were legislating these technological solutions, public welfare would be maximized and the negative impact of technology would be minimized.[47] These opportunities will be missed if engineers continue their traditional non-involvement in politics.

The engineer is entrusted with two key attributes that are critical to public policy and politics: the training of critical thinking on solving problems as well as training as to the very activities required to develop and sustain a good quality of life; and the moral and ethical obligations that they vow as part of their professional status to protect the health, safety and welfare of the public.

The engineer as politician

Contrary to stereotypes, many politicians exhibit an extraordinary sense of commitment, dedication and enthusiasm,[48] and because engineers have an obligation to further the interests of humankind, the role of the politician is a perfect fit. In addition, because of the engineers' ethical standards, engineers will be held to higher standards than the stereotyped politicians and, as such, will be held in higher regard and enlist more trust from the public. Engineers often have superior knowledge of current scientific issues (as compared to career politicians), which can be extremely useful when debating legislation regarding, say, emission guidelines from automobiles, clean water, energy policies and air pollution mandates. Since the engineer must protect the public health, safety and welfare, this moral obligation, when combined with the engineer's ability to think and devise solutions to problems, has major benefits for government and political positions. Any person in office should strive to create legislation, public policies and economic budgets that protect the public and environment while at the same time furthering progress.[49] Engineers have a unique opportunity and responsibility to the public to promote issues such as energy, clean water and sustainability, and other key global issues especially through political involvement.

Public policy, globalization and professionalism are all key areas where engineers ought to be in the forefront. If you were to have a vision of the perfect state, the perfect city where everything worked, where engineers held the top government positions, where engineers were active in public policy, where partnerships were formed with other cities or countries, where designing and building could be accomplished on budget and schedule, where innovation was key and restoration was blended with the new, where private and public investment came together for better quality of life for all, where infrastructure is maintained and developed to meet all demands, then where would you be? Many would say 'nowhere' because this scenario would only exist in an engineer's dream.

Making the transition

Engineering focuses on actions, while politics focuses on compromise and negotiation. Engineering is a profession that focuses on finding solutions rather than winning arguments. Can the engineer make a successful transition into the political arena? The engineer's thought and decision process strives to choose one solution by identifying an existing problem. The politicians follow a similar process, but select the most beneficial alternative with focus on justification and compromise relative to their constituents' desires. The political process places more emphasis on the stakeholders.[50]

However, this is where the engineer clearly holds the advantage. While a non-engineer may make decisions that may involve compromise, an engineer can ensure that the welfare of the public is not compromised, while at the same time assuring that the decisions for the government are made to the best interest of the nation. In addition, not only is government involvement essential to the engineer's responsibility, it is essential to the survival of the engineering profession as a whole. Government is vital in upholding the standards of the profession and improving the integrity of the field. Government has the power and influence to take important projects from the drawing board to reality.[51] Funding is key to critical projects that are essential for the well-being of the public. Thus, if the engineer were to take a major role in the regulatory and legislative process, the benefits would not only be to the engineering profession but to the public to whom they serve.

If engineers are to raise the bar on their profession then public policy must be viewed as a friend and not as a foe. Engineers need to be aware of the facts of what their professional engineering organizations can do in the public policy arena, as well as what they can do as individual members. While some professional organizations are not able to endorse specific candidates for office, due to government tax status, most do and actively participate in public policy and lobbying relative to legislation regarding engineering issues. However, as an individual, an engi-

47 Gassman, A. 2005. Helping Politico-Engineers off the Endangered Species List, _The American Society of Civil Engineers Journal of Professional Issues in Engineering Education and Practice, April 2005, Vol.131, No. 2.

48 Gebauer, E. 2005. Engineers and Politics: Upholding Ethical Values, The American Society of Civil Engineers Journal of Professional Issues in Engineering Education and Practice, April 2005, Vol.131, No. 2.

49 Gebauer, E. 2005. Engineers and Politics: Upholding Ethical Values, The American Society of Civil Engineers Journal of Professional Issues in Engineering Education and Practice, April 2005, Vol.131, No. 2.

50 Gassman, A. 2005. Helping Politico-Engineers off the Endangered Species List, _The American Society of Civil Engineers Journal of Professional Issues in Engineering Education and Practice, April 2005, Vol.131, No. 2.

51 Wiewiora, J. 2005. Involvement of Civil Engineers in Politics, The American Society of Civil Engineers Journal of Professional Issues in Engineering Education and Practice, April 2005, Vol.131.

neer can run for office, participate in political campaigns and make contributions that an engineer believes are in the best interest of the nation and engineering issues.

The engineering profession more globally must also dispel the perception that engineers cannot participate in public policy or politics just because they are engineers. Engineers often feel it is impossible for them to participate in public policy or hold a political position, indicating 'I would not have a chance since it is a political appointment' or 'I do not feel comfortable in presenting or writing letters to my political representative as I do not know enough about the issue at hand.' Engineers are often respected and ridiculed for their intense beliefs and interests.

In addition to engineers being more engaged, either as politicians or aiding politicians, engineering education has to revise its curriculum to highlight the importance of public policy within the engineering profession. Engineering education has arguably moved too far into purely technical content, to the detriment of elements essential to providing the tools for engineers to become leaders, both in business and in politics. Engineering education needs to include discussions on how politics influences the engineering profession. Professors need to integrate contemporary problems, global issues and indeed politicians into the technical curriculum. This will ensure, at a basic level, that engineering graduates have a grasp of public policy issues and would demonstrate that politics is an acceptable career choice. Political involvement will allow engineers to directly enhance public welfare, the environment and the society through their specialized knowledge and skills.

Conclusion

Both policymakers and the public benefit from an understanding of and appreciation for the value of the engineer. Engineers have an obligation to participate in public policy and public awareness. To maximize engineers' effectiveness in public policy and public awareness, engineering societies should work together and leverage their resource through close association. Engineering societies, on behalf of their members, should be the advocates of the engineering profession's common viewpoints on issues important to their respective nation and the profession. Engineering societies can contribute effectively in shaping public policy and public awareness by providing a forum for team-building and liaison, sharing information through collection, analysis and dissemination, and by coming to a consensus on issues. When taking action, engineering organizations should speak with a unified voice and cooperate in their respective activities and with their resources.

Life will continue without engineering leadership if we let it. However, the results of continuing the status quo will most likely not be desirable for engineers or for the public. Key engineering leadership positions will continue to be filled by

other professionals despite their lack of understanding of technology and its issues. If engineers turn their backs to the public policy process, they put their own profession in jeopardy. As is true with most areas that require change, change can only come about from those who are willing to stand up and be heard. Engineers must take a more active role in the legislative process to ensure that legislation is truly in the interest of public health, safety and welfare.

4.5.4 Transformation of national science and engineering systems

4.5.4.1 New Zealand

Andrew West, Simon J. Lovatt and Margaret Austin

In 1926, a need for solutions to problems that were specific to New Zealand's agricultural economy stimulated the creation of the Department of Scientific and Industrial Research and, shortly afterwards, research associations that were jointly-funded partnerships between government and industry in the fields of dairy processing, leather, fuel (later coal), wheat, and later wool processing, meat processing and forestry. The Ministry of Agriculture and Fisheries (MAF) also established research facilities focusing on pastoral animal research. The contribution of universities to research in New Zealand was initially small but became significant over time. This was the shape of Research in Science & Technology (RS&T) until the late 1980s.

The New Zealand economy was highly protected before 1984, through tariffs, incentives, subsidies and other government interventions – a protection which was unsustainable when combined with the oil price shocks of the 1970s. With the election of a Labour government in 1984 came a new public management model for the whole government sector, which also affected RS&T.

First was the principle of separating policy development and advice from funding mechanisms, and both of these from the provision of services. The intention was to clarify accountability and performance criteria and to allow contestability for the provision of services.

Second was the principle that the user of a service should pay for the service. This introduced market signals to force government agencies to focus on user needs. Transaction cost analysis allowed alternative means of service provision to be evaluated rather than simply assuming that a service should be provided directly by a government department. This also led to a determination to make the provision of a service subject to a written agreement or contract, whether the service was provided by an operational department or by a separate government-owned or private entity. Based on these principles, the State Owned Enterprises (SOEs) Act (1986) transformed all the trading departments of government (electricity, postal, telecommunications, railways etc.) into companies known as SOEs.

When applied to research, the 'user pays' principle was accompanied by substantial reductions in government RS&T funding, and the DSIR and MAF had to seek commercial funds to maintain staff levels. This led to an increase in private sector funding of science agencies from under 10 per cent in 1984–85 to over 27 per cent in 1990–91, but concern grew that as research organizations sought to maximize their income, duplication and overlap was occurring. There was concern too for the survival of the research associations who were now dependent on funding allocated by the DSIR. The DSIR itself introduced some internal contestability by developing a series of science activity areas for funding allocation and reporting.

The government received a working party report *The Key to Prosperity* in 1986 and set up a Science and Technology Advisory Committee (STAC). In 1988 STAC recommended that policy development and fund allocation for RS&T be separated, that funding to all research organizations be made fully contestable over five years, that research agencies be given appropriate commercial powers and further that all government RS&T funding for science and engineering, health sciences and social sciences be allocated through a single agency. Having all research organizations bid into the same pool would allow universities to play a greater role in providing research in New Zealand and would, it was argued, bring the different research providers closer together.

A bi-partisan political agreement was reached, largely in favour of the STAC recommendations. In April 1989 the government created a Cabinet portfolio for Research, Science & Technology, a Cabinet committee with responsibility for RS&T, a Ministry of RS&T (MoRST) to provide policy advice, and a Foundation for Research, Science & Technology (FRST) to purchase RS&T. Responsibility for conducting periodic in-depth reviews of science was initially placed with MoRST but was later reallocated to FRST. A significant change from the STAC recommendations was the establishment of a Health Research Council that would fund health research separately from FRST rather than as a part of the Foundation.

As an independent agency, FRST had a board, with a chair and members appointed by the government. The board appointed a chief executive who recruited the agency's staff. The government's budget set the overall level of funding for each year against the identified priority areas for funding on advice from MoRST after consultation with stakeholders, which were conveyed to FRST every year by the Minister. This created a strategy-driven approach to RS&T direction, which was a significant change from the earlier piecemeal method. All funding was to be on the basis of contestable bids for the full research cost, rather than for marginal funding, to avoid cross-subsidization and to ensure competitive neutrality.

During 1990 there was considerable debate over key aspects of how the new system would work. Some of the research carried out by government departments was to assist them in achieving their own operational goals. A Cabinet decision was required to establish which research fell into that category and should therefore be funded from departmental appropriations, and which was 'public good' research, and should therefore be administered by FRST. The term 'public good' required clarification. It was used by government policy analysts to refer to a consumer commodity while scientists saw it as research that would have positive outcome for the public. Analysts asked why government should fund the direct beneficiaries of research, and the public wanted to know why government would consider funding research that was not good for the public. All of this created some difficulties of communication between stakeholders. These issues, along with those associated with ownership of intellectual property and priority setting and also the continued role of the DSIR and other research-focused agencies, occupied the attention of the RS&T Cabinet Committee during 1990.

The election of a national government in late 1990 continued the changes as the wave of transformation moved from investment in RS&T to its provision. Early in their term of office a decision was made to restructure the existing DSIR, Ministry of Agriculture and Fisheries and other government science agencies into a series of Crown Research Institutes (CRIs). A task group was appointed to identify the number, size and specific roles of the CRIs by 30 June 1991. In accordance with the SOE model, CRIs were to be established as corporate bodies separate from the government under their own legislation (the Crown Research Institutes Act 1992). Government ownership of the CRIs would ensure that RS&T capability remained in New Zealand, that science outputs aligned to government outcomes would be delivered to required quality, relevance, timeliness and quality constraints. In response, the task group proposed that each CRI should be broadly based on a productive sector or set of natural resources, be vertically integrated, have a clear focus that was not in conflict with other CRIs, be nationally based with regional centres, and have no minimum or maximum size. External purchasing was to be important, with 60 to 90 per cent of CRI research to be purchased by FRST, with the remainder being purchased by private companies, government departments or other funding agencies. There was a debate on whether the CRIs should

◑ *Research and development in engineering is the main driver of innovation.*

provide a dividend to government, as did the SOEs, but it was decided that financial viability and a high social rate of return should be the goals.

Ten CRIs were proposed: AgResearch, HortResearch, Crop & Food Research and Forest Research (based on primary industry sectors), Industrial Research (based on the manufacturing sector), Environmental Science & Research and Social Research (for the services sector), and Landcare Research, Geological & Nuclear Sciences, and Water & Atmospheric Research (serving these three resource sectors). CRIs would be responsible for the intellectual property (IP) they created with public funding, but this IP should be exploited by the private sector, with New Zealand's private companies being given first right of refusal to take up that IP before it was offered to overseas companies. The CRI Act (1992) structured the CRIs as companies with Boards appointed by Cabinet and accountable to the Ministers of RS&T and Finance, who together held the shares of each CRI *ex officio*. Each Board was responsible for appointing a Chief Executive and supplying an annual statement of corporate intent (SCI) to the shareholding Ministers. Board members were not to be representative of sectoral interests but were to contribute a range of skills in management and application of research while understanding and promoting linkages between the CRIs and the private sector. Responsibility for providing science input to government policy was already the responsibility of MoRST. By the 1992–93 year, 75 per cent of FRST's allocations were made through 3 to 5-year contracts and, in addition, an allocation of 'Non-specific Output Funding' (NSOF) equal to 10 per cent of the public good science funds, won contestably by a CRI in the previous financial year, was made. NSOF was to be used by CRI Boards to fund science programmes that were not explicitly directed by external priorities.

The ten CRIs were established on 1 July 1992. The CRI Boards having set out their direction in their SCIs found that their research income through FRST's public good contestable sources was inadequate to retain all of the staff, and a number of redundancies resulted. The smallest CRI, Social Research, was closed in 1995 because it did not establish commercial viability, suggesting that there was in fact a minimum practical size for a CRI. The last element relating to the formation of the CRIs was put in place in 1993 when the Crown Company Monitoring and Advisory Unit (CCMAU) was established to monitor the performance and advise and report to the shareholding Ministers of government-owned companies, including CRIs.

At the same time as the CRIs were being established, a Science & Technology Expert Panel (STEP) was appointed to advise the Minister of RS&T on longer term priorities. New Zealand RS&T had 24 areas of activity and STEP recommended how the investments in each area ought to change over time, based on the potential socio-economic importance to New Zealand, the ability to capture benefits, the R&D potential and capacity and the appropriateness of government funding for each area. STEP recommended a focus on adding value to production, increased competitiveness, diversification and nurturing of selected core competencies. These recommendations received bipartisan political support and led to a government statement. As a result, some areas of traditional research such as animal production, horticulture and forage plant production, and geological structures found their funding reduced. Setting these priorities involved difficult decisions and were described soon afterwards as showing 'the political will to set zero-sum priorities' – a situation which drew comment internationally. In an effort to relieve some of the overall funding constraints, the 1993 Budget set a target of increasing investment in R&D from 0.6 per cent to 0.8 per cent of GDP by 2005–06.

In late 1992 the universities agreed to transfer NZ$10.66 million from their NZ$100 million research funding into the public good science fund, which by then totalled NZ$260 million, in exchange for being allowed to bid into that fund on an equal basis with other research organizations. The universities retained exclusive access to the remainder of their research funds, which were seen as being related to their teaching function. By the 2005–06 financial year, 68 per cent of government R&D funding was allocated through the RS&T budget, where almost all of it was available to any organization on a contestable basis and subject to national science priorities, while another 26 per cent was allocated through the education budget where it was available only to educational institutions and not prioritized.

By 1994 both the investment and delivery of publicly-funded RS&T in New Zealand had been thoroughly restructured. The government saw that allocating all of its funds based on strategic priorities left no provision to fund untargeted basic research. In response, the Marsden Fund was established with funds to be allocated on scientific excellence, as assessed by peer-review, and open to all public or private organizations and individuals. The 1995–96 budget allocated NZ$4 million, and by 2007–08 the Marsden Fund had grown to NZ$35.5 million, or about 5.5 per cent of the government's RS&T budget.

The transformation has had some negative outcomes. The high level of contestability encouraged intense competition between research organizations. Lack of collaboration across organizations and changes in investment priority over relatively short 4 to 6-year periods resulted in uncertainty for researchers and research organizations, and loss of staff. Survival meant that senior researchers had to spend increasing amounts of time engaged in writing bids to secure funds for themselves and their colleagues.

Overall, the transformation of the New Zealand RS&T system has had positive outcomes. It increased the transparency of government investment by creating an arms-length relationship between funders and providers of RS&T. This made the decision-making process more objective, reduced the influence of personal relationships on funding decisions and improved the efficiency of RS&T investment. By 2003 the New Zealand system was, by some measures, the most efficient in the OECD – producing the most papers per US$1 million basic research expenditure and the second highest number of papers per US$1 million of total research expenditure.

There is little doubt that scientists and their administrators have been challenged by the changes, and the system will continue to evolve as multi-organizational, multi-faceted longer term funding takes root and genuine productive relationships between research agencies, including universities, develop. The system is accountable and transparent with genuine decentralization and operational authority. Research managers are free to manage flexibly and to set their own commercial targets, and recent government announcements increasing investment in research will reinforce the significance of research to New Zealand's prosperity.

For further reading:

Atkinson, J. D. 1976. *DSIR's First Fifty Years*, DSIR Information Series 115, Wellington, DSIR.

Boston, J., Martin, J., Pallot, J., Walsh, P. 1996. *Public Management: The New Zealand Model*. Auckland, Oxford University Press.

MoRST. 2006. *Research and Development in New Zealand – a Decade in Review*. Available at: http://www.morst.govt.nz/publications/a-z/r/decade-in-review/report/ (Accessed: 14 May 2010).

Palmer, C. M. 1994. *The Reform of the Public Science System in New Zealand*, Ministry of Research Science & Technology, Wellington, New Zealand.

4.5.4.2 South Africa

Johann Mouton and Nelius Boshoff

Background

The National Research and Development Strategy (2002)[52] identifies one of the priorities for the country as the development of a healthy and diverse flux of 'young people seeking and finding careers in science and engineering.' The national Department of Science and Technology's (DST) most recent Strategic Plan (2007)[53] reiterates the importance of producing more engineers as an essential contribution to various flagship programmes of the country including: an initiative around the

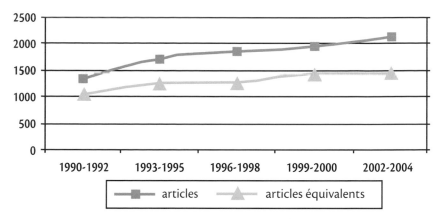

Figure 1: **Engineering output (1990–2004)**

hydrogen economy, space sciences, the Pebble Bed nuclear reactor and other major projects. The strategy document acknowledges that 'scientists, engineers and technologists remain in short supply in most sectors' and continues, 'the limited supply of scientists, engineers and technologists has also been identified as one of the constraints to the attainment of the goals of AsgiSA and is the focus of the Joint Initiative for Priority Skills Acquisition (JIPSA).' The DST has developed two strategies in this regard, the Youth into Science Strategy, and the Science, Engineering and Technology Human Capital Development Strategy for the development of a knowledge economy (DST, 2007).

The imperative to increase the supply of engineers should also be understood within the broader transformational framework of South African science. Since the transition to a democracy in 1994, this has become one of the key goals in the transformation of the national system of innovation, in at least three major ways:

1. To broaden the base of participation in science, engineering and technology by under-represented groups such as African and female scientists.

2. To ensure that knowledge production in these fields is commensurate with national socio-economic goals (such as improving the quality of life of all South Africans, to alleviate poverty, and in general to create wealth for all citizens).

3. To overcome the isolationist effects of Apartheid science by increasing international scientific collaboration, which suffered as a result of the academic boycotts in the 1970s and 1980s, and increasing the international visibility of South African science.

This contribution addresses three issues in engineering science:

---

52   Department of Science and Technology. 2002. *National R&D Strategy*. Pretoria, South Africa.

53   Department of Science and Technology. 2007. *Corporate Strategy 2007/2008*. Pretoria, South Africa.

- Research output in engineering as a proportion of overall scientific output in the country, and the broadening of the base of participation in engineering research.

- Breaking down the barriers of isolationism, increasing international scientific collaboration and shifts in the international visibility of South African engineering papers.

- Producing the next generation of engineering scientists.

Engineering research output and the broadening of participation

Research output in the field of engineering – as measured in terms of articles and article equivalents in peer reviewed journals – has increased steadily over the 15-year period between 1990 and 2004 (Figure 1) to reach just over 2,000 papers in 2004. Engineering's share of the total scientific output of the science system in South Africa over this period increased from 5 per cent in 1990 to 7 per cent in 2004 (Table 1).

As far as some transformation indicators are concerned, progress has been steady and significant. The percentage of women authors of these papers has increased from 6 per cent in 1990 to 11 per cent (nearly doubling), whereas the proportion of African authors has more than tripled, albeit from a small base. However, there is a disturbing trend as far as age is concerned with the proportion of young authors (below the age of 30) declining; conversely we witness an increase (from 26 per cent to 39 per cent) in the proportion of authors over the age of 50. This trend, which is evident in all scientific fields in the country, has major consequences for the future knowledge base of the country and requires serious and immediate attention.

Breaking down the barriers of isolationism

A standard bibliometrics measure of scientific collaboration is co-authorship of scientific papers. When analysing the fractional shares of all co-authors in the field of engineering papers, we again found a trend to greater international collaboration. In the period between 1990 and 1992 slightly more than 6 per cent of all papers were co-authored with a foreign scientist. This proportion increased to more than 14 per cent in the most recent period.

Further analysis of the origins of the foreign co-authors revealed that the majority of co-authors were from the USA, Germany, the UK and Australia in this order.

In a recent study on the citation profiles of different scientific fields, an analysis was also conducted of the international visibility of engineering papers in select fields as measured in terms of citation impact scores. In citation analysis a field-normalized citation rate of more than 1.00 is regarded as good (as it means that papers in a particular field generated more than the average number of citations for all papers in this field). The fact that none of the sub-fields of engineering achieved a score of 1.00 or higher (Table 2) means that the increased scientific collaboration reported above has not yet translated into high levels of scientific recognition. Stated differently: although South African engineers have increased their overall output over the fifteen year period since 1990, and also increased their collaboration with overseas scientists, their papers are not highly cited in the best journals in the field.

A field-normalized citation rate of 1 means that a country's citation performance is about the same as the international (western world dominated) impact standard of the field.

Producing the next generation of engineering scientists

The transformation imperative also requires that South Africa produces more engineers and engineering scientists from previously disadvantaged communities (African and female students). Table 3 presents a comparison of the graduation rates of engineering students at all qualification levels

Table 1: **South African article output in engineering and applied technologies: 1990–2004**

Year period	Engineering as % of national article output	% articles in engineering produced by female authors	% articles in engineering produced by African authors	% articles in engineering produced by authors <30 years	% articles in engineering produced by authors ≥ 50 years
1990-1992	5%	6%	3%	10%	26%
1993-1995	6%	7%	4%	9%	29%
1996-1998	6%	8%	7%	9%	36%
1999-2001	6%	10%	9%	8%	35%
2002-2004	7%	11%	10%	5%	39%

Source: South African Knowledgebase, CREST, Stellenbosch University (CREST. 2007. Human Capital and the South African Knowledgebase. Report submitted to the National Advisory Council of South Africa)

Table 2: Citation profiles for selected sub-fields in engineering and applied technologies, 1990–2004

Sub-field	Total number of ISI publications	Average number of citations per publication (excl. self-citations)	Field-normalized citation rate	% self citations	% publications not cited
Chemical engineering	980	3.75	0.85	26%	35%
Electrical & electronic engineering	831	2.23	0.56	27%	50%
Mechanical engineering	713	2.54	0.75	33%	45%
Metallurgical engineering	901	1.99	0.69	23%	56%
Materials science	1746	4.04	0.81	30%	36%

Source: Centre for Science and Technology Studies (CWTS), Leiden University

Table 3: Race-by-gender distribution of FTE graduates in engineering per qualification, 1996 and 2006

Race-by-sex group	*Professional First Bachelors Degree		Honours Degree or equivalent		Masters Degree or equivalent		Doctoral Degree or equivalent	
	1996	2006	1996	2006	1996	2006	1996	2006
African women	0.5%	11.0%	0.7%	12.4%	0.2%	4.8%	0.0%	3.8%
African men	9.3%	28.3%	14.4%	25.1%	6.1%	21.1%	0.0%	19.0%
**Coloured women	0.5%	0.8%	0.3%	1.0%	0.0%	0.8%	0.0%	0.0%
Coloured men	3.6%	4.2%	5.1%	3.7%	1.7%	2.9%	0.0%	1.9%
Indian women	0.8%	2.4%	0.3%	4.0%	0.0%	0.8%	0.0%	1.9%
Indian men	8.0%	7.3%	4.8%	8.0%	5.1%	7.0%	0.0%	6.7%
White women	7.4%	7.1%	3.0%	6.0%	9.6%	7.0%	18.9%	10.5%
White men	70.0%	38.9%	71.4%	39.6%	77.3%	55.7%	81.1%	56.2%
Total	100% (1686.02)	100% (2930.08)	100% (573.78)	100% (298.25)	100% (318.76)	100% (588.67)	100% (53.00)	100% (105.00)

Source: Own calculations based on data from the Higher Education Management Information System (HEMIS), South African Department of Education

* Professional First Bachelor's Degree = Degree qualification with a minimum duration of four years

** 'Coloured' refers to individuals of mixed race.

between 1996 and 2006. The race-by-gender analysis reveals that substantial progress has been made over this period in terms of increasing the participation and graduation rates in priority areas. Many more African female and male students as well as Indian female and male students have graduated in 2006 compared to 1996. Less progress has been made as far as coloured students are concerned. White students continue to constitute the majority of students at all four qualification levels, but their proportional share has declined significantly over this period.

Figure 2: Co-authorship patterns for engineering papers (1990–2004)

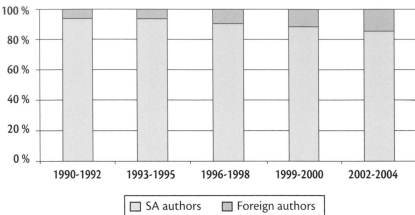

Conclusion

Engineering in South Africa has responded well to the national imperative to transform. This is evident in the demographics of its research output as well as its numbers of graduate students. It is further evidenced by its increasing internationalization, although papers in the field are not sufficiently cited. The ageing of the productive scientists in the field is a disturbing trend and requires attention. The biggest challenge remains the need to increase overall output of engineers to meet the future industrial and scientific needs of the country.

4.6 Engineering ethics and anti-corruption

4.6.1 Engineering ethics: overview

Christelle Didier

Introduction

Ethical reflection in engineering is relatively more recent than in other professions. Nevertheless, there is an area of study named 'engineering ethics' that was established as an autonomous field of academic research in the United States at the end of the 1970s, and has developed as a unique field elsewhere for example in those countries where their professional organizations have published codes of ethics. The first code was adopted in the United Kingdom in 1910 by the Institution of Civil Engineers and was followed by many others in the United States, and in other countries. However, while the codes are discussed and regularly amended in some of the associations that adopted them, in others they sometimes simply 'exist'.

While some observers question its theoretical foundations and methods, others simply doubt that the engineers' professional activities may raise specific ethical questions. Thus few seem to be surprised when philosophers and ethicists question certain aspects of technological development – technological development that is barely imaginable in the absence of engineers. Here are two established facts: first, technological development raises ethical questions; second, engineers necessarily contribute to the existence and to the deployment of technological development. For some, this confrontation compels ethical questioning in engineering. For others, the ethical challenge of techniques is not the concern of engineers.

What is the status of engineering ethics?

The concept of engineering ethics is sometimes hard to translate into languages other than English, and it is hard to understand in cultural contexts other than those developed under Anglo-American influence.

In some places, such as France, the word 'profession' can refer to any kind of job; in other countries including the United States, Canada, New Zealand, Ireland, South Africa, Australia and the United Kingdom, a profession is an area of activity whose members are provided with specific rights (or at least social recognition) and are trusted with specific responsibilities. The division of the job market between 'professions' and 'occupations' in those countries fits in with functionalist theories that have dominated the sociology of profession for decades. It also fits in with an understanding of the role and status of the professions in societies that can be traced back a long time to the early history of England.

The question 'Is engineering a profession?' can be found in all of the introductions of engineering ethics textbooks. Many scholars in this field consider it as a key question, to which the answer is affirmative. For them, engineering ethics is related to the professional status of engineering. Other scholars, also familiar to functionalist theories, consider that it is not possible to talk about engineering ethics because engineering is not a 'true' profession. These discussions about the 'essence' of engineering do not exist in countries where the demarcation between the professions and other types of activities is not an issue. Even in countries where this demarcation is meaningful, some scholars have an understanding of 'engineering ethics' (as 'professional' ethics) that is broad enough to encompass many types of ethical problems encountered at work by engineers, whether they are considered as 'true' professionals or not.

Some American scholars consider that engineering ethics rely on the fact that the engineering community has adopted standards defining what is morally permissible, which are specific to its members and go beyond the requirement of law, market and ordinary morality. They consider engineering ethics as a kind of practical wisdom in the professional practice, which can and must be transmitted. This is an interesting approach but it relies on the adoption of such standards, which is not the case all over the world. Moreover, where codes of ethics do exist, these codes often suffer from a lack of legitimacy and reinforcement procedures.

Following this approach, engineering ethics would not be so much about promoting respect of professional obligations. The focal point of engineering ethics would not be a status (a profession). Neither would it be knowledge (engineering sciences). Engineering ethics is not an ethical reflection on technical objects; it is the 'ethics of techniques'. Neither is the role of engineering ethics to evaluate technical decisions (this has been the aim of a field called 'Technology Assessment' since the 1980s). The focal point of engineering ethics is an activity. Moreover, in our engineered world, engineering ethics cannot be a preoccupation reserved for engineers only, but for all citizens concerned by the impact of engineering decisions. The expression 'engineering ethic' reminds us of the human origin of the technologies. It explicitly refers to a type of work and to a human community more in charge of this work than others: the engineers.

What is engineering?

Until recently, human social sciences and philosophy showed little interest for engineers and their practice. In the United States, the independence of the subject 'the history of technology' from 'the history of science' is very recent. Even more recently, we can mention the effort of Gary Lee Downey and Juan Lucena to attempt to trace the outlines of a specific field for engineering studies. Several characteristics of engineering are described in academic literature. Some insist on the dual nature – scientific *and* economic – of engineering; engineers are scientists but also business people because the testing of their work does not occur in laboratories but on the market place. Others underline the social dimension of this practice, which is a combination of labour and capital. The knowledge of engineers has something to do with scientific knowledge, but it remains different. Mike Martin and Roland Schinzinger have defined engineering as 'social experimentation'. Carl Mitcham insists on the fact that the product of engineering is not knowledge, but 'an object which transforms the world'.

What then are the main characteristics of engineering? Firstly, engineering takes place in a complex work environment. The agents of technical acts are engineers, but also technicians, non-technical executives and sometimes administrative and political decision-makers. Secondly, the act of engineering has the ability to transform the real world and produce consequences, which are sometimes irreversible and partially unknown. Engineering is characterized by the potential power and the partial uncertainty of its impacts, both present and future, on the natural and human environment. Finally, engineering is characterized by a central act: the act of designing. This act is a process by which objectives or functions take shape in the imagination of and plans for the creation of an object, a system or a service, with an aim to achieve the goal or function.

What about engineers' responsibility?

The moral obligations of engineers arise from the dependence of the whole of society on engineers, for certain things at least, such as the acts of technical design. Engineers have a great responsibility because if they fail to do their job with technical competency and commitment to ethics, not only can an individual be harmed or killed (as is the case if a doctor fails to do his/her job), but dozens, hundreds, even thousands of individuals may be affected.

Although the principle of proportionate care obviously forms the basis of the engineers' moral responsibility, we must keep in mind one difficulty: the phenomenon of dilution of individual responsibility in large corporations that may favor impunity. On the other hand, it may be unjust to have an individual agent bear the responsibility of the unwanted harm due to a structural failure of a collectivity. The line seems to be narrow between making the individual engineers excessively responsible and the abdication of any responsibility as a subterfuge for inaction.

In the shift from the activity to the actors, from the ethical challenges of engineering to the moral responsibility of the engineers, three questions need to be addressed: What is the moral legitimacy of engineers when taking into account the ethical issues of engineering in their decisions and actions? What is the specific knowledge that they have access to? What is their specific freedom of action within the organizations in which they are employed?

Legitimacy

For some authors, the ethical questions raised by technical development do not really concern the engineers because of its highly political dimension. Some authors are very sceptical regarding the obligations of engineers in the American codes of ethics that seek to protect the public against the bad effects of technical developments. Thus, engineers can express their point of view, with a full legitimacy, in the debates about the technical choices at different levels: within their companies, with peers and other colleagues but also with staff representatives, outside the company with local associations, standard organizations, governmental agencies, parliamentary commissions, non-governmental organizations, and so on.

Because of their position in the socio-technical system, engineers are expected to be citizens of technical democracy, more than any other member of society. Moreover, concerning their obligation within their companies or organizations, besides the role that consists of the communication of technical specifications, engineers can also (and must in certain cases) suggest alternatives to their superiors or their clients. Engineers are responsible because those who have to make the choices place trust in them.

Knowledge

The highly compartmentalized work situations of engineers and the labour division which characterizes the large corporations where they work, creates another risk-factor than just the dilution of responsibilities, such as the loss of direction and the non-retention of aims, which can result in an accepted blindness for the actors involved. There is probably a moral obligation for engineers not to be ignorant, or worse, indifferent, to the goals they are working to achieve, a well as a necessity to be able to express their positions clearly towards attaining those goals.

One cannot be held accountable for something about which one is ignorant: this has been one of the foundations of the notion of responsibility since ancient times. But there are ignorances that are more morally acceptable than others. Some people believe that the participation of engineers in decision-making is simply unknowable. Thus, their moral responsibility would be indescribable. If ethical decisions are difficult to make for engineers, ethical judgements are always possible, and they can improve.

Power

Another reason put forth for saying that there is no room for ethics in engineering is based on the engineers' status as employees, which does not afford them enough freedom. The question of the engineers' professional autonomy and of their power in decision-making in companies was studied by historians and sociologists who did not look at engineers as professionals but as workers. Although it is necessary to remind ourselves that engineers are hardly independent professionals we can wonder if their freedom of action within the organizations that employ them is as narrow as some theses on the 'proletarization' of engineers seem to suggest.

The reflections on the specificity of engineering, its impacts on the social world and its hybrid nature, social as well as technical, compel us to think of the place where the engineers exercise their power outside the most visible aspects, i.e. in the games of relationship vis-à-vis authority. Engineers are close to the 'black box' of technology; they are sometimes the princi-

pal actors of the closing of this box. But what we remember at the end are the economic and political constraints. Engineers appear then as employees among others whose only social responsibility would be to obey their hierarchy. One of the engineers' obligations may consist of, in extreme cases, blowing the whistle and taking the risk to bypass their obligation of loyalty towards their employers. But another obligation, less spectacular maybe, would consist of engineers contributing to the improvement of the structures in which they act, to turn them into more fair and responsible institutions. This point of view fits very well with Paul Ricoeur's definition of ethics as an 'aim of the good life with and for others in just institutions.'

Conclusion

Engineering ethics is a new field of contextualized ethics, far from maturity. For many years already, first in the USA, and now in some European and Asian countries, engineering ethics has started to interest a larger community of scholars. Its focus has widened from the specific nature of engineering as a 'true' profession, to the relevant characteristics of engineering as an activity at the articulation of the social, the economic, the political and the technical. We need to focus on the challenges of research in engineering ethics and stress the interest in an epistemological approach to the question, aiming at defining the outline of the activity at the heart of engineering ethics: engineering.

The most recent research works in engineering ethics also show a greater understanding of the different scales in which engineering may be questioned ethically: on the individual micro-level, on the mezzo-level of a group, a professional body or a company, and on the macro-level of the planet. Some issues related to sustainable development and corporate social responsibility, now considered as a relevant matter for engineering ethics, can merge macro and mezzo levels. Most courses in engineering ethics have long offered studying the ethical dilemmas that students could encounter in their careers. Although this approach is interesting and useful, numerous other entries can contribute to broaden the individual responsibility and ethical sensitivity of future engineers.

4.6.2 Engineering ethics: further discussion

Monique Frize

To be ethical and professional are terms that are synonymous with being an engineer. Unlike most science, the work of engineers frequently directly affects public safety and health and can influence business and even politics. The engineering profession in some countries is self-regulated, which means that it is governed by its own association of engineers. In order to join this association, engineers who apply are screened for competence, first by examining if their degree in engineering comes from an accredited program (or equivalent); if not, applicants are required to pass a number of technical exams. All applicants must complete an exam on ethical principles; and some associations require the passing of an exam on Contract Law principles. Examples of this type of regulation exist in North America (Canada and the United States). In other regions, the profession is regulated by the government, as in some countries in Europe (France and Sweden for example).

Morality is defined as what people believe to be right and good and the reasons for it. There are typical rules of conduct describing what people ought and ought not to do in various situations. Ethics is the philosophical study of morality. It is a rational examination into people's moral beliefs and behaviour, the study of right and wrong, of good and evil in human conduct. Many ethical theories exist but some are more relevant to decision-making for engineers than others. For example, theories of Subjective Relativism and Cultural Relativism have limited utility in ethical decision-making as they encourage decisions based on individual or cultural perspectives. The Divine Command Theory is based on particular religious beliefs, which can vary from one religion to another. However, theories such as Kantianism, Act Utilitarianism, Rule Utilitarianism, Social Contract (Hobbes), Rights Theory (Locke) and Rawl's Theory of Justice appear to be more helpful for decision-making related to engineering works.

Most professional engineering associations and technical societies provide their own ethical guidelines to help engineers avoid misconduct, negligence, incompetence and corruption. A complaint against an engineer can lead to discipline, which can include a fine, and/or losing the license to practice. Knowledge of the ethical decision-making process can guide engineers facing complex and difficult moral dilemmas.[54] Principles of ethics and ethical codes are at the core of the duties and responsibilities of engineers. Professional engineering associations and technical societies have their own codes of ethics. Although there are some small differences between these codes, there are many guidelines in common. Knowledge of ethical theories and the relevant codes of ethics help engineers make the most ethical decision when facing an ethical dilemma or problem.

Another important aspect of ethical behaviour in engineering is how persons from under-represented groups are treated, either by employers, peers or employees. Considering that women still make up a small proportion of the engineers in most countries, it is critically important to ensure that there is zero tolerance for harassment or discrimination in the workplace and in engineering schools. A main obstacle is that most engineers (both men and many women) are not aware of the

definition of harassment or discrimination and thus may be perpetrators without knowledge of the harm that can be done. In Ontario (Canada), the Association of Professional Engineers of Ontario (created in 1922) has made these a misconduct for which engineers can be disciplined.[55] [56]

Avoiding plagiarism, conflict of interest, fraud, and corruption are other forms of unethical behaviour that engineers must fully understand to avoid this type of misconduct.

Discussing the impact of technology on society and on people is another key component of ethical behaviour. Technological development brings major benefits and hazards in its wake.[57] [58]Each of us can do our part to ensure a positive impact for society and that our efforts help to solve some of the world's largest problems and challenges. Society must institute laws and ethical codes of conduct to guide the direction and impacts of the developments. To ensure that engineering students become socially responsible in this new century, it is essential to instruct them on how to assess the impact of their work on people and society, and teach them the process of ethical decision-making. There should be a guideline on how to include these important concepts in our engineering curriculum. An over-arching principle to keep in mind is the dynamic nature of the issues to be included in such courses. [59] [60]

On a final note, every engineer and engineering student should be aware of the United Nations Millennium Development Goals and do their best to include these whenever possible in their work, especially in developing countries. Why? Because it is within the power of the engineer to take action and thus they have an ethical responsibility to do so.

54 Andrews, G. and J. D. Kemper. 2003. *Canadian Professional Engineering Practice and Ethics*. Saunders College Canada, Harcourt Brace & Company, Canada, p.46.

55 Professional Engineers Ontario (PEO). *Final Report of the Bioengineering Sub-Group of the Engineering Disciplines Task Force (EDTG)*. 25 Sheppard Ave., Toronto, ON. Available at: http://www.peo.on.ca/ Click on Guidelines, then on Human Rights for professional practice (Accessed: 15 May 2010).

56 M. Frize. 1995. *Eradicating Harassment in Higher Education and Non-Traditional Workplaces: A Model*, CAASHHE Conference, Saskatoon, 15–18 Nov., pp. 43–47.

57 Joy, B. 2000. Why the Future doesn't need us. *Wired*. April 2000 Available at: http://www.wired.com/wired/archive/8.04/joy.html (Accessed: 15 May 2010).

58 Centre for the Study of Technology and Society. Available at: http://www.tecsoc.org/innovate/focusbilljoy.htm (Accessed: 15 May 2010).

59 Frize, M. 1996. Teaching Ethics & the Governance of the Profession: Ahead or Behind Professional Practice Realities? *Canadian Conf. on Engineering Education*, June. pp. 483–489.

60 Frize, M. 2003. Teaching Ethics for Bioengineers in the 21st Century. *Proc. of the 25th Annual International Conference of the IEEE EMBS*. Cancun, Mexico.

Brief Definitions of Ethical Theories

Subjective Relativism: Theory where there are no universal moral norms of right and wrong. Persons decide right and wrong for themselves.

Cultural Relativism: Ethical theory where the meaning of right and wrong rests with a society's actual moral guidelines.

Divine Command Theory: Theory based on the idea that good actions are those aligned with the will of God, and bad actions are those contrary to the will of God; that we owe obedience to our Creator and that God is all-good and all-knowing, the ultimate authority.

Kantianism: Theory also referred to as the categorical imperative and pertaining to actions that are universally considered to be good and involve good will and duty. Treat yourself and others as ends in themselves, never as a means to an end.

Act Utilitarianism: Theory stating that an action is good if it benefits someone and bad if it harms someone; also known as the 'greatest happiness principle' and applies to individual moral actions.

Rule Utilitarianism: Theory stating that a moral rule should be followed because its universal adoption would lead to the greatest increase in total happiness.

Social Contract Theory: Theory based on the benefits to the community, governing how people are to treat one another. It is framed in the language of individual rights and explains why rational people act out of self-interest in the absence of common agreement.

Rights Theory: Theory stating that everyone has rights arising simply from being born: The right to life, to maximum individual liberty and to human dignity. This theory is the basis for the 'Charter of Human Rights and Freedoms' in Canada.

Rawls' Theory of Justice: Theory stating that each individual may claim basic rights and liberties (e.g. freedom of thought and speech, the right to be safe from harm, and so on) as long as these claims are consistent with everyone having a claim to the same rights and liberties.

Quinn, M. 2005. *Ethics for the Information Age.* Boston: Pearson/Addison-Wesley.

Ethical decision-making process

This can be likened to the engineering design process. It consists of the following steps:

1. *Recognize* an ethical problem or dilemma that needs to be solved; gather the information needed. Determine who is involved; what can or has occurred; where, when, and what harm can occur or has happened.

2. *Define* the ethical problem. Identify what is wrong; what codes or laws have been breached, and how ethical theories define this situation.

3. *Generate alternative solutions.* Several approaches may exist and each should be listed for evaluation step.

4. *Evaluate* the possible solutions and their consequences with the help of the ethical theories and the codes of ethics; consider the legal aspects of the problem.

5. *Decision* and optimization. Select the most appropriate solution for the situation. Seek advice from experienced persons and consider all aspects.

6. *Implement* the solution. We need to keep in mind that even after a solution has been selected for action, this may require several steps and a carefully designed sequence. For example, if the problem threatens or has affected public safety, then this may call for immediate action to be taken. If the responsible party does not act, then one must escalate the ladder of authority to ensure the correcting actions are undertaken. If this does not work, then one needs to consider going public with the story if this can trigger some response from the party responsible for the problem.

7. *Corruption and fraud* refers to actions such as accepting bribes. Almost anyone in a position of authority – particularly public authority – has the potential for such wrongdoing. Similarly, use of government or corporate property or assets for personal use is fraud.

Andrews, G. and J. D. Kemper. 2003. *Canadian Professional Engineering Practice and Ethics.* Saunders College Canada, Harcourt Brace & Company, Canada. pp.142–144.

Other important concepts

■ *Secrecy* refers to the keeping of secrets; information is withheld; a breach of secrecy is an unauthorized distribution of confidential information.

■ *Privacy* refers to the freedom from intrusion or public attention; to be removed from public view or knowledge.

■ *Confidentiality* refers to being entrusted with secrets and keeping them.

■ *Intellectual Property* (IP) is defined as 'a legal entitlement which sometimes attaches to the expressed form of an idea, or to some other intangible subject matter. This legal entitlement generally enables its holder to exercise exclusive rights of use in relation to the subject matter of the IP.'

■ *Copyright* refers to 'creative and artistic works (e.g. books, movies, music, paintings, photographs and software), giving a copyright holder the exclusive right to control reproduction or adaptation of such works for a certain period of time.

■ A *patent* may be granted in relation to a new and useful invention, giving the patent holder an exclusive right to commercially exploit the invention for a certain period of time (typically twenty years from the filing date of a patent application).

■ A *trademark* is a distinctive sign used to distinguish products or services.

■ An *industrial design* refers to the form of appearance, style or design of an industrial object (e.g. spare parts, furniture or textiles, shapes).

■ A *trade secret* is an item of confidential information concerning the commercial practices or proprietary knowledge of a business.

Wikipedia.

Decew, J.W. 1997. *In Pursuit of Privacy: Law, Ethics, and the Rise of Technology,* Cornell University Press, Ithaca.

4.6.3 WFEO Model Code of Ethics

Since 1990, WFEO has worked to prepare a Code of Ethics as a model to help define and support the creation of codes in member institutions. The final version reproduced here was adopted in 2001.

Broad principles

Ethics is generally understood as the discipline or field of study dealing with moral duty or obligation. This typically gives rise to a set of governing principles or values, which in turn are used to judge the appropriateness of particular conducts or behaviours. These principles are usually presented either as broad guiding principles of an idealistic or inspirational nature or, alternatively, as a detailed and specific set of rules couched in legalistic or imperative terms to make them more enforceable. Professions that have been given the privilege and responsibility of self regulation, including the engineering profession, have tended to opt for the first alternative, espousing sets of underlying principles as codes of professional ethics which form the basis and framework for responsible professional practice. Arising from this context, professional codes of ethics have sometimes been incorrectly interpreted as a set of 'rules' of conduct intended for passive observance. A more appropriate use by practicing professionals is to interpret the essence of the underlying principles within their daily decision-making situations in a dynamic manner, responsive to the need of the situation. As a consequence, a code of professional ethics is more than a minimum standard of conduct; rather, it is a set of principles, which should guide professionals in their daily work.

In summary, the model Code presented herein expresses the expectations of engineers and society in discriminating engineers' professional responsibilities. The Code is based on broad principles of truth, honesty and trustworthiness, respect for human life and welfare, fairness, openness, competence and accountability. Some of these broader ethical principles or issues deemed more universally applicable are not specifically defined in the Code although they are understood to be applicable as well. Only those tenets deemed to be particularly applicable to the practice of professional engineering are specified. Nevertheless, certain ethical principles or issues not commonly considered to be part of professional ethics should be implicitly accepted to judge the engineer's professional performance.

Issues regarding the environment and sustainable development know no geographical boundaries. The engineers and citizens of all nations should know and respect the environmental ethic. It is desirable therefore that engineers in each nation continue to observe the philosophy of the Principles of Environmental Ethics delineated in Section III of this Code.

Practice provision ethics

Professional engineers shall:

- hold paramount the safety, health and welfare of the public and the protection of both the natural and the built environment in accordance with the Principles of Sustainable Development;

- promote health and safety within the workplace;

- offer services, advise on or undertake engineering assignments only in areas of their competence and practice in a careful and diligent manner;

- act as faithful agents of their clients or employers, maintain confidentially and disclose conflicts of interest;

- keep themselves informed in order to maintain their competence, strive to advance the body of knowledge within which they practice and provide opportunities for the professional development of their subordinates and fellow practitioners;

- conduct themselves with fairness and good faith towards clients, colleagues and others, give credit where it is due and accept, as well as give, honest and fair professional criticism;

- be aware of and ensure that clients and employers are made aware of societal and environmental consequences of actions or projects and endeavour to interpret engineering issues to the public in an objective and truthful manner;

- present clearly to employers and clients the possible consequences of overruling or disregarding of engineering decisions or judgement; and

- report to their association and/or appropriate agencies any illegal or unethical engineering decisions or practices of engineers or others.

Environmental engineering ethics

Engineers, as they develop any professional activity, shall:

- try with the best of their ability, courage, enthusiasm and dedication to obtain a superior technical achievement, which will contribute to and promote a healthy and agreeable surrounding for all people, in open spaces as well as indoors;

- strive to accomplish the beneficial objectives of their work with the lowest possible consumption of raw materials and energy and the lowest production of waste and any kind of pollution;

■ discuss in particular the consequences of their proposals and actions, direct or indirect, immediate or long term, upon the health of people, social equity and the local system of values;

■ study thoroughly the environment that will be affected, assess all the impacts that might arise in the structure, dynamics and aesthetics of the ecosystems involved, urbanized or natural, as well as in the pertinent socio-economic systems, and select the best alternative for development that is both environmentally sound and sustainable;

■ promote a clear understanding of the actions required to restore and, if possible, to improve the environment that may be disturbed, and include them in their proposals;

■ reject any kind of commitment that involves unfair damages for human surroundings and nature, and aim for the best possible technical, social, and political solution; and

■ be aware that the principles of ecosystemic interdependence, diversity maintenance, resource recovery and inter-relational harmony form the basis of humankind's continued existence and that each of these bases poses a threshold of sustainability that should not be exceeded.

Conclusion

Always remember that war, greed, misery and ignorance, plus natural disasters and human induced pollution and destruction of resources are the main causes of the progressive impairment of the environment, and that engineers, as active members of society deeply involved in the promotion of development, must use their talent, knowledge and imagination to assist society in removing those evils and improving the quality of life for all people.

Interpretation of the Code of Ethics

The interpretive articles that follow expand on and discuss some of the more difficult and interrelated components of the Code especially related to the Practice Provisions. No attempt is made to expand on all clauses of the Code, nor is the elaboration presented on a clause-by-clause basis. The objective of this approach is to broaden the interpretation, rather than narrow its focus. The ethics of professional engineering is an integrated whole and cannot be reduced to fixed 'rules'. Therefore, the issues and questions arising from the Code are discussed in a general framework, drawing on any and all portions of the Code to demonstrate their inter-relationship and to expand on the basic intent of the Code.

Sustainable development and environment

Engineers shall strive to enhance the quality of the biophysical and socio-economic urban environment of buildings and spaces, and to promote the principles of sustainable development.

Engineers shall seek opportunities to work for the enhancement of safety, health and the social welfare of both their local community and the global community through the practice of sustainable development.

Engineers whose recommendations are overruled or ignored on issues of safety, health, welfare or sustainable development shall inform their contractor or employer of the possible consequences.

Protection of the public and the environment

Professional Engineers shall hold paramount the safety, health and welfare of the public and the protection of the environment. This obligation to the safety, health and welfare of the general public, which includes one's own work environment, is often dependent upon engineering judgements, risk assessments, decisions and practices incorporated into structures, machines, products, processes and devices. Therefore, engineers must control and ensure that what they are involved with is in conformity with accepted engineering practice, standards and applicable codes, and would be considered safe based on peer adjudication. This responsibility extends to include all and any situation which an engineer encounters and includes an obligation to advise the appropriate authority if there is reason to believe that any engineering activity, or its products, processes and so on, do not conform with the above stated conditions. The meaning of paramount in this basic tenet is that all other requirements of the Code are subordinate if protection of public safety, the environment or other substantive public interests are involved.

Faithful agent of clients and employers

Engineers shall act as faithful agents or trustees of their clients and employers with objectivity, fairness and justice to all parties. With respect to the handling of confidential or proprietary information, the concept of ownership of the information and protecting that party's rights is appropriate. Engineers shall not reveal facts, data or information obtained in a professional capacity without the prior consent of its owner. The only exception to respecting confidentially and maintaining a trustee's position is in instances where the public interest or the environment is at risk, as discussed in the preceding section; but even in these circumstances, the engineer should endeavour to have the client and/or employer appropriately redress the situation, or at least, in the absence of a compelling reason to the contrary, should make every reasonable effort to contact them and explain clearly the potential risks, prior to informing the appropriate authority.

Professional Engineers shall avoid conflict of interest situations with employers and clients but, should such conflict arise, it is the engineer's responsibility to fully disclose, without delay, the nature of the conflict to the party(ies) with whom the conflict exists. In these circumstances, where full disclosure is insufficient or seen to be insufficient to protect all parties' interests as well as the public, the engineer shall withdraw totally from the issue or use extraordinary means, involving independent parties if possible, to monitor the situation. For example, it is inappropriate to act simultaneously as agent for both the provider and the recipient of professional services. If client and employer's interests are at odds, the engineer shall attempt to deal fairly with both. If the conflict of interest is between the intent of a corporate employer and a regulatory standard, the engineer must attempt to reconcile the difference and, if that is unsuccessful, it may become necessary to inform. Being a faithful agent or trustee includes the obligation of engaging, or advising to engage, experts or specialists when such services are deemed to be in the client's or employer's best interests. It also means being accurate, objective and truthful in making public statements on behalf of the client or employer when required to do so, while respecting the client's and employer's rights of confidentiality and proprietary information.

Being a faithful agent includes not using a previous employer's or client's specific privileged or proprietary information and trade practices or process information without the owner's knowledge and consent. However, general technical knowledge, experience and expertise gained by the engineer through involvement with the previous work may be freely used without consent or subsequent undertakings.

Competence and knowledge

Professional Engineers shall offer services, advise on or undertake engineering assignments only in areas of their competence by virtue of their training and experience. This includes exercising care and communicating clearly in accepting or interpreting assignments, and in setting expected outcomes. It also includes the responsibility to obtain the services of an expert if required or, if the knowledge is unknown, to proceed only with full disclosure of the circumstances and, if necessary, the experimental nature of the activity to all parties involved. Hence, this requirement is more than simply duty to a standard of care, it also involves acting with honesty and integrity with one's client or employer and one's self. Professional Engineers have the responsibility to remain abreast of developments and knowledge in their area of expertise, that is, to maintain their own competence. Should there be a technologically driven or individually motivated shift in the area of technical activity, it is the engineer's duty to attain and maintain competence in all areas of involvement including being knowledgeable with the technical and legal framework and regulations governing their work. In effect, it requires a personal commitment to ongoing professional development, continuing education and self-testing.

In addition to maintaining their own competence, Professional Engineers have an obligation to strive to contribute to the advancement of the body of knowledge within which they practice, and to the profession in general. Moreover, within the framework of the practice of their profession, they are expected to participate in providing opportunities to further the professional development of their colleagues.

This competence requirement of the Code extends to include an obligation to the public, the profession and one's peers, such that opinions on engineering issues are expressed honestly and only in areas of one's competence. It applies equally to reporting or advising on professional matters and to issuing public statements. This requires honesty with one's self to present issues fairly, accurately and with appropriate qualifiers and disclaimers, and to avoid personal, political and other non-technical biases. The latter is particularly important for public statements or when involved in a technical forum.

Fairness and integrity in the workplace

Honesty, integrity, continuously updated competence, devotion to service and dedication to enhancing the life quality of society are cornerstones of professional responsibility. Within this framework, engineers shall be objective and truthful and include all known and pertinent information on professional reports, statements and testimony. They shall accurately and objectively represent their clients, employers, associates and themselves consistent with their academic, experience and professional qualifications. This tenet is more than 'not misrepresenting'; it also implies disclosure of all relevant information and issues, especially when serving in an advisory capacity or as an expert witness. Similarly, fairness, honesty and accuracy in advertising are expected.

If called upon to verify another engineer's work, there is an obligation to inform (or make every effort to inform) the other engineer, whether the other engineer is still actively involved or not. In this situation, and in any circumstance, engineers shall give proper recognition and credit where credit is due and accept, as well as give, honest and fair criticism on professional matters, all the while maintaining dignity and respect for everyone involved.

Engineers shall not accept nor offer covert payment or other considerations for the purpose of securing, or as remuneration for, engineering assignments. Engineers should prevent their personal or political involvement from influencing or compromising their professional role or responsibility.

Consistent with the Code, and having attempted to remedy any situation within their organization, engineers are obligated to report to their association or other appropriate agency any illegal or unethical engineering decisions by engineers or others. Care must be taken not to enter into legal arrangements, which may compromise this obligation.

Professional accountability and leadership

Engineers have a duty to practice in a careful and diligent manner and accept responsibility, and be accountable for their actions. This duty is not limited to design, or its supervision and management, but applies to all areas of practice. For example, it includes construction supervision and management, preparation of shop drawings, engineering reports, feasibility studies, environmental impact assessments, engineering developmental work, and so on.

The signing and sealing of engineering documents indicates the taking of responsibility for the work. This practice is required for all types of engineering endeavour, regardless where or for whom the work is done, including, but not limited to, privately and publicly owned firms, crown corporations and government agencies/departments. There are no exceptions; signing and sealing documents is appropriate whenever engineering principles have been used and public welfare may be at risk.

Taking responsibility for engineering activity includes being accountable for one's own work and, in the case of a senior engineer, accepting responsibility for the work of a team. The latter implies responsible supervision where the engineer is actually in a position to review, modify and direct the entirety of the engineering work. This concept requires setting reasonable limits on the extent of activities, and the number of engineers and others, whose work can be supervised by the responsible engineer. The practice of a 'symbolic' responsibility or supervision is the situation where an engineer, say with the title of 'chief engineer', takes full responsibility for all engineering on behalf of a large corporation, utility or government agency/department even though the engineer may not be aware of many of the engineering activities or decisions being made daily throughout the firm or department. The essence of this approach is that the firm is taking the responsibility of default, whether engineering supervision or direction is applied or not.

Engineers have a duty to advise their employer and, if necessary, their clients and even their professional association, in that order, in situations when the overturning of an engineering decision may result in breaching their duty to safeguard the public. The initial action is to discuss the problem with the supervisor/employer. If the employer does not adequately respond to the engineer's concern, then the client must be advised in the case of a consultancy situation, or the most senior officer should be informed in the case of a manufacturing process plant or government agency. Failing this attempt to rectify the situation, the engineer must advise his professional association of his concerns, in confidence.

In the same order as mentioned above, the engineer must report unethical engineering activity undertaken by other engineers or by non-engineers. This extends to include, for example, situations in which senior officials of a firm make 'executive' decisions, which clearly and substantially alter the engineering aspects of the work, or protection of the public welfare or the environment arising from the work.

Because of the rapid advancements in technology and the increasing ability of engineering activities to impact on the environment, engineers have an obligation to be mindful of the effect their decisions will have on the environment and the well-being of society, and to report any concerns of this nature in the same manner as previously mentioned. Further to the above, with the rapid advancement of technology in today's world and the possible social impacts on large populations of people, engineers must endeavour to foster the public's understanding of technical issues and the role of engineering more than ever before.

Sustainable development is the challenge of meeting current human needs for natural resources, industrial products, energy, food, transportation, shelter, and effective waste management while conserving and, if possible, enhancing the Earth's environmental quality, natural resources, ethical, intellectual, working and affectionate capabilities of people and socio-economic bases, essential for the human needs of future generations. The proper observance to these principles will considerably help towards the eradication of world poverty.

4.6.4   Engineers against corruption Preventing corruption in the infrastructure sector – What can engineers do?

Neill Stansbury and Catherine Stansbury

It is now well understood that corruption in the infrastructure sector causes death and economic damage. Frequent examples include building collapses where bribes paid to building inspectors to overlook safety issues have resulted in deaths. Corrupt over-pricing and diversion of funds result in inadequate and defective infrastructure, and reduced funding for other social and economic needs such as schools and hospitals.

Engineers worldwide have understood the damage caused by corruption and are calling for the elimination of corruption in the infrastructure sector. The World Federation of Engineering Organizations has established an international Anti-Corruption Standing Committee to agree on appropriate anti-corruption actions. The World Economic Forum's Partnering Against

Reducing corruption in infrastructure projects at the government level

Engineers can call for action by governments in the following areas:

- **Integrity in government:** Effective national and international action must be taken to prevent corruption by government officials, to investigate and prosecute corrupt officials, and to recover their corruptly acquired assets.

- **Government approvals:** The need for government approvals, for example in the application for permits or payments, provides opportunities for corruption. Governments therefore should take the following actions:

- The number of government approvals required, and the number of people required to issue these approvals, should be reduced to the minimum necessary to ensure fair and effective government.

- Government departments should take steps to minimize extortion by their officers, to appoint a senior manager to whom complaints of extortion can be made, and to publicize a list of fees and time-scales which should properly apply to government procedures. This commitment, list of fees and time-scales should be published on a publicly acessible website.

- **Public sector projects:** In the case of public sector infrastructure projects, the government should ensure that the public sector project owner implements an effective anti-corruption system (following boxes).

- **Reporting:** Reporting systems should be maintained where details of organizations or individuals who are suspected of being involved in corruption can be reported. These reporting systems should be widely publicized. People should be able to report by telephone, letter or email. Reports should be capable of being given anonymously, and the confidentiality of sources should be protected.

- **Investigation and prosecution:** Adequate resources need to be allocated to investigation and prosecution agencies to allow them to carry out their functions effectively.

- **Asset recovery:** Greater international effort needs to be put into recovering and repatriating assets stolen through corrupt activities.

Reducing corruption in infrastructure projects at the organization level

Numerous different organizations participate in the construction of infrastructure projects: public or private sector project owners, funders, consulting engineering firms, contractors, sub-contractors and suppliers. These organizations will normally be run by engineers, or have engineers in senior management or advisory roles. Engineers can therefore either implement or recommend the implementation of a corporate anti-corruption programme by these organizations. This programme should:

- prohibit the organization's staff from engaging in any form of corrupt conduct;

- specify the organization's policy on political and charitable contributions, facilitation payments, gifts, hospitality and expenses;

- commit the organization to take all reasonable steps to prevent corruption by the organization's parent, subsidiary and associated companies, agents, joint venture and consortium partners, sub-contractors and suppliers and

- provide for effective anti-corruption management controls, audit, staff training and whistle-blowing procedures.

Several organizations have developed model codes of conduct, systems and guidance to assist companies in improving their corporate governance:

- The International Federation of Consulting Engineers (FIDIC) has developed *Guidelines for Business Integrity Management in the Consulting Industry.*

- Transparency International (TI) has developed the *Business Principles for Countering Bribery* and accompanying guidelines, implementation plan and verification module.

- The International Chamber of Commerce (ICC) has developed *Combating Extortion and Bribery: ICC Rules of Conduct and Recommendations.*

Corruption Initiative brings together over 100 major international companies from the construction and engineering, oil and gas, and mining and mineral sectors of more than thirty-five countries, with a combined turnover in excess of US$500 billion, committed not to tolerate bribery and to implement effective anti-corruption procedures. At a national level, for example, the UK Anti-Corruption Forum is an alliance of UK business associations, professional institutions and organizations with interests in the domestic and international infrastructure, construction and engineering sectors. The purpose of the UK Forum is to promote industry-led actions, which can help eliminate corruption. Numerous other initiatives worldwide are led by or involve engineers.

Engineers do not make up the complete solution to corruption prevention. Major reasons for corruption are the corrupt politicians or government officials who use infrastructure projects or military procurement contracts as their personal source of wealth creation, and also because of the inadequate level of prevention, investigation and prosecution of corruption. However, engineers are critical to the reduction of corruption in the infrastructure sector in particular, as they are represented at every stage of the process. Engineers work for or advise governments, project owners, funders, contractors and consulting engineers. They are involved in the planning, design, tendering and execution of the project. Corruption can be materially reduced if engineers work together to bring about change.

Engineers can take steps at four levels to help bring about the reduction of corruption: government, project, corporate and individual. The following boxes outline the steps at each level. Taking these steps would result in material progress towards an industry in which corruption does not kill.

Reducing corruption in infrastructure projects at the project level

Corruption on infrastructure projects is a complex problem. It may occur in the form of bribery, extortion, fraud or collusion. It can take place during any phase of a project, including project identification, planning, financing, design, tender, execution, operation and maintenance. In each project phase, corruption may involve any one or more of the government, project owner, funders, consultants, contractors, sub-contractors, suppliers, joint venture partners and agents. It may occur at any level of the contractual structure. Furthermore, corruption is concealed and those aware of it are either complicit in it or reluctant to report it. This makes it more difficult to detect.

There is no single or simple method by which to prevent such corruption. As with safety and quality issues, corruption should be addressed by the use of a comprehensive system, which combines a number of integrated measures.

All infrastructure projects involve engineers at a senior decision-making level throughout the project cycle. Engineers can therefore either implement or recommend the implementation of effective anti-corruption measures at project level. These measures should include:

- **Independent assessment:** An independent assessor should be appointed, on a full-time or part-time basis, whose duty is to detect and report corruption for the duration of the project. He/she should be suitably skilled, be nominated by an independent organization, and owe his/her duty to all participants in the project.

- **Pre-contract disclosure of information:** The major project participants should provide each other with relevant information at an early stage in the project process with the purpose of helping to reveal and so minimize the risk of corruption. Such information should relate to their principal shareholders, officers, financial status, agents, joint venture partners, major sub-contractors, criminal convictions and debarment.

- **Contractual anti-corruption commitments:** The project participants should provide anti-corruption contractual commitments to each other, which expressly cover the main types of corruption. Remedies should be specified in the event of breach of these commitments.

- **Government anti-corruption commitments:** Government departments should provide an anti-corruption commitment whereby the department agrees to take steps to minimize extortion by its officers, to appoint a senior manager to whom complaints of extortion can be made, and to publicize a list of fees and time-scales which should properly apply to government procedures.

- **Transparency:** Critical project information on the identification, financing, procurement, execution and maintenance of the project should be publicly disclosed on a website.

- **Raising awareness:** Individuals involved in the project should be made aware, through publicity and training, of what constitutes corruption, and of the risks of personal involvement in corruption.

- **Funder involvement:** Details of the funding terms and conditions, and any changes to these, should be publicly disclosed. The independent assessor should make regular reports to the funders on his activities, and report any suspected corruption to them.

- **Compliance programme:** The project participants should be required to take all reasonable steps to ensure compliance by the company and its management and staff with the project's anti-corruption requirements.

- **Reporting:** Procedures should be implemented on the project for confidential reporting by project participants and members of the public. The independent assessor should have a duty to report suspected corruption to the criminal authorities.

- **Enforcement:** There must be a real threat of enforcement. Civil enforcement should be implemented under the anti-corruption commitments. Criminal enforcement should be implemented by the criminal authorities after receiving reports from the independent assessor, project participants or members of the public.

The Project Anti-Corruption System (PACS) is an integrated and comprehensive system published by the Global Infrastructure Anti Corruption Centre (GIACC) to assist in the prevention of corruption on construction projects. It utilizes the above measures, and provides templates to enable these measures to be implemented.

Reducing corruption in infrastructure projects at the individual level

Engineers are professionals in their personal capacity. Their professional qualification is a badge not only of their skill, but also of their personal integrity. Engineers can practice and encourage integrity both individually, and through their professional institutions. At an individual level, engineers can simply refuse to become involved in any corrupt action. If all engineers refused to participate, directly or indirectly, in a corrupt act and refused to turn a blind eye to corruption, the level of corruption in the infrastructure sector would immediately and significantly fall. Most corruption on an infrastructure project could not take place without the involvement or knowledge of an engineer. However, it is often difficult for engineers to work alone, particularly when faced with corrupt government officials and, therefore, action is most powerful if taken by professional institutions on behalf of all their individual members. Professional institutions should:

- Publicly speak out against corruption.

- Increase awareness among the institutions' members of corruption and its consequences through publicity and training.

- Work in conjunction with other domestic and international business associations and professional institutions, in both the developed and developing world, so as to develop a coordinated approach to anti-corruption issues.

- Work in conjunction with government bodies to ensure that national and international efforts to curb corruption are well-founded, consistent and effective.

- Maintain and enforce an effective code of conduct, which commits the institutions' members to an anti-corruption policy. The code should provide a disciplinary mechanism under which members who breach the code are sanctioned.

Many professional institutions are already taking the above steps.

4.6.5 Business Integrity Management Systems in the consulting engineering industry

Peter Boswell

Corruption is a zero-sum game where bribery, extortion, collusion or fraud allows someone to profit at society's expense, creates unnecessary waste in the procurement of projects, undermines the values of society, breeds cynicism and demeans the individuals involved; it must be curbed for the effective functioning of a sustainable and equitable society.

Engineering consulting firms in both developing and industrialized nations confronted by corruption in everyday work at home and abroad, particularly in government procurement, wish to supply services without concerns about corruption, and be assured of competitive bidding on equal terms. Moreover, clients increasingly require assurance that consulting engineering firms operate in a corruption-free environment.

A global consensus has developed that corruption is not only wrong, but also destructive to sustainable development, quality projects and free market systems in an era of globalization. The main international anti-corruption strategy aims to create a strong legal framework that will make the cost of non-compliance an important factor, thereby increasing the commercial risk associated with corrupt practices. Only with the momentum that can be achieved by a global commitment similar to that for capacity-building and sustainable development will it be possible to make a difference. Moreover, to be controlled effectively, systemic corruption requires approaches

that encompass both the demand and supply sides of the business, and both givers and takers.

The International Federation of Consulting Engineers (FIDIC) has denounced corruption for many years in arguing that the principal criteria for selecting a consultant should be service quality and the consultant's qualifications. FIDIC considers systemic corruption as a priority issue. The FIDIC strategy is to play a proactive role in joining the worldwide effort to combat corruption by supporting legislation, promoting high ethical standards, cooperating with international agencies, offering objective advice for procurement processes, and ensuring the implementation of management practices in firms.

Efforts to identify specific courses of action that would lead to reduced corruption began in 1998 with the formulation of a strategy and action plan. The World Bank enthusiastically endorsed the initiative by establishing an Integrity Management Task Force under FIDIC's leadership, with the Inter-American Development Bank and the Pan-American Federation of Consultants (FEPAC) as members. The task force recommended the establishment of 'integrity manuals' based on a shrewd and concrete analysis of procurement procedures that went wrong or, at least, on a detailed risk analysis of hypotheti-

Implementing a BIMS

Business Integrity is an organization's ability to fulfil its commitment to a code of ethics on behalf of all its stakeholders. So Business Integrity Management – as opposed to corruption control or integrity assurance – seeks to satisfy stakeholders, internal as well as external. BIMS therefore considers the holistic implications of all elements of management on an organization's products and services. It seeks continuous integrity assurance at every transaction point along the way toward the delivery of the services offered. In other words, a BIMS is a set of interrelated elements designed for an organization that wishes to be managed by integrity principles; it is what the organization does to ensure that its work-flow is corruption free.

A BIMS for ensuring the ethical delivery of consulting services is voluntary and can be adopted by organizations of any size. An organization firm wishing to adopt BIMS

principles must implement a BIMS that complies with the FIDIC BIMS guidelines.

FIDIC's BIMS is designed so that it adds value and generates economies of scale for organizations that are committed to quality management. The BIMS principles should be compatible with the ISO 9000 family of quality management standards, and capable of being implemented independently, concurrently or in parallel with an organization's quality management system.

A commitment to quality management aims to continuously promote best practice in consulting work. FIDIC strongly recommends the development of a quality management system in member firms, where implementation is a step-by-step process requiring continuous improvement and a commitment in terms of policy and resources,

regardless of the size of the firm. Designing and implementing a BIMS involves identical considerations.

Once the BIMS is operating properly, and the organization is confident that the guidelines are met, an evaluation process should be initiated to ensure continuous compliance. This process can involve: first-party evaluation, where the management and the staff representative evaluate the BIMS; second-party evaluation based on client feedback; and third-party evaluation by an outside body. For evaluation, it can seek an external audit, a peer review by an experienced team drawn from several organizations, or certification based on having a recognized authority verify the BIMS with respect to its documentation and procedures, possibly as part of an ISO 9001:2000 quality certification process.

cal procedures, with participation by professionals working in geographically and sectorially sensitive areas. This concept became the basis for the development of a supply-side initiative for the consulting engineering industry called a Business Integrity Management System (BIMS).

BIMS recognized that many consulting firms were doing their best to define and implement anti-corruption policies. However, such approaches tend to be piecemeal. What was missing was a process that connected and transformed isolated acts of integrity assurance into a complete system, with formal procedures to identify potential risks, prevent and combat corruption, and implement policies for every project throughout an organization. The FIDIC BIMS guidelines published in 2001 provided a set of tools and a process-based approach for managing an organization's integrity, and by 2007 a FIDIC survey found that there were seventy-eight member firms reporting the implementation of a BIMS that followed the guidelines.

The consulting engineering industry has been well aware that it was not alone in addressing corruption. Supply-side initiatives now range far and wide across many industry sectors. More recently, FIDIC has proposed a Government Procurement Integrity Management System (GPIMS) for the integrity of government procurement processes for consulting services. GPIMS accommodates the fundamental principles of a government's legal system and satisfies the protocols for the government procurement anticorruption policies of the OECD's Principles for Managing Ethics in the Public Service and of the United Nations Convention against Corruption.

Steps for designing Business Integrity Management Systems

1. Formulation of a code of ethics.

2. Formulation of a business integrity policy based mainly on the OECD Anti-Bribery Convention and FIDIC's code of ethics, that must be documented, implemented, communicated internally and externally, and made publicly available.

3. Appointment of a representative, generally a senior member of the organization's management staff.

4. Identification of requirements for the BIMS that should focus on the processes which are vulnerable to corruption.

5. Analysis and evaluation of current practices.

6. An organization should use tools to support the planning and implementation of its BIMS, notably: a code of ethics, an integrity policy; the definition of roles, responsibilities and authority; integrity procedures for the main business processes; and enforcement measures.

7. Documentation: a BIMS must be well documented in order to provide evidence that all processes that may affect the business integrity of the services offered have been thoroughly anticipated.

8. Review of current practices by establishing actions to be taken in case of failure to comply with the Business Integrity Policy.

4.7 Women and gender issues in engineering

4.7.1 Women in engineering: Gender dynamics and engineering – how to attract and retain women in engineering

Wendy Faulkner

For nearly three decades, governments and industries across the industrialized world have sponsored efforts to increase the representation of women in professional engineering, recognizing the (largely) untapped pool of talent amongst women. These efforts have had some impact, but engineering remains a heavily male-dominated occupation in most countries. There is clearly room for improvement – not only in recruiting women into engineering, but also in retaining and promoting those women who do enter the profession.

Some of the issues are well understood. For example, the poor work-life balance and a lack of family-friendly policies in many engineering organizations are known to contribute to the disproportionate loss of women from the profession. But there are also more subtle dynamics at play which tend to make engineering organizations more supportive and comfortable for men than women. These dynamics were investigated in an ethnographic recent study in the UK.[61] The two-year study

---

61 This study was conducted between 2003 and 2005 with funding from the UK Economic and Social Research Council (ESRC ref: RES 000 23 0151). I gratefully acknowledge this support, and also the time and patience of all those engineers and their employers who agreed to participate in the study. A full research report can be found at http://www.issti.ed.ac.uk/publications/workingpapers (Accessed: 16 May 2010). See also Faulkner 2005 and 2007 for early academic publications of findings.

involved interviews and/or observation (through job shadowing) of sixty-six female and male engineers working in a range of industrial sectors and engineering disciplines. Its findings point to three issues that need to be addressed if we are to attract and keep more women in engineering.

What can employers do? A central aim of any diversity and equality efforts must be to nurture a workplace where everyone is comfortable and 'belongs'. There is a strong business case for sustained and sensitive diversity training, as a means of raising awareness of the kind of issues and dynamics signalled here. To be effective such efforts must involve all staff, including middle managers, and they must be tailored to the particular workforce to avoid alienating the majority group or creating a backlash. Diversity awareness must be seen to have the support of senior management. 'Top down' policies, such as the banning of pornography, can also take the pressure off individual women and men fighting offensive cultures. In some workplaces, more needs to be done to increase awareness that sexual harassment and any kind of bullying or sexist or racist behaviour is unacceptable, and of the procedures in place for handling this.

Issue 1: Attracting more women – stereotypes don't help!

The industry has a particular image problem in recruiting women. Part of the problem is that the male engineer is still very much seen as the norm. This means that many clever young women do not even consider a career in engineering. It also means that being a woman engineer marks you out as unusual, as women engineers are constantly reminded by the reactions of others. Another part of the problem is the classic stereotype of the engineer, of a man who is brilliant at, and passionate about, technology but not so good at interacting with people. This image not only says 'technology is for men', it also says being 'into technology' means not being 'into people'. As women are stereotypically 'into people', the image carries the implicit message that women engineers are not 'real women', or perhaps not 'real engineers'!

In practice, the classic stereotype of an engineer bears little or no resemblance to actual engineers, male or female. Whilst a few engineers do appear to epitomize the classic stereotype, the vast majority are more complex and more diverse than stereotypes allow. Many different 'types' of women and men enjoy engineering work. Moreover, the gender differences assumed by the classic stereotype are negligible or absent in two key areas.

First, although rather fewer women than men engineers have a 'tinkerer' background, they all get excited about, and take pride in, the technologies they work with. There are 'gadget girls' as well as 'boys and their toys'; and there also are 'non-techie' men as well as women in engineering. What draws them all to engineering is that they enjoy maths and science and want to put their problem-solving abilities to some 'practical' use.

Second, *all* engineers are socially skilled. They have to be; it simply isn't possible to do most engineering jobs without some ability to communicate and engage with others effectively! To a degree rarely understood by outsiders, the expertise required of engineers is *simultaneously* social as well as technical, for example, the need to integrate business requirements into design decisions. Perhaps for this reason, the study revealed that people skills are not obviously gender differentiated amongst engineers. This is a very significant finding, not only because it counters the classic stereotype of the engineer, but also because it counters the common assumption that women engineers have better people skills than their male counterparts.

This evidence is an important challenge to the conventional gendering of the technical-social dualism. It means that efforts to recruit more women into engineering must avoid appealing to gender stereotypes, which associate men and masculinity with 'things technical', and women and femininity with 'things social'. Rather, recruitment campaigns should 'speak to' the enthusiasm about maths, science and technology and the desire to be practical, which all would-be engineers – women and men – share. And at the same time, they should strive to reach the diverse 'types' of people which engineering needs.

The strategic aim here must be to 'normalize' engineering as a career choice for women, so that people inside and outside of engineering no longer presume that 'the engineer' will be a man. For this to happen, we need to challenge stereotypes about engineering as well as stereotypes about gender.

As we have seen, the classic stereotype is completely at odds with the reality of engineering work. Yet the image of engineering remains largely technical – in line with the more narrowly technical focus of engineering education. Indeed, many engineers cleave to a 'nuts and bolts' identity, even though their work is very socially orientated, and despite the fact that they never touch a nut or bolt. The study showed that the 'nuts and bolts' identity is a comfortably 'masculine' one for many men. But workplaces that foreground this identity can serve to exclude other engineers, including some very talented women engineers. In sum, we must avoid narrowly technical images of engineering work if we are to attract and keep talented people in engineering. Engineering has room for diverse 'types' of people because it encompasses a wide variety of jobs and roles. We need to promote and celebrate a new 'broad church' image of engineering – of useful work involving both 'technical' and 'social' expertise.

Issue 2: Good practice to help women (and men) 'become' engineers

Increasing the numbers of women recruited to engineering, though vital, is not sufficient to increase the proportion of women in engineering. Retention is a major issue – especially during the ten or so years it can take before entrants really *become* 'fully fledged' engineers. Many women, and men, are lost to the profession in the course of university education and early years on-the-job. Yet appropriate support and intervention can make a huge difference. We, therefore, need to sustain and promote good practice at university and at work if we are to keep more women and men in engineering.

Good practice in engineering education

- The engineering faculty can help to 'normalize' the female engineer amongst staff and students. In addition, they must be aware of an early confidence loss experienced by some female students.

- In terms of curricula, the provision of quality training in hands-on engineering benefits not only female students but also growing numbers of men, who do not have a 'tinkering' background. Students 'engage' more readily with engineering where the syllabus integrates practical and theoretical elements (e.g. through project work).

Good practice in supporting junior engineers on the job

- Individual supervisors, mentors, colleagues or managers can have a huge impact on how smoothly junior engineers move up the learning curve, and on whether or not they stay. There is a strong business case for employers to invest in selecting and training mentors and line managers – to build up rather than undermine the confidence of junior engineers, to create opportunities for them to prove themselves successfully, and to encourage a culture where 'there are no stupid questions'.

- Many employers ensure that graduates experience the full range of engineering work. However, women and men engineers alike can end up in jobs that do not suit their skills and interests, or which are dead ends in terms of career progression, and so they drift out of the industry or fail to progress in the company. The study found suggestive evidence that manufacturing can be particularly unsupportive of junior women engineers' careers. There is a crying need for ongoing, strategic support and advice over career development if we are to keep talented junior engineers.

- Some of the support needed during early years on the job comes from peers and, for women, from other women engineers. Employers can do much to ensure that junior engineers are not isolated, and to facilitate networking and mutual support between junior engineers and between women engineers.

Issue 3: Nurturing more 'inclusive' workplace cultures

It is frequently claimed that women who enter engineering have to fit into a masculine culture. The job shadowing conducted for this study revealed a mixed picture. Many features of engineering workplaces appear quite comfortable for all, but some feel and operate like 'men's spaces'. In a number of subtle ways which may appear trivial individually, but which cumulatively amount to a dripping tap, making many engineering workplaces undermine women's sense that they belong, for example:

Topics of conversations: Whilst non-work chat between close colleagues is quite wide-ranging and inclusive, the less routine conversations with outside associates tend to lean more readily on stereotypically 'safe' subjects – such as football and families. The more narrow the range of 'admissible' conversation, the more people (men and women) are marginalized or silenced. None of those observed was openly gay.

Humour and sex talk: Engineers generally take care to avoid potentially offensive jokes and topics of conversation. However, the humour in some workplaces is very coarse and offensive, including sexist, racist and homophobic jokes as well as 'dirty talk'. Any challenges are muted for fear of being ostracized.

Routine ways of greeting or addressing one another: In general, interactions between engineers are entirely respectful. However, routine ways of greeting or addressing one another tend to be those which men use with other men – 'mate' or 'man', even handshakes – and so are absent when men interact with women engineers. Such 'subtle absences' may mean that women engineers have to work harder than men to achieve the same level of easy acceptance with new associates or colleagues.

Gendered language: Engineers routinely use the generic 'he' when referring to other engineers. At best, expressions like 'We put our key men forward' or 'Go talk to the electrical boys' render women engineers invisible; at worst, they render the very category 'woman engineer' a non-sequitur! It is not difficult to promote gender inclusive language in engineering documentation as well as everyday talk.

Social circles and networks: There is considerable mixed-sex socializing and camaraderie amongst engineers, and most organized social activities (except the football sessions!) involve women and men. However, men-only social circles are common in engineering. Some of these have a significant influence on how the job gets done, and on who gets promoted. Breaking into the 'inner circles' can be difficult for women (and marginal men), for instance, where they bond on the golf course or over drinking sessions.

Conformity and diversity: Engineering workplace cultures accommodate a range of men – laddish blokes, family men, pranksters, macho men, nerdy men, urbane men, genteel men – and so are likely to feel comfortable to the great majority of men. Women are expected to adapt and become 'one of the lads' in order to fit in but, at the same time, not to 'lose their femininity'.

The 'in/visibility paradox' facing women engineers: Women engineers are so visible as women they are often invisible as engineers. Because the norm is a male engineer, even really experienced women engineers may have to (re)establish their engineering credentials every time they encounter a new colleague or associate – who may otherwise assume they are a secretary!

Sexual visibility and harassment: Women are also (hetero) sexually visible in a way men engineers rarely experience. Most have encountered sexual harassment and/or heavy flirting from men at some point. Often young women are unaware of procedures in place to deal with such harassment.

4.7.2 Women in engineering: The next steps

Monique Frize

The rights and position of women in many countries have improved substantially in the last century, but progress has not been linear. In certain eras, women's access to education and their ability to participate in the public domain improved, but later returned to previous conditions, with minimal educational opportunities or public role. In contrast with gains that women have made in accessing university education, relatively few choose engineering, and a representative proportion of women is still far from being reached. This is especially true in new areas of engineering, such as nanotechnology and robotics. Moreover, the increase in the enrolment of women in engineering programmes in the 1980s and 1990s has now been lost in three short years (2003–2006).

For many centuries, the participation of women in science has been cyclical with eras of advancement followed by eras of retrenchment. To break this cycle in the twenty-first century, major and concurrent efforts will be needed to reach all of the key stakeholders: girls and young women, parents and teachers, guidance counsellors, employers of engineers, role models and leaders in the scientific and professional engineering associations. We must bear in mind that outreach programmes that have been successful in the past need to be dynamic and fine-tuned for the changing teenage cultures of the new millennium; we must also reach the adults who could have some influence on their career choices.

Faculties of engineering should provide quality counselling to ensure that programme and course choices are a good fit with the student's interests and abilities. Once women make a commitment to a career in engineering, it is critical to put in place retention strategies such as providing networking opportunities for students in lower years to meet older students, or providing tutoring for those in need of help. Long-term structural and cultural changes are necessary to make engineering schools and faculties more hospitable for female students. While the environment has improved over the past decade, demeaning jokes and comments are still present and have negative effects.[62] Student newspapers appear to be more professional but they still occasionally contain inappropriate articles and sexist images. When planning group work for laboratories or design teams, it is recommended to have at least 50 per cent women in each group (resulting of course in some groups consisting of men only) since male-dominated teams tend to bring out the more traditional gender-linked behaviour in both men and women.[63] For example, the men will tend to ask the women to take the notes while they will be keen to do the hands-on work. In most programmes, the teaching style remains traditional[64] and theory is seldom connected to real life applications and contexts, which demotivates many students but women in particular.

Tobias[65] suggests that massive restructuring of the curriculum and pedagogy of elementary and secondary school science is needed to improve science literacy. In university, Tobias found some bright women and men avoid science and engineering programmes or leave after attending a few classes; others leave mid-way through their degree. Retaining this type of student could bring positive changes to the culture and make the environment friendlier for everyone. Large classes are usually taught with traditional lectures in large halls, so it is not easy to apply small group self-learning methods. Rosser[66] describes several ways to create a more 'women-friendly culture', arguing that these changes will also benefit male students.

Hiring more women faculty would help to attract an increased number of women entering into engineering graduate programmes at both the Master's and PhD levels. Moody[67] presents some of the frequent myths and easy excuses used to avoid

© Cecilia Ross

⋂ *Engineering needs more women.*

62 Ingram, Sandra and Anne Parker. 2002. The influence of gender on collaborative projects in an engineering classroom. *IEEE Transaction on Professional Communication*, Vol. 45, No. 1, pp. 7–20.

63 Ingram, Sandra and Anne Parker. 2002. The influence of gender on collaborative projects in an engineering classroom. *IEEE Transaction on Professional Communication*, Vol. 45, No. 1, pp. 7–20.

64 Anderson, Inger J. T. 2002. *The social construction of female engineers: A qualitative case study of engineering education.* Department of Sociology, University of Saskatchewan.

65 Tobias, S. 1992. *They're not dumb, they're different: Stalking the second tier.* Tucson AZ: Research Corp.

66 Rosser, Sue V. 1997. *Re-Engineering Female Friendly Science.* New York: Teachers College Press, Columbia University.

67 Moody, JoAnn. 2004. *Faculty diversity problems and solutions.* New York: Routledge.

hiring new faculty from under-represented groups; she recommends nineteen practices for university presidents, provosts, deans and departments. She also offers advice for academic search committees such as avoiding biased decision-making and snap judgements, seizing pretexts, and downgrading the institutions from which candidates obtained their degree.[68] It is frequent to hear in male-dominated departments comments such as 'we cannot lower our standards', suggesting that hiring a woman or a person from a visible minority will have this outcome. In fact, the bar is often raised for these candidates compared to the expectations from candidates from a majority group. Criteria in judging achievement, which affects hiring, tenure, promotion and the awarding of research chairs or professorships, must reflect the quality of publications instead of their number. Universities also need to create policies that allow young faculty members – female and male – to balance family and career, while looking at the potential of candidates versus what they have accomplished by the time of the interview. Biases can be reduced through education and gender sensitization programmes and ensuring a fair gender representation on decision-making committees. Proactive methods to find qualified women for positions or awards will also help.

In engineering workplaces, employers can develop objective hiring criteria, proactively seek women applicants and sensitize selection committees to recognize appropriate questions and illegal ones. Creating opportunities for women to meet and network with a fast track for women identified with management potential will provide mentors for younger women, and hopefully lead to an integration of feminine values into the culture. Instituting flexible hours can help reduce staff turnover and thus the cost of hiring and training new people. Parental leave should be available to mothers and fathers with no negative impact on their career. Access to affordable childcare is a major factor in retaining young parents in today's workplace. Providing visible assignments to people who need to build their self-confidence and credibility is important.

Progress in scientific and professional associations can be assessed by monitoring the proportion of women elected to positions on the governing body, on important committees, receiving awards and prizes, invited as keynote speakers, panelists on specialty topics and plenary sessions. Qualified women can be found, and recognizing their achievements and expertise will accelerate progress towards a fairer representation and add new perspectives in solving technological problems.

Until we get rid of stereotypes about people's aptitudes and behaviours, it will be impossible to create an atmosphere of respect and trust. The predominantly male view is not the only way to create new knowledge; the range of perspective women can bring will undoubtedly be a benefit. Integrating women's

values in a way that permeates all aspects of knowledge will have a positive impact.

One way to enhance career success is to network with colleagues in our field and with women in engineering and science. The former will be helpful to ensure that our expertise and achievements are recognized by peers, and that we have opportunities to share knowledge and learn with them. The networking available within women's organizations is also very important to share best practices on how to increase the participation of women at all levels and strategies for career advancement. Discussing how to balance work and personal life is another important aspect for everyone, women and men, in this new millennium where more men are sharing the parenting responsibilities.[69]

Effecting a change of attitudes and behaviour takes time. Equity does not just mean an equal number of women and men; it means equal chances of success and career development and having a voice at meetings. It means that average women will succeed as much as average men. If more women feel comfortable in choosing these fields, they will achieve economic independence and have more control over their lives. Women must face challenges fearlessly, discover their talents and skills, and believe in themselves. Men and women should be partners and agents of change, each in their own way.

4.7.3 Women and gender issues in engineering: an Australian perspective

Marlene Kanga

Australia is faced with an acute shortage of engineering skills, especially in electrical, mechanical, civil and mining engineering.[70] This is resulting in capacity constraints in many sectors of the economy, especially mining and infrastructure development. In such an environment, it is vital to attract both men and women to engineering and retain those who have qualified as engineers within the profession.

Women engineers currently represent less than 7 per cent of the engineering workforce in Australia – one of the lowest participation rates of women across all professions in Australia. Ensuring that more women join and remain in the profession is vital from a social equity viewpoint while providing a means to increase excellence and address the shortage of engineering skills.

68   Moody, JoAnn. 2004. *Faculty diversity problems and solutions*. New York: Routledge.

69   For more information on the International Network of Women Engineers and Scientists: http://www.inwes.org

70   *The Engineering Profession: A Statistical Review*, Engineers Australia March 2006, http://engineersaustralia.org.au

Approximately 1,500 Australian women commence engineering undergraduate degrees every year, representing approximately 13.6 per cent of all engineering students in 2006. This share has remained relatively unchanged since 1994 (13.4 per cent), although it rose to 15.7 per cent in 2001 and then declined.[71] In addition, around 500 women commence postgraduate engineering programmes annually. Approximately 1,200 foreign women students commence mainly postgraduate engineering degrees each year, up from around 200 in 1994. The overall share of women at all levels of student engineering commencements is around 15 per cent and has been at this level for the past ten years as shown in Figure 1.

Despite the relatively small numbers, women tend to complete their engineering courses with great success, representing 15 per cent of total engineering graduations, as shown in Figure 2. Retention levels for engineering students tend to be 60 per cent for women students compared to 52 per cent for men, on average. There is anecdotal evidence that women engineers tend to perform better than their male counterparts academically, and tend to achieve a higher proportion of awards and university medals and prizes.

Many women engineers tend to leave the profession within the first few years of graduating. Consequently, women engineers in Australia tend to be young. The annual survey conducted by the Association of Professional Engineers, Scientists and Managers, Australia (APESMA, 2007) reported the average age of women engineers as 31.2 years compared to 43.5 years for men.[72] The average age for women engineers is lower than the average for women scientists at 35.3 years, and for women information technology professionals at 42.8 years. The APESMA 2007 survey confirms that the retention of women in the engineering profession is an ongoing problem and that women are leaving the engineering profession at a rate 38.8 per cent faster than their male counterparts.

The statistics on membership of Engineers Australia (the national professional engineering body) shows the continuing low proportion of women engineers in the country, comprising of less than 7 per cent of its total membership in March 2008. Longitudinal analysis of these membership statistics shows that that until 2004, women tended not to progress to full qualification (so presumably were leaving while still graduate members), and that the women who were qualified were also leaving the profession. It appears that this trend may have just turned the corner and that the retention of women within Engineers Australia has started

Figure 1: **Share of women in all student commencements in Australian University engineering courses**

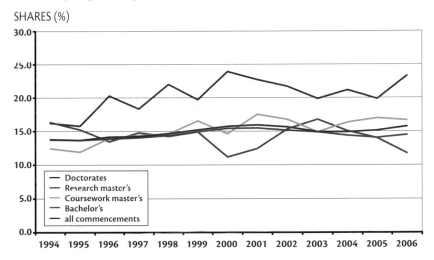

Figure 2: **Share of women in all students graduating from Australian University engineering courses**

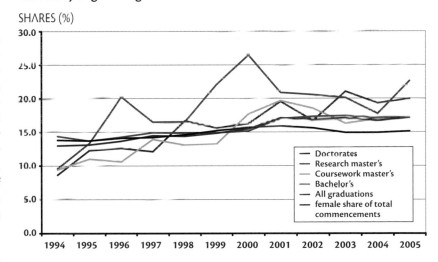

to improve. Figure 3 shows that the percentage of women members has increased steadily since 1999 from 4.0 per cent to 6.8 per cent.[73]

Women also show smaller proportions in holding positions of significant responsibility. For example, the Engineers Australia Career Review of Engineering Women (CREW, 2007) survey reports that 77.8 per cent of women engineers were in lower responsibility level positions (Levels 1 to 3 on a scale of 5). This was also reflected in their remuneration levels where 30 per cent of women earned less than AU$60,000 compared with 24 per cent of men, and that 50.6 per cent earned less than AU$75,000. At the higher end, only 10 per cent of

71 *Women in Engineering Studies in Australia*, Statistical Report prepared from data provided by the Department of Education, Science and Training (DEST), Engineers Australia, November 2007. http://www.engineersaustralia.org.au/wie (Accessed: 16 May 2010).

72 *Women in the Professions Survey Report 2007*, APESMA, Melbourne. http://www.apesma.asn.au/women (Accessed: 16 May 2010).

73 Membership Statistics, Engineers Australia, March 2008, unpublished.

Figure 3: **Total number of women members of Engineers Australia (1980–March 2008)**

Membership Grade	Total Number of Women						Percentage of Member Category (%)					
	1980	1990	2000	2003	2005	2008	1980	1990	2000	2003	2005	2008
Fellow	0	4	39	46	60	74	0	0.14	0.5	0.89	1.13	1.40
Member	46	263	496	938	1192	1613	0.3	0.9	1.8	2.94	3.73	4.78
Graduate	41	346	1741	2138	1768	1919	0.6	3.7	9.5	10.75	11.92	13.55
Student	14	467	1295	3904	4318	4760	1.4	8.2	15.0	16.83	16.00	15.72
Total	**87**	**613**	**2276**	**3122**	**3020**	**3606**	N/A	N/A	**4.0**	**5.48**	**5.79**	**6.78**

Source: Engineers Australia Membership Statistics to March 2008, unpublished

women compared to 15 per cent of men earned more than AU$121,000.[74]

Women engineers face significant barriers in comparison to other professional women in terms of an often unsupportive workplace culture. Two surveys conducted by the National Committee for Women in Engineering in Australia indicate that discrimination, bullying and harassment are common, although the incidence has reduced since the first survey (CREW Survey, 2002,[75] CREW Revisited).[76] The basis of discrimination reported was overwhelmingly gender, which was reported across all age groups but particularly by women engineers less than forty years of age. It is encouraging to note that employers have recognized the need to address work practices to modify these behaviours, just as considerable work has been done to achieve safe work practices in the past decade. The current survey shows that some engineering organizations now provide training in equity and diversity management for their employees and have developed equity and diversity policies and organizational practices to assess their equity performance that set targets for improvement.

Responsibilities for children are also a significant issue for women engineers, where 78.1 per cent of respondents to the CREW 2007 survey were not responsible for dependent children.[77] The survey also reported that 67.1 per cent of women engineering respondents did not have children, as shown in Figure 4. Both these results are significantly above the rate of 24 per cent of all women estimated by the Australian Bureau of Statistics to remain childless (in 2002), reflecting the relatively young age of women engineers and also the tendency of women to leave once they have families.

However this is beginning to be redressed in the Australian engineering profession. It is encouraging that the most significant result of the 2007 survey is the increased availability of family-friendly workplaces as shown in Figure 5.

Family-friendly practices are intended to assist employees to balance work and family commitments and consequently enhance their productivity. As women are still more frequently the primary care-givers for children, family-friendly practices should assist their retention and career progression. Engineering firms have recognized the messages about family-friendly workplace practices being critically important to attract and retain engineers and have put appropriate policies into place. Some 79 per cent of women respondents indicated that flexible work hours were available. Women respondents also indicated that paid maternity leave (72 per cent), leave without pay (91 per cent) and carer's leave (79 per cent) was available in a large majority of firms.

74   Mills, J., Mehrtens, V., Smith, E. and Adams, V, CREW Revisited in 2007. *The Year of Women in Engineering,* Engineers Australia, April 2008, http://www.engineersaustralia.org.au/wie (Accessed: 16 May 2010).

75   *Counting the losses: Career Review of Engineering Women* (CREW) Report, Engineers Australia, 2002, http://www.engineersaustralia.org.au/wie (Accessed: 16 May 2010).

76   Mills, J., Mehrtens, V., Smith, E. and Adams, V, CREW Revisited in 2007. *The Year of Women in Engineering,* Engineers Australia, April 2008, http://www.engineersaustralia.org.au/wie (Accessed: 16 May 2010).

77   Mills, J., Mehrtens, V., Smith, E. and Adams, V, CREW Revisited in 2007. *The Year of Women in Engineering,* Engineers Australia, April 2008, http://www.engineersaustralia.org.au/wie (Accessed: 16 May 2010).

Figure 4: **Percentage of women without children by professional discipline**

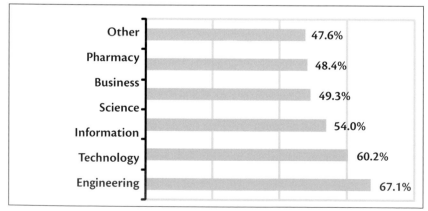

Source: APESMA Survey 2007 (see note 76).

Figure 5: **Availability and use of family-friendly employment practices in the engineering profession**

Family friendly employment practices	Percentage reporting the availability of these practices (%)		Percentage reporting having used these practices (%)	
	Women	Men	Women	Men
Flexible work hours available	79.0	78.3	75.5	79.4
Job sharing **	29.6	30.4	18.0	28.7
Part-time work **	67.7	55.5	21.2	10.1
Leave without pay **	91.4	89.1	35.8	26.3
Carer's leave	79.1	77.3	18.1	19.1
Paid maternity leave	72.4	70.0	11.7	N/A
Paid paternity leave	67.7	68.6	N/A	9.9

** Indicates a significant difference in having used these practices using the Pearson Chi-squared test with a p-value of <0.05 signifying a 95% confidence in the results.

Source: Engineers Australia CREW 2007 survey

Case studies of engagement from Engineers Australia

Engineers Australia recognizes the importance of attracting and retaining women engineers. The vision of its National Committee for Women in Engineering is that engineering becomes an inclusive profession which values, supports and celebrates the contributions of women in the engineering team. The Committee ran a very successful 'Year of Women in Engineering' campaign in 2007, which increased awareness of the achievements of women engineers within the membership of the professional institution. The committee also has strategies for attracting and retaining women in engineering which cover the entire career professional life cycle, from attracting girls to engineering, encouraging and supporting these students at university, and further support as they enter the profession. It is also encouraging employers to develop appropriate policies to retain these women as they start to have families and raise children. Examples include:

- 'GirlTalk' is a programme designed for school students to inform them about engineering as a career. A successful pilot has been delivered to more than 600 students, presented by women engineers. This programme will be delivered nationally.

- Professional development workshops specifically for women engineers are delivered to assist and support women in developing skills for dealing with a male-dominated workplace, and to prepare them for future leadership roles. These workshops and seminars include: 'Breakthrough Career Strategies for Women Engineer'; 'Managing a Diverse Workforce, What you Need to Know'; 'Women in Engineering Leadership Seminars'. These events in 2007 and 2008 reached more than 1,000 women around Australia.

- A 'Career Flexibility Policy' has been approved in principle and is being developed, recognizing the need for flexibility in maintaining chartered engineer status and ongoing registration on the National Professional Engineers Register while taking a career break or working part-time.

Engineers work in similar fields and have similar backgrounds, and engineering faces similar issues and challenges around the world, for example, in such areas as the decline of interest and enrolment of young people in engineering. However, these issues and challenges differ significantly in different regions and countries and within countries as well as in engineering resources and hence opportunities available to meet and address these issues and challenges. Because the situation of engineering is fairly comparable in similar countries and regions, and in view of limited data availability in some countries and limited space in the Report, it was decided to limit the number and size of such contributions – to be perspectives rather than country reports. This chapter presents a brief review of engineering around the world, with an introductory overview followed by regional perspectives on Africa, the Arab States, Asia and Pacific, Europe and the Americas and Caribbean. These are followed by country perspectives in Africa on Côte d'Ivoire, Ghana, Nigeria and Uganda, in the Arab States on Jordan, Lebanon and Tunisia, in Asia and the Pacific on Australia, China, India, Japan, Malaysia, and the South Pacific, in Europe on France, Germany, Poland, Russia and the United Kingdom, and in the the Americas and Caribbean on Argentina, Brazil, Canada, the USA, Venezuela, and the Caribbean.

5.1 Introductory overview

Tony Marjoram

Engineering similarities and diversities

Engineering is one of the most diverse professions in terms of fields of engineering, types and levels of engineer, where and how they are employed as well as the status of engineers and engineering, and this diversity is reflected around the world; engineering is both global and local. Most political leaders and policy-makers appear to agree that the development and application of knowledge in engineering and technology underpins and drives sustainable social and economic development, and that engineering and technology are vital in addressing the Millennium Development Goals (MDGs), basic human needs, poverty reduction and sustainable development, and in order to bridge the knowledge divide. Most would also agree that one of the major issues and challenges facing engineering is the decline of interest and enrolment of young people, especially women, in engineering in most countries around the world, which will seriously impact on capacity in engineering and the capacity of engineering to address poverty reduction, sustainable development and other MDGs. These are major concerns and challenges for engineering and the world. Despite the comments of world leaders on knowledge societies and economies, and the declarations made at international conferences and world summits, engineering is routinely overlooked in the context of development policy and planning, and is hardly mentioned in relation to the MDGs or in many Poverty Reduction Strategy Papers (PRSPs) for example.

Although engineering is both global and local, most engineers work in larger countries and economies where most engineering activity takes place in terms of the production of knowledge, patents and technology. Most technology is shaped in such societies, in accordance with perceived market and consumer needs and demands, and the associated support systems and infrastructure in engineering. This technology is then innovated and used around the world where such support systems and infrastructure may be weaker; technology transfer is a complex process. Very few countries have the engineering resources to design and manufacture jet engines for example, and few have the resources to maintain them. Similar considerations apply to the latest automobile technology – cars require increasingly sophisticated diagnostic and maintenance tools and equipment, and the home or back-street adjustment of carburettors, points and plugs of a generation ago, as with other modern 'non user serviceable' technologies, is no longer possible.

Whilst engineering faces similar issues and challenges around the world, the scale and specificity of these issues and challenges differs significantly in different regions and countries and within countries, as well as in the engineering resources and hence opportunities available to meet them. This raises important issues regarding the need for technology and engineering to be appropriate to local contexts and needs, as well as important issues and questions regarding technology policy, choice, decision making and management. These are major considerations regarding effective technology transfer, although the international focus has more often been on the protection of intellectual property as a key consideration, for example in the Agreement on Trade-Related Aspects of Intellectual Property Rights (TRIPS) – the most important instrument for the globalization of intellectual property laws and a compulsory membership requirement of the World Trade Organization. Almost gone are the days of Humphry Davy and his refusal to patent the miner's safety 'Davy lamp' for the 'cause of humanity'.

Engineering capacity, capacity-building and education

Similar and specific issues face engineering around the world including: engineering capacity and capacity-building, education, training and associated standards and accreditation;

national and international cooperation, networking and partnerships; engineering infrastructure, applications and innovation; and engineering policy and planning, information and indicators. In the context of capacity and education, although there are at present increasing numbers of young people in tertiary education, many countries are reporting a shortage of engineers, and indications that they are not producing enough engineers to maintain current capacities or meet expected increases in capacity in growing and emerging industries. Many countries also report for example, particular shortages in certain areas of engineering (e.g. mechanical, civil, medical and biochemical engineers in the manufacturing, industry, infrastructure, health and mining sectors), at certain levels (e.g. technicians and technologists), and an impending demand for engineers in such areas as nuclear power, renewable energy, and other emerging industries associated with climate change mitigation and adaptation. On top of this, many countries are concerned about a serious potential decline in engineering capacity in the medium and longer term in all areas as many engineers approach retirement, and birth rates are declining in many industrialized countries.

Universities have an obvious and important role in engineering education, training, capacity and capacity-building, continuous professional development (CPD), engineering standards and professional accreditation. Larger countries and economies usually have a diversity of universities with schools or faculties of engineering including 'research universities' with backgrounds in research and development and innovation, and supported by government and foundation funding, often linked to industry and private sector support. This is less the case in developing and especially least developing countries where there are usually only a few universities that focus particularly on undergraduate teaching. Given the attractions of research for academic staff, promotions linked to papers published and the fact that many obtained PhDs in developed country universities, the temptation to migrate felt developing country engineers are significant, as is the impact of their brain drain on engineering capacity and national development.

Almost all countries report an under-representation of women and related gender issues in engineering, which is reflected in university enrolment but begins at secondary and even primary school level. Efforts to promote the participation of women in science and engineering in many countries increased university enrolment in these areas in the 1980s and 1990s from an average of 10–15 per cent to 20 per cent and above in some countries. This relates particularly to maths, physics, chemistry and all areas of engineering. Unfortunately, since 2000, progress and enrolment appears to have declined, back to 10 per cent in some countries. In other countries the participation of women in engineering is less than this, and in a few countries there are almost no women engineers at all. Interest in women and gender issues in engineering relates not only to equity and equality, but with a shortage of engineers and an under-representation of women in engineering it makes sense to promote the role of women in engineering. This will also help attract young men into engineering, and bring a more gender-sensitive approach to engineering. We urgently need to get more women and under-represented groups into engineering to maintain and promote knowledge societies and economies, address the MDGs and reduce brain drain and associated impacts on developing countries.

Networking and partnerships

Universities and university teaching and research engineers are also vital in promoting national and international cooperation, networking and partnerships in engineering, in conjunction with practicing professional, consulting and business engineers. This often takes place and is facilitated by professional engineering societies and institutions, which may be field specific or collective for the engineering profession as a whole, or unfortunately absent in some developing and least developed countries. Professional engineering societies and institutions play a vital role in promoting engineering education, training, CPD and capacity-building, standards, accreditation, information and advocacy through the development of networking and partnerships, and national and international cooperation. The lack or limitation of engineering organizations is a further constraint on their development, and requires the full support of the national and international engineering community.

Infrastructure, applications and innovation

As regards the engineering infrastructure, applications and innovation, as mentioned elsewhere, we live in engineered technocultures where all buildings, water supply and sanitation, transportation, energy and communication systems, and other aspects of the physical and non-physical infrastructure and other applications are engineered and innovated, as were many aspects of our tangible and intangible cultural heritage. Infrastructure around the world has suffered from a lack of maintenance in recent years, especially since the economic crisis and especially in developing countries. So it is interesting to observe that one of President Obama's first announcements on taking office was that infrastructure maintenance and development would be one focus of economic recovery and regeneration. Maintenance and reliability engineering, and the design of infrastructure for reliability and ease of maintenance, are important considerations discussed elsewhere in this Report. Engineering infrastructure, applications and innovation are also vital in addressing the MDGs in the context of basic needs and poverty reduction, in sustainable development, climate change mitigation and adaptation, and also in the context of emergencies and disaster response, reconstruction and mitigation. Engineering and technology applications need to be appropriate to local contexts, and local engineers for example need to be involved in aid-supported projects involving engineering in developing countries.

© UNESCO

◔ Tidal barrage.

Engineering policy, planning and management

Engineering policy, planning and management, and associated information and indicators, are necessary to facilitate engineering education and capacity-building, the development of networks and partnerships, infrastructure, applications and innovation. Serious issues and challenges in this context relate to the fact that engineering is often be overlooked in the policy context, as is engineering as part of the broader discussion of 'science'. Although interest in science and technology studies and policy developed in the 1960s, the focus was mainly on science and technology studies, policy and planning, with little reference to engineering, and the study of engineering and

engineering policy have remained a rather neglected area of interest and emphasis. At the same time, statistics and indicators on science and engineering are aggregated in international data gathering, which is of little use in the analysis of science or engineering, or of different branches of science and engineering. There is therefore an important need, and opportunity, to develop the fields of engineering studies, engineering policy, planning and management, and to develop better statistics and indicators on engineering as an input to policy and planning. These fields need to be developed with specific reference to the role of engineering policy, planning and management for development.

5.2   Regional perspectives on engineering

Africa

Nelius Boshoff and Johann Mouton

The engineering discourse in Africa is largely focused on matters related to capacity-building and the contribution of engineering projects to sustainable development. The discourse informs engineering initiatives in Africa. The development of the African engineering profession in recent years has also benefitted from the activities of the Engineering Council of South Africa (ECSA).

For example, in 2005, ECSA signed an important memorandum of understanding with the New Partnership for Africa's Development (NEPAD). This signified the intent of ECSA and NEPAD to collaborate in building engineering capacity in Africa where ECSA, for instance, assumed responsibility for the design and quality assurance of educational programmes in engineering for African countries. However, even prior to the signing, ECSA was already providing support to African

countries as far north as Ethiopia (Poggiolini, 2004)[78]. ECSA is also collaborating with the South African Centre for Scientific and Industrial Research to create centres of excellence in the Southern African Development Community (SADC) region (ECSA, 2007).[79] Only twelve countries in Africa have national science academies (Cameroon, Egypt, Ghana, Kenya, Madagascar, Nigeria, Senegal, South Africa, Sudan, Tanzania, Zambia and Zimbabwe), and of these only South Africa has an engineering academy.

Sub-Saharan Africa, with the exception of South Africa, lags behind in terms of engineering capacity and research productivity. The building of engineering capacity-building in Africa is dependent on a number of factors and conditions such as large internationally-funded engineering projects to serve as learning sites, the prioritization of engineering education and the creation of engineering schools and even engineering academies that can provide recognition to promising engineers (Juma, 2006).[80] Existing engineering research capacity and expertise in Africa can be highlighted by looking at the publication patterns of engineering researchers, in particular the country affiliations of publications and field classifications for the journals in which the publications appear. Figure 1 shows that between the early 1990s and the most recent reporting period, African-based researchers more than doubled their total publication output (from 3170 to 7886).

The ISI Web of Science database by Thomson Scientific was used as the main data source. Publications, for our purpose,

Figure 1: **Number of publications produced by African-based researchers in engineering and applied technologies, 1990–2007**

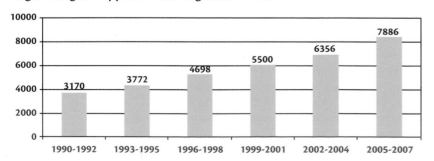

78 Poggiolini, D. 2004. Achieving new heights in professionalism. *IMIESA*, September 2004, pp.63–65.

79 ECSA. 2007. *Media Release. Engineering Council of South Africa*, 1 June 2007.

80 Juma, C. 2006. Engineering education vital for Africa's growth. *The East African*, 16 October 2006.

were taken to mean articles, reviews, notes and letters. Thus, it is possible in the ISI Web of Science database to extract only articles produced by authors in African countries, specifically for the broad field of engineering and applied technologies. We created the broad field by grouping together 33 sub-fields (agricultural engineering, automation & control systems, software engineering, etc.). Note that Figure 1 excludes publications appearing in journals not indexed by the ISI Web of Science. In the case of South Africa, about 20 per cent of the country's total publication output in engineering and applied

Figure 2: **Country breakdown of ISI publications produced by African-based researchers in Engineering and Applied Technologies, 2005-2007**

Ten most productive countries in 2005-2007 by rank	1990-1992		2005-2007	
	Publication count	Proportion of publications (out of 3170, %)	Publication count	Proportion of publications (out of 7886, %)
1. Egypt	1312	41.4%	2385	30.2%
2. South Africa	924	29.1%	1775	22.5%
3. Algeria	142	4.5%	1098	13.9%
4. Tunisia	65	2.1%	1080	13.7%
5. Morocco	176	5.6%	606	7.7%
6. Nigeria	292	9.2%	375	4.8%
7. Libya	44	1.4%	95	1.2%
8. Cameroon	13	0.4%	78	1.0%
9. Ghana	26	0.8%	53	0.7%
10. Kenya	43	1.4%	52	0.7%

Note that publication counts cannot be totalled due to multiple-country co-authorships of publications.

Figure 3: **Sub-field breakdown of ISI publications produced by African-based researchers in Engineering and Applied Technologies, 1990-1992 and 2005-2007**

Field of classification	1990-1992		2005-2007	
	Publication count	Proportion of publications (out of 3170, %)	Publication count	Proportion of publications (out of 7886, %)
Materials science	955	30.1%	2608	33.1%
Chemical engineering	337	10.6%	1290	16.4%
Electrical & electronic engineering	411	13.0%	942	11.9%
Energy & fuels	256	8.1%	617	7.8%
Mechanics	206	6.5%	586	7.4%
Nuclear science & technology	386	12.2%	510	6.5%
Metallurgy & metallurgical engineering	321	10.1%	510	6.5%
Mechanical engineering	155	4.9%	473	6.0%
Civil engineering	159	5.0%	379	4.8%
Environmental engineering	160	5.0%	337	4.3%
Instruments & instrumentation	105	3.3%	322	4.1%
Mining & mineral processing	185	5.8%	263	3.3%

Note that publication counts cannot be totalled due to multiple sub-field classifications of journals in which publications appear.

technologies can be found in national journals not indexed by the ISI – Fig.1 therefore only includes for South Africa the 80 per cent of publications appearing in ISI journals.

The fact that the total article output for Africa steadily and linearly increased between 1990–1992 and 2005–2007 does not mean that all African countries contributed equally to knowledge production activities in engineering and applied technologies. Figure 2 shows that in 2005–2007, only Egypt, South Africa, Algeria and Tunisia produced more than 10 per cent of the total publication output in this field. Of these, Egypt and South Africa are the most significant contributors accounting for 30 per cent and 23 per cent respectively of publication output. It is also clear that, besides Egypt and South Africa, Francophone countries dominate output in engineering. Algeria and Tunisia significantly increased their share of publications between 1990–1992 and 2005–2007.

Figure 3 gives a breakdown of publications in terms of subfields. Materials science, chemical engineering and electrical & electronic engineering are the three fields, which account for most papers. An interesting trend is reflected in Africa's publication in the field of nuclear science and technology: 6.5 per cent of engineering publications in 2005–2007. However, although this represents a decrease compared to the corresponding percentage for 1990–1992 (12 per cent of all engineering publications in Africa), the number of articles in this sub-field has actually increased. The same observation applies to metallurgy and metallurgical engineering.

Arab States

Federation of Arab Engineers

Since the dawn of civilization, the contributions of Arab-Islamic engineering and architecture and the achievements of Arab-Islamic civilization to the sciences of astronomy, phys-

ics, mathematics, medicine, chemistry and others, are indeed notable and undeniably significant.

In modern times (the latter part of past century and the early twenty-first century), Arab engineers have a mammoth task and an extremely important role to play in the development of their countries. Governments of various Arab countries have, to differing degrees, invested in engineering institutions and have given support for thousands of individuals, through grants and other financial assistance, to acquire engineering skills in various engineering disciplines.

Engineers – both in general and those of developing countries – have the challenge of nurturing abilities to best utilize new technologies, be conversant in foreign languages and understand the culture, issues and challenges of more developed countries. They have to conform to the appropriate utilization of natural resources, act on environmental protection and consider diverse effects of their projects in both technical and social dimensions. It is imperative that appropriate entities develop programmes of training to enhance the current capabilities of engineers.

Although statistics reveal a vast number of Arab engineers graduate in various fields, many with PhDs, the output has never been assessed. The table below shows headline data available on Arab engineers.

Europe

Lars Bytoft

Introduction

Europe is facing two main challenges. The first is globalization, which means that a new division of trade and labour is emerging and that targeted measures to keep Europe competitive

Country	Engineers per 100,000 (excluding expatriates)	Engineers per 100,000 (including expatriates)	Comments	Year
Kuwait	369	821		1997
Saudi Arabia	113	460		2005
Emirates	68	1,135		2005
Bahrain	130	385		1997
Jordan	-	1,392	Includes architects	2008
Egypt	-	2,800	May include technicians and architects	1997
Morocco	-	80		
Tunisia	300	-		2007

Source: The above statistics were extracted from material by Dr. Khalid Bin Salem Al-Sultan.

are needed. The second is solving the environmental problems facing both Europe and the world. Both European national governments and the European Commission have put forward some very ambitious plans for the handling of these challenges, but one vital obstacle may jeopardize the plans: the current shortage of engineers in many European countries, which will worsen in the future because of demography and a declining interest in science and technology studies.

Background

In order to meet the challenges of globalization and the new international division of labour, many national European governments and the European Union (EU) have set up a number of ambitious goals. Some of these goals are contained in the Lisbon agreement, where European countries have agreed to be the world's leading 'knowledge region'. This implies, amongst other things, that countries have agreed to spend at least 3% per cent of national GDP on research and development.

In addition, the threats from climatic changes and access to secure energy supply have led the EU to launch the so-called 'Climate Change and Energy Package' with some relatively ambitious goals on energy policy and renewable energy sources. To achieve these goals, and other targeted measures, the EU needs to improve the skill levels of its workforce. In engineering especially, there will be an increase in demand from both the public and the private sector. The public sector will need more engineers to meet the infrastructural challenges in energy, transport, healthcare, waste handling, education and so on. The private sector will need more engineering skills if it wants to reap the benefits of the changing international division of labour. Europe will not be able to compete within many of the labour-intensive segments of production and services, and therefore private companies need to be more technology-and-research intensive.

Until recently, the growing demand for engineering skills in both the public and private sectors in Europe was met by a complementary growth in both relative and absolute supply. In the past fifteen years however, there has been a decrease in the relative number of graduating engineers in Europe.[81] To make things even worse, the generally ageing European population and the age structure of the engineering workforce results in a massive retirement from the engineering profession within the near future. By then, the shortage of engineering skills will be a joint European problem.

European-wide statistics do not exist, but several country-specific studies have shown that the shortage of engineers is and will be severe. A German study from 2007 showed that German companies in 2006 had around 50,000 vacancies for engi-

neers that could not be filled.[82] In Denmark, a recent study has shown that by 2020 the labour market will be lacking 14,000 engineers (in comparison, there were approximately 80,000 engineers in the Danish labour market in 2008).[83] The situation seems to be similar in all European countries, but with variations in timetable.

In some countries, the lack of engineers is already severe either in general or in particular specializations. One sector that seems to be especially hard hit by the lack of engineers is the public sector. In many European countries the demography is such that the public sector within the next 10–15 years will have to recruit a disproportionately large number of new engineers because of retirements. This can be a very difficult exercise in a situation where the commodity is scarce and where the private sector in many cases will be able to offer better salaries, job opportunities and professional careers.

The opportunities for engineering graduates appear to be good, especially if compared with those of other faculties. Engineering remains the university curriculum that is most likely to provide a graduate with a job in a short period of time. However, many engineers express dissatisfaction with the quality of the job they find, as well as with the level of their salaries.[84] Furthermore engineers working in technical offices of private companies can often feel an 'inferiority complex' compared to colleagues working in the sales and marketing offices. They feel that the technical contribution does not receive enough consideration in today's production sector.

Another source of dissatisfaction comes from the now precarious nature of the labour market. This reality does not give young graduates a long-term perspective, which could somehow compensate for the decreased prestige and salary of an engineering career.[85] More attractive career prospects can be found by engineers who leave their original technical vocation in order to take up commercial or management positions. Those engineers working as freelance professionals find it difficult to compete against the technical services available from the globalized labour market.

The bottom line is that European visions about staying competitive and creating a sustainable society will be halted by an existing and growing shortage of engineering skills if nothing is done about it. The European Federation of National Engineering Associations (FEANI) therefore finds it urgent to address the 'shortage problem both within each European country and

81 Described in the OECD Policy Report Evolution of Student Interest in Science and Technology Studies, May 2006. Available at: http://www.oecd.org/dataoecd/28/55/36720580.htm (Accessed: 16 May 2010).

82 Verein Deutscher Ingenieure (Association of German Engineers, VDI), 2006.

83 Danish Society of Engineers (IDA), 2007.

84 Monastersky, R. 2004. Is there a science crisis? *The Chronicle of Higher Education*. Vol. 50, July 2004.

85 Vines, J. 2005. Engineering a crisis on the supply side. *Australian Financial Review*, March 2005.

on an overall European level. Many European countries have already taken national actions, but in FEANI we believe there will be comprehensive synergetic effects in a joint European effort to expand and utilize the pool of engineering skills.

Americas and Caribbean

Vladimir Yackovlev and Luiz Scavarda

The working group on Science, Technology and Innovation of the UN Millennium Project issued a declaration that 'developing countries will probably remain bogged down in poverty unless they do what the developed countries have done to reach sustainable growth: incorporate science, technology and innovation in their economic development strategies.' 'Engineering with social responsibility' could be added to the list, indeed, the specific importance of more and better-prepared engineers must be recognized in Latin America.

One of the reasons cited for Latin America lagging behind in its development is that practically all economists of the region have placed their hopes on the role of the market and have ignored the fundamental role played by research and engineering in the development process. The International Monetary Fund (IMF) has published data showing that the two regions of Southeast Asia and Latin America each contributed 10 per cent to the total GDP of the world in 1980, but today the contribution of South East Asia has risen to about 27 per cent whereas the Latin American contribution has fallen to about 7 per cent.

It is worth noting that, over the same period, the number of engineers in emerging Asia grew steadily whilst Latin America has a relatively small number of engineers.

Figure 1: **GDP as percentage of world total**

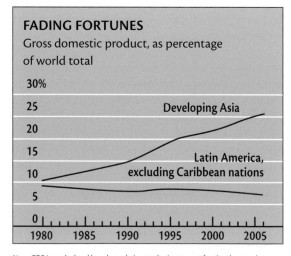

FADING FORTUNES
Gross domestic product, as percentage of world total

Note: GDP is recalculated based on relative purchasing power of national currencies.
Source: International Monetary Fund

In order to achieve sustainable development in a country or a region, certain characteristics have to be developed such as a solid basic education, high literacy rates, and the existence of well-educated professionals and highly-trained technicians who can adopt and adapt new capabilities. Such economic changes as seen in these IMF data can however be attributed to fundamental differences in national policies.

Indicators of the Latin American region fall below what might be considered desirable, perhaps because of some of the following factors:

- Public research is driven largely by scientific curiosity rather than market needs or the need to find solutions to the problems of the region.

- There is little cooperation between universities, industry and public research institutes.

- There is a lack of an innovation culture in industry, linked with demand.

- There is low investment in knowledge, with Latin America spending only around 0.6 per cent of GNP on research and development.

- Investment in research and development has diminished or remained at the same level in the region.

- The interest for the engineering profession among high school students is minimal in Latin America.

- The number of graduates with doctoral degrees and the number of researchers in the economically active population (a key indication of capacity) are several orders of magnitude below those of OECD countries and some countries in South East Asia.

Our world today is, beyond any doubt, under the influence of technology. Technology and knowledge is what determines the competitiveness of enterprise; it is technology that brings the capability for innovation and development. And it is the engineer who is the specialist in technology.

It is, therefore, not too risky to suggest that we need to increase the numbers of engineers in developing countries, especially if we look at the results achieved in countries in South East Asia. However, care must be taken not to be swayed by numbers alone – the quality of these engineers must be jealously guarded. Such numbers are merely an indication of the role of the engineer in development but they are also a call for action for state policies to develop more and better-prepared engineers.

5.3 Country perspectives

5.3.1 Africa

Côte d'Ivoire

Issié Yvonne Gueye

Introduction

In the 1960s and 1970s engineering efforts in the Côte d'Ivoire focused on civil and agricultural engineering. After the military-political crisis faced for six years, Côte d'Ivoire is now at a crossroads economically, politically and technologically. To thrive, and given the needs for reconstruction and sustainable development, it is imperative that renewed efforts are placed on engineering, particularly with regards to international standards, to allow the country to become part of the global knowledge and information society. Engineering electrical engineering has an important role to play as it adds value to long-term development and speeds up poverty reduction.

Economy

The economy of the Côte d'Ivoire is broadly split between agriculture at 22 per cent, industries at 26 per cent and services at 52 per cent of GDP. Some 34 per cent of the population is engaged in subsistence farming. The country is oriented towards private enterprise, with government participation through parastatal companies. Multinational corporations are involved in two-thirds of the largest businesses in such areas as construction, energy, petroleum, construction and food processing.

For many years, Ivorian engineers were highly regarded and enjoyed good job security, partly due to the influence and the lobbying of the Federation of Engineering Organizations (FIACI); most high positions in government as well as in public and private companies were held by engineers. For example, from 1975 to 2002 many members of the board of FIACI worked in the ministries of infrastructure, telecommunications or agriculture.

Engineers today work mainly in public and private companies and consulting firms of the country, in similar sectors such as agriculture and food processing, construction and civil engineering, energy, petroleum, chemistry and mining, computing and communications and industrial processing. According to the available data, as of 2002,[86] engineers made up 1.2 per cent of the working population.

Higher Education

Early in the 1960s, the Côte d'Ivoire developed a long-term strategy to build technological capacities to meet the challenges of national development. Professional technical centres and technical high schools were established to meet industry's demand for technicians and to prepare youth towards engineering careers. The route to higher education is through four years of secondary school and three years to baccalaureate required for entry into universities or *Grandes Ecoles*. The *Grandes Ecoles* were created to develop senior technicians and engineers, with the first of these established in 1962 for civil engineering sciences, with extensions to geology and mining available from 1973. The first national university opened in Abidjan in 1964, followed by three specialized provincial annexes. The national Institute of Technical Education, the School of Agricultural Engineering and the School of Statistics and Economy were also launched. Private universities emerged to absorb the growing number of candidates, and trained two-year degree technicians in various fields.

Data from 2005 shows that higher education in the Côte d'Ivoire comprises: three public autonomous universities with 69,436 students; six private universities with 2,209 students; four public *Grandes Ecoles* with 10,150 students; and 108 private *Grandes Ecoles* with 94,745 students. These structures fall under the remit of the Ministry of Higher Education.[87] [88] In addition, there are twenty-eight centres giving post-baccalaureate professional and technical training to 15,604 students. These are under the remit of the Ministry of Technical Education. In sum, 192,144 students are in higher education. Women make up 29.7 per cent of this total. According to national statistics, 8 per cent of the population have gone through higher education.

New and next steps

To better engage in the global economy and to accompany the industrialization process, the government has initiated policies to encourage innovation, covering areas such as taxation and intellectual property. For example, the Ivorian Office of Intellectual Property[89] (a member of the African Office of Intellectual Property and the World Organization for Intellectual Property) was created in 2005 charged with promoting inven-

---

86 Kouassi, L. and Amani, M. 2002. *Recensement général de la population et de l'habitation de 1998*. Institut National de la Statistique, Vol. IV, Analyse des résultats, août 2002.

87 Ministère de l'enseignement Supérieur: Direction de la Planification et de l'Evaluation, Statistiques 2004–2005. For more information: http://www.afristat.org/index.php?option=com_content&view=article&id=404&Itemid=58&pays=CI (Accessed: 15 May 2010).

88 Ministère de l'enseignement Supérieur: Direction des Enseignements Supérieurs Privés. Statistiques 2006–2007.

89 *Office Ivoirien de la Propriété Intellectuelle*, Documents de Présentations et Publications.

tion, protecting patents, licensing and protecting trademarks. Its statistics show that seven patents were granted in 2005, eighteen in 2006 and sixteen were granted in 2007.

Since independence, major steps have been taken in positioning engineering to face the challenge of development in the Côte d'Ivoire. Yet, much still remains to be achieved in a difficult economic environment. To move forward and to address post-war reconstruction needs, new steps that could be taken include:

- New engineering policy reforms that position the national technology and innovation system to fit new priorities and to improve the quality and relevance of technical education. These reforms should enhance educational competiveness and improve the status of engineers.

- Invest heavily in improving the quality and relevance of engineering education, which means improving continuous professional development and paying for educators, as well as improving reference materials, learning resources and laboratories to adapt them to new technologies.

- Bridge the training process with professional experience in private and public sectors to encourage employment and innovation.

- Create a better environment for women engineers.

- Develop the research and development environment of engineering educational institutions.

- Initiate more technology incubators such as technology parks in partnership with industrial partners.

- Improve engagement with engineering organizations.

- Launch a regular national survey focused on engineers, engineering and the engineering profession.

Further reading

Blanke, J. 2007. *Assessing Africa's Competitiveness in a Global Context*. World Economic Forum , Global Competitiveness Report 2008–2009.

Khelfaoui, H. *La science en Côte d'Ivoire* [in: Les sciences en Afrique], Paris, IRD, 92 p.

INP-HB. Institut National Polytechnique Félix Houphouët Boigny (INP-HB), Wassi Technologies, *Chiffres clés*.

Ministère de l'économie et des finances. 2007. *La Côte d'Ivoire en chiffres*, Vol. 2007.

List of persons met or interviewed

Nahounou, Bobouho. Former General Director of *Institut National Polytechnique Félix Houphouët Boigny* (INP-HB).

Sibi, Bonfils. Deputy Executive Director of IEPF, Québec, Canada.

D'aby, Amon. Director for the Center for Advising and Assistance to Enterprises (INP–HB).

Ouattara, Souleymane. Sous Directeur des Enseignements Supérieurs Privés.

Kouame, Kouabra. Chargé d'Etudes à l'Office Ivoirien de la Propriété Intellectuelle.

Uganda

Eriabu Lugujjo

Challenges and prospects of engineering education and training in Uganda

Education and training of graduate engineers in Uganda started in 1970 with the opening of the Faculty of Technology at Makerere University with an intake of twenty-seven students. Eight years ago, another university, Kyambogo University, began engineering programmes. These two institutions now constitute the nucleus of engineering teaching, learning and research in the country.

The Uganda Institute of Professional Engineers (UIPE) came into being in 1972. The numbers of graduate engineers trained since is approaching 3,000. These numbers are still very low to serve a population of about 29 million.

The challenges experienced so far in educating and training of engineers are both systematic and external, but derive their origin from several factors ranging from socio-economic, techno-economic, governance, demographic and institutional change. The changing role of universities over the past thirty years has also contributed to the diversification of the challenges. Besides fostering excellence in scholarship through teaching and research, universities are expected to:

- become instruments of socio-economic policy;

- become partners in community and regional development;

- on occasion, align research priority with national strategic development goals;

- be seen as tools for rural development so that they can address rural de-population; and

- produce highly-qualified graduates, who not only carry out research but also manage its applications in industry and business.

Faculties of engineering are being increasingly asked to provide value for money in terms that the public sector – rather than academics – understand, but universities are still reminded to maintain standards of excellence in teaching and research and are required to seek as much financial support as possible from sources other than government. This is the terrain under which engineering is taught, learnt and practised in Uganda. The challenges of engineering training institutions are discussed from inputs (students), delivery (human capacity, hardware, and infrastructure) and outputs (graduates, employment opportunities and linkages with industries).

Access, enrolment and opportunities

There has been increased enrolment (more than five-fold) during the past decade. This relatively high level of growth may be explained by demographic changes, gender mainstreaming, relatively more schools offering science subjects at advanced level and partly by some privatization of university education. Private universities have offered more opportunities, for students that can afford to pay, to join engineering programmes. However, maintaining the balance between the provision of greater access to engineering programmes and using the limited available facilities, without affecting the learning in view of scarce resources, is one of the challenging tasks. A number of students who join engineering programmes do so only on the strength of their grades rather than their interest or motivation. Essentially, some are not prepared for or suited to the programmes, but it is difficult to build interest and motivation in engineering given that, for example, four or five students might have to perform one experiment simultaneously, particularly in the early years of study. Such limitations in teaching resources, needless to say, compromise inquisitiveness and may hamper the potential of even the most enthusiastic students.

Staff, welfare and retention

It has become increasingly difficult to sustain a credible staff development programme in engineering faculties. The reasons are many, but the most significant are:

- The best-qualified staff must be hired on a competitive basis but pay in universities is low.

- All lecturers in engineering faculties are required to have a PhD – a requirement regarded by many as being too exclusive and unsustainable.

- The longest-serving and best-qualified staff resign in desperation and frustration, as the universities do not have incentives such as mortgages, staff transport, medical schemes or vehicle loan schemes and so on.

- Any benefits due to the lecturer are consolidated and taxed heavily.

- Offspring of those who die in-service are not catered for.

- Freezing staff recruitment, due to a lack of funds to pay staff, is common.

- Expansion of establishment, even where it is justified, meets stiff resistance, possibly because it impacts on finances.

- Vertical mobility in engineering is hampered by rigid promotional requirements at each ladder as promotion policy emphasizes papers in international journals rather the general and specifically teaching output of staff.

- Universities also experience 'brain drain' as their best graduates remain overseas after winning opportunities to go abroad for further study. Some of those who return and rejoin the workforce are forced to abandon university services due to poor working conditions such as low pay and an absence of incentives.

Delivery modes

Engineering classes have grown relatively large. It is no longer unusual to find a class of eighty-five students. With such numbers, the traditional lecturing mode of 'chalk' is still widely practised. Tutorials where students are divided into small groups are rarely conducted. This is mainly because the few staff members are excessively overloaded and there are few teaching assistants. The universities have tried to recruit part-time supporting academic staff but they are not enough to adequately cope with the problems. Timetabling for part-time staff is a very big problem as they are fully deployed elsewhere. Laboratory work has continued to suffer due to insufficient functional equipment, and obsolete ones lack spare parts. Most of the existing equipment/apparatus is obsolete. Four or five students, especially in the early years of study, perform one experiment simultaneously. This state of affairs, needless to say, compromises their inquisitiveness, enjoyment and potential.

Relevance of engineering programmes

The relevance of any programme should be analysed according to its role and place in society, its mission, relationships with the public and private sector, community and sources of funding, and its interaction with other levels and forms of education. Traditionally, relevance of engineering programmes was judged according to the appropriateness of the training to meet the needs of the government and wider public service. This has changed however, due to restructuring and the privatization of the economy. Engineering programmes have to respond positively and quickly to the demands of the marketplace and industry, whilst at the same time produce graduates who can create jobs through fast adaptability and entrepreneurship. Engineering faculties review and update their curricula once every five years or so, and do introduce electives that are deemed essential. This area, however, is still challenging.

Links with industry

Industry plays a major role in the training of engineering graduates and professionals. Students at Makerere and Kyambogo universities for example, receive industrial training at the end of the second and third years of study. Lecturers and students have to participate in looking for industrial training places, but it has become increasingly difficult to find places as most of the industries are privatized and regard training university students as being outside their mandate. Furthermore, small-scale industries are too small to run coherent training programmes. There are a numbers of weaknesses in these programmes; training programmes are not jointly developed by industries and universities, and supervision or visitation of students by lecturers is not regular enough to allow ample discussion and consultations.

Ghana

Peggy Oti-Boateng

Ghana's immediate post-independence economic history typifies the deplorable situation in which most African countries (south of the Sahara) found themselves at independence. With no peers to learn from, the early leaders had no choice but to embrace the prevailing development economics theories, which were tinted with the ideological slants of the two dominant powers of the world at the time.

Ghana tackled the problem of industrialization with a top-down approach without giving due consideration to the resources on which the ambitious projects would thrive. This led to many projects being unsustainable, factories closing down and increasing rates of unemployment. The resultant economic hardships and social agitations which followed made policy-makers in Ghana seek alternative development strategies other than the 'big push' approach of the late 1960s and early 1970s.

Ghana, like many developing countries, has suffered from international policies of trade liberalization. The indiscriminate open door policy of import without protection of local emerging industries has put many budding informal industries out of business. For example, Josbarko used to be the sole supplier of bolts and nuts to one of the largest boat building enterprises in Ghana. However, with the advent of trade liberalization, these companies had to face stiff competition from cheaper mass-produced and often poor quality imported bolts and nuts from China and South East Asia. The story is similar for many light engineering, food processing and manufacturing companies. Many of these companies have reverted to buying and selling, to the detriment of national technological capability advancement for industrial and socio-economic development. In the service industry

however, the explosion of informal industries in many parts of the country resulted in lower product quality standards to the detriment of the consumer, who developed a strong preference for imported products.

Recognizing the need to accelerate the country's industrial growth in 2000, the government initiated the 'golden age of business' policy with the aim of attracting local manufacturers to go into production. This policy, laudable though it is, has not made any difference in integrating research and the transfer of innovation for poverty reduction and enterprise development. One of the key issues identified was the slow pace at which appropriate technology innovations are used for enterprise development and working for the poor. Numerous technologies developed remain on the shelves of universities and research institutions because of the non-existence of a policy to effect this link with the informal sector. This led to a decline in market-driven internationally-competitive industrial growth in Ghana.

A cursory look at Ghana's history shows that the problem with the country's interventions in industrial development is the lack of effective mechanisms to sustain the various models that have evolved. Apart from the debilitating effect of excessive state control during the implementation of the policy of import substitution during the first republic, and of the military governments that followed, the absence of long-term thinking to ensure the sustainability of the new enterprises was the main cause of their eventual collapse.

The movers of Ghana's grassroots industrial revolution in the 1980s and 1990s had recognized the importance of harnessing the country's large human and technical capabilities as a catalyst for the country's, albeit limited, industrial take-off; as witnessed in the proliferation of secondary industries during the period. What was missing though, was a strategy to help formalize the informal enterprises which had evolved, and to help them become competitive, for example, access to reasonably cheap sources of raw materials, access to relevant technology for the manufacture of quality and competitive products, access to the benefits of favourable international trade agreements, access to favourable and innovative government and donor support. The on-going poverty alleviation programmes in Ghana have mostly used the promotion of productive enterprises as the main thrust of their interventions. In most cases though, the required impact has not been achieved because the needed purpose-built mechanisms and structures for sustainable wealth creation were missing.

Ghana is potentially a very rich country. Agricultural production and the export of primary natural resources (such as gold and timber) constitute a strong base for Ghana's economy. It is therefore not surprising that attempts to revitalize Ghana's industrial development have taken the form of adding value to the country's agricultural produce and natural resource endowments. The problem confronting these efforts has been the difficulty in getting the right mix of interventions to obtain maximum benefit from the process of adding value.

The country's poverty status is, therefore, the outcome of a management problem. In other words, with Ghana's very favourable conditions – abundant natural resources, human resources, productive enterprises and a seemingly unlimited capacity for adding value to its wide range of exports – the country's economic fortunes can be turned around and made to benefit the poorest.

Nigeria

Felix Atume

The major problem facing the growth of the engineering profession in Nigeria (and indeed in many sub-Saharan African countries) is the lack of involvement of engineers in policy matters. Political leaders, it seems, hardly take into consideration the key role that engineers and engineering can play in development. Examples abound, all tiers of government in Nigeria have embarked on massive projects to provide infrastructure but frequently without adequate engineering input. The result is that huge sums of money are spent but the desired results are not achieved. It is indeed sad that African engineers have little or no voice in their governments; they hardly influence decisions, particularly on development plans. Consequently, engineering is overlooked and development is stalled even when huge resources are committed. Engineering can only take root if engineers are involved in policy matters and therefore have a say in government.

The cumulative effect is that many young people in Africa are no longer interested in joining the engineering profession. They are running to law, economics, accountancy and marketing. The sense is that the position of engineering in society is falling. Engineering grows through challenges. African engineers must be challenged by their leaders if they are to rise to the challenge. The reasons for the decline of the engineering profession in Africa include, but are not limited to, the following:

Poor salary after graduation: A university engineering graduate, if they are lucky enough to secure employment in a Nigerian government body, will earn a monthly salary of about US$200.

Lack of future opportunities for growth: Engineering graduates in Nigeria have very few employment opportunities,

for example, there are only four oil refineries and none is working at full capacity (Nigeria is the sixth largest crude oil producer in the world) and therefore, opportunities for chemical, mechanical and civil engineers are limited. Over the last three years, more than 300 textile mills have closed down and Nigeria now relies upon massive importation of finished textile products from Japan, Europe and China. Major firms in the tyre industry have moved to South Africa, and all the car assembly plants have either closed or a working at low capacity. Because industries are not growing, there are few employment opportunities and consequently Nigerian engineers are now waiting an average of four years after graduation before getting their first jobs. Nigeria today produces an average of 3,500 engineers from universities and polytechnics. For a country of 140 million people, that is far too small, but even they cannot find work.

Maintenance of infrastructure: Whilst maintenance could provide significant employment opportunities, unfortunately there appears to be no culture of maintaining infrastructure – a problem that is more acute but that is not restricted to Nigeria or even Africa. Engineers have little support for work in this area affecting roads, bridges, airports, seaports, schools, hospitals and other key public institutions. In turn, this negatively affects society's perception of engineering and of engineers.

Low involvement of Nigerian engineers in major projects: Local engineers have not been actively involved in major engineering projects in Nigeria. In the oil and gas sector, Nigeria started producing oil at commercial quantities in the early 1960s but even now Nigerian participation in this work is still quite minimal. The proportion of Nigerian engineers in oil and gas was still less than 10 per cent in 2002, though now there is a programme to raise this to 30 per cent by the end of 2010. Similar examples can be found in major infrastructure project, being led by large multinational companies. Such situations have stalled the development of a robust indigenous engineering capacity that creates tension with local engineers. More policies that promote indigenous engineering practice are needed.

Quality of engineering education: UNESCO recommended that the government should allocate about 25 per cent of annual budgets to education but previous governments in Nigeria allocated as low as 1.8 per cent. The result is that many engineering schools are poorly equipped and use obsolete equipment that cannot promote effective learning. There's also little emphasis on entrepreneurship. How can we develop engineers in this way? Nigeria must invest more in engineering education to produce the desired capacity to take on development.

5.3.2 Arab States

Tunisia

Kamel Ayadi

Tunisia is often given as an example in the Arab Region and in Africa for its science and technology policy. By devoting 1.2 per cent of its GDP to scientific research, 2.2 per cent to higher education and around 8 per cent to education as a whole, Tunisia ranks very highly in these measures for developing countries. With limited natural resources, Tunisia has no choice but to rely on its human capital, and it prides itself on its highly-educated workforce. Education has been a priority in Tunisia since it gained independence more than half a century ago. Today primary school enrolment is at 100 per cent and access to tertiary education is approaching 40 per cent. It has been able to keep a steady GDP growth rate of 5.5 per cent over the past two decades, and GDP per capita has reached US$7,938 (purchasing-power-parity). Women constitute 51 per cent of all tertiary graduates and make up more than one-third of the total workforce.

In spite of these accomplishments, Tunisia is faced with serious challenges and, in particular, that of a relatively high unemployment rate among university graduates. Reducing unemployment to a reasonable rate would require the attainment of a new economic growth level, with a strong knowledge-based industry and value added services. Tunisia is working to change a reputation that sees it as a low-cost destination possessed of a skilled yet inexpensive workforce. This is particularly true for the textile industry dominated by off-shore activities, which emerged in the mid-1970s from the liberalization movement. Most of this industry is based on subcontracting activities with low technological added value. This provides an explanation for the modest role played by engineers in the industry sector, although engineers have been instrumental in the development of other sectors such as infrastructure and agriculture.

The number of engineers registered in the *Tableau de l'Ordre des Ingénieurs* has reached 22,000. The real number of practicing engineers far exceeds this figure, perhaps even exceeding 30,000. The engineering community increases every year by 3,000 new engineering graduates from the sixteen engineering schools and faculties in Tunisia, as well as a number of engineers trained abroad. Although the number of new graduates has doubled in the past five years, it remains low compared to other countries of similar size and comparable economic development with Tunisia. With three engineers for every thousand inhabitants (Tunisia's population is 10 million), Tunisia still falls well below the average (which ranges in developed countries from 8 to 15 and in emerging countries from 4 to 7 per thousand). The Tunisian Prime Minister recently announced the intent of his government to double the number of graduates

in engineering in the short term in order to sustain economic growth in the country, and to meet the needs of companies, particularly foreign investors.

Historically, engineering was one of the few main professions to emerge right after Tunisian independence was declared in 1956. Engineers played a crucial role in the establishment of the newly created state. They filled the void left by the departure of colonists, particularly in the running of the economy and the functioning of facilities. Engineers then easily attained positions of leadership in government and state-owned companies, which represented the main driving force of the economy. Being an engineer in Tunisia was at that time socially and financially rewarding. As a result of this inherited image, engineering became extremely attractive to the best students for two or three consecutive decades. However, this situation has changed substantially over the past years. Tunisia has observed a disturbing decline in interest in engineering studies among younger generations.

The Tunisian experience in engineering education is relatively recent, although the creation of the first Tunisian engineering school goes back more than a century. In a relatively short period of time, less than four decades, Tunisia was able to establish a network of engineering institutions across its territory and consolidate its reputation in educating well-skilled engineers. These schools were able to supply the growing economic demand for engineers, particularly up to the 1980s, where state-owned companies and government were the main employers. The role of the engineering schools was nearly confined to supplying the needs of the public sector, and curriculum was designed to meet that particular need. A few years later, when the public sector demand for engineers declined – some activities even came to saturation – employment opportunities for engineers shrank, and the engineering profession started to experience unemployment for the first time.

Economic reforms implemented at the end of the 1980s led to the emergence of the private sector as a new economic force. This transformation stimulated the job market, resulting in an increase in demand for skilled engineers, particularly from private companies who were exposed to tough competition from European companies. This diversification of the job market provided new employment opportunities for engineering graduates but also brought new requirements for skills. Criticism of the engineering education model and curriculum started to emerge for the first time. It became evident that engineers in a liberalized economy, with new private economic actors and different needs, should not continue to be taught in the same old way. Criticism concerned the focus on theoretical studies and the low exposure of students to hands-on experience. Interaction between university and industry was absent. Both had evolved in separate paths with little interaction and cooperation. Curriculum was not adapted to the evolving competencies required by companies, which resulted in low employability of new graduates. Criticism also focused on imparting analytical skills with no particular importance given to 'soft skills', including communication, management, teamwork and leadership.

Engineering schools were slow in responding to the new demand due to a lack of autonomy and preparedness to reshape their curricula to international standards. The higher engineering education system was not equipped with mechanisms that would enable it to adapt to the job market's fast-evolving needs, particularly in areas where technology changes directly affect education. Accreditation, quality control and evaluation, which could have provided the regulatory mechanisms to adjust engineering curricula, were absent.

The first attempt to address these inadequacies occurred in 1992. A major change was made to the pedagogical structure of engineering training. The engineering diploma was previously structured to create two types of engineers and one type of technician, tailored on the French model, creating a more elite corps of engineers oriented towards design and conception and a second group for the production market (under the assumption that production activities require less qualified engineers than design activities). The 1992 reform merged the two engineering diplomas into one degree of five years and the duration of technician training was lengthened to three years. The number of institutions teaching technicians was increased significantly to overcome a shortage of technicians. Before the reform, three times as many engineers as technicians were being produced. Now the pyramid was reversed. In addition, the curriculum was also revised, integrating 'soft skills', practical courses and 'alternating education'. This method alternates students' schedules between classroom work and industry internships.

Accreditation and quality control in engineering education was finally integrated for the first time in the legal tertiary education framework in February 2008 with the new Higher Education Guiding law. It is a revolutionary and progressive law in the Tunisian Higher Education regulatory landscape. It has established for the first time accountability for higher education institutions and professors, set up autonomy for universities, installed quality control, and institutionalized evaluation and accreditation. The implementation of these principles is a fundamental prerequisite for setting up an effective higher education system in accordance with international standards.

Other measures are also being implemented as part of this reform towards increasing graduates employability of graduates and adjusting curricula to meet employment market needs. This reform was initiated two years after Tunisia had decided to adopt the LMD (Licence-Masters-Doctorate) education model, following the European trend initiated by the Bologna Process. The Tunisian economy is closely tied to the European market and most Foreign Direct Investment comes from Europe, but this is changing and the education system will have to adapt further. Without such efforts, Tunisia will not be able to retain its best students and attract foreign students and academics to its institutions.

The ambition of Tunisia is to become a regional centre of high value-added services and a hub for outsourcing advanced activities. This goal will be within reach if Tunisia succeeds in becoming a regional pole in higher education.

Lebanon

Abdel Menhem Alameddine

Meeting future challenges – private engineering education in the Arab world

Universities that do not work for the best interest of their society can never claim prestige and can never be in the top leagues. The university as an institution plays a vital role in the progress of modern societies and humanity. Historically considered as intellectual shrines for academic curiosity and philosophy and a hub for an elitist group, mass education in the twentieth century has placed universities at the heart of the social and economic lives of any nation. This new trend made institutions of higher education a major key player in the development of local economies and in the strategic planning of cities and nations.

Innovation in research is synonymous with a successful university. We cannot now imagine any university providing only technical knowledge; technical schools and colleges provide this. Universities have to innovate in research and explore new ideas and tools both in science and humanities in order to progress in terms of technical knowledge. This is a core element of our system of education that is too often under-represented in the Arab world. What is important is not how many universities we have or what affiliations we have made with foreign Western universities, but how much we have invested in research and scientific and technological exploration. Research, therefore, is not an added-value but an essential asset in the success of any university in the twentieth-first century.

Colleges of engineering are not key players in the development of our nations, unlike in developed countries where engineering schools are the founders and partners in the development cycle of their societies. Indeed, both local and national development depends heavily on the expertise of engineering colleges. With the boom in the Gulf, after the historically sky-rocketing prices of oil, the Arab world is commissioning gigantic construction projects. Thousands of young engineers are hired every year to meet the market demand. There is a golden opportunity here for Arab engineering colleges to benefit from this prosperity in order to innovate in engineering. This opportunity has not yet been taken.

New private engineering schools have mushroomed in the last decade, but this should be monitored carefully. Our immediate inclination is to approve and highlight its successes, but there is also the danger of overlapping, consumerism and commercialism. The question of overlap is vital since we have private engineering institutions copying educational programmes from the West or from prestigious universities in their area. Such a tendency deteriorates quality education and leads to consumerism and commercialism; institutions of this kind are run as businesses and education is often not their top priority.

The role of the private engineering schools

Private engineering schools and colleges have to rise to the new challenges that the world is facing with the growth and mobility of capital and technology. There is a special role for private engineering education in the Arab world to foster the knowledge that the modern world is seeking. State universities in Arab regions have limited capability to adapt to the fast changes happening in the world and, therefore, private education in the field of engineering has a golden opportunity – indeed, a business opportunity – to innovate in technology and to assist in building a competitive knowledge society. The examples from Asian countries such as Singapore and Malaysia are promising in terms of partnerships that could be established between universities, the state and business.

The real challenge is therefore to innovate and not imitate in the field of engineering education in Arab countries. Historically, engineering education comprised the traditional domains that are well known: civil, electrical and mechanical. With the invention of computing and developments in information technology, these domains have expanded and specialization has become the norm. It seems that every year a new field of engineering is introduced to higher education. These fields are often created on the demands of the labour market. Such multi-disciplinarity in engineering is the approach that Arab universities will have to adopt in order to survive and create a new Arab renaissance in construction, business, telecommunications and innovation. If the Arab renaissance of the nineteenth century was a revolution for the Arab cultural identity, there is a need now for a renaissance in the teaching of engineering; and there is no place for failure because the expectations are so high and the changes are so fast.

Arab scholars should be proud of their history and could learn from their relics to build their future. One can look proudly at the Arab contribution to engineering through the inventions of the water wheel, cisterns, irrigation, water wells at fixed levels and the water clock. In the year 860, the three sons of Musa ibn Shakir published the *Book on Artifices*, which

described a hundred technical constructions. One of the earliest philosophers, al-Kindi, wrote on specific weight, tides, light reflection and optics. Al-Haytham (known in Europe as Alhazen) wrote a book in the tenth century on optics, *Kitab Al Manazir*. He explored optical illusions, the rainbow and the camera obscura (which led to the beginning of photographic instruments). Al-Haytham did not limit himself to one branch of the sciences but, like many Arab scientists and thinkers, explored and made contributions to the fields of physics, anatomy and mathematics.

So the challenges for Arab private institutions is to be inspired from a glorious history to build innovative engineering faculties that can compete in the fast world of globalization. The Arab world is not isolated and we should learn from other nations including Asian countries such as Japan, Korea, Singapore and Malaysia on how to combine theory with practice. Our responsibilities towards our nations and future generations are serious with the admission that the current situation in the engineering profession is not everything it could be and needs to be. Arab nations should have the will, through their government ministries of higher education and through their professional organizations, to give educational systems the flexibility to adopt new programmes, improve existing programmes and to monitor accreditation associations effectively so as to ensure the quality of engineering education in our private institutions.

Jordan

Jordan Engineers Association

Jordan lies among Iraq to the east, Palestine to the west, Syria to the north and Saudi Arabia to the south. It retains an historic presence as a link between cultures going back to ancient Mesopotamia and Egypt. A medium-sized country, with an area of 89,287 km², it has a population of 5.5million[90] growing at 2.8 per cent (world average is 1.3 per cent). Some 80.2 per cent of Jordan's population is under the age of 30.

The association for registering engineering professionals was founded in 1958, becoming the Jordan Engineers Association (JEA) in 1972. The association has two headquarters, in Amman and in Jerusalem where engineers living in the West Bank in the Palestinian Territories register.

The association's objectives and goals are:

■ To organize the vocation of engineering to promote its scientific and vocational level, to take benefit thereof in economic, civilization and pan-national mobilization.

---

90 Census of 2004

- To defend members' interest and dignity, and to keep the vocation's traditions and honour.

- To enhance the scientific and vocational level of the engineer, and to activate and support scientific engineering research.

- To contribute to planning and the development of engineering, industrial and vocational education programmes, and to work towards raising the effectiveness of the employees in the engineering field.

- To contribute to studying common character topics among Arab and Islamic countries and other countries, and to exchange information, expertise and engineering publications.

- To secure a good standard of living for engineers and their families in cases of disability, old age and other emergent situations.

- To work in any area that may assist the association to achieve its vocational goals.

- To cooperate and coordinate with official bodies in the kingdom in its capacity as a consulting body in its field of specialization.

- To collaborate and coordinate with Arab, Islamic and international vocational engineering unions and to be a member thereof.

The total number of men and women engineers of the association was 70,829 in 2007, increasing by about 7 per cent each year. As a proportion of the population, this is equal to eleven engineers per thousand people, and is among one of the highest rates in the world. The association includes 1,200 companies employing 6,230 people. Some 8,828 engineers work in the government while 9,950 engineers work with contracting companies, factories and private companies. Around 8,400 registered engineers are employed abroad, while the number of engineers registered with the association in Jerusalem comes to 5,000.

The increasing numbers taking interest, studying engineering sciences and joining the JEA is a result of the good standing engineers have in society. There are now more engineering educational institutions and opportunities to take engineering majors. The construction sector in particular, alongside other engineering sectors, has benefited from strong growth, including the opening of new markets for engineering work in several other countries. In addition, Arab engineers are increasingly coming to practice engineering in Jordan. Public and private sector commitment to the JEA's regulations

Table 1: **JEA members by engineering branch and nationality in 2007**

Branch/nationality	Jordanian	Arab	Foreign	Total
Civil	19,071	849	203	21,123
Architectural	5,432	469	49	5,950
Mechanical	14,368	317	45	14,730
Electrical	23,762	506	31	24,299
Mining and metallurgy	915	15	3	933
Chemist	4,728	60	6	4,794
Total	68,276	2,216	337	70,829
Rate	96.4%	3.1%	0.5%	100%

is proving effective with good cooperation in this area. The engineers salary scale, which was issued under a resolution of the association's council (and which came into effect in 2008), determined that the minimum salary for a newly graduated engineer should be JD400 (US$560), and the minimum salary for an engineer with over twelve years experience should be JD1350 (US$1,900).

5.3.3 Asia and Pacific

China

Zhong Yixin

A brief note on engineering education reform in China

According to the 2005 statistics, China has thirty-five million intellectuals among which are ten million engineers. China has 1.3 million engineering graduates per year, including 650,000 university graduates. China therefore has largest number of engineers in the world. However, there have been relatively few engineering projects contributed by Chinese engineers in these last few years, which is a matter of great concern for Chinese engineering education.

Engineering education reform has been one of the most impressive recent successes in China. Chinese engineering education is quite different from that in Western countries and the issues typically faced by Western countries, such as women's participation in engineering and the enrolment levels of students in engineering education, are not yet problems faced by China. However, in common with many other countries, the calls for reform of engineering education have been growing louder and louder in China. Such calls emphasize the strengthening of student abilities with innovation skills, and improving the performance of students with more practical training.

An engineering student in university in China has a four-year education. Students spend two years on basic courses such as mathematics, physics, chemistry, humanities, social sciences and so on, eighteen months on the fundamental courses of their major, and another six months on a practical project. The majority of the time, students learn from teachers in the classroom with some experimentation in the laboratory, so that have very little opportunity to practice their abilities, either in scientific research or hands-on projects. In addition, the coverage of engineering is very specialized. A university engineering graduate only possesses a small portion of the knowledge needed in real-world engineering.

Widely accepted proposals for the reform of engineering education in China include:

- Widening engineering education to properly cover practical engineering.

- Updating the structure of the curriculum so that it includes the latest knowledge.

- Reforming the teaching paradigm with more interaction between the teacher and the student.

- Encouraging students to raise more questions inside and outside the classroom.

- Strengthening the research and development training in university labs.

- Providing more opportunities for students to gain experience in industry.

- Recruiting new faculty members with more practical experience in engineering.

- Establishing closer links between universities and business.

India

Prem Shanker Goel and Arvind K. Poothia

Over the past few years, India has been registering 8 per cent to 9 per cent GDP growth, largely due to growth in information technology (IT), IT-enabled services and core industrial output. This can be correlated with the increased availability of a talent pool, which is young and confident. From being an importer of several goods and the recipient of aid, India has now become an exporter of finished goods and services and has offered aid to less developed countries. Globalization has opened up opportunities for India, such as outsourcing of IT and engineering services into the country.

There are enhanced expectations from engineering education. Global competitiveness places significant demands on innovation and entrepreneurship, and international accreditation demands new perspectives on engineering education, requiring timely and appropriate responses from the Indian engineering education system.

Technology denial regimes demand innovation in strategic sectors and India has performed well in developing several critical technologies: in space, defence and nuclear energy. Denial of technologies is not confined to the military sector. There is a new urgency towards technology development by Indian industry with the recognition that 'purchasable technology' is out of date, and contemporary technology is not purchasable. Managing innovation for the developing world environment must take into account special needs and circumstances, such as: appropriateness to local needs, resources and culture; easy-to-use and affordable technology; employment gaps and opportunities, and so on.

Several higher technological institutions, such as the thirteen Indian Institutes of Technology (IITs) and the twenty National Institutes of Technology (NITs), have established centres for innovation, entrepreneurship and incubation. Among their key terms of reference are phases such as 'add commercial value to academic knowledge' and 'market the intellectual and infrastructure resources for national development.'

The IITs are distributed across the country and represent higher technological institutes, declared as institutions of national importance. Admission to the IITs is made through a national examination held simultaneously at a multitude of centres across the country. About 300,000 students compete in this exam for 4,000 places, resulting in a selectivity of 1 in 75.

The Indian engineering education system is characterized by: the preponderance of private (self-financing) colleges about 80 per cent of all colleges; acute faculty shortages, a deficit of about 40,000 places; acute shortages of PhDs, about 15,000; acute shortages of MTech graduates, about 30,000; meagre production of PhDs; and an internal brain drain (particularly engineering graduates seeking employment outside the engineering profession into areas such as IT and management). Quality assurance in engineering education is achieved through the National Board of Accreditation, which is currently seeking membership of the Washington Accord.

Industry has been proactive in establishing collaboration with academia to enhance graduates' skills and employability. Employability enhancement and talent management are assuming significant importance in dealing with young engineers, whose employment preparedness and expectations are becoming serious problems. Employers are quite dissatisfied with the academic and employability education provided by the technical institutions, and several strategies have emerged to bridge the gap such as 'finishing schools', co-curricular experiences and similar. Attrition rates in several industries are high, and talent management, which involves strategies for identifying, attracting, retaining and managing talent, is important.

While the fruits of globalization have benefited the burgeoning middle class, who are able to take advantage of technological advances including the Internet and mobile phones, a large proportion of the population remains illiterate and unable to afford such technologies, and is yet to experience prosperity. This has resulted in great inequalities in education, technology, information and quality of life. Furthermore, India already faces severe shortages in several critical resources covering energy, water and qualified personnel. Future challenges exist in several areas such as ensuring balanced development that benefits as much of the population as possible, adopting a sustainable development path, ensuring access, equity and quality in all sectors of education, ensuring employment and employability for the population, and enhancing literacy and science and technology literacy among the population, among others.

Still, world-class accomplishments have been achieved in engineering, in areas such as space science and technology, information technology services, biotechnology, technology-enhanced learning, renewable energy technologies, and so on. The use of new fuels for transportation and of renewable energy technologies for power, cooking, heating and cooling is increasing. And industry is coming to appreciate the imperatives of a 'triple bottom line'. Expectations from engineering in India are indeed considerable.

Malaysia

Azni Idris and Rohani Hashim

There are significant social and economic inequalities between developed and developing countries. Many of the underlying causes of these differences are rooted in the long history of a country's development and include political, historical, social, cultural, economic and geographical factors, and also their relations with other countries.

These inequalities are also brought about by the important differences in their scientific and technological infrastructure and their implementation of science and engineering policies. An essential prerequisite to a country's technological development is the necessity of a good education system and effective human resources in engineering (key factors that, for example, contributed significantly to Japan's economic success after the Second World War).

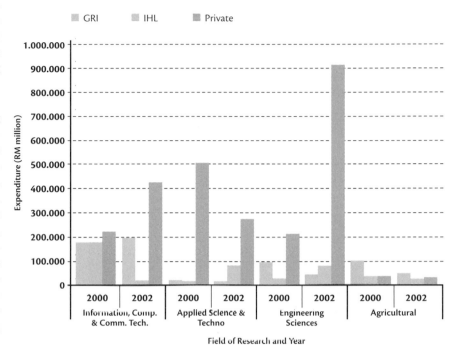

Figure 1: **R&D Expenditure by sector, 2000–2002**

Source: MOSTI, 2005
GRI: Government Research Institution, IHL: Institution of Higher Learning

In developing countries, economic growth – and, more widely, human development – can be enhanced by a comprehensive science and engineering policy. However, science and engineering can play their role in development only when the integrity of the whole sector (research institutions, universities, research priorities and human resources involving creative scientists) is preserved. Thus, the strategy in developing countries is one of increasing funding for research and development, and to set priorities for the science and engineering sectors with short, medium and long-term plans.

Many developing countries have made important contributions to the development of science and technology. The practical application of science through engineering has created an environment for the pursuit of science and engineering education in developing countries where funding scientific and engineering enterprises is widely accepted as a vital and long-term investment.

Engineering research and development

Malaysia is a country that has undergone rapid changes in the way industrial and technological research is conducted, which give birth to a strong, developing economy. Federal funding on research in Malaysia was RM1.2 billion (US$340 million) during 2001 to 2005. This is a ratio of about 0.69 per cent Gross Expenditure on Research and Development as a proportion of Gross Domestic Product (GERD/GDP). This is low in contrast to Malaysia's more developed neighbours, such as Australia

Figure 2: **Patent counts in selected countries (filed in United States), 2001**

Legend (top chart): Japan, United States

Legend (middle chart): Malaysia, Indonesia, Philipines, Thailand, Singapore

Legend (bottom chart): Australia, Germany, Netherlands, South Korea, Switzerland, Taiwan, United Kindom

Source: MOSTI, 2005

The technological development and advancement of a country is measured partly by the number of R&D outputs, and particularly the number of patent applications filed and approvals granted. The source of most of Malaysia's approved patents was the applied science and technology sector, where the field of chemistry and metallurgy has contributed 28 per cent of approved patents since 1988. In 2002, engineering related patents were about 47 per cent (MOSTI, 2005).

Productivity in patent generation can be used as a performance indicator for research innovation and to benchmark developing and developed nations. Figure 2 shows the total patent count for Malaysia, ASEAN countries and also selected developed countries for comparison. The relative patent count for ASEAN nations has not been very high, with the exception of Singapore. This could be due to low-quality research output, poor innovation strategy (whereby intellectual property protection was neglected by researchers), or poor commercialization of patents. In contrast, countries such as US, Germany, Taiwan and Singapore have achieved very significant increases in patent counts, following innovation drives and a strong focus on technological R&D.

The science and technological research programme formulated in Malaysia has achieved significant success where public funding was sufficiently given to support applied science and engineering research. The primary focus on research innovation and the drive for higher commercialization of R&D has created many new and innovative outputs that are useful to industry, employment and nation building.

Japan

Yumio Ishii

How did Japan manage to be the only nation in Asia to avoid becoming a colony of western powers and to succeed in modernizing despite having begun modernization nearly one hundred years later than western civilization? Why was Japan able to recover from the loss of the Second World War and develop its current prosperous economy? The answer lies in education and the technology transfer. However, will Japan's successes continue into the twenty-first century? What problems face Japanese society, and what are the possible solutions to such problems? These issues are from the viewpoint of a civil engineer who contributed to the development of Japan through the implementation of infrastructure.

The basis of Japan's development – science and technology in the Edo era

The Edo era (1603–1867) was a feudal era, however it was not the dark age that this term might evoke as there was progress in science and technology. As an example, survey-

with 1.53 per cent, Taiwan with 2.05 per cent and South Korea with 2.68 per cent in 2000. In relative terms, Malaysia's research and development (R&D) spending is however consistent with its level of development (MOSTI, 2005).[91]

In 2002, 39.1 per cent of R&D expenditure in Malaysia went to engineering sciences research, shown in Figure 1. In the United Kingdom, 60 per cent of R&D funding went to science and engineering, indicating the importance of industrial and technological research in the UK's economic success.

Comparing the sectors, the private sector in Malaysia spent on engineering science as a priority, followed by information and communication technology and applied science and technologies. Contributions from industry in more developed nations are high, for example about 60 per cent of Australia's R&D funding came from companies (including both cash and in-kind) and in South Korea industry contributed 75.1 per cent in 2003 (MOSTI, 2006).[92]

91 MOSTI. 2005. Ministry of Science and Technology and Innovation, *Report on Malaysian Science and Technology Indicators*, 2004 Report.

92 MOSTI. 2006. Ministry of Science and Technology and Innovation, *Report on Evaluation of R&D Projects Funded Under IRPA in 7th Malaysia Plan.*

ing techniques allowed for the completion of a map of the Japanese islands. In commerce, a money exchange system was established across the border of fief. Agriculture was the main industry; the industrial revolution was late in coming compared to western countries. The power sources available were of cattle, water mills and wind (in the sails of ships) and there was no manufacturing system. Advancements were made in river embankment construction, new paddy fields, irrigation systems, shore reclamation, port development, road building and bridge construction. At the beginning of the seventeenth century Japan's largest river, the Tone, was completely changed to protect Tokyo from flood. Tokyo had become the largest city in the world with a population of one million. The city had a sophisticated water supply system, but no sewage system – though there was an arrangement that allowed excrements to be exchanged for agricultural products so that it could be used as fertiliser. Tokyo was the cleanest city in the world at the time.

The success of modernization – the Meiji Restoration

The revolution in 1867 or the 'Meiji Restoration' transferred governing power from the Shogun to the people under the authority of the Emperor. It was the beginning of the modernization of Japan. The basis for modernization was the high standard of education of ordinary Japanese people, which allowed for the successful introduction of new technologies. Commoners paid tuition for their children to learn reading, writing and counting at *Terakoya* private schools; the commoners managed to find ways to educate their children, even when on the edge of starvation themselves. Education led to a strong sense of national identity that helped Japan to resist the invasion of western powers (as opposed to the semi-colonial status of China at the time). Government policies for technology development and transfer also contributed to modernization. The Government of Japan employed 146 foreign civil engineers as consultants. The railway network stretched across the entire nation just thirty years after the start of operations in 1872. A modern water supply and sewage systems began to be installed in large cities. Hydropower generation and a transmission network were completed. Large floodways and river improvement works allowed for the development of urban areas and industrial sites. As a result, at the beginning of the twentieth century, the Japanese industrial revolution was complete just forty years after the start of modernization and Japan was closely catching up with the West.

Reconstruction and economic growth after the Second World War

The loss of the war in 1945 was also considered a defeat in the fields of science and technology. Japan revisited its experiences from the Meiji Restoration and learned from those successes. A great deal of importance was placed on education. Junior high school education was made compulsory and more opportunities were created at high schools and universities. The western-

ization of the financial and economic system, the appointment of foreign consultants, the large numbers of students going overseas to study, and the introduction of foreign technologies in manufacturing all helped Japan's economy to recover. In 1961, the Prime Minister of Japan proposed a national scheme to double the national income in ten years in order to give the people something to strive for. The plan was actually fulfilled in just six years. The introduction of contractor and consulting engineer systems followed, brought from the West. In planning and engineering techniques, new concepts such as highway network theory, cost/benefit analysis, new designs of dams and mechanized manufacture were introduced from the USA. The development of civil engineering achieved such leading infrastructure as the Shinkansen railways, and once again formed the basis of economic growth. However, at the same time, new problems of pollution, ecosystem destruction and rapid urbanization became more prominent.

◠ *ASIMO robot by Honda.*

Current challenge: the economic crisis and lessons from the Great Depression

The Tennessee Valley Authority project, the interstate highway network and a group of dams established as a part of the New Deal solved the Great Depression and formed the basis of America's growth after the Second World War. Japan followed America's example and used 'big government' to promote public investment in infrastructure as a basis for its post-war recovery. This led to successful economic growth. However, in the 1980s, following the market fundamentalism of western countries, Japan started a shift to 'small government' with resulting reductions in public investment. Focus shifted to short-term results and inequality and social divides widened. Public investment declined after a peak in 1998, and was almost halved by 2008. This market fundamentalism is generally agreed to be the cause of the latest economic crisis facing Japan, and indeed facing the world economy.

The results of the New Deal show us that short-term economic stimulation to create domestic demand through job security and public investment coupled with long-term economic policies and infrastructure investments is the solution to this crisis. It is important that public investment flow enhances Japan's infrastructure in the long term so that they become assets that contribute to societal development.

We must simultaneously mitigate and adapt to climate change. The momentum of climate change will continue even if greenhouse gas emissions start to reduce, so the principal player in adaptation measures will be infrastructure. Infrastructural disaster prevention measures such as river banks, breakwaters, dams and early warning systems need investment, along with non-infrastructural measures such as the regulation of landuse. These measures can only be implemented by 'big government'.

Future challenges: climate change

Japan has realized one of the most energy efficient advanced economies in the world. Surviving the oil shocks twice, Japan has also reduced greenhouse gas emissions. The per capita emissions of Japan are the lowest of advanced countries and Japan consumes the smallest energy per unit GDP in the world as well. This is a new area where Japan could show leadership. It is estimated that civil engineering and construction activities account for over 40 per cent of Japan's greenhouse gas emissions. Measures such as rationalization of material (steel, cement) production, a reduction in construction processes and traffic as well as a transportation modal shift should be deployed. In adaptation work, engineers will play key roles in the implementation of both infrastructural and non-infrastructural measures.

Future challenges: demographic and generational change

In 1945, at the end of the war, Japan had a population of seventy-two million and the proportion of the population aged sixty-five and older was only 5 per cent. In 2004, the population peaked at 128 million with an aged population rate of 20 per cent. In 2050, population will decrease to 101 million with an aged rate of 36 per cent. How can Japan's economy support such change? History has shown that increasing women's participation in the workforce has at least the same effect as an increase in population; improvements to the transportation infrastructure to increase the commuting population (including visitors from overseas) also has the same effect as an increase in population; and innovative infrastructure will increase Japan's productivity and allow for increased trade in growing foreign markets, even with a smaller population.

Indifference to science by the younger generation

However, the indifference to science and technology among young people presents Japan's economy with serious problems. The roots of this problem include: the spread of a mindset where money is supreme – perhaps encouraged by market fundamentalism – leading to the decline of their interest in science and technology careers; the low social and economic status of scientists and engineers, exacerbated by a cost-driven mentality (however, the 2005 Promotion of Quality of Public Works Act provides, for the first time, that public procurement is to be evaluated on quality as well as on cost); the anonymity of people in science and technology fields, which particularly applies in civil engineering because in Japanese culture it was considered refined and polite for experts to maintain anonymity.

Promoting engineering, science and technology in Japan

Promoting the development of science and technology, particularly engineering, is crucial for Japan as a country with no abundant natural resources. Like many other developed countries, Japan is facing issues such as an ageing population with fewer children, a decline in interest in engineering among young people, the intensification of technology competition due to globalization, and growing negative perceptions regarding the ethical dimensions of science and engineering. Japan is working to tackle some of these issues, as highlighted below.

Basic Law and Basic Plans on Science and Technology

In 1995, Japan published the Basic Law on Science and Technology to emphasize and promote these areas with more effective planning, and to clarify the roles of the state and local public organizations. Based on this law, the Basic Plans on Science and Technology for five-year periods were created and implemented. The Third Basic Plan (2006–2010) primarily focuses on 'science and technology being supported by the public and to benefit society' and 'emphasis on fostering human resources and a competitive research environment.' This plan succeeds the three concepts in the Second Basic Plan, which were: 'a nation contributing to the world by creation and utilization of scientific knowledge'; 'a nation with international competitiveness and ability for sustainable development'; and 'a nation securing safety and quality of life.' The Ministry of Education, Culture, Sports, Science and Technology (MEXT) is promoting basic research and putting high priority on the fields of life sciences, information and communications, environment, nanotechnology and materials, energy, manufacturing technology, infrastructure and frontier science.

Enhancing the ethics of scientists and engineers

In 1999, the Institution of Professional Engineers, Japan (IPEJ) revised its Ethics Outline of 1911. In the same year, the Japan Society of Civil Engineers (JSCE) also renewed its Principles and Practical Guide to the Code of Ethics, and in 2007 it established a Committee on the Code of Ethics and Social Responsibility – in charge of materials used for training engineers in industry and universities and so on. In 2006, the Science Council of Japan (SCJ) issued a statement consisting of 'Code of Conduct for Scientists' and 'Toward Autonomous Implementation of the Code of Conduct for Scientists' and requested that all scientific organizations draw up their own related ethical codes of conduct. It also requested that they design and implement an ethics programme for research. The definition of 'scientists' in the statement includes engineers.

Strengthening communication and dialogue between scientists/engineers and the public

MEXT and the engineering societies have fostered and increased people's opportunities to touch, experience and learn about science and technology through exhibitions in science and technology museums, free seminars, science and technology café sessions, among others. From 1999, White Books for Children on science and technology have been published each year on selected themes (for example *The World of Particle Beams*, 2006).

Fostering the public's interest in science and technology

The Japan Science and Technology Agency has organized robot tournaments and manufacturing events in schools and universities. It has also produced broadcast programmes introducing interesting topics, science experiments and useful technologies in manner that is easy to understand for citizens or younger people. In Japan, events such as 'Science and Technology Week' and a 'Day of Civil Engineering' bring together many events nationwide to augment the public's interest.

Creating an enabling environment for wider participation

Laws have been revised and various programmes have been implemented to make the participation of youth, the elderly, women and foreigners in the activities of science, engineering and technology easier.

Adaptation to globalization

To improve the quality of engineering education in Japan and to adapt to the global environment, the Japan Accreditation Board for Engineering Education (JABEE) was established in 1999. In June 2005, JABEE was admitted as a signatory of the Washington Accord. Between 2001 and 2006, JABEE accredited 346 programmes at more than 140 educational institutions.

Professional engineer system

The Professional Engineer System in Japan (the government-licensed qualification for engineers) was established with the enactment of the Professional Engineer Law in 1957, which was revised in 1983 and 2000. Before the 2000 revision, registration as a 'P.E.Jp' was by an examination after a minimum seven years of engineering practice. After the revision, a primary examination was introduced to certify that applicants possess the academic ability equivalent to that of a four-year university graduate. Based on the Osaka Action Agenda adopted at the Asia Pacific Economic Cooperation (APEC) summit meeting of 1995, the 'APEC Engineer Mutual Recognition Project' was introduced for the mobility of engineers within the APEC region (there are currently fourteen member states participating).

Conclusion

Science and technology have made extremely significant contributions to Japan's growth. Engineering in particular, helped to support and ensure this growth. As we enter the twenty-first century, Japan is confronting a number of challenges including economic crisis, climate change, population decrease and indifference to science of younger generation, however Japan's scientists and engineers are endeavouring to overcome these challenges and they are ready to act internationally.

Australia

Peter Greenwood

Australia has a land area of 7.7 million square kilometres and jurisdiction up to 13.5 million square kilometres of ocean, in stark contrast to its population of about twenty million. Australia's size differs from many other countries with a similar population involving long transport links and major infrastructure, including communications outside urban areas, with resources and infrastructure projects absorbing engineering resources from other geographical areas. Nevertheless, Australia's contribution to world trade is considerable.

Australia has enjoyed a decade of economic growth based mainly on a long-lasting boom in minerals and energy resources – a key area of wide-ranging engineering involvement. Engineers also play a role in the international supply of goods and services, which tend to be high-value though low-volume on a world scale. Though Australia no longer relies on wool for prosperity, it still has a thriving trade in commodities. There are strong agriculture, forestry and fishing sectors supplying overseas markets in grains, timber products, wine and beer, wild and farmed fish products, and other food products including small quantities of saffron, wasabi mustard and exotic hops for beer making. In these days of diversification it is not surprising to learn how many engineers are involved in these seemingly non-technical areas. Australian engineers have worked on innovative projects as diverse as fish farm feed-control systems, satellite navigation-controlled ploughing as well as carbon sequestration.

Economic growth comes at a cost to the environment (including climate change) and places pressure on infrastructure and other community needs. Australia has a history of engineering and technical innovation that has become very important in the face of globalization. Australian scientists and engineers have established reputations as leaders in a number of areas. Australia has a small but innovative automobile and vehicle parts industry. The ship building industry is a world leader with innovative projects in military ship-building and in high-speed catamarans. A successful submarine firm has evolved, which is now capable of maintaining and developing the country's non-nuclear fleet. Australia even has a modest but highly regarded team that has achieved spectacular results in supersonic flight. Despite massive fossil fuel reserves, Australia is a world leader in photovoltaic cell research and other solar energy studies. There is a long history in the use of hydroelectricity in the country and additional resources are now going into wind power and geothermal energy. Climate change and sustainability have become key economic drivers.

The shortage of trained technical people is a dilemma. A survey of 200 organizations in 2006 by the professional body

Engineers Australia showed that more than 70 per cent of organizations in Australia employing professional engineers experienced engineering skill shortages in 2007 and 82 per cent of those reported incurred cost increases and project delays because of shortages.

In many respects, Australia shares the problems faced by other developed countries:

- Climate change including scarcity of water, increasing temperatures, rising sea levels and extreme weather events.

- Energy market restructuring and pressure to change the energy mix.

- Neglected investment in infrastructure such as roads and ports.

- Unsatisfactory health and telecommunications facilities.

- A shortage of affordable housing.

- Declining enrolments in science subjects in schools and difficulties in the tertiary education.

- An underlying skills shortage, particularly in the engineering sector.

- Skilled migration has increased, although international shortages reduce its effectiveness and emphasize the ethical dilemma of recruiting engineers from developing countries.

The engineering profession in Australia is very active internationally through the Association of Consulting Engineers Australia (ACEA) and the Association of Professional Engineers and Scientists (APESMA), as well as Engineers Australia. In the last few years we have provided the president of FIDIC and now WFEO. Australian engineers are also very active in the national Registered Engineers for Disaster Relief (RedR) and Engineers Without Borders (EWB) organizations. CSIRO, the federal government's national research organization, has divisions in many engineering-related areas such as energy, transport, communications and climate modeling. Engineers Australia is prominent internationally in engineering education accreditation through the Washington Accord and in engineers' mobility though the Engineers Mobility Forum and the APEC engineer agreement.

Major efforts are being made by government, industry and the engineering profession to resolve the problems that Australian engineering is facing, and to overcome the expected long-term effects of skills shortages.

◌ *Remains of Tonga shop after fire, the tilt-slab firewall survived but the internal concrete and steelworks collapsed.*

© A. Cleland - Arthur Budvietas & Fisilau Leone

◌ *Fire spread to timber frame of Tonga Co-operative Federation, destroying the three storey complex.*

© A. Cleland - Arthur Budvietas & Fisilau Leone

South Pacific

Andrew Cleland and Leiataua Tom Tinai

In Samoa, and the same may well apply to other nations, the term 'engineer' is generally taken to mean, say, a car mechanic or somebody that carries a pair of pliers in their back pocket. People know what a teacher does, what a lawyer does, what a medical doctor does, what an accountant does and what a policeman does. When you mention the word 'engineer', the same people hesitate (and sometimes ask 'Can you fix my car?'). This is a key challenge for the engineering profession in the islands of the Pacific and we must inform people what it is that engineers do.

South Pacific island nations vary in size from close to one million people (Fiji), through those of the order of 50,000 to 250,000 people (such as Vanuatu, Samoa and Tonga) through to small nations of less than 20,000 people (Cook Islands) and very small nations of less than 10,000 people (such as Niue). A typical South Pacific nation has one or more main islands, with a number of small islands scattered over large expanses of ocean.

The extent of engineering infrastructure varies; main islands often have reticulated water and electricity, but wastewater treatment systems can be localized. Diesel generators are a common source of electricity across the region. Telecommunications systems on main islands are generally of good quality. Radio is used between smaller islands. Airports are of generally good quality and many smaller islands have landing strips. Road quality depends on the suitability of local materials. There are few multi-storey buildings and building materials are often imported. Timber-framed houses with metal roofs are common, whereas commercial buildings are increasingly built of concrete. Port facilities are progressively being upgraded from wooden to concrete structures. The South Pacific islands often suffer major infrastructural damage during cyclones when disruptions to power and water supply, and damage to buildings, ports and roads is common.

Historically, infrastructure development was funded through foreign aid, particularly from Australia and New Zealand. Australian and New Zealand standards have been used as the de facto standard for construction projects through the supervision of projects by engineers from the donor nation. More recently, capital for infrastructure has started to come from a wider range of sources, including the private sector, and funding agencies have not necessarily required adherence to international standards. This has created a greater need for local regulation of standards.

The Pacific Island nations of Samoa, Fiji, Tonga, Vanuatu and Cook Islands (the Polynesian Pacific family) and their engineers are linked with the Institution of Professional Engineers New Zealand (IPENZ). The engineers of the Solomon Islands and Papua New Guinea are linked with Engineers Australia. Of these nations, Samoa and Fiji have passed acts of parliament for professional engineers, creating, in 1984, the Institution of Professional Engineers Samoa (IPES) and, in the 1960s, the Fiji Institution of Engineers (FIE), respectively. Nations like Tonga, Vanuatu and Cook Islands are developing a legal framework but are hindered by a lack of qualified engineers to deliver professional services and to monitor the quality of the design and construction of infrastructure.

Looking at Samoa, the present number of members in IPES is 110, compared to only sixteen when it was created. Samoa has its own Building Code NBC 1992. This code references the Australian and New Zealand codes for most of the engineering works. Other standards often used and referenced are the FIDIC and British codes. In Fiji, FIE's register had one hundred engineers in 2007, though this compares to 140 in 2000. It is however estimated that there are 300 to 400 engineers in Fiji. Tonga has no engineering body and therefore no registration system. There are fewer than twenty engineers in Tonga, of which about sixteen are academically qualified. There is no engineering body in Vanuatu or the Cook Islands, and therefore no registration systems. Most engineers in the Pacific Island nations received their qualifications from outside their home countries. A good proportion of these qualifications are obtained from other island nations like Papua New Guinea and Fiji, though there is concern of the standard of qualifications in engineering, which is also now becoming a social barrier.

The South Pacific is fundamentally different to developing countries in Africa, the Americas or even Asia in that it is people-poor and has large coastlines. Economies of scale are poor and building critical mass in engineering skills is difficult. More specifically:

- Aid-funded projects are not necessarily developing local capability or capacity; there is often no requirement to involve local firms in the projects.

- Construction capability is very low (technical and trades), and there is poor training and supervision of construction workers; some practices are unsafe.

- Access to codes of practice and relevant standards is poor. There is a lack of a practical and systematic building code for a number of nations. Furthermore, due to the small size of the nations, the capability of government and regulatory agencies to implement and enforce building regulations is insufficient. For similar reasons, the legislation, regulations or codes are often out of date or incomplete.

- The engineering workforce is ageing and there are problems in attracting young people into engineering education; those sent to study in Australia or New Zealand often do not return. The degrees offered in Fiji or Papua New Guinea are not accredited to an internationally recognized standard such as the Washington Accord or Sydney Accord.

- New engineering knowledge and knowledge of methods for handling new building materials is lacking.

- Quality and variability of materials is an ongoing issue; some imported materials are of poor quality, and local materials may not be suitable. The capability to test materials and quality-assure their reliability is poor.

- Cyclones, tsunami and earthquakes pose largely shared issues, but are not dealt with well in the design of public infrastructure and private sector construction projects across the region.

- The issue of asset degradation due to harsh tropical conditions is insufficiently well handled; some technology brought in from overseas is inappropriate.

To overcome these issues, regional approaches are preferred that cover the whole South Pacific. IPENZ provides facilitation so that engineering communities in the various nations can collaborate. All the issues are being address, and examples of specific solutions include: the creation of a professional identity for engineers through a 'South Pacific Engineers Association' (SPEA) built around the provision of professional development, adherence to the agreed competence standards and development and enforcement of technical standards (the SPEA can also assist in attracting regional funding for these activities); the development of a South Pacific Building Code, with regular updating; and benchmarking of Fijian and Papua New Guinean qualifications in relation to the competence standards.

5.3.4 Europe

Germany

Willi Fuchs

The German economy has one major card to play in the field of international competition – Germany's engineers. The contribution of engineers to the welfare of the country is huge and the engineering industry continues to be the world's number one exporter of, for example, machinery and industrial plant; in this field the annual turnover for 2007 was approximately €193 billion (€138 billion for export). Another strong industrial

Concrete block masonry wall being erected for small shop.

© A. Cleland - Arthur Budvietas & Fisilau Leone

Close up.

© A. Cleland - Arthur Budvietas & Fisilau Leone

field is the automotive sector with an annual turnover of €254 billion in 2006 (€155 billion for export). These two industrial sectors employed about 22 per cent of German engineers.

At present, there are about one million engineers in Germany. Of these, 64 per cent are national social insurance contributors and the rest are self-employed or work as civil servants. The majority of engineers work in the field of mechanical engineering (186,000), followed by electrical engineering (155,000), civil engineering (149,000) and then architecture (114,000). The rather new sector of industrial engineering (i.e. an engineering education with complementary economics studies) has 42,000 employed engineers.[93]

The status of engineers

Since the 1970s the status of engineers has been protected by the laws of engineers, (*Ingenieurgesetze*). The recognition of engineering qualifications is the responsibility of the federal states. In short, only a person who has studied engineering sciences and graduated in this field can be called an engineer.

Engineering education in Germany is delivered by forty-two universities and ninety-nine universities of applied sciences (*Fachhochschulen*). The system is changing from a one-tier diploma system into a two-tier bachelor and master system. Though many study programmes have already converted, graduate numbers are developing slowly; in the year 2006 no more than 3,181 master degrees and 1,648 bachelor degrees were awarded (in comparison to 22,599 students with a diploma from universities of applied sciences and 10,906 students with diplomas from universities in engineering science in the same year). When Germany decided to replace the highly regarded title of 'Diplom-Ingenieur' with a Bachelor and Master system, it met with a lot of resistance from the engineering associations.

In 2006 the federal government launched an excellence enhancing programme in which additional funds were made available. In a strong competition nine universities reached the status of an 'elite-university', which tends to become a major attribute for further increasing academic reputation. Each elite university will receive a total additional funding of approximately €100 million.

Regulation of the profession

The legal protection of the title 'engineer' ensures that it remains exclusive to graduated engineers, though students are entitled to use the title as well during their studies. Further regulation of the profession takes place in the field of civil engineering, where certified experience and competence is required by the authorities for engineers and architects in order to sign applications and calculations for construction works. To certify, engineers must be enrolled in the registers of the Engineers Chambers in their federal state. Around 40,000 engineers are members of the Engineers Chambers nationally. The chambers have lists of specialists for several fields, who are entitled to elaborate official opinions and assessments (for example as expert witnesses in legal disputes).

Engineering associations

Membership in an association, for most engineers, is not mandatory but many are members of *Deutscher Verband Technisch-Wissenschaftlicher Vereine* (DVT), which comprises fifty-five associations. The DVT represents Germany in international organizations such as FEANI and WFEO. Of the associations, the largest engineering association in Germany is the *Verein Deutscher Ingenieure* (VDI) with 135,000 individual members. Another, the *Verband der Elektrotechnik, Elektronik und Informationstechnik* (VDE) has 33,000 individual members. Associations also act as regulation and standards institutions in cooperation with the national standards organization. The VDI alone publishes more than 1,700 technical regulations, many of them are also in English.

The current situation

The shortage of engineers has become a serious problem for most industrial sectors in Germany. After years of positive economic development, all kinds of engineering professions are in need – even the civil construction sector, which had long suffered from having more engineers than jobs. According to the federal employment office, engineering vacancies have increased by 50 per cent in the last two years. In the same period, the number of unemployed engineers fell by 60 per cent. Due to the effects of demographic change and the more–or-less stagnant interest of students in engineering sciences, the number of available engineers may start to decrease.

For many companies the single most important factor that restricts their growth is the shortage of qualified engineers. Looking at the figures of the federal employment office, the vacancies have increased by 50 per cent in the last two years. The market demand on engineering skills can also be seen in the development of the unemployment rates. In the last two years the amount of unemployed engineers has reduced by 60 per cent.

Outlook

To solve some of these problems in the short term, Germany changed its immigration laws in 2007. The laws make it easier for more skilled personnel to enter the country and streamline and improve the process. In the longer term, engineering sciences needs to attract more students. As a result, new concepts are being discussed and introduced into universities. With the demographic trends in Germany in mind, more engineers and more companies have to be attracted into lifelong learning and other schemes to maintain their employability. The policy of allowing skilled people to take their pension somewhere between the age of fifty and sixty has come to an end.

---

93   Source: Federal Statistic Office of Germany

German engineers and German engineering have a very long history and an excellent reputation. The label 'made in Germany' still stands for high quality and innovation. Like other Western economies, Germany faces some major challenges such as demographic shifts, the change from an industrial society to a service society, and the effects of globalization, and so on. Through the activities of many major players in the technical community, German society has become aware of the important role its engineers play.

France

François-Gérard Baron

Long before the word 'engineering' was invented, the engineers' ancestors were already making large contributions to human development and culture. When Romans designed a water distribution system (for example in Nimes, where they built the Pont du Gard aqueduct), they contributed not only to higher quality of life but improved public health for all. So too did the city engineers in nineteenth century Paris when they built the sewer network; indeed, they saved many lives.

Although it is common to stress the negative effects of technology on the environment and on quality of life, and to complain about disruption to services, engineers have probably never been badly needed in our society. The scope of the challenges that engineers are being asked to face seems to be constantly enlarging. From traditional skills onwards, engineering now involves significant responsibilities in energy management, environmental issues, public and global health, poverty reduction and cultural heritage.

At a time when sustainable development is acknowledged as a priority issue, a dramatic responsibility has been placed on engineers for innovation and the development of new practices. Meanwhile, they must also take on responsibility for maintaining infrastructure that is in need of significant investment. The role of engineers is even more strategic in reducing global poverty and mitigating the effects of climate change.

Engineers also have a responsibility towards the past as well as the future. Many civil works, such as bridges, dams and ports, need to be renovated, and old and ancient monuments need to be restored. Engineers are vital for cultural heritage; the Abu Simbel temples in Southern Egypt could never have been saved without the engineer's expertise. This role is particularly important in former colonies where state governments have little financial and technical resources to prioritize these projects.

Engineering has a long tradition in France, dating from even before the medieval and renaissance periods when hundreds of castles, cathedrals and monuments were erected using tra-

ditional expertise. Formal training of engineers began during the eighteenth century. One of France's most famous engineers is Vauban, who erected a number of fortifications during the reign of Louis XIV. His works are now protected by UNESCO's World Heritage Programme.

The first school of engineers, the *Ecole Nationale des Ponts et Chaussées*, was founded by Louis XV to train civil engineers. It marked the beginning of specialized engineering education in France. Today, unlike most European countries, the majority of French engineers are still educated in schools of engineers after the baccalaureate. Very few come from universities. Of the around 160 schools of engineers, a few are called 'grand schools' such as *Polytechnique*, *Centrale*, and *Mines et des Ponts et Chaussées*. The *Grandes écoles* are backed by government ministries such as Defence, Industry and Public works. The fees are therefore very low compared to private universities (most of the other schools of engineering are private). The main way to enter a school of engineering is by examination after two or three years training following the baccalaureate. The last decade has seen the development of engineering in universities.

France has around 600,000 engineers, of which 400,000 have diplomas. They are joined by 30,000 students who receive their engineering diploma every year. French engineers are usually seen as leaders in the fields of civil engineering, aircraft and car manufacturing, chemistry and the agricultural industry. French engineers are known as highly competent in problem-solving.

There are several important points regarding the professional recognition of engineers in France:

- The title 'engineer' is not protected in France.

- According to the Bologna Declaration, French engineers are only 'long cycle', which means that most diplomas are obtained after five years of education (including two years training). However, many schools are now developing a Master's degree.

- There is no recognized professional body. However, schools of engineers are accredited by the *Commission des Titres*, which audits them periodically.

- Although many engineering schools are devoted to sectoral disciplines, there are no official statuses for these sectors (such as civil, chemical, mechanical, and so on).

Most engineering schools have launched their own alumni systems, collecting membership and providing services to current and former students, such as careers advice, events and professional development. Around 160 of them are merged into a federation called the *Conseil National des Ingenious et Scientifiques de France* (CNISF), founded in 1860 by Napoleon III. The role of this federation, which is totally independent, include representation of the profession within France and abroad,

○ *The breathtaking, record-breaking Millau viaduct in France.*

GFDL - Wikimedia - Simon Cole

231

promoting engineering skills, and disseminating scientific and technical matters. Besides CNISF, consulting engineers are represented by two main organizations, SYNTEC and CICF.

United Kingdom

Jim Birch

The Engineering Council UK and the Engineering UK jointly publish annual reports on the state of engineering in the UK.

Secondary Education

The increased number of students taking GCSE mathematics, sciences, information and communication technology, and design and technology is partly due to the increase in the size of the 16-year old cohort over the last decade. The data indicates that there has been an upward trend affecting all the aforementioned GCSE subjects in the percentage of students reaching a grade C or above. GCE A-level numbers appear to be rising again in mathematics but they are still falling in physics. GCE A-level students who achieve grades A to C have seen an encouraging growth trend over the last decade. While the overall student numbers for science, engineering and technology subjects is at best static, average grades within subjects are on the increase. There is some concern that with substantial numbers of learners being moved to single science or applied science GCSE, there will be a reduction in the cohort taking A-level subjects suitable for entry to university programmes.

Further education, vocational education and training

Research indicates that engineering technicians make up a substantial part of the UK workforce, nearly 2 million jobs, or just over 7 per cent of the total workforce. Sixteen per cent of technicians work in manufacturing and 8 per cent work in construction. It is also worth noting that many engineering technicians work in other sectors. Data suggests that the success rate for engineering, manufacturing and technology courses in further education appears to be rising, from 71 per cent in 2002–03 to 74 per cent in 2004–05. This is counterbalanced by a fall in starts, but may well indicate that the candidate capability is rising.

◑ *The annual report on engineering in the UK.*

Higher Education

In 2005 there were over 330 institutions offering higher education courses in the UK with over 306,000 undergraduate degree awards being made during the year; 85,000 of these were awarded in Science, Technology, Engineering and Mathematics (STEM) subject areas. Nearly 120,000 postgraduate degrees were awarded at masters and doctoral level in 2005, with 34,000 being awarded in STEM subjects. The last five years have seen an expansion in overall student numbers taking STEM subjects within the UK Higher Education system. STEM student numbers have increased by nearly 25 per cent

from 424,000 in 2001 to just under 529,000 in 2005. Engineering and technology as a whole has seen increases in home student numbers of 12 per cent over the past five years, rising to 17,200 home acceptances in 2005.

Graduate recruitment

Engineering and technology see the largest percentage of graduates working in finance and business (28 per cent), with the second largest group working in manufacturing (24 per cent). Whilst engineering and technology sees 28 per cent of its graduates entering the finance and business field, it is similar for social studies graduates (28 per cent) and mass communication and documentation graduates (27 per cent); the drain to finance and business is not a phenomenon specific to engineering and technology. The propensity of graduates to enter careers in professional engineering differs across the engineering disciplines. Five out of the top seventeen graduate salaries are attributed to engineering disciplines, with chemical engineering leading the way in third place with an average salary of just below £23,000.

Engineering salary levels

According to the UK Office of National Statistics data, the average annual gross earnings of professional engineers was £33,300 at the end of 2002 whereas the profession's Survey of Registered Engineers found the average annual gross earnings for registered Chartered Engineers in 2005 to be £53,000. The median Chartered Engineer salary in 2005 was £45,500 (up from £43,500 in 2003).

Professional registration

Registration is not a legal requirement in the UK but over a third of engineers who are eligible have chosen to voluntarily register with the Engineering Council. The total number of registrants has declined from just over 267,100 in 1995 to just under 243,000 in 2005, representing a fall of 9 per cent over the decade. This is partly a demographic trend as new registrations have seen positive growth over the last two years, reversing the declining trend in new registrations seen over the last decade. The median age of registered engineers in 2005 was 55 and is increasing.

Engineers in the economy

The number of top business executives with engineering qualifications in FTSE 100 companies fell from 17 in 1997 to 12 in 2004 but rose to 14 in 2006. The manufacturing sector still dominates the employment of registered engineers. The proportion of employment in manufacturing rose from 32 per cent in 1995 to 40 per cent of employment in 2003. In 2003, the remaining 60 per cent are found throughout all other sectors of the economy. The export of engineering services is a significant contributor to UK balance of trade, generating an annual surplus of US$5 billion.

Table 1: **List of UK Professional Engineering Institutions**

Name	Website	Licensed to assess
British Computer Society (BCS)	www.bcs.org	CEng, IEng
British Institute of Non-Destructive Testing (BInstNDT)	www.bindt.org	CEng, IEng, EngTech
Chartered Institution of Building Services Engineers (CIBSE)	www.cibse.org	CEng, IEng, EngTech
Chartered Institution of Highways & Transportation (CIHT)	www.ciht.org.uk	CEng, IEng
Chartered Institute of Plumbing & Heating Engineering (CIPHE)	www.ciphe.org.uk	IEng, EngTech
Chartered Institution of Water & Environmental Management (CIWEM)	www.ciwem.org.uk	CEng, IEng, EngTech
Energy Institute (EI)	www.energyinst.org.uk	CEng, IEng, EngTech
Institution of Agricultural Engineers (IAgrE)	www.iagre.org	CEng, IEng, EngTech
Institution of Civil Engineers (ICE)	www.ice.org.uk	CEng, IEng, EngTech
Institution of Chemical Engineers (IChemE)	www.icheme.org	CEng, IEng, EngTech
Institute of Cast Metals Engineers (ICME)	www.icme.org.uk	CEng, IEng, EngTech
Institution of Engineering Designers (IED)	www.ied.org.uk	CEng, IEng, EngTech
Institution of Engineering & Technology (IET)	www.theiet.org	CEng, IEng, EngTech, ICTTech
Institution of Fire Engineers (IFE)	www.ife.org.uk	CEng, IEng, EngTech
Institution of Gas Engineers & Managers (IGEM)	www.igem.org.uk	CEng, IEng, EngTech
Institute of Highway Engineers (IHE)	www.theihe.org	CEng, IEng, EngTech
Institute of Healthcare Engineering & Estate Management (IHEEM)	www.iheem.org.uk	CEng, IEng, EngTech
Institution of Lighting Engineers (ILE)	www.ile.co.uk	CEng, IEng, EngTech
Institute of Marine Engineering, Science & Technology (IMarEST)	www.imarest.org	CEng, IEng, EngTech
Institution of Mechanical Engineers (IMechE)	www.imeche.org.uk	CEng, IEng, EngTech
Institute of Measurement & Control (InstMC)	www.instmc.org.uk	CEng, IEng, EngTech
Institution of Royal Engineers (InstRE)	www.instre.org	CEng, IEng, EngTech
Institute of Acoustics (IOA)	www.ioa.org.uk	CEng, IEng
Institute of Materials, Minerals & Mining (IoM3)	www.iom3.org	CEng, IEng, EngTech
Institute of Physics (IOP)	www.iop.org	CEng
Institute of Physics & Engineering in Medicine (IPEM)	www.ipem.ac.uk	CEng, IEng, EngTech
Institution of Railway Signal Engineers (IRSE)	www.irse.org	CEng, IEng, EngTech
Institution of Structural Engineers (IStructE)	www.istructe.org	CEng, IEng, EngTech
Institute of Water (IWO)	www.instituteofwater.org.uk	CEng, IEng, EngTech
Nuclear Institute (NI)	www.nuclearinst.com	CEng, IEng, EngTech
Royal Aeronautical Society (RAeS)	www.aerosociety.com	CEng, IEng, EngTech
Royal Institution of Naval Architects (RINA)	www.rina.org.uk	CEng, IEng, EngTech
Society of Environmental Engineers (SEE)	www.environmental.org.uk	CEng, IEng, EngTech
Society of Operations Engineers (SOE)	www.soe.org.uk	CEng, IEng, EngTech
The Welding Institute (TWI)	www.twi.co.uk	CEng, IEng, EngTech

Source: Engineering Council UK

Table 2: **List of UK Professional Affiliates:**

Name	Website
Association of Cost Engineers (ACostE)	www.acoste.org.uk
Association for Project Management (APM)	www.apm.org.uk
Chartered Quality Institute (CQI)	www.thecqi.org
Institute of Automotive Engineer Assessors (IAEA)	www.iaea-online.org
Institute of Asphalt Technology (IAT)	www.instofasphalt.org
Institution of Civil Engineering Surveyors (ICES)	www.ices.org.uk
Institute of Corrosion (ICorr)	www.icorr.org
Institute of Concrete Technology (ICT)	ict.concrete.org.uk
The Institution of Diesel & Gas Turbine Engineers (IDGTE)	www.idgte.org
Institute of Explosives Engineers (IExpE)	www.iexpe.org
Institute of Mathematics & its Applications (IMA)	www.ima.org.uk
Institute of Metal Finishing (IMF)	www.uk-finishing.org.uk
International Council on Systems Engineering UK Chapter (INCOSE)	www.incose.org
The Institute of Nanotechnology (IoN)	www.nano.org.uk
Institute of Refrigeration (IoR)	www.ior.org.uk
The Institute of Telecommunications Professionals (ITP)	www.theitp.org
National Agency for Finite Element Methods & Standards (NAFEMS)	www.nafems.org
Society of Automotive Engineers (SAE-UK)	www.sae-uk.org
Safety & Reliability Society (SaRS)	www.sars.org.uk

Source: Engineering Council UK

Russia

Vladimir Sitsev

The engineering movement in Russia has evolved since the middle of the nineteenth century, through the consolidation of the scientific community, the formation of a domestic engineering corps and through representatives of business (industrialists and entrepreneurs) interested in accelerated development of domestic production. The Russian Technical Society (RTS) was established in 1866 with a charter approved by the Emperor.

○ *An Ekranoplan A-90 Orlyonok – a remarkably efficient aircraft.*

The RTS allowed individual membership and brought together prominent scientists, naturalists, members of the Russian Academy of Sciences (established in 1724), specialist practitioners and large industrialists. It covered a wide range of areas including chemical production, metallurgy, mechanical engineering, mechanics, machine building, construction, mining, architecture, shipbuilding, marine technology, artillery manufacture and weapon production as well as, later, the rapidly developing areas of aeronautics, aircraft modeling, electrical engineering and also the operation of technical devices and machinery.

Among the founders and active members of the RTS were eminent scientists, designers and engineers including A. M. Boutlerov, N. N. Zimin, D. I. Mendeleyev, D. K. Chernov, S. O. Makarov, A. N. Krylov, V. G. Shoukhov, A. S. Popov, N. E. Zhoukovskiy, and others. The first elected Chairman of the RTS was General Major of the Engineering Corps, Baron A. I. Delvig.

The RTS supported wide participation, and its scientific and technical activity has led to the creation of chemical, forestry, mining, civil, technological, water, electrotechnical, polytechnic, metallurgical engineering societies, among others. The RTS regional network grew fast; along with Saint Petersburg (where the RTS headquarters were located and the permanent Technical Exhibition was displayed) and Moscow, large branches were formed in Nizhniy Novgorod, Kiev, Kharkov, Odessa, and in a number of other industrial centres of the Russian Empire. In 1872, the Polytechnic Museum opened in Moscow and a decade later, the first in Russia Higher Engineering Courses for Workers were opened.

After the revolution of 1917 and the Civil War, such an organizational structure soon made it possible to reconstruct the scientific and technical movement, which by that time had become a mass movement, on common principles united by the All Union Council of Scientific Engineering and Technical Societies (VSNTO). The first chairman was academician, G. M. Krzhizhanovskiy, the author of the famous State Commission for Electrification of Russia plan.

The main principles for the scientific and technical movement in Russia, established as guidance by its founders, were preserved and developed over time. These included: the public creative nature of the activity; its enlightening, humanitarian purpose; the encouragement of achievements; the spread of advanced experience of engineering work; a high level of civic duty and patriotism. These principles were manifested by guiding the solutions to key scientific and technical problems, the advancement and implementation of large initiatives and the utmost strengthening of the union of education, science and production.

The RTS principles also survived the end of the USSR. They are continued by the International Union of Scientific and Engineering Public Associations (USEA) that replaced VSNTO, and which, since 1992, has brought together the creative scientific and technical unions of the former soviet republics (with the exception of the Baltic States).

At present, the USEA in Russia coordinates the work of nearly fifty scientific and technical associations (industry societies, unions, associations) and has regional branches in most of the Russian Federation. Leading associations of the country's technical higher educational institutions actively participate in its activities. The USEA was a co-founder of the Russian Engineering Academy (RIA).

The activities of the USEA, as a creative scientific and technical organization, support the Russian government's priority directions in the development of science, technologies and engineering. This covers areas as diverse as security and counter–terrorism, living systems, nanotechnology, information and telecommunication systems, prospective military equipment, environmental management, transport, aviation, space systems, power engineering and energy efficiency. The USEA also raises public awareness and recognition of the role of engineers in Russia, such as through the government-supported Engineer of the Year awards.

Poland

Jan Kaczmarek

The GDP of Poland has in recent years been reaching the average value for the EU25 countries and it is improving. Average life expectancy is comparable to that of highly developed countries. More than 40 per cent of Polish families already have personal computers with Internet access. It is also worth noting that the export and import indicators have been growing and that their balance is favourable to Poland.

Progress in engineering education is good. Poland has sixteen technical universities and nine higher education institutions. Polish students and graduates have been awarded top places in international competitions. Indeed, Polish skills have attracted firms such as Microsoft and various aviation corporations to establish branches in Poland. The achievements of Polish engineers abroad (and particularly in the European Union) must also be recognized; they have been described in detail in the recently published *Encyclopaedia of World Research and Engineering Heritage of Polish Engineers*.

Against this background, showing the distinctive nature of Polish industry, it is important to highlight the potential and activities of the Polish Federation of Engineering Associations (PFEA), which represents the Polish engineering profession, and is one of the largest civil society organizations in Poland. PFEA has 120,000 individual members from thirty-seven branches of engineering associations and two associations of Polish engineers abroad (in the UK and Canada). Its publishers offer thirty-four professional magazines for engineers, with twenty-three magazines for branch associations. PFEA also supports the 'Technical Progress Centre' and 'Science and Technology Commercialization Team'. The PFEA has significant scientific and technical potential, which positively affects all engineering activity across the country.

Despite this generally favourable evaluation of the potential of Polish engineers, unfortunately, in the EU25 statistics on innovative activity, Polish scientific and technical potential scores poorly. An analysis of possible causes of this situation has revealed two principal issues. Firstly, the funding available for the realization of innovative projects is not sufficient. The total annual expenditure per annum on research and development from the state budget and from businesses varies between 0.55 per cent and 0.60 per cent of GDP. Secondly, many multinational companies have invested in Poland but they use the innovations developed in their research and development facilities, which are often outside Poland.

The strategic goals and aspirations of Polish engineering are analogous to those of other developed countries. The significance of the above statistics is that Poland is striving to involve itself in more high- and macro- technologies. 'Niche production', characterized usually by a territorially-limited market, must supplement supply for trade flows to be balanced.

The rising changes in trade, both globally and regionally, influence national economic tactics. In Poland, the economic strategy for the next five years is additionally (if only temporarily)

© Wikimedia

⌒ *Mir Station.*

● *Warsaw University of Technology.*

© Polish Federation of Engineering Associations (NOT)

modified by preparations for the European Football Championship in 2012. The most important part of the preparations has become the building of new transport routes in accordance with the most modern engineering standards. Nevertheless, the need for housing, communications and information technology still remain social and engineering priorities.

In view of the national strategy, the Polish PFEA sets as its primary goal to continue to provide a high level of support for technological progress in small- and medium-sized businesses (which employ two-thirds of the workforce in Poland). The PFEA has taken on the constant task to strive towards a rapid increase in the level of engineering initiative, especially aimed at achieving a high rate of innovation among all engineers, particularly amongst its members, for the benefit of all society.

The leading motto of all Polish engineers, in both good and bad periods of Polish history, has remained, 'Here and now not a day goes by without progress – for the country of our fathers, for the Polish nation and for all the people of Earth.'

5.3.5 The Americas and Caribbean

USA

Charles Vest

Engineering fuelled the United States' rise to global economic and geopolitical leadership during the latter half of the nineteenth century and first half of the twentieth century. Engineering research and practice led to the creation of technologies that have increased life expectancy, driven economic growth and improved the quality of life of U.S. citizens and people around the world. The products, systems and services developed by U.S. engineers are essential to security, public health and the economic competitiveness of American business and industry. In the future, the U.S. engineering enterprise will generate technological innovations to address challenges in the areas of economic recovery – affordable healthcare, sustainable energy sources, sufficient water supplies and global security.

The strength of engineering enterprise in the U.S. has several historical roots. The production demands of two world wars and the massive government works projects during the 1930s contributed to the rapid growth of engineering capability in both practice and research, in addition to its contribution to the U.S.'s burgeoning industrial strength and economic dynamism prior to 1945. In the aftermath of the Second World War, the American government invested in basic science, engineering research and in higher education. It combined this with large-scale government expenditure on applied research and

on advanced technology development and procurement. This was mainly to meet national security needs. This approach accelerated the growth of the U.S. engineering enterprise in a large, diverse, distributed and open national innovation system, populated by a vast number of universities, government laboratories, private non-profit laboratories as well as private companies.

The role of higher education and research in the U.S.

A particular contribution to the engineering prowess of the United States was the excellence and effectiveness of its higher education system. This consists of a diverse array of institutions, ranging from two-year community colleges through to small liberal arts colleges and to research-intensive universities (both public and private). Such diversity provides a wealth of environments and opportunities for students to select a school that best matches their needs and capabilities, and also represents a wide range of funding sources. This strength was substantially leveraged by a tremendous expansion of access to higher education subsequent to the Second World War. It was a means to provide useful activity and skills training to a large number of returning soldiers, it supported economic development in the growing western states, and it supported the continued research and development needs of government and industry. This government–university partnership has transformed American universities, has been remarkably productive, and has made the country a world leader in research-intensive engineering and science education.

Strengths of the engineering workforce in the U.S.

In addition to the strength of engineering education and the productivity of American research universities, several other factors have contributed significantly to the high quality, mobility, accessibility and entrepreneurial nature of the US engineering and technical workforce. These include:

- A highly individualistic, entrepreneurial culture nurtured in U.S. industry and in many U.S. research universities by private practices, public policies and various institutional mechanisms, such as technology business incubators and venture capital firms that encourage risk-taking.

- A history of regulatory and other public policy commitments conducive to high-tech start-up companies, including the competition-oriented or technology diffusion-oriented enforcement of intellectual property rights and antitrust law (competition policy), as well as a relatively risk-friendly system of company law, particularly bankruptcy law.

- A strong indigenous talent base that has been continuously and richly augmented by a large and diverse supply of talented scientists and engineers from other countries. The openness of U.S. campuses, laboratories and companies to talented men and women from other nations in science, engineering and management has been a major factor in our academic excellence, our cultural richness and our economic success (close to 60 per cent of engineering PhD degrees awarded annually are currently earned by foreign nationals.[94] Foreign nationals residing in the United States were named as inventors or co-inventors in 24.2 per cent of the patent applications filed from the United States in 2006, up from 7.3 per cent in 1998).[95]

Global challenges to engineering practice, research and education in the U.S.

The United States has long been a leader in engineering education, especially at the graduate level, and certainly in the quality and accomplishment of our research universities overall. It has been one of the world's most technologically innovative nations thanks, in large part, to the quality and productivity of its engineering workforce. However, several factors are changing rapidly in the twenty-first century.

The last half of the twentieth century was dominated by physics, electronics, high-speed communications and high-speed long-distance transportation. It was an age of speed and power. The twenty-first century appears already to be quite different. It is increasingly dominated by biology and information, but also by macro-scale issues around energy, water and sustainability. These are issues that should be strengths of U.S. engineers, but the context is rapidly evolving.

The impact of R&D expenditures

The U.S. once had the highest national expenditure on R&D, but today North America, Europe and Asia account for about one-third of the world's R&D expenditure each. The U.S. is losing 'market share' in every quantitative category used to evaluate R&D. From 1986 to 2003, the U.S. share of global R&D spending dropped by 9 per cent. The U.S. dropped its share of scientific publications by 8 per cent, its share of new of science and engineering Bachelor's degrees by 10 per cent, its share of U.S. patents by 2 per cent and it dropped its share of new science and engineering PhDs by 30 per cent. The country graduates about 60,000 bachelor-level engineers per year, where China is now graduating about 250,000 per year. These changes reflect the global success of many other countries and we celebrate such advances. But the U.S. is recognizing that we must continue to innovate and develop our engineering and technology sectors as a nation.

Global production of engineers

The rise of production of engineers globally is tremendous. For example, China now educates about 250,000 bachelor-level engineers per year while the U.S. graduates about 60,000.

Certainly, there are definitional and quality differences, and numbers aren't everything, but Floyd Kvamme, a highly experienced high-tech venture capitalist, says that, 'venture capital is the search for smart engineers.' Therefore, for example, the U.S. needs to address the fact that fewer than 15 per cent of high school graduates have a sufficient math and science background to even have the option of entering engineering school.

Speed and changing nature of innovation

The pace of change in innovation is also presenting new challenges. Engineers must work and innovate at ever-accelerating rates. When the automobile was introduced into the market, it took fifty-five years – essentially a lifetime – until one quarter of U.S households owned one. It took about twenty-two years until one-quarter of U.S. households owned a radio. The Internet achieved this penetration in about eight years. Such acceleration drives an inexhaustible thirst for innovation and produces competitive pressures. The spread of education and technology around the world magnifies these competitive pressures.

Finally, globalization is also changing the way engineering work is organized and the way companies acquire innovation. Today, service sector employment is approaching 70 per cent of the U.S. workforce. The development and execution of IT-based service projects is usually accomplished by dividing the functions into a dozen or so components, each of which is carried out by a different group of engineers and managers. These groups are likely to be in several different locations around the world. In the manufacturing sector, this new distribution of work is even more dramatic. For example, the new Boeing 787 aeroplane reportedly has 132,500 engineered parts that are produced in 545 global locations. Indeed, the Chief Executive Officer of global IT firm IBM, Sam Palmasano, says that we have now moved beyond 'multinational corporations' to 'globally integrated enterprises'. An emerging element of this evolving engineering context is 'open innovation', where companies no longer look solely within themselves for innovation, nor do they just purchase it by acquiring small companies. Today, they obtain innovation wherever it is found – in other companies, in other countries, or even through arrangements with competitors. But, more and more often, U.S. engineers are finding themselves in competition for work with engineers from other countries who are often paid far less than what U.S. engineers expect to earn.

Working in this evolving context requires a nimble new kind of engineer and engineering organization.

More and more often, U.S. engineers are finding themselves in competition for work with engineers from other countries, and these other engineers are often paid far less – in some countries as little as one-fifth the rate of U.S. engineers. To do well in this environment, U.S. engineers not only need the sorts of analytic skills, high-level design, systems thinking and creative innovation that are normally provided in the current edu-

94   American Society for Engineering Education

95   Wadhwa, Vivek, Gary Gereffi, Ben Rissing, and Ryan Ong. 2007. Where the engineers are. *Issues in Science and Technology*, Vol. 23, No.3 (Spring), pp. 73–84.

cation system, but will also require a variety of the sorts of 'soft skills' that are often overlooked. These include communications and leadership skills, the flexibility to adapt to changing conditions, the ability to work in multicultural environments, an understanding of the business side of engineering and a commitment to lifelong learning.[96]

New Engineering Frontiers

Perhaps even more dramatic than the changes brought about by globalization and competition are the new engineering frontiers. Two emerging frontiers of engineering are 'tiny systems' and 'macro systems'. Tiny systems are those developed in the 'Bio/Nano/Info' sphere where things get increasingly smaller, faster and more complex. Here there is little distinction between engineering and natural science. Research and product development are done by teams of men and women from various scientific and engineering disciplines who rapidly move from reductionist science to synthesis and system building. Macro-systems are of ever-increasing size and complexity. Work at this frontier may be associated with systems of great societal importance: energy, water, environment, healthcare, manufacturing, communications, logistics and urbanization.

Domestic challenges

Other worrisome trends are already adversely affecting the U.S. capacity for innovation. These trends include:

- A large and growing imbalance in government research funding between the engineering and physical sciences and biomedical and life sciences.

- A near-total emphasis on highly applied research and product development in both industry-funded and government-funded research at the expense of fundamental long-term research.

- An erosion of the engineering research infrastructure due to inadequate investment over many years.

- A decline in interest of American students in engineering, science and other technical fields.

- A growing uncertainty about the ability of the United States to attract and retain gifted engineering and science students from abroad at a time when foreign nationals constitute a large and productive component of the U.S. R&D workforce.

Inspiring America's youth is a real concern as is grappling with the low level of public understanding of engineering and what can be done to improve this.[97] The predominant engineering demographic of the American white male population is in decline, yet the U.S. faces very real challenges in fully engaging women and minorities[98] in the engineering profession at levels proportionate to the representation in the population at large. Only 18.1 per cent of engineering bachelor' degrees went to women in 2006–2007, the lowest share since 1996. Female enrollment remained virtually unchanged in 2007 at 17.5 per cent. This is significantly lower than the total student body, where women comprise 58 per cent of enrolled undergraduates. African-American and Hispanic student representation has remained consistently low for the past decade. Despite comprising over 27 per cent of the U.S. population, these two groups account for only 11 per cent of engineering bachelor's degrees awarded to U.S. students.

Rising to these challenges

The only acceptable response to the aforementioned challenges is to lead. Leading will require upping the U.S. commitment to education and training at all levels. It will require increasing investments by both U.S. government and industry in R&D and innovation. Leading will require inspiring and preparing a generation of young people to push the frontiers of science and technology and to solve the real problems we face, issues like energy, environment, food, efficient delivery of healthcare, the shift to a global service economy, and world security.

In August 2007, the American Congress passed legislation, the America COMPETES Act, which would be one step in the right direction when it is fully funded by Congress. This legislation would jump-start improvement in U.S. pre-college science and math education, strengthen and sustain long-term basic research, and help to ensure that the U.S. is one of the best places to study, conduct and innovate.

Other efforts to address the current climate for engineering

Many organizations in the United States, including industry and higher education institutions, have recognized the need for and the importance of revolutionary change in engineering education, and have begun to take steps forward. The U.S. Accreditation Board for Engineering and Technology (ABET)[99] has developed a new approach that offers engineering schools more flexibility to update their curricula and to introduce innovations. Some of the key ideas that have been piloted and tested include:

---

96   National Academy of Engineering. *The Engineer of 2020: Visions of Engineering in the New Century*. 2004. Washington, DC: National Academies Press.

97   National Academy of Engineering. 2008. *Changing the Conversation: Messages for Improving Public Understanding of Engineering*, Washington, DC: National Academies Press.

98   Minority populations in the U.S. currently include African American, Asian, Hispanic, and Native American people.

99   Accreditation Board for Engineering and Technology. 2006. *Engineering Change: A Study of the Impact of EC2000*. Baltimore, MD: ABET, Inc. See also: http://www.abet.org

- Providing the flexibility in engineering curricula to pursue a variety of careers with an engineering background.

- Expanding research-based and student-centered learning approaches in the undergraduate engineering curriculum.[100]

- Educating engineers for leadership in an increasingly technological society by broadening engineering education and emphasizing communication, teamwork, policy, environment and ethics.

- Developing a variety of lifelong learning programmes in engineering, as well as the innovative use of on-line learning tools.

- Developing various initiatives to attract under-represented groups (i.e. women, African-Americans, Hispanic-Americans, Native-Americans) to engineering, and to attract domestic students to graduate studies in engineering.[101]

- Emphasizing, throughout the engineering curriculum, not just the technology, the benefits that engineers bring to society.

Action by the U.S. National Academy of Engineering

Much of what will be exciting and valuable in the twenty-first century will be the work of engineers who will move tiny systems technology into macro-systems applications. For example, the application of bio-based materials design and production, personalized predictive medicine, biofuels, and nanotechnology based energy production and storage devices. These engineers and researchers, driven by 'fire in the belly' and their obsessive concentration on solving challenging puzzles, will be the ones to take us forward. In an effort to encourage such exploration and initiative, the U.S. National Academy of Engineering announced in February 2008, fourteen grand challenges of the twenty-first century.

One of dominant themes over the next century is likely to be sustainability of the planet, and five of the grand challenges listed above relate to this theme. As our global society seeks ways to maintain itself in a sustainable way relative to the environment, it will be up to engineers to find ways to do such things as make solar power economical, provide energy from fusion, and develop methods to pull carbon dioxide out of the atmosphere and store it in the Earth's crust. Engineers will also play an important role, alongside doctors and medical researchers, in improving human health by developing better

---

> **U.S. National Academy of Engineering Grand Challenges**
>
> - Make solar energy economical
> - Provide energy from fusion
> - Develop carbon sequestration methods
> - Manage the nitrogen cycle
> - Provide access to clean water
> - Restore and improve urban infrastructure
> - Advance health informatics
> - Engineer better medicines
> - Reverse-engineer the brain
> - Prevent nuclear terror
> - Secure cyberspace
> - Enhance virtual reality
> - Advance personalized learning
> - Engineer the tools of scientific discovery

ways to store, analyse, and communicate health information, and by designing more effective drugs. Because today's powerful technologies offer many opportunities for misuse, another job of engineers will be to find ways to prevent such misuse whenever possible, for example, by thwarting terrorists who would use nuclear terror and by securing cyberspace. Finally, engineers in the coming century will have a major role to play in enhancing human capacities by advancing personalized learning and engineering tools of scientific discovery for example.

So, meeting some of these challenges is imperative for human survival. Meeting others will make us more secure against natural and human threats. Meeting any of them will improve quality of life. The twenty-first century will be very different from the twentieth century. Engineering will be enormously exciting and it will also be increasingly rich and complex in its context and importance.

Canada

Darrel John Danyluk

Engineering in Canada is a regulated profession, and all engineers responsible for engineering work require a licence from the provincial or territorial jurisdiction in which they practice. There are six engineering organizations that represent elements of the engineering profession in Canada. These are:

---

100 A National Academy of Engineering Committee, Understanding and Improving K-12 Engineering Education in the U.S., will release a report in 2009 on pre-college engineering education. Go to: http://www.nae.edu

101 National Academy of Engineering's, Engineer Your Life, is an example. Go to: http://www.engineeryourlife.org.

- Engineers Canada

- The Canadian Academy of Engineering

- The Association of Canadian Engineering Companies

- The National Council of Deans of Engineering and Applied Science

- The Engineering Institute of Canada

- The Canadian Federation of Engineering Students

These organizations are linked through the Canadian Engineering Leadership Forum, which brings together the presidents and chief executives of each body to address national engineering matters.

Established in 1936, Engineers Canada (Engineers Canada is the operating name of the Canadian Council of Professional Engineers) is the national organization of the twelve provincial and territorial associations that regulate the practice of engineering in Canada and license the country's more than 160,000 professional engineers. Engineers Canada serves members by delivering national programmes that ensure the highest standards of engineering education, professional qualifications and professional practice. It facilitates the national mobility of engineers through an inter-association mobility agreement that enables engineers to obtain a license to practice in other provinces and territories. Engineers Canada represents its members in national and international affairs, and coordinates the development of national policies, positions and guidelines on behalf of the engineering profession. It also promotes greater understanding of the nature, role and contribution of professional engineers and engineering to society, and undertakes federal government relations and national media relations.

Through its Canadian Engineering Accreditation Board, Engineers Canada accredits Canadian undergraduate engineering programs that meet the profession's high education standards. Through its Canadian Engineering Qualifications Board, Engineers Canada develops national guidelines on the qualifications, standards of practice and ethics expected of professional engineers. The International Committee is responsible for keeping Engineers Canada's Board of Directors abreast of new opportunities to maintain or enhance international mobility for Canadian engineers, and for monitoring the use and viability of Engineers Canada's existing mutual recognition agreements on the full or partial recognition of engineering qualifications

The Canadian Academy of Engineering (CAE) was founded in 1987 and was one of the highlights of the celebration of the centennial of engineering as an organized profession in

Canada. The academy is an independent, self-governing and non-profit organization established to serve Canada in matters of engineering concern, and which comprises many of the country's most accomplished engineers. In 1991, the Canadian Academy became a full and active member of the International Council of Academies of Engineering and Technological Sciences (CAETS).

The Canadian Federation of Engineering Students (CFES) is a community strengthened and enriched by a nationally diverse engineering student body. To enhance student life, the CFES facilitates communication, the sharing of ideas, and the exchange of information between member schools. To ensure that students grow both personally and professionally, the CFES keeps abreast of the changes taking place in society affecting engineering students and the engineering profession. CFES is a unified voice for students both nationally and internationally, and assists in ensuring that Canadian engineering students grow and prosper in the twent-first century.

The Engineering Institute of Canada (EIC) is an umbrella organization for twelve engineering technical societies that organize inter-society cooperation in activities such as advocacy, continuing professional development and interaction, and events such as the Canadian Conference on Climate Change Technology.

The National Council of Deans of Engineering and Applied Science represents many of the forty academic institutions in Canada that offer accredited engineering programmes. The deans meet bi-annually to exchange information on engineering trends that impact education delivery in the short, medium and long-term.

The Association of Canadian Engineering Companies was founded in 1925. ACEC is the national association of consulting firms that provide engineering and other technology-based intellectual services to the built and natural environment. Member companies offer professional engineering services worldwide to private sector and government clients. The Association's membership consists of approximately 600 independent consulting engineering firms and twelve provincial and territorial member organizations who offer, collectively, thirty-five types of services in 273 specializations.

() *The Confederation Bridge (see box).*

© Strait Crossing Bridge Limited

The Confederation Bridge has been named one of the five most significant Canadian engineering achievements of the twentieth century. The 12.9 kilometre bridge connects the eastern Canadian provinces of Prince Edward Island and New Brunswick, across the Northumberland Strait. When the bridge opened in 1997 after three and a half years of construction, it replaced the existing ferry service with a faster and more efficient transportation link. Built and operated by Strait Crossing Development Inc., the Confederation Bridge is the longest bridge over ice-covered saltwater in the world.

Brazil

Luiz Carlos Scavarda do Carmo and Cláudio Amaury Dall'Acqua

Brazil, the largest country of Latin America has 8.5 million square kilometres of territory (of which 49.3 per cent is covered by the Amazon rainforest), 190 million inhabitants and a GDP of more than US$1 trillion. It has about 9,000 kilometres of coast and one of the biggest fluvial networks on the planet. It shares borders with every South American country except for Chile and Ecuador. Brazil is now one of the four emerging global economic powers (with Russia, India and China).

Brazil has a well-developed agricultural industry, is the worlds' second biggest food producer, and its territory is very well served with fresh water resources. A robust, complete and sophisticated industry positions Brazil as a major player in some industrial fields, such as automobiles and commercial airplanes, and it is the world leader in deep water oil exploration. About 55 per cent of its annual exports (totalling US$160 billion) are manufactured products. Brazil leads ambitious aerospace and nuclear power development programmes. Additionally, of its total energy matrix of 239.4 tons of oil equivalent, 44.9 per cent is from renewable sources (14.7 per cent from hydroelectricity and 30.2 per cent of biomass). The service sector is dynamic and technologically up-to-date. The telecommunications network has more than 100 million mobile phones, and of the 6.7 million homes with computers, 4.9 million are linked to the Internet.

Brazil suffers from enormous income distribution inequalities and lacks severely in its infrastructure. Some 81 per cent of the population live in urban centres – located at the south, southeast and northeast regions along the Atlantic Ocean – with a deficit of more than 5.6 million houses. Only 52 per cent of Brazil's urban areas have sewer systems. There are significant inequalities in population distribution and large areas are informally occupied in the centre and north region of the country. The railway network is not sufficient and though there are 1.6 million kilometres of road, of which only 12 per cent are paved. The extensive coast and great network of big rivers are still only modestly explored as transport routes. This very broad picture of engineering in Brazil shows us that it is a fast-developing country, still under construction and presenting enormous potential, opportunity and challenges. Engineering in Brazil has already reached a good technical level with these advanced industries. However, engineering has not reached the status of being a strategic element of sustainable development.

Engineering as a profession faces a relatively low number of engineers, estimated at only 550,000 in the economically active population – about 6 engineers per 1,000 people. Brazil has 1,325 engineering courses with 300,000 engineering students, equivalent to 7.75 per cent of all university students, and graduates 25,000 engineers per year. In 2005, about 30,000 engineers graduated, but even this number is three times smaller than for South Korea, which has a population one-quarter of the size of Brazil. Despite the shortage of engineers in the labour market – a market that demands professionals for infrastructure construction and industrial and services expansion – there is no observed increase in youth interest for this most important profession. Indeed, statistics show that the number of students is increasing in areas of social studies but not in technical studies, meaning that technical professionals are in extreme demand.

In the 1990s, the Brazilian government promoted the opening of the commercial and industrial markets to international competition, adhering to the wave of globalization. It resulted in an enormous decrease in Brazilian consulting engineering

Projects to change engineering in Brazil

The organizational stakeholders of a process of development based on engineering are the schools of engineering, industry, government and professional societies. Though they share the same final objective, their plans and intermediary targets diverge. The great challenge in Brazil is to develop and sustain national programmes and projects that bring these stakeholders together to address engineering education, and to develop a new process to deliver new engineers, not only to reduce shortages but to innovate and create an entrepreneurial ecosystem.

Appropriate professional competencies must be forged including an interdisciplinary attitude, geographical and cultural mobility, strategic thinking and marketing wisdom, and teamwork and leadership with people from different walks of life and from other countries.

Two examples of what Brazilian projects are trying to achieve are highlighted below. Both are focused on the complexity of engineering-based development, including the integration of several stakeholders and the improvement of both higher education and secondary education. Such efforts are important for positioning engineering within the agenda of Brazilian civil society.

Project Inova: this initiative of the National Conference of Industry has received the full support of all organizational stakeholders. The project is creating a forum on the double purpose of engineering in Brazil, that is, to promote leadership in industrial innovation and to guarantee sustainable development. One of the vital aspects of Project Inova is that it stems from the limitations to strengthening engineering in Brazil. For example, the number of students enrolling at schools of engineering depends not only on intrinsic talent and interest, but also on the quality of education and motivation for engineering received in secondary schools.

Case Poli 2015: an initiative of the Polytechnic School of University of São Paulo has established a new mission for students that will graduate after 2015: 'The engineer of the future will apply scientific analysis and holistic synthesis to develop sustainable solutions which will integrate the social, environmental, cultural and economic systems.'

domestically and the denationalization of some dynamic technologically productive sectors. Many highly qualified Brazilian engineers moved or have been transferred to other countries, usually the most developed. Outside the country, although Brazilian engineering companies were doing business on all continents, they had a modest presence when compared with the presence of engineering firms from nations such as China and India.

Another Brazilian engineering challenge – and indeed a political challenge – is the necessity to increase the exports of products with a higher technological content or added value. Though more than half of Brazilian exports are manufactured products, a great proportion has low technological content or depends on imported technologies and components. This decreases national economic gains and means that job creation and private investment in the country are not reaching their potential. In a global economy, where the complexity of the interactions among distinct players is increasing at an unprecedented rate, engineering has become a special tool for sustainable development, and mainly for developing nations. The social and environmental challenges of the twenty-first century cannot be met without a new breed of professional engineers who have a broader vision for society.

Venezuela

Vladimir Yackovlev

Venezuela has an area of 916,000 square kilometres and a population of 28 million people. It has a literacy index of 93 per cent (2004), and 83 per cent (2006) of the population has access to treated water. The GNP per capita is US$6,209 with an annual growth rate of 5 per cent. The official figures for inflation and unemployment are 17.3 per cent and 10.5 per cent respectively (2008), although there is a high rate of self-employment in the informal sector of the economy. The main industrial activities are oil refining, metallurgy, iron and steel industries, food processing and the chemical industry.

The country has some 180,000 engineers and architects who, by law, have to be registered in the *Colegio de Ingenieros de Venezuela* in order to be able to work as professionals. This represents 6.5 professionals per 1,000 population. The growth of engineering professionals is 6.7 per cent annually, which is much higher than the population growth of the country at 1.3 per cent.

The *Colegio de Ingenieros de Venezuela* is the professional society that serves as the guardian of public interest, acts as an advisor to government, promotes the progress of science and technology and supervises the professional activities of its members. Engineers contribute through their professional activity in the design, construction, operation and maintenance of infrastructure, and through industry, educational institutions and engineering enterprise. However, it must be pointed out that infrastructure is deteriorating rapidly in all areas and that attention should be paid to this looming problem.

In September of 1998, the National Congress passed a law creating the 'National Academy of Engineering and the Habitat'. This is an academic corporation with thirty-five permanent members and three corresponding members from each state of the country. Its main purpose is to contribute to science and technology in the different disciplines of engineering and the habitat, and to conduct studies on the development of the country.

Undergraduate engineering studies are offered in forty universities in the country, and some of these institutions have several campuses in different cities. About 47 per cent of these universities are supported by the state and 53 per cent are private institutions. The growth of private universities is a recent phenomenon that has developed in the last quarter of a century. According to the latest statistics provided by the planning office for the university sector, there are a total of 87,020 students studying engineering. Of those, 2,906 are registered in the agricultural and forestry sectors, whilst the rest are studying in more traditional areas such as civil, mechanical, chemical engineering, among others. A noteworthy statistic is that 41.3 per cent of the total number of students studying engineering are women.

Engineering studies are normally completed in a period of five years and graduates are awarded a professional qualification, such as 'Mechanical Engineer'. Venezuelan universities offer graduate studies in engineering, leading to M.Sc., 'Specialist', Dr.Sc. or Dr.Eng. degrees. There are 290 graduate programmes currently being delivered, of which 47 per cent are programmes leading to the 'Specialist' degree, 48 per cent are M.Sc. programmes and 5 per cent are doctoral programmes.

Argentina

Conrado Bauer, Mario Telichevsky and Miguel Yadarola

Argentina is the eighth largest country in the world with an area of 2.8 million square kilometres. It has a population of around 40 million, a GDP of US$245.6 billion and GDP per capita of US$6,548 (2007). The literacy rate is 97 per cent (2003). The number of practicing engineers in Argentina is estimated at 115,000.

As the main agent of physical transformation, technological creation and productive innovation, engineering has a central role in social and economic development. However, as in many countries, this is is often not well understood by policy-makers. This is partly due to rising apathy towards politics, however a new generation of engineers is working to overcome this limitation to cooperate in national development planning and in projects with foreign financing. The main engineering challenges discussed in Argentina are:

- Improving transport infrastructure, its operation, the modes of transport used and safety.

- Urgently increasing the energy supply.

- Expansion of urban sanitation.

- Better distribution of activities and population to reduce inequality and transform informal settlements.

- Promotion of engineering enrolment, graduation and training.

Argentina has more than eighty institutions that educate and graduate engineers. Of these, seventy are public colleges or national universities (including twenty-four regional schools of the National Technological University) with free inscription for secondary school graduates, and the others are private and paid for by the students. Together they offer 395 grade courses, of which 376 grant twenty-one specialized degrees that are selected in a process of curriculum unification being conducted by the Federal Council of Engineering Deans (CONFEDI).[102] Courses are completed in five years but statistics show that only 9.6 per cent of students comply fully. The dropout rates from these studies is also very high. The total numbers of graduate engineers in the period 1998–2003 was 11,460 from national universities, 10,250 from the National Technological University and 4,090 from private universities. The main engineering fields were computer sciences and industrial, electronic, civil, chemical and mechanical engineering. It is estimated that, at present, women make up nearly 20 per cent of all engineering students. There are also many courses for postgraduate study, which are increasingly in demand.

Quality control of engineering courses is part of a system of accreditation defined by the Argentine National Law of Higher Education. The National Council of Evaluation and Accreditation (CONEAU)[103] plans evaluations and grants programmes licenses for three or six years. Accreditation guidelines and procedures are similar to those of ABET, the Washington Accord and the EMF. To improve the usefulness of the system, some engineering institutions consider that the evaluations should include the opinion of practicing engineers working in professional activities and productive sectors.

CONFEDI is analyzing, in cooperation with the Secretary of University Policies of the Ministry of Education, curricula and pedagogy[104] with a view to updating engineering education to deliver the outcomes and competences needed for 2015. Some guiding concepts for this process include: better contextualization so that engineers can meet the needs of the country; more attractive training that increases formative, creative and practical activities; closer relations with regional population, production and problems; and the consideration of social situations. Many of these concepts were postulated by UNESCO in the Delors Report105 in 1996, with inspiration for engineering education such as 'learning to know, learning to do, learning to live together and learning to be' as the four pillars of education throughout life.

In the last decades of the twentieth century, Argentina suffered a costly 'brain drain' of engineers. With economic recovery, demand is still not being satisfied by the number of new graduates. Enrolment in engineering programmes began to decline in 1990 and reached its lowest level between 1996 and 1999. Economic recovery began in 2000 with policies encouraging local production; with the result that enrolment increased 11 per cent between 2000 and 2007. There were some 30,000 enrolments of engineering students in 2005, but that same year fewer than 5,000 engineers graduated, showing that many left at intermediate level.

For this reason, the national government is encouraging engineering students to enrol and complete their studies with scholarships and funds in order to improve engineering schools. There are funds to promote the return of highly qualified Argentine engineers who have left the country. The Office of Science, Technology and Productive Innovation of the national government was upgraded to a new ministry last year, and it leads promotional programmes to expand and enhance engineering education and research, and their links with production. The national government annual budget for engineering was estimated to be just less than US$700 million in 2008, after it was increased at a rate of 16 per cent per year between 2000 and 2008. We must also add to this amount the contributions of private schools and productive enterprise to educate and train engineers.

102 Federal Council of Engineering Deans (CONFEDI). Go to: http://www.confedi.org.ar

103 National Council on Evaluation and Accreditation, Argentina. Go to: http://www.coneau.gov.ar

104 Secretary of University Policies, Ministry of Education. Go to: http://www.me.gov.ar/spu/

105 Jacques Delors. 1996. Learning: the Treasure Within. Report to UNESCO of the International Commission on Education for the Twenty-first Century. UNESCO publishing, Paris.

Investments in engineering research and development have historically been low in Argentina as the priority was to fund the sciences. In recent years, technological research has been receiving increasing support from the national government and, in smaller proportions, from the private sector. In 2003, the total investment in research and development was 0.5 per cent of the GNP, in 2008 it will be 0.8 per cent and it is planned to reach 1 per cent by 2010.

Legally, Argentine engineering is controlled by institutions called 'Professional Councils' and 'Engineering Colleges' that are governed by engineers and are located all over the country. They manage the professional registration, activities and ethics of engineering on behalf of the State. Besides those institutions, engineers are freely organized in regional associations or engineers' centres. Together, they constitute the national association UADI,[106] which is member of UPADI, the Pan-American association, and WFEO. The missions of UADI and its centres are generally to represent engineers and to improve their professional activities for the service of their country. Engineering professional practice is regulated by codes of ethics, which are approved and applied by the Professional Councils, and advised by Argentina's National Academy of Engineering.[107]

Caribbean

Gossett Oliver

Engineering and its varied products, services and insights are influential in all walks of life and in all corners of the world as a major force directing our thoughts, actions and the course of civilization. A country's ability to cope with its many challenges and to satisfy the demands of its citizens depend to a large extent on the development and application of engineering, which has its grounding in the knowledge of science and technology.

With very few exceptions, all developed nations are masters of the generation and use of science and technology (S&T), while underdeveloped nations have lesser capacity in the deployment of these instruments. It can be argued that scientific and technological capabilities are the major forces separating developed from developing countries and are, moreover, widening the gap between the rich and poor. A crucial step in closing these development gaps in the Caribbean is the willingness of the leaders to craft policies, strategies and plans to use engineering innovatively to tackle socio-economic problems and to protect their environment.

Only two of the English speaking Caribbean islands (namely Jamaica and Trinidad and Tobago, with a total population of about six million) have had a long history in scientific awareness and application. They were among the earliest Caribbean islands to craft laws to guide the use of science and technology for the exploitation of domestic natural resources. This is perhaps not surprising considering the fact that Jamaica was among the first in the American hemisphere to enjoy electricity, build a railway, establish botanical gardens as well as innovatively apply research results to boost sugar cane production.

Small countries like those in the Caribbean have a comparatively limited number of professionals and material resources, yet they will have to face most, if not all, of the challenges of larger, better equipped jurisdictions. This is forcing the Caribbean population to be more innovative in using the resources available in order to gain maximum efficiencies, and to remain flexible and adaptable to rapid change.

The Caribbean's management of science and technology has to become adept at using few skilled and trained individuals in a very considered and focused manner to achieve beneficial results. Decisions on what to tackle locally, what to acquire from the outside and how to marry the two are ineluctable and burning questions. Monitoring, evaluation and learning become essential in these endeavours.

The Caribbean realizes that it has to use existing technology and engineering knowledge to tackle chronic production problems, while meticulously building a stronger research and development base to seek answers and anticipate problems. The Caribbean therefore has to strengthen its knowledge surveillance capabilities and partnership, creating systems to cope with its limited natural resources.

Although the Caribbean has a strong university system and science pedigree, it has been difficult to translate domestic scientific results into technologies, products and services because of insufficient capital goods, funding, implementation machinery, engineering and entrepreneurship capacities. The Caribbean's private sector (perhaps with the exception of Trinidad and Tobago) is not only small but largely conservative in its approach to development; it shies away from taking risks in technological investments while taking comfort in Government papers, securities and retail trading. Many in the private sector shun innovation and technological upgrading.

Crime has become a major concern. The islands' coastlines are difficult to police without modern surveillance and detection technologies to prevent the entry of contraband, illicit drugs and weapons.

The Caribbean essentially has all the main infrastructural S&T components, except for risk and venture capital funds for tech-

106 UADI. Go to: http://www.uadi.org.ar

107 National Academy of Engineering. Go to: http://www.acadning.org.ar

nology-led projects and pilot plans facilities. Improvement in the assessment capabilities of banks to estimate risks in the knowledge economy is needed. Ways to encourage university and other tertiary graduates to commercialize knowledge and create novel products and services are also vital elements in a successful domestic economy.

Key strategic areas

Accordingly, the following strategic areas for engineers are crucial to set the Caribbean on a path of peace and prosperity:

(i)   Collection and use of vital national S&T information

In a knowledge-led world, information is the most important currency. The market does not allow for proper flows of timely information and, therefore, government must establish institutions, set policies and implement plans in order to ensure that the vital statistics of the countries are collected, analysed and distributed to inform business development and social adjustments. Also, the Caribbean has to tap into regional and global networks to follow technological trends, scientific developments and business and trade signals that may have significant impact on local enterprises and cultural norms.

The following initiatives are the minimum requirements to fulfill such purposes:

- Gather accurate information on what S&T skills, institutions, organizations and projects exist.

- Match this knowledge with the present industrial, manufacturing, service and social demands and thereby identify and fill vital gaps.

- Establish performance criteria and standards to monitor and evaluate domestic S&T and engineering activities to help their progress and ensure optimum use of resource.

- Establish a review mechanism to permit national budgeting by performance, especially S&T activities within ministries and main statutory bodies.

- Share tacit knowledge specific to the Caribbean situation, especially for the production of goods, services and recreation.

(ii)   Intelligence capabilities

Intellectual capital is the development bedrock of nations and this is fed by the development and analysis of domestic information and the pursuit of knowledge from the global arena. Consequently, the importance of effective intelligence management to promote business expansion and vitality has never been greater. Policy and planning will require high quality social intelligence from a variety of quarters, if resources are to be allocated opti-

mally and development aims achieved in a timely fashion. An information network that spans the globe is therefore of significance to the local prospects for socio-economic development. This is especially so for small states like the Caribbean.

The following objectives are therefore paramount:

- Develop social intelligence networks, engaging missions, embassies and other bodies abroad.

- Train diplomats, politicians and other government officials as well as trade union bosses and national leaders in S&T currency and their impacts.

- Develop systems for local S&T intelligence to maximize collection, analysis, dissemination and feedback.

(iii)   Deepen and expand Information and Communication Technology competence

Informatics and telecommunications are currently at the centre of the accelerated rate of globalization and increased production and trade. These technologies were the results of scientific discoveries, which led to a range of practical developments including electricity, radio waves, the laser, the transistor, the World Wide Web and the web browser. Their influences have been profound in almost all walks of life and already have provided economic benefits in states with high levels of diffusion, use and improvement of these technologies, while countries that are lagging in this field are also being left behind in knowledge sharing and application. To make these technologies work for socio-economic development, several factors are required including, liberalization and open competition, expanded infrastructures, balanced regulations, innovation in management and organization, and the use of these technologies in an increased number of firms and institutions to improve production and marketing. Accordingly, widespread competence in this field is necessary to ensure the ability to gain, share and use information constructively throughout the society. Areas where this competence is needed in the Caribbean include enhancing information and communication technology policy and skills in:

- Software Development

- Design and Hardware Assembly

- Cultural Product

- Services for the main drivers of the economy (e.g. tourism and banking)

(iv)   Environmental preservation

Socio-economic development will not be sustainable if environmental protection is not factored into the change process. This is especially true of the small tropical islands of the Carib-

↻ Trash being loaded and compacted in a landfill.

© Oliver

Effects of Hurricane Dean in 2007.

bean which have a fragile ecology and growing population, as well as transportation and industrialization pressures. To be able to strike a balance between economic development and human development, environmental protection using the best local information is required, and this will depend on astutely directed research and the creative use of its results leading to the attainment, for example, of international standards. The science of biodiversity, biosafety and bioremediation accordingly will become vital:

Policy initiatives to ensure the minimum requirements for protecting the environment and citizens must include:

- Improving R&D to reduce ecological pressures, as well as, address the exigencies of natural and man-made hazards, including droughts and floods.

- Setting up biosafety regulations and measures.

- Improving building code.

- Providing information to effect a balance between construction and agriculture.

- Zoning to ensure that flatter, more suitable lands are reserved for agriculture.

- Finding ways to successfully implement environmental preservation strategies.

- Introducing appropriate, more efficient and less polluting fuels into the region's energy mix could make a profound difference.

(iv) Technologies for coping with hazards

The Caribbean is in a hazard-prone zone and subject to frequent hurricanes, flooding and earthquakes. The Caribbean must therefore pay critical attention to modern technologies such as material and nano-technologies to improve the selection of sites, the suitability of material and the cost of construction.

More affordable and safer housing for much of the population is an urgent requirement. The island must therefore do the following:

- Conduct a survey of the various construction material and technologies that are available for building in tropical zones.

- Create awareness among R&D institutions of the opportunities for work in this area. Foster a greater engagement of professional societies in these endeavours.

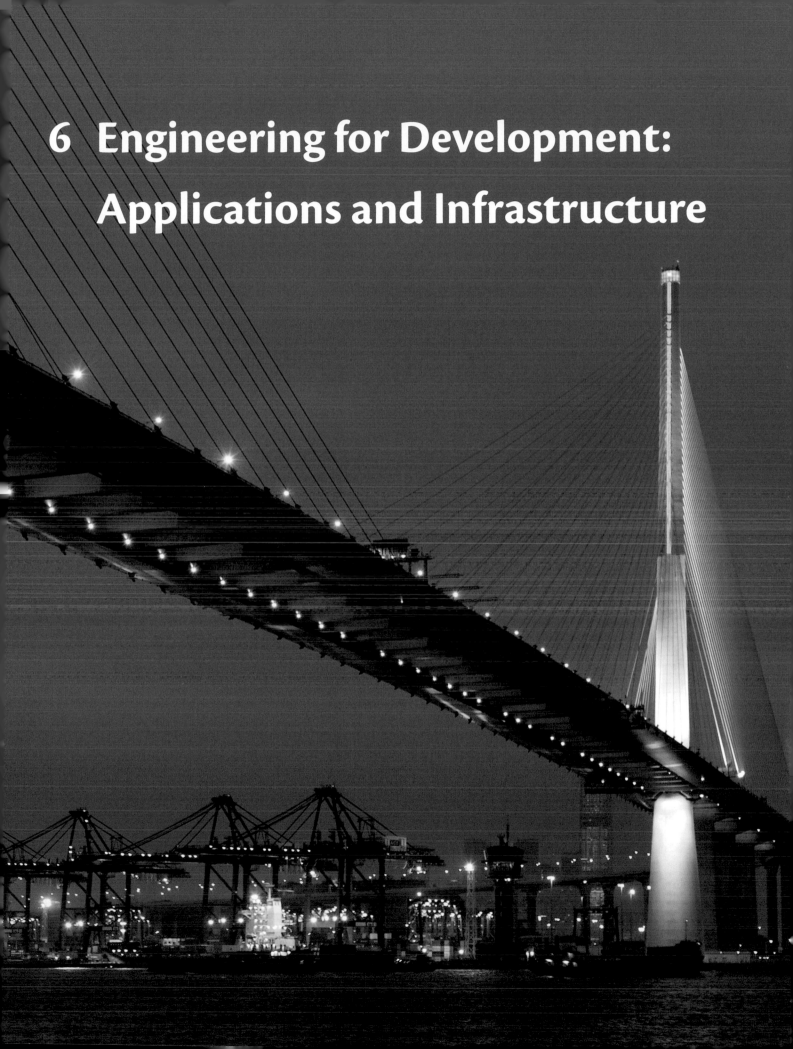

6 Engineering for Development: Applications and Infrastructure

Engineering and associated capacity building, applications and infrastructure is of vital importance in social and economic development, as indicated in the comments of world leaders on knowledge societies and economies, and in the declarations of international conferences and world summits. Yet engineering is routinely overlooked in the context of development policy and planning – it is hardly mentioned in relation to the Millennium Development Goals (MDGs), or in many Poverty Reduction Strategy Papers (PRSPs), for example. This chapter focuses on engineering for development applications and infrastructure, with particular reference to the Millennium Development Goals and related international development priorities, and the connection to engineering standards. There is an initial focus on poverty reduction, with a case study from South Africa, and sustainable development, including a study on the MDGs, sustainable development and engineering standards.

The importance of technology in climate change mitigation and adaptation has been emphasized by the IPCC and rec-ognized by many governments, and the role of engineering in this context is vital. Engineering is also vital in emergencies and disaster response, reconstruction and risk reduction, as recently evidenced by the Haiti earthquake. Technologies for development need to be appropriate to context, and the importance of 'appropriate technology' has been recognized and promoted since the 1960s, albeit with mixed reception around the world. The case for appropriate technology is presented here, with an interesting case study on the use of appropriate building technologies. Sections on engineering infrastructure include contributions on water supply and sanitation, energy, transportation, communications, reliability and maintenance management. There is a concluding section on the development of infrastructure in developing countries, including a discussion of Infrastructure Report Cards, designed to focus attention on the importance of infrastructure – with case studies from South Africa, Australia and USA.

Fiscal Stimulus Package Survey 2009

The global financial crisis has led to most major countries announcing a stimulus package – a special fiscal package of spending and tax measures meant to increase economic activity (more formally, fiscal stimulus aims to boost economic activity during periods of economic weakness by increasing short-term aggregate demand). These packages generally include a significant percentage for infrastructure projects that require consulting and engineering services. The International Federation of Consulting Engineers (FIDIC) monitors the over-all effect of this infrastructure spending on the demand for these services.

As mentioned in the Introduction, it is interesting to report here the results of the FIDIC survey of economic stimulus packages around the world – with stimulus packages totalling US$2035 billion, with US$1163 billion earmarked specifically for infrastructure, and an estimate of US$20 billion that will be spent on engineering consultancy services.

Stimulus Packages: Infrastructure Component

Country	Instrument	Date	Total	Infrastructure
European Union	European Council Agenda (includes Member Country stimulus packages given below)	11-12 Dec 08	US$ 252 billion	US$ 218 billion for extra measures
Australia	Announcement	15 Oct 08	US$ 7.4 billion	
		12 Dec 08	US$ 2.2 billion	US$ 2.2 billion
Brazil	Signed into law	23 Jan 09	US$ 20 billion	US$ 37.7 billion
Canada	Announcement	13 Jan 09	US$ 30 billion	
Chile		5 Jan 08	US$ 2.0 billion	US$ 0.7 billion

Stimulus Packages: Infrastructure Component (*continuation*)

Country	Instrument	Date	Total	Infrastructure
China	Announcement	10 Nov 08	US$ 600 billion	US$ 540 billion
China, Hong Kong			US$ 7.2 billion	
China, Taipei			US$ 1.8 billion	
Egypt		Dec 08	US$ 2.7 billion	
France			US$ 32.8 billion	US$ 13.2 billion
Germany	1st and 2nd Stimulus Packages	Dec 08 - Jan 09	US$ 64.3 billion	US$ 17.6 billion
Hungary			US$ 6.5 billion	
India		7 Dec 08 and 2 Jan 09	US$ 60 billion	US$ 33.5 billion
Israel		Nov 08	US$ 5.7 billion	US$ 2.9 billion
Italy			US$ 101 billion	US$ 20.9 billion
Japan		Aug - Dec 08 (3 packages)	US$ 133 billion	
Korea		Nov 08	US$ 11 billion	US$ 7.8 billion
Malaysia		4 Nov 08	US$ 1.9 billion	US$ 0.9 billion
Netherlands			US$ 7.6 billion	
Peru		8 Dec 08	US$ 3.3 billion	
Portugal			US$ 8.3 billion	
Russia	USD 12.7 billion		US$ 20 billion	
Singapore	Announcement	23 Jan 09	US$ 14.9 billion	US$ 3.2 billion
Spain			US$ 47.9 billion	US$ 11.3 billion
Sweden	Announcement	5 Dec 08	US$ 1.1 billion	US$ 0.1 billion
Switzerland	Government approved		US$ 0.8 billion	
Thailand	Government approved	16 Jan 09	US$ 3.6 billion	
UK	Announcement	Nov 08	US$ 30 billion	
USA	American Recovery and Reinvestment Act draft	15 Jan 09	US$ 550 billion	US$ 180 billion
Vietnam			US$ 6.0 billion	US$ 3.0 billion

The demand for consulting engineering services

Investment in infrastructure is equivalent to an increase in Gross Fixed Capital Formation (GFCF). GFCF measures the value of additions to fixed assets purchased by business, government and households less disposals of fixed assets sold off or scrapped. So it is a measure of the net new investment in fixed capital assets. Its aim is to measure the value of net additions to fixed capital stock, but somewhat confusingly, GFCF is called 'gross' because it does not include the depreciation of assets. FIDIC uses national estimates of GFCF to estimate the demand for consulting engineering services (see article PDF and FIDIC Annual Survey). Using the same methodolgy, the stimulus packages summarized above translate to an additional demand of some USD 20 billion in services.

6.1 Engineering, the MDGs and other international development goals

6.1.1 Engineering and the Millennium Development Goals

Jo da Silva and Susan Thomas

We will have time to reach the Millennium Development Goals (MDGs – a set of targets to reduce global poverty and improve living standards by 2015) worldwide and in most, or even all, individual countries, but only if we break with business as usual. Success will require sustained action between now and the deadline of 2015. It takes time to train the teachers, nurses and engineers; to build the roads, schools and hospitals; and to grow the small and large businesses able to create the jobs and income needed. So we must start now. And we must more than double global development assistance over the next few years. Nothing less will help to achieve the goals.

The role of engineering is vital in meeting the MDGs. The context of this for Arup is our Drivers of Change initiative, which includes research on poverty and other topics directly related to the Millennium Development Goals. As an example of how engineers can be proactive, British engineering firm Arup has established an International Development team. The work of this team responds to the Millennium Development Goals by seeking to maximize the long-term benefits of investment in developing countries so as to reduce poverty and vulnerability, whilst also minimizing environmental impacts.

The role of engineering

Community infrastructure is key to alleviating poverty and thus engineers have a vital role to play in all the MDGs. Without ready access to clean water and sanitation, productivity is

Drivers of change

Some five years ago, Arup began an investigation into the global areas of influence that have been identified as most likely to have a major impact on society, on our business, and on the business of our clients. The results of this research to date have been published in a series of cards that illustrate the social, technological, economic, environmental and political impacts of each driver. The topics published comprise energy, waste, climate change, water, demographics and urbanization. The topic selected for research in 2007 was poverty as a driver of change, and this reflects Arup's mission to 'shape a better world'. Globally, 2.4 billion people have no sanitation facilities; 2.3 billion lack reliable sources of energy; and 1.2 billion do not have safe drinking water. Addressing these deficiencies, and others relating to transport and communication, is essential if the Millennium Development Goals are to be achieved.

severely reduced through illness and time spent in water collection. Without roads, the poor are unable to sell their goods at market. Basic infrastructure is not a luxury that can wait for better economic times, but a precondition for creating them, and its provision is an urgent and ongoing requirement.

The Table below shows the relationship between physical infrastructure and the MDGs, indicating the importance of socio-economic inputs.

Historically, poverty alleviation strategies have focused on direct intervention to provide facilities that are lacking. Investments by international lending agencies over the past two to three decades have concentrated on solutions to deficiencies in infrastructure that are usually expensive, often with apparently limited thought to ongoing operation and maintenance.

Community infrastructure is a key to alleviating poverty.

© Joe Milligan, EWB-UK

Poverty alleviation requires interventions that involve considerable social and cultural change. Poverty has many aspects, and solutions require more than a technical or engineering basis. Provision of infrastructure alone will not alleviate poverty, without also providing access to that infrastructure.

Now is the time to focus on identifying barriers to progress. This could involve stepping to one side of the MDGs and instead looking at a needs-based approach. Understanding needs is vital for addressing those needs. But, as engineers, too often we create the stage upon which the drama of life unfolds without actually understanding the purpose of the play. As a profession and as practitioners we are not predisposed to take the time to explore an issue in breadth, to think about how the issue we are studying may relate to, or indeed be caused by, another not on the table.

The Millennium Development Goals

The eight Millennium Development Goals (MDGs), agreed at the United Nations Millennium Summit in September 2000 by nearly 190 countries to reduce global poverty and improve living standards, are as follows:

Goal 1: Eradicate extreme poverty and hunger. Halve, between 1990 and 2015, the proportion of people whose income is less than US$1 a day; halve, between 1990 and 2015, the proportion of people who suffer from hunger.

Goal 2: Achieve universal primary education. Ensure that by 2015, children everywhere, boys and girls alike, will be able to complete a full course of primary schooling.

Goal 3: Promote gender equality and empower women. Eliminate gender disparity in primary and secondary education, preferably by 2005, and in all levels of education no later than 2015.

Goal 4: Reduce child mortality. Reduce by two-thirds, between 1990 and 2015, the under-five mortality rate.

Goal 5: Improve maternal health. Reduce by three-quarters, between 1990 and 2015, the maternal mortality ratio.

Goal 6: Combat diseases including HIV/AIDS, malaria and other diseases. Have halted by 2015 and begun to reverse the spread of HIV/AIDS; have halted by 2015 and begun to reverse the incidence of malaria and other major diseases.

Goal 7: Ensure environmental sustainability. Integrate the principles of sustainable development into country policies and programmes and reverse the loss of environmental resources; halve, by 2015, the proportion of people without access to safe drinking water and basic sanitation; by 2020, to have achieved a significant improvement in the lives of at least 100 million slum dwellers.

Goal 8: Develop a global partnership for development. Address the special needs of the least developed countries and Small Island Developing States; develop further an open, rule-based, predictable, non-discriminatory trading and financial system; deal comprehensively with developing countries' debt; in cooperation with developing countries, develop and implement strategies for decent and productive work for youth; in cooperation with pharmaceutical companies, provide access to affordable and essential drugs in developing countries; in cooperation with the private sector, make available the benefits of new technologies, especially information and communications.

Looking at the shape of the MDGs, it can be seen that Goals 1 to 6 are focused on clear indicators to tackle the key poverty issues, with specific targets underpinning the goals. Goal 7 however is concerned with a limiting factor – that we only have one planet. In contrast, Goal 8 is an enabling factor – focusing on the role of business and partnership in achieving the goals.

Figure 1: **Maslow's hierarchy of needs**

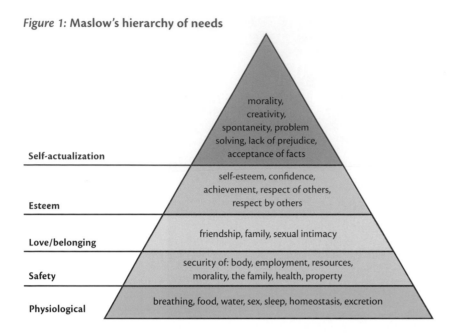

In the past there has been considerable focus on sustainability. Sustainability can be considered as a utopia, a world where the human race and the environment are in balance. Sustainable development is then the process whereby we try and get to this balance point. But this has not been reached to date and instead, the world is suffering from poor environmental health, a shortage of resources and the sickness of biosystems.

Rather than focus on the abstraction 'sustainability', we should shift our attention to securing a happier, more secure future for people. The end needs to become the future success of human society in households, neighbourhoods, communities and nations. We must become clearer that from the perspectives of rationality and morality, the elements of sustainability: economics, environmental stewardship, and civil society, can never be considered as legitimate ends in themselves. They are always means towards a preferred future that creates greater opportunity for more people over a longer period of time. Sustainability is both a physical reality and a political choice.

In a resource-constrained world – our world – a unified design approach is the most rational pathway to long-term value creation. Taken seriously, a unified approach requires us to address issues in depth, in breadth, at their intersections, and over time. Behavioural psychologists, sociologists, physicists, anthropologists, economists, and public health officials all need to be engaged in a broader definition of the design and engineering.

Within this framework, 'unified design' becomes the most robust way to seize opportunities. It also prevents any single interest from capturing the idea of design and holding it

hostage, impeding progress toward the ultimate goal: optimizing conditions for sustained human development over an extended period of time.

The challenge for the engineering profession is to move upstream; to recognize the role that engineers should play in planning projects, timescale issues and budgets. Engineers need to be seen as more than just technologists. It needs to be recognized that the engineering profession can excel at delivering integrated solutions.

Sir Ove Arup said that, 'Engineering problems are underdefined, there are many solutions, good, bad and indifferent. The art is to arrive at a good solution. This is a creative activity, involving imagination, intuition and deliberate choice.' Engineers need to be involved in that creative activity.

How can engineers help to close the infrastructure gap?

Closing the infrastructure gap represents an enormous opportunity to support the development of a sustainable built environment that supports individuals and communities to reach their full potential. Realizing this opportunity requires that the actors involved in the design and delivery of infrastructure services understand how these services will be both sustainable and pro-poor in the local context. It necessitates an understanding of the complex inter-relationships between sustainable development, poverty alleviation and infrastructure service provision, as well as appropriate mechanisms for engaging local community stakeholders in the design and delivery process.

The role of engineering in contributing to achieving the MDGs can be considered by:

- understanding the issue/opportunity;

- agreeing that the issue/opportunity should be addressed and is a priority;

- knowing what to do about the issue/opportunity and how it relates to other issues/ opportunities; and

- choosing to do what we know how to do today and improving on that tomorrow.

The most well known needs-based approach is probably Maslow's hierarchy of needs, which is often depicted as a pyramid consisting of five levels. The higher needs in this hierarchy only come into focus when the lower needs in the pyramid are satisfied. Deficiency needs must be met first. Once these are met, seeking to satisfy growth needs drives personal growth. Once an individual has moved upwards to the next level, needs in the lower level will no longer be prioritized. If a lower set of needs is no longer being met, the individual will

Relationship between physical infrastructure and the mdgs (from essential infrastructure, bottom, to advanced economic infrastructure, top)

Service	Physical infrastructure	Examples of socio-economic inputs	MDG Goal(s)	Primary/ direct MDG impact
National and international movement and Import/export of goods and people	Ports/harbours Airports Highways Railways	Trade relations and agreements	8	Global partnership
Service industries e.g. banking	Offices	Skills training External investment	8	Global partnership
Manufacturing and processing	• Factories • Industrial units	Skills training	8	Global partnership
Acute health care	Hospitals Pharmaceuticals	Medical training Affordability Accessibility	4, 5, 6, 8	Diseases
Further education	Universities Colleges Secondary schools	Academic links Curriculum development Affordability	8	Global partnership
Communications	Wireless networks Mobile networks Telephone networks Telecentres	Local skills training Private sector enterprise	3, 6, 7, 8	Global partnership
Power supply	Power stations Electricity distribution	Demand management Affordability	7, 8	Global partnership
Agriculture and food distribution	Local roads Irrigation Local markets	Training Information	1, 4, 5	Eradicate extreme poverty
Public transport and accessibility	Pedestrian/cycle routes Bus systems Water transport	Needs assessment Affordability Road safety	1, 2, 7, 8	
Primary healthcare	Health centres	Health promotion Health training	3, 4, 5, 7	Maternal health
Primary education	Primary schools	Teacher training Affordability Curriculum development	2, 3, 7	Universal Primary Education
Community mobilisation	Community centres Public buildings	Community demand Building skills	1, 3	Eradicate extreme poverty
Shelter	Houses	Building skills Siting Demand	1, 7	Eradicate extreme poverty
Disaster Risk Reduction	Communal shelters Flood defences	Community awareness Warning systems	1	Eradicate extreme poverty
Sanitation and waste management and disposal	Latrines Drainage systems Sewerage systems Solid waste transfer Landfill sites Recycling plants	Hygiene promotion Community management Community recycling	1, 2, 3, 4, 5, 7	Child mortality
Water supply	Point sources Treatment Storage Distribution systems	Hygiene promotion Community management Maintenance training Private sector enterprise	1, 2, 3, 4, 5, 7	Child mortality

temporarily re-prioritize those needs by focusing attention on the unfulfilled needs, but will not permanently regress to the lower level.

Engineering solutions are integral to mitigating poverty; however engineering is not the sole contributor to successful poverty alleviation programmes, which also entail attention to social, economic and political influences.

Sustainable engineering will be achieved when the engineering solutions adopted take into account their use of natural resources. Optimum solutions will have a positive or neutral impact on natural resource consumption. Unsound engineering solutions, by comparison, may leave the environment depleted and society poorer over time.

Lifecycle engineering takes into account the operational and maintenance cost of the engineering solution proposed, such

that the completed projects have effective and affordable operational and maintenance regimes.

Empowered engineering will take into account the capabilities of the local community, particularly its engineering and technical professions. Where possible, the solutions developed will involve local professional and technical staff and will establish an ongoing engineering and operational resource.

Appropriate engineering will consider various options that meet the engineering needs of the project, and may adopt techniques of labour-based construction, which differs significantly from labour-intensive construction. The latter basically substitutes men for machines whereas labour-based construction aims to change the technology involved to what is appropriate for manual labour.

Figure 2: **The ASPIRE model and too**

Arup, in partnership with Engineers Against Poverty, has developed a Sustainable Project Model – an integrated planning, monitoring and evaluation tool for assessing sustainability and poverty reduction performance for infrastructure projects in developing countries. The tool is called 'ASPIRE' This work has been led from Arup International Development; a team formed to provide a centre of excellence for sustainable urban development and infrastructure in developing countries. The team provides a focal point for organizations, donors and public and private sectors to more readily access the wealth of knowledge and technical expertise in the firm. The aim is to create dignified living and working conditions, which are financially viable in the long-term, and provide people with real economic opportunities to help them fulfil their potential.

ASPIRE is a software based tool for assessing the sustainability of infrastructure projects which recognises poverty reduction as an overarching objective. It provides a holistic appraisal framework encompassing the four key dimensions of environment, society, economics and institutions.

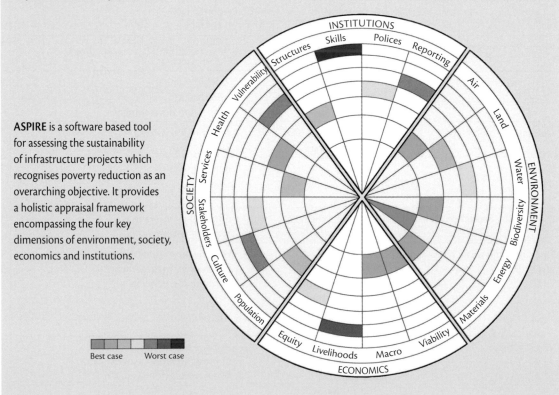

6.1.2 Poverty reduction

Tony Marjoram

Poverty is conventionally defined as living below US$2 per day and extreme poverty as living below US$1.25 per day. It therefore relates particularly to the developing and least developed countries, although not exclusively so – there are of course examples of relative poverty in most cities and countries around the world. In 2008, the World Bank estimated that 2.6 billion people lived on less than $US2 a day and 1.4 billion people lived below US$1 a day in 2005. The eradication of poverty, especially extreme poverty, is the first of the Millennium Development Goals of the United Nations. Poverty depends on social and economic context and such issues as access to land and resources, and is a measure of income and resource distribution and inequality. Poverty leads to ill health, disease and death, and is a barrier to opportunities such as education. Poverty has a gender dimension; 60 per cent of the world's poor are women, who are also in many countries mainly responsible for family care, food production, water supply, fuel gathering and cooking. At the same time, most of these women are ineligible for bank loans because they are not employed or entitled to own property.

While it is usually considered, measured and indicated financially, poverty relates essentially to the access of people to the resources with which to address their basic human needs, especially food. This depends on resource availability and population pressure; people living in poverty, closer to the poverty line, spend more of their income on basic needs such as food, and are especially vulnerable to increases in the cost of living. This in turn depends on natural factors such as drought and famine, and also on government policies regarding income and resource distribution. In the 1980s, for example, free-market policies of economic liberalization and structural adjustment cut government support of social programmes, subsidies and public financing in developing countries and lead to an increase in poverty and a substantial increase in inequality within and between countries. In the context of the deprivation of resources for an adequate standard of living, poverty is also a denial of basic human rights to food, housing, clothing, a safe environment, health and social services, education and training, decent work and the benefits of science and technology. The world has never been as rich as it is today, yet over one billion people suffer from extreme poverty even as freedom from poverty has been recognized as a fundamental human right.

Poverty reduction – access to knowledge and knowledge applications ...

The access of people to the resources with which to address their basic human needs also depends crucially on knowledge, and access to knowledge. The Industrial Revolution and devel-

opment of agricultural technologies and the steam engine in particular literally revolutionized rural and urban productivity to match increasing populations, and dramatically reduced poverty, albeit with Dickensian effects until human and political rights caught up with industrial development. This helped to break the perception, partly reflected in the Malthusian debate, that until this period, food shortages and poverty was an inevitable fact of life. Apart from food supply, production and processing, other areas of basic need include water supply and sanitation, housing, energy, transportation, communication, income generation, employment and enterprise creation.

The application of knowledge in engineering, science and technology has been and will continue to be vital in addressing basic human needs and the reduction of poverty as well as driving economic and social development, as it is vital in emergency and disaster response, reconstruction and prevention, and will be in climate change mitigation and adaptation. Engineering and technology consists of 'hardware' tools, equipment and infrastructure, and 'software' engineering knowledge that designs, produces and develops the technology that surrounds and supports people around the world. The application of engineering and technology helps address poverty at macro, meso and micro levels. At the macro, national and, increasingly, global levels, engineering and technology brought the Industrial Revolution, economic and social development, productivity and growth.

At the macro level, while classical economics ignored technological change, neo-classical and later economic growth theories paid increasing reference to technology and innovation as the main drivers of economic development and growth. Conventional economics also emphasizes economic growth as the main factor in the reduction of poverty, despite long term criticism of the 'trickle down' effect. Recent research also indicates that growth does not necessarily reduce poverty, but also requires government policies that reduce inequality.[108] Infrastructure plays a key role here.

At the meso level, many businesses in developed and developing countries are medium and small-scale enterprises with less than 250 or fifty employees respectively, while many more businesses are at the micro level with less than 10 employees. Around the world, especially in developing and least developed countries, micro, small and medium scale enterprises (MSMEs) account for the vast majority of companies and the majority of jobs, up to 50 per cent of GDP, and higher growth compared to larger industries. Many MSMEs are also focused on particular technologies and innovations. The butchers, bakers and candlestick makers of old have now been joined or dis-

○ *Community participation with slum dwellers and planning for new housing in Pune, India.*

---

108 "The Developing world's bulging (but vulnerable) middle class", *World Bank Policy Research Working Paper 4816*, January 2009.

placed by electricians, plumbers, mechanics, and TV, Internet, mobile phone and solar panel companies.

... applications of engineering and technology

It is in direct applications at the community and family level – in both villages in rural areas and in urban communities – that technologies are most vital and visible in addressing basic human needs and improving the quality of life of ordinary people. As previously mentioned, engineering and technology is vital for the provision and development of food supply, production and processing, water supply and sanitation, waste disposal, housing, energy, transportation, communication, income generation, employment and enterprise creation. Examples include the development of agriculture by women, (in what is now Papua New Guinea and Melanesia where they are still the main small farmers – in one of the few places where life expectancy for women is less than men), equipment (such as animal- and engine-powered farm machines), domestic food processing tools, equipment and techniques, the construction of wells, water tanks and improved toilets, better housing and cooking stoves, low-cost roads and, of course, almost ubiquitous mobile phone use. Technology for the poor does not have to be poor technology nor low technology. All this technology and enterprise helps create income and jobs.

Many of the engineers involved in the initial development, application and innovation of technologies that reduce poverty and human suffering on such a large scale go forgotten or unsung, as does even the fact that these technologies were created by engineers. Roman engineers created systems of water supply and sanitation that developed into systems that now serve major cities, for example in London with systems developed by people such as Joseph Bazalgette following years of cholera epidemics and 'The Great Stink' of 1858. While many millions appreciate the development of flush toilets, electric power, the motor car, the radio and television, how many of us recall the names of Thomas Crapper, Nikola Tesla, Edison, Guglielmo Marconi, Paul Gottlieb Nipkow and John Logie Baird? Hopefully, the next generation of engineers, who need to meet the great challenge of climate change mitigation and adaptation, will be inspired by their often nameless forebears.

As indicated, poverty has a gender dimension, and women contribute significantly to family survival, particularly in the use and innovation of technology in food production, water supply, fuel gathering and cooking. Poverty reduction activities relating to technological innovation, as in other areas, has to be based on a dialogue with and understanding of gender roles to be effective, not only in reducing poverty and not adding to the work of women, but also in reducing gender and related disparities. Women in many countries, for example, gather fuel and suffer higher incidence of eye and lung disease due to smoky cooking conditions; they need to be involved in the design, development and innovation of improved smoke-

less cooking stoves. Gender equality is also a human right, and the access of women to education, technology and microfinance for enterprise and job creation contributes significantly to household income, health and well-being, social and economic development and the reduction of poverty.

Applying engineering and technology to poverty reduction

Engineering and technology need to be appropriate to the social, economic, educational and knowledge situations of people living in poverty in order to facilitate and enable them to address their own basic needs, alleviate poverty and promote sustainable livelihoods and development. People living in poverty are also more vulnerable to emergencies, natural and human induced disasters, and there is an important associated role for engineering and technology in emergency and disaster preparedness, mitigation and response.

This requires effective policy formulation, implementation, and the integration of engineering and technology into Poverty Reduction Strategy Papers, as discussed elsewhere in this report. It also requires effective capacity and capacity-building, and the education and training of young engineers, particularly those in developing countries, to be aware and sensitive to the role of engineering and technology in poverty reduction. Government ministries and departments, donor agencies, universities, NGOs and other relevant organizations need to be encouraged and supported in this process with the transfer of information and experience. Groups such as Engineers Without Borders and activities such as the Daimler-UNESCO Mondialogo Engineering Award can also help facilitate this process.

6.1.3 Poverty reduction: case study of infrastructure in South Africa

Ron Watermeyer

Forecasts of the demand for new infrastructure expressed at the American Society of Civil Engineers' convention in Baltimore in 2004 indicated that approximately 80 per cent of the world's new infrastructure from 2020 to 2030 will be constructed in developing countries. The provision of such infrastructure is expected to be underpinned by poverty reduction objectives such as those relating to the stimulation of economic growth, the creation of jobs, the attainment of social progress and stability, and the promotion of the sustainable utilization of natural resources (as opposed to a strict protectionist stance).

The South African construction industry is by nature a labour intensive industry with a capacity to absorb relatively unskilled workers. The potential to deliver focused employment and business opportunities through infrastructure delivery was explored in the construction and maintenance of infrastructure in the late 1980s.

The South African post-apartheid government in 1994 recognized the potential that government procurement had for economic transformation and to address social and development issues. It accordingly embarked upon a programme of procurement reform in 1995 to focus on good governance and the use of procurement as an instrument of social and development policy. The outcome of this process was the development of a fair, equitable, transparent, competitive and cost effective procurement system that promotes objectives additional to the immediate objective of the procurement itself.

Job creation, poverty reduction and broad-based African economic empowerment remain important issues on the South African agenda for development. Approaches to the delivery of infrastructure projects include the selection of technologies, methods of construction and construction materials, as the choices made in these areas determine the quantum and nature of employment that is created and where it is generated. Emphasis is also placed on the development and nurturing of small, medium and micro-enterprises.

Lessons learned in South Africa

- The construction and maintenance of infrastructure projects can be used to provide work opportunities to vulnerable groups and business opportunities to marginalized businesses in order to address inequities within a society, and in so doing address poverty.

- Innovative procurement arrangements, appropriate technologies and construction methods are required to increase work opportunities. Accepted norms and standards need to be reconsidered and, where appropriate, reassessed using a first principle approach in order to arrive at different outcomes. Certain technologies, which have fallen into disuse in developed countries through the high cost of labour, may have to be 're-discovered' and implemented. The performance of indigenous technologies needs to be quantified and documented so that it can be applied with confidence.

- Appropriate standards and comprehensive design guidance and construction standards are needed to replicate outcomes from pilot projects at scale. National standards and best practices have an important part to play in converting research and innovation into mainstream activities, and in promoting their use.

- A uniform, flexible, predictable, rule-based procurement system is essential for increased investment in infrastructure, reducing opportunities for corrupt and fraudulent practices and ensuring that allocated budgets are spent.

- Procurement documents need to be structured in a generic manner so that procurement measures and appropriate standards aimed at reducing poverty can be readily incorporated in such documents and communicated to participants in the procurement process.

- Capacity-building is required to ensure effective and efficient implementation.

- Supply side measures need to be in place to enable those targeted to make use of the opportunity presented through the provision of infrastructure.

Linking the delivery of infrastructure delivery to the Millennium Development Goals

Procurement is fundamental to the delivery of buildings and engineering infrastructure. A wide range of tools, techniques, technologies, standards and approaches has been developed in South Africa in response to the poverty reduction imperative. These include using the procurement of infrastructure to provide work opportunities to vulnerable groups, increasing employment generated per unit of expenditure (through the promotion of small-scale enterprises and usage of labour-based technologies and methods), and providing business and work opportunities to groups of people who are socially and economically marginalized in order to address inequities within society.

This has been achieved without necessarily compromising international best practice and good governance objectives relating to procurement system requirements. They enable aspects of Chapter 7 of Agenda 21 to be implemented, namely, 'establish and strengthen indigenous building materials industry based, as much as possible, on inputs of locally available natural resources and to promote the use of labour-intensive construction and maintenance technologies which generate employment in the construction sector for the underemployed labour force found in most large cities, while at the same time promoting the development of skills in the construction sector.' As such they contribute to the reduction of the proportion of people living on less than US$1 per day and those that suffer from hunger (i.e. MDG 1: to eradicate extreme poverty and hunger).

The standards approach to implementing procurement processes which was developed in South Africa, and which is now being incorporated into ISO 10845 Construction Procurement, not only provides a practical means to root out corruption, which is placing sustainable development at risk, but also provides a rule-based trading system that improves governance and reduces poverty (i.e. MDG 8: to develop a global partnership for development).

The challenge in responding to the MDGs is to integrate the systems and techniques that have been successfully used in pilot projects in developing countries into the mainstream of public sector infrastructure delivery and to increase the capacity of the public sector to deliver in response to current increasing investment in infrastructure. The standards and best practice approach adopted in South Africa provides a workable model for mainstreaming outcomes of pilot projects and provides an excellent platform for developing capacity.

The next few decades for civil and structural engineering will not be 'business as usual'. Civil and structural engineers will need to deliver infrastructure in a manner that contributes directly to sustainable development objectives that are pertinent to developing countries, including the reduction of poverty.

6.1.4 Sustainable development

Tony Marjoram

Engineering and sustainable development

Countries around the world face increasing and daunting challenges regarding the need for their development to be environmentally sustainable and to counter climate change and the associated effects of a changing climate. Resource use needs to be sustainable for future generations, and we need to protect our environment from pollution, degradation and deterioration. Natural resource use is becoming critical in some areas, (e.g. peak production of oil and environmental 'tipping points'). Natural disasters are more frequent and affect more people. The gap between the rich and many poor countries continues to widen. All these issues are a major threat to global prosperity, security, stability and sustainable development. One cannot address issues of sustainability and climate change mitigation without first addressing issues of poverty, consumption and the distribution of resources.

⊕ Batad rice terraces.

Engineering lies at the heart of addressing the majority of these issues. All countries now recognize these issues and agree that there is an urgent and overwhelming need to reduce emissions and use resources more efficiently to minimize the catastrophic effects of climate change. The question, amid increasing population and consumerism, is how can we achieve this? Such questions were first raised in 1972, with the publication of *Limits to Growth* by the Club of Rome, which created major interest, concern and a new paradigm of debate. Many countries also understand that engineering is one of the most important activities in the context of sustainable development, climate change mitigation and adaptation. By 2009, many countries had already introduced policies and initiatives for climate change mitigation and adaptation prior to the United Nations Climate Change Conference in Copenhagen.

The Intergovernmental Panel on Climate Change has emphasized the importance of technology and finance, and hence engineering, in climate change mitigation and adaptation, and this is echoed elsewhere in this Report. Addressing these issues, and the specific outcomes and follow-up to COP15, will be one of the greatest demands and challenges that engineering has ever faced.

One of the major areas of need for engineers and the development of engineering will be in the area of sustainable or green engineering. It will also be a challenge for the engineering community to make sure that engineering and technology are at the centre of the sustainable development and climate change mitigation agenda.

The greening of engineering

To address the sustainable development agenda, investment in technology and infrastructure will need to increase significantly. It is likely that coal use will double by 2030, and so the need for carbon capture, sequestration and related technologies will be a challenge on a scale similar to that of the petrochemical and fossil fuel industry. Many countries are also looking to develop or redevelop nuclear power, which will be equally challenging because the nuclear industry has declined over the last decades. The renewable energy sector has been developing rapidly over the last decade, and will need to develop further to keep up with demand. The same applies to developments in the housing and transportation sectors. The demand for engineers will increase dramatically. While increasing market demand will help attract young people into engineering, it takes over five years to develop courses to produce graduates; so urgent government action will be required to support course development and associated R&D and innovation. Although investment in current technology is the pressing issue, R&D for new technology is also required, and governments need to invest now to encourage the development of R&D and industry in the sustainable direction and the next main wave of technological development.

An important contribution to the ongoing 'Limits to Growth' debate in 1997 was the publication of *Factor Four* on doubling wealth and halving resource use by Ernst von Weizsäcker. The debate has intensified with increasing concern over climate change, coupled with the recent financial and economic crisis and the interest of politicians around the world in a 'green new deal' to help lift economies out of recession. Von Weizsäcker[109] and the Natural Edge Project[110] have recently shown that

109 Ernst von Weizsäcker. 1997. *Factor Four: Doubling Wealth, Halving Resource Use*; and Ernst von Weizsäcker and The Natural Edge Project, Earthscan, 2009, *Factor Five: Transforming the Global Economy through 80% Improvements in Resource Productivity*.

110 The Natural Edge Project, Australia. *Critical Literacies Portfolio - Introduction to Sustainable Development for Engineering and Built Environment Professionals* (with UNESCO, 2007); *Whole System Design: An Integrated Approach to Sustainable Engineering* (with Earthscan, 2008); *Factor Five: Transforming the Global Economy through 80% Improvements in Resource Productivity* (Earthscan, 2009).

engineering and innovation makes it possible to improve resource use and wealth creation by a factor of five or an 80 per cent improvement in resource use. It is hoped that such information and advocacy will help promote political will and behavioural change toward a new wave and paradigm of green engineering and technology.

Sustainable development, climate change mitigation and adaptation will therefore need to be at the centre of the engineering agenda. The same considerations apply and are connected to engineering and related issues of poverty reduction and the other Millennium Development Goals; one cannot address issues of sustainability and climate change mitigation without addressing issues of poverty, consumption and the distribution of resources, as many of these issues are also connected.

Engineering education and capacity-building

Despite the emphasis of the Intergovernmental Panel on Climate Change (IPCC) of technology and finance, and hence engineering, in climate change mitigation and adaptation the role of engineering and technology in sustainable development is often overlooked. At the same time, as also discussed elsewhere, there is a declining interest and enrolment of young people, especially young women, in engineering. This will have

a serious impact on capacity in engineering, and our ability to address the challenges of sustainable development, poverty reduction and the other MDGs. One of the first challenges for engineering will be to make sure that there are enough appropriately qualified and experienced engineers to meet this demand and this will require the development of new courses, training materials and systems of accreditation. Young people will hopefully be attracted to such courses, and this will help to raise overall awareness of the role and importance of engineering in development. Young people need to be enthusiastically encouraged to go into engineering, as engineering will be at the very centre of efforts to build a carbon-free future.

What can we do to promote the public understanding of engineering, and the application of engineering in these vital contexts? As discussed elsewhere, it appears that the decline of interest and entry of young people into science and engineering is due to the fact that these subjects are often perceived by young people as nerdy, uninteresting and boring; that university courses are difficult and hard work; that jobs in these areas are not well paid; and that science and engineering have a negative environmental impact. There is also evidence that young people turn away from science around age ten, that good science education at primary and secondary schools is vital, as poor science teaching turns young people off science.

Action agenda for engineering

An international workshop on engineering education for sustainable development (EESD) was organized by UNESCO and Tsinghua University and held in Beijing in November, 2006. The idea for this workshop was proposed at the World Engineers' Convention, held in Shanghai in November 2004, on the theme 'Engineers Shape the Sustainable Future'. The 'Shanghai Declaration on Engineering and the Sustainable Future' called upon the engineering community, governments and international organizations to promote engineering for our sustainable future. The workshop identified and emphasized the need for:

- Engineers to take greater responsibility and commitment for shaping the sustainable future, to create and apply technology to decouple human well-being from resource consumption, waste and pollution, to preserve and enhance the health of humanity and our environment.

- High standards and ethics of professional practice, for a creative, innovative, interdisciplinary, integrative and holistic approach to EESD, promoting inclusiveness in such areas as the participation of young people, women and associated issues relating to EESD.

- Learning and teaching materials, methods and capacity in EESD, and for better incentives for engineers to work, research and publish in engineering and sustainable

development (e.g. in accreditation, work opportunities, research grants, peer-reviewed publications).

- Advocacy, lobbying, partnerships, networking and cooperation at national and international level to exchange and share knowledge and good practice to promote technology applications for health, wealth and the promotion of peace and sustainable development.

The workshop recognized and emphasized the importance of governments, intergovernmental and non-governmental organizations in this process. The workshop called upon UNESCO and the World Federation of Engineering Organizations (WFEO) to play a more active role, in conjunction with governments, international and national partners, networks and organizations, to promote the development and application of engineering to sustainable development through international cooperation. To do this, the workshop emphasized the need for activity in engineering education for sustainable development in the following areas in engineering education and sustainable development:

- Development of partnerships and networking and a network of excellence.

- Development of websites and journals for paper publication and the exchange of information.

- Development of virtual libraries (such as the virtual engineering library in Sudan created with support from UNESCO).

- Development and exchange of learning and teaching materials (such as the Natural Edge Project material on sustainable engineering supported by UNESCO).

- Promote new learning and teaching methods and approaches (such as problem- and activity-based learning).

The development and application of knowledge in engineering and technology is vital for sustainable social and economic development, climate change mitigation and adaptation, and the promotion of international cooperation and bridging the 'knowledge divide' in this area. The main challenges facing engineering are to position engineering at the centre of the sustainable development and climate change mitigation and related policy agendas, and at the same time positioning sustainable development and climate change mitigation as a central agenda for engineering.

International Workshop: Engineering Education for Sustainable Development, Tsinghua University, Beijing, November, 2006, organized by UNESCO and Tsinghua University, supported by the China Association for Science and Technology, Chinese Academy of Engineering and World Federation of Engineering Organizations, Alcoa Foundation.

There are clear needs to show that science and engineering are inherently interesting, to promote public understanding and perception of examples of this, and to make education and university courses more interesting.

The promotion of public understanding and interest in engineering is facilitated by presenting engineering as a part of the problem-solving solution to sustainable development and climate change mitigation. University courses need to be made more interesting through the transformation of curricula and pedagogy and the use of less formulaic approaches that turn students off, and with more activity-, project- and problem-based learning, just-in-time approaches and hands-on applications relating to sustainable development. These approaches promote the relevance of engineering, address contemporary concerns and help link engineering with society in the context of sustainable development, building upon rather than displacing local and indigenous knowledge.

The fact that 'relevance' works is demonstrated by the growth of Engineers Without Borders and similar groups around the world that attract students through its connection with sustainable development, and the desire expressed by the youth to 'do something' to help those in need. Engineering has changed the world, but is professionally conservative and slow to change, therefore we need innovative examples of schools, colleges and universities around the world that have pioneered activity in such areas as problem-based learning. It is also interesting to look at reform and transformation in other professions such as medicine, where some of the leading medical schools have changed to a 'patient based' approach. If the doctors can do this, when there is no enrolment pressure, then so can engineers. Engineers practice just-in-time techniques in industry, why not in education?

Systems engineering and engineering for the Earth system

Engineering is about systems, and so it should be taught. Engineers understand systems, and the natural world is the very epitome of a whole system, so it is surprising that engineers have not been more interested in holistic and whole systems approaches in the past. Engineering, however, derives from the seventeenth, eighteenth and nineteenth century knowledge models and the 'modern science' of Galileo, Descartes and Bacon, based on reductionism and the objectification and control of nature. So the rediscovery of holistic thinking is perhaps not surprising and indeed overdue, prompted, for example, by the renewed interest in biomimetics that links engineering and technology with natural life structures and systems. This marks a belated return to the biomimetics of Leonardo da Vinci in the fifteenth and sixteenth centuries, although this rediscovery has been facilitated by the development of computer science and technology and new materials. One wonders what Leonardo would have done with these technologies!

Transformation in engineering education needs to respond to rapid changes in knowledge production and application, emphasizing a cognitive, problem-solving approach, synthesis, awareness, ethics, social responsibility, experience and practice in national and global contexts. We need to learn how to learn and emphasize the importance of lifelong and distance learning, continuous professional development, adaptability, flexibility, interdisciplinarity and multiple career paths, with particular reference to engineering and sustainability.

In the context of the need for transformation in engineering education to include sustainable development and wider social and ethical issues, the work of such groups as The Natural Edge Project and their Engineering Sustainable Solutions Program is most timely and relevant, such as the publication of material on sustainable development for engineering and whole system design.

It is also important because, while the need for holistic and integrated systems approaches in engineering have been recognized and spoken about for some time, there is still a need to share information on what this means in practice, and to share pedagogical approaches and curricula developed in this context. This is particularly important for universities and colleges in developing countries who face serious constraints regarding human, financial and institutional resources to develop such curricula, learning and teaching methods. It is also timely in view of the UN Decade of Education for Sustainable Development, 2005–2014, for which UNESCO is the lead agency.

Catching the next wave of innovation for sustainability

Such transformation of engineering and engineering education is essential if engineering is to catch the 'seventh wave' of technological revolution; relating to knowledge for sustainable development, climate change mitigation and adaptation, and new modes of learning. This follows the sixth wave of new modes of knowledge generation, dissemination and application, knowledge and information societies and economies, in such areas as ICT, biotechnology, nanotechnology, new materials, robotics and systems technology, characterized by cross-fertilization and fusion, innovation, the growth of new disciplines and the decline of old disciplines, where new knowledge requires new modes of learning. The fifth wave of technological revolution was based on electronics and computers, the fourth wave of oil, automobiles and mass production, the third wave of steel, heavy engineering and electrification, the second wave of steam power, railways and mechanization, and the first wave of the technological and industrial revolution and the development of iron and water power.

The main applications challenges relate to how engineering and technology may most effectively be developed, applied and innovated to promote sustainable development and address climate change mitigation and adaptation. It is apparent that these challenges are linked to a possible solution to these challenges, and many young people and student engineers are keen to address these international issues, especially those relating to sustainable development and climate change. This is reflected, as mentioned earlier, by the interest of young people in Engineers Without Borders groups around the world, and the UNESCO-Daimler Mondialogo Engineering Award, featured elsewhere in this Report. To promote engineering and attract young people we need to emphasize these issues in teaching curricula and practice.

6.1.5 Sustainable Development and the WEHAB Agenda

Darrel Danyluk and Jorge Spitalnik

Engineering contributes to creating the groundwork for developing appropriate solutions to a wide array of issues arising from the Millennium Development Goals. The acronym 'WEHAB' comes from the following action areas recognized as being key to addressing these issues:

- Water and sanitation

- Energy

- Health

- Agriculture productivity.

- Biodiversity and ecosystem management

Issues and challenges in each one of these five areas requires strong engineering participation and action needed to:

- adopt suitable procedures based upon the development context of a given region;

- design and implement appropriate projects for assuring sustainable development; and

- ensure established standards of quality for implementation and operation.

The main issues and challenges relevant to engineering contributions to sustainable development are given in the box below, set out according to WEHAB action areas:

Special consideration is to be given in developing countries to: building human capacity and knowledge; increasing use of technologies that are appropriate to the context; improving

© Paula West Australia

operational and managerial skills; and strengthening education and training. This will require sufficient financial investment and cooperation with developed countries and international organizations.

⟨⟩ *Engineer testing repairs on steel pile.*

Notes on issues and challenges table

- Options to solve problems related to sustainable development cannot be selected on the basis of doctrine or ideology. Scientifically-sound and thoroughly-engineered solutions are needed to address sustainability matters of a technical nature. Decision-makers must be mindful of the need to analyse the feasibility and the technological availability of proposed options.

- A prime responsibility of the engineering profession is determining the feasibility of technological, economic and environmental factors of a given option and then recommending the most suitable one to decision-makers.

- Sustainable development solutions applied in developed countries are not necessarily adequate for developing ones. Solutions need to be context-specific for them to be feasible under the prevailing conditions in the given country or region.

	ISSUES	CHALLENGES
Water and sanitation	● Awareness of quality and quality features, and the importance of efficient water use and water conservation should be conveyed to all elements of the population. This will lead to more efficient water demand patterns and improve water resource management across all sectors, especially in the agriculture sector.	● Implement appropriate low-cost and environmentally sustainable water-use and supply technologies, and develop capacities in areas of water desalination, treatment of contaminants, rainwater harvesting and efficient water use. This should be achieved through technology transfers, capacity building and the sharing of best practices.
	● Irrigation projects that improve food production should be promoted. Subject to health and environmental standards and regulations, use of greywater should be encouraged for certain irrigation or industrial purposes.	● Assess the impact of natural disasters, climate change and climate variability on surface and groundwater resources, water supply, and sanitation, implement monitoring and early warning systems, and identify relevant mitigation and adaptive technologies.
	● Technology transfer on potable-water production and treatment, sanitation, wastewater treatment, effluent water reuse and residuals management is required, particularly in developing countries. In rural areas, on-site sanitation infrastructure represents a crucial contributor toward water resource-management and the safety, and security of potable water supply.	● Strengthen regulations and policies that dictate the prevention of pollution resulting from wastewater discharges, solid-waste disposal, and industrial and agricultural activities. ● Protect the ecosystems and acknowledge their critical role. Rehabilitate catchment areas by managing and regulating water flows, and improving water quality. ● Develop low-cost and efficient drinking-water and wastewater treatment technologies, including for water quality and reuse. ● Ensure effective human capacity and knowledge capability for building, operating and maintaining sanitation and sewer systems.
Energy	● Energy-supply planning should consider all sources of energy based on mature and feasible technologies, while ensuring acceptable discharge limit (GHG) emissions. Development of carbon-sequestration schemes requires urgent implementation.	● Make access to reliable and affordable energy services available to all, with particular attention to the rural and urban poor.
	● The optimal energy mix for any country depends on its available natural resource bases, population distribution, growth of energy demand, and the status of its technical and economic capability.	● Develop and use advanced and cleaner fossil-fuel technologies. Develop other clean energy sources to decrease dependence on fossil fuels.
	● Unattainable patterns of consumption – especially in the transportation sector –need to be changed to assure energy efficiency.	● Improve energy efficiency in households, the transport sector and industry. ● Innovative bio-fuel technologies can make crucial contributions to decreased dependence on fossil fuels for transportation and to lowering GHG emissions.
Health	● Health risks from environmental pollution must be dramatically reduced and, in particular, indoor-air pollution from burning biomass in confined spaces must be eliminated. In the transportation sector in developing countries, lead and sulfur must be phased out from use in gasoline.	● Minimise the human impacts of mining, and address safe and sustainable livelihood opportunities in small-scale mining ventures.
	● Pollution in agriculture should be reduced with the application of new waste treatment and management technologies.	● Thoroughly implement technologies to prevent or contain marine pollution.
	● Adequate treatment, disinfection, and proper operation and maintenance procedures are to be used to prevent waterborne diseases from entering the distribution system.	● Substantially reduce burning low-quality biomass in confined spaces. Thoroughly implement low-cost and efficient ventilation technologies for uses in the poorer communities.
Agriculture productivity	● Sustainable agriculture and rural development need to be expanded to increase food production, to enhance food security and to reduce hunger.	● Increase public and private finance for sustainable agriculture and agricultural research.
	● There is urgent need to implement programs to prevent land degradation and erosion, and to improve soil fertility and agricultural pest controls.	● Require policies for sustainable management of land and other agricultural resources in developing countries.
	● Specific technologies to allow development of small-scale aquaculture and sustainable coastal and small-scale fishing activities, mainly in small island states, will require international support.	
Biodiversity and ecosystem management	● National development policies should give high priority to technical and financial support to developing countries for conservation and sustainable use of biological resources. This should occur while ensuring fair and equitable sharing of benefits arising from utilisation of genetic resources.	● Carry out application and development of the ecosystem approach for biodiversity management.
	● A significant reduction in the current rate of loss of biological diversity is required, along with strengthened control of invasive alien species.	● Require Environmental Impact Analysis and Project Life Cycle Planning for mine development before starting extraction of mineral resources.
	● Marine environmental protection needs to be strengthened and a network of marine protected areas should be implemented worldwide. The ecosystem approach in fisheries and in marine biological diversity should be broadly applied.	● Provide financial and technical capacity to improve value-added processing, to upgrade scientific and technological information, and to reclaim and rehabilitate degraded sites.
	● The protection of ecologically sensitive areas and natural heritage requires a special worldwide treatment.	● Transfer of marine science and technology to maintain or restore depleted fish stocks to levels of sustainable yield.
	● Support natural resources management, including addressing environmental economic and social impacts of mining operations, is essential.	

6.1.6 Sustainable development and standards: the construction industry

Ron Watermeyer

The built environment

The built environment is the physical world that has been intentionally created by humans through the application of science and technology in the control and use of forces and materials of nature for the benefit of humanity. It is essential to almost every aspect of society, national infrastructure and economic activity.

The building and construction industry plays an important role in sustainable development because it is such a key sector in national economies. The built environment represents a large share of the economic assets of individuals, organizations and nations, and it is one of the single largest industrial sectors with all the consequential aspects of employment, economic importance and environmental impact. Proper housing and infrastructures are key elements in determining quality of life and it has a significant interface with poverty reduction through the provision of basic services and through the potential to engage the poor in construction, operation and maintenance activities.

Landuse and materials extraction by the building and construction industry accounts for a very large usage of natural resources. Energy use, liquid and solid waste generation, transport of construction materials, and consumption of hazardous materials are other sources of negative environmental impact from this sector. In OECD countries, buildings are responsible for 25–40 per cent of total energy use. In Europe, buildings account for 40–45 per cent of energy consumption in society, contributing to significant amounts of carbon dioxide emissions.

The evolution of standards for buildings

Buildings providing shelter for humans, animals or property of any kind are central to the built environment and the economy of any country in addition to the well-being of its people. Buildings shape and define the environment in which humans live, work and relax.

It is not surprising that building standards have been in place ever since people have been able to capture their thoughts in writing. The earliest known building code is that of Hammurabi (about 1780 BC), the sixth king of Babylon. In terms of this code, builders were required, at their own cost, to make stable any walls that appeared to be unstable prior to the completion of the house and to compensate the owner in the event of collapse.

With urbanization and the erection of many dwelling places in close proximity to each other came the scourge of fire and health risks associated with poor sanitation. Over the centuries, many cities were razed by fire and millions of people died as a result of poor sanitary conditions in highly populated areas. Lawmakers in the nineteenth century developed building laws to improve sanitation and to diminish the outbreaks and disastrous consequences of fires in cities.

In the twentieth century, minimum standards for the construction and maintenance of buildings were developed to protect public health, safety and general welfare. Issues such as structural safety and serviceability, fire safety, health and hygiene, moisture penetration, safety, accessibility and usability were addressed.

United Nations summits

Agenda 21, which establishes a conceptual framework for sustainable construction, flowed out of the 1992 Earth Summit in Rio de Janeiro. The main challenges of sustainable construction that emerged from this agenda were:

- Promoting energy efficiency: energy saving measures, extensive retrofit programmes, transport aspects and the use of renewable energies.

- Reducing use of high-quality drinking water: relying on rainwater and grey water, reducing domestic consumption with water management systems, waterless sanitation systems and the use of drought resistant plants.

- Selecting materials on environmental performance: use of renewable materials, reduction of the use of natural resources and recycling.

- Contributing to a sustainable urban development: efficient use of land, design for a long service life, the longevity of buildings through adaptability and flexibility, convert existing buildings, refurbishment, sustainable management of buildings, prevention of urban decline and reduction of sprawl, contribution to employment creation and cultural heritage preservation.

- Contribution to poverty alleviation.

- A healthy and safe working environment.

The United Nations Millennium Development Declaration, which was launched in 2000, supports the Agenda 21 principles of sustainable development. However, it acknowledges that progress is based on sustainable economic growth, which must focus on the poor, with human rights at the centre. The Declaration calls for halving the number of people who live on less than one US$1 a day by the year 2015.

The United Nations, ten years after the Rio de Janeiro Earth Summit, held a World Summit on Sustainable Development in Johannesburg. The Johannesburg World Summit in 2002 resulted in a clearer understanding of the relationship between poverty and environmental protection. It stressed that the fundamental global action associated with the international agenda for sustainable development is to fight poverty and to protect the environment.

Standards for the twentieth century

The built environment, in serving both society and economic activity, has not only positive outcomes and impacts but also detrimental ones. The balancing of these positive and detrimental aspects on the health and safety of both the public and the workforce on the physical environment, on sustainable livelihoods and on sustainability for future generations is a very important function of the built environment professional. Safeguarding the built environment against the hazards associated with development is not enough. Development must also be carried out effectively and efficiently, and solutions to negative impacts need to be rapidly communicated within the global community and replicated elsewhere. The Earth's resources are finite. Current growth rate trends indicate that the world's population will increase from 6.5 billion to 13 billion by 2067. To accommodate this growth in a sustainable manner, the built environment of 2067 will need to be very different from what we see today. Time is not on our side.

In previous centuries standards for building and construction works reflecting societal values and expectations addressed the hazards threatening communities by providing methods, procedures and systems. Today sustainability in building and construction works includes economic, environmental and social impacts, which are all interdependent and increasingly complex as the world's population grows against a background of diminishing resources. Standards, and particularly international ones, are needed to communicate new concepts, methods, procedures and processes to built environment professionals. Standards that provide the framework within which the challenges of the day may be satisfied and facilitate the rapid implementation of solutions, will improve the quality of life for this generation and the generations to come.

6.1.7 MDGs and standards

Ron Watermeyer

The Millennium Development Goals

The eight Millennium Development Goals (MDGs) to be achieved by 2015 form a blueprint accepted by all the world's countries and the world's leading development institutions. These goals – acknowledging that progress is based on sustainable economic growth and must focus on the poor with human rights at the centre – have galvanized unprecedented efforts to meet the needs of the world's poorest people and provide time-bound and quantified targets for addressing extreme poverty in its many dimensions.

Kofi Annan, during his tenure as Secretary-General of the United Nations, established the important linkages between science and technology and sustainable development. In 2002 he said, 'Let me challenge all of you to help mobilize global science and technology to tackle the interlocking crises of hunger, disease, environmental degradation and conflict that are holding back the developing world.'

Sustainability versus sustainable development

Sustainability is the state in which ecosystem components and functions are maintained for the present and future generations while meeting the current needs of people. Sustainable development is development that meets the needs of the present without compromising the ability of future generations to meet their own needs. Sustainable development is rooted in the simple concept of providing a better quality of life for all, now and for generations to come. It is a way of looking at all resources that will lead to a quality of life for the current generation, without compromising that of future generations.

The role of standards in economic development

A standard is 'a document, established by consensus and approved by a recognized body, that provides, for common and repeated use, rules, guidelines or characteristics for activities or their results, aimed at the achievement of the optimum degree of order in a given context' (ISO/IEC Guide 2).

Standards:

- facilitate the efficient and safe development, manufacturing and supply of products and services and the construction and maintenance of buildings and infrastructure;

- facilitate fair trade within and between regions or countries;

- enable suppliers, service providers and contractors to produce consistent products and outputs;

- provide a means for regulation of matters relating to health, safety and the protection of the environment;

- disseminate technical advances and innovation, new processes, procedures and methods, and good management practice;

- safeguard consumers, and users of products and services; and

- provide solutions to common problems.

Standards are accordingly fundamental to economic growth and development.

Drivers of economic development in underdeveloped countries

Engineering is underpinned by processes (successions of logically related actions occurring or performed in a definite manner) and systems (orderly or regular procedures or methods). Innovative and new engineering processes and systems brought into the mainstream of engineering practice, in either developed or developing countries, typically follow a project cycle involving:

- research and development;

- documentation of processes and systems;

- implementation on a pilot basis;

- refinement of processes and procedures;

- roll out to industry through awareness, training, skills development and capacity building;

- replication through standards, which establish a framework of acceptable and recognized engineering practice within which engineering practitioners can arrive at solutions.

This last point emphasizes that economic growth is driven by the replication at scale of knowledge, skills and systems through standards.

Regional differences in approaches to sustainable development

While the challenge of sustainable development is global, the strategies for addressing sustainability are local and differ in context and content from region to region. Such strategies need to reflect context not only in the local economy but also in the social environment, which includes social equity, cultural issues, traditions, heritage issues, human health and comfort, social infrastructure and safe and healthy environments. They may also, particularly in developing countries, include poverty reduction, job creation, access to safe, affordable and healthy shelter and mitigation of loss of livelihoods.

Given the disparity in standards of living between the developed and developing countries, their approach in general to the social component is very different. This results in different development priorities between the 'North' (developed nations) and 'South' (developing nations). In countries with dual economies such as South Africa, the priorities differ regionally, depending on where the poor or affluent live.

The so-called 'green' agenda focuses on the reduction of the environmental impact of urban-based production, consumption and water generation on natural resources and ecosystems, and ultimately on the world's life support system. As such it addresses the issue of affluence and over consumption and is generally more pertinent to affluent countries.

Figure 1: **Absolute poverty (people subsisting on up to 2 US$/day)**

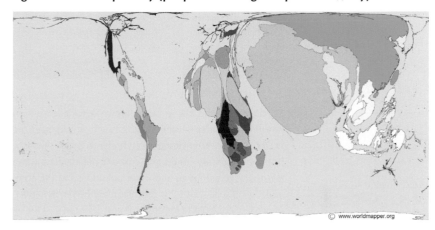

Figure 2: **Land Area for comparison**

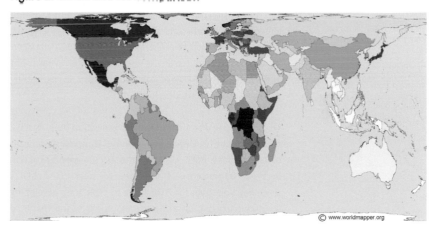

Figure 3: **Total Population for comparison**

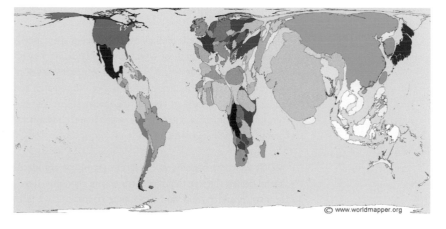

Note: Worldmapper (www.worldmapper.org/index.html) is a collection of world maps, where territories are re-sized on each map according to the subject of interest.

Figure 4: **The fundamental differences between the 'green' and 'brown' agendas**

	GREEN AGENDA		BROWN AGENDA	
NORTH	Ecosystemic well-being	**Key concern**	Human well-being	SOUTH
	Forever	Time frame	Immediate	
	Local to global	Scale	Local	
	Future generations	Concerned about	Low income groups	
	Protect an work with	Nature	Manipulated and use	
	Use less	Services	Provide more	
	Affluence and over consumption		**Poverty and underdevelopment**	

On the other hand, the so-called 'brown' agenda focuses on poverty and under development. As such, it addresses the need to reduce the environmental threats to health that arise from poor sanitary conditions, crowding, inadequate water provision, hazardous air and water pollution, and the accumulation of solid waste. It is generally more pertinent in poor, under-serviced cities or regions.

Linking the MDGs to standards

The link between the application of knowledge in engineering and technology and the reduction of poverty through sustainable economic and social development is well understood. The importance of the exchange of knowledge in engineering and technology transfer is also understood. What is not understood is the linkage of standards, indigenous engineering practice and economic development.

The International Standardization Organization (ISO) has 157 member countries. Developing countries comprise 65 per cent of its member bodies, 94 per cent of its corresponding members and 100 per cent of its subscriber members. One of ISO's seven key objectives for 2010 relate to facilitating developing country participation in the development of international standards. Yet the participation of such countries in ISO working groups and technical committees is generally very poor. Frequently standards are written without direct input from any developing country.

Standards are the tools of engineers. Engineering practice is accordingly shaped by those who draft standards, yet very little attention and investment is given to standards development in developing countries. Much is given to research and capacity-building without considering the means of communicating the practical outcomes of research and the basis for practice, namely standards.

MDGs will only become an integral part of the standards agenda when the role that standards play in economic development is understood, and developing countries have both the capability and capacity to develop their own standards and also to participate fully in the development of international standards.

6.1.8 Climate change: technology, mitigation, adaptation

Rajendra Kumar Pachauri

Background

Science, engineering and technology are of particular importance in the work of the Intergovernmental Panel on Climate Change. They are the knowledge basis on which policies and actions to mitigate and adapt to climate change are made. Science is vital in the understanding of climate change and the complex inter-relationship between human activities and the environment. Engineering and technology are vital in providing solutions for mitigation and adaptation. In terms of understanding climate change, major findings of the IPCC Fourth Assessment report indicate that the mean global temperature has unequivocally increased since the beginning of industrialization, by about 0.74°C, and that this increase has accelerated in recent years (Figure 1). Another major finding is that the sea level has risen by 17 cm in the twentieth century, most particularly over the last 10–15 years. These effects are not uniform, the Arctic for example is warming at twice the rate as the rest of the world, with higher impact on associated flora and fauna such as the polar bear.

The Fourth Assessment Report also indicated that human activity is 'very likely' the reason for global warming over the last fifty years (up from 'likely' in the Third Assessment Report). The level of carbon dioxide in the atmosphere, one of the major drivers of climate change, has increased over the last 650,000 years (Figure 2). At the observable level, glaciers have been in retreat for over a century. There are also changes in average precipitation, increasing on average in temperate regions while declining in tropical, sub-tropical and the Mediterranean regions, with a significant increase in extreme precipitation events. Changes in precipitation patterns, along with the increase in extreme temperature conditions, will have obvious impacts in terms of drought, flooding, heatwaves and fires.

Urgent need for action

Negotiations are, of course, at an advanced stage to arrive at an agreement beyond the end of the first commitment period of the Kyoto Protocol in 2012, and one important element or concern with regard to how to develop a suitable and effective agreement is contained in Article 2 of the UN framework on climate change. This Article essentially states as the ultimate objective of the Convention our ability to prevent a dangerous level of anthropogenic interference with climate change, and this would focus on issues like food security and the ability of ecosystems to be able to rebound once we create a certain level of damage through climate change. While understanding that defining 'dangerous' is a value judgement, science can certainly provide a basis by which the international community can come up with a definition of what would constitute a dangerous level of climate change.

This issue is still undecided, and while the EU has come up with the 2°C target as the maximum that should be allowed, this is not universally accepted, and there are some who are even questioning whether this might be too high, and that maybe we should think in terms of something lower, particularly since temperature increases correlate closely with some of the most threatening impacts of climate change. Climate change will reduce biodiversity and perturb the functioning of most ecosystems as well as compromising the services they provide. This will have particular impacts on the poorest communities in the world who depend particularly on nature and the land, and will also impact upon the ability of societies and communities to pursue sustainable livelihoods. IPCC has assessed that 20–30 per cent of plant and animal species are at risk of extinction if increases in global average temperature exceeds 1.5°–2.5°C. This is a serious observation that should really make the human race sit up and think, and see how we might prevent such an outcome, which could very well take place in the lifetimes of at least the young generation of today.

Turn to some projections of the future: where are temperatures likely to reach by the end of this century? IPCC has assessed a number of plausible scenarios in terms of technological changes, economic growth, social changes and institutional changes, and we find that at the lower end of these scenarios a best estimate of 1.8°C by the end of the century. At the upper end of the scenarios – if we have vigorous growth and an increase in emissions of greenhouse gases, we are likely to end up with an increase of 4.0°C as our best estimate. Therefore, the future looks something like what is shown in Figure 3, where a large range of possible temperature increases is indicated. However, if one looks at even the lower-most projection of 1.8°C, and then combines this with the 0.74°C increase that took place during the twentieth century, then it is apparent that we will likely have a temperature increase of over 2.5°C by the end of this century above that at the beginning of the century. The world has to decide how acceptable this range of possible temperature increases will be, and their likely consequences and impacts.

Expected impacts

Some ecosystems are highly vulnerable such as coral reefs, marine shell organisms, tundra, arboreal forests, mountains and Mediterranean regions. We can also identify, as we have done in the Fourth Assessment Report, some impacts that cause concern; malnutrition could be exacerbated by the reduced length of the growing season in the Sahelian region. In some countries yields from rain-fed agriculture will be particularly vulnerable given the fact that there are going to be changes in precipitation levels as well as patterns. These could be reduced by up to 50 per cent by 2020. In one projection we have made, between seventy-five million and 250 million people would be exposed to increased water stress in 2020 in Africa, and we need to remember that climate change adds

Figure 1: **Graph showing the rise in global temperatures**

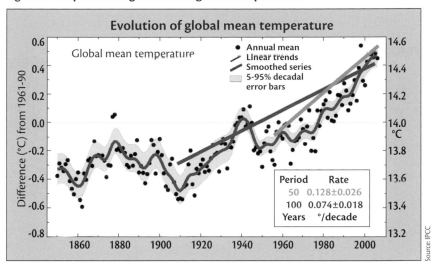

Figure 2: **Human contribution to climate change**

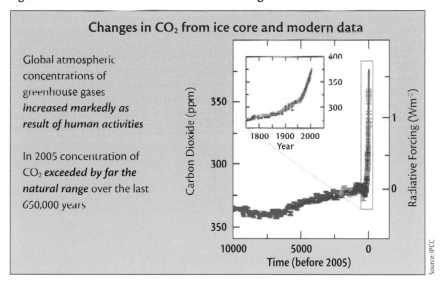

stress to societies where stresses already exist. In such cases, marginal impacts could in a sense be the last straw that breaks the camel's back.

These societies, which are poor and afflicted by several other stresses, would therefore now most likely face an additional set of stresses induced by climate change, and we need to be particularly concerned by this. As Gandhi once said, in decisions related to development, you must look at the impact on 'the last man', the most underprivileged. In the set of policies we are discussing for combating climate change, we need to have a specific and focused concern on the poorest communities in the world who will obviously face the worst impacts of climate change. Food and security and loss of livelihood would of course also be exacerbated by the loss of cultivated land and the effects on sea areas for fisheries, as well as inundation

Figure 3: **Projected temperature rises**

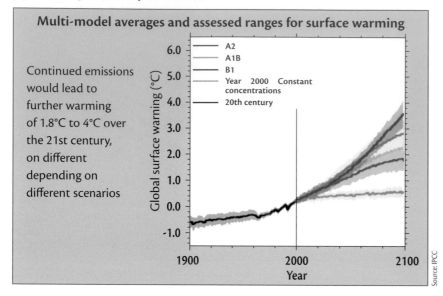

Multi-model averages and assessed ranges for surface warming

Continued emissions would lead to further warming of 1.8°C to 4°C over the 21st century, on different depending on different scenarios

Source: IPCC

and coastal erosion in low-lying areas of tropical Asia. There is already evidence in several parts of the world, and research that is being done in India, that show that climate change is already impacting unfavourably on yields, particularly wheat. This is due to the fact that during the growing cycle for wheat even a 1.0ºC change in temperature can have an unfavourable impact on productivity. Over and above that, with more frequent and more severe floods and droughts, there is an added impact on agricultural output, which raises questions of food security on a global basis. Coastal settlements are most at risk;

Figure 4 gives a picture of some major cities that are located in coastal areas. Mega-deltas in Asia are particularly vulnerable. These include Dhaka, Calcutta, Shanghai and others, and the figure shows red dots indicating those locations at extreme risk, those at high risk and others that are subject or likely to be subjected to medium level risks. The spread is quite diverse, and there is no region in the world that is immune to the dangers of coastal flooding.

Need for adaptation...

The main conclusion from the above information is that adaptation is inevitable and, given the inertia in the system and the fact that even if we were able to stabilize concentration of gases at an acceptable level today, the impacts of climate change will continue for a long period of time. The world therefore has no choice but to adapt to climate change as a necessary priority, at least to a certain level of predicted climate change. We also know that adaptation is taking place through a range of practices, and there are societies across the globe that have dealt with the vagaries of natural changes in climate and consequently have developed coping strategies in response to such changes that have been quite effective. But what is happening now will test the limits of how much these societies can cope with the changing climate. We now have to think in terms of some new sets of measures and responses. Adaptation capacity is limited and uneven across and within societies. The poor, even in the richest countries, do not have the capacity to adapt; this can be illustrated with reference to what happened with Hurricane Katrina or Hurricane Rita, where the poorest sections of society in the city

Figure 4: **Coastal settlements most at risk**

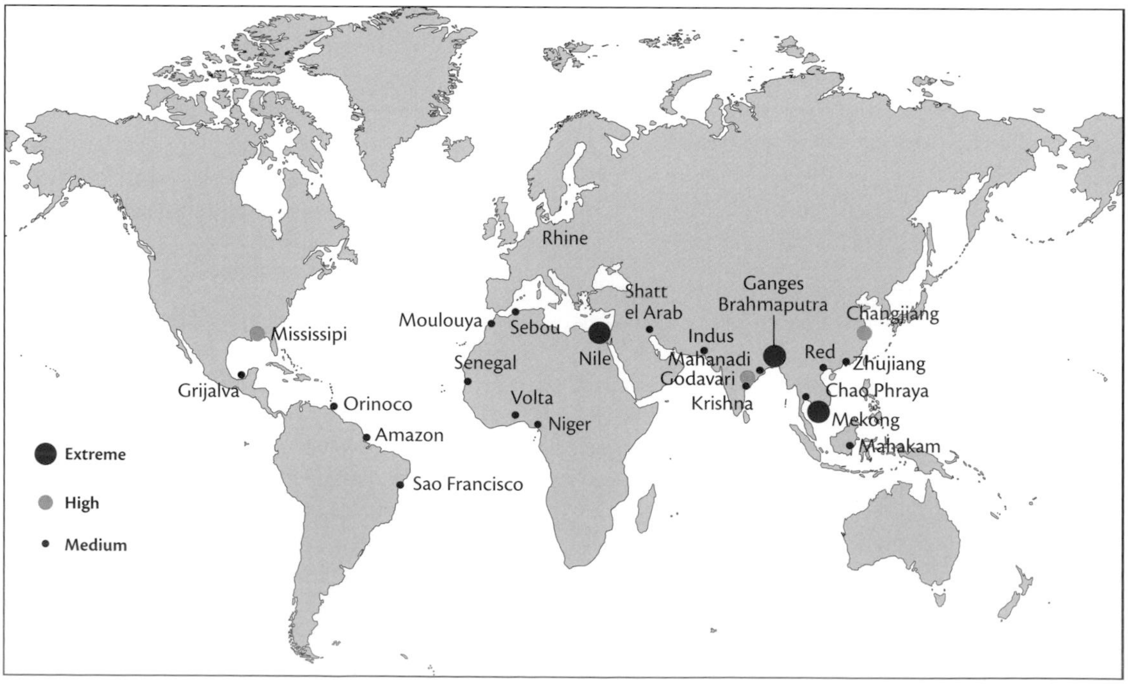

Source: IPCC

Figure 5: **Characteristics of stabilization scenarios**

Stabilization level (ppm CO₂-eq)	Global mean temp. increase at equilibrium (°C)	Year CO₂ needs to peak	Year CO₂ emissions back at 2000 level	Reduction in 2050 CO₂ emissions compared to 2000
445 – 490	2.0 – 2.4	2000 - 2015	2000 - 2030	−85 to −50
445 – 535	2.0 – 2.4	2000 - 2020	2000 - 2040	−60 to −30
535 – 590	2.8 – 3.2	2010 - 2030	2020 - 2060	−30 to +5
590 – 710	3.2 – 4.0	2020 - 2060	2050 - 2100	+10 to +60
710 – 855	4.0 – 4.9	2050 - 2080		+25 to +85
855 – 1130	4.9 – 6.1	2060 - 2090		+90 to +140
Mitigation efforts over the next txo to three decades will have a large impact on opportunites to achieve lower stabilization levels				

Source: IPCC

of New Orleans had no recourse at all to protect themselves, and suffered worst from the damage that took place. Climate change therefore poses new risks that will require new investments in adaptive responses. In the island nation of the Maldives for example, which is severely threatened by sea level rise, the capital island of Malé has a protective barrier that has certainly provided the island with some protection. However, such measures are not possible for the entire coastal region of Bangladesh for example, or other parts of the world that are so vulnerable, so there are limits that have to be appreciated in potential responses for adaptation.

Adaptation is of course necessary to address impacts resulting from global warming that are unavoidable due to past emissions and the inertia of the system. However, adaptation alone cannot cope with all the projected impacts of climate change as the impacts of climate change and cost of adaptation will increase as global temperatures increase. We therefore need to view adaptation measures though a prism of reality, beyond adaptation alone, otherwise we risk being lulled into a sense of false security based on the perception that everything will be well if we just adapt to climate change. As indicated above, this will not be a practicable or even feasible option in many cases. We therefore need a mix of strategies including adaptation, research and development into new and improved technologies, and mitigation of the main factors causing global warming and climate change, especially greenhouse gas (GHG) emissions. Mitigation and adaptation have to go together, and this will have to be the central core of strategy, policy and management in dealing with every aspect of climate change.

... and mitigation

IPCC has assessed a range of stabilization levels at which the concentration of greenhouse gases could be stabilized (Figure 5). In the top row we considered the level of 445–490 parts per million of CO₂ equivalent. Holding stabilization at this level would lead to an ultimate equilibrium temperature of 2.0°–2.4°C - which would be achieved in a time scale stretch-

ing into the twenty-second century. Based on the assessment we carried out, this clearly shows that an increase in emissions cannot be allowed any later than 2015. Beyond 2015, emissions will have to decline and the reductions that would be required to hold equilibrium temperatures at this ceiling – corresponding to levels of concentration shown in Figure 5 – show that by 2050 CO₂ emissions will need to be reduced by 85–50 per cent relative to the level in 2000. This is relevant with reference to the fact that the EU set their target at 2.0°C. Higher levels of warming could have been set as well as higher levels of concentration of these gases, which would give a little more latitude, a little more time. However, human society has to decide whether it wants to limit the damage that would take place as a result of inaction by taking suitable mitigation measures, or if we continue with 'business as usual' and allow things to reach a level where the impacts would be even more serious. It is important to emphasize that mitigation efforts have to start as soon as possible; over the next two or three decades mitigation efforts will have a major impact on the likelihood of success to achieve lower stabilization levels in the future.

Costs of mitigation

It is often reported that the costs of mitigation in terms of job losses and reduction in economic output would be crippling to economies around the world. The data presented in Figure 6 clearly contradict this. Looking at the lowermost set of numbers (44 –535 parts per million) as the level at which we can stabilize these emissions, then it is apparent that the cost in 2030 to global economic output would not exceed 3 per cent of GDP, which on an annual basis amounts to only 0.12 per cent of GDP per year. In a graphical form, Figure 7 compares GDP without mitigation and with stringent mitigation, and shows the marginal difference of shifting the growth line very slightly. Both figures indicate that the global economic output and prosperity in 2030 would hardly be affected by the adoption of stringent mitigation strategies, perhaps only postponed by a few months, which is a small price to pay when

Figure 6: **Estimated costs of mitigation**

Trajectories towards stabilization levels (ppm CO₂-eq)	Median GDP reduction (%)	Range of GDP reduction (%)	Reduction of average annual GDP growth rates (percentage points)
590 – 710	0.2	−0.6 – 1.2	< 0.06
535 – 590	0.6	0.2 – 2.5	< 0.1
445 – 535	Not available	< 3	< 0.12
Mitigation measures would induce 0.6% gain to 3% decrease of GDP in 2030			

Source: IPCC

compared to the likely costs relating to the economic impacts of climate change discussed above.

Mitigation potential

The IPCC Working Group Three report looked at a whole range of options by which emissions could be reduced, and quantified what is possible in several sectors. We looked at the energy supply, industry, transportation, household and commercial buildings, and concluded that the potential for mitigation is enormous (Figure 8).

Engineering and technological solutions

The range of stabilization levels of GHGs is something that the IPCC decided after looking at the range of technologies that are currently available or expected to be commercialized in the coming decades. The stabilization level projected by the IPCC can be achieved even with existing technologies. The news would be even better if we were to invest enough in research and development over a period of time to develop new technologies and new methods, by which there would be a substantial decline in the cost of mitigation with a corresponding substantial increase in the effectiveness of mitigation.

What are these technological solutions? If we look around the economic sectors, we can immediately see that energy supply is particularly important because this accounts for 26 per cent of greenhouse gas emissions, and we clearly need a shift in supply technologies and supply options, including renewables of course, and advanced coal, gas and nuclear technologies, super-critical steam plants, and a whole range of other technologies. Carbon dioxide capture and storage will be an important element of the solutions we apply, and combined heat and power and nuclear fusion could be a possible solution in the future. Apart from nuclear fusion, these are all technologies that are within our reach.

The transport sector accounts for 26 per cent of world energy use, and there are a whole range of possibilities that the IPCC have assessed. Air traffic is one particular segment which clearly needs attention because of its rapid growth, and improvements in air traffic efficiencies, as far as energy use is concerned, is certainly lagging behind several other sectors of the economy. Rail transport is another area where a shift to rail and an improvement in rail technology can make a significant difference.

Buildings are important because they will account for 38 per cent of baseline emissions in 2020. There is a whole range of actions that could be taken to make buildings and the use of energy within them much more efficient (these are listed on Figure 9). Engineers, architects and builders really need to apply their minds and innovate in some of these areas in order to develop some fairly dramatic solutions. In this respect, efficient appliances and heating and cooling devices are unexceptional.

Agriculture is also an area where technological solutions can and do certainly reduce emissions. The importance of efficient water management also needs to be highlighted given the fact that some parts of the world are going to encounter serious problems with water supply. We will have to move to a far more efficient system of water resource management and the use of water-efficient technologies in agriculture, as several countries in the world use 80 per cent of their water supply for agriculture alone.

Figure 7: **The costs of mitigation relative to GDP**

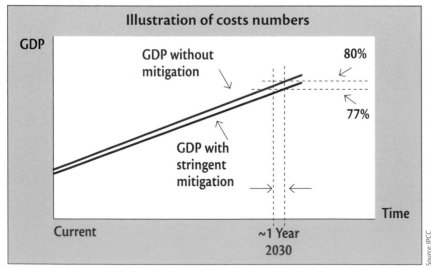

Source: IPCC

Figure 8: **Emissions reductions relative to mitigation measures**

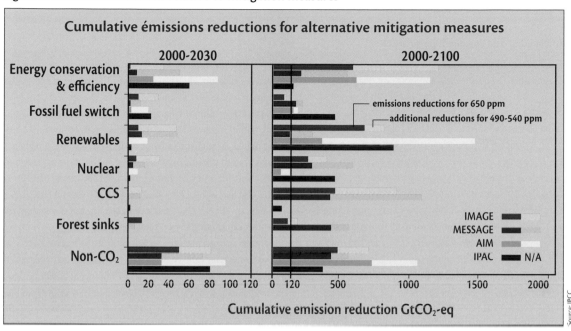

Figure 9: **Technological solutions to reduce emissions**

Improved thermal envelope	Active solar energy	Passive solar energy	Efficient appliances and heating and cooling devices
Insulation material	Photovoltaic	Sun-face glazing, airflow windows, buried pipes	Efficient lamps, cooking stoves, electric appliance
Window glazing, low-emissivity coating	Heating and water heating	Daylight sensors	Heat pumps, earth-pipe cooling

Source: IPCC

We also need to consider the fact that both livestock as well as agriculture contribute to greenhouse gas emissions. In the case of bio-energy crops, which are also potentially important solutions, there is one vital consideration (particularly in the context of biofuels): we have to be assured that there is no competition with food crops. There is a lot of criticism of policies being pursued in some parts of the world where land that has traditionally been used for producing agricultural crops is being diverted to biofuels. There is also the problem of fertiliser use and greenhouse gas emissions resulting from the use of fertilisers and chemicals.

Key policy issues

The IPCC has assessed a number of national policies and these include providing incentives for the development, acquisition, deployment and diffusion of technologies. This is absolutely critical because developing technologies alone is not going to help; we need a policy framework within which these will be deployed and utilized effectively. Information and education is essential and we also need to highlight the importance of lifestyle and behavioural changes because unless one brings

about a shift in values it is unlikely that purely technological solutions will give us the answers we are looking for.

One critical element that is missing in current policies is an effective carbon price because this would provide a signal and create incentives for producers and consumers to significantly invest in low GHG products, technologies and processes. While some may contend that technology is the answer, merely developing these technologies will not be adequate unless this is supported by a system that places an effective price on carbon because consumers and producers are obviously not going to change their patterns of behaviour in terms of production and consumption unless there is a market inducement to move to low carbon technologies. An effective price on carbon is absolutely crucial to bring about change.

As Mahatma Gandhi rightly said:

'A technological society has two choices; first it can wait until catastrophic failures expose systemic deficiencies, distortion and self-deceptions; secondly a culture can provide

social checks and balances to correct for systemic distortion prior to catastrophic failures.'

Engineering and engineering education

The engineering profession possesses the power to bring about change and can ensure that solutions are devised that really helps solve the problem of this major challenge of climate change facing the world. There are several steps that need to be taken. Firstly, engineers and scientists have to work with governments to ensure that policies are devised that have a rational basis, that they are based on adequate analysis, and that there is a clear evaluation of options and their outcomes. What is also critically important is to introduce some degree of training for engineers, perhaps right at the level of basic engineering education, by which attention can be directed to some of the critical challenges that confront the profession in meeting the threat of climate change. The same importance applies equally to measures that address mitigation and adaptation. In the case of adaptation, if we take an example such as excessive, frequent and very severe floods, then we need a totally enhanced infrastructure to protect life and property. Looking at the problem of cloudbursts and extreme precipitation events, we can see that we require more efficient drainage systems.

All of this can be introduced at the level of basic engineering education so that young people who graduate and enter the engineering professions can focus on some of these problems and possible solutions far more effectively. This is something in which the lead needs to be taken by the engineering professions themselves, and it is important that this is communicated to the engineering profession.

Conclusion

While not wanting to create a nightmare scenario, we have been very surprised by some of the facts and findings that have come out of the Fourth Assessment Report of the IPCC, and what causes most concern is the fact that there is an acceleration, not only of changes related to the climate but also the impacts that are associated with them. There is therefore a sense of urgency that we all need to accept and act on because only then will we be able to come up with solutions that are timely and effective that – as the above quotation from Gandhi suggests – will help us move away from deficiencies, distortions and, most importantly, self-deception.

This contribution is based on the 2007 international lecture by Dr R. K. Pachauri entitled *Global Climate Change: the role of Science and Technology in Mitigation And Adaptation* presented at the Royal Academy of Engineering, London, on 3 October 2007. The contribution was prepared prior to the financial/economic crisis beginning in September 2008, although the case presented above remains essentially the same over the longer term. While global GDP has declined, the impact on longer term trends, and the need for investment into improved energy, transportation and related GHG-reducing technologies in unchanged.

6.1.9 Disaster risk reduction

Badaoui Rouhban

Introduction

Natural disaster loss is on the rise. The vulnerability of the human and physical environment to the violent forces of nature is increasing. In many parts of the world, disasters caused by natural hazards (such as earthquakes, floods, windstorms, landslides, drought, wildfires, tsunami and volcanic eruptions) have caused the loss of human lives, injury, homelessness, and the destruction of economic and social infrastructure. Over the last few years, there has been an increase in the occurrence, severity and intensity of natural disasters, highlighted by the devastating Indian Ocean tsunami, the major Kashmir earthquake in Pakistan, hurricane Katrina in the USA, the Nargis cyclone in Myanmar and the Sichuan earthquake in China. Losses from human-induced disasters (such as conflict, war, structural collapses and famine) are considerably adding to the toll. Recent oil spills, plane crashes, bridge and building collapses, and so on act as frequent and tragic reminders of calamities provoked by everyday human activity.

Preparing for disaster emergencies and facing future hazards is a global source of concern. Indeed, population growth, urbanization, alteration of the natural environment, sub-standard dwellings and construction, inadequate infrastructure maintenance, global climate change and grinding poverty in numerous communities are all exacerbating the risks of disasters. Whereas natural hazards are often unexpected or uncontrollable natural events of varying magnitude, reduction of risks stemming from such events is both possible and feasible if the sciences and technologies related to natural hazards are properly applied through engineering.

Advances in the technology of disaster risk reduction

Science and technology help us to understand the mechanisms of natural hazards having atmospheric, geological, hydrological and biological origins, and to analyse the transformation of these hazards into disasters. Knowledge of the mechanisms of violent forces of nature is made up of an orderly system of facts that have been learned from study, experiment and observation of natural phenomena and their impacts on humankind and the environment. The scientific and technological disciplines involved include basic and engineering sciences, natural, social and human sciences. They relate to the hazard environment (i.e. hydrology, geology, geophysics, seismology, volcanology, meteorology and biology), to the built environment (i.e. engineering, architecture and materials) and to the policy environment (i.e. sociology, humanities, politics and management).

Engineering science has contributed considerably to disaster risk reduction. They have led to remarkable innovations in pre-

Figure 1: **Number of natural disasters per year (1900-2009)**

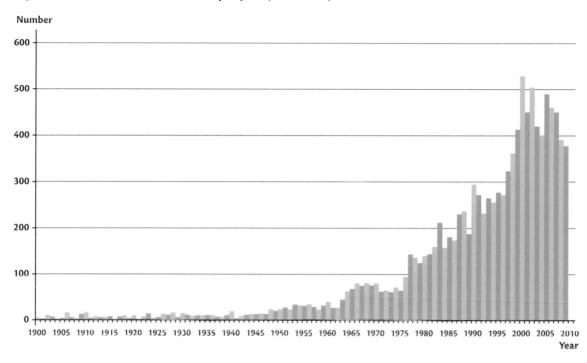

paredness, in emergency response, in rehabilitation and reconstruction as well as in long-term risk mitigation measures. Over the last three decades, knowledge of the intensity and distribution in time and space of natural hazards and the technological means of confronting them has expanded greatly. Progress in the science and technology of natural hazards and of related coping mechanisms have also made it possible to introduce significant changes in the approach to the problem of disasters. Major advances have been made in the development of global meteorological models and their application to large-scale weather prediction – enabled by the development of supercomputers. Although earthquake prediction is still not possible, considerable ability exists today to make more accurate forecasts, and to give warning, of several impending hazard events. Engineers have developed technologies and techniques that decrease the vulnerability of buildings – be they schoolhouses or skyscrapers – and other elements of socio-economic life to earthquakes and hurricanes.

Earthquake-resistant design has proven very effective, notably in some instances witnessed/demonstrated during the recent earthquakes that have occurred in Kashmir in Pakistan and Sichuan in China, where good constructions behaved quite well compared to the numerous other structures that collapsed completely. Most experts believe that better earthquake resistant-building designs and construction practices would have greatly reduced the consequences of the earthquakes in Bam, Iran; in Kashmir, Pakistan; and in Sichuan, China. The Indian Ocean tsunami's death toll could have been drastically reduced if a tsunami early warning system, similar to the one existing in the Pacific, was in place and if the warning, already

known to scientists, was disseminated quickly and effectively to the coastal populations. Warning of violent storms and of volcanic eruptions hours and days ahead save many lives and prevent significant property losses in some countries of Asia and Latin America.

In November 1970, the Bhola tropical cyclone left 500,000 dead and 1,300,000 homeless in Bangladesh. In May 1985, a cyclone of comparable strength struck the same area; the loss of life totalled less than 10,000 deaths; the death toll caused by Cyclone Sidr in 2007 was just over 4,000. The difference with the 1970 tragedy relate to improvements in hazard prediction, early warning and evacuation infrastructure in Bangladesh.

Outlook for engineering and technology in disaster risk reduction

Engineering and technology are among the principal drivers of reducing vulnerability to disasters. Modern technologies should be further applied and developed that mitigate the exposure to natural hazards of the physical and built environment, and other elements of socio-economic life. One component of the expected breakthroughs in disaster reduction, in some instances, shall be enhanced capacity to control or modify the disaster events themselves including through engineering measures. Technologies based on new methods of communication, information handling and computation bring unprecedented opportunities for the hazard-prone communities to become better prepared.

Building a culture of disaster prevention entails a great responsibility for all professionals active in engineering and technology.

Figure 2: **Pre-disaster risk, reduction phase**

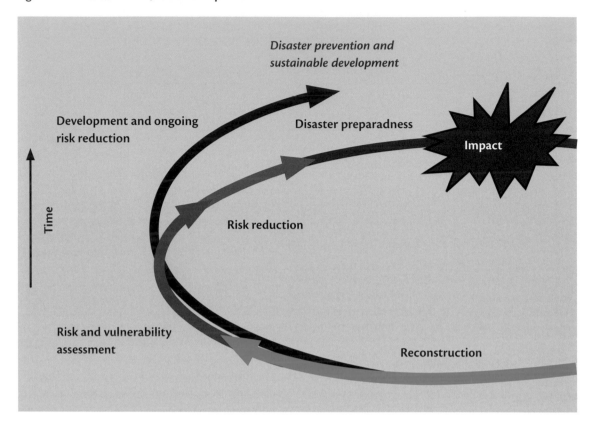

Engineers should participate in actions addressing the entire disaster cycle ranging from the long-term mitigation phase, through the preparedness phase, the emergency response, going through the post-disaster rehabilitation, reconstruction and development phases. In many countries, the need for the establishment or improvement of early warning systems remains. Hazard-zoning and risk assessment represent early tasks that require the full contribution of engineers. Mitigation of risks will rely on structural and non-structural measures that are put in place to protect communities as much as possible. Civic education, public awareness and training are necessary actions where professionals in engineering can develop robust approaches palatable to the public.

Action in these fields will increasingly depend on the active interaction between major stakeholders and engineers: gov-

The International Strategy for Disaster Reduction (ISDR) represents a global drive, sponsored by the United Nations, aimed at building disaster resilient communities. The ISDR promotes disaster reduction as an integral component of sustainable development. It is an international framework in which countries, institutions and individuals can cooperate, and is coordinated within the United Nations by an Inter-Agency Secretariat located in Geneva. A network of UN agencies, inter-governmental groups, and non-governmental or civil society organizations are teamed together as part of the ISDR. The engineering component in the activities of many of these entities represents a critical element.

UNESCO promotes disaster risk reduction through activities in education, science, culture and communication. Indeed, disaster reduction forms an integral part of UNESCO's engineering programme. The engineering and technology component of the organization's programme and its Intergovernmental Oceanographic Commission (IOC) capitalize on advances made in the science and technology of natural hazards, and have a direct bearing on disaster reduction plans. The purposes of UNESCO in the field of disaster reduction are:

■ to promote a better scientific understanding of natural hazards and of their intensity;

■ to help set up reliable observatory and early warning networks and systems;

■ to encourage the establishment of rational landuse plans;

■ to promote the adoption of suitable building design;

■ to contribute to the protection of educational buildings and cultural monuments;

■ to strengthen environmental protection for the prevention of natural disasters;

■ to enhance preparedness and public awareness through information and education;

■ to foster post-disaster investigation.

UNESCO is committed to encouraging and facilitating disaster prevention action through networking and strengthening of regional and international coordination systems, direct partnership with countries, field implementation of operational projects, preservation and dissemination of data. Networks of researchers, engineers and social scientists must be set up and undertaken to promote a combination of indigenous technology with advances in science and technology and to develop area-specific technological solutions.

ernments, the private sector and the different components of civil society including scientists, educators, parliamentarians, media, local authorities, youth, women's organizations and other non-governmental organizations. The global challenge of disaster reduction is a significant engagement on the part of engineers and technicians in an integrated approach to risk management. Enhancing cooperation among all these major groups will be imperative.

Above all, scientific and technological solutions to the complex problems of disasters must be rooted in social realities, in the fullest sense of the term. Without science and technology, and their blending with traditional modes of protection, there can be no world safe from disasters.

6.1.10 Engineering in emergencies

Andrew Lamb

Introduction

The medical profession has played a role in responding to wars since long before Henri Dunant inverted the red and white of the Swiss flag and established the Red Cross movement. The engineering profession, on the other hand, has long been associated with the prosecution of wars. Its technologies – weapons, armaments and defences – have been pivotal to military capabilities throughout history, as it is today. It is only really since the end of the colonial era following the Second World War that engineers have in significant numbers used technologies to respond to disasters and conflicts with a humanitarian motivation; saving lives through the provision of water, shelter, transport, communications and information services. It is an important but still emerging field.

Recent lessons

The human tragedies of recent disasters has re-emphasized the life-saving effects of engineering endeavour. The response to the devastating earthquake in Haiti earlier this year has drawn upon the skills of civil, structural, mechanical, electronic, electrical and software engineers to begin to address the challenge of nothing less than 200,000 fatalities, one million left homeless and a destroyed capital city. The calls to 'build back better' were immediate. The earthquake in Chile soon after quickly showed the world the difference that development makes – that a more developed infrastructure and built environment means that people are much less vulnerable to natural disaster (though the geological and geographic circumstances were different).

China's response to the devastating earthquake in Sichuan province highlighted the crucial role of military engineers in disaster relief, which has a long and proud history. The risk of the collapse of major dams, which would have caused fur-

ther substantial suffering and damage, was averted through cooperation efforts and high-level engineering expertise. Hurricane Katrina in the USA demonstrated the horrifying effects that neglect of major engineering infrastructure can have in the face of natural hazards, particularly in a society that has become dependent on advanced, and hence at times fragile, technologies. The destruction of New Orleans was in some ways the driver for a much greater focus on urban disasters (or disasters in the engineered environment). The Indian Ocean Tsunami of 2004 was a catastrophe on a global scale, and very quickly led to a focus on emergency shelter and transitional shelter in which engineers now play an important role in taking forward.

In 2007 alone, flooding affected 200 million people in China[111], displaced thirty million in India[112], Bangladesh, Nepal and Bhutan, one million in Mexico[113], 500,000 in Darfur in Sudan[114], 300,000 in North Korea[115], 125,000 in the UK[116] (with the heaviest rains since records began), 40,000 in South Africa[117] and thousands in Australia (the worst flooding for forty years)[118]. In all, about 1.5 billion people were affected by floods that year. Flooding, as with earthquakes, very quickly demands the services of engineers to redesign flood defences, rebuild bridges and roads, restore power and communications, make safe the water supply and inform future planning (such as through the use of national flood maps made using satellite data). Earthquakes destroy the infrastructure on which our lives depend, whereas floods overwhelm that infrastructure. Engineers are learning lessons very quickly as the patterns of disasters change.

Preparedness

Disaster hazards, such as extreme weather events, are increasing in periodicity and intensity. As more and more people live in densely packed cities or are forced to live on the environmental margins, the vulnerability of populations towards disaster is also increasing. Technological disasters such as train crashes and building collapses are the fifth biggest killer, following disease, famine, conflict and natural hazards.[119] Earthquakes destroy infrastructure, but they do not necessarily destroy life – it is the collapsing buildings that kill.

111 China – http://www.alertnet.org/db/blogs/36072/2007/06/23-140102-1.htm

112 www.news.bbc.co.uk/2/hi/south_asia/6941029.stm & www.en.wikipedia.org/wiki/2007_South_Asian_floods

113 www.abc.net.au/news/stories/2007/11/02/2080710.htm?section=world

114 www.alertnet.org/thenews/newsdesk/L06723272.htm

115 www.reliefweb.int/rw/rwb.nsf/db900SID/SJHG-7649NF?OpenDocument&RSS20=18-P

116 'Floods' special feature in New Civil Engineer 31st January 2008.

117 www.earthobservatory.nasa.gov/NaturalHazards/view.php?id=18817

118 www.bbc.co.uk/weather/world/news/30062007news.shtml

119 World Disaster Report 2004.

All this means that more is needed from engineers as professionals. Some engineers, with the right skills and experience, are certainly needed in disaster response to help save lives. But all engineers have an important role in reducing both the hazards people face and their vulnerability to those hazards; they can help with disaster preparedness. With a greater understanding of climatic changes, engineers can design more resilient solutions or adapt existing infrastructure. With more input into the early stages of planning and political decision making, engineers can help ensure that their work is destined only to help people, and they can also help people understand that technological solutions might not exist and that other changes are needed. With a greater emphasis on professional standards, safety and good coordination across the design, build, operation and maintenance stages, engineers can reduce the harm of technological failures. With a professional and zero-tolerance stance on corruption, particularly in construction, engineers can provide solutions that can be trusted to stand firm. Finally, as more than 95 per cent of personnel involved in disaster relief organizations are local staff, engineers can improve technical education and expertise in places where the humanitarian need is greatest and thus help build long-term capacity to cope.

Humanitarianism and Professionalization

There are strong parallels between the engineering and humanitarian communities. Engineering is a profession, and many engineers are professional in the true sense of the word; they are accountable to their peers and to the public for their actions. The humanitarian sector is trying to professionalize and is working to develop its own voluntary codes of conduct, codes of practice, field guides and manuals, training and professional development courses, methods of coordination between actors and minimum operational standards.[120] These are facilities that have long been established in the engineering profession. However, the humanitarian community does not yet have a formal professional institution of its own to spearhead similar efforts as progress in this area often lies with voluntary and poorly-funded groupings of aid agencies. This is partly because the sector is so new and so international, with its resources being directed towards particular disaster responses.

It is perhaps worth noting that there are a growing number of degree courses that teach engineering for disaster relief, which is an important indicator of a maturing sector and of the demand from engineering students to prepare appropriately for getting involved. There are more conferences on disaster issues within the engineering community as well.[121]

There has been a massive growth in recent years in the military contracting engineering companies to provide relief and deliver development projects. The wars in Afghanistan and Iraq, and the conflict that followed them, appear to many in the humanitarian sector to have produced a new military-industrial paradigm. Whilst this has had significant achievements – with new and re-built water supplies, electricity grids, hospitals, oil refineries, roads and other vital infrastructure – it has given rise to deep concerns over disaster capitalism[122] and over the public understanding of humanitarianism. It is certainly recognized that the capabilities of engineering firms to deliver large-scale reconstruction and development projects are far greater than those of humanitarian organizations, but cases have come to light regarding the way in which contracts are awarded or staff and stakeholders are treated that call into question the true motivation for such projects. In turn, this has meant that humanitarian agencies are, at the very least, hesitant to engage with the private sector in their disaster relief work. It is a serious challenge to the engineering community, particularly given the potential positive impact that engineering companies could bring (as demonstrated by successful reconstruction projects awarded to major engineering consultancies after the Indian Ocean Tsunami to help restore

---

A guide about built environmental professionals

The Royal Institution of Chartered Surveyors commissioned a report from the Max Locke Centre, published in 2009, to help non-technical decision makers in humanitarian emergencies better understand the roles of different built environmental professionals. Called *The Built Environment Professions in Disaster Risk Reduction and Response – A guide for humanitarian agencies**, it sets out the roles of architects, surveyors, planners and engineers across seven phases of disaster management. The guide demonstrates the case for greater use of built environment professionals in the humanitarian sector, and emphasizes their importance in achieving a sustainable longer term recovery.

*   Available from http://www.rics.org/site/scripts/download_info. aspx?downloadID=829&fileID=991

---

120 Examples include the Red Cross Code of Conduct, the Humanitarian Accountability Partnership, the Good Enough Guide, accredited RedR training courses, the Cluster system, and the SPHERE guidelines.

121 Examples include 'Civil Engineering Disaster Mitigation Conference: Earthquake and Tsunami' in June 2009, Istanbul (organized jointly by the World Council of Civil Engineers, the European Council of Civil Engineers and the Turkish Chamber of Civil Engineers) or 'Engineering a Better World: Relief Operations and Construction' in March 2010 in London (organized jointly by the Institution of Civil Engineers and the Commonwealth Engineers Council).

122 See the proceedings of RedR UK's 2009 Conference 'Hard Realities and Future Necessities: The Role of the Private Sector in Humanitarian Efforts' and 'The Shock Doctrine' by Naomi Klein.

infrastructure in Aceh).[123] Astonishingly successful examples of private sector contributions have also emerged from the mobile phone, logistics and finance industries[124] and even in engineering training following Hurricane Katrina.[125]

RedR

International disaster relief organizations with particular expertise in engineering have emerged. Of these, the most well known in the engineering profession is the 'Register of Engineers for Disaster Relief'. RedR was established by an engineer who, whilst working in response to the Vietnamese Boat People's Crisis in 1979, encountered serious problems in recruiting qualified engineers to help in the humanitarian response. That register has now developed into an international family with offices in the Australia, Canada, India, Malaysia, New Zealand, South Africa and the UK. The UK office has field offices in Sudan, Sri Lanka, Pakistan, Haiti and formerly in Kenya.

RedR organizations help agencies to recruit personnel, operate a peer-assessed membership scheme, produce guides (see Box) and knowledge services, deliver training courses on topics such as humanitarianism, security, management and technical skills, answer technical questions from relief workers in the field and so on. RedR has helped to build a community of trained engineers with expertise for disaster relief, a community which now reaches every major aid agency in the world. It has helped to define the skills that an engineer needs in order to be effective in responding to disaster situations (particularly in project management roles since most of those involved in disaster relief are local staff). RedR UK has applied an engineering methodology to humanitarian security issues and is now a leader in this important specialization, and it is developing its services in the health sector.

The engineering community has shown RedR a great deal of support. Companies have released their staff to go on assignments and sponsored their national organizations. Individual engineers have fundraised and donated to its cause. Engineering institutions have supported RedR through publicity, events and even office space. RedR's engineers are given as case studies to help attract more young people to study engineering, because the difference they make in their work is so clearly visible. Being associated with RedR also helps companies to recruit graduate engineers since many have a strong appetite to get involved in relief work.

RedR's members have been described by some of the world's leading engineers as true heroes of engineering.[126] They help to demonstrate how, time and again, good engineering saves lives, and how engineering can transform catastrophic situations to help people realize their own recovery and to restore dignity and peace.

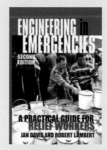

A guide for disaster relief personnel

Engineering in Emergencies is a vital publication for anyone working in the humanitarian community. Written by RedR, it is a very practical guide that covers topics from personal preparations for relief assignments, humanitarian principles, personal security, assessment and management, logistics, environmental health and sanitation, water supply and equipment maintenance, vehicles, roads and airstrips, shelter and settlements and so on. It guides relief workers in the design, construction, operation and maintenance of solutions to meet the needs of those affected by disaster, particularly those affected by complex emergencies. This handbook, which is not freely available electronically and is quite heavy to transport, is so essential to humanitarian relief workers that bootleg copies quickly circulate in disaster responses.

6.1.11 Appropriate technology

Tony Marjoram and Andrew Lamb

Interest in the idea and philosophy of 'appropriate technology' increased in the 1960s, based partly on the Ghandian notion of smaller-scale self-sufficiency and on concern for the consequences of industrialization for environmental sustainability and for the degradation that surrounded the 'limits to growth' debate in the 1960s and 1970s. The idea and philosophy of appropriate technology – or alternative technology[127] as it was also referred to – particularly in the West, relates to the use of smaller, lower cost, labour-intensive (rather than capital-intensive), easily maintained and environmentally friendly technologies, preferably using locally available materials and skills in harmony with local needs and conditions, in both developing and developed countries. The key factor is that all technology

123 See 'Royal Haskoning to rebuild tsunami-hit Aceh' in UK Association of Consulting Engineers 'Impact' magazine July/August 2007 or the New Civil Engineer / Association of Consulting Engineers Consultants of the Year 2010'Outstanding Achievement Award' given to WSP group for their work in Banda Aceh with the Canadian Red Cross.

124 See examples put forward by the World Economic Forum's Disaster Resource Network.

125 See article 'A hurricane force skills drive for the US' in New Civil Engineer 3rd July 2008.

126 An example includes Prof. Paul Jowitt's Presidential Address in November 2009, Institution of Civil Engineers.

127 David Dickson. 1974. *Alternative Technology and the Politics of Technical Change*, Fontana.

should be appropriate to economic, social and cultural contexts, as it once was when most technology was developed locally or when most situations were fairly similar in smaller scale pre-industrial days. Problems arise when technology is transferred between different economic, social and cultural contexts, even within the same country, but especially between the developed and industrial to less developed and more traditional situations. This is a relatively simple and straightforward expectation, and it is surprising that appropriate technology was a hotly debated and contentious issue in the later 1960s and 1970s in the discussion of development assistance and technology transfer (though perhaps less surprising when one considers the dominant models of economic development based on industrialization and import substitution of the time). There was particular criticism of appropriate technology in India for example, despite the Ghandian background.

Interest in appropriate technology, or AT as it often became known, increased in the context of international development and overseas aid amid concern over the transfer of larger-scale technologies to developing countries and the associated problems of operation and maintenance. Increasing interest was also driven by the work of E. F. (Fritz) Schumacher, an economist who worked with John Maynard Keynes, and who was for twenty years the Chief Economic Advisor to the National Coal Board in the UK. Schumacher was a critic of neo-classical economics, which he saw as dehumanizing, and he advocated greater attention to the workplace, decentralization and more efficient resource use – facilitated by 'intermediate' technologies more suited to the needs of developing countries. To promote such technologies and approaches, Schumacher and colleagues created the Intermediate Technology Development Group (ITDG) in 1966 (which became Practical Action in 2005) and indicated the development of the 'appropriate technology movement'. Interest in appropriate/intermediate technology increased after 1973 – the year of the first energy crisis in which Schumacher's book *Small Is Beautiful: Economics As If People Mattered*[128] was published; a critique of Western economics that was described by *The Times* as one of the hundred most influential books that helped develop the environmental movement and create environmental economics.

Interest in appropriate technology declined, together with support for international development in the later 1970s and 1980s, with the rise to power of Margaret Thatcher and Ronald Reagan in the UK and US in 1979 and 1981 respectively, and the development of structural adjustment policies in the later 1970s and 1980s based around loan conditionalities promoting market orientation and privatization. Despite this, interest in AT continued with ITDG and similar long-established organizations around the world (some also have changed names and mandates). These include the German Appropriate Tech-

nology Exchange (GATE), *Groupe de recherche et d'échanges technologiques* (GRET, France), Swiss Centre for Development Cooperation in Technology and Management (SKAT) and Volunteers in Technical Assistance (VITA, USA). These have been joined by many newcomers including the Centre for Alternative Technology (CAT, UK), Engineers Against Poverty (EAP, UK), Appropriate Technology Asia, Appropriate Technology Africa, Programme for Appropriate Technology in Health (PATH, USA), Centre for Appropriate Technology (GrAT, Austria), Aprovecho (US), Centre for Appropriate Technology (Australia), National Center for Appropriate Technology (US), Appropriate Technology Association (Thailand), the Asian Alliance of Appropriate Technology Practitioners (Approtech) and many more. In addition to this, some of the original magazines and journals still continue, including the journal *Appropriate Technology* (now published by Research Information, who took over from ITDG in 1999) and *Appropriate Technology Sourcebook* (US). The magazine *Undercurrents*, did most to promote alternative technology in the 1970s, but disappeared in 1984.

Indeed, although some of the original AT organizations, magazines, people and practitioners are no longer with us, and although the name of Fritz Schumacher is unknown by many young people today, 'Small is Beautiful' is still a well known term. They have been joined by a diversity of newer entities that, in the Internet age, help to make information about appropriate technology more accessible than ever (the online reference www.appropedia.org for example). Furthermore, AT is of increasing contemporary relevance following the financial/economic crisis of 2007–2009 and the even greater contemporary challenges of sustainable development, climate change mitigation and adaptation. The continued relevance of appropriate technology was illustrated in *Small is Working: Technology for Poverty Reduction*[129], a video and publication developed by UNESCO, ITDG and the Television Fund for the Environment in 2003 to commemorate the thirtieth anniversary of Small is Beautiful and the work of increasing numbers of Engineers Without Borders groups around the world.

Appropriate technologies can include 'high' as well as 'low', and 'soft' as well as 'hard' technologies. White, solar-powered LED lights have helped facilitate the replacement of kerosene lamps, and mobile phones and associated software systems have enabled information and communication not dreamt of before the age of electronics. This is further illustrated in the use of intermediate technologies in urban development and construction in such areas as the use of pozzolanic cement extenders and substitutes (such as rice-husk ash), adobe, rammed earth and mud brick. Housing technologies have also been enhanced with better natural passive and active solar design and ventilation systems, including such ideas as Trombe walls. Urban and rural development will both depend on

128 E. F. Schumacher. 1973. *Small Is Beautiful: Economics As If People Mattered*. Blond & Briggs, London, p.288.

129 *Small is Working: Technology for Poverty Reduction*, video/VCD and 70-page booklet, UNESCO, ITDG and TVE, 2003.

improved transportation technologies and systems, and the use of zero emission vehicles. The energy field is perhaps the most synonymous with appropriate technology, and includes photovoltaic solar panels, cogeneration and more efficient power storage, distribution and use, solar concentrators, solar absorbers and water heaters, wind- wave- and hydro-power, biofuels, biogas and biochar.

At the same time, water supply and sanitation is the most important area of appropriate technology in terms of helping save nearly two million deaths per year from preventable water-borne diseases and improving the lives of the over 900 million people who lack safe drinking water. Slow sand, porous ceramic filters and reverse osmosis facilitate this, as does chemical floc-culation chlorine and ultraviolet disinfection, improved well construction techniques, pumping systems and toilet technolo-gies. Appropriate technologies have enhanced food production with permaculture, improved irrigation, greenhouses and other techniques, and have reduced post-harvest loss with better food storage, preservation and processing. Food processing has also been enhanced with better shelling and milling machines, and the health risks of domestic cooking reduced with improved smokeless wood-burning stoves, solar cookers and related technologies. Few of the above appropriate technological innovations would be possible without appropriate systems of microfinance, and technology has also revolutionized the world of finance, including at the micro level with the use of such tech-nologies such as mobile phones.

One of the major new areas of appropriate technology are 'high-tech' such as information and communication technolo-gies. Wind-up radios, mobile phones, the US$100 Laptop, net-books and related projects, open-source software and Voice Over Internet Protocol systems – made possible by fibre-optics, satellite communications and other technologies – are revolutionizing the way we think and about appropriate tech-nology. Decentralized, distributed infrastructure systems – in many ways similar to or inspired by topography of the Internet – are becoming increasingly important as the 'traditional' path of development responds to the need for change. Industrial-ized countries are rediscovering forgotten technologies as they attempt to reduce their waste, emissions and environmental impact, and they are increasingly open to learning from tech-nologies used in developing countries.

In many ways then, the concept of appropriate technology is being re-understood for the challenges of the twenty-first century, and the image of appropriate technology is changing as well. Significant issues remain, particularly around effective knowledge sharing, commercialization, scaling-up and aware-ness. The next decade will see significant developments in information platforms, business models and in education – and will, in all likelihood, show once again that small is beauti-ful and working.

6.1.12 Appropriate technology: case study on building technologies

Solomon Mwangi

Introduction

Since the signing of the Comprehensive Peace Agreement (CPA) between the Government of Sudan and the Sudanese People Liberation Movement, only a few Sudanese refugees have returned home. The cause for this low return is due to a number of reasons, including:

- Lack of infrastructures such as schools, hospitals and houses.

- Unemployment or lack of economic activities to support normal livelihood.

- Non-existence of a dynamic private sector/enterprise cul-ture to open up business opportunities in most of the rural settings.

- Insecurity threats and rumours of war in many areas despite the CPA having been in force for three years now.

The housing and general building construction challenges in Sudan

The traditional building materials in Sudan, similar to many other countries, comprise of poles with mud for walls and thatch grass for roofing. While these traditional materials are probably the most appropriate because of their good thermal properties and affordability, its lifespan is limited to a maxi-mum of twelve years (mud is weathered by rains and wind over time and poles rot slowly or are eaten by termites). The structures are also less hygienic as they are easily infested by insects and rodents.

© S. Mwangi

↺ *Typical African hut with its mud and pole construction.*

⊃ A typical brick production site in Sudan.

Burnt bricks

Former colonial powers in Africa introduced burnt brick technology for modern construction. This technology was largely adopted in many countries, but has gone on to cause desertification and deforestation, especially in areas where trees are used as the main fuel for firing the bricks. Sudan has been no exception as the burnt brick technology is widely adopted for public buildings and permanent construction. So, whilst burnt bricks are good for the construction of permanent structures, this technology has disadvantages:

- Causes desertification with one tree required to burn every 1,000 bricks.

- Bricks made traditionally are of irregular shape, needing more mortar in construction.

- Brick makers suffer losses of 20 per cent to 50 per cent as bricks break when drying and burning.

- Bricks are not in standard sizes as different brick makers use different moulds.

- Construction with bricks takes longer in comparison to concrete blocks.

- Production requires massive pits that are often left open, degrading the land.

Construction challenges in South Sudan

Construction work in South Sudan faces several practical challenges, including:

- A lack of trained or skilled Sudanese construction workers; major construction projects are undertaken by foreign companies.

- A lack of basic building materials such as cement, sand and gravel, raising prices.

- Large regions of South Sudan are flat and susceptible to flooding in the heavy rains.

- These regions are largely made of a clay/silt soil, known as 'Black Cotton Soil', which stretches to depths of more than five metres and hence requires special, and expensive, construction designs and techniques.

- Deforestation is caused by excessive use of trees used to produce burnt bricks.

- A lack of road infrastructure makes transport very expensive and limits it to the dry seasons (in some areas, materials can only be delivered by cargo planes).

These challenges make general building construction very – sometimes prohibitively – expensive and put decent housing out of the reach of ordinary Sudanese.

Sustainable construction approach in South Sudan

Building construction in South Sudan requires innovative engineering solutions, with many regions requiring carefully tailored technologies. Challenges include:

- Manufacturing cost-effective building materials from local soils, using environmentally friendly approaches, in areas where sand and gravel are non-existent.

- Designing special foundations to be used in the unstable Black Cotton soil.

- Training youth and former soldiers in construction skills to overcome skilled labour shortages (equipping them with vital skills, helping them participate in the reconstruction of South Sudan, and curbing emerging crime caused by unemployment).

- Introducing environmentally friendly technologies that will curtail further desertification caused by cutting of local indigenous trees used for burning bricks.

- Designing affordable buildings with good thermal insulating properties to protect against the hot temperatures of South Sudan.

Local organizations have been able to develop such solutions. Stabilized soil blocks are made from soil mixed with a small amount of cement and are around 50 per cent cheaper than burnt bricks. By using cement to stabilize the soils and bind sand, no firewood is needed. Their production process requires only unskilled workers, rapidly creating employment. Special foundations have also been developed for construction in Black Cotton soil.

◊ A health centre built with Stabilised Soil Blocks in Upper Nile Sudan.

What is an Appropriate Building Technology

- Maximizes the use of locally-available materials.

- Requires locally-available equipment that does not depend on imported supplies of electricity or fuel to operate.

- Draws on skills that are easy to learn and adopt at a community level.

- Are environmental-friendly overall and will not damage the local environment.

- Is used and maintained without external assistance.

- Is safe and affordable.

- Is not necessarily 'low technology' or 'high technology', but provides a capability.

- Skills are easy to learn and adopt at village and community level

The COMAC construction programme has primarily focused on immediate public buildings needs such as schools and hospitals, working with NGOs and other development minded organizations in introducing Appropriate Building Technology (ABT) for the reconstruction of Sudan. In so doing, COMAC believes ordinary people will gradually pick up and adopt the use of these technologies in their private projects.

By using this approach, COMAC has been able to achieve and demonstrate the following:

- Introduced ABT such as Stabilized Soil Blocks (SSB) that are made from soil mixed with a small percentage of cement. The SSB technology is on average 50 per cent cheaper than burnt bricks.

- Provided employment to the unemployed. An SSB production plant employs six unskilled workers. Further employment is created for the unskilled Sudanese who are trained in construction, instead of importing a skilled labour force from neighboring Kenya or Uganda.

◖ *Black Cotton soil strata.*

- Improvized special foundations for construction in Black Cotton areas.

- Helped conserve the environment by using environmentally friendly technologies. This has been achieved by replacing burnt bricks with cement used to stabilize soils and bind sand to make building blocks. Burnt bricks also create land degradation as massive pits are left open after making bricks while SSB are made on site using soils dug from trenches dug for foundations of the intended building.

Some of the Appropriate Building Technologies used in Sudan

COMAC has been promoting the use of three construction technologies in Sudan. These are:

Stabilized soil blocks

This building material was developed in Colombia in the early 1940s and introduced into East Africa in the 1970s. The technology has benefited from developments that include:

- Robust, manually operated equipment that requires little maintenance.

- A common performance standard that conforms to international building standards for materials approved for permanent construction (such as concrete blocks).

- Wide application and adoption in Kenya, Malawi and Uganda.

- Use of interlocking blocks to further reduce costs by reducing the need for mortar.

- The blocks are made on site using soils dug from the trenches made for foundations.

Poles and Rammed Earth Technology

Poles and Rammed Earth Technology is an improvement on the traditional African construction comprising of poles and mud. In this modern technology, treated poles that protect them from termites and other insects are used as the structural framework of the building. The poles are spaced at maximum intervals of 1.5 metres, and then concreted to the ground. Barbed wire or hoop iron is then nailed horizontally between the poles at a spacing of 300 mm, helping anchor the rammed earth to the poles.

Form work support is then used, temporarily fixed on the poles both internally and externally, to support the wet mix of soil and cement used to stabilize it. On average, only 5 per cent of cement is used to stabilize and bond the stable soil type.

◖ *The wasted bricks during production.*

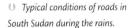

◖ *Typical conditions of roads in South Sudan during the rains.*

Manually-operated block press.

Layers of soil and cement, not exceeding 300 mm, are compacted everyday and gradually the building is completed within ten days.

Sand and cement blocks

Sand is one of the building raw materials in abundant supply in Darfur and some other parts of Sudan. Regrettably, it has not been used for building construction while desertification, caused by the use of burnt bricks, continues unabated.

COMAC undertook a Building Technologies Analysis in Darfur commissioned by Mercy Corps, an American NGO working in development projects in Darfur. The analysis revealed that the construction costs of a building would be reduced by 30 per cent with the introduction of solid sand/cement blocks, and 50 per cent with hollow sand cement blocks.

A hand mould to make sand/ cement blocks.

Reinforced ground beam foundation supported by columns in Black Cotton soil.

Special foundations for Black Cotton soil areas

Construction in Black Cotton soil is a major challenge in South Sudan. When wet, the soil swells and when it dries it shrinks and cracks. These movements can cause a building to crack unless special foundations are designed to withstand them.

In Upper Nile and Jonglei States of Southern Sudan, Black Cotton Soil covers several square kilometres of land, stretching to depths exceeding five metres. The two states also faces a major challenge due to the unavailability of raw materials suitable for construction such as sand and gravel.

COMAC has been faced with these challenges when called upon to build hospitals or police posts in this region. In fac-

ing these challenges, COMAC has come up with a number of solutions, including:

- Reinforced concrete foundations, with a ground beam supported by concrete columns.

- Special Stabilized Soil Blocks made using special soil and cement mixes.

- Laying a floating floor screed with cement/sand mortar, reinforced with chicken wire.

Accelerated dissemination of ABT's in Sudan and other developing countries

Housing, a basic human need, and unemployment are two of the major problems faced by many developing countries. As if that is not bad enough, environmental degradation is a major phenomenon in developing countries.

In all these three compounded problems (housing, unemployment and environmental degradation) one potential solution lies with the introduction, promotion and enforcement of Appropriate Building Technologies (ABT's), already mentioned. For this to happen and for the impact to be felt by the beneficiaries, deliberate policies and decisions have to be made and enforced by policy and decision-makers in governments, donor and development organizations directly or indirectly involved in development projects in the developing countries.

For this to happen in an accelerated way, donors, policy and decision-makers need to:

- Support the use of these technologies by insisting that they be given preference in the projects they fund or support.

- Support organizations and companies such as COMAC who promote these technologies by recommending their developmental construction approach be adopted by governments and development partners.

- Support a monitoring program of assessing how these technologies perform over time.

The Poles and Rammed Earth construction process.

A completed building in South Sudan.

6.2 Engineering infrastructure

6.2.1 Water supply and sanitation

Kalanithy Vairavamoorthy and
Damir Brdjanovic

Existing conditions

Water supply

The problem of water scarcity in urban areas of developing countries is a major concern. It is estimated that by 2050, half of India's population will be living in urban areas and will face acute water problems (Singh, 2000).[130] It was reported in 2002 that about 1.1 billion people were still using water from unimproved sources, and two thirds of these people live in Asia. The number of people without improved water sources in China alone is equal to the number of un-served in the whole of Africa (UNICEF/ WHO, 2004).[131] The quality of water that people receive is also questionable. In India, 85 per cent of the urban population has access to drinking water, but only 20 per cent of the available drinking water meets the health and quality standards set by the World Health Organization (WHO) (Singh, 2000).

The daily water supply rate in developing countries is very low compared to the industrial world. In India, it ranges from 16 to 300 litres per day, depending on the locality and the economic strata (Singh, 2000), whereas this figure ranges from 100 to 600 litres per day in developed countries. The populations that are not served by a piped water supply receive even smaller quantities of water. In East Africa, the daily supply rate of un-piped water was nearly a third less than for piped users of low-income communities (Thompson et al., 2001). [132]

The prevailing water stress in many developing countries is not only due to source limitations but other factors such as poor distribution efficiency through city networks and inequalities in service provision between the rich and the poor (UN-HABITAT, 1999).[133] One of the main reasons is the high rate of water loss from the distribution systems. Many studies show that water losses in cities of developing countries are at levels between 40–60 per cent of the water supplied (Arloso-

roff, 1999).[134] In many cases the water loss indicators reflect the inefficiency of the management of the water supply system. Any reduction in water losses requires coherent action to address not only the technical and operational issues but also the institutional, planning, financial and administrative issues (WHO, 2000).[135]

The design of water distribution systems in general has been based on the assumption of continuous supply. However, in most of the developing countries, the water supply system is not continuous but intermittent (Vairavamoorthy et al., 2007).[136] The Asian Development Bank has reported that, in 2001, ten of the eighteen cities studied supplied water for less than 24 hours a day (ADB, 2004).[137] The situation is similar in other regions of the world, for example in Latin America ten major cities receives rationed supplies (Choe and Varley, 1997).[138] Only 11 per cent of the consumers with a piped supply in Nigeria received water once in every two days in 1995.

Intermittent supply leads to many problems including severe supply pressure losses and great inequities in the distribution of water. Another serious problem arising from intermittent supplies, which is generally ignored, is the associated high levels of contamination. This occurs in networks where there are prolonged periods of interruption of supply due to negligible or zero pressures in the system (Vairavamoorthy and Mansoor, 2006).[139]

Sanitation

The sanitation sector is often a lower priority compared to water supply. Therefore it is not surprising that some 2.6 billion people, half of the developing world, live without improved sanitation. Sanitation coverage in developing countries (49 per cent) is half that of the developed world (98 per cent). In sub-Saharan Africa the coverage is a mere 36 per cent, and over half of this is without improved sanitation. Similarly, nearly 1.5 bil-

⌒ Stone arch construction.

130 Singh, N. 2000. Tapping Traditional Systems of Resource Management, *Habitat Debate*, UNCHS, Vol.6, No.3.

131 UNICEF/ WHO. 2004. Meeting the MDG drinking water and sanitation target - A mid term assessment of progress. United Nations Children's Fund and World Health Organization, p.36.

132 Thompson, J., Porras, I. T., Tumwine, J. K., Mujwahuzi, M. R., Katui-Katua, M., Johnstone, N. and Wood, L. 2001. Drawers of Water II. International Institute for Environment and Development, London, UK.

133 UN-HABITAT. 1999. Managing Water for African cities - Developing a Strategy for Urban Water Demand Management, Background Paper No. 1, Expert Group Meeting UNEP & UN-HABITAT.

134 Arlosoroff, S. 1999. *Water Demand Management*. International Symposium on Efficient Water Use in Urban Areas, IECT-WHO, Kobe, Japan.

135 WHO. 2000. *Global Water Supply and Sanitation Assessment Report*, World Health Organization-United Nations. Children Fund, Geneva, Switzerland.

136 Vairavamoorthy, K., Gorantiwar, S.D., and Mohan, S. 2007. Intermittent water supply under water scarcity situations. *Water International*, Vol. 32, No. 1, pp. 121–132.

137 ADB. 2004. *Second Water Utilities Data Book Asian and Pacific Region*. Asian Development Bank (ADB). Manila, Philippines.

138 Choe, K., Varley, R., and Bilani, H. 1996. Coping with Intermittent Water Supply; Problems and Prospects, Environmental Health Project. *Activity Report No. 26*, USAID, USA.

139 Vairavamoorthy, K. and Mansoor, M.A.M. 2006. Demand management in developing countries. In: Butler, D., and Memon, F. A. (Eds.) *Water Demand Management*. IWA Publishing, London, UK. pp. 180–214.

○ *A young boy in Kathmandu, Nepal, waits to collect water with a plastic bottle.*

lion people in China and India live without access to improved sanitation services (WHO/UNICEF, 2006).[140] The number of deaths attributable to poor sanitation and hygiene alone may be as high as 1.6 million a year. Statistics on wastewater treatment revealed that almost 85 per cent of global wastewater is discharged without treatment leading to serious impacts on public health and the water receiving ecosystems.

In developing countries, rapid population growth and urbanization is creating an added demand for housing and infrastructure services including sanitation services. Providing sanitation services especially for the poor living outside the designated residential areas, like informal or illegal settlements, is a challenge. The World Bank estimates that almost 26 per cent of the global urban population – over 400 million people – lack access to the simplest form of sanitation (Khatri and Vairavamoorthy, 2007).[141]

At the same time, the wastewater collection, stormwater drainage and solid waste collection services are inadequate in most of the developing countries. The systems are either poorly planned and designed or are operated without inadequate maintenance, which means that the existing services are often of poor quality. Most of the city wastes are dumped and discharged directly to the open environment. As a result, untreated urban wastes pollute surface as well as ground water sources. The situation is even worse in the area of low-income settlements. Septic tanks and feeder networks regularly discharge effluent into street gutters, open streams or drainage canals. This creates unpleasant living conditions, public health risks and environmental damage (GHK, 2002).[142]

The numbers of urban dwellers are increasing and the urban areas are becoming overcrowded. Efforts to improve basic sanitation have tended to focus on ambitious master plans that require large investments in trunk sewerage, stormwater drainage systems, centralized large-scale treatment and facilities for solid waste collection and disposal. Some of these plans either fail to be implemented due to financial and institutional constraints, or provide an inequitable service once implemented. Consequently, the effort to solve the basic sanitation problems cannot keep up with the growing population in the developing world and new and innovative approaches are

needed that lead to sustainable solutions (Khatri and Vairavamoorthy, 2007).[143]

Sustainability issues

With the achievement of the Millennium Development Goals high on the international political agenda, particularly in 2005, significant efforts are currently being made to promote and apply institutional and management approaches conducive to the sustainability and optimization of water supply and sanitation services worldwide.

In general a water supply or sanitation service is considered sustainable when it (Brdjanovic and Gijzen 2005):[144]

- is functioning and being used;

- is able to deliver an appropriate level of benefits regarding quality, quantity, convenience, continuity and health to all;

- continues to function over a prolonged period of time (which goes beyond the lifespan of the original equipment);

- has institutionalized management;

- has operation, maintenance, administrative and replacement costs covered locally;

- can be satisfactorily operated and maintained at the local level with limited, but tailor-made, external support; and,

- does not affect the environment negatively.

Furthermore, sustainable sanitation includes:

- the practice in which an essential feature is proper containment allowing for sanitation and recycling;

- closing of the nutrient and water loops;

- the ecosystem approach;

- the polluter pays principle;

- protection of the downstream health and environment;

- decentralization of the infrastructure;

140 WHO/UNICEF. 2006. *Meeting the MDG drinking water and sanitation target, The urban and rural challenge of the decade.* World Health Organization and United Nations Children's Fund, p.41

141 Khatri, K., and Vairavamoorthy, K. 2007. Challenges for urban water supply and sanitation in the developing countries. *Water for changing world: Enhancing local knowledge and capacity,* (Symposium, 13–15 June), 50th anniversary, UNESCO-IHE Institute for Water Education, Delft.

142 GHK. 2002. Effective Strategic Planning for Urban Sanitation Service, Fundamentals of good Practice, pp. 23. Go to: http://www.ghkint.com/

143 Khatri, K., and Vairavamoorthy, K. 2007. Challenges for urban water supply and sanitation in the developing countries. *Water for changing world: Enhancing local knowledge and capacity,* (Symposium, 13–15 June), 50th anniversary, UNESCO-IHE Institute for Water Education, Delft.

144 Brdjanovic, D., Gijzen, H. 2005. Challenges in Achieving a Sustainable Water Supply and Sanitation Services for Small Islands: the Caribbean Perspective. In: Proceedings: *Aqua 2005,* Cali, Colombia (31 Oct–4 Nov 2005).

- local management and financing;

- affordability; and,

- equitable services for all.

One of the hardest lessons for the water supply and sanitation sector is that making the initial capital investment is often the easiest part of the job. It is often relatively easy to find the resources (money, labour, materials and organization) for one big push to build something. It is, however, much more difficult to maintain a truly sustainable system.

The constraints identified as contributing to or causing the failure of water supply, and especially sanitation services, include:

- poor organizational structures in the responsible agency;

- lack of spare parts;

- inappropriate technology;

- lack of trained staff;

- tied funding;

- an absence of career opportunities;

- insufficient funds;

- legal framework problems;

- lack of motivation by sector personnel;

- non-involvement of the users;

- the low profile of operation and maintenance in the sector in general;

- inadequate tariff and collection systems; and,

- negative political interference.

Global challenges

Cities all over the world are facing a range of dynamic global and regional pressures, and difficulties in efficiently and transparently managing ever-scarcer water resources, delivering water supply and sanitation services. There are equal challenges on disposing of wastewater and minimizing negative impacts to the environment. In order to develop solutions to manage urban water more effectively, these global and regional pressures must be recognized and used to drive the design and management processes of urban water systems (Khatri and Vairavamoorthy, 2007).[145]

- Climate change is predicted to cause significant changes in precipitation and temperature patterns, affecting the availability of water and the effectiveness and required capacity of sanitation infrastructure.

- Population growth and urbanization are enforcing rapid changes leading to a dramatic increase in high-quality water consumption. Frequently, this demand for water cannot be satisfied by the locally available water resources, while the discharge of insufficiently treated wastewater increases costs for downstream users and has detrimental effects on the aquatic systems.

- Existing infrastructure is ageing and deteriorating. It is a technological and financial challenge to maintain and upgrade it in such a way that quality water can continue to be delivered to all sectors, and so wastewater can be adequately collected and treated.

Climate change

There is little dispute that the Earth system is undergoing very rapid changes as a result of increased human activities. As a result of these changes it is generally accepted that we have begun to witness changes in the natural cycles at the global scale. Clearly these changes will severely impact the urban water cycle and how we manage it. Components of the urban water cycle, like water supply, wastewater treatment, and urban drainage are generally planned for life spans over several decades. Hence there is a need for us to pay attention to these changes in the context of how these systems will be designed and operated in the 'city of the future'.

⋂ *Waiting at the water well at Natwarghad, India.*

Although the regional distribution is uncertain, precipitation is expected to increase in higher latitudes, particularly in winter. This conclusion extends to the mid-latitudes in most of the General Circulation Model results. Potential evapotranspiration (ET) rises with air temperature. Consequently, even in areas with increased precipitation, higher ET rates may lead to reduced runoff, implying a possible reduction in renewable water supplies. More annual runoff caused by increased precipitation is likely in the high latitudes. In contrast, some lower latitude basins may experience large reductions in runoff and increased water shortages as a result of a combination of increased evaporation and decreased precipitation.

The frequency and severity of droughts could also increase in some areas as a result of a decrease in total rainfall, more fre-

---

145 Khatri, K., and Vairavamoorthy, K. 2007. Challenges for urban water supply and sanitation in the developing countries. *Water for a changing world: Enhancing local knowledge and capacity*, (Symposium, 13–15 June), 50th anniversary, UNESCO-IHE Institute for Water Education, Delft.

quent dry spells, and higher ET. Flood frequencies are likely to increase in many areas, although the amount of increase for any given climate scenario is uncertain and impacts will vary among basins.

Water quality problems may increase where there is less flow to dilute contaminants introduced from natural and human sources. The increase in water temperature will alter the rate of operation of bio-geo-chemical processes (degrading and cleaning) and lower the dissolved oxygen concentration of water. Similarly, the increased occurrence of higher runoff will increases the load of pollutants and the overflowing of sewers. Furthermore, increased flooding frequency with overflow of treated or untreated wastewater sewer systems will seriously affect the biotic life cycle and with a higher possibility of outbreaks of waterborne diseases (such as cryptosporidium presence). The water quality matter may be more sensitive in lakes due to higher incidence of eutrophication process (Hellmuth and Kabat, 2002).[146]

The above impacts are in addition to the obvious impacts of increased risk of damage to stormwater infrastructure and facilities (e.g. underground drains, levee banks, pump stations and so on) due to higher peak flows. There are several other impacts, which we can only guess at the moment, such as an increased risk of pipe failure and collapse due to dry soil conditions.

Climate change will affect different cities in different ways with some experiencing more frequent droughts and water shortage while others will have more intense storm events with subsequent flooding issues. Flexible and adaptable solutions are hence required to reduce the vulnerability of cities to these changes.

Population growth and urbanization

Population growth and urbanization will be one of the world's most important challenges in the next few decades. The United Nations population prospects report (2006)[147] illustrates the higher rate of population growth in urban areas in developing countries. In less developed countries, urban population will grow from 1.9 billion in 2000 to 3.9 billion in 2030, averaging 2.3 per cent per year. On the other hand, in developed countries, the urban population is expected to increase from 0.9 billion in 2000 to 1 billion in 2030, an overall growth rate of 1 per cent (Brockerhoff, 2000).[148]

The numbers and sizes of cities, mostly in developing countries, are increasing due to the higher rate of urbanization. In 1950, New York City and Tokyo were the only two cities with a population of over ten million inhabitants. By 2015, it is expected that there will be twenty-three cities with a population over ten million. Of these, nineteen will be in developing countries. In 2000, there were twenty-two cities with a population of between five and ten million; 402 cities with a population of one to five million; and 433 cities in the 0.5 to one million categories.

Almost 180,000 people are added to the world's urban population each day. It is estimated that there are almost a billion people in poverty in the world; of which over 750 million live in urban areas without adequate shelters and basic services (UN, 2006).[149] Population growth and rapid urbanization will create a severe scarcity of water and will have a tremendous impact on the natural environment. In order to meet future water demand, cities will need to tap their water supply from sources situated far away from the urban area. Moreover, rapid increases in built-up areas disturbs the local hydrological cycle and environment by reducing the opportunity for natural infiltration (because the absorbing land has been sealed, for example by road or car parks), producing rapid peak stormwater flows.

Cities in developing countries are already faced with enormous backlogs in shelter, infrastructure and services as they are confronted by insufficient water supply, deteriorating sanitation and environmental pollution. Larger populations will demand larger proportions of water while simultaneously decreasing the ability of ecosystems to provide more regular and cleaner supplies.

Sustaining healthy environments in the urbanized world of the twenty-first century represents a major challenge for human settlements, development and management. Again, flexible and innovative solutions are needed to cope with sudden and substantial changes in water demand for people and their associated economic activities.

Deterioration of infrastructure systems

In order for the urban water cycle to function effectively, it needs to be supported by appropriate infrastructure in good working condition. Protecting the infrastructure used to treat and transport water (including sources, treatment plants, and distribution systems) is an important step in ensuring the safety of drinking water. However, in most cities worldwide, there has been years of neglected maintenance to water storage, treatment, and distribution systems. Poorly maintained water supply systems can generally be traced to insufficient financial resources and poor management. This deterioration

146 Hellmuth, M. and Kabat, P. 2002. Impacts. In: Appleton, B. (Ed.), *Climate changes the water rules: How water managers can cope with today's climate variability and tomorrow's climate change*. Dialogue on Water and Climate, Delft.

147 Available at: http://www.un.org/esa/population/unpop.htm (Accessed: 25 May 2010).

148 Brockerhoff, M. P. 2000. An Urbanizing World. *Population Bulletin*, A Publication of Population Reference Bureau, Vol.55, No.3, pp.1–45.

149 Available at: http://www.un.org/esa/population/unpop.htm (Accessed: 25 May 2010).

in the water infrastructure threatens the quality and reliability of all water services.

In particular there has been little or no management and maintenance of underground infrastructure. A large proportion of this infrastructure is over one hundred years old, placing it at increased risk for leaks, blockages and malfunctions due to deterioration. For example, water mains break in hundreds of thousands of locations each year in the United States, leaving water customers without a supply, or with a supply that is unsafe for consumption without special treatment (i.e. boiling or chlorination).

The escalating deterioration of water and sewer systems threatens our ability to provide safe drinking water and essential sanitation services for current and future generations. As the pipes crumble and leak, many cities are faced with an expensive water and sewer problem. The longer these problems go unresolved, the more serious they become, placing vital public assets at risk of further degradation and posing an unacceptable risk to human health and the environment, damaging public and private property, and impacting state and local economies.

The cost of rehabilitation of water infrastructure systems is increasing substantially across the world due to their accelerating deterioration. European cities are spending in the order of €5 billion per year on wastewater network rehabilitation. The United Kingdom has over 700,000 kilometres of mains supply and sewer pipes, and is implementing over 35,000 maintenance works per month on these pipes. A 5 per cent reduction in costs there would save over £20 million (Vahala, 2004).[150] In the same way, many of the infrastructure systems in Canada and the United States, worth trillions of dollars, are failing prematurely and are in need of costly repairs. The estimated capital needed for the rehabilitation of main urban water and sewer pipes, older than fifty years and in fifty largest cities of the USA, is more than US$700 billion (Yan & Vairavamoothy, 2003).[151] It will be increased significantly over the coming decades due to the combined effect of infrastructure ageing, urbanization and climate change, and therefore placing a huge burden on future generations.

These deterioration processes are more severe in developing countries, due to ageing of the systems, poor construction practices, little or no maintenance and rehabilitation activities, operation at higher capacity than designed for, and so on. There is little knowledge about specific classes of asset deterioration, the technical service life and insufficient data to know the extent and/or value of their infrastructure assets. Furthermore, there are no efficient decision support tools available to infrastructure managers and decision-makers (Misiunas, 2005).[152]

Infrastructure deterioration will impact public health, environment and institutions, including governments. Higher rates of the water leakage means higher water losses and higher chances of infiltration and exfiltration of water. This will raise the chances of drinking water contamination and the outbreak of waterborne diseases. The frequent breakdown of services, and therefore reduced water service quality and standards, will affect the willingness of consumers to pay water bills.

Conclusion

There is an urgent need for planned action to manage water resources effectively. The problems in urban areas of developing countries are of particular concern as still large sections of the community are living without a safe water supply and basic sanitation services. It has been widely acknowledged that in the past, several urban water interventions (particularly in developing countries) have failed and this has been in part due to little or no attention given to the institutional landscape within which these interventions are applied, and the lack of stakeholder involvement in the development and implementation of these interventions.

The adequate provision of an urban water supply and sanitation is likely to become more difficult in the future due to several change pressures such as urbanization, climate change and infrastructure deterioration. The challenge is to develop appropriate technical and institutional responses to these pressures that radically change the way in which urban water systems are managed. Interventions must be considered over the entire urban water cycle, recognizing interactions between the various components of the urban water system. There must also be a rethink of the way water is used and reused and the greater use of natural systems for treatment (that are likely to be more effective against emerging contaminants). The objective must be to develop urban water systems that are more robust and resilient against these uncertain future pressures.

To achieve this, appropriate engineering innovations and solutions will need to be developed. However, to ensure maximum impact of these innovations and solutions, they must be coupled with components of institutional development (through capacity-building activities), and greater stakeholder involvement, particularly with the engineers and the consumers themselves. Clearly, only if these components are included in the solutions will the process be able to substantially con-

150 Vahala, R. 2004. *European Vision for Water Supply and Sanitation in 2030*. Water Supply and Sanitation Technology Platform.

151 Yan, J. M., and Vairavamoothy, K. 2003. *Fuzzy Approach for the Pipe Condition Assessment*. Paper presented at the ASCE international conference on pipeline engineering and construction, July 13–16, Baltimore, Maryland, USA, 2, p.1817.

152 Misiunas, D. 2005. *Failure Monitoring and Asset condition assessment in water supply systems*. PhD Thesis, Lund University, Lund, Sweden.

tribute to the reduction of vulnerability of cities, and to their capacity and preparedness to cope with global changes.

6.2.2 Environmental health

James R. Mihelcic

Engineering projects do not always produce their intended effects on people's lives; the world is littered with broken down wells and unused latrines. In fact, it is estimated that as many as 60 per cent of the water systems in developing countries are non-operational (Davis and Brikké, 1995).[153] These projects may have been designed and constructed with the best of intentions, but non-technical considerations were not always taken into account. Often, community preferences and habits were ignored and the community had only a token role in the decision-making process. In other situations, initial funds for construction were provided by outside agencies but no realistic plan for supporting operation and maintenance was implemented. Furthermore, the technology selected may not have been appropriate for political, cultural, economic or geographic reasons. In short, it could be argued that these projects focused on the technology rather than on the engineering, which would have to be considered in these issues.

Engineering practice in a development setting requires technical as well as non-technical skills, and it requires an understanding of the dynamic between society, economy and the environment. It must also consider non-traditional principles of carrying capacity, equity and gender. There also needs to be recognition and understanding of the complex, interdependent and dynamic systems that comprise infrastructure that supports water, sanitation, waste disposal and air quality. Such systems also require an appreciation for the social systems, which receive the services.

In the development setting, beneficiaries are often poor and reside in under-developed communities, and the word 'project' encompasses more than the physical structure that is designed and constructed. It includes the social setting where the project is located as well as the people who will operate, manage and benefit from the project. Successful development projects thus need be collectively cared for, viewed as a public asset, and managed for the common good (Ratner and Gutiérrez, 2004).[154]

Applying a life cycle thinking approach can help assess the sustainability of a project. The five life stages of a water and sanitation project in a development setting are: needs assessment, conceptual designs and feasibility, design and action planning, implementation and operation, and maintenance. Furthermore, in the development setting, the pillars of sustainability are best viewed as five aspects: socio-cultural respect, community participation, political cohesion, economic sustainability and environmental sustainability (McConville and Mihelcic, 2007).[155]

It is also important to not separate development from improvements in public health (consider that eight of the sixteen Millennium Development Goal targets are directly related to health). For example, almost one half of the risk that contributes to the environmental burden of disease in the world is associated with poor access to drinking water and sanitation. Much of the other half results from exposure to indoor and urban air pollution. In general terms, Risk = Hazard x Exposure.

In green chemistry, risk is minimized by reducing or eliminating the hazard through use of completely benign materials or chemicals so there is no need to control exposure (Mihelcic and Zimmerman, 2008). In contrast, when considering the risk associated with indoor air pollution from burning solid fuels for cooking and heating, reducing (or eliminating) the exposure may be the preferred pathway to reduce (or eliminate) the risk even if the hazard remains high. This is because in this situation, the economic cost for a household to move up the energy ladder and use a fuel source that reduces the hazard associated with fine particulate matter may not be economically feasible.

Reducing risk in this situation can be accomplished through use of technologies such as more efficient cook stoves or improved ventilation that reduces exposure. Changes in personal behaviour can also reduce exposure but are perhaps the most difficult modification to implement, especially when they involve a practice as commonplace as cooking, watching children, or heating a home. For example, having all non-cooks stay out of the cooking space during cooking appears to be a simple way of reducing exposure, but could be complicated because of the social aspect of conversation between cooks and non-cooks or the care-giving responsibilities of women (Mihelcic et al., 2008).

In terms of solid waste management, it is common for 'scavengers' – the 'informal sector' – to participate in solid waste management activities in developing countries. Scavenging can be viewed as a form of waste processing, similar to 'hand

---

153 Davis, J., and Brikké, F. 1995. Making your water supply work: *Operation and maintenance of small water supply systems*. IRC International Water and Sanitation Centre, The Hague, Netherlands.

154 Ratner, B.D., and Gutiérrez, A. R. 2004. Reasserting community: The social challenge of wastewater management in Panajachel, Guatemala. *Human Organization*, Vol. 63, No.1, pp.47–56.

155 McConville, J.R., and Mihelcic, J.R. 2007. Adapting life-cycle thinking tools to evaluate project sustainability in international water and sanitation development work. *Environmental Engineering Science*, Vol.24, No.7, pp.937–948.

and mechanical separation' processing used in many parts of the world. However, in this case, it is critical that the engineer works with the scavenging community to ensure that their important contribution is maintained while recognizing the need to provide scavengers better access to immunizations, healthcare, education and microenterprise activities (Mihelcic et al., 2008). [156]

Engineered solutions also have a geographical context. For example, it may be that peri-urban residents better understand the need for a project compared to their rural counterparts because of the increased pollution concentration related to the high population density. Beneficiaries in rural and peri-urban locations often determine the need for, and the process to, implement, a project that directly affects them. Thus, rural and peri-urban beneficiaries may be involved in the majority of the project process. However, in urban situations the beneficiaries take on the role of a customer by paying policy-makers and the private sector to meet their needs (Ahrens and Mihelcic, 2006). [157]

Geography is of course also related to climate. For example, materials procurement is made more difficult, not only because of unreliable transportation and illness, but also from harsh weather, seasonal work and holiday calendars. Agriculture follows a strict schedule, so construction projects must incorporate flexibility to accommodate the seasonal calendar (Mihelcic and Zimmerman, 2008) [158] Water availability may also be an important barrier to selecting a particular sanitation technology (Fry et al., 2008). [159]

Lastly, many incommunicable diseases related to risk factors such as being overweight and physical inactivity can be improved by sustainable approaches to engineering. One example is for engineers to provide several mobility options to members of a community that wish to access work, goods, services and education. This means the engineer needs to think beyond personal vehicle use and consider mobility through bicycling, walking, telecommuting or the use of shared public transit and a shared personal vehicle when planning a community.

156 Mihelcic, J.R., L.M. Fry, E.A. Myre, L.D. Phillips and B.D. Barkdoll. 2008. *Field Guide in Environmental Engineering for Development Workers: Water, Sanitation, Indoor Air*, American Society of Civil Engineers (ASCE) Press, Reston, VA.

157 Ahrens, B.T., and Mihelcic, J.R. 2006. Making Wastewater Construction Projects Sustainable in Urban, Rural, and Peri-Urban Areas. *Journal of Engineering for Sustainable Development: Energy, Environment, Health*, Vol.1, No.1, pp.13–32.

158 Mihelcic, J.R., and J.B. Zimmerman. 2008. *Environmental Engineering: Fundamentals, Sustainability, Design*, John Wiley & Sons, New York.

159 Fry, L. M., J.R. Mihelcic and D.W. Watkins. 2008. Water and Nonwater-related Challenges of Achieving Global Sanitation Coverage, *Environmental Science & Technology*, Vol.42, No.12, pp.4298–4304.

6.2.3 Energy

Jorge Spitalnik, Peter Greenwood and Darrel Danyluk

The world will have to bring about a better quality of life to substantial numbers of people by providing access to affordable energy and, at the same time, it will need to mitigate and adapt to climate change. Effective and feasible choices of energy source, energy technology, and end-user efficiency will make a major contribution to addressing this challenge. These choices will have to be made in a transparent and professional manner. Several branches of engineering will play key roles even in the assessment and decision phases of this process.

Two billion people are without access to affordable and clean energy services and as many again are without reliable access. Yet, access to energy is key to achieving all of the Millennium Development Goals. To meet basic human needs, it will be necessary to provide energy for all through access to reliable and affordable energy services, giving particular attention to the urban and rural poor.

Climate change is recognized as a global sustainable development challenge with strong social, economic and environmental dimensions. Climate change is attributed to anthropogenic sources – excessive greenhouse gas emissions from human energy production and consumption.

It is widely acknowledged that existing solutions are not yet sufficient for meeting the world's growing energy needs in a sustainable manner. Though energy technologies are rapidly developing, much work and innovation are still needed to bring about substantial changes in energy for heating, transportation and electricity as well as in energy efficiency, conservation and behaviour. It is essential to change unsustainable patterns of consumption and this will require difficult cultural adjustment in some countries.

Determining the technological, economic and environmental feasibility of an energy option is one of the chief roles asked of the engineering profession. Engineers are actively involved in the development and implementation of technologies used to generate energy; indeed, engineers design, build, operate, maintain and decommission the energy systems of the world. Sustainable energy policies need to conform to realistic and factual conditions; scientifically sound and thoroughly engineered solutions are the only way to address the issues of energy sustainability.

Issues

To meet basic human needs and facilitate achievement of the Millennium Development Goals, it will be necessary to provide energy for all and access to reliable and affordable energy services, giving particular attention to the rural and urban poor.

Energy is crucial for sustainable development. A sophisticated energy mix that employs mature and feasible technologies will be needed in most countries. Ambitious but acceptable limits for greenhouse gas emissions must be managed, calling for ever-greater international cooperation. Priority should be given to exploring carbon sequestration schemes for fossil fuel utilization, ensuring the highest state-of-the-art standards of safety and non-proliferation for nuclear energy, innovation for higher efficiencies of renewable energies, designing compromises for agricultural land usage and population displacement for hydropower and developing technologies for energy efficiency and conservation. Decisions on the use of a given technology that could contribute to sustainable energy development require a thorough analysis of technological and economic feasibility; the technology of a proposed solution should be available at the time the need for it becomes apparent and the energy it provides should be affordable for the majority of the population.

There exists a relationship between quality of life and per capita consumption of energy. Indeed, the Human Development Index shows a close link between increasing quality of life in a given country and an increase in energy use per capita. In general, a high quality of life is currently achieved with a per capita consumption of 100 billion to 150 billion joules of energy. If the countries currently exceeding this level could decrease their energy consumption to within this range, their quality of life would be maintained and global resources would be better preserved and utilized, particularly among countries at different stages of development.

Significant differences exist between developed and developing countries, and energy policies must be very context-specific; they do not translate from one country to another. There is no universal solution for making sustainable energy available globally, but developing countries can learn from the lessons of developed countries. The optimal energy mix for any country will depend on, among others, its available natural resource base, population distribution, predicted growth of energy demand and its engineering and economic capacity. Energy solutions for developed countries are not always adequate in developing countries because, for example, developing countries often see much higher annual growth rates in demand. In developed countries, growth in demand is more stable, at around 1 per cent to 2 per cent per year, than in developing countries where it can reach about 4 per cent to 5 per cent. Add to this the phenomenon of strong urban migration and huge energy needs are being further concentrated in emerging mega-cities. Electricity grids in some developed countries have experienced major national and international failures due to a lack of capacity and investment; even 'stable' rates of energy demand can cause instabilities in energy supply.

Predictions of energy consumption in developed and developing countries show that, in a short space of time, demand for primary energy in developing countries will overtake that of developed countries. Sooner or later this may cause supply disturbances to developed countries, since much of the energy they are exploiting in developing countries will be taken out of the export market to satisfy local demand.

Biofuels (separate from biogas, biomass and so on) have been developing in many countries, usually as fuel additives, to increase energy security, reduce greenhouse gas emissions and stimulate rural development. However, economic, social and environmental issues limit the extent to which these goals can be met with current biofuel technologies; there are serious concerns about whether they do in fact reduce greenhouse gases overall as well as the effect they are having on landuse, biodiversity and food prices. First generation biofuels, such as bioethanol and biodiesel, are only economically competitive with fossil fuels in the most efficient agricultural production markets and under favourable market conditions of high oil prices and low feedstock prices. One of the potential new risks for drylands is growing biofuel crops using unsustainable cultivation practices, leading to accelerated soil erosion and desertification. Growing biofuel crops – using sustainable cultivation practices – on semi-arid and sub-humid lands unsuitable for food production would not compete with food production and could help rehabilitate those lands. A shift towards cellulose-based second generation biofuels, using wood and grassy crops, would offer greater net reductions emissions and use less land, but technical breakthroughs are required. The potential for second generation biofuels that are economically, environmentally and socially sustainable need to be thoroughly researched, involving modern agricultural engineering tools.

Challenges

The main challenges the world is going to face in the near future are centred on the explosion of energy demand, mainly in developing countries, and on the constraints imposed by climate change on greenhouse gases emissions that will need to be drastically abated.

Given that fossil fuels will continue to play a dominant role in the energy mix in the decades to come, the development and use of advanced and cleaner fossil fuel technologies should be increased. Hybrid technologies that use both fossil fuels and other energy sources may become more affordable and feasible on a larger scale.

There is also considerable scope for improving energy efficiency in households, transport and industry. Energy effi-

⌒ *Offshore wind turbines have enormous potential in many parts of the world.*

ciency and economy is fundamental to reducing greenhouse gas emissions, and is increasingly important for the financial economy with the cost of energy rising around the world. Many energy efficient technologies however require the use of more complex and uncommon systems and materials and have long pay-back times; these are important considerations before they can be viable for the population at large.

At present, the cost of energy from renewable and sustainable sources is higher than the cost of energy from non-renewable and unsustainable sources (although this is the subject of debate). Renewable sources (such as solar photovoltaic, wind and hydropower), even without the benefit of economies of scale, are ideal for use in situations where the energy demand is growing slowly or in places far from high-consumption centres. Engineering efforts are currently needed to lower the cost of renewable generation and also to find feasible technologies for renewable energy storage (such as hydrogen fuels cells) and distribution (such as distributed generation for small-scale renewable sources).

In the transportation sector, actions for promoting cleaner fuels and vehicles must be complemented by policies to reduce the overall demand for personal vehicle use, particularly by encouraging public transport. Modifying unsustainable transportation energy consumption patterns will require politically difficult cultural adjustments.

There is great urgency to design and implement measures for both mitigation and adaptation towards unavoidable climate change effects, including upgrading infrastructure to withstand the impacts of extreme weather events and 'climate proofing' of new projects. Development, deployment and diffusion of low-carbon energy technologies, together with energy efficiency, renewable energy and cleaner and advanced technologies for energy supply, will require intense engineering ingenuity.

Industrial development requires secure, sustainable energy and this specifically applies to the economics of developing countries. Energy efficiency is to be considered indispensable to enhancing industrial development. For addressing the serious problem of urban air pollution as well as problems of climate change, the use of cleaner energy technologies and renewable energy will be essential. Ensuring industrial competitiveness requires building the required infrastructure, including the energy supply, transport availability, trained manpower and environmental regulatory systems. Special capacity-building efforts will be required to provide engineering professionals with up-to-date knowledge on the diverse technologies for sustainable energy generation.

Engineering and civil society

Society and decision-makers must realize that analysis of the feasibility and the technological availability of energy options is necessary in any technical and engineering issue.

There is no uniform treatment for solving globally sustainable energy problems. Recognition of technical facts related to the development situation of different countries is required to achieve realistic and sustainable energy solutions.

Energy options to solve problems of sustainable development cannot be selected on the basis of doctrine or ideology. Scientifically sound and thoroughly engineered solutions are the only way to address the problems of energy sustainability.

The engineering profession is continuously generating new knowledge and adapting to new challenges. The engineering profession is, every day, anticipating, planning and preparing for these challenges. However, better engagement is still needed with civil society in general, industry and, in particular, all levels of government to respond to the energy challenges facing humankind.

6.2.4 Transportation

Tony Ridley

Transport is the movement of people and goods from multiple origins to multiple destinations by whatever means. It includes walking and cycling, shipping, pipelines and air, as well as wheeled transport. But addressing transport problems goes beyond considering the technology of transport.

All people desire access to people, activities and the resources necessary to lead a fulfilled life; access that is affordable, safe, secure, comfortable and convenient. Furthermore, no one wants to be adversely affected by other people's use of transport. Transport systems could be much better, providing greater enjoyment and quality of life to more people, with less environmental impact and far fewer deaths and injuries.

Hardy Cross was a great twentieth century American Professor of Civil Engineering and an engineering philosopher. Prof. Cross considered engineering to be part of a trilogy; pure science, applied science and engineering (Cross, 1952).[160] This trilogy is only part of a triad of trilogies into which engineering fits. The first is pure science, applied science and engineering. The second is economic theory, finance and engineering, and the third is social relations, industrial relations and engineering. Many engineering problems are as closely allied to social problems as they are to pure science. The limitations of academic classifications are notorious; the workaday world does not fit into an academic department or into so-called fields of learning. We need to consider the whole person, and the whole community in which they live and work.

Those who work in engineering are likely to find themselves in contact with almost every phase of human activity. Not only must engineers make important decisions about the mere mechanical outline of structures and machines, they are also confronted with the problems of human reactions to the environment and are constantly involved in problems of law, economics and sociology. Herein lies the challenge and the complexity of transport. Meanwhile, people and goods are travelling more, further and faster. Indeed, there is increasing concern for 'carbon miles' created by the consumption of products from around the world. My father, for example, first travelled from Northeast England to London in 1924, sailing to the Thames as a passenger on a coal boat. I first travelled to London, by car with my parents, at the age of 14. My youngest son, Michael, had already travelled twice around the world by air by the time he was 12 years old when we lived in Hong Kong.

Transport is therefore enormously complex. At any time in a transport network there is a balance between demand and supply, strongly influenced by price. Demand is influenced by a whole series of determinants: population, employment, land-use patterns, wealth and so on. As demand rises asymptotically towards capacity the flow of movement slows down and, more importantly, reliability deteriorates rapidly.

The word 'network' is central. Theoreticians carry out intricate mathematical calculations to describe the flow along a single traffic artery. Such calculations are further compounded when the moving vehicles do not have uniform behaviour characteristics and the capacity of the artery is not an absolute number. This is certainly true of roads, but also applies to rail and air transport. In terms of efficiency, and customer satisfaction, there are great advantages in finding a balance in which satisfied demand (flow) at any point in a network is within capacity by a sufficient margin to avoid congestion and to enable reliable operation. The theory of networks is a branch of applied mathematics in its own right, showing enormous complexities even when the flow of traffic can be assumed to be uniform. It can be imagined what is involved when the demand characteristics of people and goods are also taken into account, together with somewhat elastic measures of capacity and complex pricing mechanisms.

Governments must develop and implement transport strategies, not least to provide the leadership and framework within which private companies, entrepreneurs, private funding and public authorities can deliver transport services, whatever they may be. Transport strategies, also, must be clear to the entire public whether motorist, pedestrian or passenger, and whether young or old; or those working in transport, whether as a developer, contractor, financier, traffic engineer or retailer. It is vital to ensure that everyone understands that compromises are necessary. Mobility without regard for environmental protection is no more satisfactory than environmental protection without regard to the contribution of transport to quality of life.

Electronic and information technology has the possibility to transform our use of transport systems, to save lives and money, and to protect the environment. The speed of vehicles could be regulated to ensure the safety of other road users. Such control would make a major contribution to the safety of pedestrians. Much is rightly said about the divide between the rich and the poor, but worldwide, one of the greatest divides is between those inside and outside of automobiles. Transport engineers need to strive to bring safety standards on the roads towards what is achieved by public transport and air transport. Doing so would provide a boost for walking and cycling. Also, manufacturers have made major investments that are now producing automobiles with much improved fuel consumption and also reduced emissions, which is of particular

160 Cross, Hardy. 1952. *Engineers and Ivory Towers.* New York: ryci.

importance in urban areas as recent publicity about problems in developing countries, not least in Chinese cities, has been highlighted.

Actual and potential innovations in transport technology

Technology can greatly increase the capacity of roads. On main roads, convoy driving systems could be operated by automatic control over vehicle speed and direction. By these means we would significantly increase the capacity of the road system. It is also becoming increasingly possible to manage demand for road transport by the use of road user pricing, such as has been developed for Singapore and London.

Technology is increasingly being used to inform bus passengers about waiting times, and to provide dial-a-ride systems. The use of navigation systems is becoming rapidly more common in freight distribution systems, to monitor vehicle position and delivery time prediction, and for route choice guidance. Technological development is also making it increasingly possible to introduce cashless ticketing systems for public transport.

One of the most important contributions of technology to transport is the rate of cost reduction of components. Thus, cost should not be the constraint that it is in many cases of infrastructure building.

Material science is developing rapidly. New materials open the possibility for lighter, stronger, safer structures. In transport, lightweight brings the benefit of reduced energy consumption and hence reduced emission of pollutants. Materials are also being developed that work at higher temperatures, allowing power systems to convert more of the available energy into motion.

But materials must also be practical in use. Invention is not sufficient. History has many examples of failed technology, where performance gains were outweighed by maintenance or reliability problems. However there are a series of technology developments that hold out hope for all forms of transport,

© Wikimedia - Alex Needham

whether by road, rail, air or other means: self-monitoring materials by the inclusion of optical fibres in bridge or other structures; self-repairing materials; intelligent materials that have been developed by examining how dolphins and sharks are able to eliminate eddies and encourage smooth low-drag laminar flow; biodegradable materials; nano-fibres; high-strength metal alloys; super-conducting materials; and bio-engineered materials that are likely to produce significant advances for disabled people.

Manufacturers have made major investments that are now producing automobiles with much improved fuel consumption and also with reduced emissions, as previously mentioned.

The railway industry is working hard to maintain its reputation for environmental friendliness through pollution reduction and by regenerative braking, whereby the waste of energy invested in vehicle motion with ordinary braking systems is able to recycle, and thus save energy.

The energy efficiency of large marine diesels and gas turbines can exceed 30 per cent. Further improvements could be achieved with combined-cycle systems that use the waste heat

⋒ The Shanghai Airport Maglev Train is the world's fastest commercial train.

In transport, it is essential to have an understanding of the following propositions:

- transport is essentially concerned with the movement of people and goods, rather than of vehicles;

- transport is now a major environmental issue;

- transport policy should be founded on a statement of social and economic policies ;

- governments must develop, or ensure that others develop, strategic/corporate plans;

- congested and poorly coordinated transport systems are approaching a state of emergency;

- transport is, in general, too cheap;

- travel demand overall is increasing at a rate substantially faster than the capacity to absorb it;

- no major decisions on landuse should be taken without regard to the transport implications, and vice-versa;

- urban areas provide much of a county's wealth and the source of much of the growth of GDP;

- good transport is a necessary, but not sufficient, condition for urban development or regeneration;

- adequate access for freight is essential to the well-being of urban areas;

- the country, and in particular urban areas, must make the most of whatever transport infrastructure exists at any one time;

- such physical infrastructure as is justified should be put in place as expeditiously as possible;

- managerial efficiency and accountability requires transport provision by small rather than large units; and

- transport should not be the preserve of either the public sector or the private sector alone.

Transport engineering

Transport engineering can be described in terms of various characteristics: capacity, cost, demand, regularity, reliability, safety and supply. Its customers have various characteristics: age, gender, wealth, car ownership, and there are a wide variety of types of freight to be moved. A significant part of the skill and training of an engineer is having knowledge of engineering materials. The transport engineer has to deal with perhaps the most difficult material of all – the human being. Transport is conventionally, and perhaps unhappily, divided by mode: bus, rail, road, sea, air, and may also be described in terms of infrastructure and equipment such as aircraft, bridges, automobiles, signalling, tunnels and trains.

Transport is about more than technology, but what about technology? A great amount of engineering research and development is focused on improving transport, and minimizing its impact on the environment, particularly the use of electronic and information technology, materials and energy.

in the exhaust stream to power a steam turbine. In fast vessels, weight acts as a constraint. Reducing hull drag and increasing the efficiencies of propellers will make valuable contributions to energy consumption.

Aviation gas turbines can approach efficiencies of 40 per cent, and further improvements may come from raising operating temperatures through the use of ceramic components. Propulsive efficiencies of engines can be improved by using high bypass ratios with large diameter fans, and improvements in fuel consumption may be possible. Eliminating skin turbulence can, in theory, reduce total aircraft drag by up to 40 per cent. Air pollution from gas turbine emissions could be further reduced by using low sulphur fuels and introducing catalysts within the combustion chamber.

○ *The Tata Nano puts car ownership within reach of millions more in India.*

© CCBYSA - Wikimedia - Nikkul

Transport solutions must take a holistic approach to transport problems in future. Debate about single solutions makes no contribution to the problems of transport, which is, by its very nature, systemic and must be integrated. For example, there is far too much debate in many countries about road versus rail, or about demand restraint versus increasing capacity. Singapore perhaps provides a good example of the correct approach: urban railways, modern buses, demand management, effective transport interchanges, road building (including urban roads in tunnels) and landuse planning in partnership with transport planning. Transport developments will require good science and the full participation of politicians and industrialists. But, ultimately it is the engineer who will deliver progress.

6.2.5 Communications

Yixin Zhong

Communication Engineering is about implementing technologies that support information sharing and information exchange, conveniently and globally. Information Engineering concerns systems that support data and communication services, covering information collection, processing, storage and utilization, and so on.

The integration of communication and information engineering has led to a new generation of infrastructure and the emergence of the 'information society'. Such infrastructure can be seen as a huge and advanced platform for performing many of the required functions for intellectual activities, as outlined in Figure 1.

From this, we can begin to recognize the potential of communication and information engineering to provide humans with technologies that may be as intelligent as human beings themselves. At present, however, the full value of communication and information engineering is yet to be realized and there remains significant potential for discovery in this exciting area of engineering.

The capabilities that communications and information engineering currently provides us with includes almost anything related to the social and economic development such as weather forecasting, e-commerce, e-governance, healthcare, environmental monitoring and protection, disaster warnings, quality control, education and learning, research activities, enhancement of sports, contributions to culture, community development, and so on. New communication and information technologies have a particularly important role to play in situations where more traditional means of communication are impossible. A typical example of this might be found in a response to an emergency situation, where the capability

Figure 1: **The integration of communication and information engineering**

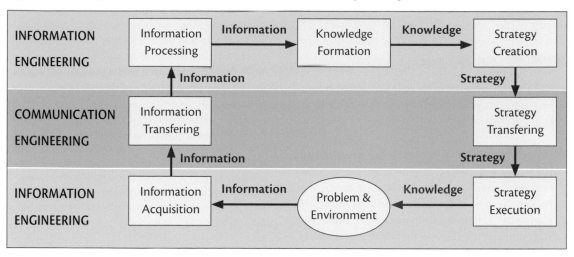

provided by communication and information engineering reduced the loss of life; in Southern and Eastern China, a disaster situation emerged in early 2008 caused by an extremely heavy snowstorm where most forms of transportation, such as railways, roads and air, were impossible, but mobile communications were still effective.

Communication and information engineering is now facing at least three grand challenges, involving technological, economic and ethical issues:

First, the technology itself is not yet mature enough, and the applications and services it can provide are far from being intelligent. Scientific research to address this challenge, particularly in the fields of artificial intelligence and enhanced networks, is being conducted around the world.

Second, any technology may be viewed as a double-edged sword. Whilst providing many good capabilities to societies, technology can also introduce severe problems as it does not discriminate with respect to its use. The Internet provides typical examples as it acts as a convenient platform for both rapid information sharing, exchange and expression, and for criminal activities and abuses. To successfully address this challenge, not only must Internet technologies become practically more secure, but an effort must be made when considering the wider ethical issues surrounding the platform (for example, the work of the Internet Governance Forum).

The third grand challenge, and perhaps the most serious, is from an economic and ethical dimension. The successful capabilities provided by communication and information engineering have led many countries into a 'knowledge society', reinforcing a high level of economic activity and a high standard of living. The rest of the world, however, are agricultural or industrializing societies that cannot develop quickly enough,

even to keep pace with the technology available. This difference is referred to as the 'Digital Divide' or 'Information Divide' as well as the 'Knowledge Divide'. The response to this challenge must go beyond simply transferring the technologies, or even the skills needed for such technologies, and economic and even cultural assistance is essential.

6.2.6 Asset, reliability and maintenance management

Yousef Ibrahim[161]

Maintenance and asset management is a multidisciplinary area that focuses on technical and administrative activities intended to ensure equipment or infrastructure is kept in a good operational state. Most large corporations and organizations are keen to enhance performance by investing in maintenance management, partly because a great deal can be achieved at limited cost. Asset management and maintenance need to be viewed as revenue generating and productive activities, rather than costs to be borne. Maintenance should also be viewed as a significant factor in enhancing the life cycle performance and productivity of equipment and infrastructure. Enhanced asset management and maintenance practice and culture is particularly required in helping least developed countries to counter problems of key equipment and infrastructure downtime and disrepair.

Traditionally, maintenance has been treated as a running cost or cost overhead, in terms of cost of maintenance, rather than cost of lost production and lost reputation. A measure of the

---

161 This material is abridged from the UNESCO Toolkit on Management of Maintenance by Yousef Ibrahim, Monash University, Melbourne, Australia, UNESCO, 2006, with additional input by Tony Marjoram.

effectiveness of maintenance practice, linking performance to maintenance, is useful in advocacy for maintenance. This is the purpose of Life Cycle Cost (LCC) and Life Cycle Profit (LCP) analysis. Terotechnology – the 'science of maintenance' from the Greek word *terin* meaning to guard or look after – links the specification, design, production, installation, operation and maintenance of equipment to life cycle analysis, and financial and economic factors to facilitate the more effective management of maintenance.

The focus here is on the need for the enhancement of asset, reliability and maintenance management, and the promotion of a culture of maintenance. The importance of maintenance management in terms of economics as well as technology will be presented in an introduction to maintenance engineering, together with a historic review of the field of 'terotechnology' – the science of looking after physical assets in the context of life cycle costs (LCC) that combines engineering, management, economics and finance. Reference will also be made to maintenance policy, planning and strategy for action, and the relationship between terotechnology and management, design and accountancy, and the costs of providing maintenance, compared to the costs of not providing maintenance – of downtime. The use of Reliability Analysis techniques is also discussed, as well as techniques of Total Productive Maintenance (TPM) and maintenance performance indices, and their impact on maintenance practice. The presentation concludes with a discussion of benchmarking and best practice in maintenance performance.

Maintenance management

Since the Industrial Revolution, maintenance has evolved through four main phases:

- First phase: up to the 1940s and the Second World War when there was less equipment that was less complex, often over-designed and more easily repairable by less qualified staff such that downtime was less critical, with less need for systematic maintenance and a 'if it ain't broken then don't fix it' approach.

- Second phase: during and after the Second World War there was an increase in mechanization, complexity and cost of machines and equipment, which was less over-designed, requiring more trained and systematic maintenance. Downtime became more critical and the cost of maintenance increased, as did the interest in preventive maintenance, maintenance planning and control systems to maximize asset performance and lifespan.

- Third phase: began in the 1970s with the increasing awareness of the complexity of asset management and interest in life cycle costs and terotechnology, including specifications, design and reliability of equipment and infrastructure.

- Fourth phase: from the mid-1980s when a change in maintenance culture took place in response to the increasing complexity of assets and asset management, with increasing expectations of better equipment and infrastructure quality, reliability, lifespan, efficiency and safety, with lower environmental impact. New techniques such as Total Productive Maintenance (TPM) and Reliability-Centred Maintenance (RCM) were developed, particularly in Japan (for example with the Toyota Production System), in response to expectations of quality, cost and reliability.

In the development of maintenance management, the following fields of interest and terminology quickly developed (some of which are familiar when one reads reports of crashes and catastrophic failures of equipment and infrastructure):

- Definitions of reliability and maintainability.

- Concepts relating to failure and modes of failure.

- Classification of failure by cause.

- Classification of failure by suddenness.

- Classification of failure by degree.

- Occurrence of failure.

- Mean life.

- Meant time to failure.

- Mean time between failures.

Maintenance costs and the life cycle approach

The Life Cycle Cost and terotechnology concepts underpin modern maintenance management and operate on the premise that every product or project, from concept to completion, has associated and changing costs that can be analysed in real time and used as part of a powerful management decision-making technique. Apart from maintenance and management, the concept of LCC and terotechnology also underpins management decisions relating to design, production, organizational performance and profitability.

In terms of maintenance economics, the costs of providing maintenance services consist of the direct costs of labour, materials/spares and overheads. The indirect costs relating to not providing maintenance services consist of downtime costs of unused labour, depreciation and other fixed operating costs, lost production, contracts and reputation, which may be significantly higher. One of the constraints facing maintenance management in companies and organizations relates to budgetary allocations and planning. The main running costs relate to the operating budget, whereas the acquisition and maintenance of equipment and infrastructure usually relate to the capital budget. In many situations the maintenance budget is regarded as a lesser priority, especially at times of economic downturn, even though this may be a false economy in the longer term. This may be countered to some degree by the use of better cost reporting of maintenance and the use of 'Z Charts' of maintenance cost information that compensate for annual fluctuations.

In a case study of a typical sugar milling industry consisting of four mills in a developing country it is estimated that approximately 25 per cent of costs are attributable to maintenance-related activities, mainly on labour costs. The company has no control over the price of sugar, so its ability to survive mainly depends on operational efficiency and the containment of cost, and fall particularly on the cost of maintenance. Maintenance activities in the four mills suffered as a result of this neglect, with maintenance activities depending mainly on the skill and inventiveness of maintenance staff at each mill; recalling to memory the 'smell of an oily rag' portrayals of the operation of ageing machines and technology in the film world. In this case, a lack of management interest was reflected in the lack of any systematic approach and absence of maintenance records. With an asset value of US$6 million, direct maintenance at the four mills cost around US$10 million per year. Indirect costs not only increased the costs of production, but also reduced total output due to wastage, and lead to lost income to the mills, the sugar cane farmers, industry, and export income and credibility. A planned and systematic approach to maintenance could have considerably reduced these losses and costs, and at less overall cost.

In an interesting study on the culture of maintenance for sustainable development in Tanzania, it was reported that the efficient and effective maintenance of production and infrastructure facilities in Tanzania and similar economies is rooted in a broad-based social appreciation of the value of the facilities in question.[162] They also identified a major challenge facing development in such economies as the need to instil, nurture, upgrade, enhance and maintain a set of social and cultural attitudes, beliefs and empowerment that attach value, significance and importance of, and care for, public and private equipment and infrastructure. This is seen as the key to efficient and effective maintenance, which in turn forms an essential condition for long-term competitiveness and sustainable development.

Maintainability and reliability

While maintenance relates to the actions required to keep equipment and infrastructure in an effective operational condition, the maintainability of equipment and infrastructure is defined by its ability to be maintained. The maintainability of equipment and infrastructure is primarily a design factor, but importantly also relates to maintenance, operability and performance, and also importantly to the human factor. Design

factors for maintainability include design specifications and materials. Maintenance factors include the ease and regularity of maintenance of the equipment required. Human factors include required skills, training and experience. Maintainability relates to the costs of downtime and labour. Maintainability requires planning in the context of design, human and system conditions and requirements. Important issues and challenges for engineering in international development relate to the maintainability of equipment and infrastructure in differing conditions of climate, available skills and maintenance resources, and in turn relate to technological appropriateness and choice, and the modes of technology transfer.

Reliability relates to the ability and probability of success of equipment and infrastructure to perform required functions under stated conditions and periods of time. The reliability of equipment relates to quality and is an important consideration for maintenance management, in so far as it is expected that better quality items are more reliable and will need less maintenance; the question then being one of balance between cost and desired reliability. Apart from quality, factors affecting reliability include production methods, operation and maintenance techniques. Reliability may be observed, assessed, extrapolated or predicted, and is the subject of mathematical analysis. Reliability-Centred Maintenance (RCM) was introduced in the late 1960s in the reliability-critical aviation industry, and has now become standard practice in many other industries. RCM focuses on system functions, function failures and consequences of failure, from which information is then used to determine appropriate maintenance tasks and procedures.

There are several techniques used in reliability analysis, the most widely used being Failure Mode, Effects and Criticality Analysis (FMECA) and Fault Tree Analysis (FTA). FMECA is the most widely used technique and is based on hardware and

The Huguenot Tunnel under construction outside Cape Town.

162 Bavu, I. K., Sheya, M. S., Mlawa, H. M., and Kawambwa, S. J. 1997. *Culture of Maintenance For Sustainable Development in Tanzania*, Institute of Technology Management, Dar es Salaam, Tanzania.

function failure analysis, both quantitative and non-quantitative, with failure modes classified according to the severity of effect. Fault Tree Analysis is a more basic form of troubleshooting to identify and localize faults in systems and equipment. Fault tree analyses are often presented as block diagrams and should be familiar with readers of motor car and consumer equipment manuals. Reliability is sometimes presented in terms of common modes of failure, material and non-material failure.

Improving maintenance management

The functions and activities of maintenance managers and engineers varies in companies, organizations and countries, in terms of economic, social and cultural conditions, climate, available skills and maintenance resources, and what is expected of maintenance management and engineering in terms of maintenance planning, organization, services and standards. Total Productive Maintenance (TPM) is an operational philosophy and methodology to enhance and optimize maintenance performance and efficiency. The main goals are to eliminate breakdowns, quality defects and losses due to set-up and adjustment, idling and minor stoppages, start-up and shutdown, reduced speed and capacity. The overall goal of TPM is to improve equipment and infrastructure efficiency and effectiveness, to improve performance, products and reliability, reduce costs, and enhance teamwork and job satisfaction.

The most important factors for the management of maintenance include maintenance scheduling and planning and the development of key performance indicators (KPIs) to monitor, evaluate and promote effective maintenance. KPIs need to have clear strategic objectives that are closely connected to core business or organizational goals, aimed at promoting success and to facilitate solutions to potential problems. KPIs, like maintenance, need to become part of a business or organizational culture. Planning indicators are useful for monitoring the efficiency of maintenance planning, and 'Maintenance

Ratios' are a useful way to present maintenance costs compared to other indicators such as the value of assets, sales and labour costs, or to compare the hours spent on maintenance with other hourly indicators.

A strategy of continuous improvement should be a cornerstone of maintenance management, and monitoring, evaluation and benchmarking are crucial factors in this activity. Benchmarking is the use of external reference for comparison to improve internal practice. KPIs are an important part of this process. Critical benchmarking factors include clear communication and understanding of staff of the role and importance of benchmarking, the linking of maintenance to performance and productivity, participation in the benchmarking process and effective implementation of results and follow-up. Benchmarking should obviously be between similar equipment, industries or infrastructure, and make allowances for differences. Steps in the benchmarking process include identifying what to benchmark, development of a benchmarking plan and choice of data to collect, choice of external references for comparison, collection of data, comparison of processes and recommendations for improvement, implementation of recommendations and recalibration of benchmarks.

Benchmarking is also useful to understand one's own activity or organization and how it works, in comparison with similar activities and organizations, in developing and implementing improvements, monitoring and evaluating results. Efficiencies gained and savings made are significant justifying and motivating factors for benchmarking and the importance of maintenance, and helps plant the seed of organizational and cultural change among staff and management.

6.2.7 Infrastructure development in developing countries

Arvind K. Poothia

The development of infrastructure required to support large populations in developing countries is lagging far behind the rate of urbanization. It is necessary to focus on integrated infrastructure development, which in turn requires a capacity-based approach to planning. The need is for the creation of modern infrastructure systems for energy, water, waste management, sanitation, drainage, transport and habitat in informal urban settlements in developing countries, while learning from the mistakes of developed countries in order to take a sustainable and affordable approach.

The transformation of land to meet housing needs should be on the basis of anticipated growth patterns and environmental constraints, supported by enabled investment and technology choice. This requires the application of sustainable

ⵔ *Concrete bridge in serious need of maintenance.*

© SAICE

technologies and, often, changes in the governing regulations; infrastructure development, economic development and environment are interdependent and, therefore, policies for infrastructure development need to be approached on the basis of all these considerations. Furthermore, the need for improving infrastructure in developing countries calls for a new scientific approach and techno-economic regime for solutions that can be implemented in these resource-poor countries.

The following broad areas might be considered when working towards ensuring proper infrastructure development in developing countries:

- **Planning and policy-making:** Policies for integrated infrastructure development have to be formulated by governments. Environmental impacts on ecology and water supplies and the long-term effects need to be understood. There is a need for multi-level planning to counter the ill-effects of urban growth (such as regional imbalances and informal settlement growth, and so on). The urban local bodies need to be strengthened further so as to generate capability to stimulate new growth centres with sufficient employment opportunities, and to plan for the process of urbanization. Strong institutional mechanisms as well as sound strategies for resource mobilization and investment are needed.

- **Providing employment and services in rural areas:** There is a need for generation of employment opportunities in the rural areas to eradicate poverty. Investments have to be made in agricultural as well as non-agricultural activities in rural areas in order to help address the inequalities between the rural and urban areas. Services that should be provided should prioritize water and sanitation, public transport, health centres, telecommunication facilities, improved access to governance structures, schools, vocational training centres, and economic facilitators such as cooperatives, local generation of distributed energy, and so on.

- **Transportation in urban areas:** Transportation is a key requirement for trade. Proper transport planning allows for the provision of an efficient and affordable transport system accessible by all communities, as well as pollution minimization and energy conservation. An integrated multi-modal transport system needs to be developed in many 'mega-cities', along with other feeder transport services to rural areas.

- **Technology intervention and knowledge networks:** The world is experiencing rapid technological innovation and there is need for disseminating knowledge between countries. A mechanism for international joint observation of infrastructure development would ensure the dissemination of knowledge and capabilities that allows lessons to be learned from projects around the world, and would raise awareness for the need for investment in infrastructure for the needs of the interdependent, globalized economy.

- **Development of financial infrastructure:** To attract Foreign Direct Investment (FDI) in the infrastructure sector, a mechanism has to be evolved to help build confidence in the durability of agreements entered into by governments, particularly since many major infrastructure projects by international institutions are seen to have failed. National capital pools need to be created for financing training and education of local bodies and technical and financial management, and to handle the difficult issues of land tenure.

The World Federation of Engineering Organizations' Committee on Engineering and the Environment (WFEO-CEE) enables the global engineering profession to address the United Nations Millennium Development Goals through the development, application and enhanced understanding of sustainable engineering practices, the adaption of infrastructure to the impacts of a changing climate, and through mitigating the risks of natural disasters.

6.2.8   Infrastructure Report Cards

Kevin Wall and Sam Amod

Infrastructure report cards: international practice

One of the earliest report cards on infrastructure was produced in the United States of America in 1988 by their National Council on Public Works Improvement. Ten years later the American Society of Civil Engineers (ASCE) took over the reins and produced the first *Report Card on America's Infrastructure*. Since then, they have produced updates in 2001, 2003, and the most recent in 2005. The reports have gradually become more detailed and broader in scope so that now reports are produced by the State and, in some instances, by the county.

In 2006, flowing from the 2005 report, ASCE produced an action plan appealing to Congress for such actions as establishing a National Commission on Infrastructure, increasing funding for specific improvements and, most notably, promoting certain Acts that are presumably under consideration by the legislators. The ASCE initiative is well funded and is an integral part of the lobbying process that is so much a part of American public participation culture, as the following excerpt testifies:

Congested highways, overflowing sewers and corroding bridges are constant reminders of the looming crisis that jeopardizes our nation's prosperity and our quality of life. With new grades for the first time since 2001, our nation's infrastructure has shown little to no improvement since receiving a collective

D+ in 2001, with some areas sliding toward failing grades. The American Society of Civil Engineers' 2005 Report Card for America's Infrastructure assessed the same 12 infrastructure categories as in 2001, and added three new categories.

In the United Kingdom, *State of the Nation* reports have been published annually since 2000. The Institution of Civil Engineers (ICE) has also progressively elaborated their product to regional reports and they have made their grading more sophisticated by incorporating trends and sustainability aspects. In his launch of the 2006 Report, ICE President Gordon Masterton stated:

'We need to start answering the questions posed in this report. How do we intend to reconcile rising demand for water with dwindling resources? Where is our electricity going to come from in the future? How can we stop our rubbish piling up on landfill sites? How do we tackle congestion on our roads and railways?

To accomplish this transformation would require changes to the law to simplify planning processes, and joined-up government with the vision to see the necessity and economic benefit of long-term infrastructure improvements. And it would need the public to be made aware that improvement programmes, that could disrupt their daily lives, will reward them, their children and generations to come.'

Engineers Australia produced a national Infrastructure Report Card in three categories in 1999 (roads, rail and water), and in 2003 and 2005 increased this to seven categories. They have also subsequently produced State and Territory report cards.

In these cases, the intention has been for engineering professionals to provide a public opinion on the condition of infrastructure in the manner of 'expert witness'. The reception to these publications has invariably been sensationalist by the media, and the reaction from much of the public sector has usually ranged from critical to denial.

South Africa

Kevin Wall and Sam Amod

Introduction

Late in 2006, the South African Institution of Civil Engineering (SAICE) released the first ever report card of the state of engineering infrastructure in South Africa. This report highlighted 'the observations of the professionals responsible for the planning, construction, operation and maintenance of our nation's life-support system.' It graded infrastructure (water, sanitation, solid waste, roads, airports, ports, rail, electricity and hospitals and clinics) on a scale from A+ through E-. Overall, it gave South Africa's infrastructure a D+ grade.

The report aimed to inform the public about the importance of infrastructure in their daily social and economic intercourse by highlighting its current condition. Furthermore, many decision-makers are technical lay-people. The report would enable better informed decisions to be made, especially regarding maintenance management and planning for new expenditure.

The publication of this first edition of the *Infrastructure Report Card for South Africa* was, by any measure, very successful and exceeded all expectations. Indeed, the report card received media coverage that exceeded SAICE's highest expectations. In addition, invitations were received from government departments and others for SAICE to engage with them in order to address issues raised in the report card. The exposure received by SAICE was the greatest it had received for many years, if not ever, all of it overwhelmingly positive. The credibility of the institution as a learned society with the authority, indeed the duty, to comment broadly on engineering infrastructure had been enhanced.

Infrastructure is a public asset. Well-maintained infrastructure underpins quality of life and economic development. All South Africans have a stake in its upkeep and operation, and all South Africans share in the expense of its construction and its ongoing maintenance. If maintenance is inadequate, social and economic growth in South Africa will be impeded, and hence the human development of the country will be reduced. The report and its subsequent versions are intended as an instrument to contribute to better-informed decisions for infrastructure development and maintenance. The purpose of the report card was to draw the attention of government, and of the public at large, to the importance of maintenance, and to factors underlying the state of repair of infrastructure – factors such as skills and finance, for example.

The report has intentionally not commented on the legacy that gave South Africa its imbalanced infrastructure distribution. Since the advent of democracy in 1994, huge strides have been made by the government to correct this balance. Ambitious plans have been made and implemented. Drinking water, sanitation, energy and transportation access have received focused attention, and – acting on its mandate – the government is continuing to invest at a rapid pace in infrastructure for disadvantaged communities.

The report has also not highlighted the stated intentions of many agencies to improve infrastructure in the future. After decades of decline, construction and infrastructure provision seem set for decades of growth, with construction forming the fastest growing sector of the economy. Construction also generates more jobs per rand spent than almost any other sector of the economy. It is imperative that we do not continue to build only to permit decay. On the contrary, adequate budgets and maintenance management plans are required for existing and new additions to the infrastructure asset base.

The answers to many issues posed in the report are neither simple nor easy. All the more reason for the public to be better informed about the serious decisions that must be taken about our infrastructure and, where appropriate, to change our behaviour.

The role of civil (and all) engineering professionals as creators and custodians of all aspects of infrastructure has been placed at centre stage. The impact has been to raise the awareness of the public, parents, learners, educators and government to the urgency of the crisis (for example, in terms of the importance of the education of engineering practitioners).

Whereas the state of South Africa's public sector infrastructure has for some while been under the spotlight, there is now broad recognition that SAICE has provided the first national-scale credible benchmark against which progress (or not) can in future years be measured. There is broad consensus that the initiative should be sustained and extended, but that at the same time the independence of the benchmarking process should not be compromised. The new *Infrastructure Report Card* will entail an even more rigorous process, with greater consultation and finer definition of the process and particularly of the grading.

Shortages

Two key themes run as a thread through all the grades:

- the extreme shortage of engineering skills and the impact of this on planning, procurement, design, construction and care of infrastructure; and

- the lack of adequate funding for the maintenance of the existing asset base and the new assets that come on-stream each day.

The consequences of inadequate maintenance are severe, affecting the quality of life and even the very lives of people, through outbreaks of waterborne disease, reduced safety on roads and rail, inconvenience and inefficient commercial activity. The allocation of maintenance funding is often thought generous at 4 per cent of capital cost per annum. However, such allocation is rare. Moreover, it is simply not sufficient, especially when it is expected to cater for a maintenance debt that usually requires upgrading, repair or refurbishment. Roads maintenance that is delayed for one year could cost three to six times more when undertaken a year or so later.

South Africa suffers an acute skills shortage in the infrastructure sector. Just two illustrations should highlight how serious these shortages are, making clear the case for transformation:

- A recent survey by SAICE showed that more than one-third of all 231 local municipalities did not have a single civil engineer, technologist or technician. Vacancies in local government for engineering practitioners exceed 1,000, a figure which is not improving.

○ *Mine, extract crystals, South Africa.*

While the link between engineering infrastructure and economic growth may be clear, it is not always clear that a similar link exists with social health. It is obvious though that cleaner drinking water, proper sanitation, better shelter, access to transport and electricity, all improve the quality of life. To millions in South Africa quality may be equated with viability. Indeed, SAICE research indicates that, in general, developing countries have more doctors than engineers, whereas the opposite is true in developed countries. The reason is obvious: proper infrastructure prevents disease and sickness. It is concerning then that South Africa has only half as many engineers as doctors. By comparison, Australia, America, Western Europe and even China or India have a similar number of engineers to doctors, or more engineers than doctors. Furthermore, the ratio of population to engineer in South Africa is of the order of 3,200 to 1, twenty times less than in some of the countries just mentioned. Furthermore, the ratio amongst the white population is approximately 300 to 1 – similar to America and Western Europe – while the ratio in the African population is in the order of 50,000 to 1, which is amongst the worst in Africa and the world.

- The case for transformation cannot be clearer.

Impact of the report card

The outcome was spectacularly successful. It was the first ever publication of a consolidated report on the state of a broad range of infrastructure in South Africa (or Africa) by a credible institution, drawing attention to its condition and importance by headlining issues in a manner understandable to technical, decision-making and lay persons. It provided the headline issues requiring attention and a benchmark for further monitoring. Whereas the state of South Africa's public sector infrastructure has for some while been under the spotlight, there is now broad recognition that SAICE has provided the first national-scale credible benchmark against which progress (or regress) can in future years be measured.

The primary objectives of informing the public and decision-makers were achieved through the numerous live interviews and presentations, print, visual and audio media exposure and discussions with client and sector organizations. Presentations were made to government departments such as National

Figure 1: **2006 report card for South Africa's built environment infrastructure**

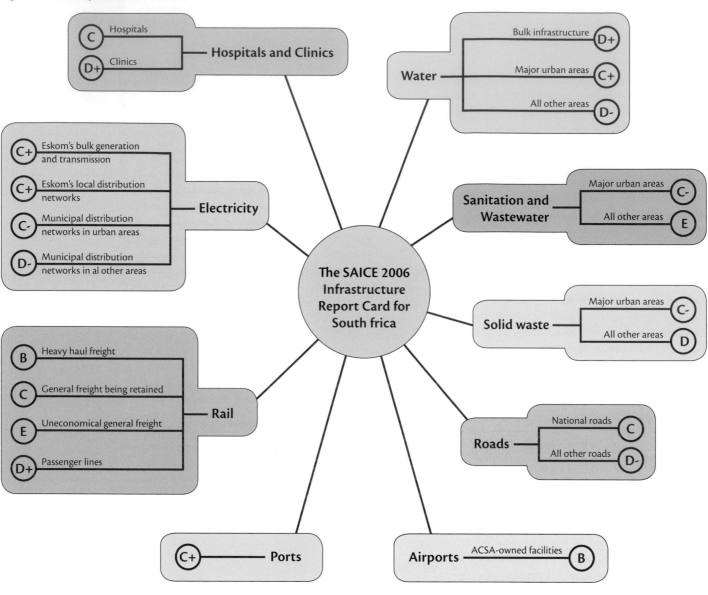

The report itself is freely available on the SAICE website (http://www.civils.org.za).

Treasury and the Department of Public Enterprises, and also to the Transport Portfolio Committee of Parliament. The authors and the Institution have been inundated with invitations to workshops and presentations by all tiers of government, parastatal agencies and industry institutions. The exposure received by SAICE was the greatest it had received for many years, if not ever, all of it overwhelmingly positive. The credibility of the Institution as a learned society with the authority, indeed the duty, to comment broadly on engineering infrastructure had been enhanced. There is broad consensus that the initiative should be sustained and extended, but that at the same time the independence of the benchmarking process should not be compromised.

The role of civil (and all) engineering professionals as creators and custodians of all aspects of infrastructure has been placed at centre stage. The impact has been to raise the awareness of the public, parents, learners, educators and government to the urgency of the crisis, e.g. in the education of engineering practitioners. However, in the midst of these positives, we need to critically analyse the shortcomings of the IRC2006 and its process. These are combined with the aspirations for future IRCs and the specific extensions and improvements identified.

Future report cards

The refinements and further development outlined below are regarded as more ambitious than can perhaps be achieved in the next edition of the IRC. Given the response to the IRC2006, and the expectations that have been created, it is clear that future reports cannot simply present an update of the IRC2006. It is considered a given that the new IRC will entail an even more rigorous process, with greater consultation and finer definition of the process and particularly the grading.

The following options are being considered. Rather than being mutually exclusive, they may also be considered as progressive elaborations:

Update and refine: Infrastructure condition does not alter significantly in the space of a year. Nonetheless, the first report card was not flawless and could do with a tweaking. So one option is to provide an interim report, incorporating a trend score (improvement, decline or unchanged grades since IRC2006) and possibly a sustainability score (the future ability of the asset to perform adequately with only routine maintenance, i.e. a refurbishment/renewal index); SAICE could also extend the IRC to include all or some of: Education, Housing, ICT, Public Works assets (Justice, police, and so on).

Extend the South African IRC to provide a detailed analysis by South African province or region. There have already been requests for assistance in compiling more regionally focused report cards. In addition, focus and comment on one or more of the following areas: rail and harbour facilities, Municipalities or just Metros. Undertake an economic analysis including a finer breakdown of the current areas, e.g. discuss backlogs and opportunity costs of doing or not doing specific maintenance or capital investments, benefits to society of various choices, and so on.

Extend the process to all Southern African countries, initially through the creation of a template that is populated through a desktop study, progressively elaborated into a nested scorecard for the region that permits examination of the infrastructure of each country individually, or the aggregated infrastructure of the region in a particular category, e.g. road transport, harbours, energy, among others, or through an examination of natural or economic corridors.

Clearly, these are ambitious objectives and some, if undertaken, go beyond the mandate of SAICE and will require external authority and especially substantial funding. It should be noted that each of these options stem from engagement with stakeholders post-IRC2006.

Conclusion

The impact of the *Infrastructure Report Card for South Africa 2006* has been extremely positive. Whereas the state of South Africa's public sector infrastructure has for some while been under the spotlight, there is now broad recognition that SAICE has provided the first national-scale credible benchmark against which progress (or regress) can in future years be measured.

There is broad consensus that the initiative should be sustained and extended, but that at the same time the independence of the benchmarking process should not be compromised.

The future of the project must also consider embracing the participation of partners such as aid agencies, SAICE's own partners such as statutory institutions, Voluntary Associations, the African Engineers Forum, the World Federation of Engineers Organization, UNESCO and others. SAICE will continue to convene the initiative through reasonable time commitment as a volunteer organization. Opinion and assistance will be sought from SAICE volunteers, but this will clearly not be sufficient. Discretion will have to be exercised regarding compensation for contributions.

USA

Alison Dickert

The report card for America's infrastructure is the signature public education and advocacy tool for the American Society of Civil Engineers (ASCE). ASCE and its members are committed to protecting the health, safety and welfare of the public, and as such, are equally committed to improving the nation's public infrastructure. To achieve that goal, the report card depicts the condition and performance of the nation's infrastructure in the familiar form of a school report card – assigning letter grades based on physical condition and needed fiscal investments for improvement. The report card can be accessed online at http://www.asce.org/reportcard.

The report card is a clear and concise document that lays out the scope of the problem in terms the average person can understand. In a world with ever increasing media clutter, the universal symbol of schoolhouse grades cuts through and leave a lasting – and sobering – impression.

Since 1998, ASCE has issued three infrastructure report cards and numerous status updates that depict the current state of the infrastructure and provide potential solutions for improvement. The report card receives widespread media coverage and has been cited in numerous academic studies. The nation's political leaders also rely on the report card to provide them with clear information, which they can use as a guide for policy decisions.

In 1988 when the report was first released, the nation's infrastructure earned a 'C', representing an average grade. Among the problems identified within the report card, titled *Fragile*

Foundations: A report on America's Public Works, were increasing congestion, deferred maintenance and age of the system; the authors of the report worried that fiscal investment was inadequate to meet the current operations costs and future demands on the system.

The Need

Public opinion research conducted in 1997 by ASCE revealed that while the general public reported a high degree of respect for engineers, they lacked a meaningful understanding of the relationship between engineering and day-to-day life. Moreover, they displayed little interest in learning more about engineering. This research did reveal strong interest in traffic, clean water, the environment and other engineering-dependent quality of life issues, coupled with a belief that engineers would be the most credible source for information and education on those issues.

To respond to the public's compelling desire for relevant information, and to position civil engineers as credible sources for that information, ASCE decided to re-examine the infrastructure report card on the tenth anniversary of its initial release.

ASCE found that in the decade since the *Fragile Foundations* report was released, the overall grade had dropped a whole letter grade to a 'D'. Moreover, a failing grade was assigned to the nation's public school infrastructure, with near failing grades in crucial areas such as drinking water, roads and dams. The grades surprised even the authors, and generated widespread public attention.

Report cards issued in 2001 and 2005, respectively, showed a slight upturn to a 'D+' in the overall grade before it sank back to a 'D'. What is most telling, however, is the fact that the concerns in the 1988 report are the same ones found subsequently, such as inadequate capacity and deferred maintenance.

The inadequate condition of the nation's infrastructure continues to be a persistent problem. Just as making the needed improvements will be a long, expensive and labour-intensive task, convincing political leaders and the public that something must be done about it is equally challenging. ASCE plans to release a new version of the report card in March 2009. Given the twenty years of age, deferred maintenance and under investment since the first report card in 1998, serious improvement is not anticipated.

The Process

To develop the report card, ASCE assembles an advisory panel of the nation's leading civil engineers, analyses hundreds of studies, reports and other sources, and surveys thousands of engineers to determine what is happening in the field. The advisory panel determines the scope of the inquiry and establishes a methodology for assigning grades.

For the 2005 report card, grades were assigned on the basis of condition and capacity, and funding versus need, generally following a traditional grading scale (e.g. if 77 per cent of roads are in good condition or better, that would earn a grade of 'C'). Base grades were then reviewed by the advisory panel and adjusted, usually with a plus or minus but sometimes as much a full letter grade, to reflect positive or negative trends or the critical consequences should a catastrophic failure occur. For example, the failure of a bridge or dam would have much more immediate and deadly consequences than a problem related to solid waste disposal.

The Benefit

In public opinion research conducted for ASCE in 2005, the public demonstrated significant recognition of the crisis facing America's infrastructure, as well as an understanding of the role of both engineers and the public in defining and adopting solutions. These findings represented a marked change from those in 1997.

The report card allows civil engineers to speak with one voice for the profession, not singular business interests. The impartiality and focus toward achieving a strategic goal for the betterment of all make ASCE a powerful advocate. With such a strong reputation, ASCE and its report card are well-respected advisors to policymakers.

Despite great accomplishments in highlighting the needs of America's infrastructure and advancing the profession of civil engineering, much still needs to be done. The report card has succeeded in convincing most people that something needs to be done, but it has yet to inspire the political leadership to effect real change. As ASCE begins its task of updating the report card for 2009, it will give particular focus to empowering the average citizen to take up this cause and fight for a better system.

During the last century, the United States saw unprecedented growth and prosperity, and at the same time experienced a corresponding build up of public infrastructure. If the nation is to keep competing in the global economy, we must have the proper infrastructure to do so. The *2009 Infrastructure Report Card* must be the catalyst to pursue that goal.

Australia

Leanne Hardwicke

Engineers Australia (EA) undertakes public policy activities at a national and state and territory level with a view to contributing to the public debate on issues that are directly engineering related, impact on the engineering profession or are in the best interest of the community from the membership's point of view. One of the most successful public policy activities to date has been the production of a series of Infrastructure Report Cards for Australia.

In producing the report cards, EA aims to raise awareness that infrastructure underpins the community's quality of life and that poor infrastructure impedes economic and social growth. EA also wants to generate debate on the quality and quantity of infrastructure to meet society's needs, and encourage best practice based on total asset management principles, sustainability and demand management.

In 2000, EA produced a basic report card on the Australia's infrastructure to highlight problem areas. That was followed with a more extensive *Australian Infrastructure Report Card* in 2001, and then a detailed state-by-state assessment. New South Wales and Queensland infrastructure report cards were published in 2003 and 2004 with the remaining state report cards completed in 2005. By weighting these results according to state and territory economies, we compiled the 2005 *Australian Infrastructure Report Card*, which provides an up-to-date strategic overview that can be used to assess the adequacy of particular classes of Australia's infrastructure and determine priorities for maintenance and capital expenditure. The report cards do not cover all infrastructure but focus on key sectors: roads (national, State and local), rail, potable water, wastewater, stormwater, irrigation, electricity, gas, ports and airports. Using ratings ranging from A (very good) to F (inadequate). Drawn from the findings of the state and territory report cards, the Australian report card also made a series of recommendations to government. The most important of these was that the planning and provision of infrastructure becoming a true partnership between the three spheres of government (including national, state and local), business and the community.

EA recommended that a 'National Infrastructure Council' be established to provide independent advice on policy, planning and delivery of infrastructure in Australia. The Council would determine priorities for nationally significant infrastructure on the basis of 20-year rolling asset and financial programmes, and would determine which infrastructure is best funded, constructed, maintained and operated by the public sector and which by the private sector. As an expert body, the National Infrastructure Council would be expected to provide advice on further reforms to regulation and taxation legislation; whole-of-life infrastructure management and alternative funding sources. Critical to its effectiveness would be programmes to increase communication with the public and key stakeholders to encourage active participation in the infrastructure debate.

The report cards have been very successful in raising awareness of infrastructure issues. Each state and territory report card received significant media attention, as did the 2005 Australian report card. After the release of the report cards, many state and territory governments produced long-term infrastructure plans and established advisory bodies or coordination offices.

At a national level, in 2007 the new government appointed a Minister of Infrastructure. In 2008, it formed a new statutory authority called 'Infrastructure Australia' to undertake a planning role for infrastructure projects of national significance. The role of this body closely mirrors Engineers Australia's recommendations.

© UNESCO/M. Borg

⌒ *Melbourne, hose for waste water.*

Infrastructure Australia is a statutory advisory council with twelve members drawn from industry, government and local government. Infrastructure Australia will: conduct audits to determine the adequacy, capacity and condition of nationally significant infrastructure, including transport, water, communications and energy; develop an infrastructure priority list to guide billions of dollars of public and private investment; and provide advice to governments, investors and owners of infrastructure on regulatory reforms that can improve the utilization of Australian infrastructure. The new government has also committed Aus$ 20 billion to a 'Building Australia Fund', which will generate funds to build critical, nationally-significant infrastructure in the future.

Challenges for Australia's infrastructure

The following provides an overview of Australia's infrastructure, as detailed in our infrastructure report cards.

⌒ *Sydney Opera House.*

© Arup

Infrastructure	2001	2005	Comments
Roads	C – D	C- – C+	• National roads are only adequate, despite upgrade work on the eastern seaboard. State roads vary greatly in quality and increased traffic is reducing local amenity. • Freight traffic and freight volumes in Australia are expected to increase, with the freight task expected to double in tonnage terms by 2020. Therefore, action must be taken to review freight routes and improve inter-modal transfers. • The highly decentralised nature of Australia's population means that the transport industry is pivotal to the effective functioning of the economy. • Improvements to substandard sections of State roads and bridges are progressing at a slower rate than desirable and local government infrastructure standards are falling behind (mainly in the rural areas).
Rail	D-	C-	• There have been notable improvements, but widespread delays remain and there are uncertainties with new investments. • There is emerging congestion in many metropolitan rail networks. As well, an integrated transport network is needed to connect regional activity centres, and to encourage the transfer of commuters from road to rail. • Improved infrastructure is required to support the transfer of inter-state freight from road to rail and rail access to ports should have an appropriate level of investment.
Ports	B	C+	• The main concerns with ports are coordination with land and air transport systems and urban encroachment, limiting the ability to expand. • Channel deepening is required for some ports to meet future growth in the size of ships, but taking into account environmental concerns.
Airports	B	B	• Airports are heavily regulated for safety and security, which tends to mean that assets are in a good condition. • Future expansion will be needed to support increased passenger movements, taking into account impacts.
Potable Water	C	B-	• Metropolitan Australia is spreading and much of the water infrastructure in metropolitan Australia is old. Catchment areas for water harvesting are limited. The barriers to providing new water solutions are generally not technical barriers, but rather political, environmental and social. • The latest rating recognised increased investment in renewing pipe networks, improved treatment, and reduced water losses from system leakage. • Spending on renewals is not keeping up with the rate of asset deterioration. Problems still exist with excess water use and encroachment on catchments by urban areas. • Record droughts in recent times have highlighted the need for new sources of supply. The magnitude of anticipated water efficiencies through demand management is ambitious and will require permanent community behavioural change.
Wastewater	C-	C+	• Rehabilitation of existing infrastructure and improved treatment have resulted in reduced discharge of pollutants into waterways. But problems still exist. • The level of water re-use has been disappointing. However, there are increasing instances of local government operating wastewater re-use schemes. • Many collection systems are old and suffering from advanced deterioration. As many sewer mains are operating at their capacity limits, and many of those systems are nearing the end of their useful service life.
Stormwater	D	C-	• The quality of stormwater infrastructure varies widely. Much stormwater infrastructure is old and funds for maintenance, repairs and renewals are lacking. • Damage from cyclones and floods damage is expensive, with flood damage averaging over Aus$300million per year. • Knowledge on the condition of many assets is limited.

Source: Engineers Australia. Full report card available at http://www.engineersaustralia.org.au

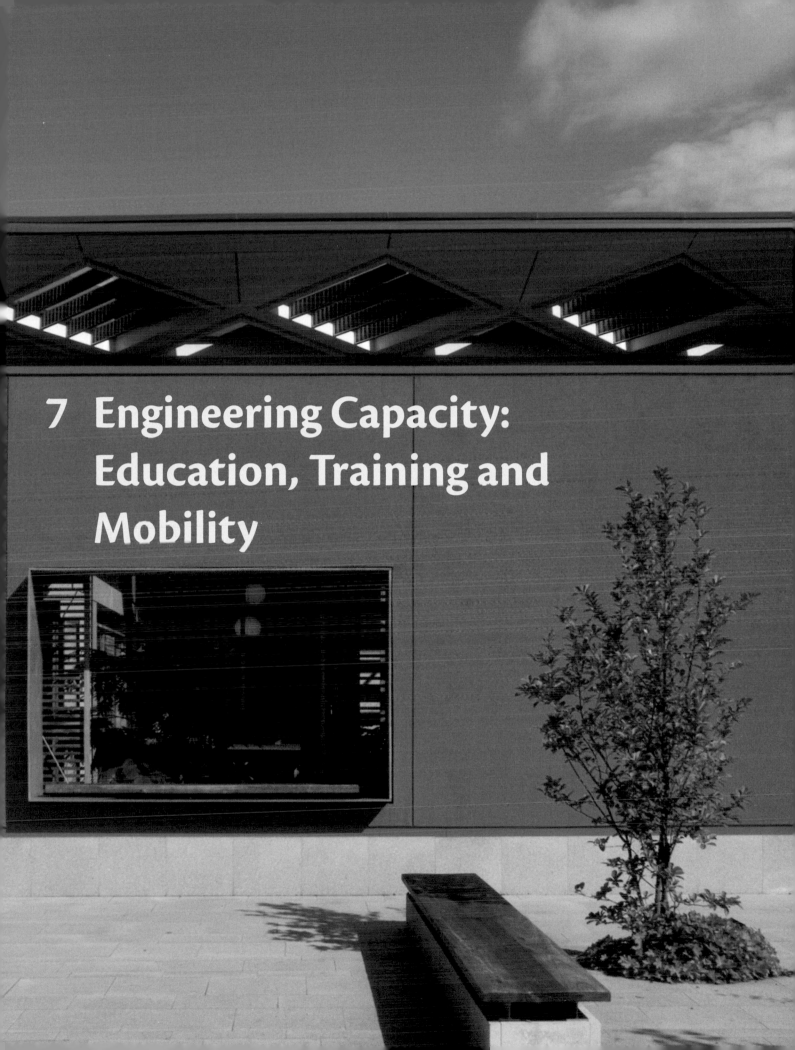

7 Engineering Capacity: Education, Training and Mobility

◌ *Engineering education begins with basic principles and hands-on experience.*

One of the most serious internal issues and challenges facing engineering is the decline of interest and enrolment of young people, especially women, in engineering in most countries around the world. This will have a serious impact on capacity in engineering, and on poverty reduction, sustainable development and the other Millennium Development Goals (MDGs) in developing countries. In view of the importance of engineering in development and the need for capacity and ongoing capacity building for adequate numbers of engineers, this is a major concern and challenge for engineering and the world. This seventh and last substantive chapter on engineering capacity focuses on engineering capacity, education, training and mobility. The chapter begins with a section on discussion of engineering capacity, and includes an introduction to needs and numbers – the demand and supply of engineers, and a contribution on technical capacity building and the role of the World Federation of Engineering Organizations (WFEO). These are followed by two case-study contributions from Africa, one on the role of capacity building for sustainability, and the other on needs and numbers in civil engineering in South Africa – based on the pioneering

work of Allyson Lawless and the South African Institution of Civil Engineers (SAICE). This section continues with contributions on enrolment and capacity in Australia, continuing engineering education and professional development, and concludes with a contribution on brain drain, gain, circulation and the diaspora of engineers. The following section focuses on the transformation of engineering education – a process that many think will be necessary to make engineering more contemporary, understandable and attractive to young people. This includes contributions on problem-based learning, sustainability and the engineering curriculum in Australia, rapid curriculum renewal, the evolution of environmental education in engineering and research in engineering education. A final section on engineering education for development includes case studies on university-based centres on engineering and technology for development in Australia, Botswana and Ghana. The chapter concludes with a discussion on engineering accreditation, standards and mobility of engineers, with particular reference to the Washington Accord, Engineers Mobility Forum, APEC Engineer and European perspective on the Eur Ing and Bologna Accord.

7.1   Engineers in education

Wlodzimierz Miszalski

Introduction

In general, the mission of engineers working in education includes:

- to disseminate technological knowledge;

- to provide society with candidates for the engineering profession who are equipped to respond to the engineering and technological challenges now and in the future;

- to increase the breadth and depth of the technological understanding of society; and

- to raise awareness of the advantages and disadvantages of technological progress.

This mission is presently the work of thousands of engineers all over the world through many different forms and programmes of engineering education starting from primary and secondary schools, through vocational or technical schools and colleges to institutes of technology, polytechnics, technical and non-technical universities as well as specific educational and training projects within professional engineering and technology organizations. It is also important to recognize the contribution of engineers teaching mathematics, physics, economics, chemistry and other disciplines, to the wider benefit of general education and knowledge in society.

Figure 1 shows the growth of science and engineering first degrees at the end of the twentieth century. More recent estimates indicate further growth of engineering graduates in Asia, for example in China with 517,000 graduates and India with 450,000 graduates per year. In 2007, 46 per cent of Chinese students graduated with engineering degrees while in the USA and Europe the proportion was 5 per cent and 15 per cent respectively.

Figure 1: Total number of first degree graduates from science and engineering studies

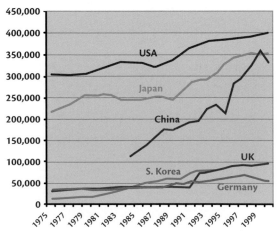

Source: James J. Duderstadt, Engineering for a Changing World, The Millennium Project, University of Michigan.

The need for a change in engineering education

Although the total educational potential in the area of engineering and technology at first might seem sufficient to satisfy the growth in and spread of technology across the world, there are great inequalities in the distribution of those engineers. This means that there is not adequate capacity, particularly to meet the challenges of sustainable development, global security, poverty reduction, environmental degradation, disaster monitoring, disaster response, and so on. The current curricula used for engineering education, the international standards that accredit them and the movements of engineering students, graduates and teachers between countries are not always equal either – and so the inequalities continue to grow. This is summarized in Figure 2.

Now, in the twenty-first century, the demand is increasing from industry and elsewhere for engineers who are able to work anywhere in the world and who can work on global engineering projects and problems. Also, the educational potential seems to be sufficient to start thinking of new models of engineering education with an international perspective. That potential can be found in: the number of academics and universities with international experience in engineering and engineering education; the volume of knowledge and lessons learned from international engineering projects; the technologies available to facilitate international education; and the growing experience with international students and the exchange of students and teachers. Such new models of education would not only satisfy the requirements of transnational companies and international engineering projects, but also the need for engineers that can work on international projects focused on, for example, poverty reduction or climate change mitigation; both require globally-thinking or globally-oriented engineers.

So recent years have brought new challenges for engineers working in the area of education. Steps forward will require greater international cooperation in technical expertise and particularly in issues of mobility, innovation, poverty reduction, management and ethics. These changing priorities in engineering practice will require corrections and perhaps more fundamental and painful transformations of educational programmes, the profiles of teaching faculty, and the organizational structures of institutions.

Key questions for engineering education

In any discussion concerning the future personal and professional profile of engineers, questions on their education are raised, including:

- What should the consecutive stages of education and training be for engineers?

- Which institutions should participate (such as: universities and institutes of technology; public and private schools;

Figure 2: **The needs for international education of engineers**

national engineering associations; international engineering federations; companies and enterprises and their training or professional development schemes; the military; the charities and non-governmental organizations)?

- What should the proportions of general and specialist technological knowledge be?

- What should the proportions of technological and non-technological knowledge be (including economics, management, ethics, humanitarianism) for a modern engineer?

WFEO-CET

The World Federation of Engineering Organizations (WFEO) has prioritized engineering education as part of its work since it was founded. The WFEO Committee on Education and Training (WFEO-CET) was established in 1970 and a Standing Committee on Education and Training was created at its second general assembly the previous year.

WFEO-CET has been engaged almost in all aspects of engineering education such as: accreditation of engineering studies; professional accreditation and practice; distance learning; management knowledge and skills; the needs of developing countries; future directions of engineering education; continuing engineering education; engineering education for mobility and innovation, and so on. This is reflected both in WFEO-CET journal *IDEAS*, intended to express the most vital issues in engineering education, professional practice and accreditation. Every three years since 1998, WFEO-CET has held a World Congress on Engineering Education. Its members have an active role in many other international organizations.

Website: www.wfeo.org

- Which domains and disciplines of technological science should be taught at what level (levels such as: polytechnical education; Bachelor degrees; Master degrees; doctorates; postgraduate education; graduate training; distance learning; self improvement)?

- How to share the total education time (e.g. 4,000 to 4,200 hours) into the general domains of fundamental knowledge necessary for engineers (such as mathematics, physics, construction and practical work)?

- How can 'traditional' areas of activity for engineers (such as mechanical, electrical, civil and structural) be adapted to the demands placed on modern engineers, particularly with respect to the traditional way that the engineering profession is organized and education is accredited?

- How are 'new' areas of activity (such as systems, nuclear, aerospace, computing, information, environmental, medical, mechatronics, robotics, acoustics, marine, energy, logistics, security, management and others) being taught and represented?

7.2 Engineering capacity

7.2.1 Needs and numbers – and the need for better numbers

Tony Marjoram

How many engineers does a country need? How many engineers does a country need to produce to keep up with this need? If a country produces more engineers – will that promote development? What types of engineer does a country need to produce, and at what levels? Are developed countries, such as the United States and Europe, failing to produce enough engineers, compared to rapidly developing countries such as China and India? Do other developing and least developed countries have enough engineers, are they producing enough or losing too many to brain drain to be able to promote development, reduce poverty and tackle major issues regarding climate change mitigation and adaptation? What are the consequences of these questions for development around the world, and what are the implications for education policy, for engineering education at tertiary level, and for science education at secondary and primary school? And what do engineers, policy-makers, planners, aid donors and international agencies, and organizations such as UNESCO need to do about it?

These questions are being asked increasingly urgently by growing numbers of people in more and more countries, for different background reasons. The problem in response is that these are also, in fact, rather complex questions, for which there are no simple or straightforward answers. This is partly, and perhaps surprisingly, because of a shortage of statistical data and indicators at national and international level with which to answer the questions and compare responses in many countries, both developed and developing. Many of the questions, are based on such widely broadcast estimates in the media, for example, that the United States only graduates 70,000 engineers a year, compared to India at 350,000 and China at 600,000. This is one reason why there is also so much reference to quantitative, qualitative and anecdotal evidence from universities, industry and professional engineering organizations regarding the supposed shortage of engineers, now and into the future. This concern was reflected in the production of the report, *Rising above the gathering storm: energizing and employing America for a brighter economic future*, by the National Academy of Engineering in the US in 2007, and the following debate (interestingly, the 'gathering storm' also alludes to the first volume of Churchill's Nobel Prize winning chronicle of the Second World War).

Background realities

The above questions are complicated not only by the fact that there are different fields, types and levels of engineers (e.g. civil, mechanical and electrical engineering, technicians and technologists, academic, professional and consulting engineers, at degree, master's or doctoral level), but also by differing needs for engineers in different sectors, fields, types and levels at different times and different places (countries and regions within them), as technologies and industries develop and decline. There are also different needs for engineers over time; for example, the increasing use of CAD software has made civil and structural engineers more productive, requiring less support staff. Engineering and technology are the drivers of incremental and disruptive change in society and in engineering, and the understanding, policy-making and planning of engineering requires a knowledge of such transverse and longitudinal changes over time.

The above questions are further complicated by different definitions and understandings of what an engineer is. In Germany, for example, there are around fifty definitions of an engineer. In many countries the term 'engineer' is also used commonly and in the media (by non-engineers) to refer to almost anybody that does anything technical such that people referred to as technicians and technologists in some countries are defined as engineers in others. This is also the case in official statistics, where, for example, degrees of different length (three or four years) may be similarly accredited, as may degrees in computer science and IT, which are not included as engineering degrees in some countries. This means that the United States, far from lagging behind India and China, may actually be producing more engineers than India, and also more than China on a per capita basis. On the other hand, this picture requires even further clarification when the numbers of overseas students studying at developed country universities are considered; university education has become a big business in many OECD countries.

The different reasons underlying such reporting may include the desire in some countries to over-represent the number of engineers to promote national status and prestige, and attract investment, whereas the desire in others may be to downplay the numbers in the lobby for increased government support to engineering education and research, or maybe to justify the outsourcing of engineering services and related overseas investment.

Structural changes and real differences

Despite this, structural rather than cyclical changes are taking place; government R&D funding in the United States and other developed countries is declining in real terms, R&D facilities are downsizing, outsourcing and offshoring to cheaper locations – as reflected in the declining publication of research papers. These changes may well have a discouraging effect on promoting the awareness of and recruitment of young people into engineering, and may also be a factor leading to the perceived shortage of engineering in developed countries. As restructuring takes place, lower level skills are displaced, with an attendant need for re-skilling, although this is counterbalanced by the greater participation of young people in education in many developed countries.

There are still significant differences, however, especially between higher and lower income countries. UNESCO data shows that developed, industrialized countries have between twenty and fifty scientists and engineers per 10,000 population, compared to around five scientists and engineers on average for developing countries, down to one or less scientist or engineer for some poorer African countries.[1] The low numbers of scientists and engineers also reflects the low investment in R&D, the low numbers of research papers published, the low level of innovation and patents, and the high level of brain drain from some countries. The engineering, science and technology capacity of many African countries has declined since

their independence. Given the importance of engineering, science and technology in development, this context will have serious consequences for the future of these countries.

For example

Governments and professional engineering bodies around the world have identified and emphasized the actual and impending shortage of engineers as a national and international priority. In the UK for example, Engineering UK (formerly the Engineering and Technology Board or ETB), has emphasized in their 2009–2010 Annual Report[2] that the UK has a shortage of engineers, is not producing enough engineers, and estimates that 600,000 new engineers will be needed over the next seven years to help build and maintain new and growing industries. While acknowledging that the UK is currently in balance in most areas, Engineering UK pointed to a particular shortage of technicians and manufacturing engineers (the UK is the sixth largest manufacturing economy in the world) and an impending decline in the medium and longer term, as well as an increasing shortage of engineers in all areas as many engineers approach retirement (30 per cent of engineering lecturers and academics have retired in recent years) and a decline in birth rate, despite increasing numbers of young people in tertiary education. Engineering UK identifies a huge demand for mechanical, civil, medical and biochemical engineers in the infrastructure, industry and health sectors, and an impending demand for engineers in (re)emerging industries associated with nuclear power, renewable energy and, particularly, climate change mitigation and adaptation. The importance of attracting the interest of parents, careers advisors as well as young people themselves to raise the status of engineering was also emphasized, and the role of practical, project-based work at school and related out-of-school activities.

Other governments and professional engineering bodies that have identified the shortage of engineers as a national priority include South Africa; a target was set in 2008 of producing up to 2,500 engineers per year, as part of the (then) government's Joint Initiative on Priority Skills Acquisition (JIPSA) launched in 2006 to help address the skills shortages that were considered to be a key constraint to economic growth. The main plan was to develop roads, electricity, water and housing, to increase economic capacity for which a dramatically increased supply of engineers was required. Engineering graduations increased from 1,200 graduations per year in 2000 to 1,500 in 2008 (the numbers and needs issue is discussed by the author, Allyson Lawless, in this Report (section 7.2.4). To counter their shortage of engineers, Morocco introduced a plan to train 10,000 engineers per year in 2007, and the President of the Institute of Engineers Malaysia, Prof. Datuk Chuah Hean Teik, emphasized

---

1   For UNESCO data, see the website of the UNESCO Institute of Statistics, http://www.uis.unesco.org/

2   Available at: http://www.engineeringuk.com/viewitem.cfm?cit_id=382740 (Accessed: 27 May 2010).

in 2009 that the present 60,000 engineers in the country would need to be increased to 200,000 engineers by 2020.[3]

The greening of engineering

Engineering is one of the most important activities in the context of climate change mitigation and adaptation, and sustainable or green engineering is one of the major areas of need and growth for engineering.[4] Many countries have already introduced policies and initiatives for climate change mitigation and adaptation prior to the 2009 United Nations Climate Change Conference in Copenhagen, and together with the specific outcomes of COP15, this will be one of the greatest demands and challenges that engineering has ever faced. One of the first challenges is to make sure that there are enough appropriately qualified and experienced engineers to meet this demand; this will require the development of new courses, training materials and systems of accreditation. Young people will hopefully be attracted to such courses, and this will help to raise overall awareness of the role and importance of engineering in development. Young people should also be encouraged to go into engineering, as engineering will be at the very centre of efforts to build a carbon-free future.

In terms of mitigation and adaptation, the investment in technology and infrastructure will be significant, and with a likely doubling of coal use by 2030, the need for carbon capture and sequestration and related technologies will be on a scale of the petrochemical and fossil-fuel industry. Many countries are looking to (re)develop nuclear power generation, which will be equally challenging, as the nuclear industry has declined over the last decades and many new engineers will be required. The renewable energy sector has been developing over the last decade, and will need to develop further to keep up with demand. The same applies to the housing and transportation sectors. The demand for engineers will increase dramatically. While increasing market demand will help attract young people into engineering, it will take over five years to develop courses to produce graduates, therefore urgent government action is required now to support course development and associated R&D and innovation. Although investment in current technology, rather than R&D for new technology, is the pressing issue, new technology will be required in the decades to come and governments need to invest now to encourage the development of R&D and industry in this direction; the next main wave of technological development. At the same time, developed country governments need to support the development of R&D and associated industries in developing countries, and to minimize brain drain, which may help address developed country human resource needs, but will make matters worse in developing countries, where increasing numbers of engineers will also be required.

Need for better numbers

The data and examples discussed above also indicate that statistics and indicators for engineering are in serious need of refining and redefining. The data for engineering is collected under guidelines developed particularly by the OECD NESTI group (National Experts on Science and Technology Indicators), and is collected and analysed at such an overall level as to be of limited usefulness in answering many of the questions relating to engineering raised above. These guidelines have been developed with particular reference to the situation in OECD countries relating to R&D (the *Frascati Manual*), innovation (the *Oslo Manual*) and human resources (the *Canberra Manual*). Other information is also used, for example, for enrolment and graduation from education data (International Standard Classification of Education, ISCED) and labour force surveys (from the International Labour Organization, ILO).

The data, for example, combine 'scientists and engineers' without disaggregating into science and engineering or the various fields of science and engineering, and focus on R&D without specifying the division of research and development and the respective roles of science and engineering. Data on patents, scientific publications and innovation are presented without reference to the identity of their authors in science or engineering (and the fact that publishing papers is less of a career priority for engineers than for scientists), as well as what constitutes innovation, who does it and where it takes place. While the origins of international trade in high-tech products in various fields of engineering should be more apparent, a clearer indication and attribution of this, and the origins and destinations of exports and imports, would also be most useful in analysing issues related to the technological balance of payments.

These present indicators are of limited use in analysing the need for, types and numbers of engineers required at national and international levels to promote development. Statistics and indicators need to be refined and in some cases redefined to allow better disaggregation between science and engineering and the various fields of engineering and engineering employment (e.g. industry, teaching or research). This will facilitate a better understanding of the role of engineers in R&D, patenting, publishing and innovation, the contribution of engineers and engineering to international trade and the role of engineering in development. It will also help dramatically in providing data for policy-makers and planners.

Considering the importance of engineering, science and technology in the knowledge society and economy, it is surprising that better data is not available on these most important driv-

---

3   Prof. Datuk Chuah Hean Teik, President of the Institute of Engineers Malaysia, at the IEM 50th anniversary in 2009.

4   Morton, Oliver. Wanted: Green Engineers, The World in 2010, *The Economist*, December 2009.

ers of social and economic development. If the data that exists can be disaggregated by gender, surely a better disaggregation into science and engineering, and various fields of science and engineering, should also be possible? The answer here is that policy-makers need to ask for such data and indicators; just as gender disaggregated data became available in response to requests from policy-makers.

Another approach to the needs and numbers issue in engineering is to look at the approach of other professions, such as doctors, lawyers and teachers, to the same issue. While the demand for lawyers is more variable and elastic around the world, and the demand for teachers more directly determined by school age populations, the need for doctors, physicians and associated senior health service professionals perhaps most closely approximates that of engineers. The numbers of doctors per capita is also similar to that for engineers – on average thirteen doctors per 10,000 people, in richer countries rising to over twenty, and in poorer countries falling to below five per 10,000. Doctors and physicians are also more in the public eye, however, as improvements in health are linked to the supply, and shortage, of healthcare workers. Models have been developed to estimate the need, demand for and supply of doctors, and the identification of potential shortages. It would be most useful to explore models and the forecasting of the need and demand for and supply of doctors and physicians with the view of developing and applying similar models to engineering so as to examine and improve the health of a nation's technology and infrastructure.

7.2.2   Technical capacity-building and WFEO

Daniel Clinton and Russell Jones

The World Federation of Engineering Organizations, through its Committee on Capacity Building, is dedicated to assisting developing countries to engage effectively in the global market place via technical capacity-building.

In the pursuit of a more secure, stable and sustainable world, developing countries seek to enhance their human, institutional and infrastructure capacity. To do so they need a solid base of technologically-prepared people to effectively improve their economies and quality of life. Such a base will facilitate the infusion of development aid and provide a basis for business partnerships and development by local entrepreneurs. In a coordinated approach, UNESCO and WFEO are mounting major efforts at technical capacity-building in developing countries.

Economic development, and indeed human development, can be stimulated by building the technical capacity of a work-

force through quality engineering education programmes. A competent technical workforce can then provide several paths to economic development: by addressing local and national technical needs; by developing small business start-ups and technically competent entrepreneurs; by the creation and attraction of technically-orientated companies that will invest; by effective utilization of foreign aid funds; and by providing a legacy of appropriate infrastructure and technically competent people capable of operating and maintaining it.

Capacity-building can be defined as, 'the building of human, institutional and infrastructure capacity to help societies develop secure, stable and sustainable economies, governments and other institutions through mentoring, training, education, physical projects, the infusion of financial and other resources and, most importantly, the motivation and inspiration of people to improve their lives.'

A simpler statement is that capacity-building in the development context is the process of assisting people to develop the technical skills to address their own needs for improving the living standards and prosperity of their own people and, from there, building a sustainable society.

Attempts to build capacity are most successful as a partnership when they are driven by the host nation working together with the supplier of assistance. Identification of key stakeholders of the host nation who have vision and drive, but also connections to key decision-makers in central and local government are essential. Those stakeholders can assist in defining and prioritizing the greatest needs, and means to achieve them. The resources of the supplier can then be used most effectively.

Responding to the needs of the developing world requires a 'paradigm shift' not only in governments, engineering associations, and charitable foundations, but also in the academic and business worlds.

In the global economy of the twenty-first century, engineers play a key role in overall economic development for countries and regions. In the well-developed countries, the role of the engineer is well understood and utilized. In many developing countries, the available pool of engineering talent is below critical mass, often to the extent that even vital and basic needs, such as the need for clean water supply and sanitation, are not being met.

Technical capacity-building efforts should therefore aim to develop a sufficient pool of skilled engineers to bring about several desirable outcomes, including:

- addressing the United Nations Millennium Development Goals including poverty reduction, safe water and sanitation, clean energy and transportation;

■ engaging effectively in the global economy through direct foreign investment, international trade, mobility of engineers and the flow of work to countries with cost-effective talent;

■ ensuring that international aid funds are utilized effectively and efficiently for initial project implementation, for long-term operation and maintenance and for the development of capacity for future work; and

■ stimulation of job creation, through entrepreneurship and enterprise, including the creation of career paths to attract and inspire future engineers.

Capacity-building should be driven by the needs of the beneficiary; there are a number of approaches that yield effective results. These include helping the key institutions: the private sector, universities and professional societies, to evolve. For externally funded infrastructure projects, having a capacity-building component explicitly included to train operators, maintenance staff and the engineers involved in the design and construction phases, is highly desirable. The intent should be to leave the local engineering community capable of executing similar projects entirely on their own, without the need for external assistance; the goal is to create the local capability, including consulting engineering practices and design-build companies, which attract capable people to grow and develop the human, institutional and infrastructure capacity within the country.

Reflections on previous efforts

In a detailed study of the results of foreign aid to developing countries over the past several decades, William Easterly concludes, in his book, *The Elusive Quest for Growth* (MIT Press, 2002):

Previous efforts have tried to use foreign aid, investment in machines, fostering education at the primary and secondary levels, controlling population growth, and giving loans and debt relief conditional on reforms to stimulate the economic growth that would allow these countries to move toward self sufficiency…

…all of these efforts over the past few decades have failed to lead to the desired economic growth…

…these massive and expensive efforts have failed because they did not hit the fundamental human behavioural chord that 'people respond to incentives'.

Having concluded that past efforts at stimulating economic growth in developing countries have failed, Easterly outlines what he thinks would work. He argues that there are two areas that can likely lead to the desired economic growth in developing countries, and can lead them toward economic self sufficiency:

1. the utilization of advanced technologies, and

2. education that leads to high skills in technological areas.

While emphasis on health and basic relief needs must continue, there is also a critical need to break the cycles of poverty through development of strong and competitive economies that can relate to world markets. The building of indigenous pools of people with quality educations in science, technology and engineering can help lead to economic growth and healthy economies.

What is needed

A large pool of high-quality, accredited engineering graduates is needed in developing countries. There is a vital need for the creation of engineering jobs. This, however, is a chicken-and-egg situation – which comes first? Increased demand for engineers will result only when there is a sufficient pool of well-qualified graduates to attract direct foreign investment, multinational corporation operations, offshore outsourcing from developed countries and entrepreneurial start-ups; but the jobs must be there in order to attract people into studying engineering. Government officials must therefore pursue effective economic development and job generation strategies in parallel with making the needed investments to enhance the quality and quantity of engineering graduates – one cannot go without the other.

At the 2004 meeting of the American Society of Civil Engineers, the South Korean delegation to the Capacity Building Forum presented the results of South Korea's investment over the past three decades in the number and quality of engineering graduates. In 1970, South Korea had about 6,000 engineering graduates. In 1980, these were increased to 14,000. By 1990, the figure had jumped to about 80,000. When plotted against South Korea's per capita GNP growth, the number of engineering graduates almost directly parallels the growth of the South Korean economy, offset by a few years. This data appears to show a direct cause and effect: investment in building a well-

qualified and sufficiently large pool of engineers leads to economic development.

In the case of India there has been a long-term effort to increase the numbers of engineering graduates and the quality of their education. Whereas in the past, many of these graduates sought employment outside the country, now many are returning and newer graduates are staying to work in India in the software and design industries, often to high-tech cities where well-paying careers and extensive numbers of colleagues await them. The growing number of technically proficient and well-educated spe-

cialists also has enabled India to become a prime location for the outsourcing technical support by the world's leading technology firms.

In China, already a major economic power, the proportion of first science and engineering degrees to all bachelor's-equivalent degrees was 59 per cent, as compared to about 33 per cent in the US in 2001 (Source: *Science and Engineering Indicators 2004*, National Science Foundation, National Science Board).

Engineering education in developing countries should include significant coverage of entrepreneurship – how to start, operate, and grow a small business. Engineering graduates should be equipped to take a path of creating jobs rather than seeking one, if they wish to do so.

Developing countries need mechanisms to apply research and development results from local universities and companies for economic gain. Such mechanisms as incubators and small business development financing are needed in the mix.

As technology-based economies grow in developing countries, one important source of top talent – in addition to new engineering graduates – is the return of previous emigrants from the diaspora. Several countries that are developing well have benefited from the return of former citizens who see new opportunities in their home countries, and bring back foreign experience and network contacts to the benefit of their home countries.

7.2.3 Capacity-building for sustainability in Africa

Dawie Botha

Introduction

The continent of Africa has vast natural and human resources that remain largely underdeveloped and untapped due to a number of issues and challenges, including:

- Large scale illiteracy, and a lack of skills and scientific and technological expertise due to a lack of education and training.

- The local political and social instability that plague many countries.

- The environmental challenges prevalent in Africa including natural disasters caused by both natural phenomena as well as human interventions.

- Large-scale illness due to poor infrastructure and pandemics including malaria and HIV/AIDS.

- Globalization issues that often marginalize African countries due to economic policies driven by the more developed countries of the world and consequential exploitation of resources and raw materials.

- Ill-advised aid and donor programmes driven by more developed countries and international funding agencies and structures, which do not necessarily take the principles of

WFEO Standing Committee on Capacity Building

Given the strong relation between creation of a critical mass of educated and skilled engineering and science graduates and economic and social development, efforts should be made to build these capacities in developing countries. This is one of the conclusions reached by both UNESCO and the World Federation of Engineers (WFEO). In keeping with its mission, WFEO created its Standing Committee on Capacity Building at the WFEO General Assembly in Tunis in 2003. The Committee focuses on several priority projects, including:

Engineering for the Americas: This project, being carried out in conjunction with the Organization of American States, is focused on developing plans for enhancing engineering education and practice throughout Latin American and the Caribbean. The focus is on upgrading engineering education and on its quality assurance for that education.

African Initiatives: Many of the societal, human and economic needs identified in the Millennium Development Goals and other similar descriptions of the situation in developing countries are present in sub-Saharan Africa. The WFEO Committee on Capacity Building (CCB) has developed programs to address a significant subset of those needs, in areas of its expertise. Activities have included: engineering education workshops; development of accreditation systems; entrepreneurial training, particularly for women; stimulation of internship programs; electronic delivery of courses; formation of Engineers Without Borders cells; and faculty and student exchanges.

South-South interactions: The CCB has collaborated in promoting South-South interactions, including technology transfer among developing countries. For example, CCB has collaborated with the South African Institution of Civil Engineers to promote meetings of the African Engineering Forum, involving a dozen countries in Southern Africa. The Institution of Professional Engineers New Zealand, a member of the CCB is similarly working with a group of low population South Pacific island nations to address their needs.

affordability, sustainability, appropriate technology, transfer of skills and lack of indigenous capacity into account.

- Poor ability to network locally and internationally with peers due to limited capacity and funding resources, impacting negatively on sharing and developing good and best practice for local and indigenous purposes and leading to isolation, an inability to keep up with technological progress and a decreasing ability to compete in world markets (which ultimately increases dependence on imported technology and goods).

- A struggle to aim for and maintain high ethical standards and adhere to anti-corruption principles in the face of imposed and implied ways to do business from a weak, negotiating position.

- A lack of basic infrastructure to use as a platform for further development.

- A widening gap in communication in spite of electronic advances (for example in Internet access and mobile telephony) that is exacerbated by backlogs in services and growing populations.

- The worldwide shortage of engineering and built environment skills has led to a skewed marketplace, which has led to 'brain drain' and still attracts huge numbers of professionals away from their home countries in Africa that educated and trained them. Indeed, a vicious circle has developed, as weakened local engineering capacity ultimately leads to the need to import skills for projects, and few international projects pay any attention to skills transfer to locals.

■ Some donor countries or funding models employ 'tied aid' where professional capacity and equipment and materials are prescribed by the donor – in many such cases little or no skills transfer takes place, and occasionally the receiving country is permanently tied to the donor country for maintenance and management of the asset.

The demands of the philosophy of sustainability can only be met if the principles of Sustainable Engineering are adhered to. This concept can be defined as striving for appropriate, affordable and sustainable engineering services and infrastructure within the local environment. This concept in turn demands the development and maintenance of indigenous scientific and technological skills and expertise supported and facilitated by the key stakeholders including government, private enterprise, academic and professional structures.

Serious challenges face all the organizations attempting to tackle capacity-building. There is for example a plethora of funding entities, each with their own preferences, rules and regulations, which in some cases make it difficult to access funding efficiently and effectively. The problem is exacerbated by the fact that the smaller organizations, institutions and NGOs have limited capacity.

A number of issues became evident during the interaction that the Africa Engineers Forum had since it developed its Protocol and actively started to engage with world bodies including the World Federation of Engineering Organizations, UNESCO, the Department for International Development UK, the African Development Bank, the World Bank and many others. These include:

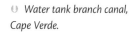

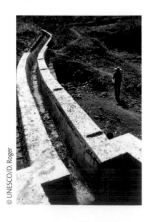

Water tank branch canal, Cape Verde.

© UNESCO/D. Roger

1. The vast differences in how the *developing* world perceives and experiences capacity-building and what it means.

2. The vast differences in how the *developed* world perceives and experiences capacity-building and what it means.

3. The vast differences in how the geographic regions perceives and experiences capacity-building and what it means.

4. The 'over-supply' of donor organizations and entities that would like to do 'good'.

5. The substantial lack of integration of effort in terms of capacity-building.

6. The measure of paternalism and turf protection evident within and among funding entities.

7. Delivery on ideas for capacity-building vanishes as quickly as the realities become evident and often ends up in talking about talks and talking in itself, which often seems to be the only outcome of hugely expensive get-togethers.

8. The initiators of ideas and the providers of resources like funding are not always aware of one another, in addition there is often a mismatch of some sorts, misunderstandings happen all the time and ultimately many, if not *most* of valuable programmes and initiatives remain on shelves or in files.

9. Even if funding becomes available for capacity-building, substantial red tape, stop-start approaches and strings attached are the order of the day and, in some cases, policy changes torpedo viable and effective programmes.

10. The principle of 'teach a man to fish' is by far not enough, since longer term sustainability of that principle is more often than not, not taken into account. The principle should not only be to teach the man to fish, but how to make his own fishing rod, how to market his fish, how to sustain fish numbers by embarking on aqua culture and so forth.

11. Many capacity-building programmes are based on what volunteers can contribute, but volunteerism only goes so far as that which will be allowed by an employer, organization or individual. The lack of continuity of volunteer members of organizations and the lack of permanent administrative capacity to support capacity-building is a serious drawback to get programmes going and to keep them going.

Components of sustainable engineering

The twenty-six items of the Protocol of the Africa Engineers Forum were expanded upon and explored to find a common understanding of the various elements that may need attention in terms of what was defined as CAPACITY.

These twenty-six items were categorized and grouped under four main headings: INDIVIDUAL, INSTITUTIONAL, TECHNICAL and DECISION MAKING. Two additional areas of crucial capacity were added, i.e. BUSINESS and RESOURCES and SUPPLIES. It must however be noted that the protocol does not address these areas of capacity since it is deemed to be outside the area in which professional societies operate. It was nevertheless agreed that these two pillars are integral elements to achieve and maintain sustainability in engineering.

In 2007, the delegates from a number of Africa Engineers Forum, signatories at the UNESCO International Policy Workshop Engineering for Poverty Eradication and the Millennium Development Goals workshop in Johannesburg, identified a number of burning issues and items that needed attention. These burning issues were categorized according to the so-called six pillars of sustainability, which was developed from the Africa Engineers Protocol. The list is not meant to be a definitive number of issues but merely points to areas of need or which need attention, or areas in which capacity or capacity-building of some sorts was deemed to be necessary or appropriate. In some cases these issues may appear under more than one 'pillar' but that must be seen as an issue that needs addressing by various entities and in various categories of capacity sectors.

Individual

- Continued Professional Development
- Productivity enhancement to facilitate international competition for investment
- Brain drain and mobility factors

Institutional

- Networks of excellence
- Regional education and training institutions for engineering
- Appropriate curricula for engineering
- Internationally accredited and recognized education and training programmes and facilities for the development of engineering professionals
- Internationally accredited and recognized professional registration systems
- Research and development
- Regional centres of excellence

Technical

- Common engineering standards

Decision-making

- Climate change
- Recycling
- Energy
- Career guidance from early ages
- Career guidance for postgraduates
- Numbers and Needs – research in the field of engineering as a tool for decision-making
- Infrastructure Report cards as a tool for decision-making
- Research and Development funding
- Engineering terminology translated for decision-makers
- Legislation for water
- The need for anecdotes
- Cross-cutting role of engineering
- Free education at secondary level
- Accountability and transparency

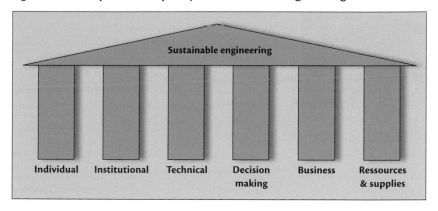

Figure 1: **The six pillars of capacity for sustainable engineering**

- Compulsory registration for engineering professionals
- Reliable statistics
- Harmonized and standardized procurement and delivery processes
- Preferential access to markets – creating a level playing field
- Engineering and HIV-AIDS
- The Health Connection – the role of engineering in health and safety of communities
- Good governance – organigrams and staff structures for governments
- Fit for purpose, affordable and appropriate infrastructure
- Benchmarking levels as a foundation to assist with decision-making
- The contribution of labour based construction
- Funding and policy regarding mathematics, science and technology teaching by government departments
- Donors – criteria and justification of projects
- Understanding the TOTAL engineering team skills need – from labourer to engineer

Business

- Mobilizing and facilitating the private sector in infrastructure
- Private sector support and funding for mathematics, science and technology teaching
- Information and Communication Technology

Resources and supplies

- Mathematics, science and technology teaching – tools for teachers and tools for learners
- Costs of raw materials

Examples of capacity-building initiatives and programmes

The following Southern African programmes or initiatives are considered to be a sample of capacity-building tools and initiatives which cover a small portion of what would be needed in terms of addressing some areas where capacity for sustainable engineering is deemed crucial. There are numerous other

*Industry - Dzamandzar
Sugar Factory, Madagascar.*

programmes from across the world that would warrant mention and many of those can be transplanted easily and implemented with very little adaptation. These examples prove an important point: effective and innovative capacity-building programmes exist and are offered in many places. The challenge is to get these programmes rolled out in all developed as well as developing countries. Other examples include activities in career guidance, harmonization of procurement, standards and guidelines.

■ *Numbers & Needs – Addressing the imbalances in the Civil Engineering Profession in South Africa (N&N1)*
This research study and suggested interventions is deemed to be world class and a world first. From the UNESCO Workshops on Poverty Alleviation it was agreed that this model should be replicated in every country in the world to facilitate decision-making regarding build environment professions.

■ *Numbers & Needs in local government – Addressing civil engineering – the critical profession for service delivery (N&N2)*
This research study and suggested interventions is a result of findings during one of the programmes that was implemented from the list of interventions in N&N1, commonly known as ENERGYS. Once more, the UNESCO Workshop delegates in Johannesburg in November 2007 agreed that this was another major contribution to the capacity-building environment.

■ *ENERGYS* – a case study in transferring of skills and accelerating experiential training for technicians and technologist students from universities of technology. The project involves mobilizing teams of retired senior engineers and students and deploying them to local authorities. In addition to the transfer of skills, teams unblocked many bottlenecks, and enhanced capacity at local authorities around RSA.

■ *Numberwise* – programme to bring the poor numeracy skills of students entering engineering studies up to acceptable levels.

■ *Tertiary Education* – a case study about the challenges facing tertiary institutions in South Africa and possibly other countries in the world.

Solutions suggested

In order to achieve effective and successful progress in capacity-building related to infrastructure, there are a number of important and crucial core components and it suggested that these issues be accepted and implemented. These include:

■ Round table integrated approaches to all elements.

■ Identification of common or generic needs and classification of areas of need.

■ A common database of funding agencies and donors and their requirements.

■ A common database of training providers.

■ A common database of training materials or programmes that are available.

■ A common administrative support system which could be accessed for purposes of capacity-building needs.

■ Well-designed templates for plans of action, roll out guidelines, clear goals, responsibilities and deadlines.

■ A networking mechanism to share ideas, get feedback on programmes and share information in general.

■ Credible and strong custodians of programmes.

■ Well-recognized and credible guarantors and non-monetary sponsors and endorsers.

■ Harmonization of processes and programmes.

It is also important that:

■ A programme to strengthen engineering in Africa is developed as an urgent priority to address the problems of serious and increasing human and institutional capacity and resource shortages in engineering in Africa.

■ A programme of human and institutional capacity-building is developed under the auspices of the Africa Engineers Forum and the proposed International Engineering Programme.

■ A programme of continuous professional development (CPD) is developed and offered in interested countries under the auspices of the Africa Engineers Forum and the proposed International Engineering Programme.

■ Activities relating to advocacy, information and communication are developed under the auspices of the Africa Engineers Forum and the proposed International Engineering Programme.

Conclusion

The Policy Statement from the UNESCO workshop on poverty alleviation should be universally accepted as a step towards building engineering capacity in developing countries. Programmes to strengthen engineering in Africa should be developed as an urgent priority to address the problems of serious and increasing human and institutional capacity and resource shortages in engineering in Africa. To achieve this an Engineering Programme for Africa and for other developing regions needs to be developed by UNESCO, in conjunction with Africa Engineers Forum and other participating organizations as a priority activity of the proposed International Engineering Programme.

7.2.4 Needs and numbers in civil engineering in South Africa

Allyson Lawless

Introduction

'Scientists discover the world that exists; engineers create the world that never was'
Theodore Von Karman, aerospace engineer

The economic well-being of any nation is dependent on growth, the availability of finance, policies conducive to sound development and capacity. It is essential that countries constantly review economic scenarios and the associated development required to maintain or improve the status quo. In much of the Western world, the engineering capacity to support growth has declined over the past twenty to thirty years posing a significant threat to long-term sustainability. Outsourcing and privatization have further depleted engineering capacity in the public sector, hence it now falls to voluntary associations such as engineering institutions and associations to review supply and demand of engineering professions to ensure that adequate training and capacity development is taking place to support their nation's well-being.

In South Africa, the accelerated development that is occurring has found the professions wanting in terms of capacity. This paper describes a comprehensive research programme carried out by the South African Institution of Civil Engineering (SAICE) that culminated in the publication of an authoritative book outlining all the interventions required to rebuild the skills base.

Background

The World Summit on Sustainable Development held in Johannesburg in 2002 focused world thinking on quality of life and the environment. Many of the goals have fallen to engineers to address. These include halving the number of people without access to safe drinking water or basic sanitation; developing and manufacturing chemicals that are more environmentally friendly than at present; and implementing poverty reduction strategies. Clearly the first two are the domain of the civil engineer, and the third falls squarely on chemists and chemical engineers. The link between poverty reduction and

engineering is not so obvious. However, J. F. Kennedy offered a clue when he said, 'It is not wealth which makes good roads possible, but good roads which make wealth possible.' Indeed, roads – again the domain of the civil engineer – offer access to education and the job market and make it possible to trade. Job creation – the escape from poverty – is also dependent on the availability of energy and machines, the domain of electrical and mechanical engineers.

Thus a sound engineering skills base is critical to the well-being of any nation. Engineers were centre stage during the pioneering era of John McAdam, Thomas Telford, the Stephensons and others in the nineteenth century who gave us surfaced roads, bridges, rail, water networks and waterborne sanitation. Even in the earlier part of the twentieth century, engineers held top public sector posts such as city engineer and director-general of infrastructure departments.

Sadly, in the latter part of the twentieth century the engineering profession found itself sidelined, playing second fiddle to the growing management and financial structures in most organizations. Engineering departments were not only sidelined, but were at the mercy of non-technical support departments for funding and permission to institute developments, upgrades and even operations that are essential to ensure sustainable services.

As a result, infrastructure development, in particular maintenance, has received inadequate attention. Furthermore, because the engineering profession had fallen from grace, fewer young people were inclined to study engineering. The result is that many countries are suffering from engineering shortages and face massive upgrading bills to restore their unmaintained infrastructure.

The world is once again starting to realize that engineers are critical for successful infrastructure service delivery, operations and maintenance. This at a time when much of the infrastructure in developing economies is inadequate and much infrastructure in the developed world is starting to fail. As a result, headlines about the need for and the shortage of engineers are being seen with increasing frequency, and capacity constraints are being cited as the most significant hindrance to development.

The challenges facing the post-1994 democratic government of South Africa have been exacerbated by the enormous development backlogs caused by the policy of apartheid, resulting in more than half the population having limited or no access to basic services. The country is thus now embarking on public sector infrastructure development to the tune of some R500 billion (US$80 billion) to ensure the desired 6 per cent growth required to stimulate job creation and alleviate poverty. The poverty relief cycle, shown in Figure 1, outlines the need for

Figure 1: Escaping the poverty trap

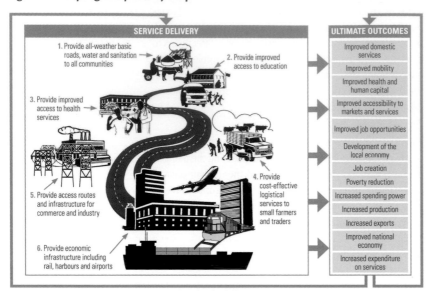

bulk and economic infrastructure to stimulate growth, and for improved domestic developments to address food security and education and health facilities to build the workforce.

However, reference to the shortage of engineers is glibly glossed over without an understanding of what is actually meant. Can countries simply poach engineers from others? Is it a matter of placing bigger, better and more adverts in the employment pages or is it a global challenge? Should new engineering faculties be opened? Or is there a systemic problem that must be addressed? Without detailed research these questions cannot easily be answered.

Figure 2: The distribution of civil engineering professionals in South Africa, April 2005

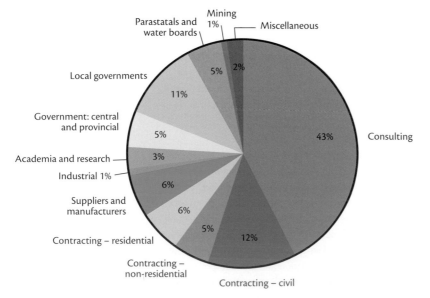

A research programme

In 2003, the South African Institution of Civil Engineering (SAICE) embarked on a comprehensive research. The programme determined the number, age, gender and racial profiles of all civil engineers, technologists and technicians in South Africa, in a bid to understand the constraints and develop solutions to address this vexing challenge. It was found that some 15,000 civil engineers, technologists and technicians were practising in the country, distributed per sector.

In October 2005, *Numbers and Needs: Addressing imbalances in the civil engineering profession*[5] was published and articulated that bottlenecks existed in the profession from pre-school to post-retirement. The findings and recommendations have been adopted by both private and public sector employers grappling with challenges of training, recruitment and retention and also by national government to guide policy development and set budgets for education, employment and infrastructure development.

Findings

Demand

Shortages in both the private and public sector were identified. For example, in 1998 a study was carried out to determine the future demand for cement. Figure 3 shows the high- and low-road scenarios projected at the time. The red line shows the actual figures at the time the book went to press in September 2005, indicating the need to increase numbers similar to those employed during the previous boom. Having suffered a 20-year decline in construction activities, many of those engineers and technicians who were trained for the boom of the 1970s and early 1980s had left the industry and often the country. Those trained in that era, who were still in the industry, were of course the baby-boomers who have started to retire and will continue to do so in significant numbers in the next five to eight years.

Supply

When analysing supply, many restrictions were identified. Weaknesses in the home environment, parental guidance and schooling were constraints to an adequate pool of learners entering tertiary institutions. In a bid to increase the number entering various institutions, entrance criteria were lowered, resulting in high dropout rates and in students taking much longer than the minimum period to complete their studies. Under-funding of tertiary institutions resulted in the appointment of fewer, and in some instances, inadequately qualified or experienced lecturing staff and inadequately equipped departments, and so on. Furthermore, the structure of the diploma course for technicians required that students spend a year in industry before completing their final semester(s). Industry, being so short of engineers, is reluctant to take on anyone with

---

5 Lawless, A. 2005. *Numbers and needs: addressing imbalances in the civil engineering profession*. Midrand: SAICE.

fewer than five years' experience, hence a catch-22 situation developed that prevents students from graduating.

Figure 4 superimposes the graduation patterns over forty years on civil spending. With the huge increase in spending shown in Figure 3, it is clear that a commensurate increase in the number of graduates is required. Sadly, inadequate workplace training, hostility towards gender, affirmative action (the existing experienced group being white males) and poor starting salaries, recorded at the time the research was carried out, resulted in poor attraction and retention at graduate level.

Experienced technical staff were found to be leaving the industry for a host of reasons including frustration (see next section), better prospects in other fields, or taking up lucrative international contracts.

Drivers and inhibitors

Drivers for economic development, a key part of human development, are:

- Growth
- Availability of finance
- Policies conducive to sound development
- Favourable interest rates, exchange rates and low inflation
- Institutional capacity

Inhibitors would obviously be the opposite. As long as all these factors are favourable, the private sector will not be held back, and indeed the towering cranes that have graced the South African skyline in recent years bear witness to private sector activity.

Although items 1 to 4 do not present significant challenges in the public sector in present-day South Africa, the same

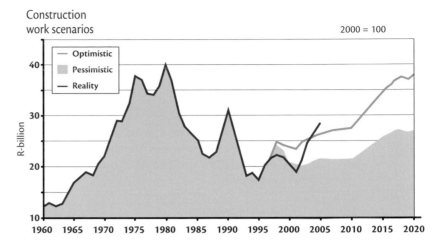

Figure 3: **Civil engineering spending and projected spending in South Africa**

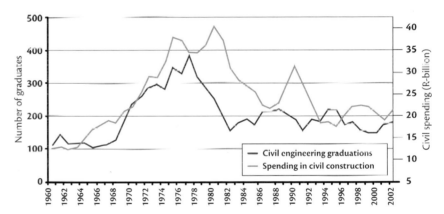

Figure 4: **Civil engineering spending versus civil engineering graduations in South Africa**

Figure 5: **The 'do nothing' approach to skills development in civil engineering**

- Immigrants
- National diploma graduate
- BSc/BEng graduate
- In industry from 2004
- Leaving the industry
- Loss due to premature dead
- Emigration
- Early retirement
- Retirement

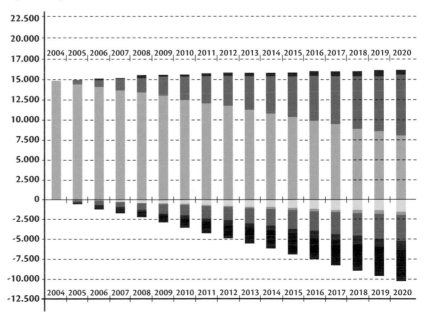

is not true of item 5 and the changing institutional environment. For example, central support departments (finance, human resources, and so on) were set up to assist technical staff. However, these support departments have taken over and developed myriads of rules, but offer no technical skills; instead of supporting delivery, they have become the cause of bottle necks as they tend to dictate how projects should be carried out. Professional skills and judgement are no longer valued or understood and technical staff are forced to accept inappropriate solutions or inaction, which flies in the face of sound engineering principles. There has thus been a slow but steady migration from the public sector to the private sector and beyond.

Recommendations

Looking at Figure 5, if nothing is done to increase the number of civil engineering graduates coming into the industry, the net figure available to the nation in 2020 will hardly be different from the current inadequate number because the gains from tertiary institutions will be balanced against the losses arising from emigration; those leaving the industry, retirement and death. Clearly many initiatives are required to increase the capacity in the industry.

Career guidance

Figure 6 shows that distribution of students studying towards a civil engineering diploma in 2005. The appalling distribution clearly needs to be addressed, as significant potential is untapped, and few engineers are likely to want to work in remote rural areas unless they have been raised in those parts. Several national departments have now committed to support career guidance in remote areas to address these gaps.

Education

Having enticed students into tertiary education, the dropout rate is very high. A change in current teaching at schools is clearly needed. The London Mathematical Society, in its document *Tackling the mathematics problem*[6] stated that:

'... recent changes in school mathematics ... have greatly disadvantaged those who need to continue their mathematical training beyond school level ... [there is] a marked decline in analytical powers when faced with simple problems requiring more than one step...'

They attributed this to the current school system approach where learners are led through set questions step-by-step rather than being taught the fundamental principles. After much campaigning the message has been heard.

With effect from January 2008, the South African Department of Education has introduced a new high school mathematics curriculum which will ensure that significantly more school leavers will have been exposed to rigorous mathematical training appropriate for engineering and other analytical tertiary courses. This represents a breakthrough for engineering education but realistically will only yield results for the profession many years from now.

Having estimated the increased number of civil engineering graduates who are required to rebuild the skills base, it was suggested to the South African government that the total number of engineering graduates per annum from universities should be increased from 1,500 to 2,500 and that output should be improved in the universities of technology. It has been gratifying to see that these recommendations have also been taken seriously. As a result most tertiary institutions have received substantial contributions (totalling in excess of R0.5 billion or US$80 million) towards expanding, updating and up-skilling their engineering departments. Enrolments have increased over the past two to three years, which augurs well for the recommended increase in graduates. During 2008, a further research project was being carried out – as an extension to the first – to assess the need for more lecturing staff, more academic development posts and so on, the outcome of which will hopefully further improve the academic environment and results.

Repatriation

The private and public sector have embarked on major international campaigns such as the 'Homecoming revolution' to encourage those who have left to return home. Several organizations have reported success with such projects.

Redeployment

Possibly the quickest wins are achieved by redeploying those who have left the industry or retired. The former can generally be encouraged to return 'if the price is right'. Salary surveys carried out at the time of the research pointed to disparities in civil engineering salaries compared with those of other engineering disciplines and particularly other professions. Salaries in the private sector have increased dramatically over the past three years, bringing many back, and the public sector is currently reviewing its levels, salary scales and the need to pay a premium for scarce skills.

The retired category presents the most interesting opportunities for redeployment, but requires a particular approach. Few retired staff actively scan employment columns for job opportunities. Many professionals keep up with technical innovations through their institutional magazines and other media, and have a strong desire to share their knowledge. Many retired engineers can be employed on a part-time or short-term contract basis simply by emailing retired members in institutional databases to offer projects that appeal to their interests.

---

6   London Mathematical Society 1995. Tackling the mathematics problem, p 42. Available at: http://www.lms.ac.uk/policy/tackling/node2.html (Accessed: 27 May 2010).